www.wadsworth.com

wadsworth.com is the World Wide Web site for
Thomson Wadsworth and is your direct source
to dozens of online resources.

At *wadsworth.com* you can find out about supplements,
demonstration software, and student resources. You can
also send e-mail to many of our authors and preview new
publications and exciting new technologies.

wadsworth.com
Changing the way the world learns®

FROM THE WADSWORTH SERIES IN SPEECH COMMUNICATION

Communication in Our Lives

■■■■■■■■

Fourth Edition

Julia T. Wood

Lineberger Distinguished Professor of Humanities
University of North Carolina at Chapel Hill

THOMSON

✦

™

WADSWORTH

Australia • Canada • Mexico • Singapore • Spain
United Kingdom • United States

THOMSON

WADSWORTH

Communication Editor: Annie Mitchell
Publisher: Holly Allen
Senior Development Editor: Renée Deljon
Assistant Editor: Aarti Jayaraman
Editorial Assistant: Trina Enriquez
Senior Technology Project Manager: Jeanette Wiseman
Senior Marketing Manager: Kimberly Russell
Marketing Assistant: Andrew Keay
Advertising Project Manager: Shemika Britt
Project Manager, Editorial Production: Jennifer Klos
Executive Art Director: Maria Epes
Print Buyer: Judy Inouye

Permissions Editor: Stephanie Lee
Production Service and Compositor: Lachina Publishing Services
Text Designer: Lisa Devenish
Photo Researcher: Jane Sanders-Miller
Copy Editor: April Wells-Hayes
Illustrator: Pam Brossia, Lachina Publishing Services
Cover Designer: Lisa Delgado
Cover Image: Frank Lobdell, *Untitled (3.25.00)* 2000, Mixed media on paper, 22-3/4 x 18 in. Photo: M. Lee Fatherree, Berkeley, CA
Printer: C&C Offset Printing Co., Ltd.

For more information about our products, contact us at
Thomson Learning Academic Resource Center
1-800-423-0563
For permission to use material from this text or product, submit a request online at
http://www.thomsonrights.com.

Any additional questions about permissions can be submitted by email to **thomsonrights@thomson.com**.

Library of Congress Control Number: 2004112876

Student Edition ISBN: 0-534-64676-X

Annotated Instructor's Edition ISBN: 0-534-62848-6

Thomson Higher Education
10 Davis Drive
Belmont, CA 94002-3098
USA

Asia (including India)
Thomson Learning
5 Shenton Way #01-01
UIC Building
Singapore 068808

Australia/New Zealand
Thomson Learning Australia
102 Dodds Street
Southbank, Victoria 3006
Australia

Canada
Thomson Nelson
1120 Birchmount Road
Toronto, Ontario M1K 5G4
Canada

UK/Europe/Middle East/Africa
Thomson Learning
High Holborn House
50–51 Bedford Row
London WC1R 4LR
United Kingdom

Latin America
Thomson Learning
Seneca, 53
Colonia Polanco
11560 Mexico D.F.
Mexico

Spain (including Portugal)
Thomson Paraninfo
Calle Magallanes, 25
28015 Madrid, Spain

For Carolyn

For so many reasons.

Brief Contents

Contents

Part II: Interpersonal, Group, and Mass Communication

Chapter 8

Foundations of Interpersonal Communication   200

Chapter 9

Communication in Personal Relationships   227

Preface

When I was an undergraduate student, I fell in love with the field of communication. My first communication course convinced me that communication was more central to my life than anything else I had studied or could study. That feeling grew stronger with each communication course I took during my undergraduate and graduate studies.

I wrote *Communication in Our Lives* to share with students my love of communication and my belief that it is critically important in our everyday lives. Because I want this book to engage students, I've tried to make it as interesting and substantive as communication itself. I use a conversational style of writing and weave into all chapters examples, reflections from students, and applications that invite students to engage material personally. Because I want this book to help students develop their competence as communicators, I emphasize concrete skills and hands-on applications.

Distinguishing Features of *Communication in Our Lives*

Communication in Our Lives has three distinct conceptual emphases. In addition, it includes a number of pedagogical features designed to increase the relevance of communication to students' everyday lives and experiences. Some of these features have been retained from the third edition, and some, as well as additional content, are new to the book's fourth edition.

Conceptual Emphases

Three conceptual goals guided my writing of this book: (1) to emphasize theories and research developed by scholars of communication, (2) to integrate coverage of social diversity as it relates to communication, and (3) to respond to student and faculty feedback about previous editions.

Emphasis on Communication Theory, Research, and Skills
One distinctive conceptual emphasis of this book is the prominence of theory, research, and skills developed by scholars of communication. The first books written for the hybrid courses in communication relied extensively on theories and research from disciplines such as psychology and sociology. To do so made sense when communication was a young field without its own base of knowledge and theories.

Although communication continues to contribute to and draw from other disciplines, it is a substantive field in its own right. Scholars of communication have developed an impressive range of theories and conducted research that shed light on the dynamics of human interaction.

Communication in Our Lives therefore highlights theories, research, and skills developed by scholars of communication. For example, Chapter 9 provides coverage of relational dialectics, a theory primarily developed by Leslie Baxter, a professor of communication at the University of Iowa. Chapter 9 also discusses research conducted by communication scholars, such as Sherryl Bowen at Villanova University, on the topic of negotiating safer sex, which is critical since HIV and AIDS continue to be serious threats to health. Chapters 13 through 17 draw on research by communication scholars that enlarges our understanding of principles of effective public communication. For instance, Clella Jaffe (2001) has identified the wave pattern as a way of organizing speeches that is more common in ethnic groups with strong oral traditions, and James McCroskey and Jason Teven (1999) have shown that speakers who demonstrate good will toward listeners tend to have higher credibility than those who don't. I emphasize the work of communication scholars both because their research is valuable and because I want students to appreciate the intellectual richness of the communication field. Although I emphasize the work of communication scholars, I don't ignore relevant research conducted by scholars in fields such as sociology, psychology, and anthropology. Thus, this book draws on research and theories in these and other related disciplines.

Integrated Attention to Social Diversity   I have woven discussion of social diversity into the basic framework of this book. I do not do this to be "politically correct" or to advance a liberal social agenda. Instead, I aim to provide integrated attention to social diversity because it is one of the most significant features of contemporary life in the United States. Our culture includes people of different ethnicities, ages, genders, physical and mental abilities, sexual orientations, economic classes, and religious or spiritual commitments (U.S. Bureau of the Census, 2002; Zachary, 2002).

The metaphor of America as a melting pot in which all differences are homogenized has given way to other metaphors such as the family quilt. Just as a family quilt consists of squares with distinct integrity, our culture consists of people with unique histories and identities; just as the individual squares in a family quilt create an exquisite whole, the different people in America make up a rich, complex overall culture.

Communication in Our Lives encourages students to appreciate social diversity as a fact of cultural life that has profound implications for our communication with others. Because social diversity affects our communication in all contexts, I weave discussion of diverse cultures and communication practices into the all chapters of this book. For example, in Chapter 10 I note how cultural values affect communication in groups and teams. In discussing personal identity in Chapter 3, I point out how social views of race, economic class, gender, and sexual orientation affect self-concept.

In addition to weaving social diversity into all chapters, Chapter 4 is devoted exclusively to communication and culture as the foundation of effective interaction in today's world. This chapter provides a sustained and focused exploration of the reciprocal relationship between culture and communication.

Evolution in Response to Student and Faculty Feedback   Like communication, books are dynamic—they evolve and change over time. This edition of *Communication in Our Lives* attempts to retain the strengths of earlier editions while also incorporating feedback from students and faculty. Before beginning work on this edition, I read feedback from hundreds of faculty members and students who used the previous edition. Their suggestions and comments led me to make a number of changes in this new edition.

Perhaps the most obvious change in this edition is the inclusion of a **new chapter on mass communication** (Chapter 12). As I've talked with faculty around the country and read written feedback from them, I've learned that an increasing number of faculty see mass communication as integral to the introductory communication course. Students today grew up in a world saturated by media, and they need to know how to think critically about media and the messages—implicit as well as explicit—that media offer. Chapter 12 focuses on developing media literacy by understanding how mass communication works.

In preparing this edition of *Communication in Our Lives,* I kept in mind the frequent complaint from instructors that each new edition of a textbook gets longer because authors add new material without taking out other material. I resisted this tendency. I have **streamlined all chapters** by deleting dated material and references and tightening prose. I have also reduced coverage of interviewing and put it in Appendix B (Chapter 12 in the previous edition).

Another significant change in this edition is **better integration of theory and skills** throughout the book. In response to requests from adopters and reviewers, I've added more hands-on activities to encourage students to apply the concepts and principles covered in the book. Also in response to feedback from teachers and students, this edition more thoroughly integrates skills and principles into various communication contexts. For example, Chapter 6's coverage of nonverbal communication notes specific ways in which nonverbal behaviors influence effectiveness in public speaking, interviewing, and group discussion.

Instructors familiar with this book's previous edition will also notice that I have integrated the **Experiencing Communication in Our Lives case studies** into each chapter. The case studies do remain the focus of an activity at the end of each chapter, but now students are prompted to read the scripts and view the case studies' multimedia scenarios as concrete examples that bring each chapter's ideas and principles to life before the chapter ends. Each new copy of the book comes with the interactive Communication in Our Lives CD-ROM that includes an enactment of the scripted interaction or student speech presented in each case study.

Because many faculty assign speeches in the first weeks of a term, and to lay a foundation for the public communication chapters that constitute Part 3, I weave **speech activities into early chapters** of the book. For instance, Chapter 1 includes a Sharpen Your Skill activity that invites students to prepare and present a short speech of introduction. By completing public speaking activities in early chapters, students gain valuable speaking experience, and they appreciate connections between public speaking and other forms of communication. I have also further integrated **Speech Builder Express** into Chapters 13–17, which focus on public speaking. Wherever appropriate within these chapters, I mention the program's speech outlining and development resources. Additionally, at the end of these chapters, I suggest specific activities designed to help students make use of this award-winning online tool. Speech Builder Express is described further in a subsequent section.

In recent years, ethical—and unethical—issues have gained renewed prominence in cultural life, and this edition of the book reflects that. Communication instructors know that they need to teach students to recognize **ethical issues** in communication, whether it be interaction in personal relationships, mass communication, or public speaking. To underline the importance of ethics, this edition calls attention to ethical issues and choices in communication. In addition to identifying ethical aspects of communication in each chapter, I include one question focused on ethics, flagged with an icon at the end of each chapter.

This edition of *Communication in Our Lives* also reflects changes in scholarship and modes of interaction. Those familiar with the third edition of this book will notice that the current edition includes **more than 150 new research sources.** I've also **amplified attention to technologies of communication** that affect interaction in a range of settings, and I've included more websites that invite students to extend coverage in the book. Finally, throughout the book I've **increased attention to communication in the workplace.**

Proven Pedagogical Features

In addition to the conceptually distinctive aspects of this book and its thorough integration of and emphasis on social diversity, several other features are designed to make it interesting and valuable to students.

First, I adopt a **conversational style of writing** rather than the more distant and formal style often used by textbook authors. I share with students some of my experiences in communicating with others, and I invite them to think with me about important issues and difficult challenges surrounding communication in our everyday lives. The accessible, informal writing style encourages students to personally engage the ideas I present.

A second feature of this book is the **student commentaries.** Every chapter is enriched by reflections on experience that were written by students in my classes and other classes around the country that adopted previous editions of this book. The questions, insights, and concerns expressed by diverse students enlarge the viewpoints represented in this book. Furthermore, they invite readers to reflect on their own experiences as communicators.

Communication in Our Lives also includes pedagogical features that promote learning and skill development. Punctuating each chapter are **Sharpen Your Skill** exercises that encourage students to apply concepts and develop skills discussed in the text. Many of these exercises end with a prompt to the *Student Companion* or the website, which offer additional opportunities for skill application. Each chapter also includes **Communication Highlights,** which call attention to interesting communication research and examples of communication issues in everyday life. **Case studies,** mentioned previously, are another central feature. These brief scenarios and speeches appear within each chapter to bring to life the ideas and principles presented. Rather than using generic case studies, I wrote the ones used in this book so that they would directly reflect chapter content and provide students with representative examples of communication theories and skills. In addition to their presentation in the book, the case studies are featured on the book's CD-ROM as short videos accompanied by interactive questions for discussion and analysis. With the multimedia enactments of the scenarios, instructors and students can analyze not only verbal messages but also non-verbal communication. Appendix A provides a collection of **annotated speeches** for student analysis in addition to the speeches presented in the case studies and within Speech Interactive on the CD-ROM (additional details appear below).

Focus questions open each chapter so that students have a preview of the main ideas to be covered, and **Communication in Our Lives Online** concludes each chapter. This substantial guide provides both an introduction to the text's many online resources, which are best accessed directly through the book's CD-ROM, and the print version of the text's learning aids—a list of **key concepts** with corresponding page numbers, and then a series of questions that encourage students to reflect on and discuss the chapter's material. Each set of these For Further Reflection and Discussion questions includes at least one question that uses **InfoTrac® College Edition,** which is explained in detail below, and, as mentioned above, a question focused on **ethics.**

After the key concepts and questions, I return to the **Experiencing Communication in Our Lives case study,** the scenario or sample speech featured within the chapter and available in multimedia format on the book's CD-ROM. Here, I again suggest that students watch the video, and then I pose additional questions that invite students to apply the material covered in the chapter to the case study. Finally, as I discussed earlier, at the very end of each chapter in Part 3, Public Communication, I suggest a related **Speech Builder Express** activity.

Resources for Instructors

The **Annotated Instructor's Edition** of *Communication in Our Lives,* prepared by Kelly Herold and Rita L. Rahoi-Gilchrest of Winona State University, can serve as the foundation for managing the extensive array of teaching resources that accompany this book.

The Annotated Instructor's Edition provides marginal annotations written exclusively for the instructor, making this a key resource for graduate teaching assistants, adjunct faculty, and experienced professors. Marginal annotations include chapter-at-a-glance notes, teaching tips, suggested class activities, discussion prompts, speech assignments, cross-references, and tips for integrating supplements such as the Communication in Our Lives CD-ROM, CNN videos, the *Student Companion,* and the *Instructor's Resource Manual.*

Carl Bishop, Clemson University, and I have written an **Instructor's Resource Manual** that describes approaches to teaching the basic course, provides a wealth of class-tested exercises including new teaching resources for the public speaking segment of your course, and provides suggested journal topics and sample test items.

ExamView® computerized testing allows you to create, deliver, and customize tests and study guides (both print and online) in minutes in its easy-to-use assessment and tutorial system. ExamView offers both a Quick Test Wizard and an Online Test Wizard that guide you step by step through the process of creating tests, while the unique "WYSIWYG" ("What You See Is What You Get") capability allows you to see the test you are creating on the screen exactly as it will print out or appear online. You can build tests of up to 250 questions using up to 12 question types. Using ExamView's complete word-processing capabilities, you can enter an unlimited number of new questions or edit existing questions.

To enhance your lecture presentations with professionally created Power-Point slides, request a copy of the *Multimedia Manager for Communication in Our Lives,* a Microsoft PowerPoint® Link Tool, from your local representative or by calling Thomson Wadsworth's Customer Service. This CD-ROM was developed and class-tested by Dan Cavanaugh. In addition to multiple text slides that highlight important concepts covered in the text, Linda includes animations of text line art and numerous video clips. All of the video clips that appear on the text CD-ROM and several CNN video clips are included in the program, so if you have a computer and LCD display, you do not also need a TV and VCR in the classroom. Because it is created in PowerPoint, the Multimedia Manager is flexible. You can add your own slides, make changes to or delete existing slides, and rearrange slide order.

The **Communication in Our Lives website** offers extensive resources and information for students and faculty. You and your students can access this site throughout the class for interactive activities, additional InfoTrac College Edition exercises, maintained and updated web links, crossword puzzles, and chapter quizzes. As an instructor, you can download a majority of the ancillary material described above, including the *Instructor's Resource Manual* and PowerPoint slides.

WebTutor Toolbox™ on *WebCT*™ and *Blackboard*™ is pre-loaded with content and available via access code. *WebTutor Toolbox* pairs all the content of this text's substantial companion website with all the sophisticated course management functionality of a *WebCT* or *Blackboard* product. You can assign materials (including online quizzes) and have the results flow automatically to your gradebook. While students only have access to student resources on the website, instructors can enter a pin code for access to password-protected Instructor Resources. For more information and to preview this program, go to http://webtutor.thomsonlearning.com. Finally, **InfoTrac**® **College Edition,** an invaluable online database of full-length articles from thousands of top academic journals and popular sources, is described in detail below.

The Teaching Assistant's Guide to the Basic Course by Katherine G. Hendrix is also available to adopters of this text. Designed specifically for the new communication teacher and based on leading teacher-training programs in communication, this guide includes general teaching and course management topics and specific strategies, such as giving performance feedback, managing sensitive class discussions, and conducting mock interviews. Instructors who adopt this book have access to Thomson Wadsworth's extensive Video Library. Included in this series are the *CNN*® *Today Videos* for Human Communication, Public Speaking and Interpersonal Communication. There are four volumes for each of these course areas, and all volumes include a number of one- to ten-minute CNN segments that directly address topics covered in this text. *Student Speeches for Critique and Analysis* and *Communication Scenarios for Critique and Analysis* are additional video series which include sample student speeches and the interpersonal and group communication scenarios featured as case studies in chapters of this text. These videos provide realistic examples of communication that allow students and teachers to identify specific communication principles, skills, and practices, and to analyze how they work in actual interaction.

I encourage you to contact your local Thomson Wadsworth representative or the Wadsworth Academic Resource Center at 1-800-423-0563 for more information, user names and passwords, examination copies, or a demonstration of these ancillary products.

Resources for Students

Completing the pedagogical support for this book are leading print and technological Student Resources. First, the *Student Companion*, co-authored by Chris North, Jamestown College, and me, provides practical exercises and inventories that guide students in applying concepts and developing skills discussed in the book. It includes chapter outlines, class-tested activities and self-tests. Student Companion icons are integrated throughout the text and signal to students opportunities to use the companion to apply text concepts and build their communication skills.

Second, the **Communication in Our Lives CD-ROM** expands student learning into a multimedia environment. This CD consists of five integrated components: the scenarios featured in the Experiencing Communication in Our Lives case studies; the text's speech videos in Speech Interactive; a direct link to premium content on the book's companion website that can only be accessed through the CD; a link to Speech Builder Express, and a link to InfoTrac College Edition. Each component of the CD-ROM is represented in the text with an icon, both throughout and at the ends of chapters, where students are directed to these and other digital learning resources.

Third, the **Communication in Our Lives website** offers extensive resources and information for students as well as faculty, including premium resources that are available only when accessed through the book's CD-ROM. Resources include interactive activities, additional InfoTrac College Edition exercises, maintained and updated web links, crossword puzzles, and chapter quizzes.

Fourth, an access code is included with every new copy of the text for four months of free access to the award-winning **Speech Builder Express**™ program. An online coach for speech development, organization, and outlining, Speech Builder Express™ prompts students to select their speech type and organizational pattern, specify their speech goal, craft thesis statements, develop the body of their speeches (including main points), integrate support material and transitions, and write their introductions and conclusions. Speech Builder Express™ also helps to format their lists of works cited, strategize about visual aids, and monitor their progress using a timeline. Among the other features the program includes are a dictionary and a thesaurus, video clips, and links to an online tutor and InfoTrac College Edition. Students can work on multiple speeches, save their work at any stage, and return to continue working as often as they like.

Fifth—and free with every new copy of this text—is a four-month subscription to **InfoTrac College Edition.** InfoTrac College Edition is a world-class online library that gives students and faculty access to the full text of articles from hundreds of well-known magazines and academic journals, such as *U.S News and World Report, Communication Quarterly,* and *Vital Speeches.* This is an incredible reference that students can use to select and refine their speech topics as well as complete their speech research. Numerous *InfoTrac College Edition Student Activities Workbooks* are published by Wadsworth and available as bundle items with this text. These 75–100-page workbooks feature individual and group activities that utilize InfoTrac College Edition to reinforce communication concepts.

Sixth, *A Guide to the Basic Course for ESL Students* by Esther Yook of Mary Washington College is an aid for non-native speakers. This guide includes strategies for accent management and overcoming speech apprehension, in addition to helpful web addresses and answers to frequently asked questions.

Finally, *The Art and Strategy of Service Learning Presentations* by Rick Isaacson and Jeff Saperstein is available bundled with this text. This handbook is an invaluable resource for students in a basic course that integrates a service learning component. The handbook provides guidelines for connecting service learning work with classroom concepts and advice for working effectively with agencies and organizations. It also provides model forms and reports and a directory of online resources.

Again, contact your Thomson Wadsworth representative or the Wadsworth Academic Resource Center at 1-800-423-0563 for more information.

Acknowledgments

All books reflect the efforts of many people, and *Communication in Our Lives* is no exception. A number of people have helped this book evolve from an early vision to the final form you hold in your hands. My greatest debt is to my editor, Annie Mitchell, and my publisher, Holly Allen. From start to finish, they have been active partners in the project. This book reflects their many insights and their generous collaboration.

Other people at Thomson Wadsworth have been remarkable in their creativity, attention to detail, and unflagging insistence on quality. Perhaps just as important is the patience they have shown in dealing with my quirks and weaknesses as an author. I am in debt to April Wells-Hayes, the most gifted and thoughtful copyeditor I've ever worked with. Thanks also to Jennifer Klos, production project manager; Mandy Hetrick, project manager, Lachina Publishing Services; Lisa Devenish, text designer; Jane Sanders-Miller, photo researcher; Maria Epes, art director; Stephanie Lee, permissions editor; Judy Inouye, print buyer; Jeanette Wiseman, our superb technology project manager; Renée Deljon, development editor; Aarti Jayaraman, assistant editor; Trina Enriquez, editorial assistant, who is uncanny in her ability to solve problems and anticipate my needs; and Kimberly Russell, our extraordinary marketing manager.

I am also grateful to the following people who reviewed previous editions of this book, who have been most generous in offering suggestions for improving the book. Reviewers for the first edition were: Robert Bohlken, Northwest Missouri State University; Tamara L. Burk, The College of William and Mary; Jamie M. Byrne, Millersville University; Diane Casagrande, West Chester University; April Chatham-Carpenter, University of Northern Iowa; Dennis Dufer, St. Louis Community College–Meramec; Lisa Goodnight, Purdue University–Calumet; Joann Keyton, University of Memphis; Bobbie

Klopp, Kirkwood Community College; Minh A. Luong, Purdue University; Kim Niemczyk, Palm Beach Community College; Nan Peck, Northern Virginia Community College–Annandale; Diane Prusank, University of Hartford; Ed Schiappa, University of Minnesota; and Ruth Wallinger, Frostburg State University.

Those who provided thoughtful reviews of the second edition of this book were: Chey Acuna, California State University, Los Angeles; Mary Allen, Valencia Community College; James Beard, University of Arkansas; Jamie Byrne, Millersville University; Diane Casagrande, West Chester University; Roberta Davilla, University of Northern Iowa; Marcia Dixson and Carol Dostal, Indiana–Purdue University at Fort Wayne; Brian Elliot, Baylor University; Edward Funkhouser, North Carolina State University; Susan Cain Giusto, Augusta State University; Lisa Goodnight, Purdue University–Calumet; Dan Hackel, Miami Dade Community College; Patrick Herbert, Northeast Louisiana University; Jodee Hobbs, Northeast Louisiana University; Joann Keyton, Memphis State University; Bobbi Klopp, Kirkwood Community College; Lynette Long, College of Charleston; Minh Luong, Purdue University; Anita McDaniel, Augusta State University; April Orcutt, College of San Mateo; Chris Paterson, Georgia State University; Jerry Phillips, Trinity Valley Community College; Phillip Powell, Valparaiso University; Karla Scott, St. Louis University; Beth Skinner, Towson State University; Tom Sullivan, Columbia College; Terry Thibodeux, Sam Houston State University; Scott Vitz, Indiana–Purdue University at Fort Wayne; Ruth Wallinger, Frostburg State University; Andrew Wood, San Jose State University; and Denice Yanni, Fairfield University.

Reviewers for the third edition were: Oluwatobin Adegbola, Howard University; Carlos Galavan Aleman, James Madison University; Laurie A. Brady, University of Arkansas; Dara N. Byrne, Howard University; Roberta A. Davilla, University of Northern Iowa; Philip Gerke, University of Arkansas; Nikita Y. Harris, Howard University; Shawn A. Lewis, Howard University; Kristi A. Schaller, University of Hawaii; and Michelle Simpson, College of Southern Maryland.

Reviewers who worked with me in developing this edition and to whom I am especially grateful are Dru C. Bookout, Richland College; John P. Hart, Hawaii Pacific University; Flora Keshishian, St. John's University; Allison Mintz, Phoenix College; Kyle Nicholas, Old Dominion University; Deleasa Randall-Griffiths, Ashland University; David Switzer, Indiana University–Purdue University Fort Wayne; Laurel Traynowicz, Boise State University; Nick Trujillo, California State University, Sacramento; Eric W. Trumbull, Northern Virginia Community College; Jayne L. Violette, Eastern Kentucky University; and Rick Wilber, University of South Florida.

I could not have written this book without the support of the Department of Communication Studies at the University of North Carolina at Chapel Hill. There, I am blessed by generous colleagues who are always willing to discuss ideas and share insights. In addition, the undergraduate and graduate students in my classes have allowed me to experiment with new approaches to teaching communication and have helped me refine ideas and activities that appear in this book. Invariably, my students teach me at least as much as I teach them, and for that I am deeply grateful.

I also thank my closest friends who are sources of personal support, insight, challenges, and experience—all of which find their way into what I write. Those people are Carolyn, Nancy, Todd, and LindaBecker.

Finally, and always, I acknowledge the support and love of my partner Robbie (Robert) Cox. Like everything else I do, this book has benefited from his presence in my life. Being married to him for 30 years has enriched my appreciation of the possibilities for love, growth, kindness, understanding, and magic between people. In addition to being the great love of my life, Robbie is my most demanding critic and my greatest fan. Both his criticism and support have shaped the final form of this book.

Julia T. Wood
Chapel Hill, NC

About the Author

JULIA T. WOOD is the Lineberger Distinguished Professor of Humanities and a professor of Communication Studies at the University of North Carolina at Chapel Hill. Since completing her Ph.D. (Pennsylvania State University) at age 24, she has conducted research and written extensively about communication in personal relationships and about gender, communication, and culture. In addition to publishing more than seventy articles and chapters, she has authored or co-authored seventeen books and edited or co-edited eight others. The recipient of eleven awards for outstanding teaching and ten awards for distinguished scholarship, Professor Wood divides her professional energies between research, writing, and teaching.

Professor Wood lives with her partner, Robert (Robbie) Cox, who is also a professor of Communication Studies at the University of North Carolina and who is actively involved with the national Sierra Club. Completing her family are Cassidy, a puppy that joined them in 2004, and two cats, Sadie Ladie and Ms. Wicca. When not writing and teaching, Professor Wood enjoys traveling, legal consulting, and spending time talking with students, friends, and family.

Courtesy of Dan Sears

Introduction

Focus Questions

1. Which aspects of your life are affected by communication?

2. How does the author's identity shape this book?

3. How do theory and practice complement each other?

A friend comes to you with a problem, and you want to show that you support him.

You've been invited to interview for your dream job, and getting it depends on communicating effectively in the interview.

A group you belong to is working on recycling programs for the campus, and you want to make group meetings productive.

At the end of the term, your romantic partner will graduate and take a job in a city 1,000 miles away, and you wonder how to stay connected across the distance.

The major project in one of your courses is an oral research report, so your grade depends on your public speaking ability.

Situations like these illustrate the importance of communication in our everyday lives. Unlike some of the subjects you study, communication is relevant to almost every aspect of your life. We communicate with ourselves when we work through ideas, psych ourselves up to meet challenges, rehearse ways to approach someone about a difficult issue, and talk ourselves into or out of various courses of action. We communicate with others to build and sustain personal relationships, to perform our jobs and advance our careers, and to participate in social and civic activities. Every facet of life involves communication.

Although we communicate all the time, we don't always communicate effectively. People who have inadequate communication knowledge and skills are hampered in their efforts to achieve personal, professional, and social goals. On the other hand, people who communicate well have a keen advantage in accomplishing their objectives. This suggests that learning about communication and learning how to communicate are keys to effective living.

Communication in Our Lives is designed to help you understand how communication works in your personal, professional, and social life. To open the book, I'll introduce myself and describe the basic approach and special features of *Communication in Our Lives*.

Introduction to the Author

As an undergraduate, I enrolled in a course much like the one you're taking now. It was an introductory class in which we studied a variety of communication forms and contexts. In that course, I began a love affair with the field of communication that has endured for 30 years. Today I am still in love with the field—more than ever, in fact. I see communication as the basis of cultural life and a primary tool for personal, social, and professional satisfaction and growth. This makes communication one of the most dynamic and important areas of study in higher education. It is a field that is both theoretically rich and pragmatically useful. I know of no discipline that offers more valuable insights, skills, and knowledge than communication.

Because communication is central to our lives, I feel fortunate to teach communication courses and conduct research in the field. Working with students allows me to help them improve their communication skills and thus their effectiveness in many arenas. Research and writing continually enlarge my understanding of communication and let me share what I learn with others like you.

Because you will be reading this book, you should know something about the person who wrote it. I am a 53-year-old, middle-class, Caucasian heterosexual with strong spiritual commitments. For 30 years I have been married to Robert (Robbie) Cox, who is also a professor of communication studies at my university. As is true for all of us, who I am affects what I know and how I think, act, interact, and write. For instance, many of the examples I share in the chapters that follow reflect my teaching and research in the areas of gendered patterns of interaction, personal relationships, and communication and cultural life. I draw from my knowledge of these areas to illustrate concepts and principles of communication.

Julia T. Wood

Other facets of my identity also influence what I know and how I write. My race, gender, social-economic class, and sexual orientation have given me certain kinds of insight and obscured others. As a woman, I understand discrimination based on sex because I've experienced it personally. I do not have personal knowledge of racial discrimination, because Western culture confers privilege on European Americans. Being middle-class has shielded me from personal experience with hunger, poverty, and class bias; and my heterosexuality has spared me from being an object of homophobic prejudice. Who you are also influences your experiences and knowledge and your ways of communicating.

Although identity limits our personal knowledge and experiences, it doesn't completely prevent insight into people and situations different from our own. From conversations with others and from reading, I have gained some understanding of people and circumstances different from my own. In our increasingly diverse world, we all need to learn about a variety of people, life circumstances, and cultures. We need to understand and communicate effectively with people whose communication styles differ from our own. What we learn by studying and interacting with people of diverse cultural heritages expands our appreciation of the richness and complexity of humanity. In addition, learning about and forming relationships with people different from ourselves enlarges our personal repertoire of communication skills and our appreciation of the range of ways to communicate.

Much of my time is spent teaching and writing, both of which I enjoy greatly. I find teaching particularly gratifying because it allows me to open students' eyes to the wonder and value of communication and to share in their pleasure as they refine their skills as communicators. Writing is another way I share my passion for communication and the knowledge I've acquired over the past three decades. To provide a context for your reading, let me share my vision of this book.

Introduction to the Book

Communication in Our Lives introduces you to many forms and functions of communication in modern life. The title reflects my belief that communication is an important part of our everyday lives. Each chapter focuses on a specific kind of communication or context of interaction.

Coverage

Because communication is a continuous part of life, we need to understand how it works—or doesn't—in a range of situations. Therefore, this book covers a broad spectrum of communication encounters, including communication with yourself, interaction with friends and romantic partners, work in groups and teams, mass communication, interaction between people with diverse cultural backgrounds, and public speaking. The breadth of communication issues and skills presented in this book can be adapted to the interests and preferences of individual classes and instructors.

Students

Communication in Our Lives is written for anyone interested in human communication. If you are a communication major, this book and the course it accompanies will provide you with a firm foundation for more advanced study. If you are majoring in another discipline, this book and the course you are taking will give you a sound basic understanding of communication and opportunities to strengthen your skills as a communicator.

Learning should be a joy, not a chore. I've written this book in an informal, personal style; for instance, I refer to myself as *I* rather than *the author,* and I use contractions (*can't* and *you're* instead of the more formal *cannot* and *you are*), as we do in normal conversation. To heighten interest, I punctuate chapters with concrete examples and insights from students at my university and other campuses around the country.

Theory and Practice

Years ago, renowned scholar Kurt Lewin said, "There is nothing so practical as a good theory." His words remain true today. In this book, I've blended theory and practice so that each draws on and enriches the other. Effective practice is theoretically informed: it is based on knowledge of how and why the communication process works and what is likely to result from different kinds of communication. At the same time, effective theories have pragmatic value: they help us understand experiences and events in our everyday lives. Each chapter in this book is informed by the theories and research generated by scholars of communication. Thus, the perspectives and skills recommended reflect current knowledge of effective communication practices.

Every facet of life involves communication.

© Tom Levy/Photo 20-20

Features

Seven key features accent this book:

Focus Questions

Each chapter opens with several focus questions that highlight important topics to be covered. Reading the questions helps you focus your attention as you study the chapter. Rereading the questions after completing the chapter allows you to check your understanding of the ideas discussed.

Experiencing Communication in Our Lives

Each chapter includes a case study, "Experiencing Communication in Our Lives." With each one, I invite you to think about how principles and skills we discuss in that chapter show up in everyday life. At the end of each chapter, I ask a few questions about the case study that allow you to apply what you have learned in a chapter to analyzing real-life communication and developing strategies for improving interaction. To see videos that depict each case study, click on the "Communication Scenarios" or "Speech Interactive" icon on the *Communication in Our Lives* CD-ROM that accompanies your textbook.

Integrated Attention to Cultural Diversity

Diversity is woven into the fabric of this book. The world and the United States have always been culturally diverse. Awareness of diversity is integral to how we communicate and think about communication; it is not an afterthought. I integrate cultural diversity into the text in several ways.

First, each chapter includes research on diverse people and highlights our commonalities and differences. For example, Chapter 9, on personal relationships, identifies general differences in women's and men's communication and provides clues about how the sexes can translate each other's language. Early chapters trace the impact of ethnicity, sexual orientation, gender, and other facets of identity on self-concept and communication practices.

You'll also notice that the photos I chose for this book include people of different races, ages, religions, and so forth. Likewise, each chapter includes examples drawn from a range of people, walks of life, and orientations, and the case studies feature diverse people.

In addition to incorporating diversity into the book as a whole, in Chapter 4 I focus exclusively on communication and culture. There you will learn about cultures and social communities (distinct groups within a single society) and the ways cultural values and norms shape how we view and practice communication. Just as important, Chapter 4 will heighten your awareness of the power of communication to shape and change cultures. This chapter will extend your insight into the intricate relationships between culture, identity, and communication. In addition, it will enhance your ability to participate effectively in a culturally diverse world.

To talk about social groups is to risk stereotyping. For instance, a substantial amount of research shows that women, in general, are more emotionally expressive than men, in general. A good deal of research also reports that Blacks, in general, speak with greater animation and force than Whites, in general. Yet, not all women are emotionally expressive, not all men are emotionally inexpressive, not all Blacks communicate forcefully, and not all Whites communicate blandly. Throughout this book, I try to provide you with reliable information on social groups while avoiding stereotyping. I rely on qualifying terms, such as *most* and *in general* to remind us that there are exceptions to generalizations.

Student Commentaries

Communication in Our Lives also features commentaries from students. In my classes, students teach me and each other by sharing their insights, experiences, and questions. Because I learn so much from students, I've included reflections written by students at my university and other campuses. As you read the student commentaries, you'll probably identify with some, disagree with others, and be puzzled by still others. Whether you agree, disagree, or are perplexed, I think you'll find that the student commentaries valuably expand the text by adding to the voices and views it represents. In the students' words, you will find much insight and much to spark thought and discussion in your classes and elsewhere.

Communication Highlights

"Communication Highlights" call your attention to especially interesting findings from communication research and news reports involving communication in everyday life. The "Communication Highlights" offer springboards for class discussions.

Sharpen Your Skill

"Sharpen Your Skill" exercises bring to life the concepts we discuss by showing you how material in the text pertains to your daily life. They invite you to apply communication principles and skills as you interact with others. Some of the "Sharpen Your Skill" features suggest ways to practice particular communication skills. Others encourage you to notice how a specific communication principle or theory shows up in your interactions. If you do the "Sharpen Your Skill" exercises, you will increase your insight into communication in general and your own communication in particular.

Critical Thinking

Communication in Our Lives strongly emphasizes on critical thinking. Competent communication demands critical thinking: distinguishing logical from illogical arguments, drawing sound conclusions from evidence, and applying concepts from one context to a different context. Each chapter calls attention to critical thinking by pointing out specific topics and issues that require critical thought.

Ethics

Finally, because ethical issues are entwined with all forms of communication, I've integrated ethics into all chapters. As you read the chapter, you'll notice that I point out particular ethical questions and considerations. Also, I've included one question focused on ethics at the end of each chapter.

I hope you enjoy reading this book as much as I've enjoyed writing it. I also hope that this book and the class it accompanies will help you develop the skills needed for communication in your life. If so, then both of us will have spent our time well.

Julia T. Wood
The University of North Carolina at Chapel Hill

For Further Reflection and Discussion

1. Think about the various forms and contexts of communication: intrapersonal communication (communication with yourself), personal relationships, groups, and public speaking. In which contexts is your communication most effective? In which contexts do you want to become more skillful? At the outset of the course, you might make a contract with yourself to focus on improving in one or two areas.

2. Do you agree that theory and practice are natural allies? As a class, discuss the importance of theories in everyday life. How do they affect your behavior and your interpretations of people, situations, and events?

3. Media today often comment on the emergence of multiculturalism in the present era. Yet in this introduction I claim that the United States and the world have always been multicultural but that this has not been widely recognized. Do you agree that multiculturalism is not new but only recently acknowledged? Do you think the current emphasis on multiculturalism is appropriate and valuable?

4. How do new technologies affect oral communication? Does personal interaction become more important, less important, or different in impor-

tance? Has the information revolution changed the nature or significance of oral communication in professional settings? How do new technologies enhance romantic relationships, group interaction, and public speaking?

5. This is a good time to familiarize yourself with InfoTrac College Edition®. Go to the site identified on the card that accompanied your book, and type in your password (also on the card). Type in the keyword *communication* and see how many articles relate to that topic. Select one to read.

6. Think critically about how your identity influences what you have experienced. Using as a model the author's introduction of herself, consider how who you are (your race-ethnicity, sex, age, spiritual commitments, economic status, and sexual orientation) both directs and limits your experience and your perspective on social issues.

7. To learn about myths and realities related to social diversity, go to http://www.jmu.edu/polisci/diversity. Before reading information on this site, did you believe any of the myths it identifies?

CHAPTER 1

The World of Communication

Focus Questions

1. Why study communication, when you've been communicating all of your life?
2. What is communication?
3. What's included in the field of communication?
4. What themes unify the field of communication?
5. What are the levels of meaning in communication?
6. What careers are open to people who have strong backgrounds in communication?

Mike hangs up the phone and shakes his head. Talking with Chris is awkward now that they live 800 miles apart. They were buddies in high school but drifted apart after they enrolled in different universities. They talk by phone every few weeks and send e-mail messages frequently, but neither is very satisfying. Mike wishes he knew how to keep the friendship going now that they can't hang out together. Shrugging, he turns on the TV while he finishes dressing for his date with Coreen. The top news story is about a shooting spree in a high school. He grimaces, thinking that the world has become a pretty mean place. Turning his thoughts back to Coreen, Mike hopes she won't want to talk about their relationship again tonight. He can't see the point of analyzing and discussing their relationship unless something is wrong, but she likes to talk about it.

As he dresses, Mike thinks about his oral presentation for Thursday's sociology class. He has some good ideas, but he doesn't know how to turn them into an effective speech. He vaguely remembers that the professor talked about how to organize a speech, but he wasn't listening. Mike also wishes he knew how to deal with a group that can't get on track. He and six other students have worked for three months to organize a student book co-op, but the group can't get its act together. By now everyone is really frustrated, and nobody listens to anyone else. When he checked his e-mail earlier today, Mike found angry messages from three of the group members. He shrugs again, turns off the TV, and leaves to meet Coreen.

Like Mike, most of us communicate continually in our daily lives. Effective communication is vital to long-distance friendships, romantic relationships, public speaking, interviewing, classroom learning, and productive group discussion. Communication opportunities and demands fill our everyday lives.

Mike—and the rest of us—rely on communication long after our college years. Even if you don't pursue a career that requires public speaking skills, such as teaching or law, communication will be essential in your work. You may need to talk with clients or patients, make progress reports, engage in public dialogues, and present proposals. You may want to persuade your boss you deserve a raise, represent your company at a press conference, or work with colleagues to develop company policies. You will have conflicts with co-workers, supervisors, and subordinates. You may need to deal with superiors who tell racist jokes or harass you sexually or with whom you simply disagree. Beyond your career, you'll communicate with family members, friends, and social acquaintances in a range of settings, each of which will call for communication skills.

Why Study Communication?

Because you've been communicating all of your life, you might wonder why you need to study communication. One answer is that formal study can improve skill. Some people have a natural aptitude for playing basketball. They become even more effective, however, if they study theories of offensive and defensive play and if they practice skills. Likewise, even if you communicate well now, learning about communication and practicing communication skills can make you more effective.

Another reason to study communication is that theories and principles help us make sense of what happens in our lives, and they help us have personal impact. For instance, learning about different gender communities would help Mike understand why Coreen, like many women, enjoys talking about relationships even when there is no problem. If Mike had better insight into the communication that sustains long-distance relationships, he might be able to enrich his friendship with Chris despite the miles between them. Mike might also be able to get his group on track if he knew how to develop an agenda. Studying public speaking could help Mike design a good presentation for his class report, and learning about interviewing would help him to impress the interviewer. Learning to listen better would help Mike retain information like his professor's tips on organizing oral reports. Communication theory and skills would help Mike maximize his effectiveness in all spheres of his life.

Sharpen Your Skill

Your Communication Activities

To find out how important communication is in your life, monitor your activities for the next 24 hours. Keep a record of the items listed here. (The activities may overlap, so your total may exceed 100%.)

1. How much time do you spend listening to others?..
   ....

2. How much time do you spend talking with yourself about ideas, plans, and options?...

3. How much time do you spend communicating with friends and romantic partners?..

4. How much of your time is devoted to group and public communication?...........
   ....

5. How much time do you spend communicating with others on the job?..............
   ....

6. How much time do you spend interacting with people of cultures different from yours?...

7. How much time do you spend using communication technologies? ....
   ....

  To identify communication skills you would like to improve, complete Activity 1.4, "Assessing Satisfaction with Communication Skills," and Activity 1.6, "Monitoring in Action," in your *Student Companion.*

To study communication is to learn about much more than communication. John Peters (2000) writes that understanding communication offers an "answer to the painful divisions between self and other, private and public, and inner thought and outer word." *Communication in Our Lives* will help you understand the profound interweaving of communication into personal, professional, social, and civic life. This book will help you become a more confident and competent communicator. Part I clarifies how communication works (or doesn't work) and explains how perception, personal identity, language, nonverbal communication, listening, and cultural factors affect the overall communication process. In Part II, we'll look at communication in five specific contexts: personal relationships, small groups, interviews, mass communication, and public settings.

This chapter lays a foundation for your study of communication. We'll first define communication. Next we'll discuss the values of communication in many spheres of your life. Then we'll examine some models of communication to clarify how the process works. In the third section of the chapter, we'll describe the breadth of the communication field and careers for communication specialists.

Defining Communication

Communication* is a systemic process in which people interact with and through symbols to create and interpret meanings. Let's elaborate the key parts of this definition.

The first important feature of this definition is **process.** Communication is a process, which means it is ongoing and always in motion, moving ever forward and changing continually. It's hard to tell when communication starts and stops, because what happened long before we talk with someone may influence interaction, and what occurs in a particular encounter may have repercussions in the future. We cannot freeze communication at any one moment.

Communication is also **systemic,** which means that it occurs in a system of interrelated parts that affect one another. In family communication, for instance, each member of the family is part of the system. In addition, the physical environment and the time of day are elements of the system that affect interaction. People interact differently in a formal living room and on a beach, and we may be more alert at certain times of day than at others.

To extend your appreciation of systems, complete Activity 1.5, "Understanding Communication Systems," in your *Student Companion.*

Different modes of communication also affect what happens between people. Recall Mike's dissatisfaction with e-mail and phone contact with his friend Chris. He found face-to-face interaction more satisfying. Communication is also affected by the history of a system. If a family has a history of listening sensitively and working out problems constructively, then saying, "There's something we need to talk about" is unlikely to cause defensiveness. On the other hand, if the family has a record of nasty conflicts and bickering, then the same comment might arouse strong defensiveness. A lingering kiss might be an appropriate way to show affection in a private setting, but the same action would raise eyebrows in an office. To interpret communication, we have to consider the system in which it takes place.

Our definition of communication also emphasizes **symbols,** which are abstract, arbitrary, and ambiguous representations of other things. Symbols

---

*Boldfaced terms are defined in the glossary at the end of the book.

include all of language and many nonverbal behaviors, as well as art and music. Anything that abstractly signifies something else can be a symbol. We might symbolize love by giving a ring, by saying "I love you," or by embracing. Later in this chapter, we'll have more to say about symbols. For now, just remember that human communication involves interaction with and through symbols.

Finally, our definition focuses on meanings, which are the heart of communication. Meanings are the significance we bestow on phenomena—what they signify to us. Meanings are not in experience itself. Instead, we use symbols to create meanings. We ask others to be sounding boards so that we can clarify our own thinking, we talk to them to figure out what things mean, we listen to them to enlarge our own perspectives, and we label feelings to give them reality. We actively construct meaning by working with symbols.

There are two levels of meaning in communication. The **content level of meaning** is the literal message. For example, if someone says, "Get lost," the content level of meaning is that you should get lost. The **relationship level of meaning** expresses the relationship between communicators. In our example, if the person who says, "Get lost" is a friend and is smiling, then you would probably interpret the relationship level of meaning as indicating that the person likes you and is kidding around. On the other hand, if the person who says, "Get lost" is your supervisor responding to your request for a raise, then you might interpret the relationship level of meaning as indicating that your supervisor regards you as inferior and dislikes your work.

To develop your ability to recognize content and relational levels of meaning, complete Activity 1.1, "Tuning in to the Relational Level of Meaning," Activity 1.2, "Identifying Levels of Meaning in Your Communication," and Activity 1.3, "Recognizing Dimensions of Relational Level Meanings" in your *Student Companion*.

Values of Communication

Now that we have a working definition of communication, let's consider its value in our lives. We spend a great deal of time communicating. We talk, listen, have dialogues with ourselves, participate in group discussions, present oral reports, watch and listen to mass communication, and so forth. From birth to death, communication shapes our personal, professional, and social lives as well as the culture in which we live.

Personal Values

George Herbert Mead (1934)[*] said that humans are "talked into" humanity. He meant that we gain personal identity as we communicate with others. In the earliest years of our lives, our parents tell us who we are: "You're smart." "You're so strong." "You're such a clown." We first see ourselves through the eyes of others, so their messages form important foundations of our self-concepts.

---

[*]I am using the American Psychological Association's (APA) method of citation. If you see "Mead (1934)," I am referring to a work by Mead that was written in 1934. If you see "Mead (1934, p. 10)" or "(Mead, 1934, p. 10)," I am specifically citing page 10 of Mead's 1934 work. The full bibliographic citations for all works may be found in the References section at the end of the book.

Later, we interact with teachers, friends, romantic partners, and co-workers who communicate their views of us. Thus, how we see ourselves reflects the views of us that others communicate.

The profound connection between identity and communication is dramatically evident in children who have been deprived of human contact. Case studies of children who were isolated from others for long periods of time reveal that they lack a firm self-concept, and their mental and psychological development is severely hindered by lack of language (Shattuck, 1980).

Communication with others not only affects our sense of identity but also directly influences our physical and emotional well-being. Consistently, research shows that communicating with others promotes health, whereas social isolation is linked to stress, disease, and early death (Baumeister & Leary, 1995; Bolger & Eckenrode, 1991; Bolger & Kelleher, 1993; Crowley, 1995). People who lack close friends have greater levels of anxiety and depression than people who are close to others (Kupfer, First, & Regier, 2002; Lane, 2000; Ornish, 1999; Segrin, 1998). One group of researchers reviewed scores of studies that traced the relationship between health and interaction with others. They reached the conclusion that social isolation is as dangerous statistically as high blood pressure, smoking, obesity, or high cholesterol (Crowley, 1995). Many doctors and researchers believe that loneliness impairs the immune system, making us more vulnerable to a range of minor and major illness (Sheehan, 1996).

Life-threatening medical problems are also affected by healthy interaction with others. Heart disease is more common among people who lack strong interpersonal relationships (Ornish, 1998; Ruberman, 1992). Heart patients who feel the least loved have 50% more arterial damage than those who feel the most loved, and those who live alone are twice as likely to die within a year of having a heart attack (Crowley, 1998). Women with metastatic breast cancer double their average survival time when they belong to support groups in which they talk with others (Crowley, 1995). Clearly, healthy interaction with others is important to our physical and mental health.

Relationship Values

Communication is also a key foundation of relationships. We build connections with others by revealing our private identities, listening to learn about others, working out problems, remembering shared history, and planning a future. Marriage counselors have long emphasized the importance of communication for healthy, enduring relationships (Beck, 1988; Gottman, 1994a, 1994b; Gottman & Carrère, 1994; Scarf, 1987). They point out that the failure of some marriages is not caused primarily by troubles and problems or even by conflict. All personal relationships encounter challenges and conflict. A major distinction between relationships that endure and those that collapse is effective communication. In fact, results of a national poll taken in 1999 showed that a majority of Americans perceive communication problems as the number one reason marriages fail—far surpassing other reasons such as sexual difficulties, money problems, and interference from family members (http://www.natcom.org/research/Poll/how_americans_communicate.htm).

Communication is important for more than solving problems or making disclosures. For most of us, everyday talk and nonverbal interaction are the

Communication Highlight

Communication and Health

Effective communication is closely linked to physical and psychological health. Humans have a basic need to interact with others and feel that they belong in communities (Baumeister & Leary, 1995; Lane, 2000). After years of studying healthy and sick people, Dr. Dean Ornish (1998) concluded that one consistent difference between them is satisfying interactions and relationships.

In an interview with Newsweek reporters, Dr. Ornish stated, "Love and intimacy are at the root of what makes us sick and what makes us well. I am not aware of any other factor in medicine—not diet, not smoking, not exercise—that has a greater impact" (Hager & Springen, 1998, p. 54).

very essence of relationships (Barnes & Duck, 1994; Duck, 1994a, 1994b; Spencer, 1994). Routine talk between intimates continually weaves their lives together. Unremarkable, everyday interaction sustains intimacy more than the big moments, such as declarations of love or major crises. By making small talk, sharing news about mutual acquaintances, and discussing clothes, furniture, and other mundane topics, partners keep up the steady pulse of their relationship. For this reason, couples involved in long-distance romances say the biggest problem is not being able to share small talk (Gerstel & Gross, 1985).

–Sandy–

When my boyfriend moved away, the hardest part wasn't missing big things in each other's life. What really bothered us was not being able to talk about little stuff or just be together. It was like we weren't part of each other's normal life when we couldn't talk about all the little things that happened or about our feelings.

Professional Values

Communication skills affect professional success. The importance of communication is obvious in professions such as teaching, business, law, sales, and counseling, where talking and listening are primary. Many attorneys, counselors, businesspeople, and teachers major or minor in communication before pursuing specialized training.

In other fields, the importance of communication is less obvious but nonetheless present. When companies are surveyed to find out what applicant qualities they consider most important, communication tops the list (Schneider, 1999; Windsor, Curtis, & Stephens, 1997). Health-care professionals must communicate effectively to explain medical problems to patients, describe courses of treatment, and gain information and cooperation from patients and their families (Berko, Wolvin, & Wolvin, 1992; Mangan, 2002). Human resource professionals say that good communication skills are critical to their on-the-job effectiveness (Morreale, 2001). Even highly technical jobs like computer programming, accounting, and system design require communication skills. Specialists have to be able to listen carefully, work in groups and teams, and explain technical ideas to people who lack their expert knowledge.

Giving a Speech of Self-introduction

This exercise serves two purposes: It gives you a first experience in public speaking, and it allows you to introduce yourself to your classmates.

Reflect on yourself and your life. Identify one interesting or unusual aspect of your identity or your life, and use that as the focus of your speech. Possible foci for your speech are experience living in another country, the origin of an unusual name, a unique event in your life, or an interesting hobby or skill. Use the following basic structure for your speech:

I. My name is.. I want to tell you this about myself:

....

II. Describe the interesting or unusual aspects of yourself or your life......................

....

III. Conclude by restating your main idea...

....

You may want to review the sample student speech of self-introduction at the beginning of this chapter and under "Speech Interactive" on your CD-ROM.

In professional life, the costs of poor communication are great. Executives in large companies report that 14% of each work week is wasted because of poor communication (Thomas, 1999). In the workplace, poor communication means that errors and misunderstandings occur, messages have to be repeated, productivity suffers, and—sometimes—people lose jobs. No matter what your career goals are, developing strong communication skills will enhance your professional success.

Cultural Values

Communication skills are important to the health of our society. To be effective, citizens in a democracy must be able to express ideas and evaluate the ideas of others. One event typical of presidential election years is a debate between or among candidates. To make informed judgments, viewers need to listen critically to candidates' arguments and their responses to criticism and questions. We also need listening skills to grasp and evaluate opposing points of view on issues such as abortion, environmental policies, and health-care reform. To be a good community member, you need skills in expressing your point of view and responding to those of others. In pluralistic cultures such as ours, we interact with people who differ from us, and we need to know how to understand and work with them. Both civic and social life depend on our ability to listen thoughtfully to a range of perspectives and to communicate in a variety of ways.

–Janet–

There are so many people from different cultures on this campus that you can't get by without knowing how to communicate in a whole lot of ways. In my classes and my dorm there are lots of Asian students and some Hispanic ones, and they

Verbal and nonverbal communication reflect cultural backgrounds and understandings.

© Bonnie Kamin/PhotoEdit

communicate differently than people raised in America. If I don't learn about their communication styles, I can't get to know them or learn about what they think.

Janet is right. When she was a student in one of my courses, she and I talked several times about the concern she expresses in her commentary. Janet realized she needed to learn to interact with people who differ from her if she is to participate fully in today's world. She has learned a lot about communicating with diverse people, and no doubt she will learn more in the years ahead. Like Janet, you can improve your ability to communicate effectively with the variety of people who make up our society.

Communication, then, is important for personal, relationship, professional, and cultural reasons. Because communication is a cornerstone of

Communication Highlight

Diversity in Social Life

America has always been socially diverse, drawing its citizens from countries all over the world. In the new millennium, social diversity is even more a fact of life in the United States. More and more people are convinced that a key function of higher education is to prepare people to function effectively and comfortably in a diverse society. In 1998, the Ford Foundation released the results of the first national poll ever taken on attitudes toward diversity and education. Two-thirds of Americans surveyed said it is very important for colleges and universities to prepare students to live and work in a society marked by diversity. Fully 94% of Americans polled said it is more important now than ever before for all of us to understand people who are

different from us. Interestingly, strong support for weaving diversity into education was not tied to political stands. Fifty-one percent of respondents said they were either conservative or very conservative politically. Still, the majority of those polled believed that every college student should be required to study different cultures and social groups in order to graduate.

 Learn more about diverse groups and their impact on America by visiting this site: http:// curry.edschool.virginia.edu/curry/centers/ multicultural.

human life, your choice to study it will serve you well. To understand what's involved in communication, let's now define the process.

Models of Communication

Theorists create models to describe how things work. Over the years, scholars in communication have developed a number of models, which reflect increasingly sophisticated understandings of the communication process.

Linear Models

Harold Laswell (1948) advanced an early model of communication that described it as a linear or one-way process in which one person acted on another person. Lasswell's verbal model consisted of five questions that described early views of how communication worked:

Who?

Says what?

In what channel?

To whom?

With what effect?

A year later, Claude Shannon and Warren Weaver (1949) extended Laswell's idea by adding that noise, or interferences, occur and may distort understanding between communicators. Figure 1.1 shows Shannon and Weaver's model. Although these early models were useful starting points, they were too simplistic to capture the complexity of most kinds of human communication. However, a linear model may accurately describe particular types of communication, such as leaving a voice mail message.

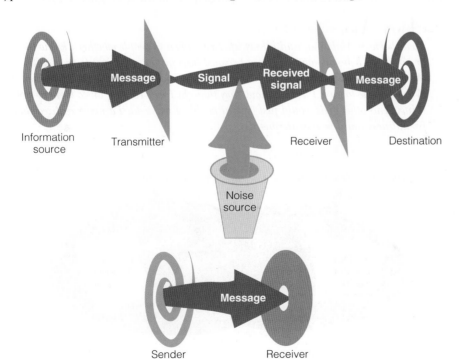

Figure 1.1
A Linear Model of Communication

Source: Adapted from Shannon, C. & Weaver, W. (1949). *The Mathematical Theory of Communication.* Urbana: University of Illinois Press.

Interactive Models

The major shortcoming of linear models was that they portrayed communication as flowing in only one direction, from a sender to a receiver. This suggests that speakers only speak and never listen. The linear model also implies that listeners only listen and never send messages. Furthermore, it suggests that listeners passively absorb senders' messages and do not respond. Clearly, this isn't how communication occurs. As you talk to friends, you notice whether they seem interested or bored. If they nod, you're likely to continue talking; if they yawn or turn away from you, you might stop. In other words, what others do affects how we communicate.

Realizing that listeners respond to senders led communication theorists to add a new feature to models. Responses to a message are called **feedback.** Feedback may be verbal, nonverbal, or both, and it may be intentional or unintentional. Wilbur Schramm (1955) depicted feedback as a second kind of message in the communication process. Research has confirmed Schramm's insight that feedback is important. Supervisors report that communication accuracy and on-the-job productivity rise when they encourage their subordinates to give feedback—ask questions, comment on supervisors' messages, and respond to supervisory communication (Deal & Kennedy, 1999).

Schramm also pointed out that communicators create and interpret messages within personal fields of experience. The more communicators' fields of experience overlap, the better they understand each other. Adding the concept of fields of experience to models clarifies why misunderstandings sometimes occur. You jokingly put down a friend; he takes it seriously and is hurt. You offer to help someone, and she feels patronized. Adding fields of experience and feedback allowed Schramm and other communication scholars to develop models of communication as an interactive process in which both senders and receivers participate actively (Figure 1.2).

–Lori Ann–

I was born in Alabama, and all my life I've spoken to people whether I know them or not. I say hello or something to a person I pass on the street just to be friendly. When I went to a junior college in Pennsylvania, I got in trouble for being so friendly. When I spoke to guys I didn't know, they thought I was coming on to them or something. And other girls would just look at me like I was odd. I'd never realized that friendliness could be misinterpreted.

Figure 1.2
An Interactive Model of Communication

Source: Adapted from Schramm, W. (1955). *The Process and Effects of Mass Communication.* Urbana: University of Illinois Press.

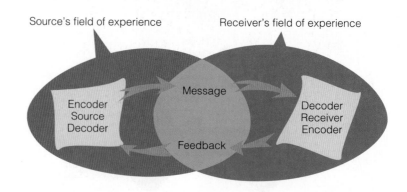

Transactional Models

A serious limitation of interactive models is that they portray communication as a sequential, linear process. One person communicates to another, who then sends feedback to the first person. This view of communication might represent e-mail conversations adequately because these tend to involve sequential turn taking. However, the interactive model doesn't recognize that everyone involved in communication both sends and receives messages, often simultaneously. While giving a press release, a speaker watches reporters to see whether they seem interested; both the speaker and the reporters are "listening," and both are "speaking."

A final shortcoming of the interactive model is that it doesn't really capture the dynamism of communication. To do this, a model would need to show that communication changes over time as a result of what happens between people. For example, Mike and Coreen communicated in more reserved and formal ways on their first date than after months of seeing each other. What they talk about and how they talk have changed as a result of interacting. An accurate model would include the feature of time and would depict features of communication as varying rather than constant. Figure 1.3 is a transactional model of communication that highlights these features and others we have discussed.

Our model also includes **noise,** which is anything that interferes with the intended communication. This includes sounds like a lawn mower or others' conversations, as well as "noises" within communicators, such as mental biases and preoccupation. In addition, our model emphasizes that communication is a continuous, constantly changing process. The feature of time reminds us that *how* people communicate varies over the history of their interaction.

The outer lines on our model emphasize that communication occurs within systems that themselves affect communication and meanings. Those

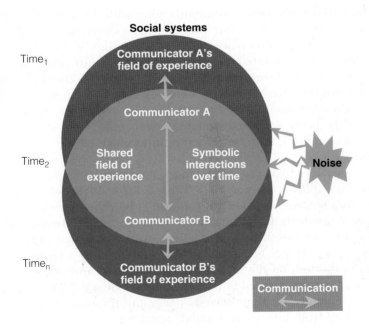

Figure 1.3
A Transactional Model of Communication

Source: Adapted from Wood, J. T. (2004). *Interpersonal Communication: Everyday Encounters* (4th ed.). Belmont, CA: Wadsworth.

systems, or contexts, include systems that both communicators share (a common campus, town, and culture, for instance) as well as each person's personal systems (family, religious associations, friends). Also notice that our model, unlike previous ones, portrays each person's field of experience and the shared field of experience between communicators as changing over time. As we encounter new people and grow personally, we change how we interact with others.

Finally, our model doesn't label one person a "sender" and the other a "receiver." Instead, both people are defined as communicators who participate actively in the communication process. This means that at a given moment in communication, you may be sending a message (speaking or nodding your head), receiving a message (listening), or doing both at the same time (interpreting what someone says while nodding to show you are interested).

The Breadth of the Communication Field

The study and teaching of communication date back more than 2,000 years. Originally, the field focused almost exclusively on public communication. Aristotle, a famous Greek philosopher, believed that effective public speaking was essential to citizens' participation in civic affairs. He taught his students how to develop and present persuasive speeches to influence public affairs.

Although public speaking remains a vital skill, it is no longer the only focus of the communication field. The modern discipline includes seven major areas of research and teaching: intrapersonal communication, interpersonal communication, group communication, public communication, mass communication and new technologies, organizational communication, and intercultural communication.

Intrapersonal Communication

Intrapersonal communication is communication with ourselves, or self-talk. We engage in self-talk to plan our lives, rehearse different ways of acting, and prompt ourselves to do or not do particular things. You might be wondering whether the term *intrapersonal communication* is just jargon for *thinking*. In one sense, it is. Intrapersonal communication is a cognitive process that goes on inside of us. Yet because thinking relies on language to name and reflect on phenomena, it is also a kind of communication. Donna Vocate's (1994) book *Intrapersonal Communication* is devoted entirely to intrapersonal communication, reflects the importance of this area of study and teaching.

Many counselors focus on enhancing self-esteem by changing how we talk to ourselves (Ellis & Harper, 1977; Rusk & Rusk, 1988; Seligman, 1990, 2002). For instance, you might say to yourself, "I blew that test, so I'm really stupid. I'll never graduate and, if I do, nobody will hire a klutz like me." Because what we say to ourselves affects our feelings, we should challenge negative self-talk by saying, "Hey, wait a minute. One test is hardly a measure of my intelligence. I did well on the other test in this course, and I have a decent overall college record. I shouldn't be so hard on myself." What we say to ourselves can enhance or diminish self-esteem and thus our effectiveness in contexts ranging from interviews to public speaking to social conversation.

Analyzing Your Self-talk

Pay attention to your self-talk for the next day. When something goes wrong, what do you say to yourself? Do you put yourself down with negative messages blaming yourself for what happened? Do you generalize beyond the specific event to describe yourself as a loser or as inadequate?

The first step in changing negative self-talk is to become aware of it. We'll say more about how to change negative self-talk in Chapter 3.

–Chiquella–

I talk to myself all the time. That's how I figure out a lot of things—by thinking them through in my head. It's like having a trial run without risk. Usually after I think through different ideas or ways of approaching someone, I can see which one would be best.

As Chiquella points out, intrapersonal communication allows us to rehearse alternative scenarios so that we can evaluate how each might turn out. To control a disruptive group member, Mike might consider (1) telling the person to shut up, (2) suggesting that the group adopt a rule that everyone should participate equally, and (3) taking the person out for coffee and privately asking him to be less domineering. Mike can think through the various ways of approaching the group member, weigh the likely consequences of each, and then choose one to put into practice. We engage in internal dialogues continually as we reflect on experiences, sort through ideas and options for communicating, and test alternative ways of acting.

Interpersonal Communication

A second major emphasis in the field of communication is **interpersonal communication,** which deals with communication between people. In one sense, everything except intrapersonal communication is interpersonal. But such a broad definition doesn't create useful boundaries for the area of study.

Interpersonal communication exists on a continuum from very impersonal to highly personal (Wood, 2004). The most impersonal kind of communication occurs when we ignore another person or treat another as an object. In the middle of the continuum is interaction with others within social roles. The most personal communication occurs in what philosopher Martin Buber (1970) called "I–Thou" relationships, in which each person treats the other as a unique and sacred person. Figure 1.4 illustrates the

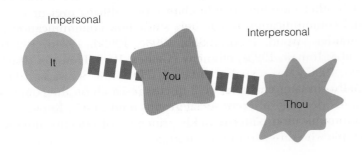

Figure 1.4
The Communication Continuum

To learn more about the field of communication, visit the National Communication Association's website at http://www.natcom.org.

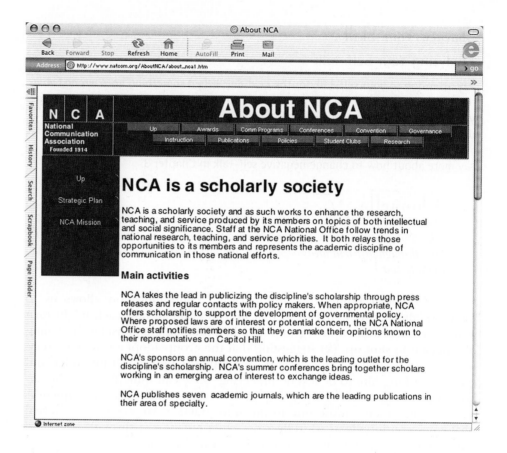

communication continuum. The more we know and interact with another person as a distinct individual, the more personal the communication is. Using this criterion, we would say that a deep conversation with a friend is more personal than a casual exchange with a salesclerk.

Since the 1960s, interest in interpersonal communication has mushroomed, making it one of the most vibrant branches of the field today. Scholars focus on how communication creates and sustains relationships and how partners communicate to deal with the normal and extraordinary challenges of maintaining intimacy over time (Canary & Stafford, 1994; Duck & Wood, 1995; Spencer, 1994; Wood & Duck, 1995a, 1995b).

Research indicates that communication is the lifeblood of close friendships and romantic relationships. Communication is the primary way people develop intimacy and continuously refashion relationships to meet their changing needs and identities. Intimates who learn how to listen sensitively and talk with each other have the greatest chance of enduring over time.

Interpersonal communication researchers study how communication is influenced by gender (Wood, 1986, 1993b, 1993c, 1993d, 1994d, 1996b, 2000, 2005; Wood & Inman, 1993), ethnicity (Gaines, 1995; Houston, 1994; Houston & Wood, 1996), and sexual orientation (Huston & Schwartz, 1995, 1996; Wood, 1994b). In later chapters, we'll discuss research on the communication goals and styles that different social groups tend to use. Knowledge about diverse communication patterns yields principles of effective interaction between people who differ from one another.

"Now let's put our heads together and see if we can get a clear picture."

Group Communication

A third important branch of communication study is small-group communication, including social groups, decision-making committees, and work teams. Small-group communication scholars study leadership, member participation, agendas for decision making, and disruptive and constructive conflict. Chapters 10 and 11 will help us understand how communication affects each of these aspects of group life and how we can participate effectively in groups.

Group communication scholars also study teams, which are special types of groups that pull together people with diverse skills and experiences and which develop especially strong cohesion. Teamwork is increasingly part of the workplace, with the average executive spending 700 hours a year in team meetings (Tubbs, 1998). Learning to communicate effectively in teams has become a criterion for success and advancement in careers.

Mass Communication and New Communication Technologies

For some time, communication scholars have studied mass communication media such as film, radio, newspapers, magazines, and television. Their research has given us insight into how media work and how they represent and influence cultural values. For instance, the cultural feminine ideal, which centers on youth and beauty, is perpetuated by the use of young, beautiful women as models in ads and as news reporters and anchors.

Media sometimes reinforce cultural stereotypes about race and ethnicity (Gutiérrez & Chao, 2003). For example, African Americans are more often cast in supporting roles than in principal roles. In addition, Black males are often portrayed as irresponsible and militant, and they are typically cast as athletes, entertainers, or criminals (Entman & Rojecki, 2000; Evans, 1993; Merritt, 2000; Wilson, Gutiérrez, & Chao, 2003). Robert Entman (1994), a communication professor at Northwestern University, points out that major

THE FAMILY CIRCUS.   By Bil Keane

11-30
©1998 Bil Keane, Inc.
Dist. by Cowles Synd., Inc.

"...lead us not into temptation,
but deliver us from e-mail..."

networks are more likely to show Black defendants in mug shots without names but to offer multiple pictures and names of White defendants. This difference may contribute to perceptions of Blacks as an undifferentiated group rather than individuals with unique identities.

─Franklin─

I hate the way television shows African Americans. Most of the time they are criminals, welfare cases, drunks, or Uncle Toms. When I watch TV, I understand why so many people still think Blacks are dumb, uneducated, and criminal. We're not, but you'd never know it from watching television.

Although the number of Asian Americans has tripled since 1970, now more than 8 million, they seldom appear on prime-time shows (Wong, 1994). Hispanics and Asians who do appear on prime time usually appear in the roles of villains, criminals, or low-paid workers (Holtzman, 2000; Merritt, 2000). One important contribution of communication scholars is heightening awareness of how media shape—and sometimes distort—our perceptions of ourselves and society.

A more recent focus of media scholars is new technologies of communication. How do new technologies influence our thinking, working, and relating? Some scholars caution that new technologies may undermine human community (Hyde, 1995), whereas others celebrate the increased social contact and productivity that technology allows (Lea & Spears, 1995; Wood & Smith, 2001). Some media experts say that new technologies give us access to unprecedented information, yet others claim that information is useless unless we also learn how to evaluate it and process it in ways that allow us to transform raw information into knowledge (Gants, 1999; Lane & Shelton, 2001; K. Young, 1998). Still others claim that new communication technologies will fundamentally transform how we think and process information (Chesebro, 1995).

─Chuck─

I live through my modem. That's how I stay in touch with friends at other schools, and I even "talk" daily with my mom, who has an e-mail system in her office. I think if I couldn't communicate with these people, the relationships would deteriorate or completely die. I think that's what happened to a lot of relationships before we had modems.

─Mele─

Sometimes I wish computers had never been invented! I'm not Luddite or anything, but I think e-mail and the web get in the way of communication as much as they help it. People read and write so fast on e-mail that they often aren't clear and they don't speak to everything in someone else's message. And they send things that they wouldn't send if they were face to face or even if they thought about it for a few minutes. People just seem to be more rude and short on e-mail and in chat rooms than when they talk in person.

Clearly, the verdict on the effects of new technologies will not be in for some time. Meanwhile, all of us struggle to keep up with our increasingly technological world. Technologies of communication pervade many aspects of our lives. Videoconferencing now makes it possible for people who are separated by many miles to talk with and see each other. Many public presentations now include PowerPoint images and other forms of technological assistance. Friends, family members, and romantic couples rely on e-mail to stay in touch. Woven into later chapters of this book are discussions of the ways in which new technologies affect how, when, and with whom we communicate.

Sharpen Your Skill

Your Mediated World

How do new technologies of communication affect your interactions? If you use the Internet, how are your electronic exchanges different from face-to-face interactions? Have you made any acquaintances or friends through electronic communication? Did those relationships develop differently from ones formed through face-to-face contact? Do you feel differently about people you have never seen and those you see?

To become familiar with Internet resources for research, complete Activity 1.7, "Introducing New Technologies," in your *Student Companion.*

Public Communication

Even though most of us may not seek careers that call for extensive formal speaking, most of us will have opportunities to speak to others. Although we may not give full speeches of self-introduction, we'll often be asked, "Say a few words about yourself," and others' first impressions of us will be based on our self-introductions.

In addition, we all will be in situations where speaking up is a responsibility. My editor speaks to her sales representatives to explain what her books are about and how to point out important features to faculty. I recently coached my doctor in public speaking so she could address her colleagues on a development in renal disease treatment. My plumber presents workshops to his

Public speaking is part of most people's lives, and when done well, it's a powerful way to communicate information, beliefs, and ideas and to foster understanding, build commitment, and motivate action.

staff to update them on new plumbing products and to teach them how to communicate effectively with customers. My sister relies on public-speaking skills when she's trying cases in court and when she's raising funds to support a center for children in need. A friend of mine recently took a leading role in organizing a union in her company. My editor, doctor, plumber, sister, and friend don't consider themselves public speakers, but public speaking is a part of their lives, and doing it effectively is important to their success.

Scholars of public communication focus on critical evaluation of speeches and on principles for speaking effectively. Rhetorical critics study important communication events such as the Reverend Martin Luther King, Jr.'s "I Have a Dream" speech and presidential speeches announcing wars. Critics often take a role in civic life by evaluating political debates and speeches to help voters understand how well candidates support their positions and respond to challenges from opponents.

Scholars of public communication also study principles of effective public speaking. As we will see in Chapters 13 through 17, we know a lot about what makes speakers seem credible to listeners and how credibility affects persuasion. Research has also enlightened us about the kinds of argument, methods of organizing ideas, and forms of proof that listeners find effective. If Mike studied this research, he could glean useful guidelines for his oral report in class.

Organizational Communication

Communication in organizations is another growing area of interest in the field of communication. As we saw earlier in this chapter, communication skills facilitate advancement in most careers. Communication scholars have identified communication skills that enhance professional success, and they have traced the impact of various kinds of communication on morale, productivity, and commitment in organizations. For many years, scholars of organizational communication have studied aspects of work life such as interviewing, listening, organizational structure, presentations, leadership, and decision making.

In addition to continuing to study these topics, organizational scholars have begun to focus substantial attention on organizational culture and personal relationships in professional settings in organizations. **Organizational culture** refers to understandings about identity and codes of thought and action shared by members of an organization (Nicotera, Clinkscales, & Walker, 2002). From this understanding emerge rules for interacting with each other, for viewing work and engaging in it. The impact of organizational culture was vividly highlighted in July 1994 when a Colorado wildfire became a raging inferno in which 14 firefighters lost their lives. A detailed investigation revealed that a primary contributor to the loss of lives was a "can-do" culture among firefighters. Trained to believe that they can do what others cannot and that they can perform heroic feats, the firefighters didn't observe critical safety regulations. Ironically, the "can-do" culture essential to such a dangerous job also led to disregard for important precautions and the subsequent loss of 14 lives.

Studies of organizational culture also shed light on the continuing problem of sexual harassment. Some institutions have developed cultures that treat sexual harassment as the normal "way we do things around here"

(Strine, 1992). A number of communication scholars have analyzed how some institutions trivialize complaints about sexual harassment and sustain an organizational culture that implies that sexual harassment is normal and acceptable (Bingham, 1994; Clair, 1993; Conrad, 1995; Strine, 1992; Taylor & Conrad, 1992).

Another area of increasing interest among organizational scholars is personal relationships between co-workers. As we increase the number of hours we spend on the job, it is natural for personal relationships between co-workers to increase. This adds both interest and complications to organizational life. In one study of personal relationships between co-workers, communication scholar Ted Zorn (1995) studied "bosses and buddies," relationships in which one friend is the boss of the other. Zorn discovered a number of ways people cope with the often contradictory rules for communication between friends and between superiors and subordinates.

−Melbourne−

It was a real hassle when my supervisor and I started going out. Before, he gave me orders like he did all the other waitstaff, and none of us thought anything about it. But after we started dating, he would sort of ask me, instead of tell me, what to do, like saying, "Mel, would you help out in Section 7?" Another problem was that if he gave me a good station where tips run high, the other waits would give me trouble because they thought he was favoring me because we go out. And when he gave me a bad station, I'd feel he was being nasty. It was a mess being his employee and his girlfriend at the same time.

Being an effective professional also requires you to understand and respect how different groups communicate. For instance, in a number of ways, women and men communicate differently, and they often misunderstand one another (Murphy & Zorn, 1996; Wood, 1993b, 1995a, 1996b, 1998, 2005). Women tend to make more "listening noises," such as "um," "uh-huh," and "go on," than most men do. If men don't make these noises when communicating with women colleagues, the women may think the men aren't listening. Conversely, men are likely to misinterpret the listening noises women make as signaling agreement rather than just interest. Such misunderstandings can hinder communication on the job (Murphy & Zorn, 1996).

Intercultural Communication

Intercultural communication is an increasingly important focus of research, teaching, and training. Although intercultural communication is not a new area of study, its importance has grown in recent years. The United States always has been made up of many peoples and cultures. Demographic shifts in the last decade have increased this, making our country richly pluralistic. Growing numbers of Asians, Indians, Eastern Europeans, Latinas and Latinos, and people of other nations are immigrating to the United States. In just the past two decades, more than 20 million people from other countries have moved legally to the United States (Zachary, 2002). Immigrants bring with them cultural values and styles of communicating that differ from those of people whose ancestors were born in the United States.

Scholars of intercultural communication increase awareness of different cultures' communication practices. For example, a Taiwanese woman in one of my classes seldom spoke up and wouldn't enter the heated debates that characterize graduate classes. One day after class, I encouraged Mei-Ling to argue for her ideas when others challenged them. She replied that that would be impolite. Her culture considers it disrespectful to argue or assert oneself and even more disrespectful to contradict others. Understood in terms of the communication values of her culture, Mei-Ling's deference did not mean she lacked confidence.

-Meikko-

What I find most odd about Americans is their focus on themselves. Here, everyone wants to be an individual who is so strong and stands out from everyone else. In Japan, it is not like that. We see ourselves as parts of families and communities, not as individuals. Here I *and* my *are the most common words, but they are not often said in Japan.*

A particularly important recent trend in the study of intercultural communication is research on different social communities within a single society. Cultural differences are obvious in communication between a Nepali and a Canadian. Less obvious are cultural differences in communication between people who speak the "same" language. Within the United States, there are distinct social communities based on race, gender, sexual orientation, and other factors. Larry Samovar and Richard Porter (2001) have identified distinctive styles of communication used by women, men, Blacks, Whites, Native Americans, homosexuals, people with disabilities, and other groups. For example, women, more than men, tend to disclose personal information and to engage in emotionally expressive talk in their friendships (Wood, 1993b, 1994a, 1994d, 2002a). African Americans belong to a communication culture that encourages dynamic talk, verbal duels, and other communication routines that have no equivalents in Caucasian speech communities (Houston, 1994; Houston & Wood, 1996). Participating effectively in a pluralistic society requires us to recognize and respect the communication practices of distinct social communities.

After reading about the major branches of the modern field of communication, you might think that the field is a collection of separate, unrelated areas of interest. Actually, this isn't the case. The field of communication is unified by a pervasive interest in language, nonverbal behavior, and the processes by which we construct meaning for ourselves and our activities.

Unifying Themes in the Field

Seemingly disparate areas such as intrapersonal, mass, and public communication are unified by central concerns with symbolic activities, meaning, critical thinking, and ethics. These four themes underlie research and teaching in different branches of the communication field.

Symbolic Activities

Symbols are the basis of language, thinking, and much nonverbal behavior. A wedding band is a symbol of marriage in Western culture; your name is a symbol for you; and a smile is a symbol of friendliness. Because symbols are abstract, they allow us to lift experiences and ourselves out of the concrete world of the here and now and reflect on our experiences and ourselves. Because symbols let us represent ideas and feelings, we can share experiences with others, even if they have not had those experiences themselves.

Whether we are interested in intrapersonal, interpersonal, mass, group, public, or intercultural communication, symbols are central to what happens. Thus, symbols and the mental activities they enable are a unifying focus of study and teaching about all forms of communication. We will discuss symbols in greater depth in Chapter 5, which deals with verbal communication, and in Chapter 6, which focuses on nonverbal communication.

Meaning

Closely related to interest in symbols is the communication field's pervasive concern with meaning. The human world is one of meaning. We don't simply exist, eat, drink, sleep, and go through motions. Instead, we imbue every aspect of our lives with significance, or meaning. When I feed my cat, Sadie, she eats her food and then returns to her feline adventures. For her, eating is a necessary and enjoyable activity. We humans layer food and eating with significance. Food often symbolizes special events or commitments. For example, kosher products reflect commitment to Jewish heritage, turkey is commonly associated with commemorating the first Thanksgiving in the United States (although vegetarians symbolize their commitment by not eating turkey), eggnog is a Christmas tradition, and mandel brot is a Hanukkah staple. Birthday cakes celebrate an individual, and we may fix special meals to express love for others.

Some families consider meals an occasion to come together and share their lives, but in other families meals are battlefields where family tensions are played out. A meal can symbolize business negotiations (power lunches, for instance), romance (candles, wine), a personal struggle to stick to a diet, or an excuse to spend two hours talking with a friend. Our experiences gain significance as a result of what we are doing and what it means.

Because we are symbol users, we don't react passively to the world. Instead, we use symbols to construct meaning. Symbols are the foundation of meaning because they enable us to name, evaluate, reflect upon, and share experiences, ideas, and feelings. Through the process of communicating with others, we define our relationships: Do we have a friendship, or is it something more? How serious are we? Do we feel the same way about each other?

–Benita–

It's funny how important a word can be. Nick and I had been going out for a long time and we really liked each other, but I didn't know if this was going to be long term. Then we said we loved each other, and that changed how we saw each other and the relationship. Just using the word love transformed who we are.

To study communication, then, is to study how we use symbols to create meaning in our lives. Communication scholars see romantic bonds, friendships, families, groups and teams, and organizations as relationships that individuals collaboratively create in the process of interaction (Andersen, 1993; Wood, 1992a, 1995b). Leslie Baxter (1987, p. 262) says that "relationships can be regarded as webs of significance" spun as partners communicate. By extension, all human activities are webs of significance spun with symbols and meaning.

Table 1.1: Critical Thinking Skills for Effective Communication

- Identify assumptions behind statements, claims, and arguments.
- Distinguish between logical and illogical reasoning.
- Separate facts from inferences.
- Evaluate evidence to determine its reliability, relevance, and value.
- Connect new information and ideas to familiar knowledge; apply concepts learned in one context to other contexts; recognize when and where specific principles are and are not appropriate.
- Distinguish between personal experience, attitudes, and behaviors and generalizations about human beings.
- Identify and consider alternative views on issues, solutions to problems, and courses of action.
- Define problems and questions clearly and precisely.
- Draw reasonable conclusions about the implications of information and argument for thought and action.
- Determine how to find answers to important questions by considering what needs to be known and what sources might provide relevant knowledge.

 Learn more by visiting the website of the Foundation for Critical Thinking: http://www .criticalthinking.org.

Critical Thinking

A third enduring concern in the communication field is **critical thinking.** To be a competent communicator, we must be able to think critically. This means that we must examine ideas carefully to decide what to believe, think, and do in particular situations (McCarthy, 1991; Wade & Tavris, 1990). Someone who thinks critically weighs ideas thoughtfully, considers evidence carefully, asks about alternative conclusions and courses of action, and connects principles and concepts across multiple contexts. Table 1.1 identifies key skills of critical thinking that affect communication competence.

The skills of critical thinking highlighted in Table 1.1 apply to all types and contexts of communication. Carol Wade and Carol Tavris (1990) wrote an entire book about the importance of critical thinking to personal relationships. They show that the skills of critical thinking can enhance communication in friendships, romantic relationships, and family relationships. Clearly, when we listen to a public speech that asks us to do something, we should ask whether the evidence is sufficient to compel our action. Yet we also need to evaluate evidence when talking to a friend who feels that his boss doesn't like him: What does the friend point to as evidence of the boss's dislike? Does the boss behave like that to other employees?

Critical thinking skills enhance your communication in all contexts. For instance, during a class lecture, your teacher states that Americans are highly individualistic and assertive. You know that you are not assertive and that you are more communal than individualistic. Should you dismiss what the teacher says as untrue? If you have critical thinking skills, you will realize that although the statement doesn't describe you accurately, it may well be true of most Americans.

Critical thinkers also work to apply concepts, skills, and principles they learn in one context to other contexts. For instance, in Chapter 8 we discuss ways to build supportive communication climates in the context of personal relationships. The same skills discussed there are relevant to developing supportive climates in small-group deliberations, public presentations, and organizational contexts. The ability to generate and evaluate solutions to a problem, which we consider in the context of group discussion (Chapter 11), is also relevant to addressing problems in personal relationships. Throughout this book, you will encounter opportunities to develop and test your critical thinking skills.

Ethics and Communication

A final theme that unifies research and teaching is ethical communication and interpretation of others' communication. Because all forms of communication involve ethical issues, this theme infuses all areas of the discipline. For instance, ethical dimensions of intrapersonal communication include the influence of stereotypes on our judgments and beliefs. In the realm of interpersonal communication, scholars who focus on ethics are concerned with issues such as honesty, compassion, and fairness in relationships. Pressures to conform that sometimes operate in groups are an ethical concern of scholars who specialize in group communication. Ethical issues also surface in public communication. For example, Linda Alcoff (1991) is concerned that people who speak for others who are oppressed may misrepresent others' experiences or even reinforce oppression by keeping others silent.

Another ethical issue relevant to a range of communication contexts concerns attitudes and actions that encourage or hinder freedom of speech: Are all members of organizations equally empowered to speak? What does it mean when audiences shout down a speaker with unpopular views? How does the balance of power between relationship partners affect each person's freedom to express himself or herself? Because ethical issues infuse all forms of communication, we will discuss ethical themes in each chapter of this book.

 In the questions at the end of each chapter, the ethics icon will call your attention to a question focused on ethics of communication.

Careers in Communication

Studying communication prepares you for a wide array of careers. As we've seen, communication skills are essential to success in most fields. In addition, people who major in communication are particularly sought after in a number of occupations.

Research

Communication research is a vital and growing field of work. A great deal of study is conducted by academics who combine teaching and research in faculty careers. In this book, you'll encounter much academic research, and you'll be able to evaluate what we learn from doing it.

In addition to academic research, communication specialists do media research on everything from message production to marketing. Companies want to know how people respond to different kinds of advertisements, logos, and labels for products. Before a new cereal or beer is named, various names are test marketed to test how customers will respond to different names. In addition, businesses research the audiences reached by different media such as newspapers, magazines, radio, and television.

Education

Clearly, I am biased toward this profession. I find nothing more exciting than opening students' eyes to the power of communication and working with them to improve their skills. Teachers are needed for communication classes and often whole curricula in secondary schools, junior colleges, colleges, universities, technical schools, and community colleges.

The level at which a person is qualified to teach depends on how extensively she or he has pursued the study of communication. Generally, a bachelor's degree in communication education and certification by the Board of Education are required of teachers in elementary and secondary schools. A master's degree in communication qualifies a person to teach at community colleges, technical schools, and some junior colleges and colleges. The doctoral degree (Ph.D.) in communication generally is required for a career in university education, although some universities offer short-term positions to people with master's degrees (NCA, 2000).

Although generalists are preferred for many teaching jobs, at the college level instructors can focus on areas of communication that particularly interest them. For instance, my research and teaching focus on interpersonal communication and gender and communication. A colleague in my department specializes in environmental advocacy and social movements. Other college faculty concentrate in areas such as oral traditions, intercultural communication, family communication, organizational dynamics, and the influence of mass media on cultural values.

Communication educators are not limited to communication departments. In recent years, more and more people with advanced degrees in communication have taken positions in medical and business schools or as communication managers in corporations. Good doctors not only have specialized medical knowledge but also know how to listen sensitively to patients, how to explain complex problems and procedures, and how to provide comfort, reassurance, and motivation. Similarly, good businesspeople know not only their businesses but also how to explain them to others, how to present themselves and their companies or products favorably, and so on. Because communication is essential for doctors and businesspeople, increasing numbers of medical and business schools are creating permanent positions for communication specialists.

Media Production, Criticism, and Analysis

Increasingly, students are attracted to careers in mass communication and new technologies of communication. There are many careers paths in media production, all of which demand good communication skills. News reporters need skill not only in presenting information clearly, but also in conducting interviews and fostering trust so that people will open up to them. To be effective, broadcasters must speak clearly and engagingly, and they must communicate credibly. Script writing and directing also require solid understanding of human communication.

Analysis and criticism of media are valuable career paths. Because our society is media saturated, we rely on people with expertise in criticism and analysis to help us understand what media are doing: whether they are representing information fairly or not, whether they are biased, whether they are offering messages that are healthy or harmful to us. One of my colleagues studies and teaches about new media, emphasizing the ways that virtual reality affects our understandings of ourselves and our expectations of relationships. A former student of mine is now pursuing graduate study in mass communication so that she can specialize in teaching media literacy to others.

Training and Consulting

Consulting is another field that welcomes people with backgrounds in communication. Businesses want to train employees in effective group communication skills, interview techniques, and group and team work. Some large corporations such as IBM have entire departments devoted to training and development. People with communication backgrounds often join these departments and work with the corporation to design and teach courses or workshops that enhance employees' communication skills.

Communication specialists may also join or form consulting firms that provide particular kinds of communication training to government and businesses. One of my colleagues consults with organizations to help them develop work teams that interact effectively. I sometimes prepare workshops for educators who want to learn how to use communication to stimulate students' interest and learning. Other communication specialists work with politicians to improve their presentation style and sometimes to write their speeches. I consult with attorneys on

A consultant is making a presentation to a group of clients. What do you notice about her nonverbal communication? Does it suggest she is confident, competent, relaxed?

© Charles Gupton/CORBIS

cases involving charges of sexual harassment and sex discrimination: I help them understand how particular communication patterns create hostile, harassing environments, and I collaborate with them to develop trial strategy. Other communication consultants work with attorneys on jury selection and advise attorneys' courtroom communication strategies.

Human Relations and Management

Because communication is the foundation of human relations, it's no surprise that many communication specialists build careers in human development or human relations departments of corporations. People with solid understandings of communication and good personal communication skills are effective in careers such as public relations, personnel, grievance management, negotiations, customer relations, and development and fundraising (NCA, 2000). In each of these areas, communication skills are the primary requirements.

Communication degrees may also open the door to careers in management. The most important qualifications for management are not technical skills but the ability to interact with others and communicate effectively. Good managers are skilled in listening, expressing their ideas, building consensus, creating supportive work environments, and balancing task and interpersonal concerns in dealing with others. Developing skills such as these gives communication majors a firm foundation for effective management.

Experiencing Communication in Our Lives

CASE STUDY: A Model Speech of Self-introduction

The following speech is featured on the *Communication in Our Lives* CD-ROM included with this book. Once you've launched the CD, click on the "Speech Interactive" icon, and, from the Speech Menu, select "Speech of Self-introduction" to watch the audiovisual presentation of Mona Bradsher's speech. Improve your own communication skills by reading, watching, listening to, evaluating, and critiquing this sample speech.

Analyze the speech by applying the principles covered in this chapter, and respond to the prompts that accompany the video, which you can access by clicking on "Evaluation" and "Critique." After answering the evaluation questions provided and writing a brief critique of the speech, you can click on the "Done" button to compare your responses with the ones I suggest. Additional analysis questions are available in print at the end of this chapter and on the book's website.

Speech of Self-introduction

My name is Mona Bradsher. I'm a junior, although I'm older than most juniors at our school. In my speech, I want to introduce you to a very persuasive 6-year-old. Through her, you'll learn why I have come back to finish my college degree after a 10-year break from school.

When I was 18, I started college like many of you. But, unlike most of you, I dropped out when I was 20—in the middle of my sophomore year. I left school because I wanted to get married to a man named Jason. I'd met him the summer before, and we had fallen in love. Jason and I did get married, and we had a daughter, Sasha.

In my case, the fairy tales were wrong: Jason and I didn't live happily ever after. We divorced just before our fifth wedding anniversary. So there I was: a 25-year-old single mom with a child to raise. My income was pretty low because I didn't have enough education to get a job that paid well. It was hard to get by on what I could make and the small amount of child support that Jason paid each month. We didn't go out for dinners or movies, but we did eat healthy meals at home. We didn't have money for a nice car, so we used the bus system. When Sasha was sick, I'd have to work extra hours to pay the doctor's bill and the cost of prescriptions. So it was tough, and I worried that as my daughter got older I wouldn't be able to support her on what I made. I felt really trapped.

Last year Sasha started school. One day she came home and told me her teacher had taught them about the importance of education. Sasha's teacher had put up a chart showing the difference between what high school graduates and college graduates make. Her teacher also talked about how education helps every person fulfill his or her individual potential and lead a fuller life. The teacher told all the children that education was the most important gift they could give themselves. So Sasha said to me, "Mommy, now that I'm going to school, why don't you go too?"

At first I told Sasha that Mommy had to work to pay for our apartment and food, but Sasha would have none of that. She insisted that I should go to school. I don't know how many of you have tried to argue with a very insistent 6-year-old, but take my word for it: You can't win! Because my daughter was so persistent, I checked around and found out there is an educational loan program specifically for older students who want to return to school and complete their education. I qualified, and I'll keep getting the loan as long as I maintain a B average. So far, my average is above that because Sasha and I have a deal: We study together for 3 hours every night.

And that's why I'm here now. That's why I've come back to finish my degree after a 10-year break. I'm here because my daughter reminded me of the importance of education. If I can learn an important lesson from a 6-year old, then I can learn other important lessons from the teachers at our university.

Chapter Summary

In this chapter, we took a first look at human communication. First, we defined communication, and then we discussed its value in our lives. Next, we considered a series of models, the most accurate of which is transactional. The transactional model emphasizes that communication is a systemic process in which people interact to create and share meanings.

Like most fields of study, communication has developed over the years. Today, communication scholars and teachers are interested in a range of communication activities. This broad range of areas is held together by abiding interests in symbolic activities, meanings, critical thinking, and ethics, which together form the foundation of personal, interpersonal, and social life.

In the final section of this chapter, we considered some career opportunities open to people who specialize in communication. The modern field of communication offers an array of exciting career paths for people who enjoy interacting with others and who want the opportunity to be part of a dynamic discipline that evolves to meet changing needs and issues in our world.

Communication in Our Lives ONLINE

In addition to presenting "Speech Interactive" and the case studies' multimedia scenarios, the *Communication in Our Lives* CD-ROM provides quick access to the *Communication in Our Lives* website and Info-Trac College Edition. The website is online at http://communication.wadsworth.com/woodciol4, but you can only access this book's premium web content when you link to the site directly through the book's CD.

 The *Communication in Our Lives* website features interactive tools for learning and reviewing the chapter's concepts and key

terms, including electronic versions of the "For Further Reflection and Discussion" questions that appear below and a review quiz.

The website also provides updated web links and additional InfoTrac College Edition activities. If required, you can e-mail completed chapter activities or the quizzes to your instructor.

Key Concepts

communication, *11*	interpersonal communication, *21*	process, *11*
content level of meaning, *12*	intrapersonal communication, *20*	relationship level of meaning, *12*
critical thinking, *30*	noise, *19*	symbol, *11*
feedback, *18*	organizational culture, *26*	systemic, *11*

For Further Reflection and Discussion

1. Using each of the models discussed in this chapter, describe communication in your family. What does each model highlight and obscure? Which model best describes and explains communication in your family?

2. Interview a professional in the field you plan to enter to discover what kinds of communication skills she or he thinks are most important for success. Which of those skills do you already have? Which skills do you need to develop or improve? How can you use this book and the course it accompanies to develop the skills you will need to be effective in your career?

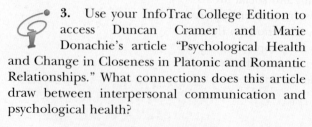 **3.** Use your InfoTrac College Edition to access Duncan Cramer and Marie Donachie's article "Psychological Health and Change in Closeness in Platonic and Romantic Relationships." What connections does this article draw between interpersonal communication and psychological health?

4. Go to the National Communication Association's website and read the association's Credo on Communication Ethics: http://www.natcom.org/conferences/ethics/ethicsconfcredo99.htm. How do the ethical principles in this credo apply to each area of the communication field?

5. Go to the placement office on your campus and examine descriptions of available positions. Record the number of job notices that call for "excellent written and oral communication skills."

6. Think critically about the impact of new technologies of communication. In what ways do you think these new technologies might improve professional, personal, and social communication? In what ways might they be counterproductive?

Experiencing Communication in Our Lives

Questions for Analysis and Discussion

Review the video of Mona Bradsher's speech of self-introduction that you watched when completing this chapter's case study (pages 34–35), or, if you haven't seen it yet, watch it for the first time. If you didn't previously finish the Evaluation questions and Critique activity included on the CD-ROM, do so now, and then respond to the following questions, which are also available on the book's website under "Activities for Chapter 1."

1. Does Mona's speech give you a sense of who she is?

2. Did Mona's introduction catch your attention and give you a road map of what she covers in her speech?

3. How did Mona create identification between herself and listeners?

4. How did examples add to the speech?

5. Was the quotation from Sasha effective?

6. Did Mona's conclusion create closure by returning to the theme of her introduction?

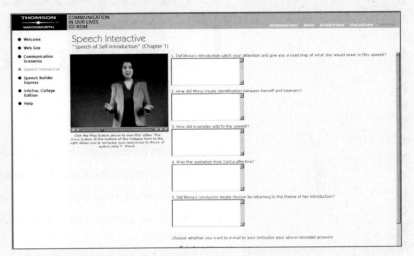

2

Perception and Communication

Focus Questions

1. How does perception affect communication?

2. How does communication affect perception?

3. How do people from different cultures perceive and communicate differently?

4. How can we increase our ability to perceive people, relationships, and situations?

5. How does the self-serving bias affect perception?

© Richard Younker

A few years ago, I interviewed male inmates in a medium-security prison as part of a research project. On the first day of interviewing, I arrived at the security station through which all visitors must pass. The guard looked at me and asked me to remove my necklace, a simple gold chain. "The inmates could use that to choke you," he explained. He then checked my purse, a standard procedure for visitors. He found my key ring, which is a 2-inch piece of metal shaped like a cat's head with pointed ears. Pointing to the ears of the cat, he said, "This could be a weapon—they could put out your eyes." For the same reason, the guard confiscated my nail clipper and file. The guard also suggested that on future visits I not wear a belt.

The guard's experience with prisoners led him to perceive dangers that I didn't notice. The necklace that I saw as a fashion accent he saw as a means of choking me. What I perceived as a key ring and manicure tools he saw as potential weapons. Our perceptions differed because we had different experiences and roles, which affected the meanings we assigned to things such as necklaces, key chains, and nail files and clippers.

This chapter focuses on **meaning,** which is the heart of communication. Meaning is the significance we attach to phenomena such as words, actions, people, objects, and events. To understand how humans create meanings for themselves and their activities, we need to explore the relationship between perception and communication. As we will see, these two processes interact so that each affects the other in an ongoing cycle of influence. In other words, perception shapes how we understand others' communication and how we ourselves communicate. At the same time, communication influences our perceptions of people and situations. The two processes are intricately intertwined. Perceptions—and the differences between people's perceptions—are major influences on human communication.

The words we use to describe others, situations, and experiences keenly affect how we perceive them. If you are going to a friend's home for a party and tell yourself in advance that it will be dull and boring, you're likely to perceive it precisely that way. If you meet someone fun at the party, you may perceive the party as fun. We communicate with others according to how we perceive and define ourselves, them, and situations; when our labels limit what we perceive, we may miss opportunities. At the same time, how we communicate may influence what happens around us and, thus, what we perceive.

To understand how perception and communication interact, we will first discuss the three-part process of perception. Next, we'll consider factors that affect our perceptions. Finally, we will explore ways to improve our abilities to perceive and communicate effectively.

Human Perception

The external world and our experiences in it do not have intrinsic meaning. They gain meaning only when we perceive and attach significance to them. **Perception** concerns how we make sense of the world and what happens in it.

Perception is an active process of selecting, organizing, and interpreting people, objects, events, situations, and activities. The first thing to notice about this definition is that perception is an active process. We don't passively receive stimuli. Instead, we actively work to make sense of ourselves, others, and interactions. To do so, we focus on only certain things, and then we organize and interpret what we have selectively noticed. What something means to us depends on which aspects of it we attend to and how we organize and interpret what we notice.

Perception consists of three processes: selecting, organizing, and interpreting. These processes are overlapping and continuous, so they blend into and influence one another. They are also interactive, so each affects the other two.

Selection

Stop for a moment and notice what is going on around you right now. Is there music in the background? Is the room warm or cold, messy or clean, large or small, light or dark? Is there laundry in the corner waiting to be washed? Can you smell anything—food cooking, the lingering odor of cigarette smoke, traces of cologne? Is anyone else in the room? Do you hear other conversations or music? Is the window open? Can you hear muted sounds of activities outside? What about this book—what do you notice about it? On what kind of paper is your book printed? Is the type large, small, easy to read? How do you like the size of the book, the colors used, the design of features in the text? Now think about what's happening inside you: Are you alert or sleepy, hungry, comfortable? Do you have a headache or an itch anywhere?

You probably weren't conscious of most of these phenomena when you began reading the chapter. Instead, you focused on reading and understanding the material in the book. You narrowed your attention to what you defined as important in this moment, and you were unaware of many other

We notice things that stand out or differ from their surroundings.

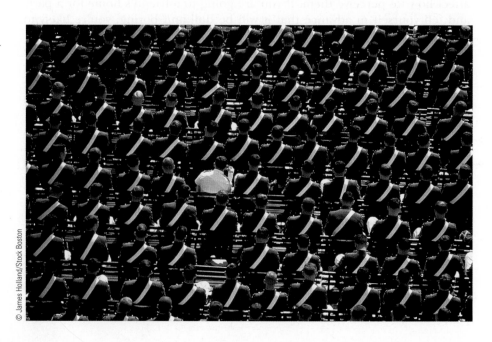

© James Holland/Stock Boston

things going on around you. This is typical of how we live our lives. We can't attend to everything in our environment, because there is simply far too much there, and most of it isn't relevant to us at a particular time.

Which stimuli we notice depends on a number of factors. First, some qualities of external phenomena draw attention. For instance, we notice things that **STAND OUT** because they are immediate, relevant, or intense. We're more likely to hear a loud voice than a soft one and to notice a bright shirt than a drab one. Second, our perceptions are influenced by the acuity of our senses. For instance, if you have a good sense of smell, you're likely to notice a person's cologne or to be enticed by the smell of freshly baked bread. People who have limited or absent vision or hearing often develop greater sensitivity in their other senses.

Third, change or variation compels attention, which is why we may take for granted all the pleasant interactions with a friend and notice only the tense moments. The impact of change is also why effective public speakers sometimes raise or lower their voices or move to a new place in a room where they are speaking: The change focuses listeners' attention on them and their message.

Sometimes we deliberately influence what we notice. Self-indication occurs when we point out certain things to ourselves. In many ways, education is a process of learning to indicate to ourselves things we hadn't seen. Right now you're learning to indicate to yourself that you perceive selectively, so in the future you will be more aware of the selectivity of your perceptions. In English courses, you learn to notice how authors craft characters and use words to create images. In French classes, you learn to notice that nouns and adjectives are ordered differently in French sentences and English ones. In every case, we learn to perceive things that previously we didn't notice.

–Abby–

Until I took a course in women's studies, I didn't realize how biased textbooks are. We learned that a lot of textbooks use more examples and pictures with men than with women and that men are described more actively. Once the teacher pointed this out, I noticed it in my chemistry and psychology books and in the texts for other classes. Now, no matter what I read, I notice whether women are underrepresented.

What we select to notice is also influenced by who we are and what is going on inside us. Our motives and needs affect what we see and don't see. If you've just broken up with someone, you're more likely to notice attractive people at a party than if you are in an established romantic relationship. Motives also explain the oasis phenomenon, in which thirsty people stranded in a desert see an oasis although none really exists.

Our expectations further affect what we notice. We are more likely to perceive what we expect to perceive. This explains the phenomenon of the **self-fulfilling prophecy,** in which a person acts in ways consistent with how they have learned to perceive themselves. Children who are told they are unlovable may perceive themselves that way and notice rejecting but not affirming communication from others. We have an ethical responsibility to consider how our communication affects others' perceptions of themselves.

Communication Highlight

—Lee Teng-hui—

Before I came to school here, I was told that Americans are very pushy, loud, and selfish. For my first few months here, I saw that was true of Americans just as I had been told it would be. It took me longer to see also that Americans are friendly and helpful, because I had not been taught to expect these qualities.

Organization

Once we have selected what to notice, we must make sense of it. We don't simply collect perceptions and string them together randomly; instead, we organize them in ways that make them meaningful to us. The most useful theory for explaining how we organize perceptions is **constructivism,** which states that we organize and interpret experience by applying cognitive structures called **schemata** (singular: *schema*). Originally developed by George Kelly in 1955, constructivism has been elaborated by scholars in communication and psychology. We use four kinds of cognitive schemata to make sense of perceptions: prototypes, personal constructs, stereotypes, and scripts (Fehr, 1993; Hewes, 1995).

Prototypes   A **prototype** is a knowledge structure that defines the clearest or most representative examples of some category (Fehr, 1993). For example, you probably have prototypes of excellent teachers, true friends, great public speakers, and perfect romantic partners. Each of these categories is exemplified by a person who is the ideal case; that's the prototype.

We use prototypes to define categories: Jane is the ideal friend, Luke is the ideal romantic interest, Robin is the ideal work associate. Prototypes exemplify categories into which we place people and other phenomena. We may then consider how close a particular phenomenon is to the prototype for that category. As Alicia's commentary points out, our prototypes can be faulty, leading us to fail to perceive someone as belonging in the appropriate category because they don't match our prototype for the category.

—Alicia—

I was working with a male nurse. Every time he met a new patient, the patient would say, "Hi, doctor." Even when he told them he was a nurse, they treated him as a doctor. No one ever confused me with a doctor. I guess patients just assume that men in white are doctors and women in white are nurses.

Personal Constructs   **Personal constructs** are mental yardsticks that allow us to position people and situations along bipolar dimensions of judgment. Examples of personal constructs are intelligent–not intelligent, responsible–not responsible, kind–not kind, and attractive–not attractive. To size up a person, we measure her or him by personal constructs that we use to think about people. How intelligent, kind, responsible, and attractive is this person? Whereas prototypes help us decide into which broad category a person or situation fits, personal constructs let us make more detailed assessments of particular qualities of phenomena we have selectively perceived. Our personal constructs shape our perceptions because we define something only in terms of how it compares to the constructs we use. Thus, we may not notice qualities of people that aren't covered by the constructs we apply.

Stereotypes   **Stereotypes** are predictive generalizations about people and situations. Based on the category in which we place a phenomenon and how the phenomenon measures up to the personal constructs we apply, we predict what it will do. For instance, if you define someone as conservative, you might stereotype the person as likely to oppose government-funded programs to help disadvantaged citizens, and so forth. You may have stereotypes of fraternity and sorority members, athletes, middle managers, and other groups of people.

Stereotypes may be accurate or inaccurate. They are generalizations, which are sometimes based on facts that are generally true of a group but sometimes on prejudice or assumptions. Even if we have accurate understandings of a group, they may not apply to particular individuals in it. Although most environmentalists don't smoke, a few do. Although college students as a group are more liberal than the population as a whole, some college students are very conservative. A particular individual may not conform to what is typical of her or his group as a whole. Ethical communicators keep in mind that stereotypes are generalizations, which can be both useful and misleading.

What stereotypes do you have of the men in this photograph? Can you identify the basis of your stereotypes of them? What would change your stereotypes of these men?

Communication Highlight

More Complexity, More Categories

Tiger Woods may be a trendsetter in more than the world of golf. When asked what his race is, he replies, "I'm Cablinasian," a term he invented to describe his multiracial heritage: part Caucasian (Ca), Black (bl), Indian (in) and Asian (Strege, 1997). The U.S. Census Bureau seems to be following Tiger's lead. In 1860, the United States had only three categories for race: Black, White, and quadroon. Today, the Census allows people to check more than one racial category. As a result, there are many more recognized racial classifications (Armas, 2001; U.S. Bureau of the Census, 2000; Schmitt, 2001b; Zachary, 2002). Nearly 7 million Americans say they belong to more than one race. The majority of people who identify themselves as multiracial are young—children and teenagers.

The number of multiracial Americans is likely to rise in the years ahead because interracial marriages and domestic partnerships are growing (Nakazawa, 2003a,b; Schmitt, 2001b). In 1970, there were 500,000 interracial unions in the United States; that number had swelled to well over a million by the turn of the century (Clemetson, 2000).

Go to http://www.census.gov to find out about current demographic statistics in the United States. Check the population reports for your state by using the search bar at the right.

© AP/Wide World Photos

Tiger Woods: "I'm Cablinasian."

—Scott—

The stereotype that really ticks me off is "dumb jock." I'm a fullback on the team, and I'm tall and big just like any good fullback. But I'm also a good student. I study, and I put a lot into papers and homework for classes. But a lot of the professors here and the students, too, assume I'm dumb just because I'm an athlete. Sometimes I say something in class, and you can just see surprise all over everyone's face because I had a good idea. When you think about it, athletes have to be smart to do all of their schoolwork plus practice and work out about 30 hours a week.

Scripts   To organize perceptions, we also use **scripts,** which are guides to action based on what we've experienced and observed. Scripts consist of a sequence of activities that define what we and others are expected to do in specific situations.

Many of our daily activities are governed by scripts, although we're often unaware of them. You have a script for greeting casual acquaintances ("Hey, how ya doing?" "Fine. See ya around."). You also have scripts for managing conflict, talking with professors, interacting with superiors on the job, dealing with clerks, and relaxing with friends. Christine Bachen and Eva Illouz (1996) studied 184 people to learn about their views of romance. They found that people have clear scripts for appropriate sequences of events for first dates and romantic dinners. In dating and most of our activities, we use scripts to organize perceptions into lines of action. Prototypes, personal constructs, stereotypes, and scripts are cognitive schemata that we use to organize our thinking about people and situations. They help us make sense of what we notice and help us anticipate how we and others will act in particular situations. Our cognitive schemata reflect our membership in a culture and in specific social groups. As we interact with others, we internalize their ways of classifying, measuring, and predicting interaction in various situations.

Social perspectives are not always accurate or constructive, so we shouldn't accept them unreflectively. For instance, many Westerners have negative and inaccurate perceptions of people from other cultures. Each of us has an ethical responsibility to assess social perspectives critically before relying on them to organize our own perceptions and direct our own activities.

Sharpen Your Skill

Perceiving Others

Pay attention to the cognitive schemata you use the next time you meet a new person. First, notice how you classify the person. Do you categorize her or him as a potential friend, date, co-worker, neighbor? Next, identify the constructs you use to assess the person. Do you focus on physical characteristics (attractive–not attractive), mental qualities (intelligent–not intelligent), psychological features (secure–not secure), or interpersonal qualities (available–not available)? Would different constructs be prominent if you used a different prototype to classify the person? Now, note how you stereotype the person. What do you expect him or her to do, according to the prototype and constructs you've applied? Finally, identify your script: How do you expect interaction to unfold between the two of you?

Interpretation

To assign meaning, we must interpret what we have noticed and organized. **Interpretation** is the subjective process of explaining perceptions to assign meaning to them.

Attributions   **Attributions** are explanations of why things happen and why people act as they do (Fehr, 1993; Fehr & Russell, 1991; Heider, 1958; Kelley, 1967). It's good to remind ourselves that the attributions we make aren't necessarily correct—they are our subjective ways of assigning meaning.

Attributions have four dimensions (Table 2.1). The first is *locus,* which attributes what a person does to either internal factors ("he's sick") or external factors ("the traffic jam frustrated him"). The second dimension is *stability,* which explains actions as resulting from either stable factors that won't change ("She's a Type A person.") or temporary, unstable factors ("She's irritable because she's just had a fight with the boss."). *Scope* is the third dimension, and it defines behavior as part of a global pattern ("He's a mean person.") or a specific instance ("He gets angry when he's tired."). Finally, the dimension of *responsibility* attributes behaviors either to factors people

Table 2.1: Dimensions of Interpersonal Attributions

Locus	Internal	External
Stability	Stable	Unstable
Scope	Global	Specific
Responsibility	Within personal control	Beyond personal control

can control ("She doesn't try to control her outbursts.") or to ones they cannot ("She has a chemical imbalance that makes her moody.").

While I was writing this book, I got an e-mail from Otis, a student who was reading this book for a class at another university. He and his classmates were debating whether scope and stability are really two different dimensions. This is a good question; most global attributions are also stable. However, there are exceptions. For example, you might say that someone is always efficient at work but inefficient during leisure time. In this case, the attribution is stable and specific. If the person were efficient in all spheres of life, the attribution would be stable and global.

Investigations have shown that happy and unhappy couples have distinct attributional styles (Bradbury & Fincham, 1990; Fletcher & Fincham, 1991; Manusov & Harvey, 2001). Happy couples make relationship-enhancing attributions. Such people attribute nice things a partner does to internal, stable, and global reasons that the partner controls ("She got the film because she is a good person who always does sweet things."). Unpleasant things a partner does are attributed to external, unstable, and specific factors and sometimes to influences beyond personal control ("He yelled at me because all the stress of the past few days made him irritable."). In contrast, unhappy couples make relationship-diminishing attributions. They explain nice actions as results of external, unstable, and specific factors ("She got the tape because she had some time to kill today."). Negative actions are seen as stemming from internal, stable, and global factors ("He yelled at me because he is a nasty person who never shows any consideration for anybody else."). Thus, we should be mindful of our attributions because they influence how we experience our relationships.

Sharpen Your Skill

Revising Attributions

Think about an attribution you recently made about a close friend or romantic partner's behavior. Did you explain it as internally or externally caused? Did you label the behavior as stable or unstable, global or specific, and within control or not? Now experiment with changing your attribution. If you attributed the behavior to internal causes (mood, personality), try thinking about it as externally caused (circumstance). If you labeled the behavior as a specific occurrence, try thinking about it as part of a larger pattern. How do changes in your attributions affect how you feel about the behavior and the person?

 To extend your insight into attributions, complete Activity 2.4, "Making Attributions," in your *Student Companion* or online under "Activities for Chapter 2" at the *Communication in Our Lives* website.

The Self-serving Bias   Research indicates that we tend to construct attributions that serve our personal interests (Hamachek, 1992; Sypher, 1984). Thus, we are inclined to make internal, stable, and global attributions for our positive actions and successes. We're also likely to claim that good results come about because of personal control we exerted. On the other hand, people tend to avoid taking responsibility for negative actions and failures by attributing them to external, unstable, and specific factors that are

Communication Highlight

I'm Right, You're Wrong

When you are in conflict with a close friend or romantic partner, how do you see your role and the other person's? Do you often think you were being reasonable and the other person was being unreasonable? Do you tend to see yourself as having good intentions and the other person as having bad ones? If so, you're not alone. In 1999, Astrid Schütz separately asked husbands and wives to describe conflicts between them. Typically, each spouse described the problem as the other's fault. Each spouse saw his or her own behavior as justified and reasonable but described the partner's behavior as unfair, inconsiderate, inappropriate, or wrong. Participants also described their own intentions

positively and their partners' intentions negatively—as unfair, irrational, mean-spirited, and so forth.

Schütz concluded that the self-serving bias is likely to affect how partners perceive themselves, each other, and conflicts between them. Resolution and positive feelings about each other are undermined when each partner perceives himself or herself as behaving well and the other as behaving wrongly. Use your InfoTrac College Edition to read Nancy Shute's brief 2001 article "A Black and White World?" What does she tell you about how people categorize others? Does her article suggest that our tendencies to classify people by race can be changed?

---

beyond personal control. In other words, we tend to attribute our misconduct to outside forces that we can't help but attribute all the good we do to our personal qualities and effort. When it comes to judging others, we tend to be less charitable. If they make mistakes, we're likely to attribute the errors to internal, not external, forces beyond their control (Sedikides et al., 1998). If we have an argument with a romantic partner, we're likely to perceive that person's behaviors as unreasonable or wrong and to see ourselves as reasonable and right (Schütz, 1999). This **self-serving bias** can distort our perceptions, leading us to take excessive credit for what we do well and to abdicate responsibility for what we do poorly.

—Nadine—

My mom wrote the book on self-serving bias. She likes to experiment with cooking, so she tries a lot of new dishes. When one turns out well, she grabs the credit, saying she used just the right touch on spices or knew how to adapt something in the original recipe. But when a dish is bad, she says the recipe was wrong or the store sold her tough meat or the stove didn't hold an even temperature. She feels proud when her dishes turn out well, but she never thinks it's her fault when one is a loser.

We've seen that perception involves three interrelated processes. The first of these, selection, allows us to notice certain things and ignore others. The second process is organization, in which we use prototypes, personal constructs, stereotypes, and scripts to order what we have selectively perceived. Finally, we engage in interpretation by using attributions to explain what we and others do. Although we discussed each of these processes separately, in reality they may occur in different order, and they interact continually.

Influences on Perception

In opening this chapter, I mentioned an incident in which a prison guard's perceptions differed from mine. His experience and priorities as a guard who dealt with dangerous men led him to perceive that certain objects could be dangerous to me or used as weapons against me or others. Being unaccustomed to prison life, I didn't perceive the same things he did. Similarly, able-bodied people may not notice the lack of elevators or ramps in a building, but someone with a physical disability quickly perceives the building as inaccessible.

European American students often don't notice that few people of color are in their classes, but the ethnic ratio is very obvious to African Americans, Native Americans, students with Asian and Hispanic heritages and others who are not European Americans. People who grew up in neighborhoods where everyone knew everyone else are more likely than people from urban areas to notice a lack of neighborliness in some big cities. As these examples illustrate, people differ in how they perceive situations and people. Let's consider some reasons for this.

Physiology

The most obvious reason perceptions vary is that people differ in sensory abilities and physiologies. Music that one person finds deafening is barely audible to another. Salsa that is painfully hot to one diner may seem mild to someone else. On a given day on my campus, students wear everything from shorts and sandals to jackets, indicating that they have different sensitivities to cold. Some people have better vision than others, and still others are color blind.

Our physiological states also influence perception. If you are tired, stressed, or sick, you're likely to perceive a comment from a co-worker as critical of you, but the comment wouldn't bother you if you felt good. If you interact with someone who is sick, you might attribute her irritability to temporary factors rather than to enduring personality. If you're a morning person, you're most alert and creative early in the day; you're likely to notice things in the morning that you don't perceive when your energy level declines later in the day.

Age also influences our perceptions. The older we get, the more complex is our perspective on life and people. Perhaps you think nothing of paying 75 cents for a can of soda, but to a 50-year-old person who recalls paying a nickel for a soda, the current prices may seem high. The extent of discrimination still experienced by women and minorities understandably discourages some young people. I am more hopeful that our society is increasingly accepting of differences because I have seen so many changes in my lifetime. When I attended college, women weren't admitted on an equal basis with men, and almost all students of color attended minority colleges. The substantial progress made during my life leads me to perceive current inequities as changeable.

Culture

The influence of culture is so pervasive that it's hard to realize how powerfully it shapes our perceptions. A **culture** consists of beliefs, values, understandings, practices, and ways of interpreting experience that are shared by a number of people. It is a set of taken-for-granted assumptions that form the pattern of our lives and guide how we think, feel, and act. One of the best ways to recognize the values and structures of a culture is to travel to places with different values, understandings, and codes of behavior.

Communication Highlight

The Burden of the Gift of Sight

Imagine that at 3 years old you contracted a disease that left you blind. Now imagine that at age 51 doctors tell you they can restore your sight. Would you want the operation? That's the question that Shirl Jennings faced, and he chose to let the doctors restore his sight. For Jennings, however, the "gift" of sight turned out to be more of a burden than a blessing.

Accustomed to seeing nothing, he was confused by all the visual images that flooded his senses. He could figure out what things were only by smelling, touching, or tasting them; these highly developed senses were the means by which he had perceived phenomena since age 3. Jennings also had no depth perception, so walking on uneven sidewalks was a challenge, and curbs were frightening. Facial expressions were enigmas to him; he didn't know

how to interpret the sight of furrowed brows or winks. Jennings had been an exceptional masseur who could feel where his clients had tensed nerves, knotted muscles, and so forth; seeing clients' bodies distracted him from feeling their pain and tensions.

Several months after regaining sight, Jennings developed another medical condition that led to deterioration of his eyes. He wasn't upset at all. He said he appreciated the brief experience of sight, but, he says, "It's really easier to be blind than see."

To learn more, see *At First Sight,* a movie based on Shirl Jennings' story.

Source: Blind man finds gift of sight also a burden. (1999, February 1). *Raleigh News and Observer,* p. 7A.

To enhance your awareness of the arbitrary nature of social categories, complete Activity 2.3, "Remaking the Social World," in your *Student Companion* or online under "Activities for Chapter 2" at the *Communication in Our Lives* website.

Consider a few aspects of modern Western culture that influence our perceptions. One characteristic of our culture is the emphasis on technology and its offspring, speed. We expect things to happen fast—almost instantly. Whether it's instant photos, 1-minute copying, or instant messaging, we live at an accelerated pace (Wood, 2000). We send letters by overnight mail, jet across the country, engage in instant messaging and paging, and microwave our meals. Does the cultural emphasis on speed diminish patience and thus our willingness to invest in long-term projects and relationships? In countries such as Nepal and Mexico, life proceeds at a more leisurely pace, and people spend more time talking, relaxing, and engaging in low-key activity.

IT USED TO BE THAT IF A CLIENT WANTED SOMETHING DONE IN A WEEK, IT WAS CONSIDERED A RUSH JOB, AND HE'D BE LUCKY TO GET IT.

NOW, WITH MODEMS, FAXES, AND CAR PHONES, EVERYBODY WANTS EVERYTHING INSTANTLY! IMPROVED TECHNOLOGY JUST INCREASES EXPECTATIONS.

THESE MACHINES DONT MAKE LIFE EASIER – THEY MAKE LIFE MORE HARASSED.

SIX MINUTES TO MICROWAVE THIS?? WHO'S GOT THAT KIND OF TIME?!

IF WE WANTED MORE LEISURE, WE'D INVENT MACHINES THAT DO THINGS *LESS* EFFICIENTLY.

Some cultures are more communal than others.

© Taxi/Getty Images

North America is also a fiercely individualistic culture in which personal initiative and independence are rewarded. Other cultures tend to be more communal, and identity is defined in terms of one's family rather than as an individual quality. In communal cultures, elders are given great respect and care, and children are looked after by the whole community.

Sharpen Your Skill

Noticing Individualism

How do the individualistic values of our culture influence our perceptions and activities? Check it out by observing the following: How is seating arranged in restaurants? Are there large, communal eating areas or private tables and booths for individuals, couples, and small groups?...
....

How are living spaces arranged? How many people live in the average house?..........
....

Do families share homes? How many common spaces and individual spaces are there in homes? ....
....

How many people share a car in your family? How many cars are there in the United States?..
....

How does the Western emphasis on individualism affect your day-to-day perceptions and activities?...
....

In recent years, scholars have realized that we are affected not only by the culture as a whole but also by our particular location, or standpoint, within the culture (Haraway, 1988; Harding, 1991). **Standpoint theory** claims that a culture includes a number of social communities, and each one distinctively shapes the perceptions, identities, and opportunities of its members. Race, ethnicity, gender, economic class, religion or spirituality, age, and sexual orientation are primary standpoints in Western culture. Although we may all realize that our society attaches unequal value to different social groups, each of us fits into only some of those groups. Our perceptions of the world and ourselves are shaped by our experiences as members of the particular groups to which we belong.

In the earliest writing on standpoint, philosopher Georg Wilhelm Friedrich Hegel (1807) pointed out that standpoints reflect power positions in social hierarchies. Hegel's original observations focused on the system of slavery, which, he noted, was perceived very differently by masters and slaves. Extending Hegel's point, we can see that those in positions of power have a vested interest in preserving the system that gives them privileges. Thus, they are unlikely to perceive its flaws and inequities or to notice how the system disadvantages others. On the other hand, those who have less power in a society are more able to discern inequities and discrimination (Collins, 1998; Harding, 1991).

Women and men, as social groups, have different standpoints. Although not every woman or man conforms to the standpoint typical of his or her sex, general patterns exist. For instance, the caregiving often associated with women results not primarily from maternal instinct but from socialization that teaches women to care for others, notice who needs what, and defer their own needs to take care of others (Ruddick, 1989; Wood, 1994d). Research shows that men who are primary caregivers also tend to become nurturing, accommodating, and sensitive to others' needs as a consequence of being in the caregiver role (Kaye & Applegate, 1990).

–Carl–

I'll admit that when Krista and I had a child, I expected Krista to stay home and take care of her. Actually, we both did, and that worked fine for three months. Then Krista got cancer, and she was in the hospital for weeks and then in and out for nearly a year for treatments. Even when she was home, she didn't have the energy to take care of little Jennie. I had to take over a lot of the child care. Doing that really changed me in basic ways. I had to learn to tolerate being interrupted when I was working. I had to tune into what Jennie needed and learn to read her. Before that experience, I thought women had a maternal instinct. What I learned is, anyone can develop a parental sensitivity.

Gendered standpoints are also evident in communication during marital conflict. Researchers have found that conflict erodes wives' love for their husbands more than it affects husbands' love for their wives (Gottman, 1994a, 1994b; Huston, McHale, & Crouter, 1986; Kelly, Huston, & Cate, 1985). This makes sense in light of related research showing that husbands generally exercise more power over decision making, so they usually prevail in conflict. Naturally, the winners of conflicts are more satisfied than the losers.

Gendered standpoints explain the difference between the amount of effort women and men, in general, invest in communication that maintains relationships. Socialized into the role of "relationship experts," women are often expected by others and themselves to take care of relationships (Tavris, 1992; Wood, 1994d, 2005). This may explain why women tend to be more aware than many men of problems in relationships and to be more

Caregiving is a skill we learn through socialization.

© Margaret Miller/Photo Researchers, Inc.

active in addressing them (Brehm, 1992). It may also shed light on why many women exercise professional leadership in more personal and relationship-oriented ways than many men do (Helgesen, 1990; Natalle, 1996).

Social Roles

Our perceptions are also shaped by social roles that others communicate to us. Messages that tell us we are expected to fulfill particular roles, as well as the actual demands of those roles, affect how we perceive and communicate.

Speakers are more likely than audience members to notice the acoustics of presentation rooms. Teachers often perceive classes in terms of how interested students seem, whether they have read material, and whether they engage in class discussion. On the other hand, many students perceive classes in terms of the number and difficulty of tests, whether papers are required, and whether the professor is interesting. In working on this book, I concentrated on ideas, information, and organization. In addition to noticing those aspects of a book, my editor focused on layout, design, and marketing issues that didn't occur to me.

The careers people choose influence what they notice and how they think and act. Doctors are trained to be highly observant of physical symptoms, and they may detect a physical problem before a person knows that she or he has it. For example, some years ago at a social gathering, a friend of mine who is a doctor asked me how long I had had a herniated disk. Shocked, I told him I didn't have one. "You do," he insisted, and sure enough, a few weeks later an MRI exam confirmed a ruptured disk in my back. His medical training enabled him to perceive subtle changes in my posture and walk that I hadn't noticed.

Cognitive Abilities

In addition to physiological, cultural, and social influences, perception is also shaped by our cognitive abilities. How elaborately we think about situations and people, and the extent of our personal knowledge of others, affect how we select, organize, and interpret experiences.

Cognitive Complexity   People differ in the number and types of knowledge schemata they use to organize and interpret people and situations. **Cognitive complexity** refers to the number of constructs used, how abstract they are, and how elaborately they interact to shape perceptions. Most children have fairly simple cognitive systems. They rely on few schemata, focus more on concrete categories than on abstract ones, and often don't perceive relationships between different perceptions. For instance, infants may call every man "Daddy" because they haven't learned more complex ways to distinguish among men.

Adults also differ in cognitive complexity. If you perceive people only as nice or mean, you have a limited range for perceiving others. Similarly, people who focus exclusively on concrete data tend to have less sophisticated understandings than people who also perceive psychological data. For example, you might notice that a co-worker is assertive, tells jokes, and talks to others easily. These are concrete perceptions. At a more abstract, psychological level, you might reason that the concrete behaviors you observe reflect a secure, self-confident personality. This is a more sophisticated cognition because it integrates three perceptions to develop an explanation of why the person acts as she or he does.

What if you later find out that the person is very reserved in one-to-one conversations? Someone with low cognitive complexity would have difficulty integrating the new information into prior observations. Either the new information would be dismissed because it doesn't fit, or the most recent information would alter the former perception, and the person would be redefined as shy. A more cognitively complex person would integrate all the information into a coherent account. Perhaps a cognitively complex thinker would conclude that the person is very confident in social situations but less secure in more personal ones.

Cognitively complex people tend to be flexible in interpreting complicated phenomena and integrating new information into their thinking about people and situations. Less cognitively complex people are likely to ignore information that doesn't fit neatly with their impressions or to use it to replace the impressions they had formed (Delia, Clark, & Switzer, 1974). Either way, they fail to recognize some of the nuances and inconsistencies that are part of human life. The complexity of our cognitive systems affects the fullness and intricacy of our perceptions of people and interpersonal situations. Cognitively complex people also tend to communicate in more flexible and appropriate ways with a range of others. This probably results from their ability to recognize differences in people and to adapt their own communication accordingly.

Person-centered Perception   **Person-centered perception** reflects cognitive complexity because it entails abstract thinking and a broad range of schemata. Person-centered perception is the ability to perceive another as a unique and distinct individual. Our ability to perceive others as unique depends both on the general ability to make cognitive distinctions and on our knowledge of particular others. As we get to know individuals, we gain insight into how they differ from others in their groups ("Rob's not like most campus politicos"; "Janet's more flexible than most managers."). The more we interact with another and the greater variety of experiences we have together, the more insight we gain into that person. As we come to understand others, we fine-tune our perceptions of them in a process that continues throughout the life of relationships.

-Dave-

First dates are the pits. It's so awkward to keep up a conversation with somebody you don't really know. You try one line of talk and it flops, so you try another. Then she starts something up, but you can't really get into that. It usually takes about three dates with a new girl before I feel comfortable about how to interact. I wish there were some easier way to get to know new people.

Person-centered perception is not the same as empathy. **Empathy** is the ability to feel with another person—to feel what she or he feels. Feeling with another is an emotional response. Because feelings are guided by our own experiences and emotions, it may be impossible to feel exactly and completely what another person feels. A more realistic goal is to try to recognize another's perspective and adapt your communication to how she or he perceives situations and people. With commitment and effort, we can learn a lot about how others see the world, even if that differs from how we see it.

When we take others' perspectives, we try to grasp what something means to them and how they perceive things. We can't really understand someone else's perspective when we're judging whether it is right or wrong, sensible or crazy. Instead, we have to let go of our own perspective and perceptions long enough to enter the thoughts and feelings of another person. Doing this allows us to understand issues from the other person's point of view so we can communicate more effectively. You might learn why your boss thinks something is important that you've been disregarding. You might find out how a friend interprets your behavior in ways inconsistent with what you intend to communicate.

At a later point in interaction, we may choose to express our own perspective or to disagree with another's views. This is appropriate and impor-

Taking the perspective of others is a foundation of effective communication.

© Stone/Getty Images

tant in honest communication, but voicing our own views is not a substitute for the equally important skill of recognizing another's perspective. In sum, differences based on physiology, culture, standpoint, social roles, and cognitive abilities affect what we perceive and how we interpret others and experiences. In the final section of the chapter, we consider ways to improve the accuracy of our perceptions.

Enhancing Communication Competence

To be a competent communicator, you need to realize how perception and communication affect each other. We'll elaborate on the connection between perception and communication and then discuss guidelines for enhancing communication competence.

Perceptions, Communication, and Abstraction

Words crystallize perceptions. When we name feelings and thoughts, we create precise ways to describe and think about them. But just as words crystallize experiences, they can also freeze thought. Once we label our perceptions, we may respond to our own labels rather than to actual phenomena. In a classic experiment, Trotter (1975) showed a film of a traffic accident to people. After seeing the film, some of the viewers were asked how fast the cars were going when they smashed into one another. Other viewers were asked how fast the same cars in the same film were going when they collided or bumped into each other. Viewers consistently perceived the cars as going faster when they smashed than when they bumped or collided.

  To replicate this experiment yourself, complete Activity 2.1, "Observing the Impact of Language on Perceptions," in your *Student Companion* or online under "Activities for Chapter 2" at the *Communication in Our Lives* website.

Just as in this experiment, the labels we use in everyday life can affect our perceptions of what is happening. Consider this situation. Suppose you get together with five others in a study group, and a student named Andrea monopolizes the whole meeting with her questions and concerns. Leaving the meeting, one person says, "Gee, Andrea is so selfish and immature! I'll never work with her again." Another person responds, "She's not really selfish. She's insecure about her grades in this course, so she was hyper in the meeting." Chances are these two people will perceive and treat Andrea differently depending on whether they label her selfish or insecure. The point is that the two people don't respond to Andrea herself but to how they label their perceptions of her.

Communication is based on a process of abstracting from complex stimuli. Our perceptions are not equivalent to the complex reality on which they are based, because total reality can never be fully described or even apprehended. This means that what we perceive is a step removed from stimuli because perceptions are always partial and subjective. We move a second step from stimuli when we label a perception. We move even further from stimuli when we respond not to behaviors or our perceptions of them but to the judgments we associate with the label we have imposed. This process can be illustrated as a ladder of abstraction, as shown in Figure 2.1 (Hayakawa, 1962, 1964; Korzybski, 1948).

Figure 2.1
Perception, Communication, and Abstraction

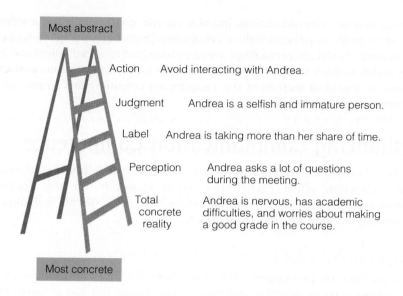

Most abstract

Action — Avoid interacting with Andrea.

Judgment — Andrea is a selfish and immature person.

Label — Andrea is taking more than her share of time.

Perception — Andrea asks a lot of questions during the meeting.

Total concrete reality — Andrea is nervous, has academic difficulties, and worries about making a good grade in the course.

Most concrete

Guidelines for Enhancing Competence

Thinking of communication as a process of abstracting suggests ways to enhance competence in interaction. Five guidelines help us avoid the problems abstraction may invite.

Recognize That All Perceptions Are Subjective

Our perceptions are partial and subjective because each of us perceives from a unique perspective. A class you find exciting may put another student to sleep. Writing is a creative, enjoyable activity for some people and a tedious grind for others. There is no truth or falsity to perceptions; they represent what things mean to individuals based on their individual social roles, cultural backgrounds, cognitive abilities, standpoints and physiology. Effective communicators realize that perceptions are subjective and don't assume that their own perceptions are the only valid ones.

Avoid Mind Reading

One of the most common problems in communication is **mind reading**—assuming we understand what another person thinks or perceives. When we mind read, we act as if we know what's on another's

mind, and this can get us into trouble. Marriage counselors identify mind reading as one of the behaviors that contributes to interpersonal tension (Gottman, 1993). According to communication scholar Fran Dickson (1995), one exception may be mind reading between spouses in long-lasting marriages. After living together for a long time, partners may be able to mind read with great accuracy.

For the most part, however, mind reading is more likely to harm than help communication. Mind reading invites problems when we say things such as "I know why you're upset" (has the person *said* she or he is upset?) or "You don't care about me" (maybe the other person is too preoccupied or worried to be as attentive as usual). We also mind read when we tell ourselves we know how somebody else will feel or react or what they'll do. The truth is we don't really know—we're only guessing. When we mind read, we impose our perceptions on others, which can lead to resentment and misunderstandings because most of us prefer to speak for ourselves.

–Pat–

I got into a lot of trouble mind reading my girlfriend. When we first started dating, I made a lot of assumptions about what Anne would or wouldn't like and then acted as if what I assumed was a fact. For example, once I got tickets for a concert that I "knew" she'd want to go to, but she had to go out of town that weekend. Another time, I "knew" she'd want to take a study break during exam week, so I got a pizza and stopped by. She was really irritated because she had eaten early and was settled in for a heavy review session. I finally realized I should ask her what she wants instead of assuming I know. We've gotten along a lot better since I figured that out.

Check Perceptions with Others   Because perceptions are subjective and mind reading is ineffective, we need to check our perceptions with others. Perception checking is an important communication skill because it helps people understand each other and their relationships. To check perceptions, you should first state what you have noticed. For example, a person might say, "Lately you've seemed less attentive to me." Second, the person should check to see whether the other perceives the same thing: "Do you feel you've been less attentive?" Third, it's appropriate to offer alternative explanations of your perceptions ("It might be that you're annoyed with me or that you're stressed out at work or that you're focused on other things."). Finally, you may ask the other person to clarify how she or he perceives the behavior and the reasons for it ("What do you think is going on?"). If the other person doesn't share your perceptions, ask him or her to explain the behaviors on which your perception is based ("Why have you wanted to be together less often and seemed distracted when we've talked lately?").

Speak tentatively when checking perceptions to minimize defensiveness and encourage open dialogue. Just let the other person know you've noticed something and would like him or her to clarify his or her perceptions of what is happening and what it means. It's also a good idea to check perceptions directly with the other person. It is more difficult to reach a shared understanding with another person when we ask someone else to act as a go-between or when we ask others whether they agree with our perceptions of a third person.

Perception Checking

Becoming skillful at checking perceptions takes practice. Enhance your skill by doing the following:

1. The next time you catch yourself mind reading, stop. Tell the other person what you are noticing and invite her or him to explain how she or he perceives what's happening. Does the person agree with you about what you noticed? If you agree, then find out how the other person interprets what you've noticed.

2. Focus on perception checking for three days so you have lots of chances to see what happens. Keep a tally of the times your mind reading was inaccurate.

Distinguish between Facts and Inferences Competent communicators know the difference between facts and inferences. A fact is a statement based on observation or other data. An inference involves an interpretation that goes beyond the facts. For example, it is a fact that my partner, Robbie, forgets a lot of things. Based on that fact, I might infer that he is thoughtless. Defining Robbie as thoughtless is an inference that goes beyond the facts. The "fact" of his forgetfulness could equally well be explained by preoccupation or general absentmindedness.

Distinguishing Facts from Inferences

Identify each of the following statements as either a fact or an inference.

1. There are fifty states in the United States. ....
2. HIV/AIDS is caused by immoral sexual activity. ....
3. Women have a maternal instinct. ....
4. German shepherds tend to suffer hip dysplasia. ....
5. Students who come to class late are disrespectful. ....
6. Acid rain destroys trees. ....
7. College students earn money to buy clothes. ....
8. Older students aren't career oriented. ....
9. Evelyn scored 378 on the LSAT exam. ....
10. Evelyn would not do well in law school. ....

Numbers 1, 4, 6, and 9 are facts; 2, 3, 5, 7, 8, and 10 are inferences.

  For additional practice distinguishing between facts and inferences, complete Activity 2.2, "Distinguishing Facts from Inferences" in your *Student Companion* or online under Activities for Chapter 2 at the *Communication in Our Lives* website.

It's easy to confuse facts and inferences because we sometimes treat the latter as the former. When we say, "He is irresponsible," we make a statement that sounds factual, and we may then regard it that way ourselves. To avoid this tendency, substitute more tentative words for "is." For instance, "Robbie's behaviors seem thoughtless" is more tentative than "Robbie is thoughtless." Tentative language helps us resist the tendency to treat inferences as facts.

Sharpen Your Skill

Using Tentative Language

For the next 24 hours, listen carefully for language that blurs facts and inferences. Listen for words such as *is* and *are*, which imply factual knowledge. When others say someone or something "is" a certain way, are they making a factual statement or an inference? When you use *is*-words, do you have a factual foundation for your statements?

Substitute tentative language for *is*-language. How does this language affect your perceptions and judgments?

Monitor the Self-serving Bias   Because the self-serving bias can distort perceptions, we need to monitor it carefully. Monitoring the self-serving bias also has implications for how we perceive others. Just as we tend to judge ourselves generously, we may also be inclined to judge others too harshly. Monitor your perceptions to see whether you attribute others' successes and admirable actions to external factors beyond their control and their short-comings and blunders to internal factors they can (should) control. If you do this, substitute more generous explanations for others' behaviors, and notice how that affects your perceptions of them.

Perceiving accurately is a communication skill that can be developed. Following the five guidelines we have discussed will allow you to perceive more carefully and accurately.

Experiencing Communication in Our Lives

CASE STUDY: College Success

The conversation scripted here is featured as a multimedia scenario on the *Communication in Our Lives* CD-ROM included with this book. Once you've launched the CD, click on the "Communication Scenarios" icon, and, from the Scenarios Menu, select "College Success" to watch the video. Improve your own communication skills by reading, watching, listening to, critiquing, and analyzing this communication encounter.

Analyze the scenario by applying the principles covered in this chapter, and respond to the prompts that accompany the video, which you can access by clicking on "Analysis." After completing the conversation analysis and answering the questions, you can click on the "Done" button to compare your responses with the ones I suggest. Additional analysis questions are available in print at the end of this chapter and on the book's website.

Jason Harris/© 2001 Wadsworth

Your friend Jim tells you about a problem he's having with his parents. According to Jim, his parents have unrealistic expectations of him. He tends to be an average student, usually making Cs, a few Bs, and an occasional D in his courses. His parents are angry that his grades aren't better. Jim tells you that when he went home last month, his father said this: "I'm not paying for you to go to school so you can party with your friends. I paid my own way and still made Phi Beta Kappa. You have a free ride, and you're still just pulling Cs. You just have to study harder."

Now, Jim says to you, "I mean, I like to hang out with my friends, but that's got nothing to do with my grades. My dad's this brilliant guy, I mean, he just cruised through college, he thinks it's easy. I don't know how it was back then, but all my classes are hard. I mean, no matter how much studying I do I'm not gonna get all As. What should I do? I mean, how do I convince them that I'm doing everything I can?"

Chapter Summary

In this chapter, we've explored human perception, which involves selecting, organizing, and interpreting experiences. These three processes are not separate in practice; they interact so that each one affects the others. What we selectively notice affects what we interpret and evaluate. In addition, our interpretations act as lenses that influence what we notice in the world around us. Selection, interpretation, and evaluation interact continuously in the process of perception.

Perception is shaped by many factors. Our physiological abilities and conditions affect what we notice and how astutely we recognize stimuli around us. In addition, our cultural backgrounds and standpoints in society shape how we see and interact with the world. Social roles are another influence on perception. Thus, professional training and roles in families affect what we notice and how we organize and interpret it. Finally, perception is influenced by cognitive abilities, including cognitive complexity, person-centered perception, and perspective taking.

Thinking about communication as a process of abstracting helps us understand how perception works. We discussed five guidelines for avoiding the problems abstraction sometimes causes. First, realize that all perceptions are subjective, so there is no absolutely correct or best understanding of a situation or a person. Second, because people perceive differently, we should avoid mind reading or assuming we know what others are perceiving. Third, it's a good idea to check perceptions, which involves stating how you perceive something and asking how another person perceives it. A fourth guideline is to distinguish facts from inferences. Finally, avoiding the self-serving bias is important because it can lead us to perceive ourselves too charitably and to perceive others too harshly.

When we label our selective perceptions, we abstract or notice only some of the stimuli around us. Consequently, we can't see aspects of ourselves and others that our labels don't highlight. Realizing this encourages us to be more sensitive to the power of language and to make more considered choices about how we use it.

Communication in Our Lives ONLINE

In addition to presenting the case studies' multimedia scenarios, the *Communication in Our Lives* CD-ROM provides quick access to the *Communication in Our Lives* website and InfoTrac College Edition. The website is online at http://communication.wadsworth.com/woodciol4, but you can only access this book's premium web content when you link to the site directly through the book's CD.

The *Communication in Our Lives* website features interactive tools for learning and reviewing the chapter's concepts and key terms, including electronic versions of the "For Further Reflection and Discussion" questions that appear below and a review quiz.

The website also provides updated web links and additional InfoTrac College Edition activities. If required, you can e-mail completed chapter activities or the quizzes to your instructor.

Key Concepts

attributions, *45*	meaning, *39*	schemata, *42*
cognitive complexity, *53*	mind reading, *56*	scripts, *44*
constructivism, *42*	perception, *39*	self-fulfilling prophecy, *41*
culture, *48*	personal constructs, *43*	self-serving bias, *47*
empathy, *54*	person-centered perception, *53*	standpoint theory, *50*
interpretation, *45*	prototype, *42*	stereotypes, *43*

For Further Reflection and Discussion

1. Identify an occasion when you engaged in the self-serving bias. Explain what you did, using the language of attributions.

2. Identify ethical issues involved in perceiving. What ethical choices do we make—perhaps unconsciously—as we selectively perceive, organize, and interpret others, particularly people whom we see as different from us in important ways?

3. Use your InfoTrac College Edition to read David DeCremer's 2000 article, "Effect of Group Identification on the Use of Attributions." How is what DeCremer calls "the group-serving bias" similar to the self-serving bias? Have you ever engaged in the group-serving bias?

4. How does electronic communication affect your perceptions of others? When you communicate electronically with someone you haven't met, what do you selectively perceive? How is that different from what you perceive when talking with someone face to face?

5. Use the ladder of abstraction to analyze your perceptions and actions in a specific communication encounter. First, identify the concrete reality, what you perceived from the totality, the labels you assigned, and the resulting inferences and judgments. Second, return to the first level of perception and substitute different perceptions—other aspects of the total situation you might have perceived selectively. What labels, inferences, and judgments do the substitute perceptions invite? With others in the class, discuss the extent to which our perceptions and labels influence "reality."

Experiencing Communication in Our Lives

Questions for Analysis and Discussion

Review the video of the scenario entitled "College Success" that you watched when completing this chapter's case study (pages 59–60), or, if you haven't seen it yet, watch it for the first time. If you didn't previously finish the Analysis questions included on the CD-ROM, do so now, and then respond to the following questions, which are also available on the book's website under "Activities for Chapter 2."

1. Both Jim and his parents make attributions to explain his grades. Describe the dimensions of Jim's attributions and those of his parents.

2. How might you assess the accuracy of Jim's attributions? What questions could you ask him to help you decide whether his perceptions are well founded or biased?

3. What constructs, prototypes, and scripts seem to operate in Jim's and his parents' thinking about college life?

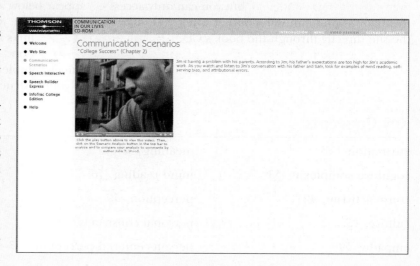

4. What could you say to Jim to help him and his parents reach a shared perspective on his academic work?

CHAPTER 3

Communication and Personal Identity

1. How does your self-concept affect your communication?

2. How does communication affect your self-concept?

3. How do cultural perspectives influence how you perceive yourself and others?

4. How can you improve your self-concept?

© Comstock

Kate is a 35-year-old mother of two children. She may also be a teacher or an attorney or a secretary. Once, she was a child. One day, she may be retired and a grandmother. Like Kate, who you are changes over time. When you were 5 or 6 you probably defined yourself as your parents' son or daughter. In doing so, you implicitly recognized sex, race, and social class as parts of your identity. In high school, you may have described yourself in terms of academic abilities ("I'm better at math than at history"), athletic achievements ("I'm on the soccer team"), leadership positions ("I'm president of the Drama Club"), your social circle ("I'm in the college-bound group" or "My best friend is Cindy"), or future plans ("I'm going to study business when I go to college").

If you entered college shortly after completing high school, you're probably starting to see yourself in terms of a major, a career path, and perhaps a relationship you hope will span the years ahead. If you worked or committed to a relationship before starting or returning to college, you probably already have a sense of yourself as a professional and a family member, and you may see the role of student as only one of many in your life. By now you've probably made some decisions about your sexual orientation, spiritual values, and political and social beliefs. Throughout your life, you'll continually create your personal identity.

As you think about the different ways you've defined yourself over the years, you'll realize that the self is not fixed firmly at one time and constant thereafter. Instead, the self is a process that evolves and changes throughout our lives. Interactions with others rank among the experiences that have the greatest impact on how we see ourselves. In this chapter, we explore how the self develops continually through communication with others.

What Is the Self?

The **self** is a process that involves internalizing and acting from social perspectives that we learn in the process of communication. At first this may seem like a complicated way to define the self. As we will see, however, this definition directs our attention to some important insights into what is very complicated: the human self.

The Self Arises in Communication with Others

The most basic insight into the self is that it isn't something we are born with. Instead, the self develops only as we communicate with others and participate in a society. From the moment we enter the world, we interact with others. We learn how they see us, and we internalize many of their views of the world and of who we are and should be. Through internal dialogues, or intrapersonal communication, we remind ourselves of the social values and the views of ourselves that we have learned in interaction with family members, peers, and our society.

Communication with Family Members For most of us, family members are the first important influence on how we see ourselves. Parents and other family members communicate who we are and what we are worth through *direct definitions, identity scripts,* and *attachment styles.*

Direct definition, as the name implies, is communication that explicitly tells us who we are by labeling us and our behaviors. For instance, parents might say, "You're my little girl" or "You're a big boy" and thus communicate to the child what sex he or she is. Having been labeled *boy* or *girl*, the child then pays attention to other communication about boys and girls to figure out what it means to be a certain sex. Parents' own gender stereotypes typically are communicated to children, so daughters are often cautioned to be careful. Girls may also be told, "Don't play rough," "Be nice to your friends," and "Don't mess up your clothes." Sons, on the other hand, are more likely to be told, "Go out and get 'em," "Stick up for yourself," and "Don't cry." As we hear these messages, we pick up our parents' and society's gender expectations. Direct definition also takes place as family members respond to children's behaviors. If a child clowns around and parents respond by saying, "What a cutup; you really are funny," the child learns to see herself or himself as funny. If instead the parents respond by saying, "Quit fooling around and be serious," the child is likely to view playfulness as negative and to try to eliminate it in himself or herself. If a child is praised for dusting furniture, being helpful is reinforced as part of the child's self-concept. Positive labels enhance our self-esteem: "You're so responsible," "You are smart," "You're sweet," "You're great at soccer." Negative labels can damage children's self-esteem: "You're a troublemaker," "You're stupid," and "You're impossible" are messages that can demolish a child's sense of self-worth.

From direct definition, children learn what parents value, and this shapes what they come to value. For instance, in my family reading was highly valued. I still have vivid memories of being shamed for a B in reading on my first-grade report card. I recall just as keenly the excessive praise heaped on me when I won a reading contest in fourth grade. By then, I had learned how to get my parents' approval. This is an example of how family members provide direct definitions of who we are and, just as important, who we are supposed to be.

Identity scripts are another way family members communicate who we are and should be. Psychologists define identity scripts as rules for how we are supposed to live and who we are supposed to be (Berne, 1964; Harris,

Communication Highlight

A Script for Raising Resilient Children

Psychologists Robert Brooks and Sam Goldstein have some advice for parents who want to raise resilient children—ones who can spring back from defeats and disappointments and become stronger (Brooks & Goldstein, 2001). They encourage parents to identify children's strengths and build on them instead of focusing on children's weaknesses. Brooks and Goldstein call this recognizing "islands of competence."

One child Brooks and Goldstein studied was having difficulty reading at school. The child's parents were fussing at their son for not reading well and pushing him to do better. With counseling, the parents learned to identify

artwork as one of their son's "islands of competence." They began praising his artwork and encouraging him to create signs for the lobby of his school. In preparing the signs, the boy had to learn to read and write, but he was able to do so because he was building from a strength, not a weakness.

 Use your InfoTrac College Edition to read Michael Myerhoff's 2001 article "Self-fulfilling Prophecy." Notice the language parents use when labeling children. Identify examples of direct definition by parents.

© Taxi/Getty Images

How we see ourselves is strongly influenced by how our family sees us.

1969). Like the scripts for plays, identity scripts define our roles, how we are to play them, and basic elements in the plot we are supposed to have for our lives. Usually, identity scripts reflect the values and heritage of our families. Think back to your childhood to identify some of the principal scripts that operated in your family. Did you learn, "We are responsible people," "Save your money for a rainy day," "Always help others," "Look out for yourself," or "Live by God's word"? These are examples of identity scripts people learn in families.

We aren't allowed to coauthor or even edit our initial identity scripts, because adults have power, and usually children aren't conscious of learning scripts. As adults, however, we are no longer passive tablets on which others can write out who we are. We have the capacity to review the identity scripts that were given to us and to challenge and change those that do not fit the selves we now choose to be.

Sharpen Your Skill

Reflecting on Your Identity Scripts

Try to recall identity scripts your parents communicated about who you were or were supposed to become. Can you hear them saying, "Our people do . . ." or "Our people don't . . ."? Can you recall messages that told you what and who they expected you to be? As a youngster, did you hear, "You'll go to college" or "You're going to be a doctor"?

Now review key identity scripts. Which ones make sense to you today? Are you still following any that are irrelevant to your present life or that are at odds with your personal values and goals? If so, then commit to changing scripts that aren't productive for you or that conflict with values you hold. You can rewrite identity scripts now that you're an adult.

  For additional insight into identity scripts that were communicated to you, complete Activity 3.6, "Identifying Your Identity Scripts," in your *Student Companion* or online under "Activities for Chapter 3" at the *Communication in Our Lives* website.

Finally, parents communicate who we are through **attachment styles,** patterns of parenting that teach us who we and others are and how to relate to others. From extensive studies of interaction between parents and children, John Bowlby (1973, 1988) developed the theory that we learn attachment styles in our first important relationship—usually with parents. They communicate how they see us, others, and relationships. In turn, we are likely to learn their views and internalize them as our own. The first relationship is especially important because it forms expectations for later relationships (Bartholomew & Horowitz, 1991; Miller, 1993). Four distinct attachment styles have been identified (Figure 3.1).

Secure attachment styles develop when the primary caregiver responds in a consistently attentive and loving way to a child. In response, the child develops a positive sense of self-worth ("I am lovable") and a positive view of others ("People are loving and can be trusted"). People with secure attachment styles tend to be outgoing, affectionate, and able to handle the challenges and disappointments of close relationships without losing self-esteem.

Fearful attachment styles are cultivated when a caregiver communicates in negative, rejecting, or abusive ways to a child. Children who are treated this way often infer that they are unworthy of love and that others are not loving. Thus, they learn to see themselves as unlovable and others as rejecting. Not surprisingly, they are apprehensive about relationships. Although they may want close bonds with others, they fear that others will not love them and that they themselves are not lovable.

Caregivers who are disinterested, rejecting, or abusive may also lead children to develop dismissive attachment styles, which make them tend to dismiss others as unworthy. Consequently, children develop a positive view of themselves and a low regard for others and relationships. This may lead them to regard relationships as unnecessary and undesirable.

Last is the anxious/ambivalent attachment style, which is the most complex of the four. Each of the other three styles results from some consistent pattern of treatment by a caregiver. However, the anxious/ambivalent style is fostered by inconsistent treatment from the caregiver. Sometimes the adult is loving and attentive, at other times indifferent or rejecting. The caregiver's communication is not only inconsistent but also unpredictable. He or she may respond positively to something a child does on Monday and react negatively to the same behavior on Tuesday. Naturally, this unpredictability creates anxiety in a child who depends on the caregiver (Miller, 1993).

© Spencer Grant/Stock Boston

We learn attachment styles in our interactions with parents.

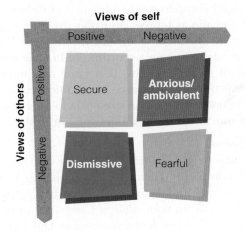

Views of self

Positive | Negative

Views of others

Positive | Secure | Anxious/ambivalent

Negative | Dismissive | Fearful

Figure 3.1
Styles of Attachment

Because children tend to assume that adults are right, they often believe they themselves are the source of any problem—that they are unlovable or deserve others' abuse.

In adult life, people who have anxious/ambivalent attachment styles know that others can be loving and affirming, but they also know that others can hurt them and be unloving. Reflecting the pattern displayed by the caregiver, people with anxious/ambivalent attachment styles often are inconsistent themselves. One day they invite affection; the next day they deny needing closeness. An interesting study by Tim Cole and Laura Leets (1999) found that people with anxious/ambivalent attachment styles often form relationships with television characters. They may feel it is safer to be in relationships with television characters than with real people. Unless we consciously work to change the attachment styles we learned in our first close relationships, they tend to affect how we communicate in our adult relationships (Bartholomew & Horowitz, 1991; Belsky & Pensky, 1988; Bowlby, 1988; Guerrero, 1996). However, we can modify our attachment styles by challenging unconstructive views of us communicated in our early years and by forming relationships that foster secure connections today.

Communication with Peers A second major influence on our self-concepts is communication with peers. From childhood playmates to work associates, friends, and romantic partners, we interact with peers throughout our lives. As we do, we gain further information about how others see us, and this refines how we see ourselves. As we communicate with peers, we engage in **social comparison,** which involves comparing ourselves with others to form judgments of our own talents, attractiveness, abilities, leadership skills, and so forth. We gauge ourselves in relation to others in two ways. First, we compare ourselves with others to decide whether we are like them or different from them. Are we the same age, color, religion? Do we have similar backgrounds and social and political beliefs?

Assessing similarity and difference allows us to decide with whom we fit. Research has shown that people generally are most comfortable with others who are like them, so we tend to gravitate toward those we regard as similar (Whitbeck & Hoyt, 1994). However, this tendency can deprive us of the diverse perspectives of people whose experiences and beliefs differ from our own. When we interact only with people who are like us, we impoverish our understandings of ourselves and the world.

We also use social comparison to measure ourselves in relation to others. Am I as good a goalie as Jenny? Do I play the guitar as well as Sam? Am I advancing as quickly as others who were hired when I was? We form and continuously refine our self-image according to how we compare with others on various criteria of judgment. This is normal and necessary if we are to develop realistic self-concepts. However, we should beware of using inappropriate standards of comparison. It isn't realistic to judge our attractiveness in relation to that of movie stars and models or our athletic ability in relation to that of professional athletes.

 To heighten insight into your own social comparisons, complete Activity 3.3, "Recognizing Your Social Comparisons," and Activity 3.1, "Comparing Your Views and Others' Views of Yourself," in your *Student Companion* or online under "Activities for Chapter 3" at the *Communication in Our Lives* website.

-Kevin-

I learned more about myself and about being White when I was assigned to room with a Black guy my freshman year. I'd never interacted much with Blacks, and I'd never had a Black friend, but I got really close with my roommate. Carl helped me see a lot of things I take for granted that he can't because of his skin. For example, people assume I'm here because I earned a good record in high school, but a lot of people think Carl got in just because he's Black and the college had to meet its minority quota. His SAT was higher than mine and so are his grades, but people believe I'm smart and he's a quota admission.

Communication with Society   A third influence on our self-concepts is interaction with society in general. The perspectives of society are revealed to us in two ways. First, they surface as we communicate with others who have internalized cultural values and express them to us. In the course of conversations, we learn how society regards our sex, race, sexual orientation, and socioeconomic class. We also learn what others regard as effective public speaking, skillful group leadership, good managerial style, and so forth.

As we interact with people, we don't simply collect their individual perspectives. Rather, we organize all of the discrete perspectives into an overall understanding of the views of society as a whole. For example, Western society encourages children to be individuals and to form separate families in adulthood. In contrast, traditional Indian culture emphasizes collective identity, and households under the same roof often include grandparents, aunts, uncles, and cousins (Lustig & Koester, 1999). Western society also encourages competition, whereas many Asian societies teach children to place priority on cooperation and teamwork (Yum, 2000).

Social perspectives are also communicated to us through media. When we read popular magazines and go to movies, we are inundated with messages about how women and men are supposed to look and act. Desirable women usually are thin, young, and beautiful, and attractive men are strong, in charge, and successful (Holtzman, 2000; Wood, 2005). Media shape teens' views of sex and sexuality—what is appropriate and cool (Brown, Steele, & Walsh-Childers, 2002).

The institutions that organize our society further communicate social perspectives by the values they uphold (Coté & Levine, 2002). For example, our judicial system reminds us that as a society we value laws and punish those who break them. The institution of marriage communicates society's view that when people marry they become a single unit. The number of schools and the levels of education inform us that as a society we value learning.

At the same time, institutions reflect prevailing social prejudices. For instance, we may be a lawful society, but wealthy defendants often can buy better "justice" than poor ones. The way our society currently defines marriage communicates that same-sex unions are not considered legitimate. Similarly, although we claim to offer equal educational opportunities to all, students whose families have money and influence often can get into better schools than students whose families lack such resources. These and other values are so thoroughly woven into the fabric of our culture that we learn them with little effort or awareness.

The Self-fulfilling Prophecy   One particularly powerful way in which communication shapes the self is the self-fulfilling prophecy, which we discussed in Chapter 2. Self-fulfilling prophecies operate when we act in ways that bring about expectations or judgments of ourselves. If you have done poorly in classes where teachers didn't seem to respect you and have done well with teachers who thought you were smart, then you know what a self-fulfilling prophecy is. The prophecies that we act to fulfill usually are first communicated to us by others. Because we often internalize others' perspectives, we may label ourselves as they do and then act to fulfill our own labels.

When I was 7 years old, my parents enrolled me in a 25-person swimming class. Unlike most of the other children, I didn't catch on quickly. The teacher modeled floating, then told us to try it. The other children floated; I sank. The teacher swam a lap, then told us to try it. The other children zipped across the water; I went under. After 3 weeks, the teacher told me I would never learn to swim. For 43 years, I believed that and didn't try to swim. When I went to the beach with friends, they'd frolic in the water and I'd stay on the beach. The few times I did venture into the water, I got in trouble and others had to rescue me. While I was writing this book, a friend of mine challenged my statement that I couldn't swim. He said he could teach me if I wanted to learn. And he did, by giving me a few hours of one-on-one coaching, which the teacher had not given me at age 7. Now I can float with ease and swim well enough to go into the ocean or a pool. For 43 years I internalized the label "nonswimmer," and it became a self-fulfilling prophecy for me.

−Terry−

I can really identify with the self-fulfilling prophecy idea. In the second grade, my family moved from our farm to a city where my dad could find work. The first week of class in my new school, we had show and tell. When it was my turn, as soon as I started talking the other kids started laughing at me. I had been raised on a farm in the rural South, and the other kids were from the city. They thought I talked funny, and they made fun of my accent—called me "hillbilly" and "redneck." From then on, I avoided public speaking like the plague. I thought I couldn't speak to others. Last year I finally took a course in public speaking, and I made a B. It took me a long time to challenge the label that I was a bad public speaker.

Like Terry and me, many of us believe things about ourselves that are inaccurate. Sometimes labels that were once true aren't any longer, but we continue to believe them and act to fulfill them. In other cases, the labels were never valid, but we are trapped by them anyway. Unfortunately, children often are labeled "slow" or "stupid" when the real problem is that they have physiological difficulties such as impaired vision or hearing. Even when the true source of difficulty is discovered, it may be too late; the children may have already internalized a destructive self-fulfilling prophecy.

The Self Is Multidimensional

Although we use the word *self* as if it referred to a single entity, in reality the self has many dimensions. You have a physical self: how large, attractive, and athletic you are, what color your skin is, and whether you are male or female. In addition, you have perceptions of your cognitive self, including your intelligence, the ways you think, and the things that interest you. You also have an emotional self-concept. Are you interpersonally sensitive? Do you have a hot temper? Are you sentimental? Are you generally optimistic or cynical?

You also have a social self. Some people are extraverted, whereas others are more reserved. Our social selves also include our roles: daughter or son, student, worker, parent, volunteer, partner in a committed relationship. Finally, each of us has a moral self that consists of ethical and spiritual principles we believe in and try to follow. As Carlyle points out, the different dimensions of ourselves sometimes seem at odds with one another.

–Carlyle–

On my own, like with friends or family, I'm pretty quiet—even shy, you could say. But my job requires me to be real outgoing and sociable. I tend bar, and people expect me to kid around and talk with them and stuff. Believe me, if I were as quiet with my customers as I am with my friends, my tips would drop to nothing. It's like when I'm in my work role, I'm Mr. Hail-fellow-well-met, but away from work I'm pretty reserved.

The Self Is a Process

The self develops over time—it is a process. We don't enter the world with a clear sense of ourselves. A baby perceives being held by the father as a unified sensation in which infant and father are one. A baby perceives no boundaries between its mouth and a nipple, or its foot and a tickle by the mother. As an infant has a range of experiences and as others respond to him or her, the child gradually begins to develop **ego boundries,** which define when the self stops and the rest of the world begins. This is the beginning of a self-concept: the realization that one is a separate entity.

–Michelle–

My daughter is 11 months old, and she's just beginning to realize she is a distinct person. Until the last month or so, she didn't recognize her hands or feet as hers. I used to point to her foot and say "Lynne's foot," and then she'd point to my hand or my foot and say "Lynne foot." She thought she was part of whatever was around her. Now she doesn't. If I ask where Lynne's foot is, she points to her foot. If I point to my foot and say Lynne's foot, she shakes her head no or giggles.

In the first years of life, infants begin to differentiate themselves from the rest of the world, and the self starts to develop. They listen to and observe others to define themselves and to become competent in the identities others assign to them (Kohlberg, 1958; Piaget, 1932/1965). For instance, children start working early on being competent females or males. They identify females and males and use them as models for their own performances of gender. In like manner, children figure out what it takes to be nice, tough, and responsible, and they work to become competent at displaying those qualities.

Of course, the ways we define ourselves vary as we mature. Struggling to be a good mud cake maker at age 4 gives way to striving for popularity in high school and succeeding in professional and family roles later in life. A person who was anxious about speaking at age 16 may become a confident speaker by age 25. (If you're interested in reducing communication anxiety, you may want to read the section in Chapter 15 that discusses it.)

Some people feel uneasy with the idea that the self is a process, not a thing. We want to believe there is some stable, enduring core that is our essence—our true, unchanging identity. Of course, we all enter the world with certain biological abilities and limits, which constrain the possibilities of who we can be. Someone without the genes to be tall and coordinated, for instance, probably is not going to be a star forward in basketball, and a person who has poor fine-motor control is unlikely to become a renowned pianist. Beyond genetic and biological limits, however, we have considerable freedom to create who we will be.

The Self Internalizes and Acts from Social Perspectives

We've already noted that in developing a self, we internalize, or take inside ourselves, others' perspectives on us. To elaborate that idea, we will now explore how we internalize both the general perspective of our society and the perspectives of particular others who are significant in our lives.

Particular Others   We first encounter the perspectives of **particular others.** As the term implies, these are the viewpoints of specific people who are significant to us. Mothers, fathers, siblings, and often day-care providers are particular others who are significant to most infants. In addition, some people include as family members aunts, uncles, grandparents, and others who live together or nearby. Hispanic and African American families, in general, are extended, so children in these families often have a great many particular others who affect how they come to see themselves (Gaines, 1995; Hecht, Jackson, & Ribeau, 2003).

–Shennoa–

My grandmother was the biggest influence on me. I lived with her while my mama worked, and she taught me to take myself seriously. She's the one who told me I should go to college and plan a career so that I wouldn't have to depend on somebody else. She's the one who told me to stand up for myself and not let others tell me what to do or believe in. But she did more than just tell me to be a strong person. That's how she was, and I learned just by watching her. A lot of who I am is modeled on my grandmother.

As children interact with particular others, they learn how others see them. This is the beginning of a self. Notice that the self starts from outside—from others' communicating their views of who we are. In other words, we must first get outside ourselves to get into ourselves. We first see ourselves in terms of how particular others define us. If parents communicate to a child that she or he is special and cherished, the child will come to see herself or himself as worthy of love. On the other hand, children whose parents communicate that the children are not wanted or loved may come to think of themselves as unlovable.

The process of seeing ourselves through others' eyes is called **reflected appraisal.** It means that we see ourselves in terms of the appraisals reflected in others' eyes. The process has also been called the "looking-glass self" because others are mirrors who reflect who we are (Cooley, 1912). Reflected appraisals are not confined to childhood but continue throughout our lives. Sometimes a teacher is the first to see potential that a student has not recognized in him- or herself. When a teacher communicates that a student is smart, the student may come to see herself that way. In professional life, co-workers and supervisors reflect their appraisals of us when they communicate that we're on the fast track, average, or not suited to our position. When we speak in public, audience responses reflect appraisals of our effectiveness. The appraisals that others communicate shape how we see ourselves. In turn, how we see ourselves affects how we communicate. Thus, if you see yourself as an interesting conversationalist, you're likely to communicate that confidence when you talk with others.

Sharpen Your Skill

Your Looking-glass Self

Identify three people who have been or are particularly important to you. For each person, identify one self-perception you have that reflects the appraisal of you communicated by that person.

Now, imagine that you'd never known each of the three people. Describe how you would be different. How would your self-image change? For instance, Shennoa (see commentary) might think she would be less independent had her grandmother not influenced how she sees herself.

Trace the way you see yourself to the appraisals that particular others have reflected.

Prepare a 2-minute presentation in which you describe one of the people you've identified as a looking glass for yourself. Explain how this person has influenced the way you see yourself. You may want to look ahead to Part Three for guidelines on preparing a speech.

The Generalized Other The second social perspective that influences how we see ourselves is called the **perspective of the generalized other.** The generalized other is the collection of rules, roles, and attitudes endorsed by the whole social community in which we live (Mead, 1934). In other words, the generalized other is overall society. In the process of socialization, most individuals internalize the perspective of the generalized other and thus

We see ourselves in the looking glass of others' eyes.

come to share that perspective. The generalized other is culture specific; the values, codes of conduct, roles, rules, and so forth of the generalized other reflect the distinct history and character of a given culture at a particular time. Modern Western culture emphasizes gender, race, sexual orientation, and economic class as central to personal identity (Andersen & Collins, 2001; Wood, 1995b, 1996b, 2004). Each of these social groupings represents a standpoint, which we discussed in Chapter 2.

North American culture views race as a primary aspect of personal identity. The Caucasian race historically has been favored and privileged in the United States. In the early years of this country, it was considered normal and right for White men to own Black women, men, and children and to require them to work for no wages and in poor conditions. Later, it was considered natural that White men could vote but Black men could not. White men had rights to education, professional jobs, ownership of property, and other basic freedoms that were denied to Blacks. Clearly, racial prejudice has diminished substantially. Even so, the upper levels of government, education, and business are dominated by Caucasian men, while people of color continue to fight overt and covert discrimination in admission, hiring, and advancement. The color of one's skin makes a difference in how society perceives and treats us and, by extension, in how we may perceive ourselves and the opportunities open to us (Lareau, 2003).

–Wen-Shu–

My family moved here when I was 9 years old. Because I look Asian, people make assumptions about me. They assume I am quiet (true), I am good at math (not true), and I defer to men and elders (true with regard to elders, but not men). People also see all Asians as the same, but Taiwanese are as different from mainland Chinese as French Caucasians are from U.S. Caucasians. The first thing people notice about me is my race, and they make too many assumptions about what it means.

Gender, another important facet of identity in Western culture, also is communicated through social practices and institutions. Historically, men—particularly White men—have been seen as more valuable and entitled to privileges than women. In the 1800s, women weren't allowed to own property, attend college, or vote. Although there has been great progress in achieving equality between the sexes, in some respects women and men still are not considered or treated as equal. From the pink and blue blankets that hospitals wrap around newborns to unequal salaries earned by women and men, gender discrimination is a persisting fact of modern life. Given the importance our society places on gender, it is no wonder that one of the first ways children learn to identify themselves is by sex (Wood, 1996b). When my niece, Michelle, was 4 years old, I asked her who she was. Her first response was, "I'm a girl." Only after identifying her sex did she describe her family, her likes and dislikes, and other parts of herself.

Western cultures have strong gender prescriptions. Girls and women are expected to be caring and cooperative, whereas boys and men are supposed to be independent, assertive, and competitive. Consequently, women who assert themselves or compete are likely to receive social disapproval, to be called "unfeminine," or to be criticized in other ways for violating gender prescriptions. Men who refuse to conform to social views of masculinity and who are gentle and caring risk being labeled "wimps." Gender prescriptions

also specify ideal body images—tall, slender and muscular for men; slender or thin and not too tall for women. Our sex, then, makes a great deal of difference in how others view us and how we may come to see ourselves.

—Erin—

I've been called "bitch" by a lot of the people I work with. My job is to schedule plumbing repairs for people. So I have to tell the crew what their schedules are each day and who has to be where when. When the guys don't like their assignments, they try to get me to change them. If I say no, they call me "bitch" or other names. Before I took this job, a guy did the scheduling and nobody ever challenged the schedules he set up, much less called him names for telling them what to do.

A third aspect of identity that cultural communication establishes as salient is sexual orientation. Our overall society communicates that heterosexuality is normal and right not only directly but also through privileges given to heterosexuals but denied to gay men, lesbians, bisexuals, transsexuals, and transgendered people. For example, a woman and man who love each other can be married and have their commitment recognized religiously and legally. Two men or two women who love each other and want to be life partners are not allowed to marry, although many localities now recognize domestic partnerships. Heterosexual spouses can obtain insurance coverage for their partners and will them money tax free, but people with other sexual orientations cannot. Although biases against sexual orientations and identities are decreasing, they still very much affect how we are viewed and treated.

Today, committed relationships between members of the same sex are viewed differently from years ago.

—Sandi—

I've known I was lesbian since I was in high school, but only in the last year have I come out to others. As soon as I tell someone I'm lesbian, they see me differently. Even people who have known me a long time act like I've developed spots or something. Some of my girlfriends don't want to hug or touch me anymore like they think I'm suddenly going to come on to them. Guys act as if I'm from another planet. It's really strange that sexual orientation makes so much difference in how others see you. I mean, relative to other things like character, personality, and intelligence, who you sleep with is pretty unimportant.

A fourth dimension of identity, socioeconomic class, is also central to the generalized other's perspective in Western culture. Our socioeconomic class affects everything from the money we make to the schools, jobs, and lifestyles we see as possibilities for ourselves (Bornstein & Bradley, 2003; Lareau, 2003). Members of the middle and upper classes assume that they will attend college and enter good professions, yet people from the working class often are directed toward vocational training regardless of their academic abilities (Langston, 1992). In such patterns, we see how the perspective of the generalized other shapes our identities and our concrete lives.

–Rochelle–

I got so mad in high school. I had a solid A average, and ever since I was 12 I had planned to go to college. But when the guidance counselor talked with me at the start of my senior year, she encouraged me to apply to a technical school that is near my home. When I said I thought my grades should get me into a good college, she did this double-take, like, "Your kind doesn't go to college." My parents both work in a mill and so do all my relatives, but does that mean that I can't have a different future? What really burned me was that a lot of girls who had average grades but came from "the right families" were told to apply to colleges.

It's important to realize that social perspectives on aspects of identity interact with one another. Race intersects gender, so women of color often experience double oppression and devaluation in our culture (Higginbotham, 1992; Lorde, 1992). Class and sexual orientation also interact: Homophobia, or fear of homosexuals, is particularly pronounced in the working class, so a lesbian or gay man in a poor community may be socially ostracized (Langston, 1992). Race and class also tend to intersect. For instance, a working-class person of a socially devalued race may suffer greater discrimination than a working-class person of a privileged race. Class and gender are also interlinked; women are far more likely than men to live at the poverty level (Stone, 1992). Intersections of race and class mean that minority members of the working class often are not treated as well as working-class Whites.

As we internalize the perspective of the generalized other, we come to share many of the views and values of our society. Shared understandings are essential for collective life. If we all made up our own rules about when to stop and go at traffic intersections, the number of accidents would skyrocket. If each of us operated by our own inclinations, there would be no shared standards regarding rape, murder, robbery and so forth.

Yet some social views are not as constructive as traffic rules and moral codes. The generalized other's unequal valuing of different races, genders, and sexual orientations fosters discrimination against whole groups of people just because they don't fit what society defines as normal or good. In a related way, social perspectives affect how we see ourselves relative to what our society currently defines as normal and right. Each of us has an ethical responsibility to exercise critical judgment about which social views we personally accept and use as guides for our own behaviors, attitudes, and values. This suggests a fourth proposition about the self.

Social Perspectives on the Self Are Constructed and Variable

The generalized other's perspective is not fixed. It is constructed and variable. This implies that it can be changed if members of a society challenge existing norms and values.

Constructed   Social perspectives are constructed in particular cultures at specific times to support dominant ideologies, or the beliefs and traditions of those in power. For example, it was advantageous to White plantation owners to define Africans as slaves and as inferior human beings. Doing so supported the privileges that White landowners enjoyed. When we reflect on social values, we realize that they are arbitrary and tend to serve the interests of those who benefit from prevailing values.

Variable   The constructed and arbitrary nature of social values becomes especially obvious when we consider how greatly values differ between cultures and within particular cultures over time. For example, in Sweden, Denmark, and Norway, marriages between members of the same sex are given legal and social recognition.

Prescriptions for femininity and masculinity also vary widely between cultures. In some places, men are emotional and dependent, and women are assertive and emotionally controlled (Wood, 2005). The meanings of femininity and masculinity also vary over time within a particular culture. In the 1700s and 1800s, women in the United States were defined as too delicate to engage in hard labor. During World Wars I and II, however, women were expected to do "men's work" while men were at war. When the men returned home, society once again decreed that women were too weak to perform in the labor market, and they were reassigned to home and hearth. Social prescriptions for men also have changed. The rugged he-man who was the ideal in the 1700s used his six-shooter to dispose of unsavory rustlers and relied on physical strength to farm. After the Industrial Revolution, physical strength and bravado gave way to business acumen, and money replaced muscle as a sign of manliness. As women, men, and families change, ideals of femininity and masculinity continue to evolve.

Some cultures recognize more than two genders and allow people to choose whether to live as women or as men (Brown, 1997; Nanda, 2004). In many countries south of the United States, mixed-race marriages are common and accepted. Even what counts as race has changed over times in societies ranging from America to South Africa (Manning, 2000). The individualistic ethic so prominent in the United States is discouraged in many countries, particularly Asian and African ones (Gudykunst & Lee, 2002; Hecht, et al, 2003).

The meaning of homosexuality has also been revised over time in Western culture. Although much prejudice still exists, it is gradually diminishing. Laws to protect lesbians and gays against housing and job discrimination have been enacted. As social views of gender, race, class, and a range of sexualities evolve, individuals' views of others and their own self-concepts will also change.

Changeable   Social perspectives are fluid and respond to individual and collective efforts to weave new meanings into the fabric of common life. From 1848 until 1920, many people fought to change social views of women, and they succeeded in gaining the rights for women to vote, to attend college, and to own property, as well as other rights enjoyed by male citizens. In the 1960s, civil rights activism launched nationwide rethinking of actions and attitudes toward non-Whites. The battle to recognize and respect gays and lesbians has begun to alter social perspectives. Changes in how we view sex, race, class, (dis)ability, and sexual orientation are negotiated in communication contexts ranging from one-to-one conversations to mass media. Each of us has an ethical responsibility to speak out against social perspectives that we perceive as wrong or harmful. By doing so, we participate in the ongoing process of refining social perspectives.

-Janine-

My husband and I have really worked to share equally in our marriage. When we got married 8 years ago, we both believed women and men were equal and should have equal responsibilities for the home and family and equal power in making decisions that affect the family. But it's a lot harder to actually live that ideal than to believe in it. Both of us have struggled against our socialization that says I should cook and clean and take care of the kids and he should make big decisions about our lives. I think we've done a pretty good job of creating and living an egalitarian marriage. A lot of our friends see us as models.

 To increase your awareness of how social perspectives change over time, complete Activity 3.4 in your *Student Companion* or online under Activity 3.4, "Tracing Changes in Social Perspective," at the *Communication in Our Lives* website.

Enhancing the Self

So far we've explained how the self forms in the process of communicating with others. Building on that knowledge, we'll now explore guidelines for encouraging personal growth as communicators.

Make a Strong Commitment to Improve Yourself

The first principle for enhancing who you are is to make a firm commitment to personal growth. This isn't as easy as it might sound. A firm commitment involves more than saying, "I want to listen better" or "I want to be less judgmental." Saying these sentences is simple, but actually investing the

Communication Highlight

Failure on the Way to Success

Who was Babe Ruth? If you know baseball history, you probably think of him as hitting 714 home runs. He did, but he also struck out 1,330 times. R. H. Macy, who founded Macy's department store, failed in his first seven efforts to start a business. Superstar Michael Jordan was cut from his high school basketball team because he wasn't good enough. Early in his career, Walt Disney was fired from a newspaper job because his editor thought he had no good or creative ideas.

Most people who succeed fail along the way; sometimes they fail many times. If Babe Ruth had let his strikeouts defeat him, he would never have been a champion batter. The same is true of most of us. Failures and defeats are inevitable. Letting them define who we are is not.

effort to change is difficult. A serious commitment requires us to keep trying even if we don't see dramatic effects immediately.

Changing ourselves takes continual effort. Because the self is a process, it is not formed in one fell swoop, and it cannot be changed in one moment. We have to be willing to invest ongoing effort. In addition, we must realize at the outset that there will be setbacks, and we can't let them derail our resolve. Last year, a student said she wanted to be more assertive, so she began speaking up more often in class. When a professor criticized one of her contributions, her resolution folded. To develop assertiveness, she needed to take that setback in stride and maintain her commitment to speak up.

-Danica-

I have always been shy, and I am more so here than I was when I lived in Croatia. But I did not like being shy, and I decided to change myself. I took a course in social dance, and I made myself carry on the conversations with other people. Next, I pushed myself to start conversations. It was very hard at first, but it is not so hard now. Now that I am not so shy, I am making many friends.

A second reason change is difficult is that the self resists change. Morris Rosenberg (1979), a psychologist who has studied the self extensively, reports that we are as likely to hold onto negative self-images as we are to keep positive ones. Apparently, consistency itself is comforting. If you realize in advance that you may struggle against change, you'll be prepared for the tension that accompanies personal growth. Because change is a process and the self resists change, a firm and continuing commitment to change essential. It's also advisable to strive for incremental, gradual improvements rather than attempt to alter yourself radically all at once.

Gain Knowledge as a Basis for Personal Change

Commitment alone is insufficient to spur changes in who you are. In addition, you need several types of knowledge. First, you need to understand how the self is formed. In this chapter, we've discussed values and views of particular others and the generalized other. You may not want to accept all the views and values you were taught. You have the right and the ethical responsibility to embrace only the values you consider worthy.

-Christina-

My parents taught me that homosexuality is a crime against nature and God, and I believed that until I came to college. Now that I've met a lot of people who are homosexuals, I just can't buy the idea that they're bad or sinful. One of my best friends is a gay man, and I think he has more integrity than most straight guys. I'm also really close to a lesbian couple, and they are as loving and normal as my boyfriend and I are. My parents grew up in a different time, and their views about homosexuals aren't going to change. But I don't have to accept their views as my own.

Second, you need to know what changes are desirable and how to bring them about. Vague goals for self-improvement usually lead nowhere because they don't indicate concrete steps toward change. For instance, "I want to be

Learning to communicate effectively enhances self-confidence and self-esteem.

better at intimate communication" is a very vague objective. You can't do anything to meet such a fuzzy goal until you know something about the talk that enhances and impedes intimacy. Books such as this one will help you pinpoint concrete skills that facilitate healthy intimate communication. For instance, Chapter 7 will help you develop empathic listening skills, and Chapters 8 and 9 will explain how communication affects personal and social relationships. Another example of an overly vague objective is "I want to be a more effective team leader." To achieve that fuzzy goal, you need to understand the communication responsibilities of group leadership and the ways to build good work teams. We will learn about these in Chapters 10 and 11.

Another important source of knowledge is other people. Perhaps you recall a time when you began a new job and didn't know the norms for interaction. If you were fortunate, you found a mentor who explained the ropes to you so that you could learn how to communicate effectively in your work context. Others can also provide useful feedback on your interpersonal skills and your progress in the process of change. Feedback from your supervisor helps you understand how she or he perceives your work and how you might improve your job performance. Finally, others can serve as models. If you know someone you think is particularly skillful in supporting others, observe her or him carefully to identify specific communication skills. Observing will make you more aware of concrete skills that you can tailor to suit your personal style.

Set Realistic Goals

Changing ourselves is most likely when we set realistic goals. If you are shy and want to be more extraverted, it is reasonable to try to speak up and socialize more often. On the other hand, it may not be reasonable to try to be the life of every party. Realistic goals are based on realistic standards.

Often, dissatisfaction with ourselves stems from unrealistic expectations. In a culture that emphasizes perfection, it's easy to be trapped into expecting more than is humanly possible. If you set a goal to become a totally perfect communicator in all situations, you set yourself up to fail. It's more constructive to establish a series of realistic small goals. You might focus first on improving one communication skill. When you're satisfied with your ability at that skill, you can work on another one.

Sharpen Your Skill

Setting Realistic Goals for Change

Apply what you've learned by completing these sentences: One important goal I have for myself is to ....

....

Specific changes in behavior that are evidence of this change would be ....
.... and ....

So that I do not set an unrealistic goal, I will not try to ....
.... or ....

With regard to our discussion of social comparison, it's also important to select reasonable measuring sticks for yourself. It isn't realistic to compare your academic work with that of a certified genius. It is reasonable to measure your academic performance against that of others similar to you in intelligence and circumstances. It isn't realistic to compare your public speaking skill with that of someone who has made public presentations for years. It is reasonable to measure your public speaking ability against that of others who have speaking experience similar to yours. Setting realistic goals and selecting appropriate standards of comparison are important in bringing about change in yourself.

-Mike-

For a long time I put myself down for not doing as well academically as a lot of my friends. They ace courses and put mega-hours into studying and writing papers. I can't do that because I work 30 hours a week. Now I see that it's unfair to compare myself to them. When I compare myself to students who work as much as I do, my record is pretty good.

Accept Yourself as Being in Process

Earlier in this chapter, we saw that one characteristic of the human self is that it is continually in process, always becoming. This implies several things. First, it means you need to accept who you are now as a starting point. You don't have to like or admire everything about yourself, but it is important to accept who you are today as a basis for going forward. The self that you are results from all the interactions, reflected appraisals, and social comparisons in your life. You cannot change your past, but you do not have to be bound by it forever. Only by realizing and accepting who you are now can you move ahead.

Accepting yourself as being in process also implies that you realize you can change. Because you are in process, you are always changing and growing.

Don't let yourself be hindered by defeating self-fulfilling prophecies or the mind trap of thinking that you can't change (Rusk & Rusk, 1988). You can change if you set realistic goals, make a genuine commitment, and then work for the changes you want. Just remember that you are not fixed as you are; you are always in the process of becoming.

Create a Supportive Context for Change

Just as it is easier to swim with the tide than against it, it is easier to change our views of ourselves when we have some support for our efforts. You can do a lot to create an environment that supports your growth by choosing contexts and people who help you realize your goals. First, think about settings. If you want to lose weight, it's better to go to restaurants that serve healthful foods and offer light choices than to go to cholesterol castles. If you want to become more extraverted, go to parties, not libraries. But libraries are a better context than parties if your goal is to improve academic performance.

−Jan−

I never cared a lot about clothes until I joined a sorority where the labels on your clothes are a measure of your worth. The girls compete with each other to dress the best and have the newest styles. When one of the sisters wears something out of style, she gets a lot of teasing, but really it's pressure on her to measure up to the sorority image. At first, I adopted my sisters' values, and I spent more money than I could afford on clothes. For a while I even quit making contributions at church so that I could have more money for clothes. When I finally realized I was becoming somebody I didn't like, I tried to change, but my sisters made me feel bad anytime I wasn't dressed well. Finally, I moved out rather than face that pressure all the time. It just wasn't a good place for me to be myself.

Communication Highlight

Uppers, Downers, and Vultures

Uppers are people who communicate positively about us and who reflect positive appraisals of our self-worth. They notice our strengths, see our progress, and accept our weaknesses and problems without discounting us. When we're around uppers, we feel more upbeat and positive about ourselves. Uppers aren't necessarily unconditionally positive in their communication; a true friend can be an upper by recognizing our weaknesses and helping us work on them. Instead of putting us down, an upper believes in us and helps us believe in ourselves and our ability to grow.

Downers are people who communicate negatively about us and our self-worth. They call attention to our flaws, emphasize our problems, and deride our dreams and goals. When we're around downers, we tend to feel down about ourselves. Reflecting their perspectives, we're more aware of our weaknesses and less confident of what we can accomplish when we're around downers.

Vultures are extreme downers. They not only communicate negative images of us but also attack our self-concepts, like the birds that prey on their victims (Simon, 1977). Sometimes vultures harshly criticize us. They say, "You're hopeless." In other cases, vultures pick up on our own self-doubts and magnify them. They pick us apart by focusing on our weak spots. By telling us we are inadequate, vultures demolish our self-esteem.

  To identify uppers, downers, and vultures in your life, complete Activity 3.2 "Recognizing the Communication of Uppers, Downers, and Vultures" in your *Student Companion* or online under "Activities for Chapter 3" at the *Communication in Our Lives* website.

Because how others view us affects how we see ourselves, you can create a supportive context by consciously choosing to be around people who believe in you and encourage your personal growth without being dishonest about your limitations. It's also important to steer clear of people who put you down or say you can't change. In other words, people who reflect positive appraisals of us enhance our ability to improve who we are.

Others aren't the only ones whose communication affects our self-concepts. We also communicate with ourselves, and our own messages influence how we see ourselves. One of the most crippling kinds of self-talk we can engage in is **self-sabotage**—telling ourselves we are no good, we'll never learn something, there's no point in trying to change. We may be repeating others' judgments of us, or we may be inventing negative self-fulfilling prophecies. Either way, self-sabotage undermines belief in ourselves.

Distinguished therapist Albert Ellis wrote a book titled *How to Stubbornly Refuse to Make Yourself Miserable About Anything—Yes, Anything* (1988). In it, he asserted that most of our negative feelings about ourselves result from negative messages we communicate to ourselves. His advice is to challenge negative statements you make to yourself and to replace them with constructive intrapersonal communication. Self-sabotage is poisonous; it destroys our motivation to change and grow. We can be downers or even vultures just as others can; in fact, we probably can do more damage to our self-concepts than others can because we are most aware of our vulnerabilities and fears. This may explain why vultures originally attack and put themselves down (Simon, 1977).

We can also be uppers for ourselves. We can affirm our worth, encourage our growth, and fortify our sense of self-worth. Positive self-talk builds motivation and belief in yourself. It is also a useful strategy to interrupt and challenge negative messages from yourself and others. The next time you hear yourself saying, "I can't do . . .," or someone else says, "You'll never change," challenge the self-defeating message with self-talk. Say out loud to yourself, "I can do it. I will change." Use positive self-talk to resist counterproductive communication about yourself. Of course, improving your self-concept is not facilitated by uncritical positive communication. None of us grows and improves when we listen only to praise, particularly if it is less than honest. The true uppers in our lives offer constructive criticism to encourage us to reach for better versions of ourselves.

  For a guide to initiating changes in yourself, complete Activity 3.5, "Improving Self-Concept," in your *Student Companion* or online under "Activities for Chapter 3" at the *Communication in Our Lives* website.

In sum, to improve your self-concept you must create contexts that support growth and change. Seek out experiences and settings that foster belief in yourself and the changes you desire. Also, recognize uppers, downers, and vultures in yourself and others, and learn which people and which kinds of communication assist you in achieving your own goals for self-improvement.

CASE STUDY: Parental Teachings

The conversation scripted here is featured as a multimedia scenario on the *Communication in Our Lives* CD-ROM included with this book. Once you've launched the CD, click on the "Communication Scenarios" icon, and, from the Scenarios Menu, select "Parental Teachings" to watch the video. Improve your own communication skills by reading, watching, listening to, critiquing, and analyzing this communication encounter.

Analyze the scenario by applying the principles covered in this chapter, and respond to the prompts that accompany the video, which you can access by clicking on "Analysis." After completing the conversation analysis and answering the questions, you can click on the "Done" button to compare your responses with the ones I suggest. Additional analysis questions are available in print at the end of this chapter, and on the book's website.

Kate McDonald is in the neighborhood park with her two children, 7-year-old Emma and 5-year-old Jeremy. The three of them walk into the park and approach the swing set.

KATE: Jeremy, why don't you push Emma so she can swing? Emma, you hang on tight.

Jeremy begins pushing his sister, who squeals with delight. Jeremy gives an extra-hard push that lands him in the dirt in front of the swing set. Laughing, Emma jumps off, falling in the dirt beside her brother.

KATE: Come here, sweetie. You've got dirt all over your knees and your pretty new dress.

Kate brushes the dirt off Emma, who then runs over to the jungle gym set that Jeremy is now climbing. Kate smiles as she watches Jeremy climb fearlessly on the bars.

KATE: You're a brave little man, aren't you? How high can you go?

Encouraged by his mother, Jeremy climbs to the top bars and holds up a fist, screaming, "Look at me, Mom! I'm king of the hill! I climbed to the very top!"

Kate laughs and claps her hands to applaud him. Jealous of the attention Jeremy is getting, Emma runs over to the jungle gym and starts climbing. Kate calls out, "Careful, honey. Don't go any higher. You could fall and hurt yourself." When Emma ignores her mother and reaches for a higher bar, Kate walks over and pulls her off, saying, "Emma, I told you that is dangerous. Time to get down. Why don't you play on the swings some more?"

Once Kate puts Emma on the ground, the girl walks over to the swings and begins swaying.

Chapter Summary

In this chapter, we explored the self as a process that evolves as we communicate with others over the course of our lives. As we interact with others, we learn and internalize social perspectives, both those of particular others and those of the generalized other, or society as a whole. Reflected appraisals, direct definitions, and social comparisons are key communication processes

Communication Highlight

The Power of Positive Thinking

A growing number of psychologists have departed from the standard model of studying what's wrong with people (such as neuroses and antisocial behavior). Instead, they think it is more productive to study and cultivate what is right with people. Labeling their school of thought "positive psychology," these scientists believe that people are uplifted by seeing good in others and by engaging in goodness themselves (Robinson, 1995). The informal leader of this new school of psychology is Martin E. P. Seligman (2002), whose research shows that optimism and pessimism aren't necessarily innate or unchangeable.

Seligman's research has demonstrated that people can learn to be optimistic by practicing cognitive skills such as

challenging negative intrapersonal communication. Positive psychologists have shown that people with medical problems who learn to be optimistic are more likely to exercise and to follow a healthful diet, and they're also more likely to attend to messages about health dangers. In other words, optimism is not the same as denial (Ruark, 1999).

 Use your InfoTrac College Edition to read B. Bower's 2001 article "Look on the Bright Side and Live Longer." How could you apply the findings of this article to your own life?

that shape how we see ourselves and how we change over time. The perspective of the generalized other includes social views of key aspects of identity, including gender, race, and sexual orientation. However, these are arbitrary social constructions that we may challenge and resist once we are adults. When we resist social views and values that we consider unethical, we promote change in both society and ourselves.

The final section of the chapter focused on ways to enhance communication competence by improving self-concept. Guidelines include making a firm commitment to personal growth, gaining knowledge about desired changes and the skills they involve, setting realistic goals, accepting yourself as in process, and creating contexts that support the changes you seek. Transforming how we see ourselves is not easy, but it is possible. We can make amazing changes in who we are and how we feel about ourselves when we commit to doing so.

 # Communication in Our Lives ONLINE

In addition to presenting the case studies' multimedia scenarios, the *Communication in Our Lives* CD-ROM provides quick access to the *Communication in Our Lives* website and InfoTrac College Edition. The website is online at http://communication .wadsworth.com/woodcio14, but you can only access this book's premium web content when you link to the site directly through the book's CD.

 The *Communication in Our Lives* website features interactive tools for learning and reviewing the chapter's concepts and key terms, including electronic versions of the "For Further Reflection and Discussion" questions that appear below and a review quiz.

 The website also provides updated web links and additional InfoTrac College Edition activities. If required, you can e-mail completed chapter activities or the quizzes to your instructor.

Key Concepts

attachment styles, *66*

direct definition, *65*

downers, *82*

ego boundaries, *71*

identity scripts, *65*

particular others, *72*

perspective of the generalized
  other, *73*

reflected appraisal, *72*

self, *64*

self-sabotage, *83*

social comparison, *68*

uppers, *82*

vultures, *82*

For Further Reflection and Discussion

1. Set one specific goal for personal growth as a communicator. Be sure to specify your goal in terms of clear behavioral changes and make it realistic. As you study different topics during the semester, apply what you learn to your personal goal.

2. Imagine that you have the authority to establish ethical social values. Would you categorize people by race, class, gender, or sexual orientation? How would you define people and differences between them? How would existing social institutions and practices have to change in response to the values you would establish?

3. What ethical issues do you perceive in the process of developing and continuously refining self-concepts, both your own and those of people around you? Is it as important to be ethical in communicating with yourself (self-talk, or intrapersonal communication) as in communicating with others?

4. How do people you meet and get to know on the Internet affect your sense of who you are? Are they significant for you? Do they represent the gen-

eralized other to you? Is it useful to distinguish between the impact of face-to-face and online communication?

5. Use your InfoTrac College Edition to read the 1998 article by Elizabeth Aries and colleagues, "Race and Gender as Components of Working Self-Concept." When are you most aware of your race and gender? Is your experience consistent with the findings in the article?

6. In what ways are your own experiences and your sense of identity consistent with generalizations about the effects of race or ethnicity, economic class, sexual orientation, and sex on self-concept? In what ways do your experiences and your sense of identity diverge from generalizations? What in your own life might account for the instances in which you do not fit generalizations?

Experiencing Communication in Our Lives

Questions for Analysis and Discussion

Review the video of the scenario entitled "Parental Teachings" that you watched when completing this chapter's case study (page 84), or, if you haven't seen it yet, watch it for the first time. If you didn't previously finish the "Analysis" questions included on the CD-ROM, do so now, and then respond to the following questions, which are also available on the book's website under "Activities for Chapter 3."

1. Identify examples of direct definition in this scenario. How does Kate define Emma and Jeremy?

2. Identify examples of reflected appraisal in this scenario. What appraisals of her son and daughter does Kate reflect to them?

3. What do Emma's and Jeremy's responses to Kate suggest about their acceptance of her views of them?

4. To what extent does Kate's communication with her children reflect conventional gender expectations in Western culture?

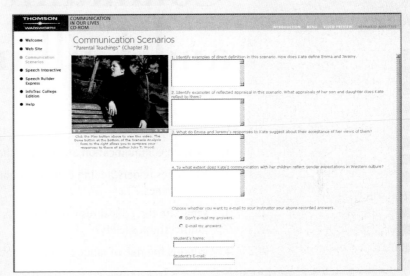

4
Communication and Culture

Focus Questions

1. How do communication and culture shape each other?

2. How does understanding cultures enhance communication effectiveness?

3. What are the ethical responsibilities for communicating in a multicultural society?

4. What is the role of language in instigating changes in cultures?

© Digital Vision/Getty Images

Concha cradles his daughter in his arms and sings her to sleep while his village wife, Bishnu, plows the small field of vegetables outside their cottage. Later today, she will repair the walls on the cottage for the harsh winter ahead. Tomorrow Concha begins the 2-day walk to Kathmandu, where he will live with his city wife, Ran Maya, and their children. That will be his home for the next 6 months between treks he leads in the Himalayas.

Halfway across the globe, John returns home after a long day at his law office. He parks his Buick in the garage and walks into the kitchen, where his wife, Ginny, is nursing their son, Daniel. After dinner she will bathe Daniel and put him to bed, and John will mow the lawn and repair a leaky faucet. Later, he'll pack a bag for tomorrow's flight to a conference 2,000 miles away. He'll be gone a week, and the au pair will help Ginny with Daniel.

More than distance separates these two families. They have different understandings of what family means and how it operates. In Nepal, gender roles are not as distinct as they are in the United States: Both women and men, as well as extended families, care for children. Both sexes engage in hard labor. The strong value attached to family in Nepal explains why some men have more than one family. Having both a village family and a city family ensures a continuous home life for many Nepalese men, who often spend half of each year based in Kathmandu, from which mountain treks and expeditions originate. Having two families is acceptable in Nepal, but no Nepalese would hire an au pair, because they believe that family and neighbors should participate in caring for children. What Concha, Bishnu, Ran Maya, John, and Ginny consider normal and right reflects the values and norms of their respective cultures.

You'll recall that when we defined communication in Chapter 1, we noted that it is a systemic process. This means that communication can be understood only within its particular systems, or contexts. Culture is one of the most important systems within which communication occurs. We are not born knowing how, when, and to whom to speak, just as we are not born with attitudes about different races, religions, sexual orientations, and other aspects of identity. We learn these as we interact with others, and we then tend to reflect cultural teachings in our own communication. For each of us, our culture directly shapes how we communicate, teaching us whether interrupting is appropriate, how much eye contact is polite, and whether argument and conflict are desirable in groups and personal relationships.

In this chapter, we explore relationships between communication and culture. In our multicultural society, being an effective citizen and professional depends on understanding different heritages and the communication practices they foster. We'll define culture and discuss the intricate ways it is entwined with communication. Then, we'll focus on guidelines for increasing the effectiveness of communication between people of different cultures and social communities.

Understanding Culture

Although the word **culture** is part of our everyday vocabulary, it's difficult to define. Culture is part of everything we think, do, feel, and believe, yet we can't point to a thing that is culture. Most simply defined, culture is a way of life. It is a system of ideas, values, beliefs, structures, and practices that is communicated by one generation to the next and that sustains a particular way of life. To understand cultures more fully, we now consider two key premises about them.

Multiple Social Communities May Coexist in a Single Society

When we speak of different cultures, we often think of societies that are geographically distinct. For instance, India, South America, Africa, and France are separate cultures. Yet geographic separation isn't what defines a culture. Instead, a culture exists when a distinct way of life shapes what a group of people believes, values, and does. Even within a culture, however, there are variations between people. Numerous social communities with distinct ways of life may coexist in a single society or physical territory.

In most societies there is a dominant, or mainstream, way of life. Although many groups may exist within a single society, not all of them identify equally and exclusively with the dominant culture. Since the colonial days, mainstream Western culture has reflected the values and experiences of Western, heterosexual, young and middle-aged, middle- and upper-class, able-bodied White men who are Christian at least in heritage if not in actual practice.

Yet Western society includes many groups outside the cultural mainstream. People in their seventies, eighties, or nineties often feel devalued or erased by America's youth-oriented culture. Gay men, lesbians, intersexuals, transsexuals, transgendered people, and bisexuals experience difficulty in a society that defines them as marginal and refuses to grant them social legitimacy or legal rights. People who have disabilities encounter countless problems as they attempt to live and work in a society that is made for able-bodied people. Prevailing customs in America often ignore the traditions and worship practices of people who follow religions such as Judaism and Buddhism. Bikers, skinheads, and punk rockers are other groups that do not fit—and often don't want to fit—within mainstream American culture.

Sharpen Your Skill

Communicating Culture

Locate a standard calendar and an academic calendar used on your campus. Check each calendar to determine which of the following holidays of different cultural groups are recognized on the calendars and which are declared as holidays by suspension of normal operations in communities and on campuses:

Christmas	Hanukkah	Kwanzaa	Elderly Day	Passover
Easter	Yom Kippur	Ramadan	Hegira	Rosh Hashanah
Saka	Seleicodae	Martin Luther King, Jr. Day		

What do calendars communicate by recognizing or not recognizing traditions of various groups?

The dominance of groups in the cultural mainstream often is evident in nonverbal communication. For example, Western culture often conveys the message that people without disabilities are normal and people with disabili-

Communication Highlight

ties are not. Notice how many buildings have no ramps and how many public presentations don't include signers for people with impaired hearing.

Most campus and business buildings feature portraits of White men, leaving people of color and women unrepresented.

Distinct cultures and social communities teach members to communicate in ways consistent with the values and norms of their communities. As Sabrina notes in her commentary, tension and misunderstanding can erupt when values and communication practices of different cultures or social communities clash.

–Sabrina–

I get hassled by a lot of White girls on campus about being dependent on my family. They say I should grow up and leave the nest. They say I'm too close to my folks and my grandparents, aunts, uncles, and cousins. But what they mean by "too close" is that I'm closer with my family than most Whites are. It's a White standard they're using, and it doesn't fit most African Americans. Strong ties with family and the Black community have always been our way.

Social communities are groups of people who live within a dominant culture yet also are members of another group or groups that are not dominant in a particular society. Social communities are distinct from dominant culture although not necessarily opposed to or entirely outside of it. For many years, social groups that lived in a dominant culture yet simultaneously belonged to a second culture were called *subcultures*. However, the prefix *sub* connotes inferiority, as if subcultures were not real cultures. Intercultural communication specialists Larry Samovar and Richard Porter (2001) call these social communities *co-cultures* to emphasize that they are equal—not sub—cultures. In this book, I use the term *culture* to refer to the way of life that is dominant for a society. I prefer the term *social community* to the term *co-culture* because members of specific social communities may also belong to and reflect the larger culture.

  To increase your awareness of facets of your identity that affect your communication, complete Activity 4.3, "Self-description," in your *Student Companion* or online under "Activities for Chapter 4" at the *Communication in Our Lives* website.

Communication styles reflect cultures and social communities.

One of the best indicators that a social community or culture exists is communication. Because we learn to communicate in the process of interacting with others, people socialized in different social communities learn to use and interpret communication in different ways. For example, many Asian cultures emphasize cooperative communication, whereas Western culture encourages a greater degree of competition (Yum, 2000). Western culture emphasizes individualism (Hofstede, 1991). By contrast, traditional Korean, Japanese, and many South Asian cultures emphasize community and interdependence of people (Diggs, 1998, 2001).

When people from different cultures and social communities interact, their different ways of communicating may cause misunderstandings. For instance, traditional Japanese people don't touch or shake hands to greet. Instead, they bow to preserve each person's personal space, which is very important in that culture. In Greece, however, touching is part of being friendly and sociable (Hargraves, 2001a, b; Kohls, 2001). In the United States, Britain, and some other societies, people form orderly lines to buy tickets, enter buildings, and board buses and planes. In India, people don't form lines—they push and rush to get a place (Spano, 2003). An American might interpret pushing for a space as rude, but in India it is an acceptable way to get a place.

Gender as a Social Community   Of the many social communities that exist, gender has received particularly intense study. Because we know more about it than about other social communities, we'll explore gender as an extended example of a social community that shapes how members communicate.

Researchers have investigated how girls and boys usually are socialized primarily in sex-segregated groups so that they learn and internalize the social prescriptions for their respective sexes. Scholars have also studied how adult men's and women's communication differs in practice. One of the earliest studies showed that children's games are a primary agent of gender

Communication Highlight

Happy New Year

For almost everyone, the new year symbolizes a new beginning and hope for the future. But when the new year begins is not universal ("A New Year's Eve Primer," 1997). Here are some of the dates on which the new year is celebrated by different cultures.

The Chinese new year begins on January 28.
The Christian new year begins on January 1.
The Grecian new year, Seleicodae, begins on September 14.
The Indian new year, Saka, begins on March 22.
The Islamic new year, Hegira, begins on April 27.
The Jewish new year, Rosh Hashanah, begins at sundown on September 20.

socialization (Maltz & Borker, 1982). Typically, children's play is sex segregated, and there are differences between the games the sexes tend to play.

Games girls traditionally favor, such as playing house and school, involve few players, rely on talk to negotiate how to play (because there aren't clear-cut guidelines), and require cooperation and sensitivity between players. Baseball, football, and war, which are typical boys' games, involve more players and have clear goals and rules, so less talk is needed. Many of the games boys typically play are highly competitive both between teams and for individual status within teams.

Interaction in games teaches boys and girls distinct understandings of why, when, and how to use talk. In general, those socialized in masculine communities learn to use talk to assert themselves, compete to gain and hold attention, and accomplish goals. People who are socialized in feminine communities typically learn to use talk to express feelings, respond to and include others, and establish relationships (Clark, 1998; Martin et al., 2000).

The rules we learn in childhood play remain with many of us as we mature. For instance, women's talk generally is more expressive and focused on feelings and relationships, whereas men's talk tends to be more instrumental and competitive (Aries, 1987; Beck, 1988; Johnson, 1989, 1996; Wood, 1993b, 1995a, 1996b, 2005). These differences sometimes show up in professional contexts. Some research reports that women leaders tend to engage in more personal communication with subordinates and peers than do men in leadership positions (Helgesen, 1990; Natalle, 1996).

Another general difference lies in what each gender regards as the primary basis of relationships. For people who have internalized masculine identities, activities tend to be a key foundation of close friendships and romantic relationships (Inman, 1996; Swain, 1989; Wood & Inman, 1993). Thus, men typically cement friendships by doing things together (playing soccer, working on cars, watching sports) and doing things for one another (trading favors, washing a car, doing laundry). People who have internalized feminine identities tend to regard communication as the crux of relationships. Thus, women often regard talking about feelings, personal issues, and daily life as the way to build and enrich relationships (Johnson, 1996; Riessman, 1990).

Given the differences between how women and men, in general, use communication, it's hardly surprising that the sexes often misunderstand one another. One clash between gendered communication styles occurs when women and men discuss problems. When women talk about something that is troubling them, they are often looking first for empathy and connection. Yet masculine socialization teaches men to use communication instrumentally, so they often offer advice or solutions (Tannen, 1990; Wood, 1998, 2005). Thus, women sometimes interpret men's advice as communicating lack of personal concern. On the other hand, men may feel frustrated when women offer empathy and support instead of advice for solving problems. In general, men also make fewer personal disclosures, whereas women regard sharing confidences as an important way to enhance closeness (Aries, 1987; Johnson, 1996).

Men and women, in general, also have different styles of listening. Socialized to be responsive and expressive, women tend to make listening noises such as "um hm," "yeah," and "I know what you mean" when others are talking (Tannen, 1990; Wood, 1998). This is how they show they are following and interested. Masculine socialization doesn't emphasize affirming others explicitly, so many men tend to make fewer listening noises than women. Thus, women sometimes feel men aren't listening to them, because some men don't show attentiveness in the ways women have learned to expect. Men may also misinterpret women's listening noises as indicating agreement (rather than attention) and are surprised when women later disagree with them.

Perhaps the most common complication in communication between the genders occurs when a woman says, "Let's talk about us." To men this often means trouble because they interpret the request as implying there is a problem in a relationship. For women, however, this is not the only—or even the main—reason to talk about a relationship. Within feminine social communities, talking is a primary way to celebrate and increase closeness (Acitelli, 1993; Riessman, 1990). The instrumental focus of masculine social communities teaches that talking about a relationship is useful only if there is some problem to be resolved (Acitelli, 1988, 1993; Wood, 1998).

—Larry—

Finally I see what happens between my girlfriend and me. She always wants to talk about us, which I think is stupid unless we have a problem. I like to go to a concert or do something together, but then she says that I don't want to be with her. We speak totally different languages.

Other Social Communities Gender isn't the only social community, and communication between men and women is not the only kind of interaction that may be plagued by misunderstandings. Research indicates that communication patterns vary between social classes. For example, working-class people tend to stay closer to and rely more on extended family than middle- and upper-class Americans (Bornstein & Bradley, 2003; Cancian, 1987).

Race and ethnicity may also shape social communities and their distinct communication patterns. Within the borders of this country, there are communities of Asian Americans, Hispanics, Latinas and Latinos, Native Americans, and Indians. Each group's values, beliefs, actions, thoughts, and communication are shaped by both mainstream Western culture and their more specific social communities (MacIel & Herrera-Sobek, 1998; Orbe, 1994).

Recent research indicates that African Americans generally communicate more assertively than European Americans (Orbe & Harris, 2001; Ribeau, Baldwin, & Hecht, 1994). What some African Americans consider authentic, powerful exchanges may be perceived as antagonistic by people from different social communities. The rapping and styling that some African Americans engage in are not practiced (or understood) by most European Americans (Houston & Wood, 1996; Wood, 1998). African American communication also tends to reflect greater commitment to collective interests such as family and community, whereas European American communication tends to be more individualistic (Gaines, 1995). As a rule, African Americans also communicate more interactively than European Americans (Weber, 1994). This explains why some African Americans call out responses such as "Tell it," "All right," and "Keep talking" during speeches, church sermons, and other public presentations. What many Caucasians regard as interruptions, some African Americans perceive as complimentary participation in communication.

Speak Out about Your Social Community

Each of us belongs to social communities that have communication practices not understood or engaged in by people outside those communities. This exercise is aimed to help you explain a communication practice in one of your social communities so that outsiders can understand and appreciate it. At the same time, you should gain from learning about communication patterns as you hear classmates explain practices in their communities.

Prepare a 3-minute speech in which you

1. Identify a specific communication practice used in one of your social communities.

2. Illustrate it by providing dialogue, a film clip, or other examples.

3. Explain what it means, using terms that outsiders to your community will understand.

  To increase your understanding of cultural differences, complete Activity 4.2, "Cultural Variations in Social Perspectives," and Activity 4.4, "Appreciating Differences among People," in your *Student Companion* or online under "Activities for Chapter 4" at the *Communication in Our Lives* website.

Notice that in discussing social communities and their communication patterns, I use qualifying words. For instance, I note that *most* women behave in certain ways and that *some* African Americans communicate more interactively than *some* European Americans. This is to remind us that not all members of a group behave in the same way. Although generalizations are useful and informative, they should not mislead us into thinking that all members of any social community think, feel, and communicate alike. We engage in stereotyping and uncritical thinking when we fail to recognize differences between individual members of social groups.

Cultures Are Systems

A culture is not a random collection of ideas, beliefs, values, and customs; rather, it is a coherent system of understandings, traditions, values, communication practices, and ways of living. As anthropologist Edward T. Hall noted years ago, "You touch a culture in one place and everything else is affected" (1977, p. 14).

You'll recall from our earlier discussion of systems that the parts of a system interact and affect one another. Because cultures are systems, aspects of a culture are interrelated and work together to create a whole. For example, one of the major changes in Western society was the Industrial Revolution. Before the mid-1800s, most families lived and worked together in one place. In agricultural regions, women, men, and children worked together to plant, tend, harvest, and store crops and to take care of livestock. In cities, family businesses were common. This preindustrial way of life promoted cooperative relationships and family togetherness. The invention of fuel-powered machines led to mass production in factories, where workers spent 8 or more hours each day. In turn, this provoked competition among workers to produce and earn more, and on-the-job communication became more competitive and individualistic. As men were hired for industrial jobs, women assumed primary responsibilities in the home, and men's roles in family life diminished. Thus, a change in work life produced reverberations throughout the culture.

The technological revolution that began in the 1970s and continues today has also had multiple and interrelated repercussions in cultural life. The Internet and the World Wide Web allow people to maintain regular communication over great distances. Computer networking, virtual conferencing, and virtual offices allow many people to work at home. Personal relationships also are affected by changes in communication. Today, many people sustain and form friendships and romantic relationships over the Internet (Swiss, 2001; Wood & Smith, 2001). New technologies change how, where, and with whom we communicate, just as they change the boundaries we use to define work and personal life. Because cultures are holistic, no change is ever isolated from the overall system.

Communication's Relationship to Culture and Social Communities

Communication and culture cannot be separated, because each influences the other. Culture is reflected in communication practices, and at the same time, communication practices shape cultural life. We'll discuss five principles that apply to social communities and cultures.

Communication Expresses and Sustains Cultures

Patterns of communication reflect cultural values and perspectives. For example, many Asian languages include numerous words to describe particular relationships (my grandmother's brother, my father's uncle, my youngest son, my oldest daughter). This reflects the cultural emphasis on family relationships (Ferrante, 2000). There are fewer English words to describe specific kinship bonds.

The respect of many Asian cultures for elderly people is reflected in language. "I will be 60 tomorrow" is an Asian saying that means, "I am old enough to deserve respect." In contrast, Western cultures tend to prize youth and to have many positive words for youthfulness (*young in spirit, fresh*)

Communication Highlight

The Haves and Have Nots in the Technological Era

Will the explosion of information and technology in our era foster a global village in which everyone has a chance to participate? Or will it create a new power and information elite and exclude those who are not part of the information revolution? Some technology experts believe that new technologies will make it more possible than in the past for all members of society to participate and to achieve greater social equality. Those who are optimistic about the potential of new technologies to lessen class divisions point out that the information superhighway gives greater access to people who previously did not have easy access to vast stores of information.

Others worry that the information infrastructure may increase, not decrease, the gap between those who have power and resources and those who do not. They caution that we could become a society in which access to technologies is based on the ability to pay for them (Poster, 2001). Will people with visual impairments be left behind by computer operating systems that rely on graphics not easily read by software designed to vocalize on-screen text

(Hagins, 1996)? Will homeless citizens be excluded from new technologies (O'Sullivan, 1995)?

Gaps in information lead to gaps in power, and those gaps will only enlarge if we do not find ways to democratize access to new technologies of communication.

Use your InfoTrac College Edition to read the full article by Patrick O'Sullivan cited in this "Communication Highlight." What does O'Sullivan's article imply is necessary to foster truly democratic participation in a technologically driven society? Also use your InfoTrac College Edition to read Peter Levine's 2001 article "Civic Renewal and the Commons of Cyberspace." What threats to a common, democratic cyberspace does Levine identify? How can individuals and government reduce those threats?

To extend your thinking about connections between technology and cultures, complete Activity 4.5, "Technology Haves and Have Nots," in your *Student Companion* or online under "Activities for Chapter 4" at the *Communication in Our Lives* website.

and negative words for seniority (*has-been, outdated, old-fashioned, over the hill*). The Western preoccupation with time and efficiency is evident in the abundance of words that refer to time (*hours, minutes, seconds, days, weeks*) and in common phrases such as "Let's not waste time." Among Buddhists, the adage "Something cannot become nothing" expresses belief that life continues in new forms after death. In the United States, "The early bird gets the worm" implies that initiative is valuable, and "Nice guys finish last" suggests that winning is important and that it's more important to be aggressive than nice.

Sharpen Your Skill

Your Culture's Sayings

What do common sayings and proverbs in the United States tell us about cultural values? What cultural values are expressed by sayings such as

"You can't be too rich or too thin."

"A stitch in time saves later nine."

"What goes around comes around."

"A watched pot never boils."

"Penny wise, pound foolish."

"You can't take it with you."

"You've made your bed, now you have to lie in it."

What other sayings can you think of that express key Western values?

Nonverbal communication also expresses cultural values. For example, some Indian women who live in the United States continue to wear traditional saris, reflecting the norms of their cultures. A Greek student in one of my classes brought exquisite pastries for everyone on her birthday, explaining that in Greece the person having a birthday thanks those who enrich her or his life. Beards worn by Orthodox and Hasidic Jews express reverence, whereas Buddhist monks often shave their faces and heads to express their spiritual commitments (Haught, 2003).

–Intan–

Eye contact is the hardest part of learning American culture. In my home we do not look at others. It would be very rude to do that. Instead, we look away or down when talking so as not to insult other persons. In America if I look down, it is thought I am hiding something or am dishonest. So I am learning to look at others when we talk, but it still feels very disrespectful to me.

Communication simultaneously reflects and sustains cultural values. Each time we express cultural values, we also perpetuate them. When some Asian Americans veil emotions in interaction, they fortify and express the value of self-restraint and the priority of reason over emotion. When Caucasians argue, push their own ideas, and compete in conversations, they uphold the values of individuality and assertiveness. Communication, then, is a mirror of a culture's values and a primary means of keeping them woven into the fabric of everyday life.

 To increase your awareness of how language can reflect cultural values, complete Activity 4.1, "Identifying Sexist and Racist Language," in your *Student Companion* or online under "Activities for Chapter 4" at the *Communication in Our Lives* website.

Cultures Consist of Material and Nonmaterial Components

Cultures include both material and nonmaterial elements. Material components are tangible objects and physical substances that have been altered by human intervention. The objects a culture invents reflect its values, needs, goals, and preoccupations. For example, a culture that creates an abun-

Communication Highlight

Proverbs Express Cultural Values

Here are examples of sayings that reflect the values of particular cultures (Gudykunst & Lee, 2002; Samovar, L. & Porter, R., 2001).

- "It is the nail that sticks out that gets hammered down." This Japanese saying reflects the idea that a person should not stand out from others but instead should conform.

- "No need to know the person, only the family." This Chinese axiom reflects the belief that individuals are less important than families.

- "A zebra does not despise its stripes." Among the African Masai, this saying encourages acceptance of things and oneself as they are.

- "The child has no owner." "It takes a whole village to raise a child." These African adages express the cultural belief that children belong to whole communities, and rearing and caring for children are the responsibility of all members of those communities, not just the children's biological parents.

dance of offensive weapons is likely to have goals of conquest. Material objects common in Western cultures include cars, phones, computers, pagers, shovels, and hammers. Each of these objects began with natural raw materials, such as metals, trees, and minerals, that were shaped into new forms for new uses. The numerous inventions to enhance speed and output in the United States reflect the Western emphasis on efficiency and productivity (Bertman, 1998; Wood, 2000).

–Raul–

In Mexico, we spend much more time doing things than people do in America. To fix food, we use only our hands and maybe knives and pots, but here kitchens have so many fancy tools. In Piste, my hometown, few people have phones, and even those who do often wait many hours to get a call through. Here, everyone has a phone—sometimes more than one—and people expect to make instant connections anywhere in the world. Most Mexicans walk or take buses; if a bus is full, no problem—we wait for the next one or the one after that. Here, everybody has his or her own car, and people do not like to wait.

Sharpen Your Skill

It's a Material World

Analyze the material symbols of your campus culture. What do statues, buildings, and landscaping say about what is valued on your campus? What do computers in most offices tell you about your campus's regard for information and efficiency? Which are the newest, largest, and nicest buildings on campus? Which buildings are the least nice and worst maintained? How do the quality and aesthetics of classrooms compare with those of administrators' offices? What can you conclude about the values of your campus culture?

Cultures also include nonmaterial components. These are intangible creations that reflect a culture's values and influence personal and social behavior. Four of the most important nonmaterial aspects of a culture are beliefs, values, norms, and language.

Beliefs   **Beliefs** are conceptions of what is true, factual, or valid. Beliefs may be rooted in faith ("God said that we live forever if we accept Him"), experience ("Storing grain in elevated places keeps it dry during the monsoons"), or science ("Penicillin cures infections"). Cultural beliefs are regarded as truths even though they are sometimes false. In the 1600s, people in the United States believed in witches and drowned or burned at the stake anyone they judged to be a witch. At one point it was widely believed that the earth was flat, so sailors did not venture beyond what they believed to be the edge of the earth. Even after that, people thought that the sun revolved around the earth. We now know that the earth is round and that it revolves around the sun. Cultural beliefs, even if inaccurate, influence personal and social conduct.

Values   **Values** are generally shared views of what is good, right, worthwhile, and important with regard to conduct and existence. Whereas beliefs have to do with what people think is true, values are concerned with what should be or what is worthy in life. For example, cultures that value families and define individuals in terms of their connections with others create laws and social policies to support family life. Many developed countries that value strong families provide paid, guaranteed family leave for all workers.

Different cultures have different values toward the natural world. Many Native American tribes valued living in harmony with nature, with other creatures, and with the earth. Thus, they adjusted their lives to the natural rhythms of seasons, created communication rituals to celebrate changes in the seasons, worked with the land, and hunted to meet needs for food and clothing but not for sport. Many Native Americans had rituals performed upon killing an animal, to honor the animal's spirit and to express thanks to it for its life. Embracing a very different value, Europeans who settled in the United States saw nature as something to be conquered and made to serve humans. The values endorsed by a culture are expressed in the communication of its members.

Norms   **Norms** are informal rules that guide how members of a culture act, as well as how they think and feel. Norms define what is considered to be normal, or appropriate, in particular situations. For instance, in the United States, salads usually are served before a main course, but in France and much of Europe, salads follow the main course. In China, defendants are presumed guilty, whereas in the United States they are presumed innocent until proven guilty. In America, children are expected to grow up and leave their families of origin to start their own families. In some Asian societies, however, children are expected to live with or near their parents and to operate as a single large family. What we view as normal reflects what our particular culture teaches us.

Norms reflect cultural values. In the United States, for instance, many norms respect the values of individuals' privacy, property, and autonomy: knocking on closed doors, asking permission to borrow others' property, having separate utensils for serving food and individual places with separate eating utensils for each person, and moving from one residence to another without consulting any authorities. In countries with collectivist values, however, different communicative norms prevail. Koreans do not set individual places, and they use the same utensils for serving and eating. In China, no citizen would change jobs or move without first getting approval from the local unit of the Communist Party (Ferrante, 2000).

The value placed on family life differs from culture to culture.

© 1998 Peter Menzel/Stock Boston

Language   Language shapes how we think about the world and ourselves. As we will see in Chapter 5, language is packed with values. Consequently, in the process of learning language, we learn our culture's beliefs, values, and norms. The value that most Asian cultures attach to age is structured into Asian languages. For instance, the Korean language makes fine distinctions between different ages, and any remark to another person must acknowledge the other's age (Ferrante, 2000). To say "I am going to school" in Korean, a teenager would say *"hakkyo-eh gahndah"* to a peer of the same age, *"hakkyo-eh gah"* to a parent, and *"hakkyo-eh gahneh"* to a grandparent (Park, 1979).

Communication Highlight

What's in a Name?

Long before the present era, some women resisted taking a man's name upon marriage. At the first Women's Rights Convention, held in 1848 at Seneca Falls, New York, Elizabeth Cady Stanton (Stanton, Anthony, & Gage, 1881/1969) said:

> When a slave escapes from a Southern plantation, he at once takes a name as the first step in liberty—the first assertion of individual identity. A woman's dignity is equally involved in a life-long name, to mark her individuality. We can not overestimate the demoralizing effect on woman herself, to say nothing of

society at large, for her to consent thus to merge her existence so wholly in that of another.

Communication scholars Karen Foss and Belle Edson (1989) studied married women's reasons for choosing their birth names, their husbands' names, or hyphenated names. Foss and Edson reported that women who took their husbands' names place greater emphasis on relationships than self. Those who retained their birth names valued self above relationships. Women who chose hyphenated names value self and relationships equally.

Language also reflects cultural views of personal identity. Western cultures tend to emphasize individuals, whereas many Eastern cultures place greater emphasis on family and community than on individuals. It's unlikely that an Eastern textbook on human communication would even include a chapter on self, which is standard in Western textbooks. If I were a Korean, I would introduce myself as Wood Julia to communicate the greater value placed on familial than personal identity.

Language, beliefs, values, and norms are cultural couriers that carry a way of life forward from day to day and generation to generation. These nonmaterial components, in combination with material ones, reflect and perpetuate cultures and social communities.

Cultures Are Shaped by Historical and Geographic Forces

The values and activities of cultures are not random or arbitrary. Many of them grow out of the history and geographic location of a society. Historically, the southern region of the United States has been more agrarian than the northern region because southern soil and climate are conducive to farming. Water is used freely in the United States but very sparingly in the hill country of Nepal, where it must be hand-carried into villages. The scarcity of oil, wood, and coal in Korea influences Koreans to use fuels conservatively. Similarly, the lack of grazing land in Korea means there are few sheep and cows for meat and dairy products. To meet needs for food, Koreans rely on resources e available in their country: rice and other grains, vegetables, fish, snakes, and soybeans. Many South American societies have siestas so that people's energy is not drained by the fierce midday heat. Cities and towns on seaboards develop maritime industries and have more seafood in their diets than inland areas do.

-Aikau-

Americans say they like Asian food, but really they do not know what it is. At home we use meat only to flavor. We have slivers of meat or chicken in a meal, but we do not have big pieces like in America. When my parents came here and opened a restaurant, they had to learn how to fix Asian food for American tastes, not like we fix it at home.

Just as our personal histories shape who we are, the traditions and history of a culture shape its character. Many Native Americans are suspicious of Caucasian Americans because of a history of exploitation and betrayal. Similarly, some African Americans may distrust Caucasians because their ancestors were enslaved and exploited by Whites. Jewish people have a painful legacy of persecution that explains why many are wary of non-Jews even today. In 1939, a ship transporting Jews from Nazi Germany docked in Miami, Florida, and was turned back. That incident is part of the history of Jewish people and helps us understand why they often distrust non-Jews and preserve their heritage within their own social communities.

Historical influences also shape the communication patterns of social groups. For instance, some African Americans know how to use standard English to fit into the dominant culture; at the same time, they know how to use more colloquial language that is typical in some traditional African American communities (Orbe, 1994; Orbe & Harris, 2001). Members of other communities, such as Jewish, Hispanic, and gay groups, also become bilingual to be effective in both mainstream culture and their social communities (Auer, 1998).

Cultural practices that originally developed for functional reasons may persist simply because "that's how we've always done it." For example, originally, women probably stayed near their homes because they had to nurse babies, and men did most of the hunting because they could leave the home and because they had larger muscles and greater physical strength. Today brains are more important than brawn for providing for a family, and infants can be fed with formula or with expressed and stored breast milk, so the mother's full-time presence is not essential. Although the original reasons for assigning women to homemaking and men to breadwinning are no longer valid, a traditionally gendered division of labor persists.

Cultural traditions shape daily activities and social life. Hindus believe that what a person is in this life reflects past lives and determines his or her fate in the next one. Thus, present behaviors are chosen with an eye toward what they are likely to bring about in the next incarnation. Cultures steeped in violence and war may regard death and battle as unremarkable parts of life. In cultures less accustomed to war and violence, elaborate communication rituals convey the extraordinariness of war and violent death.

Both verbal and nonverbal communication reflect cultural teachings. Here, an elder and a young boy wear traditional yarmulkes and partake of unleavened bread and wine as part of Passover seder.

© Bill Aron/PhotoEdit

The traditions of a culture also regulate and order life. Cultures develop traditions that dictate who does what kinds of work, where and how long people work, how much status various jobs have, and how work fits into overall life. These traditions are communicated through cultural institutions (schools, churches, synagogues) and practices (different dress for blue- and white-collar jobs, individual or team structures on the job). In the United States, for instance, people are encouraged to work a lot and to identify themselves and their worth in terms of the work they do. The cultural value attached to work in the United States encourages Americans to put in longer hours at the workplace than members of many other cultures. In a number of European countries, workers are required to take generous vacations, and extra jobs are discouraged. Hendrick, an exchange student from Germany, notes differences between U.S. and German views of work.

─Hendrick─

Americans are obsessed with work. Most students here work jobs too—sometimes 30 or 40 hours a week. I ask my American friends why they work so hard, and they tell me they need the money for their car or clothes or going out. But it seems to me that they need a car and nice clothes to go to work. If they did not work, they would not need so much of the money that they work to get.

Calendars reflect cultural traditions by designating significant days. In the United States, the Fourth of July commemorates America's independence from Britain; in France, Bastille Day celebrates the storming of the Bastille; Eastern societies have a day each year to honor the elderly. National holidays symbolize important moments in a culture's life and remind members of what the culture values. On a less obvious level, cultural calendars define who is in the mainstream of a given society and who is not. Rachael, a young woman who took several of my classes, explains this point.

─Rachael─

It is hard to be Jewish in a Christian society, especially in terms of holidays. For me, Rosh Hashanah and Yom Kippur are high holy days, but they are not holidays on the calendar. Some of my teachers give me grief for missing classes on holy days, and my friends don't accept that I can't go out on Saturday, which is our sacred day. At my job they act like I'm being a slouch and skipping work because my holidays aren't their holidays. They get Christmas and New Year's Day off, but I celebrate Hanukkah and Rosh Hashanah. And I don't have to tell you why making Easter a national holiday offends Jewish people.

We Learn Culture in the Process of Communicating

We learn a culture's views and patterns in the process of communicating. As we interact with others, we come to understand the beliefs, values, norms, and language of our culture. By observing how others communicate, we learn language (*dog*) and what it means (a pet to love or a food to eat). This allows us to participate in a social world of shared meanings.

From the moment of birth, we begin to learn the beliefs, values, norms, and language of our society. We learn our culture's values in a variety of

Communication Highlight

Life on the Color Line

Gregory Howard Williams began life as the White son in a middle-class family in Virginia. At age 10, however, he became a Black living in Muncie, Indiana. His father, James Anthony "Buster" Williams, was an olive-skinned man with some African ancestry. Buster wanted desperately to escape racism and gain the privileges that Whites have as a birthright. His son, Gregory, has pale skin, thin lips, and straight hair, which allowed others to perceive him as White.

In his autobiography, *Life on the Color Line: The True Story of a White Boy Who Discovered He Was Black* (1995), Gregory Williams provides a stunning account of the differences in how he was treated when he was considered White and Black.

Communication Highlight

communication contexts. We learn to respect our elders or not by how we see others communicate with older people and by what we hear others say about elders. We learn what body shape is valued by what we see in media and how we hear others talk about people of various physical proportions. Children enter the world without strong gender scripts, but socialization teaches most boys to be masculine and most girls to be feminine (Wood, 1996b, 1998, 2005). By the time we are old enough to appreciate the idea that culture is learned, our beliefs, values, language, and practices are already thoroughly woven into who we are and are almost invisible to us.

-Amelia-

The thing I like best about studying other cultures is how much I learn about my own culture and myself. Before I took a class in Asian culture, I would never have thought of myself as individualistic or selfish. Now I see that in a way I am, at least in comparison to people in a lot of Asian societies. Part of me thinks it would be good to be more family and community oriented, like many Asians, but I can't really imagine changing in that way.

Cultures Are Dynamic

The final principle of cultures is that they are **dynamic,** which means they evolve and change over time. Cultures must adapt to the natural world (geographic location, available natural resources, climate changes) and to human activities (inventions, war), and they must evolve in order to survive. We'll discuss four sources of cultural change.

Invention   **Invention** is the creation of tools, ideas, and practices (Samovar & Porter, 2001, p. 59). A frequently cited example of a tool is the wheel, which had far-reaching implications. Not only did its invention alter modes of transportation, it is the foundation of many machines and technologies. Other inventions that have changed cultural life are radio, television, the computer, the telephone, the airplane, the day-care center, and the automobile.

Inventions include more than machines. Societies also invent or create medicines, such as antibiotics, vaccines, and blood pressure medication. Medical inventions have dramatically extended the human life span, thereby altering our culture's views of age and of the timing of life events. For example, in the 1800s, when the average life span was around 40 years, people in the United States commonly married and had children while in their teens. Today, the average life span is around 70 years, and many people don't marry until their mid-twenties or early thirties and have children at later ages or not at all. The mid-twenties was considered middle age in 1900! As life spans lengthen, Western culture faces new challenges, including how to provide care for older citizens and how to make retirement secure. When the average life span was 60 to 65 years, someone who retired at 65 didn't have a long life expectancy. Today, a person who retires at 62 or 65 may have many more years of active life.

–Alan–

I'm not working toward a degree but just taking classes out of interest. I retired 5 years ago at 63, and at first it was nice not to have anything I had to do or anywhere I had to go. But then I got bored. After 40 years of being active, I didn't like just sitting around. A lot of my friends feel trapped in retirement. As a society, we haven't figured out how to make the later years satisfying.

Cultures also invent ideas that alter social life. For example, the concept of social diversity is a recent addition to Western thinking. As we learn to recognize and appreciate a variety of cultures and social communities, diversity changes how we interact in educational, business, and social contexts. Another concept that has changed Western life is environmental responsibility. Information about our planet's fragility has infused cultural consciousness. Terms such as *environmental responsibility* and *environmental ethics* have entered our everyday vocabularies, reshaping how we see our relationship with the environment.

Diffusion   **Diffusion** is borrowing from another culture (Samovar & Porter, 1994). Obvious examples of diffusion are borrowing language and foods from other cultures. What we call English or the American language includes a number of words imported from other cultures. Everyday conversations between Westerners are punctuated with terms such as *brocade, touché,* and *yin-yang.* The Japanese have traditionally enjoyed sushi. In recent years, many Westerners have tried and liked sushi, and sushi bars are not difficult to find in many U.S. cities. Taco Bells dot Western cities, and McDonald's has franchises throughout the world.

There are also more consequential forms of diffusion—forms that seriously alter a culture's way of life. Jagat Man Lama, a Nepalese leader, studied in India and took back what he learned to his native country. He has taught Nepalese villagers how to build water systems that provide unpolluted water. He has also taught them how to farm without harming the land. Many American businesses have adopted Japanese systems of management to improve productivity.

Cultural Calamity   **Cultural calamity** is adversity that brings about change in a culture. For example, war may devastate a country, destroying land and people alike. Losing a war can alter a culture's self-image, reshaping it into one of conquered people. Cultural calamity may also involve disasters such as hurricanes, volcanic eruptions, and plagues. Any of these can wipe out countless lives and alter patterns of life for the future.

The HIV/AIDS crisis is a recent example of a calamity that has transformed cultural life. Traditionally, many gay men were less monogamous than lesbians or heterosexual women and men, but the AIDS threat has increased long-term commitments between gay men (Huston & Schwartz, 1996). The HIV/AIDS crisis also has changed dating and sexual practices among heterosexuals, especially college students (Bowen & Michal-Johnson, 1996).

Communication A fourth source of cultural change is communication. Social communities in the United States have used communication to resist the mainstream's efforts to define their identity. Anytime a group says "No, the way you describe Americans doesn't fit me," that group initiates change in the culture's views of itself and of the range of people who make up that culture.

A primary way in which communication propels change is by naming things in ways that shape how we understand them. For instance, the term *date rape* was coined in the late 1980s. Although historically many women had been forced to have sex by men they were dating, until recently there was no term that named what happened as a violent invasion and a criminal act (Wood, 1992b). Similarly, the term *sexual harassment* names a practice that is certainly not new but only lately has been labeled and given social reality (Wood, 1994c). Myra's commentary explains how important the label is.

–Myra–

Fifteen years ago, when I was just starting college, a professor sexually harassed me, only I didn't know to call it that then. I felt guilty, like maybe I'd done something to encourage him, or I felt maybe I was overreacting to his kissing me and touching me. But after the Thomas–Hill hearings in 1991, I had a name for what happened—a name that said he was wrong, not me. Only then could I let go of that whole business.

As a primary tool of social movements, communication impels significant changes in cultural life. Thirty years ago, the civil rights movement in the United States used communication to transform laws and views of African Americans. Powerful leaders such as the Reverend Martin Luther King, Jr., and Malcolm X raised Black Americans' pride in their identity and heritage and inspired them to demand their rights in America. Simultaneously, African American leaders used communication to persuade the non-Black public to rethink its attitudes and practices.

Language also reflects changes in cultural attitudes and practices. For example, the term *homosexual* has been largely replaced by the terms *gay* and *lesbian*. The terms *boyfriend* and *girlfriend* are no longer the only ones people use to identify romantic interests; *partner, significant other,* and *special friend* are among the terms created to define romantic relations today.

In addition to bringing about change directly, communication also accompanies other sources of cultural change. Inventions such as antibiotics had to be explained to medical practitioners and to a general public that believed infections were caused by fate and accident, not viruses and bacteria. Ideas and practices borrowed from other cultures must similarly be translated into the language and culture of a particular society. Cultural calamities, too, must be defined and explained: Did the volcano erupt because of pressure in the earth or the anger of the gods? Did we lose the war because we had a weak military or because our cause was wrong? The ways a culture defines and communicates about calamities establish what these events mean and imply for future social practices and social life.

In sum, we've seen that cultures and social communities are distinct ways of life that order personal identity and social activities. Five principles about cultures capture the main points we've covered. First, communication is a primary way in which cultures are expressed and sustained. Second, cultures consist of material and nonmaterial components, including beliefs, values, norms, and language. Third, all cultures are shaped by historical and geographic forces that are carried forward through oral traditions and other forms of communication among members of a culture. The fourth principle emphasizes that we learn culture in the process of communicating with others; we are talked into membership in a society. Finally, we saw that cultures change continually in response to inventions, diffusion, calamities, and communication that challenges the status quo and argues for new ideas, roles, and patterns of life.

Actor Christopher Reeve used communication to increase public awareness of people with mobility disabilities.

Improving Communication between Cultures and Social Communities

So far we've seen that a social community's or culture's beliefs, values, and norms are reflected in the content and style of its communication. Each of us acts, speaks, and interprets others from the distinct perspective of the culture and social communities with which we identify. As long as we interact with others in our own culture, we're likely to share understandings of how to communicate and interpret one another.

But when we encounter people from other cultures and social communities, we can't count on shared guidelines. Thus, misunderstandings often occur. Although we can't eliminate misunderstandings, we can minimize them and the damage they can cause. Let's consider two principles for effective communication between members of different cultures and social communities.

Resist the Ethnocentric Bias

Most of us unreflectively use our home culture as the standard for judging other cultures. Some Taiwanese may regard many European Americans as rude for maintaining direct eye contact, whereas some European Americans may perceive some Tiawanese as evasive for averting their eyes. Many Westerners' habitual self-references may appear selfish and egocentric to some Koreans, and many Koreans' unassuming style may seem passive to some Westerners. How we view others and their communication depends more on the perspective we use to interpret them than on what others say and do.

Although it is natural to use our own culture and social communities as the standard for judging other cultures, this tendency interferes with understanding and communication. **Ethnocentrism** is the use of one's own culture and its practices as the standard for interpreting the values, beliefs, norms, and communication of other cultures. Literally, ethnocentrism means to put our own ethnicity (*ethno*) at the center (*centrism*) of the universe. Ethnocentrism fosters negative judgments of anything that differs from our own ways. In extreme form, ethnocentrism can lead one group of people to think it has the right to dominate and exploit other groups and to suppress or eliminate other cultures.

Sadly, ethnocentrism is a part of everyday experience. It occurs anytime we judge someone from a different culture or social community as less sensitive, ambitious, good, or polite than people from our own social communities or culture. It is ethnocentric to judge South Americans as lazy because they take time to do things instead of aiming for efficiency. It is ethnocentric for young people to disparage older people's values, perspectives, and behaviors. Likewise, some older people are ethnocentric when they negatively judge younger people's values, perspectives, and behaviors. Ethnocentrism leads to judgments that difference is not just different but wrong.

To reduce our tendencies to be ethnocentric, we should first remind ourselves that culture is learned. What is considered normal and right varies between cultures. In place of ethnocentrism, we can adopt the perspective of **cultural relativism,** which recognizes that cultures vary in how they think, act, and behave as well as in what they believe and value.

Cultural relativism is not the same as moral relativism. It is possible to acknowledge that a particular practice makes sense in its cultural context without approving of it. We may disapprove of clitoridectomies performed on young girls in some countries and also realize that genital surgery is rooted in long-standing traditions that have meaning in particular societies. Cultural relativism helps us remember that something that appears odd or even wrong to us may seem natural and right from the point of view of a different culture. That awareness facilitates understanding among people of different cultures and co-cultures.

Recognize That Responding to Diversity Is a Process

Developing respect for different cultures and social communities takes time. We don't move suddenly from being unaware of how people in other cultures communicate to being totally comfortable and competent interacting with them. Dealing with diversity is a gradual process that takes time, experience with a variety of people, and a commitment to participating in a world that includes a range of people and communication styles. Figure 4.1 shows five distinct responses to diversity, ranging from total rejection to complete acceptance. At particular times in our lives, we may find ourselves adopting different responses to diversity or to specific social groups. That's natural in the overall process of recognizing and responding to diversity.

Resistance   A common response to diversity is **resistance,** which occurs when we attack the cultural practices of others or proclaim that our own cultural traditions are superior. Resistance rejects the value and validity of anything that differs from what is familiar. Without education or reflection,

Figure 4.1
The Process of Responding to Multiple Cultures

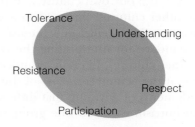

many people deal with diversity by making ethnocentric evaluations of others based on the standards of their own culture and social communities. Some people think their judgments reflect universal truths about what is normal and right. They aren't aware that they are imposing the arbitrary yardstick of their own particular social communities and culture and ignoring the yardsticks of other cultures and social communities.

-Brenda-

I overheard three of my classmates complaining about all of the mess and noise in the building where we have a class. They were saying what an inconvenience it is. The construction is to install an elevator in the building so that students like me, who are in wheelchairs, can take classes in classrooms on the second and third floor. I don't think my classmates are mean, but I do think they've never put themselves in my shoes—or my wheelchair! Every semester they pick classes according to what they want to take and when they what to take it. My first criterion is finding classes that I can get to—either first floor or in buildings that are wheelchair accessible.

Resistance may be expressed in many ways. Hate crimes pollute campuses and the broader society. Rejection of other cultures fuels racial slurs, anti-Semitic messages, and homophobic attitudes and actions. Resistance may also motivate members of a culture or social community to associate only with each other and to resist recognizing any commonalities with people from other cultures or social communities (Gitlin, 1995; Rorty, 1998).

Members of minority groups may also reject or depart from their culture or social communities to fit into the mainstream (Yamato, 2001). **Assimilation** occurs when people give up their own ways and adopt the ways of the dominant culture. For many years, assimilation was the dominant response of immigrants who came to the United States. The idea of America as a "melting pot" encouraged newcomers to melt into the mainstream by surrendering anything that made them different from native-born Americans.

Communication Highlight

Assimilation: Problem or Solution?

In *Cultures Across Borders* (1998), David Maclel and Maria Herrera-Sobek identify an increasing tension between the goals of assimilation and preservation of ethnic group identities in America. Historically, assimilation was virtually unchallenged as the "right" way for immigrants to live in America. In *Assimilation, American Style* (1998), Peter Salins notes that assimilation required three things: that immigrants adopt English as the national language, that they identify with America and take pride in its democratic principles, and that they embrace a strong work ethic of hard, honest work and self-reliance. Salins and others (Barry, 2001; Samuelson, 2001) argue that these three requirements are still critical if immigrants to the United States are to become full participants in America and if they are to help America stay united.

Not everyone agrees with Salins. According to some scholars (Collins, 1998; Fraser, 1992; West, 1992), the push for assimilation undermines distinctive ethnic identities and their expression. Another argument for preserving distinct ethnic communities is that they can serve as a check on dominant values and practices. For instance, Blacks in the 1960s critiqued the dominant racism in America, and their challenges led America to reform its laws and practices (Rorty, 1998). Women, who once held marginal positions in the United States, protested and argued for rights equal to those of men, and eventually they won those rights.

Author bell hooks seeks to affirm both commonalities and differences between us. She writes, "Community is formed not by the eradication of difference, but by its affirmation, by each of us claiming the identities and cultural legacies that shape who we are and how we live in the world" (1995, p. 265). She believes there is no necessary conflict between identifying with particular cultural groups and embracing shared traditions of a larger culture.

More recently, the Reverend Jesse Jackson proposed an alternative metaphor, the family quilt. This metaphor portrays the United States as a country in which people's unique values and customs are visible, as are the individual squares in a quilt; at the same time, each group contributes to a larger whole, just as each square in a quilt contributes to its overall beauty.

Tolerance A second response to diversity is **tolerance,** in which a person accepts differences even though she or he may not approve of or even understand them. Tolerance involves respecting others' rights to their own ways even though you may think their ways are wrong, bad, or offensive. Judgment still exists, but it's not actively imposed on others. Tolerance accepts the existence of differences, but it does not necessarily respect the value of other cultures and social communities. Although tolerance is less actively divisive than resistance, it is insufficient to foster a world in which people appreciate diversity and learn to grow from encountering differences.

–Chuck–

Until I came to college, I didn't know anyone who was gay. My parents taught me it was immoral, and I'd never questioned that. In my freshman year, I was good friends with Jim until he told me he was gay. I dropped him flat. Later I found out that a guy on my floor was gay, and this year two of my brothers at the house came out. I still don't really approve, but it doesn't bother me so much now.

Understanding A third response to diversity involves **understanding** that differences are rooted in cultural teachings and that no customs, traditions, or behaviors are intrinsically better than any others. This response grows out of cultural relativism, which we discussed earlier. Rather than assuming that whatever differs from our ways is a deviation from a universal standard (ours), a person who understands realizes that diverse values, beliefs, norms, and communication styles are rooted in distinct cultural perspectives. A person who responds to diversity with understanding might notice that a Japanese person doesn't hold eye contact, but he or she wouldn't assume that the Japanese person was devious. Instead, she or he would try to learn what eye contact means in Japanese society to understand the behavior in its native cultural context. Curiosity, rather than judgment, dominates in this stage as we make active efforts to understand others in terms of the values and traditions of their cultures.

Respect Once we move beyond judgment and begin to understand the cultural basis for practices that diverge from our own, we may come to **respect** differences. We can appreciate the value of placing family above self, of arranged marriage, and of feminine and masculine communication styles. We don't have to adopt others' ways to respect them on their own terms. Respect allows us to acknowledge differences yet remain personally anchored primarily in the values and customs of our own culture (Simons, Vázquez, & Harris, 1993). Respect for others includes the ability to see them and what they do on their terms, not ours.

Participation A final response to diversity is **participation,** in which we incorporate some of the practices and values of other groups into our own lives. More than other responses, participation encourages us to develop

Communicating with other people who differ from us fosters personal growth.

new skills and perspectives. Henry Louis Gates (1992), a Harvard professor, believes that the ideal is a society in which we build a common civic culture that celebrates both differences and commonalities.

Participation calls for us to be **multilingual,** which means we are able to speak and think in more than one language. Members of many social communities already are at least bilingual: Many African Americans know how to operate in mainstream Caucasian society and in traditional Black communities (Orbe, 1994; Orbe & Harris, 2001). Most women know how to communicate in both feminine and masculine ways, and they adapt their style to the people with whom they interact. Bilingualism is also practiced by many Asian Americans, Hispanics, lesbians and gay men, and members of other groups that are simultaneously part of a dominant culture and minority communities (Auer, 1998; Gaines, 1995).

My partner, Robbie, and I have learned how to communicate in both conventionally feminine and masculine styles. Like many men, he was socialized to be assertive, competitive, instrumental, and linear in conversation, whereas I learned to be more cooperative, relational, and inclusive in interaction. When we were first married, we often frustrated each other with our different ways of communicating. I perceived him as domineering, sometimes insensitive to feelings, and overly linear in his conversational style. He perceived me as being too focused on relationship issues and inefficient in moving from problems to solutions. Gradually, each of us learned to understand the other's ways of communicating and to respect our differences without judging them by our own standards. Still later, we came to appreciate and participate in each other's style; now both of us are fluent in both ways of communicating. This not only has improved our relationship but also has made each of us a more competent communicator in a range of settings.

Not everyone will learn to participate in a multicultural world. Some of us will become proficient at understanding but will not develop respect, or we may learn to respect cultures other than our own but not participate in them. For example, I can't engage in rapping, but I have learned to appreciate the skill involved in doing it well.

The different responses to cultural diversity that we've discussed represent a process of learning to interact with cultural groups other than our

Communication Highlight

Are racists born or made? Are sexists innately biased, or do they learn to be biased? Sociologist Phyllis Katz was so fascinated by those questions that she spent years studying children 6 months through 6 years old (Sommerville, 1999). Her research included both White and Black children. Katz found that as early as 6 months babies notice differences in sex and skin color. They first notice these in much the same way they recognize differences in hair color, height, size, and other physical characteristics of people. But by the time children begin kindergarten, they have learned how to think about sex and race differences.

Children who are taught that differences are interesting but not unequal tend to be open to people of different races, sexes, and other qualities. On the other hand, children who are taught that different sexes and skin colors represent unequal worth tend to devalue women and minority races. To raise children who respect differences, Katz encourages parents to talk openly and nonjudgmentally with their children about differences; pretending there are no differences doesn't work because children can see them. She also advises parents to expose their children to other people of different races, sexes, religious backgrounds, and so forth. The more children experience diversity, the less likely they are to be ethnocentric.

own. In the course of our lives, many of us move in and out of various responses as we interact with people from multiple cultures and social communities. At specific times, we may find we are tolerant of one cultural group and respectful of another, and those responses may change over time.

Experiencing Communication in Our Lives

CASE STUDY: The Job Interview

The conversation scripted here is featured as a multimedia scenario on the *Communication in Our Lives* CD-ROM included with this book. Once you've launched the CD, click on the "Communication Scenarios" icon, and, from the Scenarios Menu, select "The Job Interview" to watch the video. Improve your own communication skills by reading, watching, listening to, critiquing, and analyzing this communication encounter.

Analyze the scenario by applying the principles covered in this chapter, and respond to the prompts that accompany the video, which you can access by clicking on "Analysis." After completing the conversation analysis and answering the questions, you can click on the "Done" button to compare your responses with the ones I suggest. Additional analysis questions are available in print at the end of this chapter and on the book's website.

Mei-ying Yung is a senior who has majored in computer programming. Mei-ying's aptitude for computer programming has earned her much attention at her college. She has developed and installed complex new programs to make advising more efficient and to reduce the frustration and errors in registration for courses. Although she has been in the United States for 6 years, in many ways Mei-ying reflects the Chinese culture into which she was born and in which she spent the first 15 years of her life. Today Mei-ying is interviewing for a position at New Thinking, a fast-growing tech company that specializes in developing programs tailored to the needs of individual companies. The interviewer, Barton Hingham, is 32 years old and a native of California, where New Thinking is based. As the scenario opens, Ms. Yung walks into the small room where Mr. Hingham is seated behind a desk. He rises to greet her and walks over with his hand stretched out to shake hers.

Jason Harris/© 2001 Wadsworth

HINGHAM: Good morning, Ms. Yung. I've been looking forward to meeting you. Your résumé is most impressive.

Ms. Yung looks downward, smiles, and limply shakes Mr. Hingham's hand. He gestures to a chair, and she sits down in it.

HINGHAM: I hope this interview will allow us to get to know each other a bit and decide whether there is a good fit between you and New Thinking. I'll be asking you some questions about your background and interests. And you should feel free to ask me any questions you have. Okay?

YUNG: Yes.

HINGHAM: I see from your transcript that you majored in computer programming and did very well. I certainly didn't have this many As on my college transcript!

YUNG: Thank you. I am very fortunate to have good teachers.

HINGHAM: Tell me a little about your experience in writing original programs for business applications.

YUNG: I do not have great experience, but I have been grateful to help the college with some of its work.

HINGHAM: Tell me about how you've helped the college. I see you designed a program for advising. Can you explain to me what you did to develop that program?

YUNG: Not really so much. I could see that much of advising is based on rules, so I only need to write the rules into a program so advisors could do their jobs more better.

HINGHAM: Perhaps you're being too modest. I've done enough programming myself to know how difficult it is to develop a program for something with as many details as advising. There are so many majors, each with different requirements and regulations. How did you program all of that variation?

YUNG: I read the handbook on advising and the regulations on each major and then programmed decision trees into an advising template. Not so hard.

HINGHAM: Well that's exactly the kind of project we do at New Thinking. People come to us with problems in their jobs, and we write programs to solve them. Does that sound like the kind of thing you would enjoy doing?

YUNG: Yes. I very much like to solve problems to help others.

HINGHAM: What was your favorite course during college?

YUNG: They are all very valuable. I enjoy all.

HINGHAM: Did you have one course in which you did especially well?

YUNG: [blushing, looking down] I would not say that. I try to do well in all my courses, to learn from them.

Later Barton Hingham and Molly Cannett, another interviewer for New Thinking, are discussing the day's interviews over dinner.

CANNETT: Did you find any good prospects today?

HINGHAM: Not really. I thought I was going to be bowled over by this one woman—name's Mei-ying Yung—who has done some incredibly intricate programming on her own while in college.

CANNETT: Sounds like just the kind of person we're looking for.

HINGHAM: I thought so too, until the interview. She just didn't seem to have the gusto we want. She showed no confidence or initiative in the interview. It was like the transcript and the person were totally different.

CANNETT: Hmmm, that's odd. Usually when we see someone who looks that good on paper, the interview is just a formality.

HINGHAM: Yeah, but I guess the formality is more important than we realized—Yung was a real dud in the interview. I still don't know what to make of it.

Chapter Summary

In this chapter, we've learned about the close connections between communication and cultures. Our communication reflects our culture's values and norms; at the same time, our communication sustains those values and norms and the perception that they are natural and right. In elaborating this view of culture, we saw that cultures consist of both material and nonmaterial components, that they are shaped by historical and geographic forces, that they are learned through socialization, and that they are dynamic, always evolving and changing.

The final section of the chapter emphasized the importance of learning to communicate effectively in a multicultural society. We need to understand and respect the ways in which we differ from one another if we are to communicate effectively and if we are to live and work together in a diverse social world. Moving beyond ethnocentric judgments based on our own culture allows us to understand, respect, and sometimes participate in a diverse world and to enlarge ourselves in the process.

But differences between us are only part of the story. It would be a mistake to be so aware of differences that we overlook our commonalities. We all have feelings, dreams, ideas, hopes, fears, and values. Our common humanness transcends many of our differences, an idea beautifully expressed in a poem by Maya Angelou (1990, p. 5).

> **Human Family**
> I note the obvious differences
> between each sort and type,
> but we are more alike, my friends,
> than we are unalike.
> We are more alike, my friends,
> than we are unalike.

"Human Family" from *I Shall Not Be Moved* by Maya Angelou, copyright © 1990 by Maya Angelou. Used by permission of Random House, Inc.

Communication in Our Lives ONLINE

In addition to presenting the case studies' multimedia scenarios, the *Communication in Our Lives* CD-ROM provides quick access to the *Communication in Our Lives* website and InfoTrac College Edition. The website is online at http://communication .wadsworth.com/woodciol4, but you can only access this book's premium web content when you link to the site directly through the book's CD.

The *Communication in Our Lives* website features interactive tools for learning and reviewing the chapter's concepts and key terms, including electronic versions of the "For Further Reflection and Discussion" questions that appear below and a review quiz.

The website also provides updated web links and additional InfoTrac College Edition activities. If required, you can e-mail completed chapter activities or the quizzes to your instructor.

Key Concepts

assimilation, *109*	dynamic, *104*	resistance, *108*
beliefs, *99*	ethnocentrism, *107*	respect, *110*
culture, *89*	invention, *104*	social communities, *91*
cultural calamity, *105*	multilingual, *111*	tolerance, *110*
cultural relativism, *108*	norms, *100*	understanding, *110*
diffusion, *105*	participation, *110*	values, *99*

For Further Reflection and Discussion

1. Some scholars claim that there are many distinct social communities in the United States. Examples are deaf people, people with disabilities, and elderly people. Do you agree that these groups qualify as distinct social communities? What is needed for a group to be considered a specific and distinctive social community?

2. Continue the exercise started on page 97 by listing common sayings or adages in your culture and social communities. Decide what each saying reflects about the beliefs, values, and concerns of your culture.

3. Are the different styles of communication typical of distinct social communities evident in online interaction? For instance, do you see patterned differences between messages written by women and men? If you see differences, are they consistent with the generalizations about gendered social communities that we discussed in this chapter?

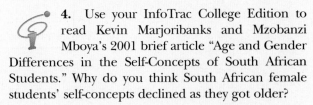 **4.** Use your InfoTrac College Edition to read Kevin Marjoribanks and Mzobanzi Mboya's 2001 brief article "Age and Gender Differences in the Self-Concepts of South African Students." Why do you think South African female students' self-concepts declined as they got older?

5. Consider metaphors for U.S. society. For many years, it was described as "the melting pot," a metaphor that suggested that all the differences between people from various cultures would be melted down and merged into a uniform culture. In recent years, however, the idea of a melting pot has been criticized for tending to obliterate differences rather than respect them. The Reverend Jesse Jackson refers to the United States as a family quilt; others say it's a collage or a rainbow in which differences exist and are noted as parts of the overall diverse society. Flora Davis (1991) calls the United States a salad bowl. What do you think she means by the metaphor of salad bowl? What metaphor would you recommend? On what do you base your metaphor?

6. Think critically about how you do and do not fit generalizations about your racial or ethnic group. Identify three ways in which you reflect what is generally true of your group. Identify three ways in which you personally diverge from generalizations about your group. Extend this exercise by thinking critically about how people in racial or ethnic groups other than your own do and do not fit generalizations about their group.

7. Reflect on the different responses to diversity that we discussed in the last section of this chapter. What ethical values do you perceive in each response?

Experiencing Communication in Our Lives

Questions for Analysis and Discussion

Review the video of the scenario entitled "The Job Interview" that you watched when completing this chapter's case study (pages 112–114), or, if you haven't seen it yet, watch it for the first time. If you didn't previously finish the analysis questions included on the CD-ROM, do so now, and then respond to the following questions, which are also available on the book's website under "Activities for Chapter 4."

1. How does Mei-ying Yung's communication reflect her socialization in Chinese culture?

2. How could Mei-ying be more effective without abandoning the values of her native culture?

3. What could enhance Barton Hingham's ability to communicate effectively with people who were raised in non-Western cultures?

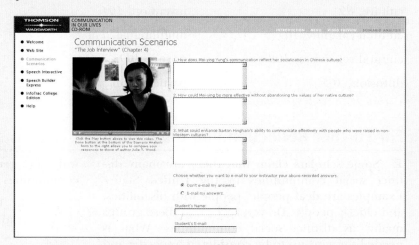

CHAPTER 5

The Verbal Dimension of Communication

Focus Questions

1. How can words hurt people?
2. To what extent is bias inevitable in language?
3. Can we think without symbols?
4. How does using *I*-language improve communication?

"I do."

"You're terrible."

"He's a drunk."

"The war on the environment is stealing our children's future."

The four sentences you have just read illustrate the power of words. Words name experiences, shape attitudes, and define our identities. The two little words *I do*, for instance, have the power to change people's lives personally, legally, socially, and spiritually. Parents who say, "You're terrible" can devastate a child's self-concept (Vachss, 1998a, 1998b). It's more dramatic and memorable to give a speech about the "war on the environment" than to speak against "opening public lands to mining and drilling." Likewise, the phrase "stealing our children's future" is more powerful than saying, "Environmental losses will have long-range consequences."

You may also have noticed that these opening examples illustrate difficulties arising from the abstractness of language, which we discussed in Chapter 2. "He's a drunk" is an abstract generalization based on concrete behaviors that may or may not justify the label. People who suffer from certain medical conditions often behave much like people who are intoxicated. Furthermore, someone who has drunk too much on a specific occasion is not necessarily a drunk. It is harsher to say, "He's a drunk" than "He drank too much last night" or "Sometimes he drinks too much."

In this chapter, we take a close look at the verbal dimension of communication. We begin by defining symbols, which are the basis of language. Second, we explore principles of verbal communication. Next, we consider what language allows us to do. The final section of the chapter focuses on guidelines for effective use of language.

Symbols and Meaning

As we discovered in our discussion of perception, we don't interact with phenomena in their complete, concrete detail. Instead, we abstract only certain parts of phenomena to notice and label. After we label them, we tend to respond to our labels, not to the phenomena themselves. This means that our perceptions are shaped by symbols. The semantic triangle (Figure 5.1) illustrates the indirect relationship between symbols and the phenomena they represent. Notice that the line between the symbol *cat* and the physical referent of a cat is dotted to indicate that the symbol and its referent are only indirectly related. The lines between the thought and the symbol *cat*

Figure 5.1
The Semantic Triangle

Source: Adapted from Wood, J. T. (2004). *Communication Theories in Action* (3rd ed.). Belmont, CA: Wadsworth. Reprinted with permission of Wadsworth, a division of Thomson Learning, Inc.

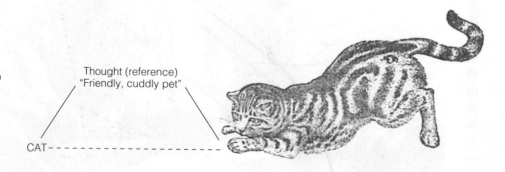

Thought (reference)
"Friendly, cuddly pet"

CAT -

and between the thought and the actual cat are unbroken, indicating that our thoughts are directly related to symbols and their referents.

Symbols represent phenomena. For instance, the word *house* is a symbol that stands for a type of building. *Total quality management* is a verbal symbol that represents a specific managerial philosophy. *Cyberspace, hyperlink, instant messaging, chat rooms,* and *Internet* are words we have coined to represent phenomena that accompany computer technologies.

All words are symbols, but not all symbols are words. Art, music, company logos, and objects also can be symbols that stand for feelings, thoughts, and experiences. The key to understanding symbols is to realize that they are arbitrary, ambiguous, abstract ways of representing things.

Symbols Are Arbitrary

Symbols are **arbitrary,** which means they are not intrinsically connected to what they represent. For instance, the word *book* has no necessary or natural connection to what you are reading now. We could substitute a different word as long as we agreed it would stand for what we now call a book. Certain words seem right because as a society we agree to use them in particular ways, but they have no natural correspondence to their referents.

The high-tech industry provides dramatic examples of the ways symbols function as private codes that are understood by insiders and exclude outsiders.

Because language is arbitrary, we can create private codes that only certain people know. For example, in most organizations employees use some specialized terms that are not understood by outsiders. Similarly, most couples have terms that are not understood, and are not meant to be understood, by people outside the relationship. This allows them to pass private messages in public settings. Coded language also allows people to communicate confidential information. Two primary tasks of military intelligence are to invent secret, unbreakable codes and to break the secret codes of others.

Language and meanings change over time. In the 1950s, *gay* meant "lighthearted and merry"; today it is generally understood to mean men who are sexually oriented toward men. Until the 1980s, the word *apple* was assumed to refer to a fruit, but today it is equally likely to refer to a computer company and its products. College students are particularly creative in making up new language. The first time a student told me my class was "da bomb," I was offended. I thought he meant that the course was really bad! He explained that "da bomb" is a compliment. Students also seem to be the originators of "101" as a generic description of something elementary. Apparently the fact that "101" generally signifies introductory courses (Comm 101, Psych 101) has been generalized to expressions such as "dating 101" and "recycling 101."

© Mark Richards/PhotoEdit

Communication Highlight

Code Talkers

During World War II, a special group of soldiers serving on Iwo Jima developed a private code that was never broken by enemy intelligence. Because all the soldiers in this group were Navajo Indians, the code they devised was based on the Navajo language, an oral language that had never been written down and was not understood by non-Navajos. Dubbed "the code talkers," these soldiers invented a 400-word code that was extremely secure. Drawing on the strong nature theme in Navajo life and language, the code included the Navajo words for owl (observer), hawk (dive bomber), and egg (bomb).

To learn more about the code talkers, go to http:www.history.navy.mil/faqs/faq61-2.htm. This site provides facts about the history and work of the Navajo code talkers, as well as related links, including a dictionary of terms used by the code talkers.

© AP/Wide World Photos

President George W. Bush honors a Navajo code talker.

Many words and terms were coined in response to changes in business and the professions. *Heads up* means "I'm giving you some information in advance so you'll be prepared for something that's coming later." Today, many people work out of *virtual offices,* a term nobody had heard 20 years ago. The word *downsize* didn't exist 15 years ago, yet today it is commonly used. We used to hear that companies laid people off; today we hear that companies have *downsized* or *rightsized.*

Politics is another rich source of new words. In 1994, Newt Gingrich proposed "the contract with America," a phrase that symbolized the newly elected Republican majority's plans to restrict or reverse much of the work of Democratic leaders. George W. Bush campaigned for the presidency with the slogan "compassionate conservatism." Later, as president, he launched "the war on terrorism." *The moral majority, big-spending liberals,* and *battleground states* are other terms that were coined by politicians and have entered into popular language.

Symbols Are Ambiguous

Symbols are also **ambiguous,** which means their meanings aren't clear cut or fixed. The meanings of words vary, even words we have agreed to use in specific ways. *Government regulation* may mean positive assistance to citizens who are suffering from pollutants emitted by a chemical factory. To owners of the chemical company, however, *government regulation* may mean costly and undesired requirements to reduce pollution. To one person, a *good friend* means someone to hang out with; to another person, it means someone to confide in. *Affirmative action* means different things to people who have experienced racial or sexual discrimination and to those who haven't. Although the words are the same, their meanings vary according to individuals' identities and experiences.

Although words don't mean exactly the same thing to everyone, many symbols have an agreed-on range of meanings within a culture. Thus, we all understand that *dog* means a four-footed creature, but each of us also has personal meanings for the word based on dogs we have known and our experiences with them. We've all experienced dynamic speakers, yet we may differ in our notions of what concrete attitudes and behaviors would lead us to label a speaker *dynamic* (remember the abstraction ladder we discussed in Chapter 2). Because we learn meanings by interacting in our society, intercultural communication often involves misunderstandings.

The ambiguity of symbols explains why misunderstandings so often occur. At work, team members may have different meanings for the same words. In personal relationships, too, the ambiguity of words is a source of frequent misunderstandings. When my niece, Michelle, visited me this year, I told her we were going to go to bed early one night because we had to leave at 5 A.M. to catch a plane the next day. When Michelle was still reading and hadn't changed to her nightgown at 10:30 P.M., I reminded her we were

Communication Highlight

New Language for New Experiences

Any new technology demands new language to describe its parts and the experiences it makes possible. With the invention of the automobile, we coined words such as *gearshift* and *carburetor*. With cable and satellite television came terms such as *pay-per-view* and *channel surfing*. Online communication and web interaction also have given birth to many new terms or new meanings for existing terms (Higgins, 1996; Stone, 1998):

buddy list	A feature available from some online service providers that alerts you when a friend of yours signs on
IM	Abbreviation for "instant message," usually from someone on your buddy list
punting	Causing another user's screen to freeze, which forces the other user to log off

wbasayc	Abbreviation for "write back as soon as you can"
scrolling	Rapid-fire repetition of nonsense phrases to disrupt an online discussion
meatspace	The physical world, as distinct from the virtual world
hamster	A wireless mouse
treeware	Manuals and documentation for computer programs
cobweb	A website that is never updated

To learn more terms in net-language, go to http://www.netlingo.com.

Communication Highlight

The Dynamism of Language

If you think you have trouble keeping up with new words, pity the *Oxford English Dictionary's* new words team. To prepare the latest dictionary, the team screened more than 216,000 proposed new words and terms to decide which ones would gain legitimacy by appearing in the new dictionaries (Smith, 1999). Here's a sampling of new words and terms they accepted:

analysisparalysis — paralysis of the ability to make a decision because of overwhelming information that one feels the need to analyze

ego-surfing — searching the Internet for instances of your own name

exformation — information that is known to everyone so it doesn't need to be explicitly stated when communicating

elk test — testing a car's ability to stay upright and on the road when making high-speed turns

uplift anxiety — psychological difficulties that result from being cured of depression and starting to feel more positive

irritainment — very irritating programming that one nonetheless watches compulsively

microphobes — opponents of Microsoft who think the software company has created an unfair monopoly in the industry

fashionista — a devotee to the cutting edge of fashion

dot govs — government employees in Washington, D.C., because ".gov" is part of their e-mail addresses

 If you want to learn more about slang and idioms, some of which may appear in dictionaries, check out this website: http://www.owlnet.rice.edu/~ling215/NewWords.

going to bed early. She replied "I know. I'll be in bed by midnight." I'd meant 10 P.M. when I said early!

Ambiguity often surfaces in friendships and romantic relationships. Martina tells her boyfriend that he's not being attentive, meaning that she wants him to listen more closely to what she says. However, he infers that she wants him to call more often. Similarly, spouses often have different meanings for "doing their share" of home chores. To most women, it means doing half of the work, but some men may see it as doing more than their fathers did (Hochschild & Machung, 2003; Wood, 1998).

To minimize the problems that ambiguity can cause, we should be as clear as possible in communication. In the earlier example, Martina asked her boyfriend to be more attentive, but she and he had different ideas about what that meant. Thus, it's more effective to say, "I would like you to look at me and give feedback when I'm talking" than "I wish you'd be more attentive."

Sharpen Your Skill

Clarifying Meaning

The next time someone you're close to uses an ambiguous word such as *successful* or *thoughtful,* ask what she or he means by the word. Invite the person to tell you in concrete terms what she or he sees as successful or thoughtful. Is that what it means to you?

Now apply the same principle to your own communication. When you use an abstract, ambiguous word, ask whomever you're talking with what he or she thinks it means. Are your meanings the same?

To develop your ability to recognize the ambiguity of language, complete Activity 5.1, "Recognizing Ambiguity in Verbal Language," and Activity 5.9, "The Personal Nature of Meanings," in your *Student Companion* or online under "Activities for Chapter 5" at the *Communication in Our Lives* website.

The ambiguity of language may also cause problems in groups, organizations, and public speaking. A team leader who asks members to be "more responsible" may get a variety of responses, depending on what the ambiguous term *responsible* means to different members. The term *restructuring* may be interpreted to mean firing employees, closing locations, or reducing bonuses and salaries. Your supervisor tells you it's important to be "a team player," which you assume means you should cooperate with co-workers. However, your supervisor may mean that you are expected to initiate and participate in project teams on the job. After you give a public presentation, someone suggests you should be "more forceful," but does that mean you should use more facial expressions, greater vocal inflection, stronger evidence, more motion? Effective communicators realize that different people may attribute different meanings to the same words.

Communication Highlight

(Not) Saying "I'm Sorry"

In April 2001, a Chinese plane and a U.S. survey plane collided in international airspace. The Chinese plane crashed, killing the pilot, its only occupant. The badly damaged U.S. plane sent out Mayday calls asking permission to make an emergency landing, but these were ignored in violation of international policy. Seeing no other choice, the pilot of the U.S. plane landed without permission. The U.S. pilot and crew were safe, but Chinese officials took possession of the plane and crew and refused to release them until the United States issued a formal apology acknowledging that it was at fault in causing the death of the Chinese pilot and landing without permission. The U.S. government believed it had no reason to apologize.

For weeks, high tensions marked negotiations and relations between the United States and China. Finally, a letter was written that made use of the ambiguity of language. The letter, written in English, stated that the United States was "very sorry" about the missing Chinese pilot, Wang Wei, and the loss to his family. The Chinese embassy trans-

lated the phrase *very sorry* as *shenbiao qianyi,* an expression of sincere apology that connotes acknowledgment of error and acceptance of responsibility for harm done. But the U.S. Embassy translated *very sorry* as *feichang wanxi,* which means extreme sympathy for the Chinese people and the family of Wang Wei and does not connote fault or acceptance of responsibility. The varying translations of "very sorry" allowed both countries to save face.

Symbols Are Abstract

Finally, symbols are **abstract,** which means not concrete or tangible. They stand for ideas, people, events, objects, feelings, and so forth, but they are not the things they represent. In Chapter 2, we discussed the abstraction ladder, whereby we move farther and farther away from concrete reality. The symbols we use vary in abstractness. *Managerial potential* is a very abstract term. *Organizational and presentational skill* is less abstract. Even more concrete expressions are *experience in collaborating with others, speaking to large groups,* and *organizing project teams.*

–Adiva–

Non-native speakers have much difficulty with abstract language. My resident assistant told us we must observe "quiet hours" from 7 to 10 each night so that people can study. But everyone on my hall plays music and talks during quiet hours. My adviser told me I needed to take courses in social diversity, so I took a class in oral traditions of Asian cultures. Then my adviser told me that is a non-Western civilization course, not one in social diversity.

As our symbols become increasingly abstract, the potential for confusion mushrooms. One way this happens is through overgeneralization. Public speakers sometimes make very general claims that critical listeners won't accept without clarification. For example, the assertion that "environmentalists despise big business" is overly general. Few environmentalists dislike all big business; many respect the goals and the efforts to protect the environment made by a substantial number of large businesses and industries.

Overly abstract language can also complicate personal relationships. Couple counselor Aaron Beck (1988) reports that generalizations can distort how partners think about a relationship. Statements such as "You never go along with my preferences" or "You always interrupt me" are overgeneralizations that are not entirely accurate. Yet the symbols partners use them to frame how they think about their experiences. We are more likely to notice behaviors that are consistent with our labels for people than behaviors that are inconsistent (Fincham & Bradbury, 1987). When we say that a partner never listens, we're likely to notice the times he or she doesn't seem to listen, and not to perceive all the times when he or she listens carefully.

Communication Highlight

Lost in Translation

Language doesn't always translate well. Consider these examples of English terms that turned out to mean something very different in other cultures (Leaper, 1999).

When the U.S. manufacturer of the soft drink Fresca decided to export the product to Mexico, sales were dismal. It turned out the word *fresca* in Spanish sometimes is used to describe a woman who is aggressive, brash, or unfeminine in her behavior—hardly an image that prompts buying a soft drink.

Don't say, "I'm a Pepper" in the United Kingdom. Dr. Pepper discovered that this didn't work, because *pepper* is British slang for prostitute.

When General Motors exported its popular Chevrolet Nova to South America, there were problems. In Spanish, *no va* means "does not go"—not a very good advertisement for a car!

For years, Allstate has run an ad that shows a person holding out his or her hands while the voice-over promises, "You're in good hands with Allstate." This ad didn't work in Germany; there, two hands held out signify begging, not offering security and protection.

Jargon and Gobbledygook

Make a list of ambiguous and abstract language used in your present workplace or a previous one. List jargon—specialized terms that are clear to professionals in the area. Next, list words and phrases that aren't necessary for specialized concepts but seem only to cause confusion and ambiguity.

Do you see the following phrases as clear or as ambiguous? Would they invite confusion and lack of shared understanding among employees?

cash flow problems

teamwork

negative revenues

aggressive accounting

 To develop your ability to reduce the abstractness of language, complete Activity 5.6, "Reducing the Abstractness of Language," in your *Student Companion* or online under "Activities for Chapter 5" at the *Communication in Our Lives* website.

Because symbols are arbitrary, ambiguous, and abstract, they can represent complex ideas and feelings in ways that allow us to share our ideas with others. At the same time, symbols have the potential to create misunderstandings. When we understand that symbols are ambiguous, arbitrary, and abstract, we can guard against their potential to hinder communication.

Principles of Verbal Communication

Now that we understand what symbols are, we can consider three principles that further explain how we use verbal communication and how it affects us.

Interpretation Creates Meaning

Because symbols are abstract, ambiguous, and arbitrary, their meanings aren't self-evident or absolute. Instead, we have to interpret the meaning of symbols. We construct meanings in the process of interacting with others

and through dialogues we carry on in our own heads (Duck, 1994a, 1994b; Shotter, 1993). The process of constructing meaning is itself symbolic because we rely on words in thinking about what things mean.

If a work associate says, "Let's go to dinner after work," the comment could mean a variety of things. It could be an invitation to explore transforming the work relationship into a friendship. It could be a veiled request for a strategy session regarding some issue in the workplace. It might also indicate that the person issuing the invitation is interested in a romantic relationship. "Let's go to dinner after work" doesn't mean the same thing at all times. Does "I'm sorry" mean I am sorry for something I did? Or does it mean I'm sorry about something that happened, even though it wasn't my fault? We have to invest effort to interpret words and assign meanings to them. By extension, effective communicators are alert to possible misunderstandings, and they check with others to see whether meanings match.

Communication Is Rule Guided

Verbal communication is patterned by unspoken but broadly understood rules (Argyle & Henderson, 1985; Shimanoff, 1980). **Communication rules** are shared understandings of what communication means and what kinds of communication are and are not appropriate in various situations. For the most part, rules aren't explicit or intentionally constructed. In the course of interacting with our families and others, we unconsciously absorb rules that guide how we communicate and how we interpret others' communication. Children begin to understand and follow communication rules by the time they are 1 or 2 years old (Miller, 1993).

Two kinds of rules guide communication (Cronen, Pearce, & Snavely, 1979; Pearce, Cronen, & Conklin, 1979). **Regulative rules** specify when, how, where, and with whom to talk about certain things. For instance, we follow regulative rules for turn taking in conversation. In formal contexts, we usually know not to interrupt when someone else is speaking, but in more informal settings interruptions may be appropriate. Talking during formal speeches is appropriate in some contexts, as in traditional African American churches and meetings, where feedback usually is regarded as evidence of interest. Some families have a rule that people can't argue at the dinner table or that conflict should be avoided (Honeycutt, Woods, & Fontenot, 1993; Jones & Gallois, 1989).

Regulative rules also define when, where, and with whom it's appropriate or necessary to communicate in particular ways. Some people have the rule that it's okay to kiss intimates in private but not in public. On the job, there are often unwritten regulative rules that specify that people with higher positions may interrupt subordinates but that subordinates may not interrupt organizational superiors. Regulative rules in the workplace may also stipulate that employees are expected to show interest and respect when higher-ups communicate.

Constitutive rules define what communication means by telling us how to count certain kinds of communication. We learn what counts as showing respect (paying attention), demonstrating affection (kisses, hugs), and being rude (yawning, talking over others). We also learn what communication is expected of a friend (expressing support), a professional (being assertive), and a romantic partner (expressing trust). We learn it is appropriate to applaud when a speaker is introduced and after she or he finishes a presentation.

Communication Rules in Families

Identify constitutive and regulative rules you follow when interacting with your family.

Constitutive Rules

What counts as being attentive in a team meeting at work?

What counts as being attentive to a romantic partner?

What counts as being respectful of parents?

What counts as being responsible?

What counts as showing affection?

Regulative Rules

When is it appropriate to interrupt parents, friends, co-workers?

What topics are appropriate during family dinner conversation?

With whom can you talk about personal issues?

With whom do you talk about money problems?

  To increase your awareness of communication rules, complete Activity 5.3, "Understanding Communication Rules," in your *Student Companion* or online under "Activities for Chapter 5" at the *Communication in Our Lives* website.

Social interactions tend to follow rules that are widely shared in a specific society. Interaction between intimates also follows rules, but these may not be shared by the culture as a whole. Intimate partners negotiate private

What regulative and constitutive rules guided mealtime conversation in your family when you were growing up?

© Taxi/Getty Images

Communication Highlight

Rules for Communication Using Technologies

Have you ever been in church when your cell phone rang? Have you ever been disturbed in a theater by another person's pager? If so, you understand the potential for irritation that accompanies new technologies of communication. One funeral director explained that he asks people to turn off their pagers and cell phones before entering funeral services. Even so, more than once he has had to ask people to leave a graveside service when their communication equipment went off (Boudreau, 2000). On a less somber note, restaurant managers report that more and more customers are complaining about cell phones ringing during their meals. One exasperated diner nearly got into a food fight when his meal was disturbed by eight cell phones clanging around him.

Today, millions of Americans use cell phones and smart phones (a cross between the wireless phone and the personal digital assistant or PDA). Yet we haven't developed any consensual rules for when to use them—and when not to use them. What should the rules be?

Should people be required to turn off cell phones and pagers in restaurants, at funerals, in classrooms, in church, at public meetings?

Should people interrupt face-to-face conversations to answer cell phones or pages?

Is it impolite, not to mention dangerous, to talk on a phone while you are driving?

 To read a summary of a national report on the use and safety of wireless phones and some states' efforts to pass laws limiting their use, go to http://www.nhtsa.dot.gov/people/injury/research/wireless/#rep.

rules to guide how they communicate and what certain things mean (Wood, 2000). Couples craft personal rules that specify how to argue, express love, make decisions, request favors, and spend time together (Beck, 1988; Fitzpatrick, 1988).

In the process of interacting with others, we learn communication rules, often without even realizing it. New employees learn the rules for communicating with each other and with superiors as they interact with co-workers and internalize the organizational culture. They learn which supervisors are open to suggestions, whether teamwork or individual initiatives are rewarded, and what degree of socializing is expected on the job. We may not realize that rules exist until one is broken and we become aware that we had an expectation. A study by Victoria DeFrancisco (1991) revealed that husbands consistently interrupted wives and were unresponsive to topics wives initiated. The couples were unaware of the rules, but their communication nonetheless followed the pattern. Becoming aware of communication rules empowers you to change those that don't promote healthy interaction and relationships.

  To discover what happens when you violate communication rules, complete Activity 5.10, "Breaking the Rules of Gendered Communication," in your *Student Companion* or online under "Activities for Chapter 5" at the *Communication in Our Lives* website.

–Milan–

There's this funny pattern with the guys I hang out with. It starts when one of us says, "Let's go get something to eat." Then somebody suggests Mexican food, and someone else says he hates it. Another guy says we should get a pizza, and someone else says they're too expensive. Somebody says burgers, and one of the others groans. Then we decide to fix something at the apartment. Honestly, we go through this routine two or three times a week, and it's always the same.

Punctuation Affects Meaning

We punctuate communication to create meaning. In writing, we use periods to define where ideas stop and start. Similarly, in interpersonal communication, **punctuation** is the mental mark of the beginnings and endings of particular interactions (Watzlawick, Beavin, & Jackson, 1967). For example, when a teacher steps to the front of a classroom, that punctuates the beginning of the class. When the CEO enters a room, that punctuates the beginning of a meeting. When a speaker says, "Thank you for your attention" and folds notes, that punctuates the end of the formal speech.

When we don't agree on punctuation, problems may arise. A common instance of conflicting punctuation is the demand–withdraw pattern (Bergner & Bergner, 1990; Caughlin & Vangelisti, 2000) (Figure 5.2). This occurs when one person tries to express closeness and the other strives to maintain autonomy by avoiding interaction. The more one partner pushes for personal talk, the further the other withdraws. Each partner punctuates the beginning of the interaction with the other's behavior. Thus, the demander thinks, "I pursue because you withdraw," and the withdrawer thinks, "I withdraw because you pursue."

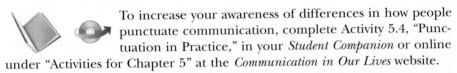 To increase your awareness of differences in how people punctuate communication, complete Activity 5.4, "Punctuation in Practice," in your *Student Companion* or online under "Activities for Chapter 5" at the *Communication in Our Lives* website.

Effective communicators realize that people don't always agree on punctuation. When they punctuate differently, they ascribe different meanings to what is happening between them. To break out of destructive cycles such as demand–withdraw, partners need to discuss how each of them is punctuating the experience. This reminds us of a guideline discussed earlier: Effective communication includes perspective taking. Steven's comment illustrates the demand–withdraw pattern and a lack of perspective taking between him and his parents.

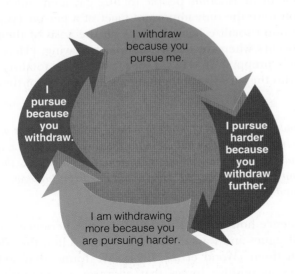

Figure 5.2
The Demand–Withdraw Pattern

I withdraw because you pursue me.

I pursue because you withdraw.

I pursue harder because you withdraw further.

I am withdrawing more because you are pursuing harder.

My parents say I am irresponsible if I don't tell them about something I do. So then they probe me and call more often to check up on me. I hate that kind of intrusion, so I don't return their calls and I sidestep questions. That makes them call more and ask more questions. That makes me clam up more. And we just keep going in circles.

Symbolic Abilities

Because we use symbols, we live in a world of ideas and meanings. Instead of just reacting to our concrete environments, we think about them and sometimes transform them. In much the same way, we don't simply accept ourselves as we are but continuously work to change and grow. Philosophers of language have identified five ways symbolic capacities affect our lives (Cassirer, 1944; Langer, 1953, 1979). As we discuss each, we'll consider how to realize the constructive power of symbols and minimize the problems they can generate.

Symbols Define

The most basic symbolic ability is definition. We use symbols to define experiences, people, relationships, feelings, and thoughts. As we saw in Chapter 2, the definitions we impose on phenomena shape what they mean to us. When we label people, we focus attention on particular aspects of them, and we necessarily obscure other aspects of who they are. We might define a person as an environmentalist, a teacher, a gourmet cook, and a father. Each way of classifying the person directs our attention to certain, and not other, aspects of identity. We might discuss wilderness legislation with the environmentalist, talk about testing with the teacher, swap recipes with the cook, and exchange stories about children with the father. We tend to interact with people according to how we define and classify them.

Totalizing is using a single label to represent the totality of a person. We fixate on one symbol to define someone and fail to recognize many other aspects of who she or he is. Some people totalize gay men and lesbians as if sexual orientation were the only important facet of a person (Wood, 1998). Interestingly, we don't totalize heterosexuals on the basis of their sexuality. Totalizing also occurs when we dismiss people by saying, "He's a liberal," "She's old," "She's preppy," or "He's a jock." When we totalize others, we negate most of who they are by spotlighting a single aspect of their identity.

I'm Indian, and that's all a lot of people here see in me. They see that my skin is dark and I wear a sari, and they put me in the category "foreigner" or, if they are observant, "Indian." They mark me off as different, foreign, not like them, and they can't see anything else about me. How would they feel if I categorized them as "Americans" and didn't see their individual qualities?

Symbols influence how we think and feel about experiences and people. In one study, colleagues and I asked romantic couples how they defined differences between them (Wood et al., 1994). We found that some people define differences as positive forces that energize a relationship. Others define differences as problems or barriers to closeness. There was a direct connection between how partners defined differences and how they dealt with them. Partners who labeled differences as constructive approached disagreements with curiosity and a belief that they would grow by discussing differences. On the other hand, partners who labeled differences as problems tended to deny differences or avoid talking about them.

How we think about relationships directly affects what happens in them (Duck, 1994a, 1994b; Honeycutt, Woods, & Fontenot, 1993; Spencer, 1994). People who dwell on negative thoughts about relationships heighten awareness of relationship flaws and diminish perceptions of strengths (Cloven & Roloff, 1991). Conversely, partners who focus on good facets of their relationships are more conscious of positive qualities of partners and relationships and less aware of imperfections (Bradbury & Fincham, 1990; Fletcher & Fincham, 1991; Seligman, 2002).

The power of symbols to define and evaluate phenomena is evident in the nonverbal communication at public events, such as this one at President Reagan's funeral.

–Cheryl–

About 3 years ago, my husband and I were seriously considering divorce. We decided to try marital counseling first, and that saved our marriage. The counselor helped us see that we noticed problems, aggravations, and faults in each other and didn't see all of the good qualities in each other and our relationship. Now we have a "warts-and-all" philosophy, which means we accept each other, warts and all. Changing how we think about our marriage really has changed what it is for us.

As Cheryl's commentary indicates, our definitions of relationships can create self-fulfilling prophecies. Because verbal language is ambiguous, arbitrary, and abstract, there are multiple ways we can define any experience, person, relationship, policy, or idea. Once we select a label, we tend to see what our label spotlights and to overlook what it doesn't highlight. This suggests an ethical principle for using and interpreting language: We should consider what the language that we and others use includes as well as what it excludes.

Symbols Evaluate

Symbols are not neutral. They are laden with values. This is an intrinsic quality of symbols. We tend to describe people we like with language that

Communication Highlight

Blaxicans

What do you call yourself when language has no name that fits you? That didn't stump a young woman from San Diego whose mother was Mexican and father was African. She coined the term *Blaxican* to describe her ethnicity (Rodriguez, 2003). We're likely to see more creative language as multiracial children decide how to name themselves.

Language Shapes Our Realities

Language shapes our perceptions in ways that reflect a culture's values (Whorf, 1956). The language of the Hopi Indians makes no distinction between stationary objects and moving processes, whereas English uses nouns and verbs, respectively. In one part of Australia people speak Guugu Timithirr, a language that does not include the terms *right* and *left.* In Guugu Timithirr, special locations are described in relation to a compass. Thus, a person speaking this language might ask to have the pepper passed north (Monastersky, 2002).

accents their good qualities and downplays their flaws. The reverse is generally true of descriptions of people we don't like. My friend is *casual;* someone I don't like is *sloppy.* Restaurants use positive words to heighten the attractiveness of menu items. "Tender lobster accented with drawn butter" sounds more appetizing than "crustacean murdered by being boiled alive and then drenched in saturated fat."

 To extend your insight into the power of language, complete Activity 5.2, "Good Enough to Eat," in your *Student Companion* or online under "Activities for Chapter 5" at the *Communication in Our Lives* website.

Of course, there are degrees of evaluation in language. We might describe people who speak their minds as *assertive, outspoken, straightforward, blunt,* or *rude.* Each word has a distinct connotation. In recent years, we have become more sensitive to how the evaluative nature of symbols can hurt people. Most people with disabilities prefer not to be called *disabled* because that tends to totalize them in terms of a disability (Braithwaite & Braithwaite, 1997). The term *African American* emphasizes cultural heritage, whereas *Black* focuses on skin color. The word *Hispanic* emphasizes the Spanish language spoken in the home countries, whereas *Latino* and *Latina* highlight the geographic origin of Latin American men and women, respectively (Glascock, 1998). People with roots in Spanish-speaking Caribbean countries tend to refer to themselves as *Latinos* and *Latinas* or to use more specific labels such as *Cubano, Peruvian,* and *Mexican* (Rodriquez, 2003).

Language referring to homosexuals is in transition. Some gays and lesbians use the term *sexual orientation* to suggest that they didn't choose their sexuality. Others use the term *sexual preference* to indicate that their sexuality is a matter of choice, not genetics. Still others speak of *affectional preference* to signal that their commitment concerns the entire realm of affection, not just sexual activity. An ethical guideline for using language is to try to learn and respect others' preferences for describing their identities.

Loaded language consists of words that strongly slant perceptions and thus meanings. For example, conservative television and radio commentators sometimes disparage people with liberal social and political values as *knee-jerk liberals* and call environmentalists *tree-huggers.* At the same time, liberal commentators sometimes describe people with conservative social and political values as *country club fat cats* and describe people who oppose environmental regulations as *maiming nature.* Loaded language also fosters negative views of older citizens. Terms such as *geezer* and *old fogey* incline us to regard older people with contempt or pity. Alternatives such as *senior citizen* and *elderly person* encourage more respectful attitudes.

Symbols Organize Perceptions

We use symbols to organize our perceptions. As we saw in Chapter 2, we rely on cognitive schemata to classify and evaluate experiences. How we organize experiences affects what they mean to us. For example, your prototype of a good friend affects how you judge particular friends. When we place someone in the category of friend, the category influences how we interpret that person's communication. An insult is likely to be viewed as teasing if made by a friend but a call to battle if made by an enemy. The words don't change, but their meaning varies, depending on how we classify the person uttering them.

Because symbols organize thought, they allow us to think about abstract concepts such as the work ethic, democracy, morality, good citizenship, and healthy family life. We use broad concepts to transcend specific, concrete activities and to enter the world of conceptual thought and ideals. Thinking abstractly relieves us of having to consider every specific object and experience individually.

Our capacity to abstract can also distort thinking. A primary way this occurs is in stereotyping—thinking in broad generalizations about a whole class of people or experiences. Examples of stereotypes are "Sorority women are yuppies," "Ph.D.s are smart," and "Democrats tax and spend." Notice that stereotypes can be positive or negative. Another example of stereotyping is racial profiling, a practice in which law enforcement officers are more likely to be suspicious of people who aren't White. Racial profiling can make officers more likely to stop cars driven by Blacks and Hispanics than by Whites to check for drinking or drugs.

—Reggie—

People say racism no longer exists, but I know it does. If I'm out walking at night, White girls cross the street because they think I'll mug them. They don't cross the street if they see a White guy. One of the guys on my hall asked me whether I thought the Bridge Program was helpful. I didn't go through it because I had a good high school record. Does he think every Black needs special help?

Common to all stereotypes is classifying experiences or people into a single category based on general knowledge or beliefs about a group. When we do this, we obscure the uniqueness of the individual person or a specific

Communication Highlight

"Come In; This Place Is for Everyone"

Adopted by the World Congress in 1969, the stylized wheelchair has become the international symbol of access for people with disabilities. Critics, however, say it is not the ideal symbol. One problem with the wheelchair symbol is that it doesn't represent many forms of disabilities; a visually impaired person couldn't even see the symbol. According to graphic designer Brendan Murphy, another problem is that the stylized wheelchair depicts a disabled person who is dependent and helpless (Pierson, 1995).

Murphy has proposed an alternative new symbol that he thinks communicates, "Come in; this place is for everyone." "Everyone" includes the 43 million Americans who currently have disabilities, as well as those who will develop disabilities during their lives. Murphy's open-door symbol applies to all impairments: ones that affect sight, hearing, physical motion, and learning.

experience. Clearly, we have to generalize. We can't think about each thing in our lives as a specific instance. However, stereotypes can discourage us from recognizing important differences among the phenomena we lump together. Thus, we have an ethical responsibility to reflect on stereotypes and to stay alert to differences among the things and people that we place in a single category.

Sharpen Your Skill

Assessing Your Stereotypes

Identify a stereotype you use, and consider ten people to whom you might apply it. Identify differences between the people. At first, this may be difficult because stereotypes gloss over differences. What do you discover as you look for individual variations in the people you lumped together under a single symbol?

Symbols Allow Hypothetical Thought

Who was your best friend when you were 5 years old? What would you do if you won the lottery? To answer these questions, you must think hypothetically, which means thinking about experiences and ideas that are not part of your concrete, present situation. Because we can think hypothetically, we can plan, dream, remember, fantasize, set goals, and weigh alternative courses of action.

Hypothetical thought is possible because we use symbols. When we symbolize, we name ideas so that we can hold them in our minds and reflect on them. We can contemplate things that currently have no real existence, and we can remember ourselves in the past and project ourselves into the future. Our ability to live simultaneously in all three dimensions of time explains why we can set goals and work toward them even though there is nothing tangible about them in the moment (Dixson & Duck, 1993). For example, you've invested many hours in studying and writing papers because you imagine having a college degree. The degree is not real now, nor is the self that you will become once you have the degree. Yet the idea is sufficiently real to motivate you to work hard for many years.

Close relationships rely on ideas of history and future. One of the strongest glues for intimacy is a history of shared experiences (Bellah et al., 1985; Wood, 2000). Just knowing that they have weathered rough times in

Communication Highlight

Hate Speech Online

Many companies have message boards to allow employees to discuss issues relevant to the company. However, that's not the only reason employees are using them. Increasingly, message boards for specific companies are becoming sites of vicious gossip, innuendo, and hateful speech (Abelson, 2001). In some cases, employees engage in racist, sexist, or homophobic attacks or spread damaging rumors about co-workers' sexual activities. Disgruntled employees sometimes use message boards to harass co-workers or bosses. Some employees even represent themselves as others. In one case, a worker posted a message that claimed to be from a female co-worker in which the message writer offered to have sex with others.

 To learn more about hate speech and differing opinions about whether it should be regulated, go to http://www.netfreedom.org. Do you agree with this site's position?

the past helps partners get through current trials. Belief in a future also sustains intimacy. We interact differently with people we don't expect to see again and people who are continuing parts of our lives. Talking about the future also enhances intimacy because it suggests that more lies ahead (Acitelli, 1993; Duck, 1990).

Hypothetical thought can help us improve. In Chapter 3, we noted that improving self-concept begins with accepting yourself as in process. This requires you to remember how you were at an earlier time, to appreciate progress you've made, and to create an image of how you want to be, to motivate your continued growth.

Symbols Allow Self-reflection

Just as we use symbols to reflect on what goes on outside of us, we also use them to reflect on ourselves. There are two aspects to the self (Mead, 1934). First, there is the *I*, which is the spontaneous, creative self (Table 5.1). The *I* acts impulsively in response to inner needs and desires, regardless of social norms. The *me* is the socially conscious part of the self that monitors and moderates the *I*'s impulses. The *me* reflects on the *I* from the social perspectives of others. The *I* is impervious to social conventions and expectations, but the *me* is keenly aware of them. In an argument, your *I* may want to hurl a biting insult at a co-worker who has criticized you, but your *me* censors that impulse and reminds you that it's impolite to put others down and that doing so might create future problems with that co-worker.

The *me* is the reflective part of the self. The *me* reflects on the *I*, so we simultaneously author our lives and reflect on them. This means we can think about who we want to be and set goals for becoming the self we desire. We can feel shame, pride, and regret for our actions—emotions that are

Self-reflection is a foundation of personal identity and communication.

Table 5.1: Two Aspects of the Self

I	*Me*
Impulsive	Reflective
Individualistic	Social
Creative	Conventional
Active	Analytical
Spontaneous	Controlled
Socially naive	Socially sophisticated
Motivated by urges	Edits urges

possible because we self-reflect. We can control what we do in the present by casting ourselves forward in time to consider how we might later feel about our actions.

Self-reflection also empowers us to monitor ourselves and our actions. When we monitor ourselves, we (the *me*) notice and evaluate our (the *I*'s) actions and may modify them based on our (the *me*'s) judgments. For instance, while giving a speech, you might notice that quite a few members of the audience are looking around or slouching. You think to yourself, "They seem bored. Perhaps I've been using too many statistics. Maybe I could regain their interest by mentioning some personal examples." In this case, monitoring allowed you to gauge your speaking effectiveness and make adjustments.

Self-reflection also allows us to manage our image, or the identity we present to others. Because we reflect on ourselves from social perspectives, we are able to consider how we appear in others' eyes. Our ability to manage how we appear sometimes is called *facework* because it involves controlling the face we present to others. When talking with teachers, you may consciously present yourself as a respectful, attentive student. When interacting with parents, you may repress some of the language that surfaces in discussions with your friends. When communicating with someone you'd like to date, you may choose to be more attentive and social than you are in other circumstances. In work situations, you may do facework to create an image of yourself as responsible, ambitious, and dependable. Continuously, we adjust how we present ourselves so that we sculpt our image to fit particular situations and people.

Summing up, we use symbols to define, evaluate, and organize experiences, think hypothetically, and self-reflect. Each of these abilities helps us create meaning in our lives.

Sharpen Your Skill

I–me Dialogues

Monitor your *I–me* dialogues as you talk with a close friend, a teacher, and a person with whom you work. What creative ideas and desires does your *I* initiate? What social controls does your *me* impose? What whims occur to your *I*? What social norms does your *me* remind you of? How do the *I* and the *me* work together? What would be lost if your *I* became silent? What would be missing if your *me* disappeared?

Enhancing Effectiveness in Verbal Communication

We've explored what symbols are and how they may be used differently in distinct social communities. Building on these understandings, we can now consider ways to improve the effectiveness of our verbal communication.

Engage in Dual Perspective

The single most important guideline for effective verbal communication is to engage in **dual perspective.** Dual perspective involves recognizing another person's point of view and taking that into account as you communicate. Effective communication is not a solo performance but interaction between people. Awareness of others and their viewpoints should be reflected in how we speak. For instance, a person using dual perspective when talking with a woman who has a problem might realize that many women appreciate empathy and supportive listening more than advice (Wood, 1998, 2005). Public speakers should respect listeners' values.

We don't need to abandon our own perspectives to recognize those of others. In fact, it would be just as unethical to stifle your own views as to dismiss those of others. Dual perspective, as the term implies, consists of two perspectives. It entails understanding both our own and another's point of view and acknowledging each when we communicate. For example, you and your supervisor may disagree about a performance review. It's important that you understand why your supervisor assigns the ratings he or she does, even if you don't share his or her perceptions. By understanding the supervisor's perceptions and ratings, you enhance your ability to have a good working relationship and to perform effectively on the job. Most of us can accept and grow from differences, but we don't feel affirmed if we feel unheard or disregarded.

Dual perspective is a foundation of effective communication.

© Bonnie Kamin/PhotoEdit, Inc.

Sharpen Your Skill

Dual Perspective in Public Speaking

Identify a position you hold that you could advocate in a public speech in your class. For instance, you might be for or against gun control, stricter environmental regulations, or stem cell research. Now consider reasons why some of your class-mates might hold different, even opposing, positions on the topic. List three reasons some of your classmates might disagree with your opinion. Next to each reason, indicate one way you could acknowledge and respect listeners' views in your speech. You may want to look ahead to Chapters 13 and 17, which provide detailed information about analyzing and adapting to listeners.

Reason	Way to Acknowledge and Respect It in Your Speech
1.	....
2.	....
3.	....

© AP/Wide World Photos

Effective communicators acknowledge and respect others.

Own Your Feelings and Thoughts

We sometimes use language that obscures our responsibility for how we feel and what we think. For instance, people say, "You made me mad," "You made me feel inadequate about my job performance," or "You hurt me," as if what they feel is caused by someone else. On a more subtle level, we sometimes blame others for our responses to what they say. "You're so demanding" really means that you don't like what someone else wants or expects. The sense of feeling pressured by another's expectations is in you; it is not cre-ated by the other person. In reality, others seldom directly cause our feelings.

Our feelings and thoughts result from how we interpret others' communication, not from their communication itself. Others sometimes exert a great deal of influence on how we feel and how we see ourselves. Yet they do not directly cause our feelings. Although how we interpret what others say may lead us to feel certain ways, we can't hold them responsible for our feelings. In relationships with manipulative or dysfunctional people, you may find it useful either to communicate in ways that don't enable the other and that do preserve your integrity or to leave the relationship before it jeopardizes your own well-being.

Effective communicators take responsibility for themselves by using language that owns their thoughts and feelings. They own their feelings and do not blame others for what happens in themselves. To take responsibility for your own feelings, rely on *I*-language instead of *you*-language. Table 5.2 gives examples of the difference.

In my work with inmates who have violent histories, one of the key skills they learn is using *I*-language. At the outset, the inmates say things such as, "She made me hit her by what she did," and "I shot him because he made me mad by what he said." Through instruction, exercises, and practice, they learn to change their *you*-language to *I*-language, saying, "I hit her because I didn't like how she was acting," and "I shot him because I got upset about what he said." The inmates tell me that learning *I*-language is empowering because it helps them see that they have a lot more control in many situations than they had realized.

There are two differences between *I*-language and *you*-language. First, *I*-statements own responsibility, whereas *you*-statements project it onto another person. *You*-language tells others that they make you feel some way. This is likely to arouse defensiveness, which doesn't facilitate healthy communication. Second, *I*-statements offer more description than *you*-statements. *You*-statements tend to be abstract accusations, which is one reason they're ineffective in promoting change. *I*-statements, on the other hand, provide concrete descriptions of behaviors and feelings without directly blaming another person for how we feel.

Some people feel awkward when they first start using *I*-language. This is natural because most of us are accustomed to using *you*-language. With commitment and practice, however, you can learn to communicate using *I*-language. Once you feel comfortable using it, you will find that *I*-language has many advantages. It is less likely than *you*-language to make others defensive, so *I*-language opens the doors for dialogue.

Table 5.2: *You*-language and *I*-language

You-language	*I*-language
You hurt me.	I feel hurt when you ignore what I say.
You make me feel small.	I feel small when you tell me that I'm selfish.
My boss intimidates me.	When my boss criticizes my work, I feel intimidated.
You're really domineering.	When you shout at me, I feel dominated.
The speaker made me feel dumb.	I felt uninformed when the speaker discussed such complex information.
You humiliated me.	I felt humiliated when you mentioned my problems in front of our friends.

I-language is also more honest. We deceive ourselves when we say, "You made me feel . . ." because others don't control how we feel. Finally, *I*-language is more empowering than *you*-language. When we say, "You hurt me," or "You made me feel bad," we give control of our emotions to others. This reduces our personal sense of agency and, by extension, our motivation to change what is happening. Using *I*-language allows us to own our feelings while also explaining to others how we interpret their behaviors.

 To practice using *I*-language, complete Activity 5.5, "Learning to Use *I*-Language," in your *Student Companion* or online under "Activities for Chapter 5" at the *Communication in Our Lives* website.

–Roth–

I never realized how often I use you-*language. I'm always saying my girlfriend makes me feel happy or my father makes me feel like a failure. What I'm beginning to see is that they really don't control my feelings. I do.*

Respect What Others Say about Their Feelings and Ideas

Has anyone ever said to you, "You shouldn't feel that way"? If so, you know how infuriating it can be to be told that your feelings aren't valid, appropriate, or acceptable. It's equally destructive to be told our thoughts are wrong. When someone says, "How can you think something so stupid?" we feel devalued. Effective communicators don't disparage what others say about what they feel and think. Even if you don't feel or think the same way, you can still respect another person as the expert on her or his perspective.

We also disrespect others when we speak for them instead of letting them speak for themselves. Recently, I had a conversation with a couple at a party in which one person spoke for another. In response to questions that I asked the man, the woman said, "He's having trouble balancing career and family responsibilities," "He's proud of sticking with his exercise program," and "He's worried about how to take care of his parents now that their health is declining." She didn't allow her husband to speak for himself. By automatically answering questions I addressed to him, she left him voiceless. Parents sometimes speak for children by responding to questions the children could answer. Generally, it's arrogant and disempowering to speak for others.

Just as we should not speak for others, we also should not assume that we understand how they feel or think. We called this mind reading in Chapter 2, and it is relevant to this discussion as well. As we have seen, our distinct experiences and ways of interpreting life make each of us unique. We seldom, if ever, completely grasp what another person feels or thinks. Although it is supportive to engage in dual perspective, it isn't supportive to presume that we fully understand someone else's feelings or thoughts, especially when he or she differs from us in important ways.

It's particularly important not to assume we understand people from other cultures or social communities (Fussell, 2002; Houston, 2003). Recently, a woman from Nigeria in one of my classes commented on discrimination she faces, and a Caucasian man in the class said, "I know what you mean. Prejudice really hurts." Although he meant to be supportive, his response angered the woman, who retorted, "You have no idea how I feel, and you have no right to act like you do until you've been female and non-

White." When we claim to understand what we haven't experienced, others may feel we're taking away from their lives and identities.

Respecting what others say about what they feel and think is a cornerstone of effective communication. We also grow when we open ourselves to perspectives, feelings, and thoughts that differ from our own. If you don't understand what others say, ask them to elaborate. This shows you are interested and respect their expertise and experience.

Strive for Accuracy and Clarity

Because symbols are arbitrary, abstract, and ambiguous, the potential for misunderstanding always exists. In addition, individual and cultural differences may lead to misunderstandings. Although we cannot entirely eliminate misunderstandings, we can minimize them.

Be Aware of Levels of Abstraction Misunderstanding is less likely when we are conscious of levels of abstraction. Much confusion results from language that is excessively abstract. For instance, suppose a professor says, "Your papers should demonstrate a sophisticated conceptual grasp of material and its pragmatic implications." Would you know how to write a paper to satisfy the professor? You probably would not, because the language is very abstract and unclear. Here's a more concrete description: "Your papers should include definitions of the concepts and specific examples that show how they apply in real life." With this less abstract statement, you would have a better idea of what the professor expected.

Abstract language is not always inadvisable. As we have seen, abstract language allows us to generalize, which is necessary and useful. The goal is to use a level of abstraction that suits particular communication objectives and situations. Abstract words are appropriate when speakers and listeners have similar concrete knowledge about what is being discussed. For example, a couple that has been dating for a year might talk about "light movies" and "heavy movies" as shorthand ways to refer to two kinds of films. Because they have seen many movies together, they have shared referents for the abstract terms *light* and *heavy*. Similarly, long-term friends can say "Let's just hang out," and they will each understand the kinds of concrete activities implied by the abstract term *hang out.*

More concrete language is advisable when communicators don't have shared experiences and interpretations. For example, early in a friendship the suggestion to "hang out" would be more effective if it included specifics: "Let's hang out today—maybe watch the game and go out for pizza." Providing concrete examples for general terms clarifies meanings.

Abstract language is particularly likely to lead to misunderstandings when people talk about how they want one another to change. Concrete language and specific examples help people share understandings of which behaviors are unwelcome and which ones are wanted. For example, "I want you to be more responsible about your job" does not explain what would count as being more responsible. Is it arriving on time, taking on extra assignments, or something else? It isn't clear what the speaker wants unless more concrete

Reprinted by permission of Marjorie Bakken.

"Well, then, if 'commandments' seems too harsh to me, and 'guidelines' seems to wishy-washy to you, how about 'The 10 Policy Statements'?"

Ron Sachs-Pool/Getty Images

Politicians are often criticized for using very abstract language. Why might politicians prefer to speak in the abstract instead of using concrete language?

descriptions are supplied. Likewise, "I want to be closer" could mean the speaker wants to spend more time together, talk about the relationship, do things together, or any number of other things. Vague abstractions promote misunderstanding if people don't share concrete referents.

Qualify Language   Another way to increase the clarity of communication is to qualify language. Two types of language should be qualified. First, we should qualify generalizations so we don't mislead ourselves or others. "Politicians are crooked" is a false statement because it overgeneralizes. A more accurate statement would be, "A number of politicians have been shown to have accepted paybacks for favors." Qualifying reminds us of the limitations of what we say.

  To develop your skill in using qualified language, complete Activity 5.7, "Practicing Using Qualified Language," in your *Student Companion* or online under "Activities for Chapter 5" at the *Communication in Our Lives* website.

We should also qualify language when describing and evaluating people. **Static evaluation** consists of assessments that suggest that something is unchanging or frozen in time. These are particularly troublesome when applied to people: "Ann is selfish," "Don is irresponsible," "Bob is generous." Whenever we use the word *is*, we suggest that something is inherent and fixed. In reality, we aren't static but continuously changing. A person who is selfish at one time may not be at another. A person who is irresponsible on one occasion may be responsible in other situations.

  To develop skill in avoiding static language, complete Activity 5.8, "Guarding against Static Language," in your *Student Companion* or online under "Activities for Chapter 5" at the *Communication in Our Lives* website.

Indexing is a technique developed by early communication scholars that allows us to note that our statements reflect only specific times and circumstances (Korzybski, 1948). To index, we would say "Ann$_{June 6, 1997}$ acted selfishly," "Don$_{on the task committee}$ was irresponsible," Bob$_{in college}$ was generous." See how indexing ties description to a specific time and circumstance? Mental indexing reminds us that we and others are able to change in remarkable ways.

—Roy—

I had a couple of accidents right after I got my driver's license. Most teenagers do, right? But to hear my father, you'd think I am a bad driver today. Those accidents were 5 years ago, and I haven't even had a ticket since then. But he still talks about "reckless Roy."

We've considered four principles for improving the effectiveness of verbal communication. Engaging in dual perspective is the first principle and a foundation for all others. A second guideline is to take responsibility for our own feelings and thoughts by using *I*-language. Third, we should respect others as the experts on what they feel and think and not speak for them or presume we know what they think and feel. The fourth principle is to strive for clarity by choosing appropriate degrees of abstraction, qualifying generalizations, and indexing evaluations, particularly ones applied to people.

CASE STUDY: The Roommates

The conversation scripted here is featured as a multimedia scenario on the Communication in Our Lives CD-ROM included with this book. Once you've launched the CD, click on the "Communication Scenarios" icon, and, from the Scenarios Menu, select "The Roommates" to watch the video. Improve your own communication skills by reading, watching, listening to, critiquing, and analyzing this communication encounter.

Analyze the scenario by applying the principles covered in this chapter, and respond to the prompts that accompany the video, which you can access by clicking on "Analysis." After conversation analysis and answering the questions, you can click on the "Done" button to compare your responses with the ones I suggest. Additional analysis questions are available in print at the end of this chapter and on the book's website.

Bernadette and Celia were assigned to be roommates a month ago when the school year began. Both were initially pleased with the match because they discovered commonalities in their interests and backgrounds. They are both sophomores from small towns, they have similar tastes in music and television programs, and they both like to stay up late and sleep in.

Lately, however, Bernadette has been irritated by Celia's housekeeping—or lack of it. Celia leaves her clothes lying all over the room. If they cook in, Celia often leaves the pans and dishes for hours, and then it's usually Bernadette who cleans them. Bernadette feels she has to talk to Celia about this problem, but she hasn't figured out how or when to talk. When Celia gets in from classes, Bernadette is sitting and reading a textbook on her bed.

Jason Harris/© 2001 Wadsworth

CELIA: Hey Bernie, how's it going?

Celia drops her book bag in the middle of the floor, flops on the bed, and kicks her shoes off on the floor. As Bernadette watches, she feels her frustration peaking and decides now is the time to talk to Celia about the problem.

BERNADETTE: You shouldn't do that. You make me nuts the way you just throw your stuff all over the room.

CELIA: I don't "throw my stuff all over the room." I just took off my shoes and put my books down, like I do every day.

BERNADETTE: No, you didn't. You dropped your bag right in the middle of the room, and you kicked your shoes where they happen to fall without ever noticing how messy they look. And you're right—that is what you do every day.

CELIA: There's nothing wrong with wanting to be comfortable in my own room. Are we suddenly going for the Good Housekeeping Seal of Approval?

BERNADETTE: Comfortable is one thing. But you're so messy. Your mess makes me really miserable.

CELIA: Since when? This is the first I've heard about it.

BERNADETTE: Since we started rooming together, but I didn't want to say anything about how angry you make me. I just can't stand it any more. You shouldn't be so messy.

CELIA: Sounds to me like you've got a problem—you, not me.

BERNADETTE: Well it's you and your mess that are my problem. Do you have to be such a slob?

Chapter Summary

In this chapter, we've discussed the world of words and meaning, which make up the uniquely human universe of symbol users. Because symbols are arbitrary, ambiguous, and abstract, they have no inherent meanings. Instead, we actively construct meaning by interpreting symbols based on perspectives gleaned through interaction with others and our personal experiences. We also punctuate to create meaning in communication.

We use symbols to define, evaluate, and organize our experiences. In addition, we use symbols to think hypothetically so we can consider alternatives and inhabit all three dimensions of time. Finally, symbols allow us to self-reflect so we can monitor our own behaviors.

Because symbols are abstract, arbitrary, and ambiguous, misunderstandings can occur between communicators. We can reduce the likelihood of misunderstandings by being sensitive to levels of abstraction. In addition, we should engage in dual perspective, own our thoughts and feelings, respect what others say about how they think and feel, and monitor abstractness, generalizations, and static evaluations. In Chapter 6, we continue our discussion of the world of human communication by exploring the fascinating realm of nonverbal behavior.

 ## Communication in Our Lives ONLINE

In addition to presenting the case studies' multimedia scenarios, the *Communication in Our Lives* CD-ROM provides quick access to the *Communication in Our Lives* website and InfoTrac College Edition. The website is online at http://communication .wadsworth.com/woodciol4, but you can only access this book's premium web content when you link to the site directly through the book's CD.

 The *Communication in Our Lives* website features interactive tools for learning and reviewing the chapter's concepts and key terms, including electronic versions of the "For Further Reflection and Discussion" questions that follow and a review quiz.

The website also provides updated web links and additional InfoTrac College Edition activities. If required, you can e-mail completed chapter activities or the quizzes to your instructor.

Key Concepts

abstract, *124*

ambiguous, *121*

arbitrary, *119*

communication rules, *126*

constitutive rules, *126*

dual perspective, *137*

hypothetical thought, *134*

indexing, *142*

loaded language, *132*

punctuation, *129*

regulative rules, *126*

static evaluation, *142*

totalizing, *130*

For Further Reflection and Discussion

1. Pay attention to *I-* and *you*-language in your own communication and that of others. What happens when you switch a *you*-statement to an *I*-statement? Does it change how you feel or what happens in interaction?

2. Can you think of experiences, feelings, or other phenomena for which we don't currently have names? What might we call a lesbian or gay couple with children? Are both parents *mommies* in lesbian couples and *daddies* in gay ones? What is a good term for describing someone with whom you have a serious romance? *Boyfriend* and *girlfriend* no longer work for many people. Do you prefer *significant other, romantic partner, special friend,* or another term?

3. Use your InfoTrac College Edition to read the 2001 article by Jennifer Piccolo, Rachel Lioi, and Jerry Seper entitled "The Trend Spotter: Insight's Summary of Savvy Surveys." If you had been included in the poll reported in this article, what responses would you have given? What ethical responsibilities should accompany the right to free speech?

4. Identify communication rules for online conversations. What counts as joking (how do you indicate you're joking)? What counts as flaming? How is interaction regulated with rules for turn taking and length of comment?

Experiencing Communication in Our Lives

Questions for Analysis and Discussion

Review the video of the scenario entitled "The Roommate" that you watched when completing this chapter's case study (pages 143–144), or, if you haven't seen it yet, watch it for the first time. If you didn't previously finish the analysis questions included on the CD-ROM, do so now, and then respond to the following questions, which are also available on the book's website under "Activities for Chapter 5."

1. Identify examples of *you*-language in this conversation. How would you change it to *I*-language?

2. Identify examples of loaded language and ambiguous language.

3. Do you agree with Celia that the problem is Bernadette's, not hers?

4. Do Celia and Bernadette seem to engage in dual perspective to understand each other?

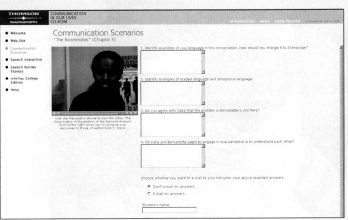

The Nonverbal Dimension of Communication

Focus Questions

1. Is nonverbal communication learned or instinctual?

2. How is nonverbal communication like and different from verbal communication?

3. What are the types of nonverbal communication?

4. How does nonverbal communication express power relationships?

5. Do facial expressions have universal meanings

Ben Thompson had traveled to Japan to negotiate a joint business venture with Haru Watanabe. They seemed to see the mutual benefit of combining their resources, yet Thompson felt something was wrong in their negotiations. Every time they talked, Watanabe seemed uneasy and refused to hold eye contact. Thompson wondered whether Watanabe was trying to hide something. Meanwhile, Watanabe wondered why Thompson was so rude if he wanted them to work together.

Maria noticed a nice-looking guy who was studying two tables away from hers in the library. When he looked up at her, she lowered her eyes. After a moment, she looked back at him just for a second. A few minutes later he came over, sat down beside her, and introduced himself.

Liz Fitzgerald gave a final glance to be sure the dining-room table was just right for dinner: The placemats and blue linen napkins were set out, the silver and the crystal sparkled, the bowl of flowers in the middle of the table added color, and the serving dishes were warmed and ready to be filled with roast, buttered new potatoes, and steamed snow peas with mushrooms.

Across town, Benita Bradsher was also preparing dinner for her family. She stirred the pot of mashed potatoes and transferred it from the stove to the kitchen table. Next, she piled plates, paper napkins, knives, spoons, and forks in the middle of the table for her husband and children. She took the ground beef casserole from the oven, put it on a potholder on the table, and called her family to dinner.

These examples illustrate the power of nonverbal communication. In the first case, Thompson and Watanabe have difficulty because of different nonverbal communication norms in Japan and the United States. Thompson has learned that eye contact is a sign of honesty and respect, so he looks directly at Watanabe when they talk. In Watanabe's culture, however, direct eye contact is considered rude and intrusive, so he doesn't meet Thompson's gaze and feels uncomfortable when Thompson looks directly at him.

In the library scene, we see a gendered pattern of nonverbal communication. Maria follows feminine communication norms by indirectly signaling her interest and waiting for the man to initiate contact. In turn, he enacts the rules of masculine communication culture by gazing directly at her and moving to her table.

In the final example, nonverbal communication reflects differences in socioeconomic class. Whereas Liz Fitzgerald sets her table with cloth napkins, placemats, silver, crystal, and a vase of flowers, Benita Bradsher sets her table with pans off the stove and a pile of utensils and paper napkins for family members to take. Notice also the different foods the two women serve: roast, new potatoes, and snow peas with mushrooms for the Fitzgerald family; mashed potatoes and casserole for the Bradshers. What each woman serves and how she sets her table reflect the customs of the social group to which she belongs.

Gender, ethnicity, sexual orientation, and socioeconomic class are identities that we create and sustain by performing them day in and day out. Candice West and Don Zimmerman (1987) note that we "do gender" all the time by behaving in ways that announce that we are feminine or masculine. We also communicate nonverbally to perform, or "do," race, class, and sexual orientation. In this sense, nonverbal communication, like language, is a primary way in which we announce who we are. The intricate system of nonverbal communication helps us establish identity, negotiate relationships, and create environments we enjoy.

Nonverbal behavior is a major dimension of human communication. The nonverbal system accounts for 65% to 93% of the total meaning of communication (Birdwhistell, 1970; Mehrabian, 1981). One reason for the impact of nonverbal communication is the breadth of what it includes: everything from dress and eye contact to body posture and vocal inflection. In this chapter, we explore the fascinating realm of nonverbal interaction. We will identify principles of nonverbal communication and then discuss types of nonverbal behavior and ways to improve our effectiveness in nonverbal communication.

Principles of Nonverbal Communication

Nonverbal communication is all aspects of communication other than words themselves. It includes how we utter words (inflection, volume), features of environments that affect interaction (temperature, lighting), and objects that influence personal images and interaction patterns (dress, jewelry, furniture). Five key points highlight the power of nonverbal communication to affect meaning.

Verbal and Nonverbal: Similar Yet Different

Nonverbal communication and verbal communication are similar in some ways and different in others. We'll identify both the similarities and the differences.

Similarities   Like verbal communication, nonverbal behavior is symbolic, which means it is ambiguous, abstract, and arbitrary. Thus, we can't be sure what a smile or gesture means, and we can't guarantee that others understand the meanings we intend to express with our own nonverbal behaviors.

Different cultures prescribe different styles of dress.

© The Image Bank/Getty Images

Also like verbal communication, our nonverbal behavior and our interpretations of others' nonverbal behaviors are guided by constitutive and regulative rules. In the United States, a handshake counts as a proper way to greet business acquaintances.

A third similarity between the two communication systems is that both are culture bound. Our nonverbal communication reflects and reproduces values and norms of the particular culture and social communities to which we belong (Hickson, Stacks, & Moore, 2003). For instance, dress considered appropriate for women varies across cultures: Some women in the United States wear miniskirts; women in some other countries wear veils. Dress also reflects organizational identities: Bankers, attorneys, and many other professionals are expected to wear business suits or dresses; carpenters and plumbers usually wear jeans.

Lastly, both verbal and nonverbal communication may be either intentional or unintentional. Sometimes we carefully sculpt our appearance, just as we sometimes control our verbal communication. For instance, in a job interview we are highly conscious of our dress and posture as well as the words we use. At other times, our verbal and nonverbal communication may be unintentional. If the interviewer asks you a difficult question, your facial expression may reveal that you are caught off guard, or you may speak ungrammatically.

Differences   There are also differences between the two systems of communication. First, nonverbal communication is perceived as more honest. If verbal and nonverbal behaviors are inconsistent, most people trust the nonverbal behavior. There is little evidence that nonverbal behavior actually *is* more trustworthy than verbal communication; after all, we often control it quite consciously. Nonetheless, it is *perceived* as more trustworthy (Andersen, 1999).

Second, unlike verbal communication, nonverbal communication is multichanneled. Verbal communication usually occurs within a single channel; oral verbal communication is received through hearing, and written verbal communication and Sign Language are received through sight. In contrast, nonverbal communication may be seen, felt, heard, smelled, and tasted. We often receive nonverbal communication simultaneously through two or more channels, as when we feel and see a hug while hearing a whispered "I love you."

Finally, verbal communication is discrete, whereas nonverbal is more continuous. Verbal symbols start and stop; we begin speaking at one moment and stop speaking at another moment. In contrast, nonverbal communication tends to flow continually. Before we speak, our facial expressions and posture express our feelings; as we speak, our body movements and appearance communicate; and after we speak our posture changes, perhaps relaxing.

Supplements or Replaces Verbal Communication

Communication researchers have identified five ways in which nonverbal behaviors interact with verbal communication (Andersen, 1999; Malandro & Barker, 1983; Richmond & McCroskey, 1995b). First, nonverbal behaviors may repeat verbal messages. For example, you might say "yes" while nodding your head. In making a public presentation, a speaker might hold up first one, then two, and then three fingers to signal to listeners that she or he is moving from the first to the second to the third points of a speech.

Second, nonverbal behaviors may highlight verbal communication, as when you use inflection to emphasize certain words ("This is the *most* serious consequence of the policy that I oppose"). Third, nonverbal behaviors may complement or add to words. When you see a friend, you might say, "I'm glad to see you" and underline the verbal message with a smile. Public speakers often emphasize verbal statements with forceful gestures and increases in volume and inflection. Fourth, nonverbal behaviors may contradict verbal messages, as when a group member says, "Nothing's wrong" in a hostile tone of voice. Finally, we sometimes substitute nonverbal behaviors for verbal ones. For instance, you might roll your eyes to indicate that you are exasperated by something.

Regulates Interaction

You generally know when someone else has finished speaking, when a professor welcomes discussion from students, and when someone expects you to speak. Seldom do explicit, verbal cues tell us when to speak and keep silent. Instead, conversations usually are regulated nonverbally. When talking, friends don't say, "It's your turn to talk"; work associates don't point to one another to switch speaking roles; and professors don't hold up signs saying, "I am through now." We use our eyes and body posture to indicate that we want to enter conversations, and speakers step back from a podium to indicate that they have finished a speech. We invite people to speak by looking directly at them, often after asking a question (Drummond & Hopper, 1993; Wiemann & Harrison, 1983).

–Darcy–

I know one guy who dominates every conversation. I'd never noticed this until we studied how nonverbal behaviors regulate turn taking. This guy won't look at others when he's talking. He looks out into space, or sometimes he gives you a hard stare, but he never looks at anyone like he's saying, "Okay, your turn now."

Establishes Relational-level Meanings

In Chapter 1, we noted that there are two levels of meaning in communication. To review: The content level of meaning concerns actual information or literal meaning; the relational level of meaning defines people's identities and relationships. Nonverbal communication is often more powerful than verbal language in conveying relational-level meanings (Keeley & Hart,

Communication Highlight

Cross-cultural Nonverbal Clashes

Cross-cultural misunderstandings aren't limited to verbal communication, according to Siu Wa Tang, chair of the Department of Psychiatry at the University of California at Irvine (Emmons, 1998). When Dr. Tang and a colleague visited pharmaceutical plants in Changchun, China, Tang was well accepted but his colleague was not. The Chinese took an immediate and strong dislike to the colleague. Tang says the problem was facial expressions. His American colleague used facial expressions that Americans would interpret as showing honesty and directness, but the Chinese people interpreted the colleague as aggressive and rude.

Based on this experience, Tang conducted experiments to test the universality of facial expressions. He found that a few basic feelings and expressions were understood across cultures. Happiness and sadness, for example, were nonverbally expressed in similar ways. However, other facial expressions did not translate so well. Nine out of ten Americans interpreted a photograph of a face as showing fear, yet six of ten Japanese identified the same photograph as expressing surprise or sadness. A photo that nine of ten Americans identified as showing

anger was interpreted by 75% of Japanese as expressing disgust or contempt. Another source of cross-cultural nonverbal misunderstandings is eye contact. Americans generally consider it polite to look another person in the eye when conversing, but Japanese look at each other's cheeks; to look another in the eyes is perceived as very aggressive.

Cross-cultural communication clashes may also occur over gift giving (Axtell, 1990a, 1990b). An American might offend a Chinese person with the gift of a clock because clocks symbolize death in China. Giving a gift to an Arab person on first meeting would be interpreted as a bribe. Bringing flowers to a dinner hosted by a person from Kenya would puzzle the host because in Kenya flowers are given only to express sympathy over a loss. And the Swiss consider even numbers of flowers bad luck, so giving a dozen is inappropriate, and the recipient would probably interpret the gift as reflecting ill will.

 Use your InfoTrac College Edition to read Deborah Blum's 1998 article in *Psychology Today* entitled "Face It." What intercultural differences in reading facial expressions does Blum identify?

1994). In fact, some communication scholars call nonverbal communication the "relationship language" because it so often expresses the overall feeling about relationships (Burgoon et al., 1984; Richmond & McCroskey, 1995b; Sallinen-Kuparinen, 1992).

Nonverbal communication is used to convey three dimensions of relationship level meanings: responsiveness, liking, and power (Mehrabian, 1981). Yet how we convey relationship meanings and what specific nonverbal behaviors mean depends on the communication rules we've learned in our particular cultures.

Responsiveness   One facet of relational level meaning is responsiveness. We use eye contact, facial expressions, and body posture to indicate interest in others, as Maria did in one of the examples that opened this chapter. We signal interest by holding eye contact and assuming an attentive posture. But as the example with Haru Watanabe and Ben Thompson reveals, eye contact doesn't mean the same thing in all cultures. To express disinterest, Westerners tend to avoid or decrease visual contact and adopt a passive body position or turn away from another person. In the case study that opened this chapter, Bill's lack of eye contact with other group members signaled his disinterest. Also, harmony between people's postures and facial expressions may reflect how comfortable they are with each other (Berg, 1987; Capella, 1991). In cohesive groups, there is typically a great deal of nonverbal communication indicating responsiveness. Less cohesive groups include fewer nonverbal indicators of engagement.

-Maryam-
Americans do more than one thing at a time. In Nepal, when we talk with someone, we are with that person. We do not also write on paper or have the television on. We talk with the person. It is hard for me to accept the custom of giving only some attention to each other in conversation.

As Maryam's observation indicates, different cultures teach members distinct rules for showing responsiveness. In the West, feminine speech communities emphasize sensitivity to others, so women generally display greater emotional responsiveness and interest in what others say than do men (Montgomery, 1988). In addition to communicating their own feelings nonverbally, women are generally more skilled than men in interpreting others' emotions (Burgoon & Le Poire, 1999; Noller, 1986, 1987). Prisoners also develop astute abilities to decode nonverbal behaviors (Wood, 1994d). Decoding may be a survival strategy for people in subordinate standpoints. The well-being and sometimes physical safety of those with low power depend on being able to decipher the feelings and intentions of those with greater power.

-Ellen-
Secretaries are the best decoders. They can read their bosses' moods in a heartbeat. I am a secretary, part time now that I'm taking courses, and I can tell exactly what my boss is thinking. Sometimes I know what he feels or will do before he does. I have to know when he can be interrupted, when he feels generous, and when not to cross his path.

Posture and other nonverbal behaviors can indicate power relations.

© Michael Newman/PhotoEdit, Inc.

Liking A second dimension of relational meaning is liking. Smiles and friendly touching usually indicate positive feelings, whereas frowns and belligerent postures express antagonism (Keeley & Hart, 1994). Have you ever noticed how often political candidates shake hands, slap backs, and otherwise touch people whose votes they want? Masculine speech communities tend to emphasize emotional control and independence, so men are less likely than women to use nonverbal behaviors that reveal feelings. Reflecting the values of feminine speech communities, women generally are more likely than men to initiate hand holding and affectionate touches. Happy couples sit closer together and engage in more eye contact than unhappy couples (Miller & Parks, 1982; Noller, 1986, 1987). Similarly, in work settings, people who like one another often sit together, exchange eye contact, and smile at one another.

Power The third aspect of relational level meanings is power, or control. We use nonverbal behaviors to assert dominance, express deference, and negotiate status and influence (Andersen, 1999; Henley, 1977; Remland, 2000). In general, men assume more space and use greater volume and more forceful gestures than women (Hall, 1987; Major, Schmidlin, & Williams, 1990). Men are also more likely than women to move into others' space, as the man in the library moved to Maria's table in the example at the beginning of this chapter. In addition, men tend to use gestures and touch to exert control (Leathers, 1986). Powerful people, such as bosses, touch those with less power, such as secretaries, more than those with less power touch those with more power (Spain, 1992).

–Ramona–

In my home, my father sits at the head of the table, and he has his chair in the family room and his workroom. My mother does not have her chair anywhere in the house, and she has no room of her own either. This accurately reflects the power dynamics between them.

As Ramona observes, the amount of space a person has often directly reflects her or his power. The connection between power and space is evident in the fact that CEOs usually have large, spacious offices, entry- and midlevel professionals have smaller offices, and secretaries often have minuscule workstations, even though secretaries often store and manage more material than those higher in the organizational chain of command. Regulative communication rules also tacitly specify that people with status or power have the right to enter the space of people with less power, but the converse is not true. Space also reflects power differences between family members. Adults usually have more space than children; like Ramona's father, men more often than women have their own rooms and sit at the head of the table.

Control can also be exerted through silence, a powerful form of nonverbal communication. We sometimes use silence to stifle others' conversation. Silence accompanied by a glare is doubly powerful in conveying disapproval. In extreme form, power is nonverbally enacted through physical violence and abuse (May, 1998; Wood, 2001b, in press).

Reflects Cultural Values

Like verbal communication, nonverbal patterns reflect communication rules of specific cultures and social communities (Andersen, Hecht, Hoobler, & Smallwood, 2002). This implies that most nonverbal behavior isn't instinctual but learned in the process of socialization. Nonverbal behaviors vary across cultures and social communities.

Have you ever seen the bumper sticker that says, "If you can read this, you're too close"? That slogan proclaims North Americans' fierce territoriality. We value our private spaces, and we resent—and sometimes fight—anyone who trespasses on what we consider our turf. We want to have private homes, and many people want large lots to protect their privacy. On the job, a reserved parking space and a private office with a door mark status; employees with lower status often park in satellite lots and share offices or have workstations without doors. In cultures where individuality is less valued, people are less territorial. For instance, Brazilians routinely stand close together in shops, buses, and elevators, and when they bump into each other, they don't apologize or draw back. Similarly, in countries such as Hong Kong people are used to living and working in very close quarters, so territoriality is uncommon (Andersen, et al., 2002; Chan, 1999). In some cultures—Italy, for example—dramatic nonverbal displays of emotion are typical, but other cultures consider more reserved displays of emotion appropriate (Matsumoto, Franklin, Choi, Rogers, & Tatani, 2002).

Look at the man at the left. What do his facial expression and kinesics tell you about how he relates to the homeless man at the right?

© Bob Daemmrich/Stock Boston

—Sucheng—

In United States, each person has so much room. Every individual has a separate room in which to sleep and sometimes another separate room in which to work. Also, I see that each family here lives in a separate house. People have much less space in China. Families live together, with sons bringing their families into their parents' home and all sharing the same space. At first when I came here it felt strange to have so much space, but now I sometimes feel very crowded when I go home.

Patterns of eye contact also reflect cultural values. In the United States, frankness and assertion are valued, so meeting another's eyes is considered appropriate and a demonstration of personal honesty. Yet, as we've noted, in many Asian and northern European countries, direct eye contact is considered abrasive and disrespectful (Axtell, 1990a, 1990b; Samovar & Porter, 2001). In Brazil, eye contact often is so intense that people from the United States consider it rude staring. As the example with Mr. Watanabe and Mr. Thompson suggests, this cultural difference can cause misunderstandings in intercultural business negotiations.

Greeting behaviors also vary across cultures. In the United States and many other Western countries, the handshake is the most common way to greet. Arab men are more likely to kiss each other on both cheeks as a form of greeting. Embraces are typical greetings in Mexico. Bowing is the standard form of greeting in some Asian cultures (Samovar & Porter, 2001).

  To develop insight into nonverbal expression of cultural values, complete Activity 6.2, "Nonverbal Exclusions," in your *Student Companion* or online under "Activities for Chapter 6" at the *Communication in Our Lives* website.

In sum, we've noted five was in which nonverbal communication affects meaning. First, there are similarities and differences between nonverbal and verbal communication. Second, nonverbal behavior can supplement or replace verbal communication. Third, nonverbal behaviors regulate interaction. Fourth, nonverbal communication is often especially powerful in establishing and expressing relational meanings. Finally, nonverbal behaviors reflect cultural values and are learned, not instinctive. We're now ready to explore the many types of behavior in the intricate nonverbal communication system.

Types of Nonverbal Communication

In this section, we will consider nine forms of nonverbal behavior, noticing how we use each to communicate.

Kinesics

Kinesics is body position and body motions, including those of the face. Our bodies express a great deal about how we see ourselves. A speaker who stands erect and appears confident announces self-assurance, whereas someone who slouches and shuffles may seem to say, "I'm not very sure of myself." A person who walks quickly with a resolute facial expression appears more determined than someone who saunters along with an unfocused gaze. We sit rigidly when we are nervous and adopt a relaxed posture when we feel at ease. Audiences and groups indicate attentiveness and interest by body posture.

Body postures and gestures may signal whether we are open to interaction and how we feel about others. Someone who sits with arms crossed and looks downward seems to say, "Don't bother me." That's a nonverbal strategy students sometimes use to dissuade teachers from calling on them in classes. To signal that we'd like to interact, we look at others and sometimes smile. We use one hand gesture to say okay and another to communicate contempt.

The world of sports provides some interesting examples of nonverbal communication—and its consequences. At the 1968 Olympic Games in Mexico City, a group of African American athletes raised clenched fists to symbolize Black power, a politically radical gesture in that country and era. The athletes were punished for their communication by having their medals taken away. Nonverbal communication has been costly for some sports stars ("Be Civil," 1994). When German midfielder Stefan Effenberg made an obscene gesture to fans during a World Cup match in the summer of 1994, his coach promptly kicked him off the squad. The season before, Miami Dolphins linebacker Bryan Cox flipped an obscene gesture; the National Football League slapped him with a $10,000 fine (later reduced to $3,000).

Private companies such as athletic teams can make their own rules. In the United States, however, nonverbal behavior is protected by freedom of speech laws. Thus, Louis Sirkin, a First Amendment attorney, successfully defended a motorist who insulted a traffic officer by making an obscene hand gesture. Sirkin argued that his client's gesture was a form of communication protected by the Constitutional guarantee of free speech.

Communication Highlight

Communicating Hand to Mouth

Robert Krauss's career as a researcher of nonverbal communication may have been launched by a story his grandfather told him when he was a young boy. According to Krauss, his grandfather told him about two men who were taking a walk on a very cold day. One man chattered continually. The other kept his hands stuffed in his pockets and said little. Finally, the talkative man asked, "Why aren't you saying anything?" His friend replied, "I forgot my gloves." Without gloves, the quiet man kept his hands in his pockets to protect them from the frigid winter air. And without being able to use his hands to gesture, he couldn't talk.

Now, some 50 years after hearing that story, Krauss is fascinated by the connections between gestures and speech. His research shows that gestures do more than amplify or accent verbal communication (Begley, 1998). They also seem to help people retrieve ideas and words, unlocking what Krauss calls the "lexical memory." In one

study, Krauss found that people tend to use gestures when they are trying to define words that have spatial meanings (*under, beside, nearby*) and when defining abstract words (*evil, mysterious*). Does this mean that people who are unable to gesture might have trouble communicating?

That's exactly what scientists are finding. In one experiment, half of the participants held a bar to keep their hands still and were then asked to name words to match definitions read by a researcher. Compared with participants whose hands were free, those holding the bar either took longer or couldn't name the word.

 Use your InfoTrac College Edition to read a follow-up article written by Sharon Begley. The article, which appeared in 1999, is entitled "Talking from Hand to Mouth." Based on this article, do you consider gestures to be a language with rules of syntax and grammar?

Our faces are intricate messengers (Carroll & Russell, 1996). The human face is capable of more than 1,000 distinct expressions. Our eyes can shoot daggers of anger, issue challenges, express skepticism, or radiate love. With our faces we can indicate disapproval (scowls), doubt (raised eyebrows), love (eye gazes), and challenge (stares). The face is particularly powerful in conveying responsiveness and liking (Keeley & Hart, 1994; Patterson, 1992). Speakers often use facial expressions to suggest that they are open and friendly.

How we position ourselves relative to others may express our feelings toward them. On work teams, friends and allies often sit together, and competitors typically maintain distance. We communicate dissatisfaction by moving away from others and by decreasing smiles and eye contact (Miller & Parks, 1982; Walker & Trimboli, 1989). Americans often cross their legs, but this is perceived as offensive in Ghana and Turkey (Samovar & Porter, 2001).

For good reason, poets call the eyes "the mirrors of the soul." Our eyes communicate some of the most important and complex messages about how we feel. If you watch infants, you'll notice that they focus on others' eyes. As adults, we often look at eyes to judge emotions, honesty, interest, and self-confidence. This explains why strong eye contact tends to heighten the credibility of public speakers. Eye contact tends to make us feel closer to others and more positive about them. This may explain the recent research finding that customers leave larger tips when servers maintain eye contact with them (Davis & Kieffer, 1998).

Haptics

Haptics is physical touch. Touch is the first of our senses to develop, and many communication scholars believe that touching and being touched are essential to a healthy life (Whitman et al., 1999). Research reveals that mothers in dysfunctional families touch their babies less often and less affectionately than mothers in healthy families do. Conversely, research shows that massage helps babies thrive (Mwakalye & DeAngelis, 1995).

Sharpen Your Skill

Communicating Closeness

What do your nonverbal behaviors say about how you feel toward others? To find out, observe yourself with (a) someone you really like and feel comfortable with, (b) a stranger, and (c) someone you don't trust or like. How closely do you sit or stand to each of the three people? How does your posture differ? What facial expressions and eye contact do you use with each person?

 Extend this exercise by completing Activity 6.5, "Identifying Nonverbal Cues," in your *Student Companion* or online under "Activities for Chapter 6" at the *Communication in Our Lives* website.

Touching also communicates power and status. People of high status touch others and enter others' spaces more than people with less status (Henley, 1977). Cultural views of women as more touchable than men are reflected in gendered patterns. Parents touch sons less often and more roughly than they touch daughters (Condry, Condry, & Pogatshnik, 1983). These patterns early in life teach the sexes different rules for using touch and interpreting the touches of others. As adults, women tend to touch others to show liking and intimacy (Montgomery, 1988), whereas men more typically rely on touch to assert power and control (Jhally & Katz, 2001; Leathers, 1986; Le Poire, Burgoon, & Parrott, 1992).

-Yvette-

When I was pregnant, total strangers would walk up to me and touch my belly. It was amazing—and disturbing. They seemed to think they had a right to touch me or that the baby wasn't me, so they could touch him. Amazing!

Physical Appearance

Western culture places an extremely high value on **physical appearance.** For this reason, most of us notice how others look, and we form initial evaluations based on their appearance. We first notice obvious physical qualities such as sex, skin color, size, and features. What we notice about others' appearance leads us to form judgments of how attractive they are and to make inferences about their personalities. Although our judgments and inferences may be inaccurate, they can affect our decisions about friendships, dating, hiring, and promotion.

Cultures stipulate ideals for physical form. Currently, cultural ideals in the West emphasize thinness and softness in women and muscularity and height in men (Hicks, 1998; "The Wrong Weight," 1997). In an effort to meet these ideals, many people, particularly women, develop eating disorders. Men are more likely to engage in excessive body building or use steroids. Both sexes are increasingly turning to plastic surgery (Bordo, 1999; Gilman, 1999). In 1995, more than 800,000 people elected to have cosmetic surgery on their faces (Gross, 2000; Sharlet, 1999). In 2004, two television programs, *Extreme Makeover* and *The Swan,* glorified radical plastic surgery to enhance women's physical attractiveness. An extreme example of having plastic surgery is the case of Cindy Jackson. She has had twenty-nine plastic surgeries to change her face and body to match Barbie's as closely as surgery can achieve. To learn more about Cindy Jackson's efforts to embody Barbie, visit her website: http://www.cindyjackson.com.

General Western standards for attractiveness are qualified by ethnic identity. In traditional African societies, full-figured bodies are perceived as symbolizing health, prosperity, and wealth, which are all desirable (Villarosa, 1994). African Americans who embrace this value accept or prefer women who weigh more than the current ideal for European American women (Root, 1990; Thomas, 1989).

-Cass-

I found out how much appearance matters when I was in an auto accident. It messed up my face so that I had scars all over one side and on my forehead. All of a sudden, nobody was asking me out. All these guys who had been so crazy about me before the accident lost interest. Some of my girlfriends seemed uneasy about being seen with me. When I first had the wreck, I was so glad to be alive that I didn't even think about plastic surgery. After a couple of months of seeing how others treated me, however, I had the surgery.

Class membership further modifies ethnic values concerning weight. In 1994, *Essence* magazine reported that African American women who are either rich or poor are likely to have strong Black identities that allow them to resist Caucasian preoccupations with thinness. On the other hand, middle-class African American women who are upwardly mobile are more inclined to de-emphasize their ethnic identities, and they are more susceptible to eating disorders and obsessions with weight (Villarosa, 1994).

Artifacts

Artifacts are personal objects with which we announce our identities and personalize our environments. We craft our <u>image</u> by how we dress, the jewelry we wear, and the objects we carry and use. Nurses and doctors wear white and often drape stethoscopes around their necks; professors travel with briefcases, whereas students more often tote backpacks. White-collar professionals tend to wear tailored outfits and dress shoes, whereas blue-collar workers often wear jeans or uniforms and boots. Military uniforms define individuals as members of the group. In addition, stripes, medals, and insignia signify rank and accomplishments.

Sharpen Your Skill

Artifactual Gender Messages

What do your artifacts say about you? Are your clothes casual or formal? Are they traditional, the latest fad, or uniquely your style? Does your jewelry suggest that you are playful (novelty jewelry), rich (real gold and precious stones), or ethnically identified? What do the objects in your room convey about your values, interests, and the important people in your life?

Extend this exercise by completing Activity 6.3, "Portrait of Myself," and Activity 6.7, "Sculpting Personal Image with Nonverbal Communication," in your *Student Companion* or online under "Activities for Chapter 6" at the *Communication in Our Lives* website.

Have you ever noticed that how you're dressed affects how you behave? If so, you're not alone. Roughly a decade ago, some businesses instituted a practice called "casual Friday" that allowed employees to dress informally on Fridays. This practice was intended to make employees more comfortable on the job. However, many businesses have found that casual dress tends to lead employees to be too laid-back. A number of businesses report that when

employees dress casually, they are less productive, polite, and punctual ("New Wrinkles," 1999).

We also use artifacts to define settings and personal territories. When the president of the United States speaks, the setting is usually replete with symbols of national identity and pride, such as the flag. At annual meetings of companies, the chair usually speaks from a podium that bears the company logo. In much the same manner, we claim our private spaces by filling them with objects that matter to us and reflect our experiences and values. Lovers of art adorn their homes with paintings and sculptures. Religious families display pictures of holy scenes and the Bible, the Koran, or another sacred text. Our artifacts also symbolize important relationships and experiences. Pictures of family members decorate many offices. I've personalized my writing desk with a photograph of my sister, Carolyn; an item that belonged to my father; the first card Robbie ever gave me; and a jar of rocks from my favorite beach. These artifacts personalize my desk with reminders of people and experiences I cherish.

−Naomi−

I've moved a lot since coming to college—dorm, apartment, another apartment, and another apartment. I never feel a place is home until I put a photograph of my grandmother holding me on my dresser. Then it's home.

In her book *Composing a Life,* Mary Catherine Bateson (1990) comments that we turn houses into homes by filling them with objects that matter to us. With our artifacts, we make impersonal spaces familiar and comfortable. We use mugs given to us by special people, nurture plants to enliven indoor spaces, surround ourselves with books and magazines that announce our interests, and sprinkle our world with material reflections of what we care about.

Artifacts communicate important relational meanings. We use them to express our personal identities. For instance, body piercing has become popular, particularly among people under 25. Because some people find it unappetizing, however, restaurant chains such as Chili's have established policies to limit piercings that might offend customers: Ears are the only visible body part that employees may pierce ("Business Bulletin," 1996).

Communication Highlight

Dress for Success

Does what you wear have anything to do with getting a job or promotion? According to image consultants, how you dress definitely affects your success on the job. One of the best-known dress consultants is John Molloy, who wrote *The New Dress for Success* (1988) and *The New Women's Dress for Success Book* (1996). The colors most appropriate for business settings are black, brown, navy, gray, and beige. Darker colors usually are associated with higher status and greater authority, so wearing navy or black may increase others' perceptions of your rank (Greenleaf, 1998). What about bolder colors such as red or

purple? A splash of color, such as a bright scarf on a navy dress or a red tie with a dark suit, can indicate confidence: others may assume that you are sure enough of yourself not to stick rigidly to the "safe" colors. However, wearing a bright red dress or a purple jacket may communicate just the opposite message: that you don't know what is appropriate in a work setting.

 To learn more about norms for dressing, visit http://www.dressingwell.com.

Although clothing has become more unisex in recent years, once you venture beyond the campus context, gendered styles are evident (Abdullah, 1999). To perform gender, we dress to meet cultural expectations for men and women. Thus, women sometimes wear makeup, dresses that may have lace or other softening touches, skirts, high-heeled shoes, jewelry, and hosiery. Typically, men wear less jewelry, although Western men increasingly wear necklaces or bracelets or pierce ears and other body parts (Klein, 2001). Men's clothes and shoes tend to be less confining and more functional than women's (Johnson, Roberts, & Warell, 2002). Flat shoes allow a person to walk comfortably or run if necessary; high heels don't. Men's clothing usually is looser and less binding than women's clothing, and it includes pockets for wallets, change, keys, and so forth. In contrast, women's clothing tends to be more tailored and often doesn't include pockets, so women have to carry purses to hold personal items.

We also use artifacts to express ethnic identity. Kwanzaa is an African American holiday tradition that celebrates the centrality of home, family, and community. Hanukkah is a Jewish holiday tradition, and Christmas is a European American, Christian tradition. The kinara is a branched candleholder that holds seven candles, one of which is lit during each day of Kwanzaa (Bellamy, 1996; George, 1995). The menorah is a candleholder used during Hanukkah, and Christmas trees and manger scenes are artifacts used in conjunction with Christmas. In recent years, marketers have offered more ethnic clothing and jewelry so people of color can more easily acquire artifacts that express their cultural heritage.

Artifacts chosen by others can express how they see us. Parents and especially fathers tend to give sons toys that encourage rough play (trucks) and competitiveness (baseball gloves, toy weapons), whereas they tend to give daughters toys that cultivate nurturing (dolls, play stoves) and attention to appearance (makeup kits, frilly clothes) (Caldera, Huston, & O'Brien, 1989; Lytton & Romney, 1991). We give gifts to say, "You matter to me." Artifacts such as engagement rings and wedding bands signify commitment. We also symbolize that we're connected to others by wearing their clothes, as when women wear male partners' shirts.

Proxemics

Proxemics is space and how we use it. Every culture has norms for using space and for how close people should be to one another (Afifi & Burgoon, 2000). In the United States, we interact with social acquaintances from a distance of 4 to 12 feet but are comfortable with 18 inches or less between us and close friends or romantic partners (Hall, 1966). Confirming that space reflects intimacy, research shows that spouses who are dissatisfied typically maintain greater distance than do happy partners (Crane, 1987; Miller & Parks, 1982). When we are angry with someone, we tend to move away from him or her and to resent it if he or she approaches us.

Space also signals status; greater space is assumed by those of higher status. Research shows that in our society women and minorities generally have less space than Caucasian men. (Andersen, 1999; Spain, 1992). The prerogative to enter someone else's personal space is also linked to power; those with greater power are most likely to trespass into others' territory. Responses to invasions of space also reflect the relationship between gender

Communication Highlight

and power: Many men respond aggressively when their space is invaded, whereas women are more likely to yield space to the aggressor (Le Poire, Burgoon, & Parrott, 1992).

How people arrange space reflects how close they are and whether they want interaction. Rigidly organized businesses may have private offices with doors and little common space. In contrast, more open businesses are likely to have fewer doors and more common space, to invite interaction between employees. Couples who are very interdependent tend to have greater amounts of common space and less individual space in their homes than do couples who are more independent (Fitzpatrick, 1988; Fitzpatrick & Best, 1979; Werner, Altman, & Oxley, 1985). Families that enjoy interaction arrange furniture to invite conversation and eye contact. In families that

What does this executive's space convey about his power and openness to others?

© Taxi/Getty Images

Communication Highlight

seek less interaction, chairs may be far apart and may face televisions instead of each other (Burgoon, Buller, & Woodhall, 1989; Keeley & Hart, 1994).

People also invite or discourage interaction by how they arrange office spaces. Some professors and executives have desks that face the door, and a chair beside the desk for open communication with people who come to their offices; other professionals turn desks away from the door and position chairs across from their desks to preserve status and distance.

Environmental Factors

Environmental factors are elements of settings that affect how we feel and act. For instance, we respond to architecture, colors, room design, temperature, sounds, smells, and lighting. Rooms with comfortable chairs invite relaxation, whereas rooms with stiff chairs prompt formality. Research shows that students perceive professors as more credible and approachable if the professors have attractively decorated offices (Taylor et al., 1998). Dimly lit rooms can enhance romantic feelings, although dark rooms can be depressing. We feel solemn in churches and synagogues with their somber colors and sacred symbols such as crosses and menorahs.

We tend to feel more lethargic on sultry summer days and more alert on crisp fall days. In settings where people work at night, extra lighting and even artificial skylights sometimes are installed to stimulate alertness. A study conducted by the Rocky Mountain Institute found that increased daylight in work spaces results in less absenteeism and fewer errors. Similarly, Wal-Mart discovered that in areas with skylights, customers bought more and employees were more productive than in artificially lit areas (Pierson, 1995).

Restaurants use environmental features to control how long people linger over meals. For example, low lights, comfortable chairs or booths, and soft music often are part of the environment in upscale restaurants. On the other hand, fast-food eateries have hard plastic booths and bright lights, which encourage diners to eat and move on. To make a profit, restaurants have to get people in and out as quickly as possible. Studies indicate that faster music in the background speeds up the pace of eating ("Bites," 1998; Bozzi, 1986).

Environmental Awareness

Think of one place where you feel rushed and one where you linger. Describe the following about each place:

How is furniture arranged?

What kind of lighting is used?

What sort of music is played, and what other sounds are there?

How comfortable is the furniture for sitting or lounging?

What colors and art are there?

Based on your observations, can you make generalizations about environmental features that promote relaxation and ones that do not?

  You can extend this exercise by completing Activity 6.4, "Nonverbal Designs," in your *Student Companion* or online under "Activities for Chapter 6" at the *Communication in Our Lives* website.

Feng shui is the ancient Chinese art of placement that arranges furniture, objects, colors, and walls in harmony with the earth. Dating back more than 3,000 years, *feng shui* aims to balance life energy, called *chi*, so that a setting promotes a harmonious flow of energies. Many *feng shui* principles are consistent with research on nonverbal communication: Don't put large furniture in the path to a door; stairways should not be visible from the front door; use colors to stimulate feelings such as creativity and calmness (Cozart, 1996; O'Neill, 1997; Spear, 1995).

Chronemics

Chronemics is how we perceive and use time to define identities and interaction. In an early study of how and what time communicates, Nancy Henley (1977) identified a cultural rule: Important people with high status can keep others waiting. Conversely, people with low status are expected to be punctual in Western society. More recent research validates Henley's finding that time and status are related (Levine & Norenzayan, 1999; Richmond & McCroskey, 1995b). It is standard practice to have to wait, sometimes a long while, to see a doctor, even if you have an appointment. This carries the

Communication Highlight

Environmental Racism

According to Robert Cox (2004), former president of the Sierra Club, the term *environmental racism* arose to describe a pattern whereby toxic waste dumps and hazardous industrial plants are located in low-income neighborhoods and communities of color. The pattern is very clear: The space of minorities and poor people can be invaded and contaminated, but the territory of more affluent citizens cannot be.

 To learn more about environmental justice and environmental racism, go to http://www.ejrc .cau.edu. This site provides information on the Environmental Protection Agency's strategies for preventing environmental racism.

message that the doctor's time is more valuable than ours. Professors can be late to class, and students are expected to wait, but students sometimes are reprimanded if they arrive after a class begins. Subordinates are expected to report punctually to meetings, but bosses are allowed to be tardy.

Chronemics express cultural attitudes toward time. In Western societies, time is valuable, so speed is highly valued (Bertman, 1998; Hochschild, 1997; Keyes, 1992; Schwartz, 1989). Thus, we want computers, not typewriters, and we replace our computers and modems as soon as faster models hit the market. We often try to do several things at once to get more done, rely on the microwave to cook faster, and take for granted speed systems such as instant copying and photofinishing (Urgo, 2000). Many other cultures have far more relaxed attitudes toward time and punctuality. It's not impolite in many South American countries to come late to meetings or classes, and it's not assumed that people will leave at the scheduled ending time (Levine & Norenzayan, 1999). Whether time is treated casually, or closely watched and measured out, reflects larger cultural attitudes toward living.

The amount of time we spend with different people reflects our interpersonal priorities. A manager spends more time with a new employee who seems to have executive potential than with one who seems less impressive. A speaker spends more time responding to a question from a high-status member of the audience than to a person of lower status. We spend more time with people we like than with those we don't like or who bore us. Increasing time together is one of the most important ways college students intensify relationships, and reducing time together signals decreasing interest (Baxter, 1985; Dindia, 1994; Tolhuizen, 1989).

Expectations of time are established by social norms. For example, you expect a class to last 50 to 75 minutes. Several minutes before the end of a class period, many students close their notebooks and start gathering their belongings, signaling the teacher that time is up. A parallel pattern often is evident in business meetings. We expect religious services to last approximately an hour, and we might be upset if a rabbi or minister talked for 2 hours. These

Whispered secrets reflect special intimacy between people.

expectations reflect our culture's view that time is a precious commodity to be saved and invested carefully (Lakoff & Johnson, 1980). Many everyday expressions reflect the cultural view that time is like money, a valuable and limited resource to be used wisely: "You're *wasting* my time." "This will *save* some time." "I don't *have* any time to *give* you." "That mistake *cost* me 3 hours." "I've *invested* a lot of time in this class, and now I'm *running out of time.*"

Paralanguage

Paralanguage is vocal communication that does not involve words. It includes sounds, such as murmurs and gasps, and vocal qualities, such as volume, rhythm, pitch, and inflection. Our voices are versatile instruments that tell others how to interpret us and what we say. Vocal cues signal others to interpret what we say as a joke,

© Antony Nagelmann/Getty Images/FPG

threat, statement of fact, question, and so forth. Vocal cues also express irritation. Effective public speakers know how to modulate inflection, volume, and rhythm to enhance their verbal messages.

Sharpen Your Skill

Practicing Paralanguage

Say "really" so that it means

> I don't believe you.
>
> Wow! That's amazing.
>
> That doesn't square with what I've heard.
>
> I totally agree.

Say "get lost" so that it means

> I want you out of here.
>
> That's a dumb idea.
>
> I'm crazy about you.

We use our voices to communicate feelings. Whispering, for instance, often signals secrecy, and shouting conveys anger. Depending on the context, sighing may communicate empathy, boredom, or contentment. Research indicates that tone of voice is a powerful clue to feelings between marital partners. Negative vocal tones are among the most important symbols of marital dissatisfaction (Gottman, 1994b; Gottman, Markman, & Notarius, 1977; Noller, 1987). Negative intonation may also signal dissatisfaction or disapproval in work settings. The reverse is also true: A warm voice conveys liking, and a playful lilt suggests friendliness.

We use our voices to communicate how we see ourselves and wish to be seen by others. For instance, we use a firm, confident voice in job interviews or when explaining why we deserve a raise. The president adopts a strong, serious voice when announcing military actions. We also know how to make ourselves sound apologetic, seductive, or angry when it suits us. In addition to the ways we intentionally use our voices to project an image, vocal qualities we don't deliberately choose can affect how others perceive us. Pace of speaking may influence perceptions. For instance, research shows that people who speak at a slow to moderate rate are perceived as having greater control over interaction than people who speak rapidly (Tusing & Dillard, 2000). Accents, too, may affect perceptions. A person with a pronounced Bronx accent may be perceived as brash, and someone with a Southern drawl may be perceived as lazy. People for whom English is a second language often are falsely perceived by Americans as less intelligent than native English speakers.

—Rayna—

When I first moved to the United States, I didn't understand many words and idioms. I did not understand that "A bird in the hand is worth two in the bush" meant it is smart to hold on to what is sure. I did not understand that "Hang a right" meant to turn right. So when I did not understand, I would ask people to explain. Most times they would say the very same thing over, just louder and more slowly, like I was deaf or stupid. I felt like saying to them in a very loud, slow voice, "I am Indian, not stupid. You are stupid."

Paralanguage also reflects our cultural heritage. For example, many African Americans' speech has more vocal range, inflection, and tonal quality than that of most European Americans (Garner, 1994). In addition, among themselves some African Americans engage in highly rhythmic rapping and "high talk" to create desired identities (Ribeau, Baldwin, & Hecht, 1994). We also use paralanguage to perform gender. To perform masculinity, men use strong volume, low pitch, and limited inflection, all of which conform to cultural prescriptions for men to be assertive and emotionally controlled. To perform femininity, women tend to use higher pitch, softer volume, and more inflection. We also perform class by our pronunciation of words, our accents, and the complexity of our sentences.

Silence

A final type of nonverbal behavior is **silence,** which can communicate powerful messages. The assertion "I'm not speaking to you" actually speaks volumes. We use silence to communicate different meanings. For instance, silence indicates contentment when intimates are so comfortable they don't need to talk. Silence can also communicate awkwardness, as you know if you've ever had trouble keeping conversation going with a new acquaintance. We feel pressured to fill the void.

Silence can also disconfirm others. In some families, children are disciplined by being ignored. No matter what the child says or does, parents refuse to acknowledge his or her existence. In later life, the silencing strategy may also surface. You know how disconfirming silence can be if you've ever said "Hello" to someone and gotten no reply. Even if the other person didn't deliberately ignore you, you felt slighted. We sometimes deliberately freeze out others when we're angry with them. In some military academies, such as West Point, silencing is a recognized method of stripping a cadet of personhood if he or she is perceived as having broken the academy code. Whistle-blowers and union-busters often are shunned by peers. Similarly, the Catholic Church excommunicates people who violate its canons.

Sharpen Your Skill

Observing Nonverbal Communication

To find out whether research findings about nonverbal communication apply in real life, observe two of the contexts listed here. Describe environmental features and artifacts in the settings. Also, identify patterns of proxemics, kinesics, chronemics, haptics, and paralanguage. Do your observations concur with research findings discussed in this chapter?

Expensive retail stores and discount stores

Executive and secretarial offices

Faculty clubs and student cafeterias

Libraries and student unions

College administrative buildings and classroom buildings on campus

Describe how nonverbal factors reflect the different identities of these contexts and the kinds of activities and interactions each context invites and discourages.

The complex system of nonverbal communication includes kinesics, haptics, physical appearance, artifacts, proxemics, environmental features, chronemics, paralanguage, and silence. We use these nonverbal behaviors to announce our identities and to communicate how we feel about relationships with others. In the final section of this chapter, we consider guidelines for improving the effectiveness of our nonverbal communication.

Improving Nonverbal Communication

Nonverbal communication, like its verbal cousin, can be misinterpreted. You can reduce the likelihood of misunderstandings in nonverbal communication by following two guidelines.

Monitor Your Nonverbal Communication

The monitoring skills we have stressed in other chapters are also important for competent nonverbal communication. Think about the ways we use nonverbal behaviors to announce our identities. Are you projecting the image you desire? Do your facial and body movements represent how you see yourself and how you want others to perceive you? Do people ever tell you that you seem uninterested when they are talking to you? If so, you can monitor your nonverbal actions and modify them to more clearly communicate involvement and interest. You can also set up your spaces to invite the kind of interaction you prefer.

To increase your awareness of how others may misinterpret you nonverbal behaviors, complete Activity 6.6, "Monitoring Your Nonverbal Communication," in your *Student Companion* or online under "Activities for Chapter 6" at the *Communication in Our Lives* website.

Interpret Others' Nonverbal Communication Tentatively

In this chapter, we've discussed findings about the meanings people tend to attach to nonverbal behaviors. It's important to realize that these are only generalizations about how we interpret nonverbal communication. We cannot state what any particular behavior means to specific people in a particular context. For instance, we've said that satisfied couples tend to sit closer together than unhappy couples. As a general rule, this is true. However, sometimes very contented couples prefer autonomy and like occasional distance between each other. In addition, someone may maintain distance because she or he has a cold and doesn't want a partner to catch it. The generalizations we've discussed may not apply to people from non-Western cultures. Ethical communicators qualify their interpretations of nonverbal behavior by considering personal and contextual considerations.

Personal Qualifications Nonverbal patterns that accurately describe most people may not apply to particular individuals. Although eye contact generally indicates responsiveness, some people close their eyes to concentrate when listening. In such cases, it would be inaccurate to conclude that a person who doesn't look at us isn't listening. Similarly, people who cross their arms and condense into a tight posture may be expressing hostility or lack of interest in interaction. However, the same behaviors might mean a person is cold. Most people use less inflection, fewer gestures, and a slack posture when they're not really interested in what they're talking about. However, fatigue can result in the same behaviors.

–Derrick–

I'd like to tell off those jerks who write the popular books on reading nonverbal behavior. One of the things they say is that crossing your legs a certain way means you're closed or hostile. Well, I have a bum knee from football, and there's only one way I can cross my legs. It doesn't mean anything about whether I'm closed. It means my knee doesn't work.

To avoid misinterpreting others' nonverbal communication, you can check perceptions and use *I*-language, not *you*-language, which we discussed in Chapter 5. You can check perceptions to find out whether the way you interpret another's nonverbal behavior is what that other person means: "I sense that you're not really involved in this conversation; is that how you feel?" In addition, you can rely on *I*-language. *You*-language might lead us to inaccurately say of someone who doesn't look at us, "You're communicating lack of interest." A more responsible statement would use *I*-language to say, "When you don't look at me, I feel you're not interested in what I'm saying." Using *I*-language reminds us to take responsibility for our judgments and feelings. In addition, it reduces the likelihood that we will make others defensive by inaccurately interpreting their nonverbal behavior.

Contextual Qualifications   Like the meaning of verbal communication, the significance of nonverbal behaviors depends on the contexts in which they occur. Most people are more at ease on their own turf than on someone else's, so we tend to be more friendly and outgoing in our homes than in business meetings and public spaces. We also dress according to context. When I am on campus or in business meetings, I dress professionally, but at home I usually wear jeans or running clothes.

In addition to our immediate physical settings, nonverbal communication reflects particular cultures. We are likely to misinterpret people from other cultures when we impose the norms and rules of our culture on them. An Arabic man who stands practically on top of others to talk with them is not being rude, according to his culture's standards, although Westerners might interpret him as rude.

–Eleni–

I have been misinterpreted very much in this country. My first semester here, a professor told me he wanted me to be more assertive and to speak up in class. I could not do that, I told him. He said I should put myself forward, but I have been brought up not to do that. In Taiwan, that is very rude and ugly, and we are taught not to speak up to teachers. Now that I have been here for 3 years, I sometimes speak in classes, but I am still more quiet than Americans. I know my professors think I am not so smart because I am quiet, but that is the teaching of my country.

Even within a single culture, different social communities have distinct rules for nonverbal behavior. A man who doesn't make "listening noises" may be listening intently according to the rules of masculine speech communities. Similarly, when women nod and make listening noises while another is talking, men may misperceive them as agreeing. According to the rules typically learned in feminine social communities, ongoing feedback is a way of signaling interest, not necessarily agreement. We should adopt dual perspective when interpreting others, especially when they belong to cultures or communities that are different from ours.

CASE STUDY: Nonverbal Cues

The conversation scripted here is featured as a multimedia scenario on the *Communication in Our Lives* CD-ROM included with this book. Once you've launched the CD, click on the "Communication Scenarios" icon, and, from the Scenarios Menu, select "Nonverbal Cues" to watch the video. Improve your own communication skills by reading, watching, listening to, critiquing, and analyzing this communication encounter.

Analyze the scenario by applying the principles covered in this chapter, and respond to the prompts that accompany the video, which you can access by clicking on "Analysis." After completing the conversation analysis and answering the questions, you can click on the "Done" button to compare your responses with the ones I suggest. Additional analysis questions are available in print at the end of this chapter and on the book's website.

Jason Harris/© 2001 Wadsworth

A project team is meeting to discuss the most effective way to present its recommendations for implementing a flextime policy on a trial basis. Members of the team are Jason Brown, team leader; Erika Filene; Victoria Lawrence; Bill Williams; and Jensen Chen. They are seated around a rectangular table with Jason at the head.

JASON: So we've decided to recommend trying flextime for a 2-month period and with a number of procedures to make sure that people's new schedules don't interfere with productivity. There's a lot of information to communicate to employees, so how can we do that best?

VICTORIA: I think it would be good to use PowerPoint to highlight the key aspects of the new procedures. People always seem to remember better if they see something.

BILL: Oh, come on. PowerPoint is so overused. Everyone is tired of it by now. Can't we do something more creative?

VICTORIA: Well, I like it. It's a good teaching tool.

BILL: I didn't know we were teaching. I thought our job was to report recommendations.

VICTORIA: So what do you suggest, Bill? [She nervously pulls on her bracelet as she speaks.]

BILL: I don't have a suggestion. I'm just against PowerPoint. [He doesn't look up as he speaks.]

JASON: Okay, let's not bicker among ourselves. [He pauses, gazes directly at Bill, then continues.] Lots of people like PowerPoint, lots don't. Instead of arguing about its value, let's ask what it is we want to communicate to the employees here. Maybe talking about our goal first will help us decide on the best means of achieving it.

ERIKA: Good idea. I'd like us to focus first on getting everyone excited about the benefits of flextime. If they understand those, they'll be motivated to learn the procedures, even if there are a lot of them.

JENSEN: Erika is right. That's a good way to start. Maybe we could create a handout or PowerPoint slide—either would work—to summarize the benefits of flextime we've identified in our research.

JASON: Good, okay now we're cooking. Victoria, will you make notes on the ideas as we discuss them?

Victoria opens a notebook and begins writing notes. Noticing that Bill is typing into his personal digital assistant (PDA), Jason looks directly at Bill and says,

JASON: Are you with us on how we lead off in our presentation?

BILL: Sure, fine with me. [He puts the PDA aside but keeps his eyes on it.]

ERIKA: So maybe then we should say that the only way flextime can work is if we make sure that everyone agrees on procedures so that no division is ever missing more than one person during key production hours.

JENSEN: Very good. That would add to people's motivation to learn and follow the procedures we've found are effective in other companies like ours. I think it would be great if Erika could present that topic because she did most of the research on it. [He smiles at Erika, and she pantomimes tipping her hat to him.]

JASON: [He looks at Erika with a raised brow, and she nods.] Good. Okay, Erika's in charge of that. What's next?

VICTORIA: Then it's time to spell out the procedures and. . .

BILL: You can't just spell them out. You have to explain each one—give people a rationale for them—or they won't follow them.

Victoria glares at Bill, then looks across the table at Erika, who shrugs as if to say, "I don't know what's bothering Bill today."

JASON: Bill, why don't you lead off, then, and tell us the first procedure we should mention and the rationale we should provide for it.

Bill looks up from his PDA, which he's been using again. He shrugs and says harshly, "Just spell out the rules, that's all."

VICTORIA: Would it be too much trouble for you to cut off your gadget and join us in this meeting, Bill?

BILL: Would it be too much trouble for you to quit hassling me?

JASON: [He turns his chair to face Bill squarely.] Look, I don't know what's eating you, but you're really being a jerk. If you've got a problem with this meeting or someone here, put it on the table. Otherwise, be a team player.

Chapter Summary

In this chapter, we've explored the world beyond words. We learned that there are similarities and differences between nonverbal communication and verbal communication. Next, we noted that nonverbal communication supplements or replaces verbal messages, regulates interaction, reflects and establishes relational-level meanings, and expresses cultural membership.

We discussed nine types of nonverbal communication: kinesics, haptics, physical appearance, artifacts, proxemics, environmental features, chronemics, paralanguage, and silence. Each form of nonverbal communication reflects cultural understandings and values and also expresses our personal identities and feelings toward others.

Because nonverbal communication, like verbal communication, is symbolic, it has no inherent, universal meaning. Instead, we construct meaning as we notice, organize, and interpret nonverbal behaviors.

 Communication in Our Lives ONLINE

In addition to presenting the case studies' multimedia scenarios, the *Communication in Our Lives* CD-ROM provides quick access to the *Communication in Our Lives* website and InfoTrac College Edition. The website is online at http://communication.wadsworth.com/woodciol4, but you can only access this book's premium web content when you link to the site directly through the book's CD.

 The *Communication in Our Lives* website features interactive tools for learning and reviewing the chapter's concepts and key terms, including electronic versions of the "For Further Reflection and Discussion" questions that follow and a review quiz.

The website also provides updated web links and additional InfoTrac College Edition activities. If required, you can e-mail completed chapter activities or the quizzes to your instructor.

Key Concepts

artifacts, *158*	kinesics, *154*	proxemics, *160*
chronemics, *163*	nonverbal communication, *148*	silence, *166*
environmental factors, *162*	paralanguage, *164*	
haptics, *156*	physical appearance, *157*	

For Further Reflection and Discussion

1. Attend a gathering of people who belong to a social community different from yours. Observe nonverbal behaviors of the people there: How do they greet one another, how much eye contact accompanies interaction, and how close to one another do people stand and sit?

 2. Using your InfoTrac College Edition, read Simon Bullock's 2001 article "Polluting the Poor." According to Bullock, which ethnic groups in America are most frequently the victims of environmental injustice?

3. Make a survey of restaurants near campus. Describe the kinds of seats, lighting, music (if any), and distance between tables. Do you find any connections between nonverbal patterns and expensiveness of restaurants?

4. Describe the spatial arrangements in the home of your family of origin. Was there a room in which family members interacted a good deal? How was furniture arranged in that room? Who had separate space and personal chairs in your family? What do the nonverbal patterns reflect about your family's communication style?

 5. What ethical issues are entailed in interpreting others' nonverbal communication from our own perspectives?

Experiencing Communication in Our Lives

Questions for Analysis and Discussion

Review the video of the scenario entitled "Nonverbal Cues" that you watched when completing this chapter's case study (pages 169–170), or, if you haven't seen it yet, watch it for the first time. If you didn't previously finish the analysis questions included on the CD-ROM, do so now, and then respond to the following questions, which are also available on the book's website under "Activities for Chapter 6."

1. Identify nonverbal behaviors that regulate turn taking within the team.

2. Identify nonverbal behaviors that express relational-level meanings of communication. What aspects of team members' nonverbal communication express liking or disliking, responsiveness or lack of responsiveness, and power?

3. How do artifacts affect interaction between members of the team?

4. If you were the sixth member of this team, what kinds of communication might you enact to help relieve tension in the group?

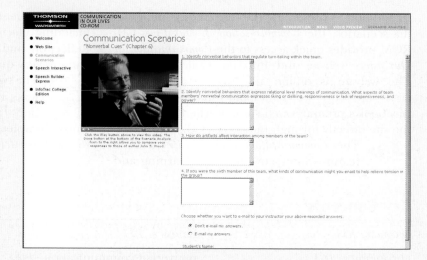

CHAPTER 7

Listening Effectively

Focus Questions

1. What's the difference between hearing and listening?

2. What are the most common obstacles to effective listening?

3. What specific skills enhance listening for information, listening critically, listening to support others, and listening for pleasure?

4. How can you improve your recall of messages?

© Jose Galvez/PhotoEdit

"D o you have a minute to talk?" Joanne asks her friend Elly as she enters her dorm room.

"Sure," Elly agrees without looking up from the e-mail she is writing to her mother. Lately her mother has been criticizing her for not studying enough, and Elly's trying to explain that college is more than academics.

"I'm worried about what's happening between Drew and me," Joanne begins. "He takes me for granted all the time. He never asks what I want to do or where I'd like to go. He just assumes I'll go along with whatever he wants."

"Yeah, I know that routine. Steve does it to me, too," Elly says with exasperation as she looks up from the computer. "Last weekend he insisted we go to this stupid war movie that I wouldn't have chosen to see in a million years. But what I wanted didn't make a lot of difference to him."

"That's exactly what I'm talking about," Joanne agrees. "I don't like it when Drew treats me that way, and I want to know how to get him to be more considerate."

"What I told Steve last weekend was that I'd had it, and from now on we decide together what we're doing, or we don't do it together," Elly says forcefully. "We've had this talk before, but this time I think I really got through to him that I was serious."

"So are you saying that's what I should do with Drew?"

"Sure. You have to stand up for your rights, or he'll walk all over you," Elly says while typing on the keyboard. "Take it from me, subtlety won't work. Remember last year when I was dating Larry? Well, he started this routine, and I tried to be subtle and hint that I'd like to be consulted about things. What I said to him went in one ear and out the other. If you're not firm, they'll run over you."

"But Drew's not like Larry or Steve. He's not trying to run over me. I think he just doesn't understand how I feel when he makes all the decisions," Joanne says.

"Well, I really don't think Steve's 'like that' either. He's just as good a guy as Drew," Elly snaps.

"That's not what I meant," Joanne says. "I just meant that I don't think I need to hit Drew over the head with a two-by-four."

"And I suppose you think Steve does need that?"

"I don't know. I'm just thinking that maybe our relationships are different," Joanne says.

How would you describe the communication between Elly and Joanne? Is Elly a good listener? Usually, when we think about communication, we focus on talking. Yet talking is not the only part—or even the greatest part—of communication. Effective communication also involves listening. As obvious as this is, few of us devote as much energy to listening as we do to talking.

Poor listening is evident in the conversation between Elly and Joanne. The first obstacle to effective listening is Elly's initial preoccupation with the e-mail she's writing to her mother. If she really wants to listen to Joanne, she should postpone the e-mail. A second problem is Elly's tendency to monopolize the conversation by focusing on her problems and her boyfriends instead of on Joanne's concerns about the relationship with Drew. Third, Elly listens defensively, taking offense when Joanne suggests that their rela-

Communication Highlight

tionships may differ. Like Elly, most of us often don't listen as well as we could. When we listen poorly, we are not communicating well.

Think about your normal day. You spend more time listening—or trying to—than talking. Studies of people from college students to professionals indicate that the average person spends 45% to 75% of waking time listening to others (Barker et al., 1981; Nichols, 1995; Steil, 1997). If we don't listen effectively, we're communicating poorly much of the time!

When people don't listen carefully on the job, they often miss important information that affects their work and their advancement (Deal & Kennedy, 1999; What Work Requires, 1991). In a recent survey of ideal qualities of effective managers, 1,000 human resource professionals ranked listening as number one (Windsor, Curtis, & Stephens, 1997). Workers who listen better (as measured by listening comprehension tests) hold higher-level positions and are promoted more frequently than workers who listen less well (Sypher, Bostrom, & Siebert, 1989). Effective listening is also important in resolving conflicts: People who grasp different viewpoints and the reasons behind them are likely to find constructive solutions to disputes (Van Styke, 1999).

Listening well is also critical to success in school and other learning environments. Effective listening in the classroom increases your learning as well as your performance on tests and other assignments. In personal relationships, good listening helps us minimize misunderstandings with people we care about and allows us to affirm them with our attention.

This chapter explores what listening is and how to listen effectively. First, we'll consider what's involved in listening, which is more than most of us realize. Next, we'll discuss obstacles to effective listening and how to minimize them. Third, we'll consider common forms of nonlistening. The fourth section of the chapter explains different types of listening and the skills needed for each. In our discussion, we'll identify principles for improving listening effectiveness.

The Listening Process

Although we often use the words *listening* and *hearing* as if they were synonyms, actually they're not. **Hearing** is a physiological activity that occurs when sound waves hit our eardrums. Hearing is passive; we don't have to invest any energy to hear. Listening, on the other hand, is an active process that requires energy (International Listening Association, 1995). Listening involves more than just hearing or receiving messages through sight, as when we notice nonverbal behaviors or when people with hearing impairments read lips or use American Sign Language (ASL).

Figure 7.1
The Chinese Character
for *Listening*

Eyes

Ears

Heart

Listening

Listening is an active, complex process that includes being mindful, physically receiving messages, selecting and organizing information, interpreting communication, responding, and remembering. The complexity of listening is represented in the Chinese character for listening, which includes symbols for eyes, ears, and heart (Figure 7.1). As the character suggests, to listen effectively, we use not only our ears, but also our eyes and hearts.

Being Mindful

The first step in listening is making a decision to be mindful. **Mindfulness** is being fully engaged in the moment. Your mind is focused on what is happening in the here and now. When you are mindful, you don't let your thoughts wander from what is happening in the present conversation. You don't think about what you did yesterday or about a letter you're writing to your mother, and you don't think about your own feelings and issues. Instead, when you listen mindfully, you tune in fully to another person and try to hear that person without imposing your own ideas, judgments, or feelings on him or her. You may later express your feelings and ideas, but when we listen mindfully, we attend to another fully. You demonstrate mindfulness by paying attention, indicating interest, and responding to what another expresses (Bolton, 1986; Deal & Kennedy, 1999).

Mindfulness enhances communication in two ways. First, attending mindfully to others increases our understanding of how they feel and think about what they are saying. In addition, mindfulness can enhance others' communication. When we really listen to others, they engage us more fully, elaborate their ideas, and express themselves in greater depth.

Being mindful is a choice we make. It is a personal commitment to attend fully and without diversion to another person. No amount of skill will make you a good listener if you do not choose to attend mindfully to others. Thus, your own choice to be mindful or not is the foundation of how well you listen—or fail to.

Being Mindful

Mindfulness is a skill that develops with commitment and practice. Follow these guidelines to develop skill in mindful listening:

1. Empty your mind of thoughts, ideas, and plans so that you are open to listening to another.

2. Concentrate on the person with whom you are communicating. Say to yourself, "I want to focus on this person and what she or he is saying and feeling."

3. Don't be surprised if distracting thoughts come up or you find yourself thinking about your responses instead of what the other person is saying. This is natural. Just push away diversionary thoughts and refocus on the person with whom you are talking.

4. Evaluate how well you listened when you were focusing on being mindful. If you aren't as fully engaged as you want to be, remind yourself that mindfulness is a habit of mind and a way of living. Developing it takes practice.

Physically Receiving Messages

In addition to being mindful, listening involves physically receiving oral messages. For many people, this happens through hearing. People who are deaf, however, receive messages by reading lips or by reading sign language (Carl, 1998). As we noted earlier, hearing is a physiological process in which sound waves hit our eardrums so that we become aware of noises, such as music or human voices. Similarly, we read lips and see ASL when our eyes register light waves and images.

Our ability to receive messages may decline when we are fatigued or when we have to be attentive for extended times without breaks. You may have noticed that it's harder to sustain attention in long classes than in shorter ones. Physical reception of messages may also be impeded by background noises, such as a blaring television or others talking nearby, or by competing visual cues. Thus, it's a good idea to control distractions that hinder listening.

—Jimmy—

It's impossible to listen well in my apartment. Four of us live there, and at least two different stereos are on all the time. Also, a TV is usually on, and there may be conversations or phone calls, too. It's crazy when we try to talk to each other in the middle of all the racket. We're always asking each other to repeat something or skipping over whatever we don't hear. If we go out to a bar or something, the noise there is just as bad. Sometimes I think we don't really want to talk with each other and all the distractions protect us from having to.

Other physiological factors influence how and how well we listen. For instance, our sex seems to affect how we listen. As a rule, women are more receptive than men to what is happening around them, including surrounding noises and activities. As a rule, men tend to focus, shape, and direct

Communication Highlight

Selective listening starts early in life. Babies are born with the ability to hear all the sounds in the full range of languages, but by age 1—if not sooner—they can hear and distinguish only among the sounds of the language or languages spoken around them (Monastersky, 2001). For instance, native English speakers have difficulty distinguishing between two sounds in Mandarin Chinese: *qi*, which is approximately like the *ch* sound; and *xi*, which is approximately like the *sh* sound. Native Japanese speakers have a hard time distinguishing between two English sounds: *ra* and *la*. In learning a language, we learn its distinctive sounds and rhythms. Simultaneously, it seems, we also learn not to hear sounds and rhythms that aren't part of our language.

their hearing in instrumental ways, whereas women are more likely to attend to the whole of communication, noticing details and tangents as well as major themes ("Men Use," 2000). Judy Pearson (1985), a communication researcher, suggests that this could result from different hemispheric specialization of the brain. Women usually have better-developed right lobes, which govern creative and holistic thinking, whereas men typically have better-developed left lobes, which control analytic and linear processing of information. Women also have better-developed corpus callosa, the bundles of nerves that connect the two hemispheres of the brain. The difference in listening styles can complicate interaction between women and men. Sometimes men think women's communication is unfocused and burdened with irrelevant details, but to many women, the details and sideline topics are part of the overall interaction (Johnson, 2000). Women, on the other hand, sometimes think the linear, undetailed communication that is more typical of men is too abbreviated to foster maximum understanding.

Selecting and Organizing Material

The third part of listening is selecting and organizing material. As we noted in Chapter 2, we don't perceive everything around us. Instead, we selectively attend to some messages and elements of our environments and disregard others. What we select to attend to depends on many factors, including our interests, cognitive structures, and expectations. If we realize that our own preoccupations can hamper listening, we can curb interferences.

We can monitor our tendencies to attend selectively by remembering that we are more likely to notice stimuli that are intense, loud, or unusual. Thus, we may overlook communicators who don't call attention to themselves with strong volume and bold gestures. If we're aware of this tendency, we can guard against it so that we don't miss out on people and messages that may be important. Once again, mindfulness comes into play. Choosing to be mindful doesn't necessarily mean that our minds won't stray when we try to listen, but it does mean that we will return to a focus on what the other is saying.

Once we've selected what to notice, we organize what we've received. As you'll recall from Chapter 2, we use cognitive schemata to organize our perceptions. As you listen to others, you decide how to categorize them by asking which of your prototypes they most closely resemble (friend, supervisor, teacher, and so forth). You then apply personal constructs to define others and their messages more fully. You evaluate whether they are smart or not smart, reasonable or not reasonable, honest or not honest, and so on. Based on how you construct others, you apply stereotypes to predict what they will do. Finally, based on the meanings you have constructed, you choose which script to follow in interaction.

When a friend is upset, you can reasonably predict that he may not want advice until he has first had a chance to express his feelings. On the other hand, when a co-worker comes to you with a problem that must be solved quickly, you assume she might welcome concrete advice or collaboration. Your script for responding to the distraught friend might be to say, "Tell me more about what you're feeling" or "You sound really upset—let's talk." With a work team that is facing a deadline, you might adopt a more directive script and say, "Here's what we need to do" or "Maybe we can work together and get it all done." In a public speaking situation, you might follow a script that specifies that you should compliment listeners and engage their interest before you move into the substance of your speech.

—Elliot—

I never realized how much I affect communication by listening—or sometimes by not listening. Like when I'm in a class, I used to think it was the teacher's job to communicate effectively. Now I see that if I want to learn it's my job to actively work to take in what the teacher says. I still think teachers should try to make material interesting, but I also think I need to put in some effort.

Elliott has realized that listeners play active roles in constructing the meaning of interaction. The schemata we use to create meaning help us figure out how to respond to others. In other words, the meaning we attribute to communication depends on how we select and organize what others say and do. This reminds us to keep our perceptions tentative. In the course of interaction, we may revise our initial perceptions.

Interpreting Communication

The fourth part of listening is interpreting others' communication. When we interpret, we put together all that we have selected and organized to make sense of the overall situation. The most important principle in this process is to interpret others on their own terms. Certainly, you won't always agree with other people and how they see themselves, others, issues, and situations. However, if you want to listen well, you have an ethical responsibility to make an earnest effort to understand others' perspectives.

To interpret someone with respect for their perspective is one of the greatest gifts we can give. Too often, we impose our meanings on others, we try to correct them or argue with them about what they feel, or we crowd out their words with our own (Bolton, 1986).

—Maggie—

Don and I didn't understand each other's perspective, and we didn't even understand that we didn't understand. Once I told him I was really upset about a friend of mine who needed money for an emergency. Don told me she had no right to expect me to bail her out, but that had nothing to do with what I was feeling. He saw the situation in terms of what rights my friend had, but to me it was about feeling concerned for someone I like. Only after we got counseling did we learn to really listen to each other instead of listening through ourselves.

10-24

©2003 Bil Keane, Inc.
Dist. by King Features Synd.
www.familycircus.com

"Sam's my best friend. He never talks
about himself, and he listens while
I talk about me."

Responding

Effective listening includes responding, which is communicating attention and interest as well as voicing our own views (Purdy, 1997). Skillful listeners give outward signs that they are interested and involved. We don't respond only when others finish speaking, but throughout interaction. This is what makes listening such an active process. The only way others know we are listening is through our feedback. Indicators of engagement include attentive posture, head nods, eye contact, and vocal responses such as "um hmm," "okay," and "go on." When we respond with interest, we communicate that we care about the other person and what she or he says.

Remembering

The final part of effective listening is remembering, or retaining what you have heard. According to communication professors Ron Adler and Neil Towne (1993), we remember less than half of a message immediately after we hear it. As time goes by, retention decreases further; we recall only about 35% of most messages 8 hours after we hear them. Because we forget about two thirds of what we hear, it's important to make sure we hang onto the most important third. Effective listeners let go of many details in order to retain basic ideas and general impressions (Cooper, Seibold, & Suchner, 1997; Fisher, 1987). Later in this chapter, we'll discuss strategies for retaining material in communication.

Obstacles to Effective Listening

There are two broad types of obstacles to good listening: those external to us and those inside of us.

External Obstacles

 There are many hindrances to effective listening in communication situations. Although we can't always control external obstacles, knowing what situational factors hinder listening can help us guard against them or compensate for the interference they create.

Message Overload   The sheer amount of communication in our lives makes it impossible to listen fully to all of it. As communication technologies have grown, so has the amount of information we are expected to process. When we're not talking face-to-face with someone, we're likely to be on a phone or participating in a videoconference. We simply aren't able to listen mindfully all of the time. Instead, we have to screen the talk around us, much as we screen calls on our answering machines, to decide when to listen carefully.

Communication Highlight

Information Overload Can Be Toxic

There's a good reason why our time has been dubbed "the information age": We are inundated with information. *Newsweek* reporter Jennifer Tanaka (1997) writes that a single weekday edition of a national newspaper today supplies more information than the average person of the seventeenth-century would have encountered in an entire lifetime.

And it's likely to get worse, not better, because technologies are speeding up the flow of information. You've probably experienced e-mail overload, which is a growing problem for many companies (Hymowitz, 2000; Imperato, 1999; Salopek, 1999). In *Data Smog*, author David Shenk (1997) asserts that many people are feeling overwhelmed by the information they receive and are expected to process. Faxes, e-mail, cell phone calls, pages, and so on—it's nonstop. According to Shenk, this creates a toxic environment of continuous overstimulation that can cause stress. Accustomed to overstimulation, more and more people are finding it difficult or impossible to unwind, even on weekends and vacations.

Message overload often occurs in academic settings, in which readings and class discussions are packed with detailed information. If you're taking four or five classes, you confront mountains of information. Message overload may also occur when communication takes place simultaneously in two channels. For instance, you might suffer information overload if a speaker presents information verbally while also showing a graph with complex statistical data. It's difficult to know whether to focus your listening energy on the visual message or the verbal one.

Message Complexity   Listening is also impeded by the difficulty of some messages. The more detailed and complicated ideas are, the harder it is to follow and retain them. Many jobs today are highly specialized; hence much on-the-job communication is very complex and increasingly rapid (Cooper, 1997; Hacker, Goss, & Townley, 1998). It's tempting to tune out people who use technical vocabularies, focus on specifics, and use complex sentences. When we have to listen to messages that are dense with information, taking notes can improve retention.

 To increase your awareness of how complex messages can be distorted in the process of listening, complete Activity 7.1, "Rumor Clinic," in your *Student Companion* or online under "Activities for Chapter 7" at the *Communication in Our Lives* website.

Environmental Distractions   Effective listening is also impeded by distractions in the environment. Sounds around us can divert our attention or make it difficult to hear clearly. Perhaps you've been part of a crowd at a rally or a game. If so, you probably had to shout to the person next to you just to be heard. Although most sounds aren't as overwhelming as the roar of crowds, there is always some noise in communication situations. It might be music or television in the background, side

Environmental distractions interfere with effective listening.

© David Young Wolff/PhotoEdit, Inc.

conversations in a class, or muffled traffic sounds from outside. Increasingly, the rings of cell phones and pagers intrude on face-to-face communication.

Good listeners try to reduce environmental distractions. It's considerate to turn off a television or turn down music if someone wants to talk with you. In the example that opened this chapter, Elly should have put aside the e-mail she was writing to listen mindfully to Joanne. Similarly, when meeting with others it's advisable to defer private comments until after the meeting so they don't interfere with listening. Professionals hold incoming phone calls when they want to give undivided attention to a client or business associate. It's also appropriate to suggest moving away from a noisy area to talk. Even if we can't always eliminate distractions, we can usually reduce them or change our location to one more conducive to good communication.

Internal Obstacles

In addition to external interferences, listening may be hindered by four psychological obstacles.

Preoccupation   A common obstacle to listening is preoccupation. When we are absorbed in our own thoughts and concerns, we can't focus on what someone else is saying. Perhaps you've attended a class right before taking a test in another class and later realized you got almost nothing out of the first class. That's because you were preoccupied with the upcoming test. If you are preoccupied with a report you need to prepare, you may not listen effectively to what a colleague says. If your cell phone or pager rings or vibrates, your mind is diverted from listening to others. When we are preoccupied with something other than what another person is saying, we aren't listening mindfully.

> ## –Auturro–
>
> *Last week I got a letter from my family in which my mother said the monsoons had hurt their crops and so they would not make much money at the market. I was very worried because my family does not have savings—we live year to year, crop to crop. After a couple of days, I realized that I did not know what had happened in any of my classes. I read my notebooks and I had good notes, but I didn't remember ever hearing the lectures in class.*

Prejudgments   Another obstacle to effective listening is prejudgment of others or ideas. Anna Deavere Smith, who teaches listening to students in law and medical school, says that to listen, "I empty out myself. While I'm listening, my own judgments and prejudices certainly come up. But I know I won't get anything unless I get those things out of the way" (Arenson, 2002, p. 25).

Sometimes we decide in advance that others have nothing to offer us, so we tune them out. If a co-worker's ideas have not impressed you in the past, you might assume he or she will contribute nothing of value to a present conversation. The risk is that you might miss a good idea simply because you prejudged the other person. It's also important to keep an open mind when listening to speeches that present ideas about which you already have opinions. You might miss important information and perspectives if you don't suspend prejudgments about the topic.

Another kind of prejudgment occurs when we impose our preconceptions of a message on the person who is communicating. When this happens, we assume we know what another feels, thinks, and is going to say, and we then assimilate her or his message into our preconceptions. This can lead us to misunderstand what the person means because we haven't really listened on her or his own terms.

−Keith−

My parents need a course in listening! They are so quick to tell me what I think and feel, or should think and feel, that they never hear what I do feel or think. Last year I approached them with the idea of taking a year off from school. Before I could even explain why I wanted to do this, Dad was all over me about being responsible and getting ahead in a career. Mom jumped on me about looking for an easy out and not having the gumption to stick with my studies. The whole point was that I wanted to work as an intern to get some hands-on experience in media production, which is my major. It had nothing to do with wanting an easy out or not trying to get ahead, but they couldn't even hear me through their own ideas about what I felt.

Prejudgments disconfirm others by forcing their words into our own preconceived mind-set. This devalues others and their messages. When we impose our prejudgments on others' words, at the relational level of meaning we express a disregard for them and what they say. It may also deprive us of information, which can be costly in the workplace.

Lack of Effort It takes a lot of effort to listen well, and sometimes we aren't willing to invest it. It's hard work to be mindful—to focus closely on what others are saying, try to grasp their meanings, ask questions, and give responses so they know we are interested and involved. In addition to these activities, we have to control distractions inside ourselves, monitor external noise, and perhaps fight fatigue or hunger (Isaacs, 1999).

Because active listening takes so much effort, we're not always able or willing to do it well. Sometimes we make a decision not to listen fully, perhaps because the person or topic isn't important to us. There are also times when we really want to listen but have trouble marshaling the necessary energy. If you can't summon the effort to listen well, you might suggest postponing interaction until a time when you will be able to invest effort in listening. If you explain to the other that you want to defer communication because you really are interested and want to be able to listen well, she or he is likely to appreciate your honesty and commitment to listening.

Not Accommodating Diverse Listening Styles A final internal obstacle to effective listening is not respecting and adjusting to different listening styles that reflect diverse communities and cultures. The more we understand about different people's rules for listening, the more effectively we can signal our attention in ways they appreciate. For example, in the United States, it is considered polite to make frequent but not continuous eye contact in conversation. Yet in some cultures, continuous eye contact is normative, and in others almost any eye contact is considered intrusive and inappropriate.

Different cultures have different norms for listening. These Nepalese villagers have been socialized to be quiet and attentive when another person is talking.

© Julia T. Wood

Even within the United States, there are differences in listening rules based on membership in racial, gender, and other social communities. Some African Americans engage in a more participative listening style than is typical of European Americans. Blacks who grew up attending traditional Black churches may have learned to call out responses to a speaker as a way of showing their interest. A speaker who doesn't understand that this is a compliment in some African American communities is likely to misinterpret responses as interruptions (Houston & Wood, 1996). In general, men provide fewer verbal and nonverbal clues that they are interested in what another person is saying. They may also respond primarily to the content level of meaning and tune in less to the relationship level of meaning. If you understand these general differences, you can adapt your listening style to particular people with whom you communicate. In addition, understanding diverse listening styles will improve your accuracy in interpreting what others mean by the ways they listen and signal interest.

–Lavonda–

My boyfriend is the worst listener ever. Whenever I try to tell him about some problem I have, he becomes Mr. Answer Man. He tells me what to do or how to handle a situation. That doesn't do anything to help me with my feelings or even to let me know he hears what I'm feeling.

We have seen that there are many obstacles to effective listening. Ones inherent in messages and situations include message overload, message complexity, and environmental distractions. In addition, there are four potential interferences inside us: preoccupation, prejudgment, lack of effort, and failure to recognize and adapt to diverse expectations of listening.

© 1995 United Feature Syndicate, Inc.

Forms of Nonlistening

Now that we've discussed obstacles to effective listening, let's consider some forms of nonlistening. As you read about these six types of nonlistening, they may seem familiar because you and others probably engage in them at times.

Pseudolistening

Pseudolistening is pretending to listen. When we pseudolisten, we appear to be attentive, but really our minds are elsewhere. Sometimes we pseudolisten because we don't want to hurt a friend who is sharing experiences, even though we are not really interested. We also pseudolisten when communication bores us but we have to appear interested. Superficial talk in social situations and boring lectures are two communication situations in which we may consciously choose to pseudolisten so that we seem polite even though we really aren't involved. On the job, we often have to appear interested in what others say because of their positions.

Monopolizing

Monopolizing is hogging the stage by continually focusing communication on ourselves instead of on the person talking. Two tactics are typical of monopolizing. One is conversational rerouting, in which a person shifts the topic of talk to himself or herself. For example, if Ellen tells her friend Marla that she's having trouble with her roommate, Marla could respond empathically by showing interest in Ellen's problem and feelings. Instead, however, Marla might reroute the conversation by saying, "I know what you

Communication Highlight

Listen Up, Doctors!

Have you ever felt that your doctor wasn't listening to you? If so, you're not alone. Communication researcher Michael Nyquist (1992) studied interactions between doctors and patients. He found that after patients had spoken for an average of only 18 seconds, doctors interrupted and took charge of the conversation. The doctors assumed they understood the medical problem and so they didn't encourage patients to give relevant background on life circumstances and symptoms that could affect diagnosis and treatment. According to consultant Sheila Bentley, doctors need to be taught how to listen (Crossen, 1997). The workshops she presents to doctors focus on effective listening because she thinks that not listening well is the most common and most expensive mistake doctors make.

mean. My roommate is a real jerk." Then Marla would go off on an extended description of her own roommate problems. Rerouting takes the conversation away from the person who is talking.

Another monopolizing tactic is diversionary interrupting, which is interrupting in ways that disrupt the person speaking. Often interrupting occurs in combination with rerouting, so that a person interrupts and then directs the conversation to a new topic. In other cases, monopolizers fire questions that express doubt about what a speaker says ("What makes you think that?" "How can you be sure?" "Did anyone else see what you did?") or prematurely offer advice to show how much they know ("What you should do is . . . ," "You really blew that," "What I would have done is . . ."). Both rerouting and diversionary interrupting are techniques to monopolize a conversation. They are the antithesis of good listening.

It's important to realize that not all interruptions are monopolizing tactics. We also interrupt to show interest, voice support, and ask for elaboration. Interrupting for these reasons affirms the person who is speaking and keeps the focus on her or him. Some research indicates that women are more likely than men to use interruptions to show interest and support (Anderson & Leaper, 1998; James & Clark, 1993). Although it has been claimed that men use interruptions to assert themselves and gain control of conversations, existing research doesn't provide a clear picture of men's reasons for interrupting (Aires, 1996; Goldsmith & Fulfs, 1999).

Selective Listening

Selective listening is focusing on only particular parts of messages. We listen selectively when we screen out parts of a message that make us uncomfortable, don't interest us, or conflict with our views. We also listen selectively when we isolate for attention the parts of communication that especially interest us or with which we agree.

One form of selective listening is focusing only on aspects of communication that interest us or correspond with our values. If you are worried about a storm, you will listen attentively to weather reports while screening out news and commercials. Students often become highly attentive when teachers say, "This is important for the test." We also listen selectively when we tune in only to topics that interest us and tune out the rest of what others say. For example, we might give only half an ear to a friend until the friend mentions spring break, and then we tune in fully. In the workplace, we may become more attentive when communication addresses topics such as raises, layoffs, and other matters that may affect us directly.

Selective listening also occurs when we reject communication that bores us or makes us uncomfortable. For instance, we may not listen when others criticize us, because we don't like what they say. We all have subjects that bore or bother us, and we may be tempted to avoid listening to communication about them. You can resist this temptation by being mindful and monitoring your tendencies to tune out messages you find boring or uncomfortable.

Sharpen Your Skill

Anticipating Selective Listening in Public Speaking

Effective public speakers know that selective listening can undermine their impact. They anticipate parts of a speech in which listeners may screen out information that they disagree with or that makes them uncomfortable. They take steps to keep listeners attentive and focused. Think about how you could use the following techniques of discouraging selective listening to keep your listeners from selectively screening out parts of your message.

Highlighting: "This next point is very important."

Forewarning: "I know you may find this argument difficult to accept, but please hear me through before you dismiss it."

Showing empathy: "I know some of this information can be boring, but please stick with me so you don't miss something that will matter to you."

Repetition: "Let me restate this idea, because I want you to remember it."

Defensive Listening

Defensive listening involves perceiving personal attacks, criticisms, or hostile undertones in communication when no offense is intended. When we listen defensively, we read unkind motives into whatever others say. Some people are generally defensive, expecting insults and criticism from all quarters (a global, stable attribution). They hear threats and negative judgments in almost anything said to them. Thus, an innocent remark such as, "Have you finished your report yet?" may be perceived as suspicion that you aren't doing your work.

Ambushing

Ambushing is listening carefully for the purpose of attacking. Unlike the other kinds of nonlistening we've discussed, ambushing involves very careful listening, but it isn't motivated by interest in another. Instead, ambushers listen intently to gather ammunition, which they then use to attack a speaker. Political candidates routinely do this. Each person listens carefully to the other for the sole purpose of later undercutting the opponent. Ambushing may be common in organizations that have a competitive culture in which employees feel they must outdo one another. There is no openness, no effort to understand the other's meaning, no interest in recognizing value in what another says, and no interest in genuine dialogue.

—Eric—

One of the brothers at my house is a real ambusher. He's a pre-law major, and he loves to debate and win arguments. No matter what somebody talks about, this guy just listens long enough to mount a counterattack. He doesn't care about understanding others, just about beating them. I've quit talking when he's around.

Literal Listening

The final form of nonlistening is **literal listening,** which is listening to only the content level of meaning and ignoring the relationship level of meaning. All communication includes both content, or literal, meaning and relational meaning that pertains to the power, responsiveness, and liking between people. When we listen literally, we attend only to the content meaning and overlook what's being communicated about the other person or our relationship with that person. When we listen only literally, we are insensitive to others' feelings and to our connections with them.

Nonlistening, as we have seen, comes in many forms, including pseudo-listening, ambushing speakers, monopolizing the stage, responding defensively, attending selectively, and listening literally. Being aware of forms of nonlistening enables you to exercise control over how you listen and thus how fully and mindfully you participate in communication with others.

  To increase your ability to recognize forms of nonlistening, complete Activity 7.2, "Noticing Forms of Ineffective Listening," in your *Student Companion* or online under "Activities for Chapter 7" at the *Communication in Our Lives* website.

Adapting Listening to Communication Goals

Effective listening is tailored to specific purposes. Informational listening, critical listening, and relational listening entail different listening styles and behaviors. We'll discuss the specific attitudes and skills that support each type of listening.

Informational and Critical Listening

Much of the time, we listen to gain and evaluate information. We listen for information in classes, at political debates, in professional meetings, when important news stories are reported, and when we need guidance on everything from medical treatment to directions to a new place. In all of these cases, the primary purpose of **informational listening** is to gain and understand information.

Closely related to informational listening is **critical listening,** in which we listen to form opinions, make judgments, or evaluate people and ideas. Critical listening goes beyond gaining information; it requires us to analyze and evaluate information and the people who express it. We decide whether a speaker is credible and ethical by judging the thoroughness of a presentation, the accuracy of quotes and statistics, and the carefulness of reasoning. In Chapter 14, we discuss ways to evaluate evidence in depth. Both informational and critical listening require us to be mindful and to organize and retain information.

Be Mindful Our discussion of obstacles to listening suggests some important clues to listening critically to information. First, it's important to decide to be mindful, choosing to attend carefully even if material is complex and difficult. Don't let your mind wander when information gets complicated or confusing. Avoid going off on tangents; instead, stay focused on gaining as much information as you can. Later, you may want to ask questions if material wasn't clear even though you listened mindfully.

Control Obstacles You can also minimize distractions in communication situations. You might shut a window to block out traffic noises or adjust a thermostat so that the room temperature is

A park ranger is communicating important information about safety. Visitors who listen well will gain the knowledge they need to enjoy a mishap-free visit to the park.

© James D. Wilson/Woodfin Camp & Associates

comfortable. In addition, you should minimize psychological distractions by emptying your mind of preoccupations and prejudgments that can interfere with effective listening.

Ask Questions   It is also important to pose questions to speakers. Asking speakers to clarify or elaborate on their messages allows you to understand information you didn't grasp at first and enhances insight into content that you did comprehend. Questions are also compliments to speakers because they indicate that you are interested and want to know more.

When listening critically, it's appropriate to ask probing questions of speakers: "What is the source of your statistics on the rate of unemployment?" "What is the date of the statistics you cited?" "Have you met with any policy-makers who hold a point of view contrary to yours? What is their response to your proposals?" "I noticed that all of the sources you quoted were fiscal conservatives. Does this mean that your conclusions are biased?" It's especially important and appropriate for non-native speakers to ask questions if they don't understand language (Lee, 1994, 2000). The English language is ambiguous, and it contains many colloquial phrases and slang expressions. People whose native language is not English may not understand idioms such as "in a heartbeat" (fast), "not on your life" (very unlikely), or "hang a right" (turn right). Sensitive communicators explain any idioms they use if non-native speakers are present. If speakers don't offer explanations, listeners should request them.

Use Aids to Recall   To understand and remember important information, we can apply the principles of perception we discussed in Chapter 2. For instance, we learned that we tend to notice and recall stimuli that are repeated. To use this principle in everyday communication, repeat important ideas to yourself immediately after hearing them. This moves the ideas from short-term to long-term memory (Estes, 1989). Repetition can save you the embarrassment of having to ask people you just met to repeat their names.

Another way to increase retention is to use mnemonic (pronounced "nemonic," rhymes with *demonic*) devices, which are memory aids that create patterns for what you've heard. You probably already do this in studying. For instance, you could create the mnemonic MPSIRR, which is made up of the first letter of one word for each of the six parts of listening (Mindfulness,

Communication Highlight

Between a Rock and a Hard Spot

Most of us have had the experience of being frustrated by a speaker who used highly specialized language that we couldn't understand. That experience is very common for people in the United States for whom English is a second language.

Colloquial English words and phrases often are difficult or impossible for non-native speakers to understand. According to communication scholar Wen-Shu Lee (1994, 2000), phrases that often defy understanding for non-native speakers include "miss the boat" (Where is the boat? I don't see a boat.), "kick the bucket" (Who's kicking what bucket?), "chew the fat" (Why would you want to chew fat?), "between a rock and a hard place" (Why is someone in such a position?), and "hit the road" (Why would anybody hit a road?).

When native English speakers communicate with people for whom English is a second language, they should be cautious about using colloquial phrases and slang.

 To learn more about English slang and people for whom English is a second language, go to http://www.eslcafe.com/slang/slang.cgi.

Physically receiving, Selecting and organizing, Interpreting, Responding, Remembering). You can also invent mnemonics to help you recall personal information in communication. For example, KIM is a mnemonic to remember that Kim from Iowa is going into Medicine.

Organize Information Another technique to increase retention is to organize information. For example, suppose a friend tells you he is confused about long-range goals, doesn't know what he can do with a math major, wants to locate in the Midwest, wonders whether graduate school is necessary, likes small towns, needs some internships to try out different options, and wants a family eventually. You could regroup this stream of concerns into two categories: academic information (careers for math majors, graduate school, internship opportunities) and lifestyle preferences (Midwest, small town, family). Remembering those two categories allows you to retain the essence of your friend's concerns, even if you forget many of the specifics.

Sharpen Your Skill

Improving Recall

Apply the principles we've discussed to enhance memory.

1. The next time you meet someone, repeat his or her name to yourself three times after you are introduced. Do you remember the name?

2. After your next class, take 15 minutes to review your notes in a quiet place. Read them aloud so that you hear as well as see the main ideas. Does this increase your retention of material?

3. Invent mnemonics to create patterns that help you remember basic information in a message.

4. Organize ideas into categories. To remember the main ideas of this chapter, you might use major subheadings to form categories: listening process, obstacles to listening, and listening goals. The mnemonic LOG (Listening, Obstacles, Goals) could help you remember those topics.

Relational Listening

Listening for information focuses on the content level of meaning in communication. Yet in some listening situations we're as concerned or even more concerned with the relational level of meaning. We engage in **relational listening** when we listen to a friend's worries, let a romantic partner tell us about problems, counsel a co-worker, or talk with a parent about health concerns. Whenever supporting a person and maintaining a relationship are important, we should use skills that advance relational listening.

Be Mindful The first requirement for effective relational listening is to be mindful. You'll recall that this was also the first step in informational and critical listening. When we're interested in relational meanings, however, a different kind of mindfulness is needed. Instead of focusing our minds on information, we need to concentrate on understanding feelings that may not be communicated explicitly. Thus, mindful relational listening calls on us to pay attention to what lies "between the words," the subtle clues to feelings and perceptions. As listening scholar Gerald Egan (1973, p. 228) notes, "Total listening is more than attending to another person's words. It is also listening to the meanings that are buried in the words and between the words and in the silences in communication."

Suspend Judgment   When listening to provide support, it's important to avoid highly judgmental responses. Although Western culture emphasizes evaluation, often we really don't need to judge others or what they feel, think, and do. Judgments add our evaluations to the others' experiences. When we do this, we move away from them and their feelings. To curb evaluative tendencies, ask whether you really need to pass judgment in the present moment.

Only if someone asks for our judgment should we offer it when we are listening to support. Even if our opinion is sought, we should express it in a way that doesn't devalue others. Sometimes people excuse strongly judgmental comments by saying, "You asked me to be honest" or "I mean this as constructive criticism." Too often, however, the judgments are not constructive and are harsher than candor requires. Good relational listening includes responses that support others.

—José—

My best friend makes it so easy for me to tell whatever is on my mind. She never puts me down or makes me feel stupid or weird. Sometimes I ask her what she thinks, and she has this way of telling me without making me feel wrong if I think differently. What it boils down to is respect. She respects me and herself, so she doesn't have to prove anything by acting better than me.

Understand the Other's Perspective   One of the most important principles for effective relational listening is to grasp the other person's perspective. We can't respond sensitively to others until we understand their perspective and meanings. This means we have to step outside of our own point of view, at least long enough to understand how another person sees things.

Paraphrasing is a method of clarifying another's meaning or needs by reflecting our interpretations of his or her communication back to him or her. For example, a friend might confide, "I'm really scared my kid brother is messing around with drugs." We could paraphrase this way: "It sounds as if you think your brother may be experimenting with drugs." This paraphrase allows us to clarify whether the friend has any evidence of the brother's drug involvement. The response might be, "No, I don't have any real reason to suspect him, but I just worry because drugs are so pervasive in high schools now." This tells us that the friend's worries are more the issue than any evidence that her brother is experimenting with drugs.

Paraphrasing can help us figure out what others feel. If someone screams, "I can't believe he did that to me!" it's not clear whether he is angry, hurt, or upset. We could find out what he's feeling by saying, "You seem really angry." If anger is the emotion, the speaker could agree; if not, he could clarify what he is feeling. Paraphrasing also allows us to check whether we understand another person's meaning: "Let me see if I followed you. What you're saying is . . .".

Practicing Paraphrasing

Developing skill in paraphrasing others' messages is important in effective communication. Practice your paraphrasing skill by creating paraphrases of the following comments:

1. "I don't know how they expect me to get my work done, when they don't give me the information I need and there's no training on how to use this new software program."

2. "I've got three midterms and a paper due next week, and I'm behind in my reading."

3. "Can you believe it? This is the fifth rejection letter I've received. I thought all the time I spent interviewing would produce better results."

4. "My parents don't understand why I need to go to summer school, and they won't help with the expenses."

5. "My son wants to go to summer school and expects us to come up with the money. Doesn't he understand what we're already paying for the regular school year?"

For further practice in paraphrasing, complete Activity 7.3, "Learning to Paraphrase," in your *Student Companion* or online under "Activities for Chapter 7" at the *Communication in Our Lives* website.

Another skill to help you understand others is the use of **minimal encouragers.** These are responses that express interest in hearing more and thus gently invite another person to elaborate. Examples of minimal encouragers are "Tell me more," "Really?" "Go on," "I'm with you," "Then what happened?" "Yeah?" and "I see." We can also use nonverbal minimal encouragers, such as a raised eyebrow to show we're involved, a nod to indicate we understand, or widened eyes to indicate we're fascinated.

Minimal encouragers indicate that we are listening, following, and interested. They encourage others to keep talking so that we can more fully understand what they mean. Keep in mind that these are *minimal* encouragers. They shouldn't interrupt or take the focus away from another. Effective minimal encouragers are very brief interjections that prompt, but do not interfere with, the flow of another's talk.

A third way to enhance understanding of what another feels or needs is to ask questions. For instance, we might ask, "How do you feel about that?" "What do you plan to do?" or "How are you working this through?" Another reason we ask questions is to find out what a person wants from us. Sometimes it isn't clear whether someone wants advice, a shoulder to cry on, or a safe place to vent feelings. If we can't figure out what's wanted, it's appropriate to ask, "Are you looking for advice or a sounding board?" "Do you want to talk about how to handle the situation, or do you just want to air the issues?" Asking directly signals that we really want to help and allows others to tell us how we can best do that.

Express Support Once you have understood another's meanings and perspective, then relational listening should focus on communicating support. This doesn't necessarily require us to agree with another's perspective or ideas. What it does call on us to do is to communicate support for the person. To illustrate how we can support a person even if we don't agree with her or his position, consider the following exchange between a son and his father.

SON: Dad, I'm changing my major from business to drama.

FATHER: Oh.

SON: Yeah, I've wanted to do it for some time, but I kept holding back because acting isn't as safe as accounting.

FATHER: That's certainly true.

SON: Yeah, but I've decided to do it anyway. I'd like to know what you think about the idea.

FATHER: It worries me. Starving actors are a dime a dozen. It just won't provide you with any economic future or security.

SON: I understand acting isn't as secure as business, but it's what I really want to do.

FATHER: Tell me what you feel about acting—why it matters so much to you.

SON: It's the most creative, totally fulfilling thing I do. I've tried to get interested in business, but I just don't love that like I do acting. I feel like I have to give this a try, or I'll always wonder if I could have made it. If I don't get somewhere in 5 or 6 years, I'll rethink my career options.

FATHER: Couldn't you finish your business degree and get a job and act on the side?

SON: No. I've got to give acting a full shot—give it everything I have, to see if I can make it.

FATHER: Well, I still have reservations, but I guess I can understand having to try something that matters this much to you. I'm just concerned that you'll lose years of your life to something that doesn't work out.

SON: Well, I'm kinda concerned about that too, but I'm more worried about wasting years of my life in a career that doesn't turn me on than about trying to make a go of the one that does.

FATHER: That makes sense. I wouldn't make the choice you're making, but I respect your decision and your guts for taking a big gamble.

This dialogue illustrates several principles of effective relational listening. First, notice that the father's first two comments are minimal encouragers that invite his son to elaborate thoughts and feelings. The father also encourages his son to explain how he feels. Later, the father suggests a compromise solution, but his son rejects that, and the father respects the son's position. Importantly, the father makes his own position clear, but he separates his personal stance from his respect for his son's right to make his own choices. Sometimes it's difficult to listen openly and nonjudgmentally, particularly if we don't agree with the person speaking, as in the example. However, if your goal is to support another person, then sensitive, responsive involvement without evaluation is key to effective listening.

Sharpen Your Skill

Relational Listening

Practice your skills in relational listening. The next time a friend talks to you, focus mindfully on him or her. While listening, suspend judgment at least long enough to understand your friend's perspective on his or her terms (not your own). While your friend talks, signal interest by keeping eye contact, nodding your head, paraphrasing, and offering minimal responses. Express support by acknowledging, confirming, and—if you honestly can—endorsing what your friend says. How does your friend react? How is her or his communication affected by your responsiveness?

Repeat this exercise in a team situation. When other members of the team speak, express your interest and attention through nonverbal communication that signals involvement. Offer responses that show you acknowledge and confirm team members and that you are attending to what they say. How do various members of the group respond?

  You can extend this exercise by completing Activity 7.5, "Identifying Effective Behaviors for Relational Listening," and Activity 7.4, "Listening to Support Others," in your *Student Companion* or online under "Activities for Chapter 7" at the *Communication in Our Lives* website.

Listening to discriminate is vital when doctors communicate with patients.

Other Purposes of Listening

Listening for information and to evaluate critically and listening to support others are two major listening purposes. In addition, we will briefly discuss other listening goals.

Listening for Pleasure Sometimes we listen for pleasure, as when we attend concerts or play CDs. Listening for enjoyment is also a primary purpose when we go to comedy shows or pay attention to jokes an acquaintance tells. When we are listening for pleasure, we don't need to concentrate on organizing and remembering as much as when we listen for information, although retention is important if you want to be able to tell a joke to someone else later. Yet listening for pleasure does require mindfulness, hearing, and interpretation.

Listening to Discriminate In some situations, we listen to make fine discriminations in sounds in order to draw valid conclusions and act appropriately in response. For example, doctors listen to discriminate when they use stethoscopes to diagnose heart functioning or chest congestion. Parents listen to discriminate among a baby's cries for atten-

© Frank Siteman/Index Stock Imagery

tion, food, or a diaper change. Subtle differences in crying signal distinct needs in infants, and parents need to be able to discriminate accurately. Skilled mechanics can distinguish between engine sounds that most people cannot detect. Mindfulness and keen hearing abilities are particularly important when listening to discriminate.

Sharpen Your Skill

Learn from the Pros

One way to improve your listening skills is to observe people who are experts at effective listening. Watch a television program that features interviews—Sunday morning news shows and programs such as "20/20" and "60 Minutes." Select one interview to observe, and answer the following questions about it:

> How does the interviewer phrase questions to encourage the interviewee to talk? Are questions open or closed, biased or unbiased?

> How is the interviewer seated in relation to the interviewee—how close, at what angle?

> Does the interviewer paraphrase the interviewee's responses?

> Does the interviewer make minimal responses?

> How, if at all, does the interviewer show that she or he understands and respects the interviewee's perspective?

> How, if at all, does the interviewer demonstrate attentiveness?

Experiencing Communication in Our Lives

CASE STUDY: Family Hour

The conversation scripted here is featured as a multimedia scenario on the *Communication in Our Lives* CD-ROM included with this book. Once you've launched the CD, click on the "Communication Scenarios" icon, and, from the Scenarios Menu, select "Family Hour" to watch the video. Improve your own communication skills by reading, watching, listening to, critiquing, and analyzing this communication encounter.

Analyze the scenario by applying the principles covered in this chapter, and respond to the prompts that accompany the video, which you can access by clicking on "Analysis." After completing the conversation analysis and answering the questions, you can click on the "Done" button to compare your responses with the ones I suggest. Additional analysis questions are available in print at the end of this chapter and on the book's website.

Over spring break, 20-year-old Josh visits his father. He wants to convince his family to support him in joining a fraternity that has given him a bid. On his second day home, after dinner Josh decides to broach the topic. His dad is watching the evening news on television when Josh walks into the living room. Josh sits down and opens the conversation.

Jason Harris/© 2001 Wadsworth

JOSH: Well, something pretty interesting has happened at school this semester.

DAD: I'll bet you found a girlfriend, right? I was about your age when your mother and I started dating, and that was the best part of college. I still remember how she looked on our first date. She was young, and then she was very slender and pretty. I saw her and thought she was the loveliest thing I'd ever seen. Before long, we were a regular item. Yep, it was about when I was 20, like you are now.

JOSH: Well, I haven't found a girlfriend, but I did get a bid from Sigma Chi.

DAD: Sigma Chi. What is that—a fraternity?

JOSH: Yeah, it's probably the coolest fraternity on campus. I attended some rush parties this semester—mainly out of curiosity, just to see what they were like.

DAD: Why'd you do that? Before you ever went to college, I told you to steer clear of fraternities. They cost a lot of money, and they distract you from your studies.

JOSH: Well, I know you told me to steer clear of fraternities, but I did check a few out. I'd be willing to take a job to help pay the membership fee and monthly dues. Besides, it's not that much more expensive when you figure I'd be eating at the house, and . . .

DAD: Do you realize how much it costs just for you to go to that school? I'm paying $14,000 a year! When I went to school, I had to go to state college because my parents couldn't afford to send me to the school of my choice. You have no idea how lucky you are to be going to the school you wanted to go to and have me footing all the bills.

JOSH: But we could work it out so that a fraternity wouldn't cost you anything. Like I said, I . . .

DAD: If you want to take a job, fine. I could use some help paying your tuition and fees. But you're not taking a job just so you can belong to a party house.

JOSH: I thought they were just party houses too, until I attended rush. Now, I went to several houses that were that way, but Sigma Chi isn't. I really liked the brothers at Sigma Chi. They're interesting and friendly and fun, so I was thrilled when . . .

DAD: I don't want to hear about it. You're not joining a fraternity. I told you what happened when I was in college. I joined one, and pretty soon my Dean's List grades dropped to "C"s and "D"s. When you live in a fraternity house, you can't study like you can in your dorm room or the library. I should know. I tried it and found out the hard way. There's no need for you to repeat my mistake.

JOSH: But, Dad, I'm not you. Joining a fraternity wouldn't necessarily mean that my grades . . .

DAD: What do you mean you're not me? You think I wasn't a good student before I joined the fraternity? You think you're so smart you can party all the time and still make good grades? Let me tell you something, I thought that too, and, boy! was I ever wrong. As soon as I joined the house, it was party time all the time. There was always music blaring and girls in the house and poker games—anything but studying. I wasn't stupid. It's just not an atmosphere that encourages academic work.

JOSH: I'd like to give it a try. I really like these guys, and I think I can handle being in Sigma Chi and still . . .

DAD: Well, you think wrong!

Chapter Summary

According to Zeno of Citium, an ancient philosopher, "We have been given two ears and but a single mouth, in order that we may hear more and talk less." Thousands of years later, we can still learn from his comment. Listening is a major and vital part of communication, yet too often we don't consider it as important as talking. In this chapter, we've explored the complex and demanding process of listening.

We began by distinguishing between hearing—physically receiving messages—and listening. The former is a straightforward physiological process that doesn't take effort on our part. Listening, in contrast, is a complicated and active process involving being mindful, hearing, selecting and organizing, interpreting, responding, and remembering. Listening well takes commitment and skill.

To understand what interferes with effective listening, we discussed obstacles in situations and messages and obstacles in us. Listening is hindered by message overload, complexity of material, and external noise in communication contexts. In addition, listening can be hampered by our preoccupations and prejudgments, lack of effort, and failure to recognize differences in listening styles. These obstacles to listening give rise to various types of nonlistening, including pseudolistening, monopolizing, selective listening, defensive listening, ambushing, and literal listening. Each of these forms of nonlistening signals that we aren't fully present in interaction.

We also discussed different purposes for listening and identified the skills and attitudes that advance each purpose. Informational and critical listening requires us to adopt a mindful attitude and to think critically, organize and evaluate information, clarify understanding by asking questions, and develop aids to retention of complex material. Relational listening also requires mindfulness, but it calls for other, distinct listening skills. Suspending judgment, paraphrasing, giving minimal encouragers, and expressing support enhance the effectiveness of relational listening.

Communication in Our Lives ONLINE

In addition to presenting the case studies' multimedia scenarios, the *Communication in Our Lives* CD-ROM provides quick access to the *Communication in Our Lives* website and InfoTrac College Edition. The website is online at http://communication.wadsworth.com/woodciol4, but you can only access this book's premium web content when you link to the site directly through the book's CD.

The *Communication in Our Lives* website features interactive tools for learning and reviewing the chapter's key concepts and terms, including electronic versions of the "For Further Reflection and Discussion" questions following and a review quiz.

The website also provides updated web links and additional InfoTrac College Edition activities. If required, you can e-mail completed chapter activities or the quizzes to your instructor.

Key Concepts

ambushing, *187*	listening, *176*	paraphrasing, *191*
critical listening, *188*	literal listening, *187*	pseudolistening, *185*
defensive listening, *187*	mindfulness, *176*	relational listening, *190*
hearing, *175*	minimal encouragers, *192*	selective listening, *186*
informational listening, *188*	monopolizing, *185*	

For Further Reflection and Discussion

1. Select one type of nonlistening in which you engage, and work to minimize its occurrence.

2. Apply the strategies for remembering discussed in this chapter to aid your retention of material covered in one of your classes. Does this increase your understanding and retention?

3. How does listening online differ from listening in face-to-face conversations? How do you know whether someone is really listening to you when you are talking online? What signals mindful listening in these settings? Are there differences in how you organize and interpret others' messages when you are online, as opposed to when you are interacting face-to-face?

4. What ethical principles guide different listening purposes? What different moral goals and responsibilities accompany listening for information and listening relationally?

5. To learn more about good communication between doctors and patients, use your InfoTrac College Edition to read John Portman's 2000 article "Physician–Patient Relationships: A Marriage Without the Romance." Are your expectations of your personal physician consistent with those that Portman advocates?

6. Who is your prototype of an excellent listener? Describe what the person does that makes him or her effective. Do the person's listening behaviors fit with the guidelines offered in this chapter?

Experiencing Communication in Our Lives

Questions for Analysis and Discussion

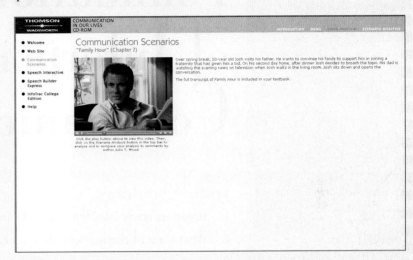 Review the video of the scenario entitled "Family Hour" that you watched when completing this chapter's case study (pages 195–196), or, if you haven't seen it yet, watch it for the first time. If you didn't previously finish the analysis questions included on the CD-ROM, do so now, and then respond to the following questions, which are also available on the book's website under "Activities for Chapter 7."

1. What forms of ineffective listening are evident in this dialogue?

2. If you could advise Josh's father on listening effectively, what would you tell him to do differently?

3. Would you offer any advice to Josh on how he could listen to his father more effectively?

8

Foundations of Interpersonal Communication

Focus Questions

1. How does communication shape the interpersonal climates of relationships?
2. What kinds of communication foster constructive conflict?
3. How can we assert ourselves while also respecting others?
4. Is self-disclosure always constructive?

You have scheduled a performance review with Jenette, an employee assigned to your project team. You need to call her attention to some problems in her work while also communicating that you support her and value her in the company.

You know your neighbor is worried about losing his job because his company has announced substantial layoffs. You want to let him know that you are open to talking with him about his worries.

You're concerned about reports of drugs at the school your 13-year-old son attends. You want to warn him about the dangers of drugs without making him feel you're judging him. You also want to establish open lines of communication between the two of you so he feels free to talk with you about drugs and other issues.

You have been appointed to represent your firm at a press conference. You know that some of the reporters and stockholders are angry because they've heard rumors that the company has not observed adequate safety regulations. You want to establish your credibility and create an open atmosphere so you and attendees can talk productively.

In each of these situations, achieving your goals depends on your ability to create an effective climate for communication. Your goals—to offer criticism in a supportive manner, to make it comfortable for others to disclose private feelings, to open lines of communication, and to promote productive interaction—are likely to be met only if you first cultivate a climate that fosters openness and trust between people.

Perhaps you feel foggy-headed or down when the sky is overcast, and upbeat when it's sunny. Do you feel more energetic and positive in some seasons than in others? Most of us are affected by aspects of the physical climate. In much the same way that physical climates influence how we feel, interpersonal climates affect how we communicate with others. We feel on guard when a supervisor is manipulative, when a co-worker is in a stormy mood, or when a friend judges us. In each case, the communication climate is cloudy.

Interpersonal climate is the overall feeling between people that arises largely out of the ways people communicate with each other. Interpersonal climate isn't something we can see or measure objectively, and it isn't just the sum of what people do together. Instead, it is the overall feeling or emotional mood between people. In interacting in some situations and with some people, we feel tense and on guard. In other interactions, we feel comfortable, at ease, and open.

Interpersonal climate is an important foundation of communication in all contexts. On the job, we need to know how to create supportive, productive climates that foster good work relationships and outcomes. In public speaking contexts, speakers want to create climates that lead listeners to trust them and attend to what they say. In social relationships, we try to build climates that allow us and others to feel at ease. In personal relationships, we want to develop climates that allow us to disclose private feelings and thoughts without fear of criticism or ridicule.

This chapter focuses on interpersonal climate as a cornerstone of effective communication in all contexts. We'll begin by discussing self-disclosure, a form of communication that can promote an open climate of communication if used appropriately. Next, we'll explore how specific kinds of communication foster distinct climates. Third, we'll consider the role of conflict in relationships, and we'll see that creating healthy climates helps us manage conflict constructively. The final section of the chapter identifies guidelines for creating and sustaining healthy interpersonal climates. To extend this chapter's discussion of foundations for interpersonal communication, Chapter 9 will explore communication in close friendships and romantic relationships.

Self-disclosure

Self-disclosure is revealing personal information about ourselves that others are unlikely to discover on their own. We self-disclose when we share private information about ourselves with others—our hopes, fears, feelings, thoughts, and experiences. Although we don't reveal our private selves to everyone and don't do it often, even with intimates, self-disclosure is an important kind of communication.

Self-disclosure has notable values. First, sharing personal feelings, thoughts, and experiences often enhances closeness between people. By extension, when others understand our personal sides, they may respond to us more sensitively, as unique individuals. Self-disclosing also tends to invite others to self-disclose, so we may learn more about them. Finally, self-disclosure can affect what we know about ourselves and how we feel about who we are. For example, if we reveal a weakness or an incident of which we're ashamed, and another person accepts the disclosure without judging us negatively, we may find it easier to accept ourselves.

Self-disclosure and Personal Growth

A number of years ago, Joseph Luft and Harry Ingham created a model that describes different kinds of knowledge related to individual growth and the development of relationships with others (Luft, 1969). They called the model the Johari Window (Figure 8.1), which is a combination of their first names, Joe and Harry.

The Johari Window includes four types of information. Open, or public, information is known both to us and to others. Your name, height, academic major, and tastes in food and music are information that you share easily with many people. Listeners usually are aware of a speaker's professional title and some of his or her accomplishments. Our co-workers and casual

Figure 8.1
The Johari Window

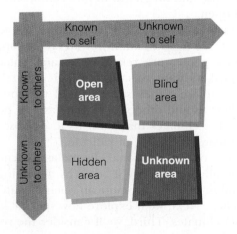

acquaintances often know information about us that is in our *open area*.

The *blind area* contains information that others know about us but we don't know about ourselves. For example, others may see that we are insecure in new situations, even though we don't realize we are. Others may also recognize needs or feelings that we haven't acknowledged to ourselves. Co-workers and supervisors may recognize in us strengths, weaknesses, and potentials of which we are unaware.

The third area in the Johari Window, the *hidden area*, consists of information that we know about ourselves but choose not to reveal to most others. You might not tell many people about your vulnerabilities or about traumatic experiences, because you consider this private information. You might not reveal blemishes in your work history to employers. Politicians want audiences to think they are speaking their own minds, so they seldom reveal that their speeches were written mostly or completely by others.

© Norbert Schaefer/CORBIS

Disclosing private thoughts and feelings tends to enhance closeness.

The *unknown area* is made up of information about ourselves that neither we nor others know. This area includes our untapped resources, untried talents, and unknown reactions to experiences we've never had. Nobody knows how you will manage a crisis until you've been in one; nobody can tell what kind of parent you would be until you've had a child; nobody knows whether you have managerial aptitude until you are in a management role.

  To apply the Johari Window to yourself, complete Activity 8.1, "Your Many Windows," in your *Student Companion* or online under "Activities for Chapter 8" at the *Communication in Our Lives* website.

Because a healthy self-concept begins with knowing yourself, it's valuable to learn about what's in your blind area and to explore your unknown area. Some ways to do this are to enter unfamiliar situations, to try novel things, and to experiment with new kinds of communication. Another way to increase self-knowledge is to ask how others see you, and then reflect on what they say.

  To become aware of changes in the blind and unknown areas of yourself, complete Activity 8.2, "Changing Windows of Yourself," in your *Student Companion* or online under "Activities for Chapter 8" at the *Communication in Our Lives* website.

The areas in your Johari Window are neither static nor the same for all relationships. They may change over time. For example, if you enter new situations and see yourself doing things you've never done, your unknown area shrinks. If you do something you are ashamed of, or if something disturbing happens to you, your hidden area may expand. The size of the panes of the window may also vary across different relationships. For example, my hidden area in my relationship with Robbie is much smaller than with casual acquaintances. I also have a smaller blind area in the relationship with Robbie because he has given me lots of feedback on how he perceives me.

Self-disclosure and Closeness

At least among Westerners, self-disclosure is a key gauge of closeness (Derlega & Berg, 1987). Satisfaction with romantic relationships is closely tied to appropriate self-disclosure (Fitzpatrick & Sollie, 1999; Vito, 1999). As people share their private selves with each other, trust and understanding tend to grow.

Self-disclosure should take place gradually and with appropriate caution. It's unwise to tell anyone too much about ourselves too quickly, especially if revelations could be used against us (Petronio, 2000). We begin by disclosing information that is somewhat private but not likely to make us too vulnerable ("I haven't had much experience in this kind of assignment," "I'm from a small town," "I'm anxious about speaking in public"). If a person responds with acceptance to early and limited disclosures, and if the person keeps our confidences, we're likely to reveal progressively more intimate information as the relationship continues ("I was let go from my last job because I couldn't handle the stress," "I'm having marital difficulties"). If these disclosures are also met with understanding and confidentiality, trust and intimacy grow.

In the early stages of relationships, disclosures are more frequent, and reciprocity is important. If you mention a personal weakness to a new acquaintance, you'll be more comfortable if the other person responds by revealing private information about herself or himself (Cunningham, Strassberg, & Haan, 1986; Dindia, 2000). Sharing personal information also tends to foster an interpersonal climate of trust and comfort.

–Jan–

Josh and I have been married for 15 years. At first we shared a lot of personal information and private thoughts with each other, but we don't do that much now. Yet I feel so close to Josh because he knows me in ways no one else does. All the experiences and feelings we shared earlier help us understand the significance of things that happen now. We don't even have to talk, because we know layers and layers of each other.

The need to reciprocate disclosures recedes in importance once trust is established. Partners in established friendships and romances generally don't feel the need to reciprocate disclosures immediately. Further, in relationships that endure over time, disclosures make up very little of the total communication between partners (Wood & Duck, 1995a). Although disclosure wanes over time, partners continue to reap the benefits of the trust and depth of personal knowledge created by early disclosures. Of course, partners in established relationships continue to disclose new experiences and insights to one another; it's just that significant disclosures tend to be less frequent in established relationships.

When closeness declines, the frequency and depth of disclosures typically decrease (Baxter, 1987). The normal level of disclosure, whatever it may have been, diminishes as intimacy wanes. We are reluctant to entrust another with our secrets and personal emotions when we no longer want closeness or when we sense that the other is pulling away.

Communication Highlight

Self-disclosure and Relationship Satisfaction

Does self-disclosure influence satisfaction with romantic relationships? That's the question that Brenda Meeks, Susan Hendrick, and Clyde Hendrick (1998) wanted to answer. Studying 140 dating couples, they discovered that satisfaction with a relationship is strongly related to a person's rating of his or her own self-disclosure and his or her perceptions of a partner's self-disclosure. In other words, the more a person perceives herself or himself as disclosing and a partner as disclosing, the more satisfied with the relationship the person is likely to be. This study and others (Harter et al., 1997; McKinney, Kelly, & Duran, 1997) also show that satisfaction is strongly and positively related to perceived perspective taking skills by both partners.

–Sid–

For 3 years, Tom and I worked together, and we were really close. We'd even talked about starting up our own company and being partners. Tom and I knew everything about each other, and it was easy to talk about anything, even problems or failures, with him. But last year he stopped talking about himself. At first I didn't notice and just kept telling him what was going on with me, but then I got to feel kind of awkward, like it was one-way, and I was more exposed than he was. I asked Tom if anything was wrong, and he said no, but he didn't talk to me like he used to. Finally, I found out he was working with another guy to start a franchise. When he stopped talking openly with me, it was a signal that our relationship was over.

Communication to Build Supportive Climates

One of the greatest influences on interpersonal climate is communication that is confirming and supportive. Philosopher Martin Buber (1957, 1970) believed that to be healthy and to grow, each of us needs confirmation. The essence of confirmation is valuing. We all want to feel valued for who we are and what we do. When others confirm us, we feel cherished and respected. When they disconfirm us, we feel disregarded.

Interpersonal climates exist on a continuum from confirming to disconfirming (Figure 8.2). Of course, few relationships are purely confirming or disconfirming. In reality, most relationships fall between the two endpoints of the continuum. In these, some communication is confirming, and other messages are disconfirming; or the communication cycles between basically confirming and basically disconfirming.

Levels of Confirmation and Disconfirmation

Communication scholars (Cissna & Sieburg, 1986) have identified specific kinds of communication that confirm or disconfirm others on three levels

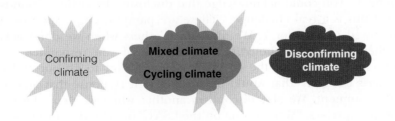

Figure 8.2
Continuum of Interpersonal Climates

Table 8.1: Levels of Confirmation and Disconfirmation

	Confirming Messages	Disconfirming Messages
Recognition	"You exist." "Hello."	"You don't exist." Silence, no eye contact
Acknowledgment	"You matter to me." "We are a team." "I'm sorry you're hurt."	"You don't matter." "We are not a team." "You'll get over it."
Endorsement	"What you think is true." "What you feel is okay." "I feel the same way."	"You are wrong." "You shouldn't feel that way." "Your feeling doesn't make sense."

(Table 8.1). The most basic form of confirmation is **recognition** that another person exists. We do this with nonverbal behaviors (offering a smile, hug, or handshake; maintaining eye contact when speaking in public; looking up when someone enters our office) and verbal communication ("Hello," "Good to meet you," "Thank you for coming to my presentation today"). We disconfirm others at a fundamental level when we don't acknowledge their existence. For example, you might not speak to or look at a person when you enter a room or look at a teammate who comes late to a meeting. Not responding to another's comments also disconfirms his or her presence. Parents who punish a child by refusing to speak to her or him disconfirm the child's existence. In Chapter 6, we discussed "the silent treatment" as a way to disconfirm another's existence.

-Reggie-

Any African American knows what it means to have your existence denied. The law may forbid segregation now, but it still exists. When I go to an upscale restaurant, sometimes people just look away. They ignore me, like I'm not there. I've even been ignored by waiters in restaurants. This is especially true in the South, where a lot of Whites still don't want us in their clubs and schools.

A second level of confirmation is **acknowledgment** of what another feels, thinks, or says. Nonverbally, we acknowledge others by nodding our heads or using facial expressions to indicate that we are listening. Verbal acknowledgments are direct responses to others' communication. If a friend says, "I'm really worried that I blew the LSAT exam," you could acknowledge that by responding, "So you're scared that you didn't test well on it, huh?" If a co-worker tells you, "I'm not sure I have the experience to handle this assignment," you could acknowledge that disclosure by saying, "Sounds as if you feel this is a real challenge." These are paraphrasing responses, which we discussed in Chapter 7. We disconfirm others when we don't acknowledge their feelings or thoughts. For instance, if you responded to your friend's statement about the LSAT by saying, "Want to go out and throw some darts tonight?" that would be an irrelevant response that ignores the friend's comment. We also disconfirm another when we deny the feelings she or he expresses: "You did fine on the LSAT," or "Oh, don't worry—you'll handle the assignment fine."

−Lisa−

I'm amazed by how often people won't acknowledge what I tell them. A hundred times I've been walking across campus and someone's come up and offered to guide me. I tell them I know the way and don't need help, and they still put an arm under my elbow to guide me. I may be blind, but there's nothing wrong with my mind. I know if I need help. Why can't others acknowledge that?

Lisa makes an important point. We shouldn't assume we know more than others about what they want or need. When we don't acknowledge what another says, we disconfirm him or her. You may recall that in previous chapters we've cautioned against speaking for others. It is fundamentally disconfirming to have others deny us our own voices.

The final level of confirmation is **endorsement.** Endorsement involves accepting another's feelings or thoughts as valid. You could endorse the friend who is worried about the LSAT by saying, "It's natural to be worried about the LSAT when you have so much riding on it." We disconfirm others when we don't accept their thoughts and feelings. For example, it would be disconfirming to say, "How can you worry about whether you can do this assignment, when so many people are being laid off? You should be glad to have a job." This response rejects the validity of the other person's expressed feelings and is likely to close the lines of communication between the two of you.

In summary, confirmation and disconfirmation occur on levels. The most basic confirmation is recognizing that another exists. On the second level, we confirm others by acknowledging their ideas and feelings, which carries the relational-level meaning that they matter to us. In essence, we say, "I am paying attention because your feelings and ideas matter to me." The highest form of confirmation is acceptance of others and what they communicate. We feel validated when others accept what we think and feel.

Disconfirmation is not mere disagreement. After all, disagreements can be productive and healthy, and they imply that people matter enough to each other to argue. It is disconfirming to be told that we or our ideas are crazy, wrong, stupid, or deviant. If you think about what we've discussed, you'll probably find that the relationships in which you feel most valued and comfortable are ones in which you feel confirmed.

Sharpen Your Skill

Analyze Your Relationships

Think about two relationships in your life. One should be a relationship in which you feel good about yourself and accepted by the other person. The second relationship should be one in which you feel disregarded or not valued. Identify instances of each level of confirmation and disconfirmation in each relationship. Does this give you insight into why these relationships are so different?

  To practice communicating different levels of confirmation, complete Activity 8.8, "Communicating Levels of Confirmation," in your *Student Companion* or online under "Activities for Chapter 8" at the *Communication in Our Lives* website.

Communication Highlight

Defensive and Supportive Climates

Confirming and disconfirming messages are one important influence on the climate of relationships. Other kinds of communication also contribute to interpersonal climate. Communication researcher Jack Gibb (1961, 1964, 1970) studied the relationship between communication and interpersonal climates. He began by noting that in some relationships we feel defensive and on guard, whereas in others we feel safe and supported. Of course, the climate of many relationships is in between the extremes of defensive and supportive. Gibb, however, was interested in understanding the specific kinds of communication that foster defensive climates and supportive climates. He identified six types of communication that promote each kind of climate.

−Wayne−

I've gotten a lot of disconfirmation since I came out. When I told my parents I was gay, Mom said, "No, you're not." I told her I was, and she and Dad both said I was just confused, but I wasn't gay. They refuse to acknowledge I'm gay, which means they reject me. My older brother isn't any better. His view is that being gay is a sin against God. Now, what could be more disconfirming than that?

Evaluation versus Description

We tend to become defensive when we believe others are evaluating us. Few of us feel what Gibb called "psychologically safe" when we are the targets of judgments. This is as true in professional relationships as in personal ones (Conrad & Poole, 2002; Eadie, 1982). In his commentary, Wayne expressed feeling disconfirmed by his family when he told them he was gay. His parents and brother made evaluations—very negative ones—of him and of gayness. Yet even positive evaluations may provoke defensiveness because they imply that another person feels entitled to judge us. We may feel that if our supervisor makes positive judgments, he or she may also render negative ones. Examples of evaluative statements are "You have no discipline," "It's dumb to feel that way," "I approve," "You shouldn't have done that," "You did the right thing," and "That's a stupid idea."

An alternative to evaluation is description. Descriptive communication describes behaviors without passing judgment. I-language, which we learned about in Chapter 5, describes what the person speaking feels or thinks, but it doesn't evaluate. For example, "I wish you hadn't done that" describes your feelings, whereas "You shouldn't have done that" evaluates another's behavior. Descriptive language may describe another's behavior in a nonjudgmental way: "You seem to be sleeping more lately" (versus "You're sleeping too much"), "You've shouted three times today" (versus "Quit flying off the handle").

Sharpen Your Skill

Using Descriptive Language

To develop skill in supportive communication, translate the following evaluative statements into descriptive ones.

Evaluative	Descriptive
This report is poorly done.	This report doesn't include background information.
You're lazy.	....
I hate the way you dominate conversations with me.	....
Stop obsessing about the problem.	....
You're too involved.	....

Certainty versus Provisionalism

Language characterized by certainty is absolute and often dogmatic. It suggests there is one and only one right answer, valid point of view, or reasonable course of action. Because communication laced with certainty proclaims an absolutely correct position, it fosters a climate that is not conducive to collaboration (Wilmot & Hocker, 2001). A leader who expresses certainty about what a team should generate is likely to stifle creativity and openness. Similarly, supervisors who communicate that their minds are made up often miss critical feedback (Fisher, 1998). There's no point in talking with people whose minds are made up and who demean any point of view other than their own. Certainty is also expressed by, "This is the only idea that makes sense," "My mind can't be changed because I'm right," "Only a fool would vote for that person," or "There's no point in discussing it further." People who restate their own positions in response to others' ideas also express certainty.

One form of communication characterized by certainty is ethnocentrism, which we discussed in Chapter 4. Ethnocentrism is an attitude based on the assumption that our culture and its norms are the only right ones. For instance, someone who says, "It's disrespectful to be late" reveals a lack of awareness of cultures that are less concerned with speed and efficiency than the United States.

–Monika–

My father is a classic case of close-mindedness. He has his ideas, and everything else is crazy. I told him I was majoring in communication studies, and he hit the roof. He said there was no future in learning to write speeches and told me I should go into business so that I could get a good job. He never asked me to describe communication studies. If he had, I would have told him it's a lot more than speech writing. He starts off sure that he knows everything about whatever is being discussed. He has no interest in exploring other points of view or learning something new. He just locks his mind and throws away the key. We've all learned just to keep our ideas to ourselves around him—there's no communication.

An alternative to certainty is provisionalism, which expresses tentativeness about our own ideas and openness to other points of view. When we speak provisionally, we indicate that we have a point of view, yet our minds aren't closed. We signal that we're willing to consider alternative positions, and this encourages others to voice their ideas. Provisional communication includes statements such as "The way I tend to see the issue is . . . ," or "One way to approach the problem is . . . ." Notice how these comments signal that the speaker realizes there could be other positions that are also reasonable. Tentative communication reflects an open mind, which is why it invites continued conversation.

Strategy versus Spontaneity

Most of us feel on guard when we think others are manipulating us or being less than up-front about what's on their minds. For instance, employees are likely to feel defensive if they think management is trying to trick them into doing extra work or giving up benefits (Conrad & Poole, 2002). An example of strategic communication is this: "Would you do something for me if I told

you it really mattered?" If the speaker doesn't tell us what we're expected to do, it feels like a setup.

We're also likely to feel that another is trying to manipulate us with a comment such as "Remember when I helped you with your math last term and when I did your chores last week because you were busy?" With a preamble like that, we suspect a trap of some sort is being set. We also get defensive when we suspect others of using openness to manipulate how we feel about them. For instance, people who disclose highly personal information early in a relationship may be trying to win our trust so that we self-disclose in return. Nonverbal behaviors may also convey strategy, as when a person pauses for a long time before answering or refuses to look at us when she or he speaks. A sense of deception pollutes the communication climate.

© PhotoDisc

Based on nonverbal behaviors, what kind of climate do you think is present in this photograph?

— Sandy —

This guy I dated last year was a real con artist, but it took me a while to figure that out. He would look me straight in the eye and tell me he really felt he could trust me. Then he'd say he was going to tell me something he'd never told anyone else in his life, and he'd tell me about fights with his father or how he didn't make the soccer team in high school. The stuff wasn't really that personal, but the way he said it made it seem that way. So I found myself telling him a lot more than I usually disclose and a lot more than I should have. He started using some of the information against me, which was when I started getting wise to him. Later on, I found out he ran through the same song and dance with every girl he dated. It was quite an act!

Spontaneity is a counterpoint to strategy. Spontaneous communication may be thought out, yet it is also open, honest, and uncontrived. "I really need your help with this computer glitch" is a more spontaneous comment than "Would you do something for me if I told you it really mattered?" Likewise, it is more spontaneous to ask for a favor in a straightforward way ("Would you help me?") than to preface a request with a recitation of all we've done for someone else.

Control versus Problem Orientation

Controlling communication tends to trigger defensiveness (Wilmot & Hocker, 2001). Controlling communication overtly attempts to dominate others or force them to defer. A common instance of controlling communication is a person's insistence that her or his solution or preference should prevail. In the workplace, employees tend to feel defensive if supervisors are overly controlling, or micromanaging (Conrad & Poole, 2002). The relational meaning is that the person exerting control thinks she or he has greater power, rights, or ideas than others. It's disconfirming to be told that our ideas are wrong or that we can't do our job without micromanagement from a supervisor.

A study by Escudero Valentin, Edna Rogers, and Emilio Gutierrez (1997) found that there were more attempts to dominate and control in unsatisfying marriages than in satisfying ones. For example, a wife who earns a higher salary than her husband might say to him, "I like the Honda more than the Ford you want, and it's my money that's going to pay for it." The wife not only pushes her preference but also tells her husband that she has more power than he does because she makes more money. This disconfirms and disrespects him.

Rather than imposing a preference, problem-oriented communication cooperatively focuses on finding answers that satisfy everyone (Sonnentag, 2001). The goal is to come up with a solution that all parties find acceptable. Here's an example of problem-oriented communication: "It seems that we have really different preferences about a car. Let's talk through what we like and dislike about the two models and see if that helps us decide." Notice how this statement invites collaboration and confirms the other and the relationship by expressing a desire to meet both people's needs. Problem-oriented communication tends to reduce unproductive conflict and keep lines of communication open (McKinney, Kelly, & Duran, 1997). One of the strengths of focusing on problems is that the relational level of meaning emphasizes the importance of the relationship between communicators. In contrast, controlling behaviors aim for one person to triumph over the other, an outcome that undercuts interpersonal harmony.

Neutrality versus Empathy

People tend to become defensive when others act in a neutral, or detached, manner. It's easy to understand why we might feel uneasy with people who seem uninvolved, especially if we are talking about personal matters. In interviews, defensiveness arises when an interviewer appears withdrawn and distant (Civickly, Pace, & Krause, 1977). Neutral communication implies a lack of regard and caring for others. Consequently, it may be interpreted as disconfirming.

In contrast to neutrality, expressed empathy confirms the worth of others and our concern for their thoughts and feelings. Empathy is communicated when we say, "I can understand why you feel that way," or "I don't blame you for being worried about the situation." Empathy doesn't necessarily mean agreement; instead, it acknowledges others and their perspectives and demonstrates that we want to understand them (Hall & Bernieri, 2001).

Superiority versus Equality

It's normal to feel on guard when talking with people who act as if they are better than we are. Consider several messages that convey superiority: "I know a lot more about this than you." "You just don't have my experience." "You really should go to my hairdresser." Each of these messages says, loud and clear, "You aren't as good (smart, savvy, competent, attractive) as I am." Predictably, the result is that we protect our self-esteem by defensively shutting out the people and messages that belittle us.

–Carl–

I am really uncomfortable with one of the guys on my team at work. He always acts like he knows best and all the rest of us aren't as smart or experienced or whatever. The other day, I suggested a way we might improve our team's productivity and he said, "I remember when I used to think that." What a putdown! I feel uneasy saying anything around him.

We feel more relaxed and comfortable communicating with people who treat us as equals. At the relational level of meaning, expressed equality communicates respect and equivalent status between people. This promotes an open climate. Creating a climate of equality allows everyone to be involved without fear of being judged inadequate.

Sharpen Your Skill

Assessing Climate

Use the behaviors we've discussed as a checklist for assessing climates. The next time you feel defensive, ask whether others are communicating superiority, control, strategy, certainty, neutrality, or evaluation. Chances are that one or more of these laces communication.

For a communication climate you find supportive, check to see whether others are communicating spontaneity, equality, provisionalism, problem orientation, empathy, and description.

If you find yourself in a defensive climate, try to resist the normal tendency to respond defensively. Instead, try to make the climate less defensive by being empathic, descriptive, and spontaneous, showing equality and tentativeness, and solving problems.

  To extend this exercise, complete Activity 8.3, "Using Supportive Communication," and Activity 8.6, "Rating the Supportiveness of Communication Climates," in your *Student Companion* or online under "Activities for Chapter 8" at the *Communication in Our Lives* website.

We've seen that specific kinds of communication express confirmation or disconfirmation and foster climates that are more or less defensive or supportive. Establishing a confirming, supportive climate is especially important as a foundation for managing conflict in our personal, social,

Communication Highlight

What Goes Around Comes Around

Have you ever heard the expression, "What goes around comes around"? It's an adage—a kind of folk wisdom—that reminds us that whatever we do, good or bad, to others tends to come back to us. It turns out that this is equally true in relationships. Researchers who study relationships have noted the principle of reciprocity in relationships. It means that people tend to act in reciprocal ways, giving back to others what others give to them. Communication scholars Beth Le Poire and Stephen Yoshimura (1999) had research participants participate in a practice medical interview. They found that pleasant behaviors were consistently reciprocated.

Reciprocity appears to be especially likely with positive behaviors. If you accept a friend's flaws, the friend is likely to reciprocate by accepting yours. If you try to understand a partner's perspective during a conflict, it's likely your partner will also try to understand yours.

 Use your InfoTrac College Edition to read the 2001 article by Eline Van Der Heijden, Jan Nelissen, Jan Potters, and Harrie Verbon entitled "Simple and Complex Gift Exchange in the Laboratory." According to their report, what is the role of trust in simple and complex reciprocity?

and professional relationships. Building on what we've discussed so far, let's now explore how communication allows us to manage it productively.

Conflict in Relationships

Conflict exists when people who depend on each other have different views, interests, or goals and perceive their differences as incompatible. Conflict is a normal, inevitable part of all relationships. You like to eat meat, and your roommate is a strict vegetarian. You believe money should be enjoyed, and your partner believes in saving for a rainy day. You favor one way of organizing a work team, and your colleague thinks another is better. Again and again, we find ourselves seemingly at odds with others. When this happens, we either part ways or resolve the differences, preferably in a way that doesn't harm the relationship.

–Yih-Tang Lin–

I had a very bad conflict with my ex-girlfriend. When we disagreed, she wanted to argue about problems, but I couldn't do that. I was brought up to see conflict as bad. I learned to smooth over problems. So I would avoid conflict and say everything was okay when it was not. I think this kept us from working out problems.

The presence of conflict doesn't indicate that a relationship is in trouble, although how people manage conflict does influence relational health. Conflict is a sign that people are involved with each other. If they weren't, it wouldn't matter if they differed, and they wouldn't need to resolve differences. This is a good point to keep in mind as we discuss four principles of conflict.

Conflict May Be Overt or Covert

Overt conflict exists when people express differences in a straightforward manner. They might discuss their disagreement, honestly identify their different points of view, argue about ideas, or engage in a shouting match. In each case, differences are out in the open.

Yet much conflict isn't overt. **Covert conflict** exists when partners deny or camouflage disagreement or anger and express it indirectly. For instance, if you're annoyed that your roommate left the kitchen a mess, you might play the stereo when she or he is sleeping. A man who is angry with his wife might deliberately be half an hour late to meet her when he knows she hates to be kept waiting. Covert aggression sidesteps the real problems and issues, which makes it almost impossible to resolve the problems.

–Carlotta–

My roommate will never say when she's mad or hurt or whatever. Instead, she plays games that drive me crazy. Sometimes she'll just refuse to talk to me and deny anything is wrong. Other times she forgets some of my stuff when she gets our groceries and pretends it was an accident. I have to guess what is wrong because she won't just come out and tell me. It really strains our friendship.

Conflict May Be Managed Well or Poorly

Because conflict is natural and inevitable, we need to learn to deal with it in ways that benefit us and our relationships. Depending on how we handle disagreements, conflict can strengthen a relationship or poison it. We're most able to realize conflict's potential to enhance relationships when we understand the different parts of the conflict process. Clyde Feldman and Carl Ridley (2000) identify four components of conflict:

- *Conflicts of interest.* These are the seemingly incompatible opinions, viewpoints, goals, or interests that the conflict addresses.
- *Conflict orientations.* These include attitudes toward conflict: whether people think conflict is healthy, how people are characteristically inclined to regard conflict (e.g., win–win, win–lose, lose–lose).
- *Conflict responses.* These are each person's overt behavioral responses to conflict, methods of addressing conflict, and conflict strategies, which may sustain, escalate, defuse, or resolve conflict.
- *Conflict outcomes.* Included as outcomes are whether and how the conflict of interest is resolved, how mutual the process is, and how the conflict process affects emotional closeness in a relationship.

We've already discussed the first component of the conflict model. The second one refers to our typical ways of thinking about and approaching conflict. Do you tend to think conflict is bad, period? Do you typically think that everyone loses in conflict, or that one person wins and the other loses, or that both can win? Your orientations toward conflict can act as a self-fulfilling prophecy, shaping how you communicate and what happens in the situation.

  To increase your awareness of how your family may have shaped your orientation to conflict, complete Activity 8.11, "Understanding Your Conflict Script," in your *Student Companion* or online under "Activities for Chapter 8" at the *Communication in Our Lives* website.

The third component of the conflict process is responses: how we actually respond when conflict occurs. Caryl Rusbult and her colleagues conducted a series of studies that allowed them to identify four distinct ways Westerners respond to relational distress (Rusbult, 1987; Rusbult, Johnson, & Morrow, 1986; Rusbult & Zembrodt, 1983; Rusbult, Zembrodt, & Iwaniszek, 1986). These are represented in Figure 8.3. According to this model, responses to conflict can be either active or passive, depending on how emphatically they address problems. Responses can also be constructive or destructive in their capacity to resolve tension and to preserve relationships.

  To assess your styles of responding to conflict, complete Activity 8.9, "Identifying Your Style(s) of Responding to Conflict," in your *Student Companion* or online under "Activities for Chapter 8" at the *Communication in Our Lives* website.

The *exit* response involves leaving a relationship, either by walking out or by withdrawing psychologically. Because exiting doesn't address problems, it is destructive. Because it is forceful, it is active. The *neglect* response occurs when a person denies or minimizes problems. "You're making a mountain out of a molehill" denies that a serious issue exists. The neglect response is also disconfirming because it fails to acknowledge and respect another person's opinion that the issue *is* serious. Neglect is destructive because it evades difficulties, but it does so passively, by avoiding discussion.

Figure 8.3
The Exit–Voice–Loyalty–
Neglect Model

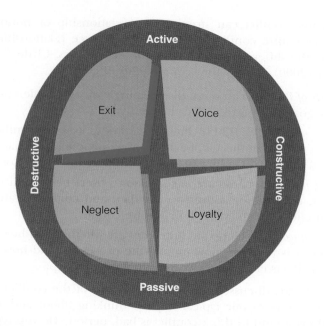

The *loyalty* response is staying committed to a relationship despite differences. Loyalty might be expressed by hoping that conflicts will blow over. Loyalty is silent allegiance, so it is a passive response. Because it doesn't end a relationship and preserves the option of addressing tension later, loyalty is considered constructive. Finally, *voice* is an active, constructive strategy that responds to conflict by talking about problems, offering sincere apologies, or trying to resolve differences so that a relationship remains healthy (Fincham & Beach, 2002).

The final component of the conflict process is *outcomes*. In addition to the obvious outcome of how the issue is resolved, another consequence is impact on the relationship between people. Our choices of how to communicate during conflict shape how conflict affects our feelings toward others and our relationships with them.

What responses to conflict do the people in this photo seem to be employing?

Although each of us has characteristic conflict orientations and responses, we can develop skill in other orientations and alternative ways of responding. Constructive strategies (voice and loyalty) are advisable for relationships that you want to maintain. Of those two, voice is preferable because it actively intervenes to resolve conflict. Loyalty may be useful as an interim strategy when partners need time to reflect or cool off before dealing with tension directly. Once you understand your current tendencies for responding to conflict, you can consider whether you want to develop skill in alternatives to them.

 To practice different ways of responding to conflict, complete Activity 8.10, "Generating Different Responses to Conflict," in your *Student Companion* or online under "Activities for Chapter 8" at the *Communication in Our Lives* website.

Conflict Reflects and Expresses Cultures and Social Communities

How we perceive conflict and how we act during conflict are shaped by our membership in particular cultures and social communities. For example, most Mediterranean cultures regard conflict as a normal part of everyday life. In contrast, many Asian cultures discourage open expression of conflict or disagreement (Gangwish, 1999).

Our views of conflict and ways of dealing with it are also influenced by the social communities to which we belong. For instance, there are general differences between women's and men's responses to conflict. Although the generalizations don't apply to all women and all men, in general, women are more likely to adopt a voice response to conflict, whereas men are more likely to choose the exit response, often by refusing to discuss problems (Jacobson & Gottman, 1998; Stafford, Dutton & Hass, 2000). One reason that men may seek to avoid conflict is that, in general, they tend to experience greater and longer-lasting physical responses to conflict than women (Jacobson & Gottman, 1998). Membership in racial and ethnic groups may also affect how people feel about conflict and how it affects relationships. Terri Orbuch and Joseph Veroff (2002) report that spirited verbal arguments can be harmful to White couples, but they aren't necessarily damaging to Black couples.

Conflict May Be Good for Individuals and Relationships

One outcome of conflict is impact on relationships. Although many people think conflict is negative, it can benefit us and our relationships in several ways. When managed constructively, conflict can help us grow as individuals and strengthen our relationships. We can enlarge our personal perspectives when we express them and consider critical responses from others. Conflict

Communication Highlight

The Four Horsemen of the Apocalypse

Psychologist John Gottman has spent more than twenty years studying marriages and counseling couples (Gottman, 1994a, 1994b, 1999; Gottman & Silver, 1994). He concludes that there is no difference in the amount of conflict between happily married couples and couples who divorce or have unhappy marriages.

Healthy and unhealthy marriages do differ in two important respects. First, partners who are unhappy together and who often divorce tend to engage in what Gottman calls "corrosive communication patterns." Gottman views these destructive communication practices as "the four horsemen of the apocalypse":

complaint and criticism

defensiveness and denial of responsibility

expressions of contempt

stonewalling

These "four horsemen of the apocalypse" foster negative feelings, including anger, fear, sadness, and dissatisfaction. Gottman thinks the most corrosive of the four is **stonewalling**, which is relying on the exit response to conflict and refusing to discuss issues. When people stonewall, they block the possibility of resolving conflicts. In addition, on the relationship level of meaning they communicate that problems in the relationship aren't worth dealing with. Gottman has found that husbands are more likely than wives to stonewall.

The second major difference between marriages that succeed and those that fail is not bad moments, but a predominance of good moments. Happy couples have as many conflicts and tensions as unhappy ones, but they have more enjoyable times together. Says Gottman, a positive balance is everything.

allows us to consider points of view different from our own. Based on what we learn, we may change our opinions, behaviors, or goals. Conflict can also allow people to work through and resolve differences that have been interfering with their relationships.

Guidelines for Creating and Sustaining Healthy Climates

We've seen that communication plays a vital role in creating the climate of relationships in general, and the climate for dealing with conflict in particular. To translate what we've learned into practical information, we'll discuss five guidelines for building and sustaining healthy climates in social, professional, and personal relationships.

Actively Use Communication to Shape Climates

We have seen that communication influences the climate of relationships. Thus, we want to use communication to foster effective, supportive climates. Several principles suggest themselves. First, we want to recognize and acknowledge others and to endorse them when we honestly can. A study of more than 3,000 adults found that people felt least validated and least able to express their authentic selves when their partners were self-focused and didn't acknowledge them. The people who felt most validated in their relationships focused on self and other, as did their partners (Harter et al., 1997). This finding was confirmed by Bruce McKinney, Lynne Kelly, and Robert Duran (1997), who reported that the most competent communicators balance attention to their own issues and those of their partners.

Second, we should use communication that fosters confirming, supportive climates because they make it more likely that conflict will be overt and constructive. What you've learned about defensive and supportive climates should allow you to monitor your communication to make sure it contributes to open, positive interaction. You can identify and avoid disconfirming patterns of talk, such as evaluation and superiority. In addition, you can actively work to use supportive communication, such as problem orientation and tentativeness.

Third, use skills we've discussed in previous chapters to shape climates effectively. For example, being mindful, engaging in dual perspective, checking perceptions, using *I*-language, and paraphrasing are important skills when conflict arises.

 To practice using communication to shape climates, complete Activity 8.4, "Transforming Defensive Communication into Supportive Communications" in your *Student Companion* or online under "Activities for Chapter 8" at the *Communication in Our Lives* website.

Fourth, actively shaping climates involves accepting and growing from the tension generated by conflicting needs and desires in relationships. For instance, you may want private time, but your partner wants to do something together. You might learn something new about yourself or your partner if you honor his or her preference or if the two of you collaborate to create both individual and couple time during a day. Although friction between contradictory needs can make us uncomfortable, we should recognize its constructive potential. The discomfort of tension pushes us to transform our relationships so that they—and we—continue to grow.

Do these women seem to be engaged in supportive, confirming communication?

Accept and Confirm Others

Throughout this chapter, we've seen that confirmation is a cornerstone of healthy climates and fulfilling communication. Although we can understand how important confirmation is, it isn't always easy to give it. Sometimes we disagree with others or don't like certain things they do. Being honest with others is important because it enhances trust between people. Communication research indicates that people expect real friends to be sources of honest feedback, even if it isn't always pleasant to hear (Rawlins, 1994). This implies that we should express honest misgivings about our friends' behaviors or other aspects of their identity. It is false friends who tell us only what we want to hear.

The same is true in professional relationships. To build good working relationships with subordinates, managers must demonstrate that they give honest feedback (Fisher, 1998). The key is to communicate in ways that express respect for others as people, even if we disagree with them on some matters. As Aaron's commentary explains, we can offer honest feedback within a context that assures others that we value and respect them.

When I first came to school here, I got in with a crowd that drank a lot. At first I drank only on weekends, but then it got so I was drinking every night and drinking more and more. My classes were suffering, but I didn't seem able to stop on my own. Then my friend Betsy told me she was worried about me and wanted to help me stop drinking so much. I'd have been angry if most people had said that, but Betsy talked to me in a way that said she really cared about me. I saw that she was a better friend than all my drinking buddies because she cared enough not to stand by when I was hurting myself. All my other so-called friends just stood by and said nothing.

In satisfying, healthy relationships, people feel confirmed. This doesn't mean that you always agree with others or that you defer your own needs. Instead, the point is to recognize and respect others' needs just as you want them to respect yours. Listening mindfully and engaging in dual perspective are primary ways to communicate respect and affirmation of others (McKinney, Kelly, & Duran, 1997; Weisinger, 1996). Although personal talk may make you feel most close to another person, you should also realize that some people feel closer when they do things together. To meet both of your needs, you could take turns honoring each other's preferred paths to closeness. Alternatively, you might combine the two styles of intimacy by doing things together that invite conversation. For example, backpacking is an activity in which talking naturally occurs.

Accept and Confirm Yourself

It is just as important to accept and confirm yourself as to do that for others. You are no less valuable; your needs are no less important; your preferences are no less valid than those of others. It is a misunderstanding to think that communication principles we've discussed concern only how we should behave toward others. They pertain equally to how we should treat ourselves. Ethical communicators respect both their own and others' needs, preferences, and ways of creating intimacy.

Although we can't always meet the needs of all parties in relationships, it is possible and desirable to give voice to everyone, including yourself. If your partner favors greater autonomy than you, you need to recognize that preference and also assert your own. If you don't express your feelings, there's no way others can know them and thus no way they can confirm you.

–Liz–

Ever since I was a kid, I have muffled my own needs and concentrated on pleasing others. I thought I was taking care of relationships, but actually I was hurting them because I felt neglected. My resentment poisoned relationships in subtle ways, so it was really destructive. I've been developing my skills in telling others what I want and need, and that's improving my relationships.

Unlike aggression, assertion doesn't involve putting your needs above those of others. But unlike deference, assertion doesn't subordinate your needs to those of others. Assertion is a matter of clearly and nonjudgmentally stating what you feel, need, or want. You should do this without disparaging others and what they want. You should simply make your feelings known in an open, descriptive manner. Table 8.2 illustrates aggressive, assertive, and deferential responses.

 To develop your awareness of differences between assertion, aggression, and deference, complete Activity 8.5, "Distinguishing Aggressive, Assertive, and Deferential Forms of Communication," in your *Student Companion* or online under "Activities for Chapter 8" at the *Communication in Our Lives* website.

Table 8.2: Aggression, Assertion, and Deference

Aggressive	Assertive	Deferential
We are going to spend the weekend together.	I'd like to spend the weekend together.	If you don't want to spend time together this weekend, it's okay.
Tell me what you're feeling.	I'd like to know what you are feeling.	If you don't want to talk about your feelings, it's okay.
I refuse to take the assignment.	That assignment doesn't interest me. Can we find another one for which I'm better suited?	If you want me to take that assignment, okay. I'll do it.

Communication Highlight

Responding to Anger in the Workplace

What should you do if you are the target of anger from a co-worker or supervisor? In his book *Anger at Work*, Dr. Hendrie Weisinger (1996) suggests two ways to respond.

First, try to defuse the conflict by improving the climate. Use your communication to relax the angry person and to foster a more relaxed, cooperative climate. For instance, you might offer the person a glass of water or invite the person to sit down and talk. Another strategy is to suggest a "time out"—tell the person that you want to discuss the issue but need 10 minutes to return a call or finish a report. It may also help to move to a different environment, out of the office or room where the conflict erupted. Strategies such as these interrupt the angry moment and the other person's tendencies to attack.

Second, says Dr. Weisinger, listen mindfully to the other person. Although this is difficult when someone seems to be attacking you, listening is a key way to acknowledge

and affirm the other person. Make a sincere effort to understand what she or he is angry about. Don't interrupt when she or he is talking: Interruptions communicate that you are more interested in what you have to say than what the other person has to say. Also, avoid mind reading. Let the other person talk, concentrate on understanding her or his perspective, acknowledge what the other person says, and look for points of agreement. Only then should you think about responding with questions, paraphrases, and expressions of your own point of view.

 To learn more about the problems of anger in the workplace and ways to manage it, visit the website of the Centre for Conflict Resolution International at http://www.conflictatwork.com. On that site, you can take an interactive quiz to assess your own style of managing conflict.

We can tolerate sometimes not getting what we want as long as we don't feel personally devalued. However, it is disconfirming when our needs and our worth are not acknowledged. Even when people disagree or have conflicting needs, each person can state his or her feelings and express awareness of the other's perspective. Usually, there are ways to acknowledge both viewpoints, as Dan's comments illustrate.

–Dan–

My supervisor did an excellent job of letting me know I was valued even when I got passed over for a promotion last year. I'd worked hard and felt I had earned it. Jake, my supervisor, came to my office to talk to me before the promotion was announced. He told me that both I and the other guy were qualified, but that the other person had seniority and also field experience I didn't have. Then Jake told me he was assigning me to a field position for 6 months so that I could get the experience I needed to get promoted the next time a position opened up. Jake communicated that he understood how I felt and that he was supporting me even if I didn't get the promotion. His talk made all the difference in how I felt about staying with the company.

Self-disclose When Appropriate

As we noted earlier, self-disclosure allows people to know each other in greater depth. For this reason, it's an important communication skill, especially in the early stages of relationships. Research indicates that appropriate self-disclosure tends to increase trust and feelings of closeness (Cosby, 1973; Dindia, 2000; Meeks, Hendrick, & Hendrick, 1998). In addition, self-disclosure can enhance self-esteem and security in relationships because we feel that others accept our most private selves. Finally, self-disclosure is an important way to learn about ourselves. As we reveal our hopes, fears, dreams, and feelings, we get responses from others that give us new perspectives on who we are. In addition, we gain insight into ourselves by seeing how we interact with others in new situations.

Although self-disclosure has many potential values, it's wise to be cautious about when and to whom we reveal ourselves. As we have seen, self-disclosures necessarily involve risk—the risk that others will not accept private information or that they might use it against us (Petronio, 2000). Appropriate self-disclosure minimizes these risks by proceeding slowly and establishing trust. It's wise to test the waters gradually before plunging into major self-disclosures. Begin by revealing information that is personal but not highly intimate or able to damage you if exploited. Before disclosing further, observe how the other person responds to your communication and what she or he does with it. You might also pay attention to whether the other person reciprocates by disclosing personal information to you.

Respect Diversity in Relationships

Just as individuals differ, so do relationships. There is tremendous variety in what people find comfortable, affirming, and satisfying in interpersonal interaction. You may have one friend who enjoys a lot of verbal disclosure and another who prefers less. There's no need to try to persuade the first friend to disclose less or the second one to be more revealing. Similarly, you may be comfortable with greater closeness in some of your relationships and more autonomy in others. The differences between people create a rich variety of relationships.

Research indicates that people vary in how they create closeness with others. Most of us enjoy talking intimately with close friends and romantic partners, and most of us enjoy doing things with and for people we care about. However, research suggests that people differ somewhat in the emphasis they place on talk and activity. Some people—usually women rather than men—rely primarily on talking to create closeness with others. This is called **closeness in dialogue.** Other people—usually men rather than women—see doing things with and for others as a primary (but not the only) means of creating closeness (Clark & Delia, 1997; Inman, 1996; Johnson, 1996, 2000; Wood & Inman, 1993). This mode is called **closeness in the doing.** The two ways of expressing and experiencing closeness are different but not necessarily of different value. Most of us engage in and appreciate both modes, although we may differ in how much of each we prefer.

Because people and relationships are diverse, we should strive to respect a range of communicative choices and relationship patterns. In addition, we should be cautious about interpreting others' communication through our own perspectives. People from distinct cultures and social communities have learned different communication styles. What Westerners consider openness and healthy self-disclosure may feel offensive and intrusive to people

Men often prefer a side-by-side style of friendship in which closeness is expressed through doing things together, such as fishing.

© IPA/The Image Works

from some Asian societies. To improve your understanding of others, ask them what they mean by certain behaviors. This conveys the relational message that they matter to you, and it allows you to gain insight into the interesting differences between us.

CASE STUDY: Cloudy Climate

The conversation scripted here is featured as a multimedia scenario on the *Communication in Our Lives* CD-ROM included with this book. Once you've launched the CD, click on the "Communication Scenarios" icon, and, from the Scenarios Menu, select "Cloudy Climate" to watch the video. Improve your own communication skills by reading, watching, listening to, critiquing, and analyzing this communication encounter.

Jason Harris/© 2001 Wadsworth

Analyze the scenario by applying the principles covered in this chapter, and respond to the prompts that accompany the video, which you can access by clicking on "Analysis." After completing the conversation analysis and answering the questions, you can click on the "Done" button to compare your responses with the ones I suggest. Additional analysis questions are available in print at the end of this chapter and on the book's website.

Andy and Martha married 5 years ago when both completed graduate school. Last week, Andy got the job offer of his dreams—with one problem: He would have to move 1,500 miles away. Martha loves her current job and has no interest in moving or in living apart. Andy sees this job as one that could really advance his career. For the past week they have talked and argued continually about the job offer. Tonight, while they are preparing dinner in their kitchen, they have returned to the topic once again. We join them midway through their discussion, just as it is heating up.

ANDY: So, today I was checking on the costs for flights from here to Seattle. If we plan ahead for visits, we can get round-trip flights for around $300.00. That's not too bad.

MARTHA: While you're thinking about finances, you might consider renting a second apartment out there. We agreed last night that it would be too expensive to live apart.

ANDY: I never agreed to that. Martha, can't you understand how important this job is to my career?

MARTHA: And what about our marriage? I suppose that's not important?

ANDY: [He grabs a knife and begins cutting an onion] I never said that! If you'd pull with me on this, our marriage would be fine. You're just not . . .

MARTHA: [She slams a pot on the stove.] Not what? Not willing to be the traditional supportive wife, I assume.

ANDY: [He grimaces, puts down the knife, and turns to face Martha.] That isn't what I was going to say. I never asked you to be a traditional wife or to be anything other than who you are, but I want you to let me be myself too.

MARTHA: If you want to be yourself, then why did you get married? Marriage is about more than just yourself—it's about both of us and what's good for the two of us. You're not thinking of us at all.

ANDY: And I suppose you are? You're only thinking about what you want. You don't seem to give a darn what I want. You're being incredibly selfish.

MARTHA: [She slams her hand against the counter and shouts.] Selfish?! I'm selfish to care about our marriage?

ANDY: You're using that to manipulate me as if I don't care about the marriage and you do. If you really cared about it, maybe you'd consider moving to Seattle so we could be together.

MARTHA: [She raises her eyebrows and speaks in a sarcastic tone.] And just a minute ago you said you weren't asking me to be a traditional wife. Now you want me to be the trailing spouse so you can do what you please. Dandy!

ANDY: I didn't say that. You're putting words in my mouth. What I said was . . .

MARTHA: What you said was I should move to Seattle and support whatever it is you want to do.

ANDY: [He slams the knife into the cutting board.] I did not say that. Quit telling me what I said! [He takes a deep breath, lowers his voice, then continues.] Look, Martha, can we just step back from this argument and try to look at the options with a fresh eye?

MARTHA: I've looked all I want to look. I've heard all I want to hear. You know where I stand on this, and you know I'm right, even if you don't want to admit it.

Chapter Summary

In this chapter, we've explored self-disclosure and climates as foundations of interpersonal communication. A basic requirement for healthy communication climates is confirmation. Each of us wants to feel valued, especially by those for whom we care most deeply. When partners recognize, acknowledge, and endorse each other, they communicate, "You matter to me." Confirmation is also fostered by communication that fosters supportive climates and discourages defensive ones. Defensiveness is fueled by evaluation, certainty, superiority, strategies, control, and neutrality. More supportive climates arise from communication that is descriptive, provisional, equal, spontaneous, empathic, and problem oriented.

The communication skills that confirm others and build supportive climates also help us manage conflict constructively so that it enriches, rather than harms, relationships. By creating affirming, healthy climates, we establish foundations that allow us to deal with tensions openly and to communicate in ways that enhance the likelihood that we can resolve differences or find ways of accepting them with grace.

We closed the chapter by discussing five guidelines for building healthy communication climates. The first one is to use communication to create healthy climates. Second, we should accept and confirm others, communicating that we respect them, even though we may not always agree with them or feel the same as they do. The third guideline is a companion to the second one: We should accept and assert ourselves. A fourth guideline is to self-disclose when appropriate so that we increase our security in relationships and so that we add to the information we have about ourselves and others.

Finally, embracing diversity in relationships is a source of personal and interpersonal growth. People vary widely, as do the relationship patterns and forms they prefer. By respecting differences between us, we expand our insights into the fascinating range of ways in which humans form and sustain relationships. In Chapter 9, we'll continue thinking about interpersonal communication by exploring how it influences friendships and romantic relationships.

 ## Communication in Our Lives ONLINE

In addition to presenting the case studies' multimedia scenarios, the *Communication in Our Lives* CD-ROM provides quick access to the *Communication in Our Lives* website and InfoTrac College Edition. The website is online at http://communication .wadsworth.com/woodciol4, but you can only access this book's premium web content when you link to the site directly through the book's CD.

 The *Communication in Our Lives* website features interactive tools for learning and reviewing the chapter's concepts and key terms, including electronic versions of the "For Further Reflection and Discussion" questions following and a review quiz.

 The website also provides updated web links and additional InfoTrac College Edition activities. If required, you can e-mail completed chapter activities or the quizzes to your instructor.

Key Concepts

acknowledgment, *206*	covert conflict, *214*	recognition, *206*
closeness in dialogue, *222*	endorsement, *207*	self-disclosure, *202*
closeness in the doing, *222*	interpersonal climate, *201*	stonewalling, *217*
conflict, *214*	overt conflict, *214*	

For Further Reflection and Discussion

1. Develop ethical guidelines for building confirming, supportive climates in one relationship in your life. It might be a personal relationship or a workplace relationship. Identify the ethical values that communication should serve to build and maintain a healthy climate.

2. Use your InfoTrac College Edition to read Christine Kemp-Longmore's 2000 article "Conflict Resolution in the Workplace." What communication skills does she identify as important to effective resolution of conflict in the workplace? To what extent are her recommendations consistent with information and advice in this chapter?

3. Using the six categories for defensive and supportive styles of communication, describe communication in a place where you have worked or currently work. Do the categories allow you to analyze why that workplace feels supportive or defensive?

4. How often do you rely on exit, voice, loyalty, and neglect styles when responding to conflict or tension in relationships? What does your response style achieve and prevent?

Experiencing Communication in Our Lives

Questions for Analysis and Discussion

Review the video of the scenario entitled "Cloudy Climate" that you watched when completing this chapter's case study (pages 223–224), or, if you haven't seen it yet, watch it for the first time. If you didn't previously finish the analysis questions included on the CD-ROM, do so now, and then respond to the questions below, which are also available on the book's website under "Activities for Chapter 8."

1. Identify examples of mind reading, and describe their impact on Martha and Andy's discussion.

2. Identify communication that fosters a defensive interpersonal climate.

3. To what extent do you think Andy and Martha feel listened to by the other?

4. Do you perceive any relational-level meanings that aren't being addressed in this conversation?

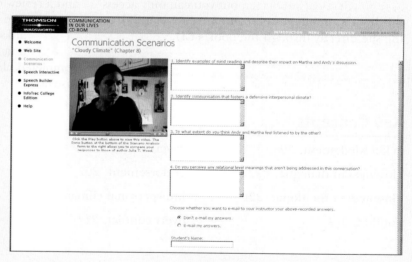

CHAPTER 9

Communication in Personal Relationships

Focus Questions

1. How do friendships and romantic relationships typically develop?

2. How do couples handle their competing needs for time together and independence?

3. What communication strategies help people maintain long-distance relationships?

4. What is the *cycle of abuse*?

I t's been a rough semester. You're not doing well in your classes, and you're having trouble balancing work and school. You feel overwhelmed by all of it. Then, you talk to your best friend about your problems. She listens and sympathizes with all the stress you feel. Even though you haven't solved your troubles, you feel better because you've shared your feelings with someone who cares about you.

Your partner graduated last term and took a job 500 miles away. You call and e-mail a lot, but that's no substitute for seeing each other every day. After 8 weeks apart, you're finally together for a long weekend. Just being together makes you feel more complete and happier. You can't imagine not having this person in your life.

How would your life be different if you had no close relationships? If you're like most people, a great deal would be missing. We need people we care about and who care about us. You have many relationships, but only a few are close, or intimate. Your relationships with co-workers, other students, cashiers at stores where you frequently shop, and people who live near you are **social relationships.** This chapter builds on what we learned in Chapter 8 by focusing on communication in two special types of personal relationships: friendships and romantic relationships. To launch the discussion, we'll define personal relationships. Next, we'll consider how communication guides the development of friendships and romances over time. Finally, we'll examine some of the special challenges for personal relationships in our era.

Defining Personal Relationships

Personal relationships are unique commitments between irreplaceable individuals who are influenced by rules, relational dialectics, and surrounding contexts. We'll discuss each part of this definition.

Uniqueness

Most of our relationships are social, not personal. In social relationships, participants adhere to social roles rather than interacting as unique individuals. For instance, you might exchange class notes with a classmate, play racquetball each week with another person, and talk about politics with a neighbor. In each case, the other person could be replaced by someone else taking the same role. The value of social relationships lies more in what participants do than in who they are, because a variety of people could fulfill the same functions.

In personal relationships, however, the particular people—who they are and what they think, feel, and do—define the value of the connection. I'm not committed to marriage in the abstract, but I am deeply committed to a particular man named Robbie and the unique ways in which we have fitted ourselves together. Nobody else could replace him. When one person in a personal relationship leaves the relationship or dies, that relationship ends. We may later have other intimates, but a new romantic partner or best friend will not replace the former one.

Commitment

For most of us, passion is what first springs to mind when we think about romantic intimacy. **Passion** involves intensely positive feelings and desires for another person. The sparks and the emotional high of being in love or discovering a new friend stem from passion. It's why we feel "butterflies in the stomach" and fall "head over heels." Despite its excitement, passion isn't the primary building block of enduring relationships.

Passion is a feeling based on the rewards of involvement with a person. **Commitment,** in contrast, is a decision to remain in a relationship. The hallmark of commitment is the intention to share the future. Committed friends and romantic partners assume they will stay together. Because a committed relationship assumes a future, partners are unlikely to bail out if the going gets rough. Instead, they weather bad times (Lund, 1985; Wood, 2000). Commitment is a decision to stay together in spite of trouble, disappointments, sporadic boredom, restlessness, and lulls in passion.

Commitment grows out of **investments,** that which we put into relationships that we could not retrieve if the relationship were to end. When we care about another person, we invest material things, such as money and possessions. Even more important, we invest time, energy, thought, and feelings. In doing this, we invest *ourselves.* We can't get back the feelings and energy and material investments; we can't recover history shared with another. For good or ill, investments bind us to relationships.

In personal relationships, partners invest themselves.

 To extend your understanding of the distinction between love and commitment, complete Activity 9.1, "Distinguishing Between Love and Commitment," in your *Student Companion* or online under "Activities for Chapter 9" at the *Communication in Our Lives* website.

Relationship Rules

All relationships have **rules** that guide how partners communicate and interpret each other's communication. As in other contexts, relationship rules define what is expected, what is not allowed, and when and how to do various things. Typically, relationship rules are unspoken understandings between partners. As you may recall from our discussion in Chapter 5, two kinds of rules guide our communication. Constitutive rules define the meaning of various types of communication in personal relationships. For instance, women friends often count listening to problems as demonstrating care, whereas many men are more likely to count hanging out and doing things together as showing care (Tavris, 1992; Wood, 1998, 2005). Friends work out a number of constitutive rules to define what kinds of communication count as loyalty, support, rudeness, love, joking, acceptance, and so forth.

Regulative rules influence interaction by specifying when and with whom to engage in various kinds of communication. For example, friends often have a regulative rule that says it's okay to criticize each other in private but not okay to do so in front of others. Many men regard interrupting as a normal part of conversation between friends, whereas women sometimes interpret interruptions as rude (Tannen, 1990; Wood, 1998, 2005). Some romantic partners limit physical displays of affection to private settings.

Friends and romantic partners develop rules for what they want and expect of each other, as well as rules for what will not be tolerated (Argyle & Henderson, 1984). For example, you would probably consider it a betrayal if your best friend dated your romantic partner, and you would end one or both relationships. On the other hand, not interrupting may be a rule, but breaking it probably won't destroy a good friendship.

Affected by Contexts

Personal relationships are not isolated from the social world. Instead, the surroundings of relationships influence interaction between partners (Klein & Milardo, 2000). Friendships and romances are affected by neighborhoods, social circles, family units, and society as a whole. For instance, Western culture values marriage, which means that men and women who marry generally receive more social support than do cohabiting partners or gay and lesbian couples (Strasser, 1997). Our families of origin shaped what we look for in intimates—the importance we place on social status, faith, intelligence, and so on. Our social circles establish norms for activities such as drinking, involvement with community groups, studying, and partying. In many ways, families, friends, and society shape the rules we form in our relationships.

−Kaya−

I had never drunk much until I started going out with Steve. He was 10 years older than me. We usually spent time with his friends, who were also older and in business. All of them drank—not like a whole lot or anything, but several drinks a night. Pretty soon, I was doing that too—it was just part of the relationship with Steve.

Personal and social contexts affect relationships in other ways. Families may voice approval or disapproval of our choices of intimates or of how we run our private relationships. Technological advances and mobility make long-distance relationships more possible today than they were in earlier times. The increasing number of people involved in dual-career relationships is revising expectations about each partner's participation in earning income, homemaking, and child care. As our society becomes more diverse, interracial and interethnic relationships are more common and more socially accepted. Thus, both our social circles and the larger society are contexts that affect the kinds of relationships we form and the ways we communicate within them.

Relational Dialectics

A final feature of personal relationships is **relational dialectics**—the opposing and continual tensions that are normal in personal relationships. Scholars have identified three relational dialectics (Baxter, 1990, 1993; Baxter & Montgomery, 1996; Erbert, 2000).

Autonomy/Connection   Intimates experience tension between wanting autonomy and wanting connection. Because we want to be deeply linked to intimates, we cherish time with them and the sharing of experiences, thoughts, and feelings. At the same time, each of us needs some independence. We don't want our individuality to be swallowed up by relationships, so we seek some privacy and distance, even from the people we love most.

In most close relationships there is frequent—sometimes continuous—friction arising from the contradictory impulses for autonomy and connection (Beck, 1988; Erbert, 2000; Scarf, 1987). Friends and romantic partners may vacation together and be with each other almost all the time for a week or more. Yet the intense closeness leads them to crave time apart once they return home. Both autonomy and closeness are natural human needs. The challenge is to preserve individuality while also creating intimacy.

–Stanley–

For a long time, I've been stressed about my feelings. Sometimes I can't get enough of Annie, and then I feel crowded and don't want to see her at all. I never understood these switches, and I was afraid I was unstable or something. Now I see that I'm pretty normal after all.

Novelty/Predictability   The second dialectic is a tension between wanting familiar routines and wanting novelty. We like a certain amount of routine to provide security and predictability to our lives. Friends often have standard times to get together, and they develop preferred interaction rituals. Romantic couples develop preferred times and places for going out, and they establish patterns for interacting. Yet too much routine is boring, so friends occasionally explore a new restaurant, and romantic couples periodically do something spontaneous and different to introduce variety into their customary routines.

Openness/Closedness The third dialectic is tension between the desire for openness and the desire for privacy. Although intimate relationships sometimes are idealized as totally open and honest, in reality complete openness would be intolerable (Baxter, 1993; Petronio, 1991, 2000). We want to share our inner selves with our intimates, yet there are times when we don't feel like sharing and topics that we don't want to talk about. All of us need some privacy, and our partners need to respect that. Wanting some privacy doesn't mean that the relationship is in trouble. It means only that we need both openness and closedness in our lives.

Sharpen Your Skill

Understanding Dialectics in Your Relationships

Trace the presence of the three dialectics in a close relationship of your own. How do you ensure enough of both autonomy and connection, openness and privacy, and novelty and predictability? What happens when you feel too much or too little fulfillment of any of these six human needs?

  To extend this exercise, complete Activity 9.3, "Recognizing Relational Dialectics," in your *Student Companion* or online under "Activities for Chapter 9" at the *Communication in Our Lives* website.

Managing Dialectics Leslie Baxter (1990) identifies four ways intimates deal with dialectical tensions. One response, called **neutralization,** negotiates a balance between dialectical needs. This involves striking a compromise in which both needs are met to an extent but neither is fully satisfied. A couple might agree to be somewhat open but not intensely so. The **separation** response favors one need in a dialectic and ignores the other. For example, friends might agree to make novelty a priority and suppress their needs for routine. Separation also occurs when partners cycle between dialectical poles to favor each pole alternately. For example, a couple could spend weekends together and have little contact during the week.

A third way to manage dialectics is **segmentation,** in which partners assign each need to certain spheres, issues, activities, or times. For instance, friends might be open about many topics but respect each other's privacy and not pry into one or two areas. Romantic partners might be autonomous in their professional activities yet very connected in their interaction in the home and their involvement with their children.

—Marianne—

Bart and I used to be spontaneous all the time. There was always room for something unexpected and unplanned. That changed when we had the twins last year. Now our home life is totally regulated, planned to the last nanosecond. If we get off schedule in getting the boys dressed and fed in the morning, then we're late getting to day care, which means we have to talk with the supervisor there, and then we're late getting to work. We try to have some spontaneity times when Bart's folks take the boys for a weekend, but it's a lot harder now that the boys are in our life.

The final method of dealing with dialectics is **reframing.** This is a complex strategy that redefines apparently contradictory needs as not really in opposition. My colleagues and I found examples of reframing in a study of romantic partners (Wood et al., 1994). Some of the couples said that their autonomy enhanced closeness because knowing they were separate in some ways allowed them to feel safer being connected. Instead of viewing autonomy and closeness as opposing, these partners transcended the apparent tension between the two to define the needs as mutually enhancing.

Research suggests that separation by fulfilling one need and squelching the other is generally the least satisfying response to dialectical tensions (Baxter, 1990). Repressing any natural human impulse diminishes us. The challenge is to find ways to honor and satisfy the variety of needs that humans have. Understanding that dialectics are natural and constructive allows us to accept and grow from the tensions they generate.

The Evolutionary Course of Personal Relationships

Each relationship develops at its own pace and in unique ways. Yet there are commonalities in the evolutionary course of most friendships and romances. We'll explore prototypical patterns for the evolution of personal relationships.

© Laurence Monneret/Getty Images/Stone

Partners in enduring, intimate relationships accept dialectics as natural and create constructive ways to respond to them.

Friendships

Although friendships sometimes jump to life quickly, usually they unfold through a series of stages. Bill Rawlins (1981, 1994), an interpersonal communication researcher, developed a six-stage model of how friendships develop (Figure 9.1).

Role-limited Interaction Friendships begin with an encounter. We might meet a new person at work, through membership on an athletic team or club, or by chance in an airport, restaurant, or class. During initial encounters, we rely on standard social rules and roles. We tend to be polite and careful about what we disclose, and we are keenly alert to signs that interest in a relationship is not mutual (Snapp & Leary, 2001). One exception to this generalization is electronically conducted relationships, in which people often venture into more personal, disclosive communication in the early stages of acquaintance. Willingness to take some risks early in relationships may be greater when people aren't interacting face to face.

—Lewis—

I met Stan over the Internet. We were both in the same chat room, and it was like we were on the same wavelength, so we started e-mailing each other privately. After a couple of months, it was like I knew Stan better than any of my close friends here, and he knew me too—inside and out. It seemed safer or easier to open up online than in person. Maybe that's why we got so close so fast.

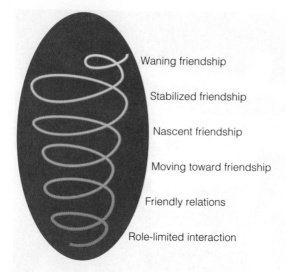

Figure 9.1
Stages of Friendship

Waning friendship

Stabilized friendship

Nascent friendship

Moving toward friendship

Friendly relations

Role-limited interaction

Friendly Relations   The second stage of friendship is friendly relations, in which each person checks the other out to see whether common ground and interests exist. Communication during this stage allows people not only to discover whether they have shared interests but also whether they have similar or compatible perspectives on life and ways of interacting (Weinstock & Bond, 2000). Riddick tells Jason that he really likes adventure movies. If Jason says he does too, then they've found a shared interest. A businessperson talks to an associate about running to find out whether the associate is also a runner and might want to set up a running schedule. Although friendly exchanges are not dramatic, they are important in allowing us to explore the potential for a deeper relationship with another person.

Moving toward Friendship   Moving toward friendship involves stepping beyond social roles. To signal that we're interested in being friends, we could introduce a more personal topic than we've discussed so far. We also move toward friendship when we set up times to get together. Maria might ask Raul to go to lunch after class. Sometimes we involve others to lessen the potential awkwardness of being with someone we don't yet know well. For instance, you might invite a new acquaintance to a party where others will be present. People who have gotten to know each other over the Internet may decide to meet in person. As people interact more personally, they begin to form a foundation for friendship.

Nascent Friendship   During the stage of nascent friendship, people may begin to think of themselves as friends or as becoming friends. At this point, social norms and roles become less important, and friends begin to work out their own private ways of relating. When my friend Sue and I were in graduate school, we developed a ritual of calling each day between 5 and 6 o'clock to catch up while we cooked our dinners. Some friends settle into patterns of getting together for specific things (watching games, discussing books, walking, playing bridge). Other friends share a wider range of times and activities. The milestones of this stage are that people begin to think of themselves as friends and to work out private roles and

rules. Thus, interaction between nascent friends establishes basic patterns and climate for the friendship.

Stabilized Friendship   When friends feel established in each other's lives, friendship stabilizes. The benchmarks of this stage are the assumptions of continuity and trust. Whereas in earlier stages the friends didn't count on getting together unless they made a specific plan, stabilized friends assume they'll keep seeing each other. They no longer have to ask whether they'll get together, because they are committed to continuing the relationship. Stabilized friends communicate their assumption of ongoing closeness by asking, "Where do you want to have lunch this Friday?" instead of, "Do you want to have lunch on Friday?" The former question assumes they will see each other.

Stabilized friends also have developed considerable trust based on disclosing private information and responding with acceptance. In turn, they feel safe sharing even more intimate information and revealing vulnerabilities they normally conceal from others. As trust and knowledge of each other expands, friends become more deeply woven into each other's life. Stabilized friendships may continue indefinitely, in some cases lasting a lifetime.

 To identify how key features of personal relationships apply to your friendships, complete Activity 9.4, "Features of Friendships," in your *Student Companion* or online under "Activities for Chapter 9" at the *Communication in Our Lives* website.

Waning Friendship   Friendship withers when one or both people cease to be committed to it. Sometimes, friends drift apart because each is pulled in a different direction by personal or career demands. In other cases, friendships deteriorate because they've become boring. Breaking relationship rules can also end friendships. Telling a friend's secrets to a third person or being dishonest may violate the rules of the friendship.

When friendships deteriorate, communication changes in predictable ways. Defensiveness and uncertainty rise, causing people to be more guarded and less open. Communication may also become more strategic as people try to protect themselves from further exposure and hurt. Even when serious violations occur between friends, relationships can sometimes be repaired. For this to happen, both friends must be committed to rebuilding trust and talking openly about their feelings and needs.

Sharpen Your Skill

Faded Friendships

Remember three friendships that were once very close but have faded away. Describe the reasons they ended. How did boredom, differences, external circumstances, or violations contribute to the decay of the friendships? How did communication patterns change as the friendships waned?

 Extend this exercise by completing Activity 9.7, "Why Friendships Wane," in your *Student Companion* or online under "Activities for Chapter 9" at the *Communication in Our Lives* website.

Romantic Relationships

Like friendships, romances also have a typical—but not a universal—evolutionary path. For most of us, romance progresses through the stages of escalation, navigation, and deterioration. Within these three broad stages are a number of more specific moments.

Escalation Six stages of interaction progressively move two people toward the point of commitment. At any point in this process, one or both people may decide to end the relationship. In the first stage, we aren't interacting. We are **individuals** who are aware of ourselves as such, with particular needs, goals, experiences, and qualities that affect what we look for in others and relationships. Before forming romantic relationships, we also have learned a number of constitutive and regulative communication rules that affect how we interact with others and how we interpret their communication (Bachen & Illouz, 1996).

The second stage is **invitational communication,** in which people express interest in interacting. This stage involves both making invitations to others and responding to invitations they make to us. "Want to dance?" "Where are you from?" "Hi, my name's Shelby," and "Did you just start working here?" are examples of invitations to interact. Invitational communication usually follows a conventional script for social conversation. The meaning of invitational communication is found on the relational level, not the content level, of meaning. "Want to dance?" literally means that a person is inviting you to dance. On the relational level of meaning, however, the message is "I'm available and possibly interested. Are you?"

Out of all the people we meet, we are attracted romantically to only a few. The three greatest influences on initial attraction are self-concept, proximity, and similarity. Our self-concept affects our choices of candidates for romance. How we define our sexual orientation, for example, is a primary influence on our consideration of potential romantic partners, as are race and social class. The myth that the United States is color blind and classless is disproven by the fact that most people pair with others of their race and social class. In fact, social prestige influences dating patterns now more than it did in the 1950s (Whitbeck & Hoyt, 1994).

In addition to self-concept, proximity influences initial attraction. We can interact only with people we meet, whether in person or in cyberspace. Social and economic class affect whom we meet. For example, people in lower economic strata are less likely to use the Internet, so they have less opportunity to meet people and develop relationships online (Flanagin, Farinola, & Metzger, 2000). Consequently, where we live, work, and socialize, as well as the electronic networks in which we participate, constrain the possibilities for relationships. This reminds us that communication is systemic, a principle we noted in Chapter 1. Some contexts, such as college campuses, promote meeting potential romantic partners, whereas other contexts are less conducive to meeting and dating. Specialized electronic networks and web pages are set up for people who want to talk about particular topics, develop friendships, or meet potential romantic partners. Each year, 61% of American singles look for a date on the Internet (Fagan, 2001; Fein & Schneider, 2002), and some people who meet online have long term romances or marry (Clement & McLean, 2000).

Similarity is also important in romantic relationships. Most of us are attracted to people whose values, attitudes, and lifestyles are similar to ours. Similarity of personality is also linked to long-term marital happiness (Caspi & Harbener, 1990). In general, people also tend to match themselves with others who are about as physically attractive as they are. We may fantasize about relationships with movie stars and devastatingly attractive people, but when reality settles in, we're likely to pass them by for someone who is about as attractive as we are. In general, we seek romantic partners who are similar to us in many respects. To enhance attractiveness, similarities between people must be recognized and communicated (Duck, 1994a, 1994b). In other words, attraction grows when people discuss common feelings, experiences, values, beliefs, and goals.

 To learn more about bases of attraction in romantic relationships, complete Activity 9.9, "Let's Get Personal," in your *Student Companion* or online under "Activities for Chapter 9" at the *Communication in Our Lives* website.

Explorational communication is a stage in which we explore the possibilities for a relationship. We communicate to announce our identities and to learn about others. As in the early stages of friendship, potential romantic partners fish for common interests: "Do you like jazz?" "What's your family like?" "Do you follow politics?" As we continue to interact with others, both breadth and depth of information increase. Self-disclosure tends to escalate intimacy (Berger & Bell, 1988) because we perceive it as a sign of trust. During escalation, reciprocity of disclosure is expected so that neither person is more vulnerable than the other (Duck, 1982; Miell & Duck, 1986).

If early interaction increases attraction, then we may escalate the relationship. **Intensifying communication** increases the depth of a relationship by increasing the amount and intimacy of interaction. My students nicknamed this stage "euphoria" to emphasize the intensity and happiness it typically embodies. During this phase, partners spend more and more time together, and they rely less on external structures such as movies or parties. Instead, they immerse themselves in the budding relationship and may feel they can't be together enough. Additional and more personal disclosures are exchanged, and partners increasingly learn how the other feels and thinks.

Sharpen Your Skill

Private Language

What are the special words and nonverbal codes in a close relationship of yours? Do you have a way to signal each other when you're bored at a party and ready to leave? Do you use nicknames and private words? Would you feel any loss if you had no private language in your relationship?

The intensifying stage often involves idealizing and personalized communication. Idealizing occurs when we see a relationship and a partner as more wonderful, exciting, and perfect than they really are (Hendrick & Hendrick, 1988). During euphoria, partners often exaggerate each other's virtues, downplay or don't notice vices, and overlook problems in the relationship. It is also during euphoria that partners begin to develop relationship vocabularies that include nicknames and private codes. Just as private language within a group increases cohesiveness (Bolman & Deal, 1992; Fisher, 2000), private language between intimates increases the sense of "we-ness," or pair identity. Sometimes Robbie and I greet each other by saying, *"Namaste."* This is a Nepalese greeting that expresses good will. Saying it reminds us of our trek in the mountains of Nepal. Private language heightens partners' sense of being a special couple. Partners make up words and nicknames for each other, and they develop ways to send private messages in public settings. Private language not only reflects intimacy but also enhances it ("Public Pillow Talk," 1987).

Revising communication, although not part of escalation in all romantic relationships, occurs often enough to merit our consideration. During this stage, partners come down out of the clouds to talk about their relationship's strengths, problems, and potential for the future. With the rush of euphoria over, partners consider whether they want the relationship to be permanent or at least extended. If so, they work through problems and obstacles to long-term viability. In same-sex relationships, partners often have to resolve differences about openness regarding their sexual orientations. Couples may also need to work out differences in religions and conflicts in locations and career goals.

–Kyle–

When Todd and I got together, I knew he was the one for me—the man I wanted to spend the rest of my life with. But we had a huge problem. He is totally out, and I'm not. If I came out at my job, I'd be off the fast track immediately, and I'd probably be fired. It was a huge issue between us because he wanted me to be as out as he is—like to take him with me to the holiday parties at my company. I can't do that. It's still a real tension between us.

As you might expect, during this phase of romance, communication often involves negotiation and even conflict. Issues that weren't problems in a dating relationship may have to be resolved if partners are to commit to a long-term future. Many couples are able to revise their relationships in ways that make the long term possible. Other couples find they cannot resolve problems. It is entirely possible to love a person with whom we don't want to share our life.

Communication Highlight

Mixed Matches

Although similarity clearly is a major influence on romantic attraction, it isn't the whole story. As society becomes more ethnically diverse, people of different races and cultural heritages are finding each other and building relationships together (Crohn, 1995; Dicks, 1993; Moran, 2001; Schmitt, 2001b).

To create enduring and satisfying relationships, people with different cultural backgrounds need to understand each other and work out accommodations. An American man who married an Italian woman reports that his greatest difficulty was adjusting to the closeness of Italian families. A German woman and Portuguese man found it difficult to establish a mutually acceptable level of emotional expressiveness. In Mediterranean cultures, free and often dramatic expression of feelings is normal, but German culture emphasizes greater emotional restraint. An American woman who married a Turkish man was astonished by his and his family's expectations that women should be highly deferential and cater to husbands and in-laws.

Commitment is a decision to stay with a relationship permanently. This decision transforms a romantic relationship from one based on past and present experiences and feelings into one with a future. Before making a commitment, partners don't view the relationship as continuing forever. With commitment, the relationship becomes a given around which they arrange other aspects of their lives. This stage is analogous to stabilized friendship because the basis of both is assumed continuity.

Romantic relationships escalate for different reasons and with different effects (Surra, Arizzi, & Amussen, 1988). Some relationships are driven by external events and circumstances that push a couple toward commitment. Timing, approval from friends and family, good jobs, and so forth are events that can drive relationships forward. Other relationships seem to be driven by factors internal to the relationship. Trust, compatibility, history, shared values, and self-disclosure are examples of relationship factors that can drive romance forward. Long-term satisfaction with marriage is more positively associated with relationship-driven commitments than with event-driven ones. Here are examples of both escalation processes.

Bizarro

GROK LOOK AT CHONK, GROK FEEL DIZZY. GROK WANT CHONK STAY AT GROK'S CAVE ALWAYS. HERE PRETTY ROCK.

ORIGIN OF THE WEDDING RING

© Dan Piraro. Reprinted with permission of King Features Syndicate.

Emeka and Fred met and started dating in their senior year of college. Both families supported the relationship, and Emeka and Fred felt it was time to settle down. They married a month after graduation but separated a year later.

Tyrone and Ella dated for 3 years. By the time they walked down the aisle, they knew each other well, they shared the same values and faith, and they had developed trust. Three years later, they are very satisfied with the marriage.

Navigation   Navigation is the ongoing process of communicating to sustain intimacy over time and in the face of changes in oneself and one's partner, the relationship, and surrounding contexts. Although navigation can be an extended stage in romantic intimacy, it is not stable but very dynamic (Canary & Dainton, 2003). Couples continuously work through new problems, revisit old ones, and accommodate changes in their individual and joint lives. To use an automotive analogy, navigation involves both preventive maintenance and periodic repairs (Canary & Stafford, 1994). Navigating communication aims to keep intimacy satisfying and healthy and to deal with any problems and tensions that arise (Harvey & Wenzel, 2001).

The nucleus of intimacy is **relational culture,** a private world of rules, understandings, meanings, and patterns of interacting that partners create for their relationship (Wood, 1982). Relational culture includes how a couple manages relational dialectics. Mei-Ling and Gregory may do a great many things together, whereas Lana and Kaya emphasize autonomy. Brent and Carmella may be open and expressive, whereas Marion and Senona prefer more privacy. There aren't right and wrong ways to manage dialectics, because individuals and couples differ in what they need. The unique character of each relationship culture reflects how partners deal with tensions

"How do I love thee? Let me count the ways." In opening one of her best-known poems with these lines, Elizabeth Barrett Browning foresaw what social scientists would later discover: There are many ways of loving (Swidler, 2001). Just as people differ in their tastes in food and styles of dress, we differ in how we love. Researchers have identified six different styles of loving, each of which is valid in its own right, although not all styles are compatible with one another (Hendrick & Hendrick, 1996; Hendrick et al., 1984; Lee, 1973, 1988). See whether you can identify your style of loving in the descriptions below.

**Figure 9.2
The Colors
of Love**

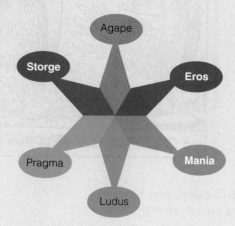

Eros is a style of loving that is passionate, intense, and fast moving. Not confined to sexual passion, eros may be expressed in spiritual, intellectual, or emotional ways.

Storge (pronounced "store-gay") is a comfortable, best-friends kind of love that grows gradually to create a stable and even-keeled companionship.

Ludus is a playful, sometimes manipulative style of loving. For ludic lovers, love is a challenge, a puzzle, a game to be relished but not one to lead to commitment.

Mania is a style of loving marked by emotional extremes. Manic lovers often are insecure about their value and their partners' commitment.

Agape is a selfless kind of love in which a beloved's happiness is more important than one's own. Agapic lovers are generous, unselfish, and devoted.

Pragma is a pragmatic and goal-oriented style of loving. Pragmas rely on reason and practical considerations to select people to love.

  To enhance your ability to recognize communication that reflects different styles of love, complete Activity 9.11, "Recognizing Styles of Love," in your *Student Companion* or online under "Activities for Chapter 9" at the *Communication in Our Lives* website.

---

between autonomy and connection, openness and privacy, and novelty and routine (Fitzpatrick & Best, 1979; Wood, 1995b).

Relational culture also includes communication rules. Couples develop agreements, usually unspoken, about how to signal anger, love, sexual interest, and so forth. They also develop routines for contact. Robbie and I catch up while we're fixing dinner each evening. Other couples reserve weekends for staying in touch. Especially important in navigation is small talk, through which partners weave together the fabric of their history and their current lives, experiences, and dreams.

Not all intimately bonded relationships endure. Despite popular belief that love is forever, often it isn't forever and may not even be for very long. Tensions within a relationship, as well as pressures and problems in surrounding contexts, may contribute to the end of intimacy.

Deterioration Processes   Steve Duck (1982) proposed a five-phase model of relationship deterioration. Working with me (Duck & Wood, in press) and Stephanie Rollie (Rollie & Duck, in press), Duck recently revised his original model to emphasize the processual nature of relationship decline.

Instead of representing relationship deterioration as a sequence of stages, Duck and his colleagues emphasize that relationships decline through a series of processes, each of which is complex and dynamic.

Intrapsychic processes launch relational deterioration. During these processes, one or both partners reflect and sometimes brood about dissatisfaction with the relationship. It's easy for intrapsychic processes to become self-fulfilling prophecies: As gloomy thoughts snowball and awareness of positive features of the relationship ebbs, partners may actually bring about the failure of their relationship. There are some general sex and gender differences in what partners brood about when a relationship begins to deteriorate (Duck & Wood, in press). For women, unhappiness with a relationship most often arises when communication declines in quality or quantity. Men are more likely to be dissatisfied by specific behaviors or the lack of valued behaviors, such as preparation of special meals (Riessman, 1990). For many men, dissatisfaction also arises if they have domestic responsibilities that they feel aren't a man's job (Gottman & Carrère, 1994). Because many women are socialized to be sensitive to interpersonal nuances, they are generally more likely than men to notice tensions and early symptoms of relationship distress (Cancian, 1989; Tavris, 1992).

Dyadic Processes usually—but not always—come next. These processes first may involve the breakdown of established patterns, understandings, and rules that have been part of the relationship. Partners may stop talking after dinner, no longer bother to call when they are running late, and in other ways depart from rules and patterns that have defined their relational culture. As the relational culture weakens, dissatisfaction mounts.

Communication scholars report that many people avoid talking about problems, refuse to return calls from partners, and in other ways evade confronting the difficulties (Baxter, 1984; Metts, Cupach, & Bejlovec, 1989). Although it is painful to talk about problems, avoiding discussion does nothing to resolve them and may make them worse. What happens during dyadic processes depends on how committed the partners are, on whether they perceive attractive alternatives to the relationship, and on whether they have the communication skills to work through problems constructively. A recent study (Battaglia, Richard, Datter, & Lord, 1998) found that many college undergraduates follow a cyclical pattern when breaking up. They pull apart and get back together several times before actually ending the relationship.

If partners lack commitment or the communication skills they need to restore intimacy, they enter into **social support processes,** which involve telling others about problems in the relationship and seeking support from others. Friends and family members can provide support by being available and by listening. Partners may give self-serving accounts of the breakup to save face and secure sympathy from others. Thus, Vera may tell her friends all the ways in which Frank was at fault and portray herself as the innocent party. Each partner may criticize the other and expect friends to take sides. Although self-serving explanations of breakups are common, they aren't necessarily constructive. We have an ethical responsibility to monitor communication during this period so that we don't say things we'll later regret.

If partners decide they will definitely part ways, they move into **grave dressing processes**. One important part of grave dressing is that either separately or in collaboration, partners decide how to explain their problems to

Communication Highlight

Fifty Ways to Leave Your Lover

Some years ago, musician Paul Simon scored a hit with his song "Fifty Ways to Leave Your Lover." More recently, a similar point emerged from a study by relationship scholars Dina Battaglia, Francis Richard, Darcee Datteri, and Charles Lord (1998). They found that most people don't break up on the first try. Instead, couples routinely follow a cyclical pattern of pulling apart and trying to get back together before officially declaring the relationship over. The researchers identified a 16-part script that the couples they studied followed. See how closely the script they identified matches your experiences:

1. Feel less interested in your partner
2. Start noticing other people you might date
3. Act distant with your partner
4. Try to work things out with your partner
5. See less of partner or even avoid partner
6. Feel interest declining further
7. Consider breaking up
8. Communicate dissatisfaction to your partner
9. Try to work things out with your partner
10. Notice other people you might like to date
11. Act distant with your partner
12. Date other people (sometimes still date your partner as well)
13. Get back together
14. Consider breaking up
15. Move on emotionally by accepting the ending of the relationship
16. Officially break up

friends, co-workers, children, in-laws, and social acquaintances. When partners don't craft a joint explanation for breaking up, friends may take sides, gossip, and disparage one or the other partner as the bad guy (La Gaipa, 1982). During grave dressing, each partner also works individually to make sense of the relationship: what it meant, why it failed, and how it affected him or her. Typically, partners mourn the failure to realize that which once seemed possible.

Yet mourning and sadness may be accompanied by other, more positive outcomes from breakups. Ty Tashiro and Patricia Frazier (2003) surveyed undergraduates who had recently broken up with a romantic partner. They found that breakups generate not only distress but also personal growth. People reported that breaking up gave them new insights into themselves, improved family relationships, and gave them more clear ideas about future partners. Grave dressing processes allow partners to put the relationship to rest so they can get on with their individual lives.

The final part of relationship deterioration is **resurrection processes,** which involve each ex-partner's moving ahead to a future without the former partner. Each person prepares himself or herself to live without a partner, either for the short or long term, or to seek new romantic relationships.

The stages we've discussed describe how most people experience the evolu-

Figure 9.3
Typical Evolution of Romantic Relationships

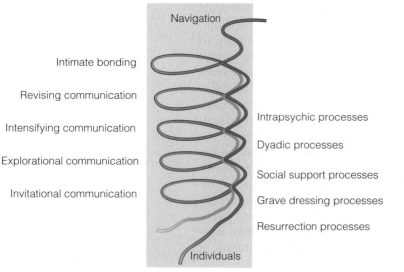

Navigation

Intimate bonding

Revising communication

Intensifying communication

Explorational communication

Invitational communication

Intrapsychic processes

Dyadic processes

Social support processes

Grave dressing processes

Resurrection processes

Individuals

tion of romance (Figure 9.3). However, not all couples follow the standard pattern. Some couples skip one or more stages or cycle more than once through certain stages. For example, a couple might soar through euphoria, work out some tough issues in revising, then go through euphoria a second time. It's also normal for long-term partners to move out of navigation periodically as they experience both euphoric seasons and intervals of dyadic breakdown. In the ebb and flow of enduring romantic relationships, there is a great deal of movement. As long as intimacy exists, what remains constant is partners' commitment to a future and investments in the relationship.

Sharpen Your Skill

Your Relationship's Evolution

Recall a romantic relationship of yours that ended. Trace how it evolved from first meeting through final encounter. Describe the unique relational culture you created. Do the stages we've discussed apply to the evolution of your romantic relationship? If not, how would you change or add to the stages we've described?

  To increase your ability to identify stages in romantic relationships, complete Activity 9.12, "Identifying Stages in Romantic Relationships," in your *Student Companion* or online under "Activities for Chapter 9" at the *Communication in Our Lives* website.

Challenges in Personal Relationships

To sustain fulfilling personal relationships, partners rely on communication to deal with internal tensions between themselves and external pressures. The skill with which we manage these challenges is a major influence on the endurance and quality of personal relationships. We'll consider five specific challenges that many friends and romantic partners face.

Adapting to Diverse Communication Styles

Personal relationships may be strained when friends and romantic partners have different ways of communicating that reflect their different cultures. A range of communication styles is common in a diverse society such as ours.

For instance, a native Japanese man might perceive a friend from Milwaukee as arrogant for saying, "Let's go out to celebrate my job offer." A Thai woman might not get the support she wants from a friend from Brooklyn because she learned not to assert her needs, whereas the Brooklyn friend was taught that people speak up for themselves.

In the United States, misunderstandings also arise from differences between social communities. Joe, who is White, might feel hurt if Markus, a Black friend, turns down going to a concert in order to go home to care for an ailing aunt. Joe might interpret this as meaning that Markus really doesn't want to be with him. Joe would interpret Markus differently if he realized that, as a rule, African Americans are more communal than Caucasians, so taking care of extended family members is a priority (Gaines, 1995). Ellen may feel that her friend Jed isn't being supportive when, instead of listening to her problems, he offers advice or suggests they go out to take her mind off her troubles. Yet he is showing support according to

Communication Highlight

What Counts as Support?

Communication researchers Ruth Anne Clark and Jesse Delia (1997) wanted to know what people in distressing situations wanted from their friends. It turns out that people have a range of constitutive rules for what counts as support. Some people appreciated having friends talk openly about the problems or unhappiness they were experiencing. Others preferred that friends not initiate discussion of troubles. And many people wanted different things at different times: At times, they found it helpful to talk about their worries; at other times, they wanted some space. Clark and Delia concluded that the standard advice to talk about problems is not always useful.

masculine rules of communication. Jed, on the other hand, may feel that Ellen is intruding on his autonomy when she pushes him to talk about his feelings. According to feminine rules of communication, however, Ellen is showing interest and concern (Wood, 1998, 2005).

Differences themselves usually aren't the cause of problems between intimates. Instead, how we interpret and judge diverse communication styles is the root of much tension and hurt (remember the abstraction ladder we discussed in Chapter 2?). Jed interpreted Ellen according to his communication rules, not hers, and she interpreted Jed according to her communication rules, not his. The tension between them results from how they interpret each other's behaviors, not from the behaviors themselves.

Dealing with Distance

Geographic separation can be difficult for friends and romantic couples. Fully 70% of college students are or have been in long-distance romances (Rohlfing, 1995). An even greater percentage of students have one or more long-distance friendships. The number of long-distance romantic relationships is also rising because partners pursue independent careers (McGrane, 2000).

One of the greatest problems for long-distance commitments is the lack of daily communication about small events and issues. The first problem—not being able to share small talk and daily routines—is a major loss, especially for partners who can't communicate over the Internet. As we have seen, communication about the ordinary comings and goings of days helps partners keep their lives woven together. The mundane conversations of romantic partners and friends form the basic fabric of their relationship. Many long-distance friends and romantic couples rely on e-mail to stay in daily touch so they don't give up small talk.

A second common problem is unrealistic expectations for time together. Because friends and partners have so little time when they are physically together, they often believe every moment must be perfect. They may feel that there should be no conflict and that they should be with each other all of the time they have together. Yet this is a very unrealistic expectation. Conflict and needs for autonomy are natural in all relationships. They may be even more likely in long-distance relationships because friends and partners are used to living alone and have established independent rhythms that may not mesh well.

The good news is that these problems don't necessarily sabotage long-distance romance. Many people maintain satisfying commitments despite geographic separation. To overcome the difficulties of distance, many couples engage in creative communication to sustain intimacy (Guldner, 2003; McGrane, 2000). In the last two decades, electronic communication has mushroomed, making it one of the primary ways many couples who are apart stay in touch.

To apply principles discussed in this section to a long-distance friendship in your life, complete Activity 9.8, "Long-Distance Friendship," in your *Student Companion* or online under "Activities for Chapter 9" at the *Communication in Our Lives* website.

Creating Equitable Romantic Relationships

Equity between partners affects satisfaction with relationships. On the job, we expect equity—to be treated the same as other employees at our level. If we are asked to do more work than our peers, we can appeal to a manager or supervisor. In romantic relationships, however, there is no supervisor to ensure equity. Researchers report that the happiest dating and married couples believe both partners invest equally (Buunk & Mutsaers, 1999; Hecht, Marston, & Larkey, 1994). When we think we are investing more than our partner is, we tend to be resentful. When it seems our partner is investing more than we are, we may feel guilty. Imbalance of either sort erodes satisfaction.

Although few partners demand moment-to-moment equality, most of us want our relationships to be equitable over time. Equity has multiple dimensions. We may evaluate the fairness of financial, emotional, physical, and other contributions to a relationship. One area that strongly affects satisfaction of

Communication Highlight

Coping with Geographic Separation

Reports on long-distance romance shed light on some of the common advantages, disadvantages, and coping strategies perceived by partners who live apart (Franklin & Ramage, 1999; Justice, 1999, Sutton, 2001):

Advantages	Disadvantages	Coping Strategies
Career development	Lack of companionship	Develop good support system of friends for each partner
Increased appreciation of one another (not taking each other for granted)	Reduced emotional support	Stay positive; talk with each other and others about what is good about the relationship and the separation
	Missing small talk and moments	Communicate creatively to have small talk; e-mail daily or more often; call often

Advantages	Disadvantages	Coping Strategies
Independence	Expenses of two places to live, travel, and phone bills	Maintain trust by following mutually agreed-upon ground rules; for instance, phone when you say you will
Greater range of people and interests in each person's life	No one to share chores with	Set a time limit for how long you'll live apart

Use your InfoTrac College Edition to read the article on long-distance relationships that appeared in the May 21, 2001, issue of *Jet.* How does the advice in this article reflect and extend the strategies listed in this box?

Couples who share equitably in domestic responsibilities are happier than couples who don't.

spouses and cohabiting partners is equity in housework and child care. Inequitable division of domestic obligations fuels dissatisfaction and resentment, both of which harm intimacy (Anderson & Guerrero, 1998; Gottman & Carrère, 1994; Steil, 2000). Marital stability is more closely linked to equitable divisions of child care and housework than to income or sex life (Oakley, 2002; Risman & Godwin, 2001).

A majority of marriages today include two wage earners. Unfortunately, divisions of family and home responsibilities have not changed much in response to changing employment patterns. Even when both partners in heterosexual relationships work outside the home, in 80% of dual-worker families, women do most of the child care and homemaking. In only 20% of dual-worker families do men assume equal domestic responsibilities (Hochschild with Machung, 2003).

How are domestic responsibilities managed in same-sex couples? Lesbian couples create more egalitarian relationships than either heterosexuals or gay men. More than any other type of couple, lesbians are likely to communicate collaboratively to make decisions about domestic work and parenting (Huston & Schwartz, 1995). Consequently, lesbians are least likely to have negative feelings of inequity (Kurdek, 1993). In many gay couples, the man who makes more money has and uses more power, both in making decisions that affect the relationship and in avoiding housework (Huston & Schwartz, 1995, 1996).

As a rule, women assume **psychological responsibility** for relationships, which involves remembering, planning, and coordinating domestic activities (Hochschild with Machung, 2003; Steil, 2000). Parents may alternate who takes children to the doctor, but it is usually the mother who remembers when check-ups are needed, makes appointments, and reminds the father to take the child. Both partners may sign cards and gifts, but women typically assume the burden of remembering birthdays and buying cards and gifts. Successful long-term relationships in our era require partners to communicate collaboratively to design equitable divisions of responsibility.

-Molly-

It really isn't fair when both spouses work outside of the home but only one of them takes care of the home and kids. For years, that was how Sean's and my marriage worked, no matter how much I tried to talk with him about a more fair arrangement. Finally, I had just had it, so I quit doing everything. Groceries didn't get bought, laundry piled up and he didn't have clean shirts, he didn't remember his mother's birthday (and for the first time ever, I didn't remind him), and bills didn't get paid. After a while he suggested we talk about a system we could both live with.

Resisting Violence and Abuse between Intimates

Sadly, violence is common between romantic partners. Over 4 million incidents of intimate partner violence are reported each year in the United States alone (Feldman & Ridley, 2000; Johnson, 2001; National Coalition Against Domestic Violence, 1999) and they cut across lines of class, race, and ethnicity (Harvey & Weber, 2002; West, 1995). Intimate partner violence is high not only in heterosexual marriages but also in dating and cohabiting relationships (Goode, 2001; Stets, 1990; Thompson, 1991; Wood, 2001b). In addition to physical abuse, verbal and emotional brutality poison all too many relationships. Too often, people don't leave abusive relationships because they feel trapped by economic pressures or by relatives and clergy who counsel them to stay (Jacobson & Gottman, 1998; West, 1995).

Most of reported intimate partner violence is committed by men against women (Johnson, 2001; Johnson & Ferraro, 2000). Researchers have found that many men who engage in intimate partner violence have low-self esteem (Boyd, 2002; Faludi, 1999). Using physical force against others is a sign of weakness—an admission that a person must resort to the crudest, least imaginative methods of control. Men who resort to violence against wives and girlfriends tend to feel they have little control in their worlds. Hurting intimates is a way they try to regain a sense of control. In harming intimates, however, they further diminish their self-esteem. I work with male inmates who have committed violence against women and who want to stop being violent (Wood, in press). These men's self-esteem grows as they learn how to express anger, frustration, and other feelings without becoming violent.

Intimate partner violence tends to follow a predictable cycle: Tension mounts in the abuser, the abuser explodes by being violent, the abuser then is remorseful and loving, the victim feels loved and reassured that the relationship is working, and then tension mounts anew and the cycle begins again. Without intervention, the cycle of violence is unlikely to stop. Abusive relationships are unhealthy for everyone involved. They violate the trust that is a foundation of intimacy, and they jeopardize the comfort, health, and sometimes the lives of victims of violence.

Communication is related to intimate partner violence in two ways. Most obviously, patterns of communication between couples and the intrapersonal communication of abusers can fuel tendencies toward violence. Some partners deliberately annoy and taunt each other. Also, the language abusers use to describe physical assaults on partners includes denial, trivializing the harm, and blaming the partner or circumstances for "making me do it" (Stamp & Sabourin, 1995; Wood, 2001b, in press). These intrapersonal communication patterns allow abusers to deny their offenses, justify violence, and cast responsibility outside themselves.

Intimate partner violence is also promoted by cultural communication practices that normalize violence. Media are saturated with incidents of rape and physical violation of women. From magazines to films to MTV, domination of women and violence against them are pervasive in media. News accounts that refer to "loving

Figure 9.4
The Cycle of Abuse

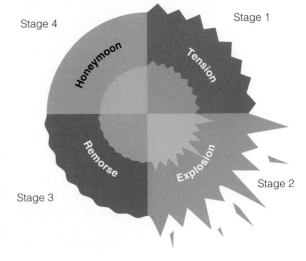

her too much" and "love that gets out of hand" camouflage the brutality and unloving nature of violence (Meyers, 1994, 1997).

Violent relationships are not the fault of victims. A person cannot earn battering, nor do victims encourage it. If you know or suspect that someone you care about is a victim of abuse, don't ignore the situation, and don't assume it's none of your business. It is an act of friendship to notice and offer to help. Victims of violence must make the ultimate decisions about what to do, but the support and concern of friends can help them.

Negotiating Safer Sex

In the HIV and AIDS era, sexual activities pose serious, even deadly threats to sexual partners—heterosexuals as well as gays and lesbians (Greene, Frey, & Derlega, 2002). In the United States alone, nearly one million people have HIV (Maugh, 2002).

Despite vigorous public education campaigns, a great many people still don't practice safer sex, which includes abstinence, restriction of sexual activity to a single partner who has been tested for HIV, and use of latex condoms (Reel & Thompson, 1994). For people who choose to engage in sexual activities, not practicing safer sex puts both partners at grave risk for early death.

Intimate partner violence tends to follow a predictable cycle.

Researchers have identified three primary reasons why many people don't practice safer sex. First, ironically, many people find it more embarrassing to talk about sex than to engage in it. They find it awkward to ask direct questions of partners ("Have you been tested for HIV?" "Are you having sex with anyone else?") or to make direct requests of partners ("I want you to wear a condom," "I would like you to be tested for HIV before we have sex"). Naturally, it's difficult to talk explicitly about sex and the dangers of HIV. However, it is far more difficult to live with HIV or the knowledge that you have infected someone else.

A second reason some people don't practice safer sex is that they hold erroneous and dangerous misperceptions. Among these are the assumption that you are safe if you and your partner are monogamous, the belief that you can recognize "the kind of person" who might have HIV, and the idea that planning for sex destroys the spontaneity (Reel & Thompson, 1994). Some of my students have told me that they think the new treatments for HIV reduce the seriousness of the disease and that soon a cure will be found. All of these are dangerous beliefs that can put you and your partners at grave risk.

A third reason people sometimes fail to practice safer sex is that their rational thought and control are debilitated by alcohol and other drugs. In a series of studies of college students' sexual activities, communication researchers Sheryl Bowen and Paula Michal-Johnson (1996) found that safer sex precautions are especially likely to be neglected when people drink heavily.

© Rubberball Productions/Getty Images

Communication Highlight

Romance Narratives

In a recent study, I talked with women who had been in violent romantic relationships (Wood, 2001b). Among my findings was the fact that these women's relationships were shaped by culturally endorsed narratives of romance that they had learned from their families and friends as well as from the media (Meyers, 1997). Participants in my study made sense of their violent relationships by relying on one or both of two romance narratives established in Western culture.

The first is most familiar to many people. It is the Fairy Tale Romance Narrative, in which Prince Charming rescues the damsel in distress, and they live happily ever after. Children's fairy tales, television, films, and popular romance novels tutor people in the fairy tale narrative. Women in violent relationships consistently described their relation-ships as starting off like the fairy tale: "He swept me off my feet," "He was totally adoring—just like Prince Charming," "He showered me with gifts," "I was just in the clouds."

The second narrative is the Dark Romance Narrative, which claims that it's normal for men to be domineering or even violent and that good women stand by their men. The Dark Romance Narrative also claims that a woman needs a man to be successful, so she should hang onto the one she has, even if he hurts her. Tammy Wynette's country song "Stand by Your Man" exemplifies the idea that no matter what a man does, a good woman stands by him. When women in my study could not sustain belief in the Fairy Tale Romance Narrative, they turned to the Dark Romance Narrative, which is also entrenched in cultural life.

Discussing and practicing safer sex may be awkward, but there is no sensible alternative. Good communication skills can help you negotiate safer sex. It is more constructive to say, "I feel unsafe having unprotected sex" than, "Without a condom, you could give me AIDS." (Notice that the first statement uses *I*-language, whereas the second one relies on *you*-language.) A positive communication climate is fostered by relational language, such as *we*, *us*, and *our relationship* to talk about sex (Reel & Thompson, 1994). People who care about themselves and their partners are honest about their sexual histories and careful in their sex practices.

Experiencing Communication in Our Lives

CASE STUDY: Wedding Bells?

The conversation scripted below is featured as a multimedia scenario on the *Communication in Our Lives* CD-ROM included with this book. Once you've launched the CD, click on the "Communication Scenarios" icon; from the Scenarios Menu, select "Wedding Bells?" to watch the video. Improve your own communication skills by reading, watching, listening to, critiquing, and analyzing this communication encounter.

Analyze the scenario by applying the principles covered in this chapter, and respond to the prompts that accompany the video, which you can access by clicking on "Analysis." After completing the conversation analysis and answering the

Jason Harris/© 2001 Wadsworth

questions, you can click on the "Done" button to compare your responses with the ones I suggest. Additional analysis questions are available in print at the end of this chapter and on the book's website.

After meeting at a New Year's party in the spring of their senior year at Agora College, Trevor and Meg quickly developed an exclusive dating relationship. Now, four months later, they are trying to figure out what to do about their relationship.

TREVOR: Do you realize that half our friends are planning weddings? Maybe we should start thinking about ours.

MEG: Don't start this again. You know how I feel about that. It's just too soon. We need to know a lot more before we even think about marriage.

TREVOR: Why? I'm crazy in love with you, and you are with me, right?

MEG: (Nods)

TREVOR: So what's too soon? What else do we need to know?

MEG: First of all, I'll be starting law school in the fall, and that's a whole new thing for me. You haven't decided on a job yet. We don't even know if we'll be in the same city!

TREVOR: Sure we do. You'll be going to law school at State, and I can get a job near there. One good thing about being a business major is that I can get a job anywhere.

MEG: See, right there is a problem: I'm much more concerned about my career than you are about yours. Your whole attitude toward it is just so casual.

TREVOR: I am not casual about us. I love you enough to arrange the rest of my life around our relationship. So why aren't you willing to do the same?

MEG: 'Cause it's just too soon. Law school will be very demanding, and I don't want to try starting that and a marriage at the same time.

TREVOR (grins): I'll help you study. Any other problems?

MEG: What about eating? We do okay now because we don't live together. But I'm a vegan, and you'll eat anything. I think we'd have problems if we lived together.

TREVOR: Just keep your tofu away from my chicken in the refrigerator, and we'll be fine.

MEG: I'm serious, Trevor.

TREVOR: So am I. I mean, just because we live together doesn't mean we have to eat the same things. That's not a problem.

MEG: You and I have different values and goals. You think I'm nuts to want a Mercedes, and I don't know how you can be happy with that old truck you drive. And you think I'm extravagant any time I buy anything for myself.

TREVOR: Okay, so we'll have separate accounts, and that way each of us can decide how to spend our own money. Next problem?

MEG: What about children?

TREVOR: What about children? I don't see any children. No problem there.

MEG: Quit kidding around, you know what I mean. You definitely want children; I don't know if I do. That's a big issue, one we should settle before we even think about marriage.

TREVOR: Meggie, if we wait until we've settled every issue, you know, solved every problem, we'll never get married. I totally love you, and I believe in us. I think that we can resolve any issue as it comes along. That's what love is.

MEG: I'm just not comfortable with that. I'd like a lot more of these issues settled before I marry anyone. Love is great, but it's not enough.

Chapter Summary

In this chapter, we've explored communication in personal relationships, which are defined by uniqueness, commitment, relational dialectics, relationship rules, and interaction with surrounding contexts. We traced the typical evolutionary paths of friendships and romances by noting how partners communicate during escalating, stabilizing, and declining stages of personal relationships.

In the final section of the chapter, we considered five challenges that friends and romantic partners face. The communication principles and skills we have discussed in this and previous chapters can help us meet the challenges of adapting to diverse communication styles, sustaining intimacy across geographic distance, creating equitable relationships, resisting violence, and negotiating safer sex. Good communication skills enable us to meet these challenges so that we, our intimates, and our relationships survive and thrive over time.

 ## Communication in Our Lives ONLINE

In addition to presenting the case studies' multimedia scenarios, the *Communication in Our Lives* CD-ROM provides quick access to the *Communication in Our Lives* website and InfoTrac College Edition. The website is online at http://communication .wadsworth.com/woodciol4, but you can only access this book's premium web content when you link to the site directly through the book's CD.

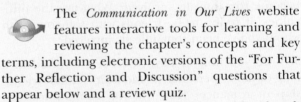 The *Communication in Our Lives* website features interactive tools for learning and reviewing the chapter's concepts and key terms, including electronic versions of the "For Further Reflection and Discussion" questions that appear below and a review quiz.

The website also provides updated web links and additional InfoTrac College Edition activities. If required, you can e-mail completed chapter activities or the quizzes to your instructor.

Key Concepts

For Further Reflection and Discussion

1. Think about the distinction between love and commitment in personal relationships. Describe relationships in which commitment is present but love is not. Describe relationships in which love exists but not commitment. What can you conclude about the values of each?

2. Think about differences in the goals and rules for friendships and romantic relationships. Does comparing the two kinds of relationship give you any insight into the difficulties that commonly arise when two people who have been friends become romantically involved? What are the difficulties of trying to be friends with someone with whom you've been romantically involved?

3. Are you now or have you been involved in a long-distance personal relationship, either friendship or romance? How did you communicate to bridge the distance? Do your experiences parallel the chapter's discussion of challenges in long-distance relationships?

4. Does a person who wants to end a serious romantic relationship have an ethical responsibility to talk with his or her partner about why he or she is no longer interested in maintaining the relationship? Under what conditions are we ethically obligated to help a partner through a breakup?

5. Use your InfoTrac College Edition to read Stacy Rogers' and Paul Amato's 2001 article, "Have Changes in Gender Relations Affected Marital Quality?" How do gender roles differ for couples married before 1980 and after 1980? You may also want to complete Activity 9.6, "Gendered Styles of Friendship," in your *Student Companion* or online in the activities listed for Chapter 9.

Experiencing Communication in Our Lives

Questions for Analysis and Discussion

Review the video "Wedding Bells?" that you watched when completing this chapter's case study (pages 249–251), or, if you haven't seen it yet, watch it for the first time. If you didn't previously finish the "Analysis" questions included on the CD-ROM, do so now, and then respond to the questions below, which are also available on the book's website under "Activities for Chapter 9."

1. Based on the scenario, which styles of loving do you think Meg and Trevor have? What communication by each of them leads you to perceive particular styles of loving?

2. Based on their conversation, what do you perceive to be Meg's and Trevor's levels of commitment to the relationship?

3. What aspects of context seem to influence Meg's and Trevor's preferences for how the relationship should proceed?

10
Foundations of Group and Team Communication

Focus Questions

1. How do groups and teams differ?

2. What are the potential limitations of groups and teams?

3. What are the potential strengths of groups and teams?

4. How do cultural values influence communication in groups and teams?

5. How does egocentric communication affect group cohesion and progress?

6. How do new and converging technologies of communication affect group work?

© Bruce Ayers/Tony Stone Images

"Teams take too much time to decide anything."

"Working in groups increases creativity and commitment."

"Groups suppress individuality."

"Teams make better decisions than individuals do."

With which of these statements do you agree? People who enjoy working in groups would tend to agree with the second and fourth statements. The first and third claims are more likely to ring true to people who find group work difficult or unrewarding. Actually, there's some truth to each statement. Groups generally do take more time to reach decisions than individuals, yet group decisions often are superior to those made by one person. Although group interaction stimulates creativity, it may also suppress individual opinions.

Communication is a major influence on whether groups and teams are productive and enjoyable or inefficient and unpleasant. Communication in groups and teams calls for many of the skills and understandings that we've discussed in previous chapters. For example, constructive group communication requires that members express themselves clearly, check perceptions, support others, respect differences between people, build good climates, and listen mindfully. This chapter and Chapter 11 will help you discover how to communicate effectively when you work in groups and teams. Reading these two chapters will enlarge your appreciation of the ways communication shapes and is shaped by the distinct context of small groups. That insight will enhance your ability to participate in and lead groups and teams effectively.

The chapter opens by defining groups and teams. Next, we discuss potential weaknesses and strengths of groups. We then examine influences on interaction between members of groups and teams. Finally, we identify various kinds of group communication and consider how each affects collective climate and productivity.

What Are Groups and Teams?

Pick up any newspaper, and you will see announcements and advertisements for social groups, volunteer service committees, personal support groups, health teams, focus groups sought by companies trying out new products, and political action coalitions. It is a rare person in the United States who hasn't had a wealth of group experiences.

The tendency toward group work is especially pronounced in the workplace. Although groups and teams have gained increased prominence in today's organizations, they actually have a long history in the workforce. Miners, seafarers, and other skilled tradespeople relied on groups to accomplish their jobs and often to survive harsh and dangerous working conditions (Hodson & Sullivan, 2002).

Today groups and teams are an even greater part of work life (Ortiz, 1998; Pfeffer, 1997). The average business executive spends about 700 hours a year in group and team meetings (Tubbs, 1998). Whether you are an attorney working with a litigation team, a health-care professional who participates in health delivery teams, or a factory worker on a team assigned to find ways to reduce production time, working with others probably will be part of your career. It's likely that your raises and advancement will depend significantly on how well you work in groups. The reason for increasing reliance on groups and teams is that they often do better work than individuals. As members of a team communicate, thinking is stimulated and creativity is stoked. Often, the results are better ideas and greater personal satisfaction with work. In this chapter, we'll cover some of the foundations for participating in many types of groups and teams; in Chapter 11, we will focus in greater depth on communication within task teams.

Sharpen Your Skill

Groups in Your Life

To how many groups do you belong? List the groups in which you currently participate.

Social groups:

Personal support groups:

Work groups:

On-the-job teams:

Volunteer service committees:

  To gain insight into features of groups that affect the quality of group experiences, complete Activity 10.3, "Assessing Group Discussion," in your *Student Companion* or online under "Activities for Chapter 10" at the *Communication in Our Lives* website.

Thus far in this chapter, we've mentioned *groups* and *teams* several times. But what are groups and teams? Are six people standing together on a street corner waiting to cross the street a group? Are five people studying in a library a group? Are four students standing in line to buy books a group? The answer is no in each case. These are collections of individuals, but they are not groups.

For a group to exist, there must be interaction and interdependence between individuals, a common goal, and shared rules of conduct. Thus, we can define a **group** as three or more people who interact over time, depend on each other, and follow shared rules of conduct to reach a common goal. To be a group, members must perceive themselves as interdependent—as somehow needing one another and counting on one another (Gordon, 1998; Lumsden & Lumsden, 2004). Group interdependence and interaction tend to generate cohesion, or a feeling of group identity. Later in this chapter, we'll discuss cohesion in greater detail.

A **team** is a special kind of group that is characterized by different and complementary resources of members and a strong sense of collective identity. Like all other groups, teams involve interaction, interdependence, shared rules, and common goals. Yet a team is a distinct kind of group in two respects. First, teams consist of people with diverse skills. Whereas a group may consist of several people, each of whom contributes to all aspects of group work, a team usually consists of people who bring specialized and different resources to a common project (Kelley & Littman, 2001). Second, teams develop greater interdependence and a stronger sense of collective identity than most groups (Hoover, 2002; Lumsden & Lumsden, 2004). One way to remember the difference between groups and teams is to realize that all teams are groups, but not all groups are teams.

Teams and other groups consist of individuals who are interdependent and who interact over time. People who are in one place but not interacting are not a group, nor does a group exist if people have only a fleeting exchange that is insufficient to generate cohesion or interdependence. Groups and teams also develop rules that members understand and follow. You'll recall from earlier chapters that constitutive rules state what counts as what. For example, in some groups, disagreement counts as a positive sign of involvement, whereas other groups regard disagreement as negative. Regulative rules regulate how, when, and with whom we interact. For instance, a group might have regulative rules stipulating that members don't interrupt each other and that it's okay to be a few minutes late but more than 10 minutes is a sign of disregard for other group members. Groups generate rules over time in the process of interacting and figuring out what works for them.

Teams have become increasingly popular in today's business world. Team members must communicate continuously (and well!) to meet their shared goals.

−Mieko−

When I first came here to go to school, I felt very alone. I met some other students from Japan, and we formed a group to help us feel at home in America. For the first year, that group was most important to me and the others because we felt uprooted. The second year it was good, but not so important, because we'd all started finding ways to fit in here and we felt more at home. When we met the first time of the third year, we decided not to be a group anymore. The reason we wanted a group no longer existed.

Groups are also characterized by shared goals. Some common objective or objectives bring and hold members together. Citizens form groups to

Communication Highlight

Team Spirit and Career Growth

Whether you love or hate working with others, your career may depend on how well you do it (Rothwell, 2004). Two-thirds of U.S. employers rely on work teams to accomplish objectives (Lancaster, 1996). At Xerox, for instance, more than 75% of workers are actively involved in one or more teams (Bowles, 1990). The most common type of team is a temporary unit made up of members from different departments and job levels.

Teams can facilitate career advancement. Because teams include employees at different levels, new members of an organization can interact with higher-ups they wouldn't otherwise meet. Take the case of Shaunna Sowell, who was in the design department of Texas Instruments when she was asked to join a product quality team. After one meeting, she thought to herself, "I've ruined my career. . . . I've just told a guy four levels above me he was wrong." As it turns out, the man whom she called wrong was looking for new executive talent, and he was impressed by Sowell's knowledge and assertiveness. Before long, she was promoted to the position of general manager of one of eight regional divisions.

accomplish political goals, establish social and art programs, protest zoning decisions, and protect the security of neighborhoods. Workers form teams to develop and market products, evaluate and refine company programs, and improve productivity. Other groups form around goals such as promoting personal growth (therapy groups), sharing a life (families), socializing (singles clubs), having fun and fitting in (peer groups), or participating in sports (intramural teams). As Mieko explains in her commentary, without a common goal, a group doesn't exist. Groups end if the common objective has been achieved or if it ceases to matter to members. To better understand small groups, we'll now consider their potential values and limits, features that affect participation, and the influence of culture on group communication.

Potential Limitations and Strengths of Groups

A great deal of research has compared individual and group decision making. As you might expect, the research identifies both potential weaknesses and strengths of groups.

Potential Limitations of Groups

Two significant disadvantages of group discussion are the time needed for the group process and the potential for pressure to conform; both can interfere with high-quality work from groups.

Time   If you've ever worked in a group—and who hasn't?—you know that a group takes much longer to decide something than an individual does. Operating solo, an individual can think through ideas efficiently and choose the one she or he considers best. In group discussion, however, all members must have an opportunity to voice their ideas and to respond to the ideas others put forward.

It takes substantial time for each person to describe ideas, clarify misunderstandings, and respond to questions or criticisms. In addition, groups need time to deliberate about alternative courses of action. Thus, group discussion probably is not a wise choice for routine policy making and emergency tasks. When creativity and thoroughness are important, however, the values of groups may outweigh the disadvantage of time.

Conformity Pressures   Groups also have the potential to suppress individuals and encourage conformity. This can happen in two ways. The most obvious is that conformity pressures may exist when a majority of members have an opinion different from that of a minority of members or a single member. It's hard to hold out for your point of view when most of your peers have a different one. In effective groups, however, all members understand and resist conformity pressures. They realize that the majority is sometimes wrong, and the minority, even a minority of one, is sometimes right. This implies that members should communicate in ways that encourage expression of diverse ideas and open debate about different viewpoints. Chapter 8's discussion of communication that creates an open climate can be applied to group contexts to help you create climates that are sufficiently open and supportive to encourage expression of differences.

Conformity pressures may also arise when one member is extremely charismatic, has high prestige, or has greater power than other members. Even if that person is all alone in a point of view, he or she has sufficient status to pressure others to go along. Sometimes a high-status member doesn't intend to influence others and may not overtly exert pressure. However, the status is still there and influential. For example, President Kennedy often tried not to shape the views of his advisers, but they regarded him so highly that in some cases they suspended their individual critical thinking and agreed with whatever he said (Janis, 1977). As this example illustrates, often neither a high-status person nor others are conscious of conformity pressures. Effective discussion occurs when members guard against the potential to conform uncritically.

−Lance−

I used to belong to a creative writing group where all of us helped each other improve our writing. We were all equally vocal, and we had a lot of good discussions and even disagreements when the group first started. But then one member of the group got a story of hers accepted by a big magazine, and all of a sudden we thought of her as a better writer than any of us. She didn't act any different, but we saw her as more accomplished, so when she said something, everybody listened and nobody disagreed. It was like a wet blanket on our creativity because her opinion just carried too much weight once she got published.

Potential Strengths of Groups

In comparison to individuals, groups generally have greater resources, are more thorough and more creative, and generate greater commitment to decisions.

Greater Resources   A group obviously exceeds any individual member in the number of ideas, perspectives, experiences, and expertise it can bring to bear on solving a problem. Especially in teams, the different resources of individual members are a key to effectiveness (Kelley & Littman, 2001). One member knows the technical aspects of a product, another understands market psychology, a third has expertise in cost analysis, and so forth. When my father was hospitalized after a series of strokes, we had a health-care team that included a neurologist, a cardiologist, a physical therapist, a social worker, and a registered nurse. Each member of the team had distinct expertise, and they coordinated their specific skills and knowledge to provide him with integrated care.

Greater Thoroughness   Groups also tend to be more thorough than individuals, probably because members act as a check-and-balance system for each other (Rothwell, 2004; Salazar, 1995). The parts of an issue one member doesn't understand, another person does; the details of a plan that bore one person interest another; the holes in a proposal that one member doesn't see will be recognized by others.

The greater thoroughness of groups isn't simply the result of more people. It also reflects interaction among members. Discussion itself promotes more critical and careful analysis because members propel each other's thinking. **Synergy** is a special kind of energy that combines and goes beyond the energies, talents, and strengths of individual members (Lumsden & Lumsden, 2004).

Greater Creativity A third value of groups is that they are generally more creative than most individuals. Again, the reason seems to lie in the synergetic communication in groups. When members know how to communicate effectively, they interact in ways that spark good ideas, integrative thinking, and creativity. Any individual eventually runs out of new ideas, but groups seem to have almost infinite generative ability. As members talk, they build on each other's ideas, refine proposals, see new possibilities in each other's comments, and so forth. Often, the result is a greater number of ideas and more creative final solutions.

–Laura–

The first time I heard about brainstorming was on my job, when the supervisor said all of us in my department were to meet and brainstorm ways to cut costs for the company. I thought it was silly to take time to discuss cost saving when each person could just submit suggestions individually. But I was wrong. When my group started, each of us had one or two ideas—only that many. But the six of us came up with more than twenty-five ideas after we'd talked for an hour.

Greater Commitment Finally, an important strength of groups is their ability to generate commitment to decisions. The greater commitment fostered by group discussion arises from two sources. First, participation in the decision-making process enhances commitment to decisions. Thus, groups build commitment among members, which is especially important if members are to be involved in implementing the decision. Second, because groups have greater resources than the individual decision maker, their decisions are more likely to take into account the points of view of various people whose cooperation is needed to implement a decision. This is critical because a decision can be sabotaged if the people it affects dislike it or believe their perspectives weren't considered.

Greater resources, thoroughness, creativity, and commitment to group goals are powerful values of group decision making. To realize these values, however, members must be aware of the trade-off of time needed for group discussion and must resist pressures to conform or to induce others to conform without critical thought.

Interaction between team members often heightens commitment to collective goals.

© Craig Aurness/Woodfin Camp & Associates

Features of Small Groups

The group strengths we've identified are realized only if members participate effectively. If members don't participate or lack the communication skills to participate effectively, a group can't achieve its potential for creativity, thoroughness, resourcefulness, and commitment. Thus, we need to know what influences communication in small groups and how communication itself influences the nature and quality of group work. We'll consider five features of small groups that directly affect participation.

Cohesion

Cohesion is the degree of closeness, esprit de corps, and group identity. In highly cohesive groups, members see themselves linked tightly together and unified in their goals. This increases members' satisfaction with the group and, in turn, their productivity (Gammage, Carron, & Estabrooks, 2001). High cohesion and the satisfaction it generates tend to increase members' commitment to a group and to achieving common goals (Langfred, 1998; Wech, Mossholder, Streel, & Bennett, 1998). Consequently, cohesiveness is important to effective and satisfying group communication.

Perhaps you wonder whether you can foster cohesion in groups. The answer is yes; your communication can foster or inhibit cohesiveness. To help build cohesiveness, it's important to engage in communication that emphasizes the group or team and the common objectives of all members. Comments that stress pulling together to promote collective interests build cohesion by reinforcing group identity. Cohesion is also fostered by communication that highlights similarities between members: the interests, goals, experiences, and ways of thinking that are common to different people in the group (Donnellon, 1996; Wilmot & Hocker, 2001). A third way to enhance cohesion is by expressing affection, respect, and inclusion so that all members feel valued and part of the group (Fisher, 1998; Hoover, 2002).

Sharpen Your Skill

Communication and Cohesion

Select a group to which you belong, and rate its level of cohesion as high, moderate, or low. Next, pay attention to the communication between members of the group during one meeting. Based on the discussion, answer these five questions:

1. To what extent does communication focus on the group or team?

2. To what extent does talk between members emphasize collective goals?

3. To what degree do members talk about pulling together and collaborating?

4. To what extent do members comment on similarities in their goals, interests, experiences, and so on?

5. To what degree do members communicate affection and respect for one another?

Cohesion and participation influence each other reciprocally. Cohesion is promoted when all members participate. At the same time, because cohesion generates a feeling of identity and involvement, once established, it fosters participation. Thus, high levels of participation tend to build cohesion, and strong cohesion generally fosters vigorous participation. Encouraging all members to be involved in discussion and attending responsively to everyone's contributions generally foster cohesion and continued participation.

Although cohesion is important for effective group communication, too much cohesion can undermine sound group work (Mullen, 1994). When members are extremely close, they may be less critical of each other's ideas and less willing to engage in the analysis and arguments necessary to the best outcomes. When groups are too cohesive, they may experience **groupthink,** which occurs when members cease to think critically and independently about ideas generated by a group. Groupthink has occurred in high-level groups such as presidential advisory boards and national decision-making bodies (Janis, 1977, 1989; Young, Wood, Phillips, & Pedersen, 2001). Members perceive their group so positively that they share the illusion that it cannot make bad decisions. Consequently, they are less careful in evaluating ideas generated in the group. The predictable result is inferior group outcomes.

Group Size

The sheer number of people in a group affects the amount of communication. Consider the difference between communication between two people and among five people. When only two individuals talk, two people send and receive messages. In a group of five, there are five people doing the same thing! Each idea that's expressed must be understood by four others, who may also choose to respond. Consequently, the greater the number of people in a group, the fewer the contributions any individual may make. Because participation is linked to satisfaction and commitment, larger groups may generate less satisfaction and commitment to decisions than smaller ones. Groups with nine or more members may also be less cohesive than smaller ones (Benenson, Gordon, & Roy, 2000; Carletta, Garrod, & Fraser-Krauss, 1998). Larger groups may also encourage formation of cliques, which undermine cohesiveness (Carron & Spink, 1995).

Because of the disadvantages of large groups, you might assume that small groups would be the most effective. However, groups can be too small as well as too large. With too few members, a group has limited resources, which eliminates a primary advantage of groups for decision making. Also, in very small groups, members may be unwilling to disagree or criticize each other's ideas because alienating one person in a two- or three-person group would dramatically diminish the group. Most researchers agree that five to seven members is the ideal size for a small group (Hamilton & Parker, 2001; Lumsden & Lumsden, 2004).

-Yolanda-

The worst group I was ever in had three members. We were supposed to have five, but two dropped out after the first meeting, so there were three of us to come up with proposals for artistic programs for the campus. Nobody would say anything against anybody else's ideas, even if we thought they were bad. For myself, I know I held back from criticizing a lot of times because I didn't want to offend either of the other two. We came up with some really bad ideas because we were so small we couldn't risk arguing.

Power Structure

Power structure is a third feature that influences participation in small groups. **Power** is the ability to influence others (Rothwell, 2004; Young et al., 2001). There are different kinds of power, or ways of influencing others.

Power over is the ability to help or harm others. This form of power usually is expressed in ways that highlight the status and visibility of the person wielding influence. A group leader might exert positive *power over* a member by providing mentoring, positive reports to superiors, and visibility in the group. A leader could also exert negative *power over* a member by withholding these benefits, assigning unpleasant tasks, and responding negatively to the member's communication during group meetings.

Power to is the ability to empower others to reach their goals (Boulding, 1990; Conrad & Poole, 2002). People who empower others do not broadcast their own influence. Instead, they act behind the scenes to enlarge others' influence and help others succeed. *Power to* is expressed in creating opportunities for others, recognizing achievements, and arranging circumstances to facilitate others in accomplishing their goals. In small groups, *power to* involves the capacity to create community, inspire loyalty, and build team spirit so that members of groups are productive and satisfied (Boulding, 1990). Group members who use *power to* help each other foster a win–win group climate in which each member's success is seen as advancing collective work. Members perceive themselves as a unit that benefits from the successes of each individual member.

All those in favor, say, "I'D LIKE TO KEEP MY JOB." Those opposed, say, "FIRE ME."

Bizzaro © Dan Piraro. Reprinted with permission of King Features Syndicate.

  To heighten your awareness of the difference between *power to* and *power over,* complete Activity 10.2, "Distinguishing Power Over and Power To," in your *Student Companion* or online under "Activities for Chapter 10" at the *Communication in Our Lives* website.

–Stanley–

The different kinds of power we discussed make me think of my high school. The principal came over the intercom to make announcements or lecture us on improper behaviors and threaten us about what was going to happen if we misbehaved. The teachers were the ones with power to. *Most of them worked to empower us. They were the ones who gave us encouragement and praise. They were the ones who helped us believe in ourselves and reach our goals.*

The power structure of a group refers to the distribution of power among various members. Power may result from position (CEO, president, professor) or it may be earned (demonstrated competence or expertise). Ideally, a person who holds a powerful position will have earned that position through competence. If all members of a group have equal power, the group has a *distributed power structure.* On the other hand, if one or more members have greater power than others, the group has a *hierarchical power structure.* In some cases, hierarchy takes the form of one person who is more

Communication Highlight

Five Bases of Power

What is power? How does a person get it? There is more than one answer to each of those questions, because there are different sources of power (Arnold & Feldman, 1986).

Reward power   The ability to give people things they value, such as attention, approval, public praise, promotions, and raises

Coercive power   The ability to punish others through demotions, firing, and undesirable assignments

Legitimate power   The organizational role, such as manager, supervisor, or CEO, that results in others' compliance

Expert power   Influence derived from expert knowledge or experience

Referent power   Influence based on personal charisma and personality

powerful than all others, who are equal in power to each other. In other cases, hierarchy may be more complicated, with more than two levels of power. A leader might have the greatest power, three others might have power equal to each other's but less than the leader's, and four other members might have little power.

How are individual power and group power structure related to participation? First, members with high power tend to be the centers of group communication: They talk more, and others talk more to them. **Social climbing** is the attempt to increase personal status in a group by winning the approval of high-status members. If social climbing doesn't work to increase the status of the climber he or she may become a marginal participant in the group. In addition, members with a great deal of power often have greater influence on group decisions. Not surprisingly, high-power members tend to find group discussion more satisfying than members with less power (Young et al., 2001). This makes sense because those with power get to participate more and get their way more often.

Aspects of nonverbal communication, such as seating patterns, both reflect and shape the power structure of groups.

© LeDuc/Stock Boston

Power not only influences communication but also is influenced by communication. In other words, how members communicate can affect the power they acquire. People who demonstrate expertise in the group's task tend to acquire power quickly (Hawkins, 1995). This is an example of earned power, which is gained when a member provides skills valued by the group.

Interaction Patterns

Another important influence on participation is the group's interaction patterns. Some groups are centralized; one or two people have key positions, and most or all communication is funneled through them (Figure 10.1). Other groups have decentralized patterns, in which communication is more balanced and thus more satisfying to

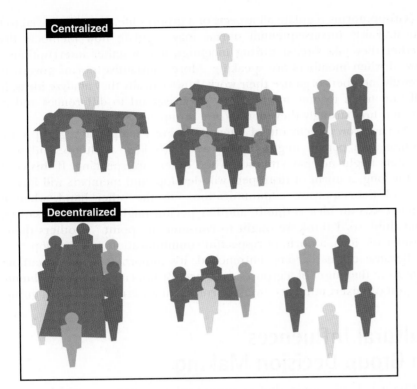

Figure 10.1
Group Interaction Patterns

everyone. As you might suspect, the power of individual members and the power structure of the group often affect interaction patterns. If one or two members have greater power than others, a centralized pattern of interaction is likely to emerge.

Decentralized patterns are more typical when members have relatively equal power. One strategy for controlling communication in groups is to manage nonverbal influences on interaction. If you want a centralized communication structure (and hierarchical power), you might arrange chairs so that one person is more central than the others. On the other hand, if you want a decentralized structure, you would arrange chairs so that no one person was more central than any other. Equalized participation directly enhances satisfaction with belonging to a group and commitment to a group's decisions.

Group Norms

A final feature of small groups that affects communication is **norms.** Norms are standardized guidelines that regulate how members act and how they interact with each other. Our definition of a small group, in fact, emphasizes that individuals must share understandings about their conduct in order to be a group. Like rules in relationships, a group's norms define what is allowed and not allowed and what kind of participation is rewarded. A group meets for the first time, and one member brings popcorn for everyone. A different member brings pretzels to the next meeting. By the third meeting, it's likely that members will expect some snack and that someone will bring it. A norm has developed for the group.

Group norms regulate all aspects of a group's life, from the trivial to the critical. Fairly inconsequential norms may regulate how members dress, whether they take breaks during meetings, and whether interruptions are allowed when members are speaking. More substantive norms govern how carefully members organize their work, how critically they analyze ideas, how well they listen to one another, how they respond to differences and conflict, and how strongly they identify as a group.

Norms grow directly out of interaction. For example, at a group's initial meeting, one person might dismiss another's idea as dumb, and several members might not pay attention when others are speaking. If this continues for long, a norm of disrespect will develop, and members will form the habit of nonresponsive communication. On the other hand, when one member says an idea is dumb, another person might counter by saying, "I don't think so. I think we ought to consider the point." If others then do consider the idea, a norm of respectful communication may develop.

Because norms become entrenched, it's important to pay attention to them from the outset of a group's existence. By noticing patterns and tendencies, you can exert influence over the rules that govern conduct in a group.

Cultural Influences on Group Decision Making

In Chapter 1, we noted that communication is systemic, which means it occurs within systems, or contexts, that influence the character of communication. Like other forms of communication, small-group communication is embedded in larger social and cultural systems that affect how groups are perceived and how members interact in them (Gupta, Hanges, & Dorfman, 2002; House, Javidan, Hanges, & Dorfman, 2002; Hirokawa, Cathcart, Samovar, & Henman, 2004). In Chapter 4, we noted that communication reflects culture; that principle pertains to groups as well as to individuals and relationships. Although Western society is increasingly diverse, work groups in the United States still tend to reflect primarily Western values and styles of communicating. For example, the democratic ideology of our society is reflected in the widespread tendency toward democratic leadership in groups. Let's consider several pronounced Western values that shape group communication in the West.

Individualism

One of the most strongly held values of Western society is **individualism,** which holds that each person is unique and important and should be recognized for her or his personal activities (Hofstede, 1980; Samovar & Porter, 2001; Triandis, 1990). It means that individual achievement and personal freedom are greatly respected. In group discussions, individualism is evident in the extent to which Western groups acknowledge the individuals who make contributions, and in the assumption that each individual has the right to express himself or herself freely and fully. In addition, an individualist orientation leads people to be loyal primarily to themselves rather than to a group or employer (Goleman, 1990). Contrast this with the greater emphasis on collectivism in countries such as Japan, Pakistan, Nepal, and

Figure 10.2
Ranking Individualism across Cultures
Source: Hofstede (1991)

Most individualistic	
1	United States
5	Netherlands
8	Belgium
11	France
15	Germany
19	Israel
24	Iran
30	Portugal
34	Singapore
37	Peru
Most collectivist	
40	Venezuela

Colombia. In those societies, groups are less likely to spotlight individual members and more likely to consider everything contributed to be part of the group (Figure 10.2).

Assertiveness

Perhaps because most Westerners place such high value on individualism, they also tend to admire assertiveness. People are expected to speak up, to assert their ideas, and to stand up for their rights. Like other cultural values, this one is not universal. In Thailand, the Philippines, and Japan, assertiveness not only is not admired but may be considered offensive. Filipinos regard bluntness as extremely rude and disrespectful (Gochenour, 1990) and instead admire *pakikisma,* or harmonious interaction. Cultural differences in perceptions of assertiveness explain why intercultural discussions sometimes are frustrating. A person from Chicago may argue forcefully for her position and offend a Japanese member of the group. The American regards the Japanese member as uninterested and uncommitted because he won't take a firm position.

–Betsy–

I think I really misjudged a guy in a class project group I was in last term. No matter what anyone said, Park Jin Kean nodded and praised the idea. When we asked him what he thought, he would say stuff like, "I do not have an opinion to advance" or "I will support whatever others want." I just thought he was a real wimp, but now I see that he just had a different point of view on how to communicate as a good group member.

Equality

A second strong Western value is equality. The United States was founded on the belief that all people are created equal. Even though there are clear status markers and much class division in the United States, the idea of equality is strongly endorsed in Western society, and this value influences communication in small groups. In small groups, the value placed on equality is reflected in the assumption that every member has an equal right to speak and that no member is better than others. In a number of other cultures, hierarchies are used to order people according to particular criteria. Even in Western society, the ideal of equality is qualified in specific ways. For example, men often are more assertive and more likely to put themselves forward than women, so male members of groups may speak more, and their comments may be given greater respect (Mapstone, 1998).

Progress, Change, and Speed

Westerners also tend to value progress, change, and speed, especially in the area of technology. We like a quick pace, rapid answers, fast action. Communication scholars Larry Samovar and Richard Porter (2001) explain that the Western emphasis on progress is not a specific belief or activity but a basic mind-set by which Westerners operate. Valuing change and progress leads Westerners to focus on the future and to believe they can (and should) control almost all things. The mind-set favoring progress is obvious in the ways Western groups define problems and the kinds of solutions they seek. The typical Western decision-making committee would be likely to feel it had accomplished nothing if it did not recommend changes in existing policies. The goal is to produce change and move forward. In societies such as Japan and China, history is more revered, and traditions are more likely to be sustained by group decisions.

Risk and Uncertainty

The importance Westerners place on progress also explains why they tend to be more tolerant of risk than members of many other cultures. Embarking on new paths, trying bold innovations, and experimenting with untested ideas take daring and willingness to take risks. Associated with risk is acceptance of uncertainty as a normal part of life and of moving forward. Countries such as the United States, Sweden, Ireland, and Finland accept uncertainty more easily than do countries such as Greece, Germany, Peru, and Japan (Samovar & Porter, 2001).

One implication of the value placed on risk taking is that Western groups are more likely to accept new ideas if such ideas promise to con-

Communication Highlight

Speeding Along

David Brooks is a writer and an observer of social trends. One that has caught his attention lately is Americans' growing love affair with technology and its offspring, speed. Brooks thinks that communication technologies are teaching us to crave speed and to be impatient with even the slightest delays in getting information or service. "Wireless Man," says Brooks, "craves his next data fix. He's a speed freak" (2001b, p. 71). Brooks also notes that twenty-first-century Westerners are addicted to whatever is new, cool, and cutting edge (2001a). We want to do more and do it faster. But the quest for speed may undermine real creativity. When we're accustomed to doing everything in high gear, reflection and the time for thinking in fresh ways become rare.

To learn more about Americans' addiction to speed, go to http://www.alternet.org/ story/ 9809 to read Tamara Straus's article on addiction to high-tech speed.

tribute to what they regard as progress. Ironically, valuing newness and change doesn't always translate into appreciating people or ideas that depart from Western cultural values. Westerners' generally high regard for change is in tension with resistance, sometimes quite strong, to people and ideas that challenge Western conventions.

Informality

Another Western cultural value is informality. People generally treat each other directly and in a relaxed way. How often have you heard someone say, after a formal introduction, "Please call me by my first name"? College classes tend to feature informal interaction between professors and students. In contrast, classes in a number of cultures are rigidly organized, with the teacher at the center and perhaps on a stage or raised platform; sometimes the teacher's voice is almost the only one to be heard. Once initial introductions have been made, Americans largely avoid titles and the formal rituals of conduct followed in other countries such as Japan, Egypt, Turkey, and Germany (Javidi & Javidi, 1994).

Sharpen Your Skill

Assessing the Values of Your Group

Select one group to which you belong that has existed for an extended period of time. Identify communication that reflects the values discussed in this section:

Communication that reflects individuality: ....

Communication that reflects assertiveness: ....

Communication that values risk taking: ....

Communication that expresses equality: ....

Communication that fosters informality: ....

Let's summarize what we've discussed so far in this chapter. We've seen that a small group is three or more people who interact over time, have a common purpose, and share understandings about their conduct. Teams are a special kind of group, in which members have specific and different resources and in which cohesion and a sense of collective identity exceed those typical of most groups. The advantages of groups and teams for problem solving are that they have greater resources and tend to be more thorough, creative, and powerful in generating commitment to decisions than individuals are. The amount of time discussion takes and the possibility of conformity pressure are potential weaknesses that should be curbed. We've also identified cohesion, size, power structure, interaction patterns, and norms as features of groups that affect participation. Finally, we've noted that small groups exist in particular cultural contexts that shape how members communicate and work together.

Communication in Small Groups

We've seen that effective small group discussion entails knowing when groups are likely to be superior to individuals and understanding how group

What can you infer about this group from members' dress, seating patterns, and postures?

features affect participation. We're now ready to consider the variety of ways in which members communicate within groups. We'll discuss ways group members contribute, decision-making methods, and communication responsibilities of leadership.

Forms of Group Communication

Because communication is the heart of all groups, the ways members communicate are extremely important to the effectiveness of group process. There are four kinds of communication in groups (Mudrack & Farrell, 1995) (Table 10.1). The first three—task, procedural, and climate communication—are constructive because they foster good group process and outcomes. The fourth kind of communication is egocentric, or dysfunctional, communication. It tends to detract from group cohesion and effective decision making.

These forms of communication shape group climate and productivity for groups and teams that meet face to face as well as those that interact by videoconferencing. As technologies become increasingly sophisticated, videoconferencing is becoming more popular, especially for group discussions between people who do not work in the same area.

Communication Highlight

Virtual Groups

Technologies are allowing more and more groups and teams to work without getting together in the same physical space. Increasingly, businesses are holding virtual conferences in which people who are separated by distance interact in simultaneous time in videoconferences or computer-mediated conferences (Cragan, Wright, & Kasch, 2004). All that's needed is the correct software, a computer with a video monitor, and a modem hooked to a telephone line.

Videoconferencing saves travel time and expense for individual members of groups and teams, yet it preserves the benefits of interaction (Marion, 1997). Electronic brainstorming groups are increasingly effective because members can remain anonymous and so are more willing to take risks in venturing creative ideas (Dennis et al., 1999; Pinsonneault & Barki, 1999). And virtual conferences aren't necessarily one-time events. Virtual teams are becoming more and more common in the workplace (Crandall & Wallace, 1998; Hartzler & Henry, 1998).

One gauge of the growth of virtual teams is the increasing number of workers who have Internet access in their home offices. In 1996, only 26% of home offices had Internet access. In 1999, 81% did (Stroup, 2001). Today, nearly 100% do. More and more workers today choose to work out of their homes, where they've equipped their offices with computers, fax machines, modems, and video-conferencing technology (Dash, 1998; Shellenbarger, 1995). This enables them to do their work and stay in contact—even visually—with colleagues and supervisors at other virtual offices or the main office. The growth in telecommuters is striking. In 1991, only 1.4% of U.S. workers were telecommuters. In 1999, 5% were, and that number is expected to increase to 20% in 2005 and 40% by 2020 (Stroup, 2001).

If you have a group or team and want to create a virtual conference room for it, try the voice-enabled Web service CentraNow. The first five members are free; there's a charge for members six through twenty. Visit the site at http://www .centranow.com.

Table 10.1: Types of Communication in Groups

Task Communication	Climate Communication
Initiates ideas	Establishes and maintains healthy climate
Seeks information	Energizes group process
Gives information	Harmonizes ideas
Elaborates ideas	Recognizes others
Evaluates, offers critical analysis	Reconciles conflicts
	Builds enthusiasm for group

Procedural Communication	Egocentric Communication
Establishes agenda	Aggresses toward others
Provides orientation	Blocks ideas
Curbs digressions	Seeks personal recognition (brags)
Guides participation	Dominates interaction
Coordinates ideas	Pleads for special interest
Summarizes others' contributions	Confesses, self-discloses, seeks personal help
Records group progress	Disrupts task
	Devalues others
	Trivializes group and its work

Task Communication **Task communication** focuses on the problems, issues, or information before a group. It provides ideas and information, ensures members' understanding, and uses reasoning to evaluate ideas and information. Task contributions may initiate ideas, respond to others' ideas, or provide critical evaluation of information before the group. Task contributions also include asking for ideas and evaluation from others. Task comments emphasize the content of a group's work.

Procedural Communication If you've ever participated in a disorganized group, you understand the importance of **procedural communication,** which helps a group get organized and stay on track in its decision making. Procedural contributions establish an agenda, coordinate the comments of different members, and record group progress. In addition, procedural contributions may curb digressions and tangents, summarize progress, and regulate participation so that everyone has opportunities to speak and nobody dominates.

Climate Communication A group is more than a task unit. It also includes people who are involved in a relationship that can be more or less pleasant and open. **Climate communication** focuses on creating and maintaining a constructive climate that encourages members to contribute cooperatively and evaluate ideas critically. Climate comments emphasize a group's strengths and progress, encourage cooperative interaction, recognize others' contributions, reconcile conflicts, and build enthusiasm for the group and its work (Sonnentag, 2001).

Egocentric Communication   The final kind of group communication is not recommended but does sometimes surface in groups. **Egocentric communication,** or dysfunctional communication, is used to block others or to call attention to oneself. It detracts from group progress because it is self-centered rather than group centered. Examples of egocentric talk are devaluing another member's ideas, trivializing the group's efforts, aggressing toward other members, bragging about one's own accomplishments, dominating, disrupting group work, and pleading for special causes that aren't in a group's interest. Another form of egocentric communication is cynical remarks, which undermine group cohesion and enthusiasm (LaFasto & Larson, 2001).

Sharpen Your Skill

Your Communication in Groups

1. How do you contribute to small group discussions? ....

2. Do you specialize in task, procedural, or climate communication? ....

3. Observe yourself in a small group setting, and record the focus of your comments. ....

Which kinds of group communication do you do well? In which areas do you want to develop greater skill? ....

  To extend this exercise, complete Activity 10.1, "Identifying Kinds of Communication in Groups," in your *Student Companion* or online at the *Communication in Our Lives* website.

Task, procedural, and climate communication work together to foster productive, organized, and comfortable group discussion. Most of us are particularly skilled in one or two kinds of communication. For instance, some people have a gift for reconciling conflicts and using humor to break tension. Other people are very organized and become procedural leaders. Still others are especially skillful in task matters, knowing how to evaluate data and determine what information is needed to make decisions. All three communication emphases contribute to effective groups. The kinds of communication that you associate with yourself reflect your self-concept, which we discussed in Chapter 3. Interacting in groups and making a commitment to enlarge your current communication skills should allow you to broaden your repertoire for contributing to group work.

Egocentric communication, on the other hand, does not contribute to enjoyable group interaction or high-quality outcomes. Egocentric participation can sabotage a group's climate and hinder its progress. If it occurs, others in the group should intervene to discourage it. Communicating clearly that egocentric behavior will not be tolerated in your group fosters norms for effective interaction.

The following excerpt from a group discussion will give you concrete examples of each type of group communication. Each comment is coded as one of the four types of communication we have identified.

ED: We might start by discussing what we see as the goal of this group. (*procedural*)

JAN: That's a good idea. (*climate*)

BOB: I think our goal is to come up with a better meal plan for students on campus. (*task*)

ED: What do you mean by "better"? Do you mean cheaper or more varied or more tasteful? (*task*)

ANN: I think we need to consider all three. (*task*)

ED: Well, we probably do care about all three, but maybe we should talk about one at a time so that we can keep our discussion focused. (*procedural*)

BOB: Okay, I vote we focus first on taste—like it would be good if there were some taste to the food on campus! (*task and climate [humor]*)

JAN: Do you mean taste itself or quality of food, which might also consider nutrition? (*task*)

BOB: Pure taste! When I'm hungry, I don't think about what's good for me, just what tastes good. (*task*)

JAN: Well, maybe that's a reason why we might want the food service to think about nutrition—because we don't. (*task*)

BOB: If you're a health food nut, that's your problem. I don't think nutrition is something that's important in the food service on campus. (*task; possibly also egocentric if his tone toward Jan was snide*)

ED: Let's do this: Let's talk first about what we would like in terms of taste itself. (*procedural*) Before we meet next time, it might be a good idea for one of us to talk with the manager of the cafeteria to see whether they have to meet any nutritional guidelines in what they serve. (*task*)

ANN: I'll volunteer to do that. (*task*)

ED: Great. Thanks, Ann. (*climate*)

BOB: I'll volunteer to do taste testing! (*climate [humor]*)

JAN: With your weight, you'd better not. (*egocentric*)

BOB: Yeah, like you have a right to criticize me. (*egocentric*)

ANN: Look, none of us is here to criticize anyone else. We're here because we want to improve the food service on campus. (*climate*) We've decided we want to focus first on taste (*procedural*), so who has an idea of how we go about studying that? (*task*)

This dialogue includes all four kinds of communication that we have discussed. It's particularly noteworthy to recognize how skillfully Ann communicates to defuse tension between Bob and Jan before it disrupts the group. You might also notice that Ed provides the primary procedural leadership

The most effective work teams spend a good deal of time on task communication; however, they also find time to laugh and enjoy interaction.

© J. Wilson/Woodfin Camp & Associates

for the group, and Bob is effective in interjecting humor. Several members recognize contributions to the discussion.

In effective group discussion, communication meets the task, procedural, and climate demands of teamwork and avoids egocentrism that detracts from group progress and cohesion. By understanding how varied types of communication affect collective work, you can decide when to use each type of communication in your own participation in groups. Although you may not be proficient in all three valuable kinds of group communication right now, with commitment and practice, you can develop skill.

Experiencing Communication in Our Lives

CASE STUDY: Group Communication

The conversation scripted here is featured as a multimedia scenario on the *Communication in Our Lives* CD-ROM included with this book. Once you've launched the CD, click on the "Communication Scenarios" icon, and, from the Scenarios Menu, select "Group Communication" to watch the video. Improve your own communication skills by reading, watching, listening to, critiquing, and analyzing this communication encounter.

Analyze the scenario by applying the principles covered in this chapter, and respond to the prompts that accompany the video, which you can access by clicking on "Analysis." After completing the conversation analysis and answering the questions, you can click on the "Done" button to compare your responses with the ones I suggest. Additional analysis questions are available in print at the end of this chapter and on the book's website.

Jason Harris/© 2001 Wadsworth

As members of the Student Government Financial Committee, Davinia, Joyce, Thomas, and Pat make decisions on how much funding, if any, to give to various student groups that request support from the funds collected from student fees. They are meeting for the first time in a campus cafeteria.

THOMAS: Well, we've got twenty-three applications for funding and a total of $19,000 that we can distribute.

DAVINIA: Maybe we should start by listing how much each of the twenty-three groups wants.

JOYCE: It might be better to start by determining the criteria that we will use to decide if groups get any funding from student fees.

DAVINIA: Yeah, right. We should set up our criteria before we look at applications.

THOMAS: Sounds good to me. Pat, what do you think?

PAT: I'm on board. Let's set up criteria first and then review the applications against those.

JOYCE: Okay, we might start by looking at the criteria used last year by the Financial Committee. Does anyone have a copy of those?

THOMAS: I do. [He passes out copies to the other three people.] They had three criteria: service to a significant number of students, compliance with the college's nondiscrimination policies, and educational benefit.

DAVINIA: What counts as "educational benefit"? Did last year's committee specify that?

JOYCE: Good question. Thomas, you were on the committee last year. Do you remember what they counted as educational benefit?

THOMAS: The main thing I remember is that it was distinguished from artistic benefit—like a concert or art exhibit or something like that.

PAT: But can't art be educational?

DAVINIA: Yeah, I think so. Thomas, Joyce, do you?

THOMAS: I guess, but it's like art's primary purpose isn't to educate.

JOYCE: I agree. It's kind of hard to put into words, but I think educational benefit has more to do with information and the mind, and art has more to do with the soul. Does that sound too hokey?

[Laughter.]

PAT: Okay, so we want to say that we don't distribute funds to any hokey groups, right?

[More laughter.]

DAVINIA: It's not like we're against art or anything. It's just that the funding we can distribute is for educational benefit, right?

[Everyone nods.]

JOYCE: Okay, let's move onto another criterion. What is a significant number of students?

THOMAS: Last year we said that the proposals for using money had to be of potential interest to at least 20% of students to get funding. How does that sound to you?

PAT: Sounds okay as long as we remember that something can be of potential interest to students who aren't members of specific groups. Like, for instance, I might want to attend a program on Native American customs even though I'm not a Native American. See what I mean?

DAVINIA: Good point—we don't want to define student interest as student identity or anything like that.

[Nods of agreement.]

THOMAS: Okay, so are we agreed that 20% is about right with the understanding that the 20% can include students who aren't in a group applying for funding? [Nods.] Okay, then do we need to discuss the criterion of compliance with the college's policies on nondiscrimination?

Chapter Summary

In this chapter, we've considered what small groups are and how they operate. We defined groups as three or more people who meet over time, share understandings of how to interact, and have a common goal. The potential weaknesses of group discussion, notably conformity pressures and time, must be recognized and managed in order to realize the important advantages of group decision making.

Communication in groups and teams is influenced by cohesion, group size, power, norms, interaction patterns, and cultural values. Each of these features shapes the small-group system within which communication transpires. At the same time, how members communicate affects the nature and functioning of groups by encouraging or inhibiting cohesion, power, and norms. Effective communication in groups and teams requires that members be aware of and exert control over features that make up the group system. By managing these influences, you should be able to enhance the content and climate of communication, the outcomes of group deliberation, and members' feelings about participation.

The final section of the chapter focused on the kinds of communication that occur in small groups. We saw that effective group interaction includes task, climate, and procedural contributions and is hindered by egocentric communication. Developing skill in the three constructive types of communication and avoiding egocentric comments will make you a valuable member of any group.

In Chapter 11, we will build on what we have learned in this chapter. We will identify the kinds of task teams that dot the contemporary landscape, and we will discuss leadership, organization of group discussion, and ways of managing conflict so that it benefits group work.

Communication in Our Lives ONLINE

In addition to presenting the case studies' multimedia scenarios, the *Communication in Our Lives* CD-ROM provides quick access to the *Communication in Our Lives* website and InfoTrac College Edition. The website is online at http://communication.wadsworth.com/woodciol4, but you can only access this book's premium web content when you link to the site directly through the book's CD.

 The *Communication in Our Lives* website features interactive tools for learning and reviewing the chapter's concepts and key terms, including electronic versions of the "For Further Reflection and Discussion" questions that appear below and a review quiz.

 The website also provides updated web links and additional InfoTrac College Edition activities. If required, you can e-mail completed chapter activities or the quizzes to your instructor.

Key Concepts

climate communication, *271*	individualism, *266*	procedural communication, *271*
cohesion, *261*	norms, *265*	social climbing, *264*
egocentric communication, *272*	power, *262*	synergy, *260*
group, *256*	power over, *263*	task communication, *271*
groupthink, *262*	power to, *263*	team, *256*

For Further Reflection and Discussion

1. Recall the last group in which you participated. Did you find it effective in achieving its task goals? Was the climate comfortable? Now describe your group according to key features discussed in this chapter: size, interaction patterns, cohesion, power, rules, and cultural influences. Do these features explain the climate and task effectiveness of your group?

2. What ethical responsibilities accompany having power in a group? What are ethical and unethical uses of power in group and team situations?

3. Observe a group discussion on your campus or in your town. Record members' contributions by classifying them as task, climate, procedural, or egocentric. Does the communication you observe explain the effectiveness or ineffectiveness of the group?

4. Talk with several people who have lived in non-Western cultures. Ask them whether the cultural values that affect group communication in the United States are present in the countries where they lived. In your conversation, explore differences in cultural values and how these differences affect small group interaction.

5. Use your InfoTrac College Edition to read Linda Larson's 2001 article, "How to Defuse Other People's Anger." Is her advice consistent with what you have learned about creating supportive communication climates? Can you apply her advice to group and team situations?

 6. To learn more about groupthink, visit this site: http://www.orst.edu/instruct/theory/grpthink.html.

Questions for Analysis and Discussion

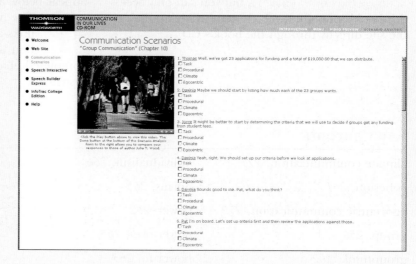

Review the video of the scenario entitled "Group Communication" that you watched when completing this chapter's case study (pages 274–276), or, if you haven't seen it yet, watch it for the first time. If you didn't previously finish the "Analysis" questions included on the CD-ROM, do so now, and then respond to the following questions, which are also available on the book's website under "Activities for Chapter 10."

1. Classify each statement in this scenario as one of the forms of group communication (task, procedural, climate, egocentric). Is the balance between forms appropriate for a decision-making group?

2. Based on this discussion, does this group seem to have a single leader, or do different members lead the group?

3. How do you perceive the interaction pattern among members? Does everyone seem to be involved and participating?

4. Are any of the potential values of group versus individual decision making evident in this discussion?

CHAPTER 11

Effective Communication in Task Groups and Teams

Focus Questions

1. What kinds of task groups are common in professional life?
2. Do groups work better when there is only one leader?
3. How do different leadership styles affect productivity and group climate?
4. How can group members organize discussion for high-quality results?
5. How can conflict be managed effectively in groups?

© Bill Bachmann/PhotoEdit, Inc.

There are many kinds of groups, and each kind has distinctive goals and communication patterns. Social groups provide us with recreation and the stimulation of conversation with people we enjoy. Communication in social groups tends to be relaxed, informal, and more focused on interpersonal climate than on task goals. Personal growth groups enable people to deal with significant issues and worries in a context of interpersonal support. In personal growth groups, communication generally is personal in topic and tone, and its goals are to support members and to help them clarify and address issues in their lives. Task groups, such as project teams and decision-making groups, focus on accomplishing a particular objective, such as improving the quality of work, generating policy, or resolving problems.

Although groups differ in their primary purpose and focus, most groups include interaction that goes beyond their basic purpose. For example, social groups often move into task discussion, as when one friend asks another for advice in solving a problem. Groups that exist to accomplish a task typically include some social communication, and therapy groups usually involve both task and social dimensions that contribute to the primary goal of personal growth.

One of the most prominent types of groups in modern life is the task group or team, which aims to accomplish some defined objective, such as creating a policy, making a decision on expansion, solving a marketing problem, advising others about handling a public relations concern, or generating ideas for improving customer service.

Because task groups and teams are extensively relied on in professional and civic life, this chapter concentrates on communication in task-oriented groups and teams that manage projects, develop ideas, and make decisions or recommendations. We'll begin by identifying types of task groups. Next, we'll discuss leadership in task groups. We'll then consider a method of organizing efficient and productive discussion. In the fourth section of this chapter, we'll consider alternative methods of making decisions in groups. Finally, we'll return to the topic of conflict, which we first discussed in Chapter 8. We will focus on the constructive potential of conflict and ways to manage it effectively in task groups and teams.

Task Groups

The task group, which is often a team, has emerged as a major feature of modern life. Earlier in this century, most people worked fairly independently. Each person had his or her individual job responsibilities and coordinated with others only when necessary. Increasingly, however, recognition of the values of group communication has led to reliance on group work in business and civic life (Hoover, 2002). There are several types of task groups, each with a specific purpose and value. We'll discuss six common types here.

Project Teams

Project teams are becoming increasingly popular in business and professional life (LaFasto & Larson, 2001; Maxwell, 2001). Project teams consist of a number of people who have special expertise in relation to some project and who work together over a period of time to combine their knowledge and skills to accomplish a common goal. Typically, project teams exist to deal with one-time tasks (Jossi, 2001), such as establishing a training system for a company, creating a public relations campaign for a new product, or determining the public image of a corporation in a community.

Communication in project teams allows each member to draw on the resources of other members and coordinate their different areas of experience and talent. To launch a new product, pharmaceutical companies often compose product teams that include scientists, who understand the technical character of the new drug, and personnel from marketing, product design, advertising, and customer relations. Working together, these people develop a coherent plan for testing, packaging, advertising, and marketing the new product to the public. If the individuals worked separately in their specific areas, they would generate a less well-coordinated, less effective plan: Marketing wouldn't know what advertising was planned, advertising wouldn't understand the overall image of the product, and customer relations wouldn't have informed advertising and marketing of salient issues in the product's target market.

A project team is valuable when many people will work on a single project and when each person's actions have implications for other members of the team. Wadsworth Publishing Company put together a project team for this book. Besides me, the team included a communications editor, who oversaw all aspects of development and production; a production editor, who coordinated the efforts of the copy editor, photo research, art manager, and permissions editor; a marketing manager, who matched information about this book with interests of faculty and students; a designer, who created page layout and visual features for the book; and sales representatives, who were involved from the early stages to provide feedback on faculty and student needs. The team was able to develop a holistic vision of the book and to infuse every aspect of the book's development and marketing with that vision.

Members of a project team bring specialized expertise that allows them to approach a task in an integrated manner.

Focus Groups

Also popular in the workplace is the focus group, which is used to find out what people think about a specific idea, product, issue, or person. Focus groups are a mainstay of advertisers, who want to understand the attitudes, preferences, and responses of the people most likely to buy their product: What do 18- to 25-year-olds think of a new light beer? How do retirees respond to a draft advertising campaign for cruises? Focus groups are also popular in political life: What do middle-class women and men think of a politician's record on social issues? How do young voters

© David Young-Wolff/PhotoEdit

Non Sequitur

feel about economic issues? Do Latinos and Latinas regard Candidate Y as trustworthy?

A focus group is guided by a leader or facilitator, who encourages members to communicate their ideas, beliefs, feelings, and perceptions relevant to the topic. The contributions of group members serve as the foundation for later decisions, such as how to refine the recipe for the light beer, increase perceptions of Incumbent Y's trustworthiness, and tailor the advertising for the cruises. The facilitator doesn't offer personal judgments and opinions but guides group members to express themselves, respond to each other's communication, and analyze the reasons for their thoughts, feelings, and responses.

To prepare for leading a focus group, the facilitator usually develops a list of questions and probes that can be used to encourage participants to elaborate responses (Lederman, 1990). Facilitators also keep a steady eye on group dynamics so that they can keep participants on track and ensure maximum input and efficiency (Kruger & Casey, 2000).

Brainstorming Groups

Brainstorming groups harness group discussion's creative potential. **Brainstorming** groups—or a brainstorming phase in other types of groups—are used to generate ideas and to stimulate "outside-the-box" thinking.

Communication Highlight

The Verdict on Focus Groups

When the term *focus group* comes up, most people think of groups of people companies put together to test the appeal of a new product, political candidate, or ad campaign. But that's not the only use of focus groups. Increasingly, attorneys rely on focus groups to test trial strategies and get feedback from people who are similar to the jurors who will decide the case.

A recent case in North Carolina involved an 8-year-old girl who suffered severe internal injuries when she was sucked halfway down a pool drain (Saker, 1996). The girl's family sued the company that manufactured the pool drain. Attorneys on both sides used focus groups to gauge people's reactions to various arguments and ways of presenting the sides of the case. The attorneys also relied on the groups to tell them what to concentrate on, or—as the term implies—how to focus the case.

Table 11.1: Rules for Brainstorming

- Do not evaluate ideas that are volunteered. Both verbal and nonverbal criticism are inappropriate.
- Record ideas on a blackboard or easel pad so that all members of the group can see them.
- Go for quantity: The more ideas, the better.
- Build on ideas. An idea presented by one member of the group may stimulate an extension by another member. This is desirable.
- Encourage creativity. Wild, even preposterous, ideas should be welcomed. An idea that seems wacky may lead to other ideas that are more workable.

In brainstorming, the goal is to come up with as many ideas as possible. Because criticism tends to stifle creativity, no criticism is allowed while brainstorming is in progress. Creativity and even wild thinking are encouraged in order to come up with the most imaginative ideas possible. When group members start to run out of ideas, a leader or leaders can prompt further brainstorming by suggesting extensions of ideas already generated and new dimensions of the topic. Table 11.1 lists the rules for brainstorming.

Perhaps you're concerned that brainstorming can produce unrealistic ideas or ideas that are not well analyzed. That's not really a problem, because brainstorming is followed by evaluative discussion. During evaluation, members work together to appraise all the ideas that were generated in brainstorming. Criticism is now appropriate and constructive because the group must decide which idea or ideas merit more attention. However, the first priority is to get some good ideas on the table. Once that has happened through brainstorming, impractical ideas are discarded, weak or undeveloped ideas are improved, related ones are consolidated, and promising ones are discussed further.

The leader or facilitator of a brainstorming group should set a tone for creative communication. To do this, leaders should show energy, respond enthusiastically to members' ideas, and communicate excitement. Leaders may also need to stoke members' imaginations if they hit a dry spell. This can be done by making encouraging comments, such as "Who can add to the list of ideas?" "Imagine that we have unlimited money and time. What else might be possible under those conditions?" "Let's think about extending and combining some of the ideas we already have," "We're being too restrained—think outside the box," and "Let's generate about five more ideas before we move on."

Sharpen Your Skill

Brainstorming

To discover the value of brainstorming, try this: First, for each of the numbered questions, write down as many ideas as you can think of by yourself. Then, with 4 to 6 other students in your class, spend 10 minutes generating responses to the same question. Be sure to follow the rules for brainstorming that appear in Table 11.1.

1. Identify ways to make your campus more environmentally sensitive.

2. List ways to improve your campus newspaper.

3. Develop ideas for your class's graduation gift to the university or college.

What do you conclude about the value of brainstorming as a method of promoting creative communication in groups?

Advisory Groups

As the name suggests, advisory groups provide advice to others. They are probably the most common type of task group. Advisory groups do not actually make policies or decisions. Instead, they inform and recommend to others who make the actual decisions. Advisory groups are formed when a person wants to be briefed by experts on a topic about which she or he must make a decision. For example, at my university we have an Academy of Distinguished Teachers, who provide advice to various campus units and administrators. Our committee has been consulted about the role of technology in teaching, the criteria for teaching awards, and other matters relevant to teaching and learning. As a basis for our advice, our committee gathers and analyzes information from our campus and other institutions.

In 1995, Vice President Gore worked with an advisory group consisting of leaders of major environmental organizations in the United States. Bringing together a handful of key players to discuss national environmental policy accomplished two objectives. First, it informed the vice president about environmental issues that national policies should address. Second, the interaction between members of the advisory group generated understandings and ideas that none of the individuals had before working together as a group.

Advisory groups may also consist of peers who advise each other. In a *Wall Street Journal* column addressed to small business owners, management consultant Howard Upton (1995) described a system of peer advisory groups developed by chief executives of the Petroleum Equipment Institute. The executives created groups of ten to twelve presidents of the 700 distributorships in the United States and Canada. By conferring regularly with peers, these presidents were able to advise each other on common problems, practices, and goals. The members found that by pooling experience and reports on methods of problem solving, they were able to inform each other in ways that enhanced everyone's effectiveness.

In business and civic affairs, executives are seldom experts on the range of issues relevant to decisions they must make. According to Howard Upton, "It is impossible for the head of any company, large or small, to succeed without benefit of outside advice" (1995, p. A14). The solitary manager, president, or CEO who relies only on his or her own ideas is seldom effective on the whole range of issues he or she needs to handle. Advisory groups allow individuals to use other experts' information and advice in developing effective policies and making informed decisions.

Quality Improvement Teams

A **quality improvement team** (also called a *continuous quality improvement team*) is three or more people from different areas of an organization who work together to improve quality in the organization (Lumsden & Lumsden, 2004). Originally, quality circles were part of a management approach called *total quality management* (Deming, 1982), in which intensive teamwork and highly participative work structures are used to maximize the quality of an organization's output. The original quality circles have evolved into quality improvement teams, which are used in a variety of organizations whether or not they embrace total quality management as an overall organizational philosophy.

Typically, quality improvement teams mix not just people from different areas of expertise but also people from different levels of an organization's hierarchy. Thus, a secretary may contribute as much as a managing partner to a discussion of ways to improve office productivity. A line worker in a cafeteria may have a better understanding of waste and ways to reduce it than the manager of the cafeteria.

The first few meetings of a quality improvement team typically involve a lot of complaining about problems ("Quality Circles," 1991). This is natural, and it helps members become comfortable with one another because they create common ground over shared frustrations. In addition, this opening talk generally alerts the group to the special concerns and knowledge of each member. After initial venting of frustrations, discussion focuses on solving problems. Communication concentrates on identifying needs, on areas in which organizational functioning could be improved, and on areas of stress or discontent for employees.

To be effective, quality improvement teams must be given the power to solve problems (Hyatt & Ruddy, 1997). Nothing is more frustrating than to be asked to work on a problem but be denied the authority to implement changes or the assurance that others will implement them. This means that quality circles should be formed only if organizational leaders are receptive to implementing solutions the groups devise. When given appropriate authority, quality improvement teams often generate impressive and creative solutions to organizational concerns such as lowering expenses, improving safety, and recognizing accomplishments. These teams usually make regular reports (weekly or monthly) to keep management informed of the group's insights, progress, and intentions.

Decision-making Groups

A sixth kind of task group exists to solve problems or make decisions. In some cases, decision-making groups and teams are formed to render a specific decision or policy: What should be Corporation X's policy on medical leave? How should we determine raises for employees? What operations and personnel should we reduce or eliminate to achieve a 15% decrease in annual expenses?

In other cases, ongoing groups are charged with making decisions and solving problems in particular areas. Many organizations have standing committees that assume responsibility for budget, public relations, external communication, and other matters. In my department, standing committees are in charge of decisions related to curricula, teaching quality, tenure and promotion, and advising. Because these are ongoing committees, members have acquired expertise in the particular issues within the groups' purview.

Leaders of decision-making groups are responsible for creating a supportive communication climate for group work, organizing discussions productively, and ensuring constructive communication among members. Later in this chapter, we will discuss a method for organizing decision making, and we will also discuss leadership in more detail.

Task groups are becoming more and more prominent in professional and civic life. When members and leaders know how to communicate effectively, these task groups maximize the strengths of group communication we discussed in Chapter 10. They allow diverse people with varying experience, expertise, interests, and talents to interact and generate ideas, understandings, plans, and decisions that often are more creative and better informed than those an individual could devise.

 To test your understanding of different types of groups and teams, complete Activity 11.1, "The Many Types of Task Groups," in your *Student Companion* or online under "Activities for Chapter 11" at the *Communication in Our Lives* website.

Leadership Communication

For decades, it was assumed that leaders were born, not made. In following this assumption, researchers attempted to identify the traits of effective leaders. Personal qualities ranging from intelligence and height to emotional balance and physical energy were studied in an effort to understand the traits of born leaders. This line of study was unsuccessful in discovering any consistent traits that mark leaders. However, it was effective in shifting our understanding of leadership. The lack of identifiable leader traits led researchers to realize that leadership is not a person or a set of personal qualities. Instead, leadership is a set of functions that assist groups in accomplishing tasks efficiently while maintaining a good climate. What is considered effective leadership varies across cultures and between organizations. Westerners' general preference for democratic leadership isn't shared by more authoritarian cultures.

Leadership, Not Leader

Leadership may be provided by one individual or by several members who contribute to guiding the process and ensuring effective communication within the group. Leadership exists when one or more members communicate to establish a good working climate, organize group processes, and focus discussion productively on the task at hand. Recalling our discussion in Chapter 10, you may realize that the functions of leadership we've just identified parallel the three types of constructive communication that group members make in discussions. A fourth function of leadership is to control disruptive members who engage in egocentric communication.

When one person provides leadership, he or she performs the functions necessary for effective group discussion. When leadership is not vested in one person, several members share responsibilities (McCauley & Van Velsor, 2003; Lumsden & Lumsden, 2004). Whether there is one leader or shared leadership, the primary responsibilities are to organize discussion, to ensure critical thinking, to create a productive working climate, to build group morale, to promote effective communication between members, and to discourage egocentric communication that detracts from group efforts.

–Krystal–

The most effective group I've ever been in had three leaders. I was the person who understood our task best, so I contributed the most to critical thinking about the

Communication Highlight

According to David Herbert Donald, the Charles Warren Professor of American History at Harvard University, Abraham Lincoln's ability to lead well resulted largely from his skills as a communicator (Donald, 1996). Donald concludes that two principles were especially prominent in Lincoln's leadership:

- **Encourage criticism from others and listen carefully to it.** Without the public opinion polls that are common today, Lincoln stayed in touch with citizens and learned what mattered to them and what they thought of his actions and plans. Nearly every day of his presidency, Lincoln opened the doors to the White House for what he called his "public opinion baths." Ordinary citizens poured in to voice their opinions, and Lincoln listened intently.

- **Communicate clearly and concisely.** Lincoln believed that any effective leader had to be able to speak and write clearly in ways that ordinary citizens could understand. He abhorred jargon, preferring to speak naturally and informally. He worked to create language that brought ideas alive: vivid words and phrases, concrete analogies, everyday examples.

In seeking feedback, Lincoln followed a principle that is central to contemporary leadership training—to actively encourage feedback from peers, subordinates, and supervisors (McCauley & Van Velsor, 2003). It's vital to understanding how others perceive your effectiveness as a leader.

Use your InfoTrac College Edition to learn more about leadership. Type the keyword "leadership" into the search screen, and read several of the articles that the search generates. Use your InfoTrac College Edition to read Alan Yuspeh's speech (in "Vital Speeches") "Principled Leadership," which was given on August 15, 2001. What three things does Yuspeh say are needed for principled leadership?

---

issues. But Belinda was the one who kept us organized. She really knew how to see tangents and get us off of them, and she knew when it was time to move on from one stage of work to the next. She also pulled ideas together to coordinate our thinking. Kevin was the climate leader. He could always tell a joke if things got tense, and he was the best person I ever saw for recognizing others' contributions. I couldn't point to any one leader in that group, but we sure did have good leadership.

When we realize that leadership is a series of functions that move groups along, it becomes clear that more than one person may provide leadership to a group or team. Sometimes, one member communicates to provide guidance on tasks and procedures and another member communicates to build a healthy group climate. A group needs both climate and task leadership to be maximally effective. It is also possible for various people to provide leadership at different times in a group's life. The person who guides the group at the outset may not be the one who advances the group's work in later phases. A person who is skilled in prompting critical analysis may not be talented at stimulating brainstorming, which requires a very different mind-set.

Depending on what a group needs at any given time, different leadership functions are appropriate and may come from different members. Even when an official leader exists, other members may contribute much of the communication that provides leadership to a group. Although the official leader has the responsibility for a group's decision (and gets the credit or blame), others often contribute to running a group.

Styles of Leadership

Think about the groups in which you've participated. Some of them probably operated casually and were even unfocused at times; others may have been productive and participative, while still others were regimented and tightly controlled by one person who had and exerted power. If these three portraits of groups seem familiar, then you already have an experiential understanding of different styles of leadership.

Although leadership can't be reduced to a set of traits, it can be understood as an overall style of communication. The different styles of leadership have different impacts on group productivity and climate (Lewin, Lippitt, & White, 1939). Styles may be enacted by a single person who is a group leader or by several members. Researchers have identified three primary styles of leadership, each of which involves distinctive forms of communication and each of which has a unique impact on group climate and productivity. In many cases, a group's leadership cannot be classified neatly into one of the three styles. Instead, leadership may be a blend of the styles, and the blend may change over time.

Laissez–faire Leadership

Laissez-faire is a French phrase that roughly translates as "do nothing." **Laissez-faire leadership** is laid-back and nondirective. The laissez-faire leader doesn't provide guidance or suggest directions in which the group should move. Laissez-faire leaders also don't exert authority, preferring to let the group set its own goals and at its own speed. If problems develop in a group, the laissez-faire leader is unlikely to intervene to get the group back on track.

Laissez-faire leadership is not always undesirable. When a group consists of members who are mature, experienced, and self-directed, there may be little need for control by one or more leaders. Yet this is more the exception than the rule. Most groups need guidance, at least at times, to develop and sustain a good climate and to be productive. For this reason, laissez-faire leadership generally is not recommended. It tends to cultivate unfocused discussion and inefficient work. Thus, laissez-faire leadership may hinder productivity or decision making (Bass, 1990). In addition, laissez-faire leadership typically fosters an unproductive climate because lack of direction generates frustration among members. Inefficiency is perhaps the most common characteristic of laissez-faire leadership (White & Lippitt, 1960).

Authoritarian Leadership

As the name suggests, **authoritarian leadership** is directive and dictatorial. It may vary in how directive and domineering it is. This style of leadership tends to be used by a lone leader rather than by several members who share leadership. Authoritarian leaders may announce directions for discussion, assign specific tasks to members, make decisions without consulting others in the group, and otherwise exert control over the group process. As you might suspect, groups that have authoritarian leadership often are very efficient, but members' morale and work quality may not be optimal (Van Oostrum & Rabbie, 1995).

Highly authoritarian leadership generally discourages interaction between members and fosters a centralized pattern of leader-to-member, member-to-leader communication. The paucity of communication among members interferes with the development of group morale and a sense of cohesive identity. Although groups with authoritarian leaders sometimes produce good decisions, this style of leadership seldom promotes satisfaction and cohesion among members. Furthermore, authoritarian leadership doesn't cultivate initiative and commitment among members, so group climate and morale are not ideal. Dependence, apathy, low cohesion, and resentment are common responses to highly authoritarian leadership (Gibb, 1969; Kouzes & Posner, 1999; Lewin, Lippitt, & White, 1939).

Before you dismiss authoritarian leadership altogether, you should realize that it can be effective, even ideal, in some circumstances (Yanes, 1990). The movie *Vertical Limit* is an adventure tale about high-risk mountain climbers. In the film, one group of climbers falls into a crevasse while attempting to reach the summit of K-2 in Pakistan. Another group of climbers decides to mount a rescue effort. When disagreement about how to proceed breaks out among the rescuers, the most seasoned and expert climber tells the others, "This is not a democracy. You'll do what I say." This autocratic style of leading was appropriate for two reasons. First, the leader had the most experience and probably the best judgment about how to proceed. Second, the first group of climbers could have died from edema, hypothermia, or other conditions if the rescue team had taken the time to discuss all ideas and democratically decide what to do.

−Doug−

It took me a while to learn that my boss doesn't want any of us to take initiative or state our ideas unless we agree with him. He is a classic authoritarian leader who tells us what to do as well as what answers and decisions he wants us to produce. He blasts anyone who doesn't play "yes man" to him. By now, none of us cares what happens in our project group. We don't even try to think of ways to improve our work. He's taught us not to take any initiative by penalizing us anytime we depart from his agenda and his prejudgments.

Democratic Leadership **Democratic leadership** provides direction and guidance but does not impose rigid authority. Democratic leadership, whether provided by one individual or by several members, fosters members'

Communication Highlight

Empowering Leadership

In recent years, the term *empowerment* has gained increasing currency in the workplace. Leaders and managers are realizing that employees tend to be maximally productive, satisfied, and committed when they feel empowered in their jobs, which happens when they believe that they have the ability to accomplish things and that they and their work matters. What makes employees feel empowered? That's the question addressed in two books by highly accomplished leadership scholars and consultants.

Ken Blanchard, John Carlos, and Alan Randolph wrote *Empowerment Takes More Than a Minute* (1998) to give working tools to people who want to be empowering leaders. The book is organized in story form, relying on an extended case study to provide hands-on advice, tools, and exercises to increase employees' sense of empowerment.

They emphasize the importance of personal contact, encouragement, and feedback between leaders and employees. James Kouzes and Barry Posner wrote *Encouraging the Heart: A Leader's Guide to Recognizing and Rewarding Others* (1999). Their book aims to guide leaders in building skills for empowering others. Kouzes and Posner think that employees are empowered by stretching to meet high goals and standards. At the same time, leaders must provide appropriate support if they want employees to stretch. Appropriate support includes being clear about goals, giving continuous feedback (more feedback early in a new stretch, less later), and recognizing progress and accomplishments privately and publicly. When leaders are effective in empowering others, eventually those people become self-empowering.

What leadership style seems to be operating in this group? Identify aspects of nonverbal communication that affect your perceptions of leadership style.

development by encouraging them to formulate their own goals and procedures and to take initiative within a group. This style of leadership tends to generate high, generally balanced communication among members who have been socialized in democratic cultures. In turn, high participation fuels group cohesion and members' satisfaction with belonging to a group (Gastil, 1994; Gibb, 1969). Finally, democratic leadership tends to yield high-quality task outcomes that are generally more original and creative than those produced by groups with authoritarian or laissez-faire leadership (Blanchard, Carlos, & Raldolph, 1998; White & Lippitt, 1960).

Before concluding this discussion, we should emphasize that effective leadership cannot be reduced to a one-size-fits-all formula. Although researchers have found that in Western cultures the democratic style of leadership is linked to good group climate and productivity, that research was conducted in societies committed to democratic values. In societies that place higher value on authoritarian structures, an autocratic style of leadership might well be more acceptable and effective. Furthermore, authoritarian leadership may be effective in certain contexts in democratic societies (for instance, when it is nearing 5 P.M. and a group hasn't finished its work). Laissez-faire leadership can be effective when groups have the expertise, commitment, and self-direction they need to perform a task. Like other forms of communication, good leadership is responsive to particular members, situations, circumstances, and cultures.

 To develop skill in determining the style of leadership appropriate in a situation, complete Activity 11.4, "Fitting Leadership to Group Situations," in your *Student Companion* or online under "Activities for Chapter 11" at the *Communication in Our Lives* website.

Effective leadership often changes over time. What a group needs to be productive varies at different points in a group's life cycle and in relation to the maturity of members (Hershey & Blanchard, 1993). When a group first begins to work, direction in framing the issues and determining the group's objectives is vital, and the person who supplies this is performing the critical leadership at that time. As a group continues to work, however, it often matures and no longer needs strong task guidance. At that point, the most effective leadership communication may focus on consideration or climate contributions.

Recognizing the group's progress and the efforts of individual members heightens morale and motivates further commitment to the task. As members invest in group work, the person who initially provided leadership may delegate more and more responsibility. This acknowledges group members' abilities, increases satisfaction, and heightens their loyalty to the group and its decisions (Johnson & Johnson, 1991).

Communication Highlight

Emotionally Intelligent Leadership

Psychologist Daniel Goleman (1995, 1998) says that one aspect of intelligence that standard IQ tests don't measure is **emotional intelligence.** Goleman defines emotional intelligence as the ability to recognize which feelings are appropriate in which situations and the ability to communicate those feelings effectively. Goleman's research indicates that people who have high emotional intelligence are comfortable with themselves and are able to create satisfying personal relationships.

But that's not all. According to Goleman (1998; Goleman, McKee, & Boyatzis, 2002), emotionally intelligent

people are also more effective leaders. They have keen awareness of their own feelings and can recognize and respond to the feelings of others. Thus, they are both self-confident and sensitive—a winning combination, particularly when groups are under stress. Does this mean we have finally found a leadership "trait"? Not according to Goleman. He maintains that emotional intelligence is learned, just as leadership is. Both are skills that can be acquired with commitment and practice.

In sum, leadership is a dynamic process of meeting the changing and multiple needs of effective communication in small groups. Whether provided by one or several members, effective leadership involves communication that advances a group's task, organizes deliberations, builds group morale, controls disruptions, and fosters a constructive climate.

Decision-making Methods

Task groups make decisions: They develop plans for new products, generate recommendations for others, create policies, and solve problems. To accomplish these objectives, task groups must have methods of making decisions. Four common methods of group decision making have been identified. Each involves distinct communication styles and has particular strengths and limitations (Wood & Phillips, 1990). We'll describe each method and consider when it is most likely to be constructive and appropriate.

Consensus

Perhaps the most popular decision-making method in Western societies is **consensus,** which occurs when all members of a group express their ideas and agree on a decision. Members may differ in how enthusiastically they support a decision, but everyone agrees to it. Communication to achieve

Non Sequitur

consensus involves wide participation and often prolonged discussion. For everyone to support the decision, everyone must be involved in crafting it.

The strength of the consensus method is that it involves all members; thus, consensus decisions tend to have strong support. In addition, consensus tends to increase cohesion and member satisfaction because the method generates commitment to both the process and its outcome. As you probably realize, the greatest disadvantage of the consensus method is the time needed to hear all members and to secure everyone's commitment to a single decision. This makes consensus inappropriate for trivial decisions, emergency issues, or decisions on which members cannot agree even after extended discussion (Wood & Phillips, 1990).

Voting

A second method of making decisions is **voting,** by which a decision is made based on the support of a certain number of group members. Some groups have simple majority rule; others require two-thirds or three-fourths support before a decision can be accepted. The obvious drawback of voting is that it can lead to a decision that doesn't have everyone's support. For instance, the majority rule method allows 51% of members to win a vote, leaving 49% dissatisfied. Voting has the potential to foster dissatisfaction and reduce group cohesion. Also, voting may preclude thorough analysis, clarification of issues, and evaluation of different possibilities. Yet voting also has advantages, notably its efficiency and resolution. Thus, when time is short, when a decision is not major, or when a group needs to move on, voting may be advisable.

Compromise

A third method of decision making is **compromise,** in which members work out a solution that satisfies each person's minimum criteria but may not fully satisfy all members. When decisions are made by compromise, the purposes of communication are to clarify what each member or subgroup of members needs in order to accept a decision and to identify issues on which members are willing to bend. Compromise decisions often involve trading and bargaining—"I'll give on this point if you'll give on that one" (Wood & Phillips, 1990). Sometimes compromise results in an effective decision that combines the strong points advocated by different members. In other cases, members hammer out a decision that meets each person's bottom line but may not inspire great enthusiasm from anyone.

The shortcomings of the compromise method are obvious. One is that decisions often are less coherent than decisions made by consensus. This is because compromises may involve a series of separate considerations designed to satisfy particular members. Thus, the parts of a decision may not come together into a fully integrated whole. Also, as we've noted, compromise decisions don't always have enthusiastic support from all members. So why would any group use compromise? The answer is that sometimes it seems the only way to make a decision. If members are deadlocked even after extensive discussion, they may be unable reach consensus. Also, if members represent outside constituencies, as in labor–management negotiations, they have conflicting interests and goals that make consensus unlikely.

Authority Rule

A final method of group decision making actually doesn't involve a decision made by a group. Instead, **authority rule** occurs when an individual or group with power tells a group what to do and the group ratifies the authority's decision. In some cases, the authority is a high-status member of the group (the group leader, for example). In other cases, the authority is someone outside the group who appoints the group to give the appearance of a democratic method and to distribute responsibility for what may be an unpopular decision. Sometimes an authority announces a decision after first allowing a group to discuss issues. Authority rule can also be implemented without prior discussion when a person tells a group what it will decide.

You probably can guess the drawbacks of this decision-making method. It can generate resentment in members, who may dislike being forced to ratify a decision of which they don't approve or being used to camouflage an autocratic process. Equally important, this method short-circuits the potential of group discussion to generate outcomes superior to those of individuals. Exerting authority over a group undermines the special values of group discussion such as increased resources, creativity, and thoroughness. Finally, authority rule can dampen participation in the long run if members think their ideas make no difference in decisions made. On the other hand, authority rule, like autocratic leadership, has advantages in some situations (Yanes, 1990). Obviously, this method is very efficient, so it has the virtue of saving time. Also, it may be useful for routine decisions that could take more time to discuss than their importance justifies.

—Cedric—

I wish someone would teach my work group about authority rule. There are eight of us who meet as a group to decide everything that affects our department. Each of us likes to have our say and to talk things through, and that makes a lot of sense for big decisions like how to assign projects or evaluate subordinates or design new policies. But we talk just as long about trivial decisions. Last week we had a 40-minute discussion about whether to give our secretary individual gifts or pool our money to buy one large gift for the holidays. Forty minutes! We talked just as long about new carpeting for our office. Everyone had a different color preference, and we never did agree. We should let one person make a decision on these things.

There is no single best method of making group decisions. Instead, what is appropriate varies according to factors such as the nature of the decision, preferences of group members, time available for reaching decisions, and cultural values and norms. Many ongoing groups rely on multiple methods of decision making and attempt to use the method most appropriate in each particular situation.

Govennor Arnold Schwarzenegger meets with citizens to discuss issues that are important to them. Reaching consensus on each issue would be difficult and extremely time-consuming with a group this large.

© Tim Wimborne/Reuters/Corbis

Figure 11.1
Stages in the Standard Agenda

I.   Define the problem
     A. Define terms
     B. Phrase a question to guide deliberation
II. Analyze the issues
     A. Gather information on history, how issues have
        been addressed elsewhere, and so on
     B. Analyze causes of problem or need
     C. Discuss desired outcomes of decision
III. Establish criteria
IV. Generate possible solutions
     A. Review research
     B. Brainstorm
V.   Evaluate possible solutions
VI. Select and implement solution
VII. Develop an action plan to monitor solution

Organizing Group Discussion

Perhaps the biggest complaint about group work is that it often seems disorganized. Groups often *are* disorganized, primarily because members don't know how to move efficiently through decision making. Individuals vary greatly in their approach to issues and decisions, so it's unlikely that a group of individuals will share procedural tendencies. One particularly effective method of organizing group discussion is the **standard agenda** (Rothwell, 2004; Young et al., 2001). The standard agenda is a logical, seven-step method for making decisions. In our discussion, we'll focus on the kinds of communication that occur during each of the stages in the standard agenda. Figure 11.1 summarizes the stages.

Stage One: Define the Problem

One of the most common errors groups make is to assume that all members agree on the problem or issue to be resolved and turn immediately to discussing possible solutions. This is a mistake because in reality people often don't agree on what the problem is or what decision they must make. For instance, I once served on a group that was instructed to review the undergraduate curriculum in my department. I assumed this meant we were to consider whether the courses we offered reflected the communication field. Another member thought our job was to decide on the requirements for a major. A third person believed we were to evaluate whether we offered a sufficiently broad range of courses sufficiently often. Each of these views of the task made sense, but they weren't equivalent. Our first task as a group was to define exactly what we were to do.

Decision-making groups often find it useful to decide whether they are dealing with issues of fact, value, or policy. Each type of issue necessitates a different sort of analysis and decision, so groups need to agree on their focus (Lumsden & Lumsden, 2004). Factual tasks involve finding out what is the case, what is true or untrue, and what exists. Usually, factual group reports are descriptive. For instance, the group I mentioned previously could address the factual question, "What are the undergraduate courses taught in our department, and how often are they offered?" Answering this question requires only that the group consult records on departmental offerings and count the number of times each course has been offered.

Value questions have to do with the worth, ethicality, or importance of a policy, procedure, concept or action. For example, "Which courses offer the most valuable educational experiences to undergraduates?" Answering this question would require members to consider and evaluate the alternative values of education (broadening the mind, developing skills, increasing understanding). What are the standards for judging educational value: national trends, student evaluations of courses, faculty competencies, or the overall mission of a particular college (liberal arts, for example)? Deciding how to define valuable educational experiences allows a group to proceed with common understandings.

A policy focus requires a group to decide what actions or positions to take and who will be responsible for taking them. For example, my group might have concentrated on recommending what courses should be offered each term and which ones should be offered only yearly. Alternatively, we might have focused on recommending what requirements the dean or college should make about undergraduate courses in our department. Policy issues revolve around questions of viability, feasibility, need, and responsibility for implementation. Groups must identify the needs at stake, evaluate the viability of different ways to meet needs, and determine who can most effectively implement their recommendations (Young et al., 2001).

Sharpen Your Skill

Clarifying Questions

Phrase a question of fact, a question of value, and a question of policy for each of the following topics:

Class Attendance

Fact ....

Value ....

Policy ....

Graduation Requirements at Your School

Fact ....

Value ....

Policy ....

Allowing Students to Take Grades of Incomplete in Courses

Fact ....

Value ....

Policy ....

Although groups should decide whether their primary purpose is to make a factual, value, or policy decision, most task deliberations involve all three types of questions. We often need facts to design policy (for example, how many students currently enroll in each class we offer?), and values are at stake in almost every decision, no matter how objective or factual it may appear.

Whether a group is dealing with facts, values, or policies, part of the work in stage one is to define all terms in the group's question. As we learned in Chapter 5, language is ambiguous. Because meanings vary among people, it's unwise to assume that key words in a group's mission mean the same thing to all members. We've already seen that a word such as *should* must be clarified by identifying the standards for what ought to be the case. Other ambiguous words also must be defined in the initial meetings of a group. For example, "What is the most meaningful way to structure a curriculum?" cannot be answered until the word *meaningful* is defined clearly.

In clarifying its focus, a group should attempt to minimize bias. Asking, "How can we give students the classes they want?" is obviously biased toward students' perspectives. Likewise, "How can we let faculty teach the courses they want?" is biased toward faculty interests. Once members have decided whether they are dealing with issues of fact, value, or policy and have clarified key terms, the group is ready to move to stage two.

Stage Two: Analyze the Issues

The focus of this stage is gathering and analyzing information about the issues confronting a group. Initially, members must decide what information they need: Reports from prior groups dealing with this issue, existing records, opinion polls, interviews with experts, information about how others handle the problem, and research are all valuable sources of information that may shed light on issues before the group. (Chapter 14 discusses ways to gather and evaluate research.)

During this phase, communication between members focuses on presenting and evaluating information. Members should be critical of information, to screen out what isn't accurate or helpful. Asking about the credentials and bias of any interviewee or source is important, as is questioning the methods used to conduct opinion polls. To do a good job of analyzing information, members may want to consult books that cover principles of logic and reasoning.

Stage Three: Establish Criteria

What would a good decision look like? That's the question members deal with during stage three of the standard agenda. **Criteria** are standards members use to evaluate alternative solutions or decisions. Without clear criteria, it's easy for groups to make decisions that don't meet needs or that create new problems. Establishing clear criteria before considering solutions helps a group avoid these pitfalls.

The curriculum group on which I served established four criteria: The recommended curriculum had to (1) allow all majors to meet requirements for the major within 4 years, (2) include only courses that our faculty were qualified to teach, (3) offer courses that have high student demands most often, and (4) conform to the university's requirements for an undergraduate major and for faculty teaching loads. These criteria provided us with a blueprint for evaluating possible decisions in the next phase of our work.

Stage Four: Generate Solutions

Once a group understands the issues surrounding its topic and has agreed on criteria for assessing resolutions, the group's focus turns to generating possible decisions. The research conducted during stage two often uncovers a number of possible solutions. My curriculum group's research revealed how curricula were designed in communication departments around the country, so all of those were possible solutions for us. We also learned about prior curricular reforms in the department and why they hadn't worked, so we were spared the embarrassment of repeating past mistakes.

A second source of alternative solutions is brainstorming, which encourages the free flow of ideas without immediate criticism. In brainstorming, the goal is to generate as many and as creative solutions as possible. Members should volunteer any ideas that occur to them, even ones that seem outrageous. Also, they should prompt each other to think imaginatively. For brainstorming to work, members must refrain from criticizing ideas when they are contributed. Evaluation is appropriate later, but at this point it can inhibit participation. One member records each idea so that the group has a complete list of possibilities.

Stage Five: Evaluate Solutions

Once members have a good list of solutions based on research and brainstorming, the goal is to evaluate each one against the criteria established in stage three of the standard agenda. Solutions that don't meet all criteria are discarded. Remaining are those that satisfy all of the standards members consider important for a good decision. Sometimes only a single solution meets all criteria. In other cases, members must decide which one of several solutions most fully meets the criteria.

© Michael Heron/Woodfin Camp & Associates

Members of a zoning board analyze information pertinent to reaching a sound decision about future growth in their community. What can you tell from the members' nonverbal communication? Do they look involved in the task and responsive to one another?

Ideally, by this point members can arrive at a consensus on the best decision. Sometimes consensus doesn't develop, however, and members must rely on other methods of decision making. If there is sufficient time, it's worthwhile to keep talking in the hope of reaching a consensus. If time is limited or extensive discussion indicates that consensus is not possible, then voting and compromise are viable options. Occasionally, rule by authority is exercised, although this should be a last resort.

Stage Six: Choose and Implement the Best Decision

In stage six, the group implements its decision. Implementation may involve announcing its decision—perhaps a new policy or set of procedures. More often, implementing a decision involves writing a formal report to the individual or body that initially charged the group. This is how advisory groups implement their decisions, because the goal is to generate advice for another person or group.

Many groups who effectively work through the first five stages of the standard agenda stumble in the final stage by saying, "We recommend that such-and-such decision be implemented." A vague recommendation such as this does not specify what is necessary to ensure that a decision will be implemented effectively. Because group members are the experts on the issues, they need to make very specific recommendations about who is to do what when and by what means. Should the decision be implemented by the CEO, the department chair, the group itself, or some other person or group? Is the decision to be forwarded to some governing body, circulated for comment, announced to others, or added to a handbook of policies? When should the decision take effect, and how should those affected be notified of the decision? Specifying the logistics of implementation is an important group responsibility.

Stage Seven: Develop an Action Plan to Monitor the Solution

The final responsibility of decision-making groups is to develop an action plan for monitoring the effectiveness of their solution and, if necessary, modifying it. This involves designating ways to assess the impact of a decision and ways to determine whether the decision achieves the intended result without creating any new problems. The point here is to check on the effectiveness of the solution once it has been put into effect. Even with very careful group work, decisions usually need some fine-tuning. That's why it's a good idea to develop ways to evaluate the impact of your decision and to check on its implementation.

Members should specify how they will measure the success of their decision. My curricular group recommended that it conduct a poll of majors and faculty one year after the new curriculum was implemented to find out whether students were able to get the courses they needed and whether faculty thought teaching assignments were fair. Without monitoring, even a sound decision can go awry or produce side effects nobody envisioned. By specifying monitoring provisions and who is to implement them, a group ensures that what seems like a good decision in theory actually works in practice. If it doesn't work, modifications must be made to achieve the desired goal. Thus, the action plan should identify a person or group to make modifications, if any are needed.

—Sibby—

A student group I was in came up with a great plan for printing student evaluations of all courses so that students could decide which ones to take. We got funding for the project, collected the data, and printed up the booklets. It wasn't until a year later that we figured out most students weren't reading the booklets because we weren't distributing them to the places students are likely to be when they sign up for courses—advisers' offices, for instance. If we had monitored our solution from the start, it would have worked better.

The standard agenda guides groups through the stages and issues that allow members to develop, implement, and assess decisions. Many groups use the standard agenda to schedule meetings. One or more meetings are devoted to each stage, which allows members to think ahead and to keep focused.

  To test your understanding of the phases in the standard agenda, complete Activity 11.2, "Organizing Group Discussion," in your *Student Companion* or online under "Activities for Chapter 11" at the *Communication in Our Lives* website.

Understanding and Managing Conflict in Groups

Conflict exists when people who are interdependent have different views, interests, or goals that seem incompatible. In Chapter 8, we learned that conflict is a natural and productive part of relationships. Likewise, conflict is normal and can be productive in groups. Conflict stimulates thinking, ensures that different perspectives are considered, and enlarges members' grasp of issues involved in making decisions and developing policies.

To achieve the potential values of conflict, however, members must manage it carefully. In this section, we build on Chapter 8's discussion of conflict to consider how to manage it constructively so that it enriches the processes and outcomes of collective endeavors.

—Trey—

I used to think conflict was terrible and hurt groups, but last year I was a member of a group that had no—I mean, zero—conflict. A couple of times I tried to bring up an idea different from what had been suggested, but my idea wouldn't even get a hearing. The whole goal was not to disagree. As a result, we didn't do a very thorough job of analyzing the issues, and we didn't subject the solution we developed to critical scrutiny. When our recommendation was put into practice, it bombed. We could have foreseen and avoided the failure if we had been willing to argue and disagree in order to test our idea before we put it forward.

Trey's commentary is instructive. Although many of us do not enjoy conflict, we can nonetheless recognize its value—even its necessity—to effective group work. Just as conflict in relationships can enlarge perspectives

Table 11.2: Characteristics of Group Conflict

Disruptive Conflict	Constructive Conflict
Competitive	Cooperate
Self-interested	Collective focus
Win–lose approach	Win–win approach
Screens out opposing ideas	Listens to opposing ideas
Closed climate	Open climate
Defensive communication	Supportive communication
Personal attacks	Issue focus

and increase understanding, conflict in groups can foster critical, thorough, and insightful deliberations.

Types of Conflict

Depending on how it is handled, conflict may be disruptive or constructive. Effective leadership helps groups communicate in ways that allow constructive conflict about the substance of the group's work. At the same time, effective leadership helps group members avoid or control communication that fosters disruptive conflict over personal differences or matters not relevant to the task. Table 11.2 summarizes the differences between these two basic forms of group conflict.

Disruptive Conflict Disruptive conflict exists when disagreements interfere with the effective work and healthy communication climate of a group. Typically, disruptive conflict is marked by communication that is domineering, rigid, and competitive (Wilmot & Hocker, 2001). Accompanying the competitive tone of communication is a self-interested focus in which members talk only about their ideas, their solutions, their points of view. The competitive and self-centered communication in disruptive conflict fosters a win–lose orientation. Members express the belief that only one or some members can win and others will lose.

Disruptive conflict harms group climate and undercuts members' satisfaction (Anderson & Martin, 1995). A closed atmosphere often develops in which members feel defensive and apprehensive. They may feel it's unsafe to volunteer ideas because they might be harshly evaluated or scorned by others. Personal attacks may occur as members criticize one another's motives or attack one another personally.

Disruptive conflict results from communication that produces defensiveness and draws members' attention from collective concerns and goals. In Chapter 8, we saw that defensive climates are promoted by communication that expresses evaluation, superiority, control orientation, neutrality, certainty, and closed-mindedness. Just as these forms of communication undermine personal relationships, they also interfere with group climate and productivity.

Constructive Conflict Constructive conflict occurs when members understand that disagreements are natural and can help them achieve their goals. This attitude is reflected in collaborative communication. Each person listens respectfully to others' opinions and voices her or his own ideas. Members also emphasize shared interests and goals. Collaborative communication encourages a win–win orientation. Discussion is open and supportive of differences, and disagreements focus on issues, not personalities.

Communication that fosters constructive conflict expresses interest in hearing differing ideas, openness to others' points of view, willingness to alter opinions, and respect for the integrity of other members and the views they express. As we learned in Chapter 8, these forms of communication build supportive communication climates in which individuals feel free to speak.

  To extend this discussion by examining different orientations to conflict in group and team situations, complete Activity 11.3, "Orientations to Conflict," in your *Student Companion* or online under "Activities for Chapter 11" at the *Communication in Our Lives* website.

Constructive conflict allows members to broaden their understandings, generate a range of possible decisions or solutions, and subject all ideas to careful, cooperative analysis. Constructive conflict is most likely to occur when the appropriate groundwork has been established by creating a supportive, open climate. Group climate is built throughout the life of a group, beginning with the first meeting. Thus, it's important to communicate in ways that build a strong climate from the start so that it is established when conflict arises.

CASE STUDY: Teamwork

The conversation scripted here is featured as a multimedia scenario on the *Communication in Our Lives* CD-ROM included with this book. Once you've launched the CD, click on the "Communication Scenarios" icon, and, from the Scenarios Menu, select "Teamwork" to watch the video. You'll recognize this video because you watched it before in Chapter 6. When you view it this time, focus on group dynamics and communication.

Analyze the scenario by applying the principles covered in this chapter, and respond to the prompts that accompany the video, which you can access by clicking on "Analysis." After completing the conversation analysis and answering the questions, you can click on the "Done" button to compare your responses with the ones I suggest. Additional analysis questions are available in print at the end of this chapter and on the book's website.

Jason Harris/© 2001 Wadsworth

A project team is meeting to discuss the most effective way to present its recommendations for implementing a flextime policy on a trial basis. Members of the team are team leader Jason Brown, Erika Filene, Victoria Lawrence,

Bill Williams, and Jensen Chen. They are sitting around a rectangular table with Jason at the head.

JASON: So we've decided to recommend trying flextime for a 2-month period and with a number of procedures to make sure that people's new schedules don't interfere with productivity.

There's a lot of information to communicate to employees, so how can we do that best?

VICTORIA: I think it would be good to use PowerPoint to highlight the key aspects of the new procedures. People always seem to remember better if they see something.

BILL: Oh, come on. PowerPoint is so overused. Everyone is tired of it by now. Can't we do something more creative?

VICTORIA: Well, I like it. It's a good teaching tool.

BILL: I didn't know we were teaching. I thought our job was to report recommendations.

VICTORIA: So what do you suggest, Bill? [She nervously pulls on her bracelet as she speaks.]

BILL: I don't have a suggestion. I'm just against PowerPoint. [He doesn't look up as he speaks.]

JASON: Okay, let's not bicker among ourselves. [He pauses, gazes directly at Bill, then continues.] Lots of people like PowerPoint, lots don't. Instead of arguing about its value, let's ask what it is we want to communicate to the employees here. Maybe talking about our goal first will help us decide on the best means of achieving it.

ERIKA: Good idea. I'd like us to focus first on getting everyone excited about the benefits of flextime. If they understand those, they'll be motivated to learn the procedures, even if there are a lot of them.

JENSEN: Erika is right. That's a good way to start. Maybe we could create a handout or PowerPoint slide—either would work—to summarize the benefits of flextime that we've identified in our research.

JASON: Good, okay now we're cooking. Victoria, will you make notes on the ideas as we discuss them?

Victoria opens a notebook and begins writing notes. Noticing that Bill is typing into his personal digital assistant (PDA), Jason looks directly at Bill and says,

JASON: Are you with us on how we lead off in our presentation?

BILL: Sure, fine with me. [He puts the PDA aside but keeps his eyes on it.]

ERIKA: So maybe then we should say that the only way flextime can work is if we make sure that everyone agrees on procedures so that no division is ever missing more than one person during key production hours.

JENSEN: Very good. That would add to people's motivation to learn and follow the procedures we've found are effective in other companies like ours. I think it would be great if Erika could present that topic, because she did most of the research on it. [He smiles at Erika, and she pantomimes tipping her hat to him.]

JASON: [He looks at Erika with a raised brow, and she nods.] Good. Okay, Erika's in charge of that. What's next?

VICTORIA: Then it's time to spell out the procedures and . . .

BILL: You can't just spell them out. You have to explain each one—give people a rationale for them, or they won't follow them.

Victoria glares at Bill, then looks across the table at Erika, who shrugs as if to say, "I don't know what's bothering Bill today."

JASON: Bill, why don't you lead off, then, and tell us the first procedure we should mention and the rationale we should provide for it.

Bill looks up from his PDA, which he's been using again. He shrugs and says harshly, "Just spell out the rules, that's all."

VICTORIA: Would it be too much trouble for you to cut off your gadget and join us in this meeting, Bill?

BILL: Would it be too much trouble for you to quit hassling me?

JASON: [He turns his chair to face Bill squarely.] Look, I don't know what's eating you, but you're really being a jerk. If you've got a problem with this meeting or someone here, put it on the table. Otherwise, be a team player.

Chapter Summary

In this chapter, we focused on task teams, groups that communicate to provide responses to ideas, people, and products; to inform and advise; to improve work continually; to generate ideas; and to make decisions. Task teams are increasingly popular in modern professional life because they are often more effective than individuals in producing creative, high-quality decisions.

To be effective, task teams need leadership. As we have seen, leadership may be provided by a single person or by a group of members. What matters is that one or more members communicate to organize discussion, ensure careful work on the task, and build cohesion, morale, and an effective climate for collective work. Meeting the task and climate responsibilities of leadership may be achieved by different styles of leadership. After discussing the laissez-faire, authoritarian, and democratic styles of leading, we noted that effective leadership style depends on the particular circumstances of a group, including the values of the culture and organization in which the group exists.

We also examined the advantages and limitations of consensus, voting, negotiation, and authority rule as methods of making decisions. No one decision-making method is best for all situations, because what will be effective varies according to particular group circumstances, tasks, and members. Thus, groups should consider their situations and needs to choose the most effective decision-making methods.

In this chapter, we also discussed the standard agenda, a well-tested and effective way of organizing discussion so that it is thorough, efficient, and effective. The standard agenda also allows groups to break down decision making into units that can be managed in a series of separate meetings. What we covered in this chapter should give you a good general understanding of how task teams work and how to be an effective member of groups in which you participate. Finally, we considered the role of conflict in enhancing group work, and we identified communication that fosters constructive conflict and improves the quality of group decision making. Constructive conflict in groups, as we have seen, grows out of a supportive communication climate that is built over the course of a group's life.

Communication in Our Lives ONLINE

In addition to presenting the case studies' multimedia scenarios, the *Communication in Our Lives* CD-ROM provides quick access to the *Communication in Our Lives* website and InfoTrac College Edition. The website is online at http://communication .wadsworth.com/woodciol4, but you can access this book's premium web content only when you link to the site directly through the book's CD.

The *Communication in Our Lives* website features interactive tools for learning and reviewing the chapter's concepts and key terms, including electronic versions of the "For Further Reflection and Discussion" questions that appear below and a review quiz.

The website also provides updated web links and additional InfoTrac College Edition activities. If required, you can e-mail completed chapter activities or the quizzes to your instructor.

Key Concepts

authoritarian leadership, *288*	consensus, *291*	laissez-faire leadership, *288*
authority rule, *293*	criteria, *296*	quality improvement team, *284*
brainstorming, *282*	democratic leadership, *289*	standard agenda, *294*
compromise, *292*	emotional intelligence, *291*	voting, *292*

For Further Reflection and Discussion

1. Interview a professional in the field you hope to enter after college. Ask her or him to identify ways in which the various task groups and teams discussed in this chapter are used on the job. What can you conclude about the prevalence of task teams in modern professional life?

2. Reread the Communication Highlight on page 287. Do you think all leaders should follow Lincoln's practice of taking "public opinion baths"? What ethical responsibility do leaders have to listen to the views and ideas of subordinates?

3. Form groups of five to seven members in your class to use the standard agenda to work on a problem. You might address the question, "What is the

best method of testing knowledge in this course?" or another question that you and your instructor select. Move through the standard agenda, and record your key ideas and conclusions for each stage. For example, if you addressed the suggested question, in stage one you would need to define *best* and *knowledge*. After the process is completed, assess the value of the standard agenda as a problem-solving method.

4. Use your InfoTrac College Edition to read David Varney's speech (in "Vital Speeches"), "Personal Reflections on Leadership," which was presented on March 1, 2001. How did Varney's personal experiences shape his philosophy and practice of leadership?

5. Review guidelines for creating effective climates in personal relationships that we discussed in Chapter 8. How would you modify the guidelines to apply them to group and team work?

6. Use your InfoTrac College Edition to access Carla Joinson's 2002 article, "Managing Virtual Teams: Keeping Members on the Same Page Without Being in the Same Place Poses Challenges for Managers." How would you adapt the principles of effective group communication and leadership that we have discussed to the context of virtual groups?

Experiencing Communication in Our Lives

Questions for Analysis and Discussion

Review the video of the scenario entitled "Teamwork" that you watched when completing this chapter's case study (pages 301–303), or, if you haven't seen it yet, watch it for the first time. If you didn't previously finish the analysis questions included on the CD-ROM, do so now, and then respond to the following questions, which are also available on the book's website under "Activities for Chapter 11."

1. Identify leadership behaviors on the team. Is Jason the single leader, or do other team members contribute leadership to the group?

2. Is the conflict on this team constructive, disruptive, or both? If you were a member of the team, how might you communicate to enhance the constructiveness of disagreements?

3. Judging from Jason's comments, what leadership style does he seem to use?

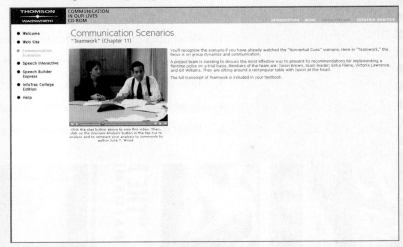

CHAPTER 12

Mass Communication and Media Literacy

Focus Questions

1. What does mass communication include?
2. What is the distinction between mass communication and mass media?
3. How does mass communication affect our perspectives?
4. To what extent is news constructed, or created?
5. What is media literacy, and how can you develop it?

To launch our discussion of mass communication, answer these three questions:

1. In an average week, what is the chance that you will be involved in some form of violence?
   A. one in 100
   B. ten in 100
   C. twenty-five in 100
   D. one in 200

2. What percentage of crimes in the United States are violent crimes, such as murder, rape, robbery, and assault?
   A. 75%
   B. 50%
   C. 25%
   D. 10%

3. During the 2004 presidential primaries, Democratic contender Howard Dean did which of the following after coming in third in the Iowa primary?
   A. gave a speech that was out of control
   B. delivered a maniacal shriek vowing he would yet win the nomination
   C. gave a speech in which he sounded like a prairie dog on speed
   D. gave a rally-the-troops speech to his supporters

The correct answer for each item is D. The more time you spend watching television, the more likely you are to have answered one or more questions incorrectly. Mass media, especially television, exaggerate the extent of violence in the world. The more television you watch, the more likely you are to overestimate the amount of violent crime in the United States (question 2) and the probability that you personally will be a victim of violent crime (question 1).

Mass communication also shapes (or misshapes) our perceptions of events. Which answer did you select for question 3? Most people who followed television and talk radio coverage of the 2004 Democratic presidential primaries would choose A, B, or C. Television coverage of the candidates after the January 20, 2004, Iowa primary repeatedly showed close-up footage in which Howard Dean appeared to be screaming wildly that he would win the Democratic nomination despite having come in third in the Iowa primary. Talk radio programs replayed Dean's yell, labeling it "the maniacal shriek," and saying Dean was "out of control" and sounded like "a prairie dog on speed" (Dean yell, 2004). What mass media did not emphasize was that Dean was speaking before a large group of his supporters who were shouting at such a volume that Dean had to scream to be heard. Also not emphasized was that Dean's speech was intended to address his loyal supporters—a speaking occasion that calls for passion and confidence. Because a unidirectional microphone was used by reporters covering the speech, the deafening screams of his supporters were barely audible, making Dean's volume seem excessive and inappropriate. Mass media coverage of the event encouraged viewers to perceive Dean as a wild man who was out of control.

The chapter begins by defining mass communication and discussing its significance in our lives. Next, we consider four theories that help us understand how mass communication affects our views of the world, as well as how we think, feel, and act. In the second section of this chapter, we discuss ways of developing media literacy, a critical skill in our media-saturated era.

The Nature and Scope of Mass Communication

You've heard the term *mass communication* often, but you may not have a precise definition of it. So that we have a clear and shared understanding, we'll start by defining mass communication and exploring its prevalence in our lives.

Defining Mass Communication

Mass communication is messages that are transmitted by a source through a mass medium to a large group of people who may not be in direct contact with the source of the messages. Sources include television stations, film companies, newspapers, and so forth. Technologies include audio and visual equipment, printing presses, and so forth. Mass media include newspapers, radios, books, and so forth. Television programs such as *Sex and the City, The Oprah Show, Who Wants to Marry a Millionaire?* and *Queer Eye for the Straight Guy* attract millions of viewers; mass mailed advertisements reach millions of people each week; millions of people rely on newspapers and the web for daily news updates. Each of these reaches a mass audience.

Mass media are channels of mass communication. Books, film, television, radio, newspapers, magazines, CDs are examples of channels, or media, by which mass communication reaches great numbers of people. Mass communication also includes computer technologies such as the web and WebTV that reach many people. However, mass communication does not include e-mail messages exchanged between friends, closed-circuit television programs, small list serves, and small blogs, which reach few people. But the lines between personal and mass communication are not really clear cut. For instance, if you send an e-mail to a list serve with 10,000 members, is that interpersonal or mass communication? Stanley Baran and Dennis Davis (2003) believe it is more appropriate to think of mediated communication as a continuum that ranges from clearly interpersonal to clearly mass, with a lot of in-between forms of communication between those two extreme ends (Figure 12.1).

What does mass communication offer us? Clearly, it is a major source of information, companionship, and entertainment. Yet, if we look more closely, we realize that mass communication does more than report information, provide characters with whom we identify, and entertain us. It also

Figure 12.1
The Continuum
of Communication

Interpersonal   **Mass**

Telephone   E-mail   List serves   Blogs   Network TV

Communication Highlight

shapes our attitudes, values, and perceptions of people, situations, places, and events. Mass communication presents us with particular and partial views of human beings, social groups, events, issues, and cultural life. Mass communication also gives greater coverage (time and attention) to some people and points of view than to others.

The Prevalence of Mass Communication

Because mass communication reaches so many people, it is a significant influence on individual and cultural life. We rely on newspapers, radio, magazines, the web, and television to provide us with information about national and world events and public figures. We watch political candidates debate on television and decide which ones we support and do not support. We listen to interviews with celebrities to learn who they are and what their lives are like. In times of national crisis, such as after September 11, 2001, we count on mass communication to give us nearly instant coverage of events. In the days after the attacks on the Pentagon and the World Trade Center, most of us were glued to our televisions and the web as we sought information that might help us grasp what had happened and what it meant.

–Meggan–

I think the web has done more to expand individuals than anything ever invented. You can browse and learn all kinds of things and get involved with an amazing range of people that you would never meet in person. Computers have opened so many new doors for communication among people.

–Shelton–

My 6-year-old spends more time with his computer than he does with family or friends. He's on the Internet each morning before he goes to school. He refuses to be in extracurricular activities because after-school meetings would reduce his time in chat rooms. I worry he won't develop social skills and learn to adjust to different people.

Children are heavy viewers of television. By the time the average child in the United States enters first grade, she or he is watching about three hours

Communication Highlight

The Prevalence of Mass Communication in Americans' Lives

How prevalent is mass communication in the United States? Consider these statistics:

- 99% of U.S. households have at least one radio.

- 98% of U.S. households have at least one television.

- 80% of U.S. households have VCRs.

- 66% of U.S. households have cable.

- There are 140.8 million cell phone users in the United States.

- Three quarters of American homes have at least one computer.

- There are more than 206,900,000 online users in the United States.

- 55.2 million U.S. households subscribe to at least one daily newspaper.

- In the average U.S. home, at least one television is on at least 7 hours a day.

- MTV is the number one cable network for 12- to 24-year-olds in America.

- The average American spends about 10 hours a day engaged with mass media.

Sources: Kilbourne, 1999; Samuelson, 2002; *Statistical Abstract of the United States*, 2002; U.S. Bureau of the Census, 2003.

---

of television each day. By age 6, the average child in the United States has watched 3,000 to 5,000 hours of television. By the age of 8, children watch, on average, at least four hours of television each day (Baran & Davis, 2003). Viewing time soars to 19,000 hours by the age of 18.

In addition to consuming programs, music, and articles, we are also exposed to countless ads every day—on the radio and on billboards as we drive, on pop-up screens when we are on the web, on posters in buildings, as part of the packaging for products we buy, and so forth. Each of us encounters hundreds of ads every day of our lives. We also interact with mass com-

Does mass communication discourage face-to-face interaction? How many families share a meal without talking?

© Spencer Grant/PhotoEdit, Inc.

munication when we listen to CDs, watch films, and read magazines, books, and newspapers. Children under 18 average 38 hours a week interacting with mass communication—roughly the amount of time spent in a full-time job ("Study finds," 1999). That's a lot of time with mass communication!

The Functions and Effects of Mass Communication

How does mass communication work? How does it affect us? How do we use it? Four theories help us understand the functions and effects of mass communication. As we will see, each theory offers valuable insight into how mass communication works and what it does.

Uses and Gratification

Think about the last time you went to a movie. Did you go because the story mattered to you? Were you using the movie to escape from problems and worries? Did you attend because it featured stars you like? According to **uses and gratification theory,** we choose to attend to mass communication to gratify ourselves. If you are bored and want excitement, you might watch an action film or an episode of *The Sopranos*. If you are stressed and want some light-hearted diversion, perhaps you watch an episode of *Everybody Loves Raymond*. If you are interested in national affairs, you might listen to National Public Radio. If you are concerned that a game may be rained out, you might tune into the Weather Channel. Uses and gratification theory says we make conscious choices of media to fulfill our needs and desires.

If people use media such as television to gratify themselves, then we might expect that people will also create media if existing media do not satisfy them and others in their communities. That's exactly what happens. Most national newspapers in the United States primarily reflect the interests, concerns, and biases of middle-class Caucasian heterosexuals. Typically, they don't offer many stories that speak to the particular concerns of Hispanics, gays, Asian Americans, or other groups (Shim, 1997). To address the issues of concern to nonmajority groups, local newspapers and other printed materials are published. For instance, more than 200 Spanish-language newspapers and 350 Native American newspapers have been created (Campbell, 1999). These newspapers serve the interests of specific groups that are neglected by mainstream media. Similarly, webmasters set up new websites to meet needs and preferences that existing websites don't fulfill.

New and converging media of mass communication also expand our options for choosing media that gratify us. The exploding number of satellite and cable channels and the convenience of e-mail (Boneva, Kraut, & Frohlich, 2001) offer us more ways to engage with others and to choose sources of mass communication that we enjoy. In addition, the interactivity of new and converging computer-mediated mass communication increases our ability to use mass communication in gratifying ways (Ruggiero, 2000).

In sum, uses and gratification theory assumes that people are active agents who make deliberate choices among media to gratify themselves. We use media to gain information, alleviate loneliness, divert us from problems, and so forth. In other words, uses and gratification theory assumes that people exercise control over their interaction with mediated mass communication. As we look at the next theory, we'll see that not everyone agrees that people are active, deliberate consumers of mass communication.

Agenda Setting

A second view of mass communication asserts that it establishes an agenda for us by spotlighting some issues, events, and people and downplaying others. **Agenda setting** is selecting and calling to the public's attention ideas, events, and people (Agee, Ault, & Emery, 1996; McCombs & Ghanem, 2001; Scheufele, 2000). In the case of cadets who withdrew from the Citadel in 1995, mass communication focused on Shannon Faulkner and called her to the public's attention. Therefore, many people were aware of her departure from the military school but didn't realize that a number of male cadets also left.

Mass communication keenly affects the events, people, and issues that reach public consciousness. For instance, television and newspaper reports make us very aware of the sexual activities (real or rumored) of public figures, especially politicians. Historical accounts have documented the extramarital sexual activities of many past presidents, but at the time, those activities were not put on the public agenda. In our era, mass communication does call the sexual lives of public figures to our attention, making us more aware of this issue than the public was in previous times. In the first years of the new millennium, mass media called to Americans' attention businesspeople and financial institutions that had violated laws to profit themselves. Surely this happened before 2000, but it became part of the public agenda when media made it a story.

But mass media also divert attention from many topics. Ralph Nader (1996) criticizes media for what they do *not* cover. Nader notes that there is no national television program that highlights nonathletic issues and accomplishments at colleges and universities. Nader also points out that we have many programs devoted to business profits and growth but no television or radio program that focuses on workers and labor issues. Nader urges us to think critically about what media do and do not offer us and how media foci affect our knowledge and sense of what's happening in the world.

Within agenda-setting theory, **gatekeeper** is a key concept. A gatekeeper is a person or group that decides which messages pass through the gates of media to reach consumers. Gatekeepers are people who manage mass media—producers, editors, webmasters, and so forth. Gatekeepers screen messages, stories, and perspectives to create messages (programs, interviews, articles) and to shape our perceptions of what is happening and what is and is not significant. Which stories make the front page of a newspaper, and which are placed on a back page of Section C? Which stories lead nightly television news broadcasts, which are appended at the end, and which are not covered at all? Which stories are the cover stories for national magazines such as *Newsweek* and *U.S. News & World Reports*? When a controversial issue is covered, do spokespeople for all sides get equal time or space to present their points of view, or are spokespeople for some points of view given more or all of the time or space devoted to the story? Each of these gatekeeping decisions shapes what we perceive to be significant and what knowledge and attitudes we form.

The media have many gatekeepers:

- Reporters decide whose perspectives on a story to present and whose to ignore.
- Editors of newspapers, books, and magazines screen the information that gets to readers and decide where to place stories and other material.
- Owners, executives, and producers filter information for radio and television programs.
- Government agencies may put pressure on the press and television and radio stations not to broadcast certain information.
- Advertisers and political groups may influence which messages get through.

Obviously, gatekeepers serve an important purpose—we could never digest *all* the news in a given day, so someone must decide which stories are covered. Although we clearly need gatekeepers, we should also be aware that the choices they make regarding media affect our knowledge and perspectives. For example, America Online (AOL), a major Internet service provider, chooses which companies, groups, and issues to highlight on the pop-up menus that besiege users while they are online. This gives visibility to the groups, people, and issues that AOL—not users—decides to emphasize.

Gatekeepers screen not only information content but also sources of information. Writers, producers, and others who control programming decide which experts to feature, which people in the news to cover, and which perspectives on events to include. An example of bias in mass communication is the tendency to use members of minority groups almost exclusively as authorities on issues involving race. This can foster the misperception that members of minorities have expertise only about minority issues.

There is also evidence of racial bias in media accounts of crime stories. According to some media scholars (Gandy, 1994; James, 2000), newspapers present minority citizens as violent criminals more often than they present European Americans as violent criminals and more often than they present minorities in positive stories. This pattern may lead us to inaccurate perceptions of the extent to which members of different races perpetrate violent crimes. As Gandy notes (1994), how stories are presented "influences what we understand about the world in which we live" (p. 47).

Racial bias may also be evident in whose perspectives are covered and whose are not. In 1999, an Associated Press story carried this headline: "Unemployment rate for youths is lowest in thirty years" ("Unemployment rate for youths," 1999). The story emphasized the fact that summer unemployment for Americans between the ages of 16 and 24 was the lowest since 1969. Buried at the end of the article was the fact that unemployment for

Many Americans rely on nightly news programs to understand major issues and events.

© David Young-Wolff/PhotoEdit, Inc.

Communication Highlight

Media's Representation of Race

Do television news programs equitably represent different races, political views, and sexes? Consider these facts:

- Total number of U.S. sources interviewed by the three major networks on evening news broadcasts in 2001 (the latest year for which data are available) 14,632

- Percentage of U.S. sources interviewed who were White 92%

- Percentage of U.S. sources interviewed who were male 85%

- Percentage of U.S. sources interviewed who were Republican when party affiliations were revealed 75%

- Number (not percentage) of Native Americans interviewed 1

Source: "View," *Utne Reader,* November/December 2002.

African Americans between the ages of 16 and 24 was more than twice as high as the national average.

Racial bias also occurs in programming on major commercial television networks. Black defendants are more likely than White ones to be unnamed and to be shown in mug shots, which places them in a context associated with criminality. White defendants are more likely to be named as individuals and to be portrayed in a series of videos and still photos that provide less criminal and more individual visions of them (Entman, 1994).

Latino and Latina actors are underrepresented in commercial programming. When Latina and Latino actors do appear, often they are typically portrayed as low-level workers, criminals, or other undesirable characters. Latino and Latina actors who are presented positively seem assimilated into mainstream White culture, and their racial and ethnic heritage is seldom evident in story lines (National Council of La Raza, 1998).

Historically, gays and lesbians have been virtually invisible in mass media. One interesting change in commercial programming is the increased presence of gays and lesbians who are portrayed positively in prime-time shows and major films. In the blockbuster hit *Philadelphia*, Tom Hanks gave a compelling and positive portrayal of a gay man. Other films such as *As Good As It Gets, Midnight in the Garden of Good and Evil,* and *Angels in America* prominently featured characters who demonstrated the complexity and humanity of gays and lesbians. Since Ellen DeGeneres came out on her television program *Ellen* in 1997, more gay and lesbian characters have been included and sometimes featured as lead characters in popular television programs. *Will & Grace* and *Queer Eye for the Straight Guy,* which is a runaway success with viewers of all sexual orientations, are two good examples. Showtime's recently debuted *The L Word* indicates the continuing appeal of shows featuring gay and lesbian characters.

Cultivating Worldviews

Additional insight into how mass communication works and affects us comes from **cultivation theory,** which claims that television promotes a worldview that is inaccurate but that viewers nonetheless assume reflects real life. This theory is concerned exclusively with the medium of television, which it claims creates a synthetic reality that shapes heavy viewers' perspectives and beliefs about the world (Gerbner, 1990; Gerbner et al., 1986; Shanahan & Jones, 1999; Signorielli & Morgan, 1990).

Cultivation is the cumulative process by which television fosters beliefs about social reality. According to the theory, television fosters particular and often unrealistic understandings of the world as being more violent and dangerous than statistics on actual violence show it is. Thus, goes the reasoning, watching television promotes distorted views of life. The word *cumulative* is important to understanding cultivation. Researchers don't argue that a particular program has a significant effect on viewers' beliefs. However, they claim that watching a lot of television over a long period of time affects viewers' basic views of the world. By extension, the theory claims that the more television people watch, the more distorted their views of the world are likely to be. Simply put, the theory claims that television cumulatively cultivates a synthetic worldview that heavy viewers are likely to assume represents reality.

Cultivation theorists identify two means by which cultivation occurs: **mainstreaming** and **resonance.** Mainstreaming is a process by which mass communication stabilizes and homogenizes social perspectives. For example, if commercial programming consistently portrays Hispanics as unambitious, African Americans as criminals and uneducated, and European Americans as upstanding citizens, viewers may come to accept these representations as factual. If television programs, from Saturday morning cartoons to prime-time dramas, feature extensive violence, viewers may come to believe that violence is common. As they interact with others, heavy viewers communicate their attitudes and thus affect the attitudes of others who watch little or no television. According to some media scholars (Gerbner, et al., 1986) "television has become the primary common source of socialization and everyday information (mostly in the form of entertainment) of an otherwise heterogeneous population" (p. 18).

The second explanation for television's capacity to cultivate worldviews is resonance, which is the extent to which media representations are congruent with personal experience. For instance, a person who has been robbed or assaulted is likely to identify with televised violence and to watch shows that feature it. When media representations correspond with our personal experiences, we are more likely to assume that they accurately represent the world in general.

People who watch a lot of television are more likely than people who watch little or no television to have beliefs that reflect the worldview portrayed by television, which is not equivalent to a worldview based on empirical data. In television entertainment programming, 57% of all programs include some violence,

The prevalence of violence in mass communication can make the world seem more violent than it is.

© AFP/Getty Images

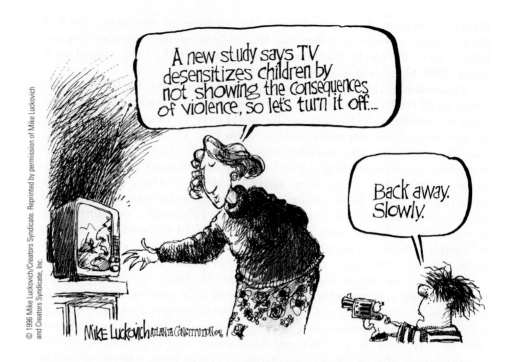

and 77% of major characters who commit crimes perpetrate acts of violence. Compare this with the fact that roughly 10% of reported real crimes are violent. In prime-time entertainment programming on commercial networks, 86% of the depictions of the criminal justice system in the United States portray criminals as never being brought to trial or as getting off at trial (National Television Violence Study, 1996; Silverblatt, 2001). Yet of the nearly 11,000 felony arrests in California in one year, 80% went to trial, and 88% of the trials resulted in convictions. Prime-time entertainment programs portray 64% of characters as involved in violence, so heavy viewing of television is likely to cultivate the belief that being a victim of violence is common. In the real world, however, the average person has a 1 in 200 chance of being involved in a violent crime in any week.

The world of television teems with violence. The Annenberg Public Policy center reports that 28% of children's shows include four or more acts of violence, and fully 75% of these programs do not carry the FV (fantasy violence) rating ("Value of Children's Shows," 1999). Most children watch television without parents present and without any enforced rules for what they may view (Rideout et al., 1999). The average 18-year-old in the United States has viewed 200,000 separate acts of violence on television, including 40,000 murders (Zuckerman, 1993). Given the extent of violence on television, it's no wonder that many heavy viewers think the world is more violent than crime reports show it is.

–Kelly–

I didn't think much about sex and violence on TV until my daughter was old enough to watch. When she was 4, I found her watching an MTV program that was absolutely pornographic. What does seeing that do to the mind of a 4-year-old girl? We don't let her watch TV now unless we can monitor what she sees.

Communication Highlight

Mediated Violence and Real-life Violence

Does watching violence increase viewers' aggression? Not necessarily. Whether watching violence increases viewers' actual violence depends on many factors. James Potter (1997) identified aspects of televised violence that make it more likely that viewers will become more aggressive themselves.

- Reward/punishment: Aggression that is rewarded is more likely to be modeled by viewers than aggression that is punished.

- Motivation: If a character's aggression is portrayed as justified, viewers are more likely to model that aggression than if it is portrayed as unjustified.

- Realism: Realistic aggression by characters is perceived as applicable to real life and thus is more

likely to be modeled by viewers. This is especially true of young male viewers.

- Humor: Media violence that is presented humorously (for instance, in cartoons) increases the likelihood that viewers will behave aggressively.

- Identification: Viewers who identify positively with mediated characters who engage in violence are more likely to use the behaviors that those characters use.

- Arousal: The more arousing mediated violence is, the more likely it is that viewers will engage in aggressive behavior in real life.

The high incidence of violence in news programming reflects in part the fact that the abnormal is more newsworthy than the normal (Mander, 1999). It isn't news that 99.9% of couples are either getting along or working out their problems in nonviolent ways; it was news when Lorena Bobbitt amputated her husband's penis and when O.J. Simpson's wife was murdered (Hunt, 1999). It isn't news that most of us grumble about big government but refrain from violent protest; it is news when someone blows up the Federal Building in Oklahoma City and cites dissatisfaction with big government as a motive. Simply put, violence is news.

News programs aren't the only television shows that feature high levels of violence. In one of the classic studies that established cultivation theory, Nancy Signorielli (1990) found that 71% of prime-time and 94% of weekend programs included acts of violence. Each hour of prime-time programming averaged more than five acts of violence, and weekend programming averaged more than six. Signorielli then surveyed people at five different times to learn their views of the world. Consistent with cultivation theory, she found that heavy viewers are more likely than lighter viewers to see the world as a mean place and people as untrustworthy.

In his 1985 book *Amusing Ourselves to Death,* cultural critic Neil Postman argued that the fast and furious format of news programming creates the overall impression that the world is unmanageable, beyond our control, and filled with danger and violence. In an effort to present as many stories as possible, news programs offer little analysis, depth, or reflection (Ferrante, 2000; Gitlin, 2002). Consequently, reports on crime and violence may do less to enhance understanding and informed response than to agitate and frighten us.

Perhaps you are thinking that few people confuse what they see on television with real life. Research shows that this may not be the case. Children's sex-role stereotypes seem directly related to the amount of commercial television (but not educational television) they watch. In a comparison

Sexualized images are increasingly common in mass media.

© Reuters/CORBIS

of communities that did not have television with ones that did, one researcher (Kimball, 1986) found that children who watched commercial television had more sex-stereotypical views of women and men than children who didn't view television. When television was introduced into the communities that had not had it, children's sex-stereotypical attitudes increased.

Media portrayals of relationships may also cultivate unrealistic views of what a normal relationship is. MTV programming strongly emphasizes eroticism and sublime sex, and people who watch a lot of MTV have been shown to have higher expectations for sexual perfection in their relationships (Shapiro & Kroeger, 1991). Relatedly, people who read a lot of self-help books tend to have less realistic views of relationships than people who read few or no self-help guides. Investigations have also shown that both males and females who watch sexually violent MTV are more likely to regard sexual violence as normal in relationships (Dieter, 1989; Weimann, 2000).

Sharpen Your Skill

Testing the Mean World Hypothesis

The basic worldview studied by cultivation theorists is exemplified in research on the **mean world syndrome** (Gerbner et al., 1986). The mean world syndrome is the belief that the world is a dangerous place, full of mean people who cannot be trusted and who are likely to harm us. Although less than 1% of the U.S. population is victimized by violent crime in any year, television presents the world as a dangerous place in which everyone is at risk.

To test this theory, ask ten people whether they basically agree or disagree with the following five statements, which are adapted from the mean world index used in research. After respondents have answered, ask them how much television they watch on an average day. Do your results support the claim that television cultivates a mean world syndrome?

1. Most public officials are not interested in the plight of the average person.

2. Despite what some people say, the lot of the average person is getting worse, not better.

3. Most people mostly look out for themselves rather than trying to help others.

4. Most people would try to take advantage of you if they had a chance.

5. You can't be too careful in dealing with people.

—Kasheta—

To earn money, I babysit two little boys four days a week. One day they got into a fight, and I broke it up. When I told them that physical violence isn't a good way to solve problems, they reeled off a list of TV characters that beat up on each other. Another day, one of them referred to the little girl next door as a "ho." When I asked why he called her that, he started singing the lyrics from an MTV video he'd been watching. In that video women were called "hos." It's scary what kids absorb.

Ideological Control

Critical media scholars focus on identifying and challenging the ways that media function as tools that represent the dominant ideology in a culture as normal and right (Potter, 2001, Urgo, 2000). In other words, critical media scholars study how cultural elites use media to maintain their dominant positions in society (Baran & Davis, 2003). Because individuals and groups that have benefited from the existing social structure tend to control mass communication, they have a vested interest in promoting their own views and values as normal and right. Thus, it is unsurprising that mass communication is more likely to portray White men as good, powerful, and successful than it is to describe White women or minority men or women in those ways.

In his book *Rich Media, Poor Democracy* (1999), Robert McChesney argues that media primarily benefit wealthy individuals, corporations, advertisers, and organizations, including media themselves. Advertising is a primary means of increasing profits for a sliver of Americans while depleting the resources of many. Media scholar W. James Potter (2001) reports that money spent on advertising has grown from $500 million in 1900 to more than $220 billion today. To introduce a new product and stimulate consumer interest, an advertiser will spend about $50 million (Potter, 2001). Each year, the average child in America views more than 30,000 television commercials (Numbers, 1999). If elite groups control mass communication, it is unsurprising that capitalism tends to be presented positively, and consumers are encouraged to want more and buy more, which will benefit the elite group that profits from capitalism.

Mass media are particularly powerful in representing the ideology of privileged groups as natural and good (Hall, 1986, 1989; McChesney, 1999). Television programs, from children's shows to prime-time news, represent White, heterosexual, able-bodied males as the norm in the United States, although they are actually not the majority. Magazine covers and ads, as well as billboards, portray young, able-bodied, attractive White people as the norm. Minorities continue to be portrayed most often as criminals, victims, subordinates, or otherwise less than respectable people (Braxton, 1999;

Communication Highlight

Media's Shaping of Body Images

A recent research report (Becker, Burwell, Gilman, Herzog, & Hamburg, 2002) suggests that media are very powerful in shaping—or distorting—body images. For centuries, the people of Fiji had been a food-loving society. People enjoyed eating and considered fleshy bodies attractive in both women and men. In fact, when someone seemed to be losing weight, acquaintances chided her or him for "going thin."

All of that changed in 1995, when television stations in Fiji began broadcasting American programs such as *Melrose Place, Seinfeld,* and *Beverly Hills 90210.* Within three years, a high number of Fijian women began dieting and developing eating disorders. When asked why they were trying to lose weight, young Fijian woman cited characters such as Amanda (Heather Locklear) on *Melrose Place* as their model.

Entman, 1994; Gandy, 1994; James, 2000). Even scantier in the world of television are Latinos and Latinas, who are the fastest growing ethnic–racial group in the United States (Haubegger, 1999).

Sharpen Your Skill

Detecting Dominant Values in Media

Watch two hours of prime-time commercial television. Pay attention to the dominant ideology that is represented and normalized in the programming. Who are the good and bad characters? Which personal qualities are represented as admirable, and which are represented as objectionable? Who are the victims and victors, the heroes and villains? What goals and values are endorsed?

Think about the ways in which media tend to represent social movements. When college students protested the Communist government in China at Tiananmen Square, they were portrayed as "heroes of democracy," but when people protested the World Trade Organization in Seattle, Washington, they were portrayed as "extremists" and "radical anarchists" (Baran & Davis, 2003, p. 226; FAIR, 2000). In the first case, the protesters' views were consistent with elites who control media; in the second case, the protesters' views challenged elite interests.

We've considered four theories of mass communication. Probably each view has some validity. Surely, we make some fairly conscious choices about how to use media, as uses and gratification theory claims. At the same time, mass communication probably influences us in ways that we don't notice, as agenda setting and cultivation theories assert. And critical scholars probably are correct in describing mass communication as a conservative force that supports dominant ideologies. Keep each of these theories in mind as we consider how we improve our ability to interact with mass communication.

Developing Media Literacy

Because mass communication surrounds and influences us, we need to be responsible and thoughtful consumers. This requires us to develop **media literacy,** which is the ability to understand the influence of mass media and to access, analyze, evaluate, and respond actively to mass media in informed, critical ways. Figure 12.2 shows the components of media literacy.

Just as it takes work to become literate in written and oral communication, it takes effort to develop literacy in interacting with media. Instead of passively absorbing media, you want to cultivate your abilities to access, analyze, evaluate, and respond thoughtfully to media. Figure 12.3 describes stages in the development of media literacy. How literate we become, however, depends on the extent to which we work to develop and apply critical skills.

Understand the Influence of Mass Communication

Media literacy begins with deciding how much mass communication influences us. Does mass communication determine individual attitudes and social perspectives, or is it only one of many influences on

Figure 12.2
The Components of Media Literacy

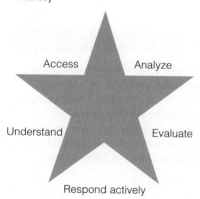

Access

Analyze

Understand

Evaluate

Respond actively

6 Months	3 Years	4 Years	7–8 Years	Throughout Life
Children pay attention to television.	Children engage in exploratory viewing.	Children search for preferred viewing.	Children make clear distinctions between ads and programs.	People who commit to media literacy learn to recognize puffery, hooks, and other devices for directing their attention and behavior.
	Children establish preferred patterns of viewing.	Children develop a viewing agenda.		
	Children do not distinguish between programs and ads.	Children's attention is held by a story line.	Children become skeptical of ads for products with which they are familiar; they are less skeptical of ads for products they haven't tried or don't own.	People who commit to media literacy learn to use media in sophisticated ways to meet their needs and to compensate for media bias and techniques.
		Children begin to distinguish between ads and programs.		
		Children do not realize that ads seek profits.		

Figure 12.3
Stages in the Development of Media Literacy

Source: Adapted from Potter, 2001.

individual attitudes and social perspectives? The first view is both naive and overstated. It obscures the complex, multiple influences on how we think as individuals and how we organize social life. It also assumes that mass communication is linear—that we passively receive whatever gatekeepers send us.

The second view represents a thoughtful, qualified assessment of the influence of mass communication and our ability to exercise control over its effects. Mass media, individuals, and society interact in complex ways. We are not unthinking sponges that absorb whatever is poured on us. Instead, we can interact thoughtfully and critically with mass communication to mediate its impact on us and our assent—or resistance—to what it encourages us to believe, think, feel, and do.

Access Mass Communication

The second component of media literacy is access to mass communication. This is the capacity to own and use televisions, radios, computers and so forth. You may be thinking that access is not an issue. After all, you probably have a television, radio, and computer (among other products that allow you to access mass communication), and you know how to use them. But not everyone does.

Democratic Access We must to be aware of the fact that people do not have equal access to mass communication, especially technologies of mass communication. Technologies of mass communication may magnify existing

Communication Highlight

The Digital Divide

Not everyone in the United States has equal access to communication technologies. In 1999, the National Telecommunications and Information Administration, which is part of the U.S. Commerce Department, released a report entitled "Falling Through the Net." You can read the full report at http://www.ntia.doc.gov/ntiahome/digitaldivide. The report detailed disturbing trends in use of the Internet. Age, rural versus urban setting, and education are all factors that affect who has access to telecommunication. Among the many factors, two stand out: income and race. At that time, only 12.1% of people with annual incomes under $10,000 used the Internet, whereas 58.9% of people with incomes of $75,000 or more used the Internet.

In 2001, the Census Bureau reported that the gap in computer use is narrowing between different ethnic and socioeconomic groups, leading some people to think there is no digital divide (Samuelson, 2002). Decide for yourself how real the digital divide is by reading the following summary comparing 1997 and 2001 statistics on who has one or more computers in the home.

	1997	2001
Asian Americans	58%	71%
Blacks	44	56
Hispanics	38	49
Whites	58	70
Families with incomes below $25,000	37	47
Families with incomes above $75,000	81	88

 Go to the website listed in this box to read the full report.

social divisions because some people have better access to new technologies. An information elite could easily develop because access to new technologies requires both knowledge and resources that not everyone has. For example, fiber optic networks are so costly that they might be laid between two prosperous urban areas but not routed into poorer rural communities. Hence, people living in the already advantaged urban areas would have better access to video, audio, and computer technologies, whereas members of rural communities would be relegated to the margins of the information revolution and the personal and professional enrichment it allows. According to Ken Freed (2002), "We need to understand interactive media simply to function and flourish in our interactive world" (p. 2). Thus, people who do not have access to interactive media may be excluded from full participation in society.

As citizens, workers, and voters, we have an ethical responsibility to identify and work to realize the potential of communication technologies to enrich us as individuals and as members of a common world. America's pledge of equal opportunity for all will not be honored in the information age if access to new and converging technologies is limited to individuals and groups that are already privileged by their social, professional, and economic status. In the short run, it would be expensive to provide access and training to people who cannot afford to purchase it for themselves. In the long run, however, it might be far less costly than the problems of a society in which a small technology elite is privileged and many citizens are excluded from full participation.

Expose Yourself to a Range of Media Sources In addition to the issue of democratic access to mass communication, each of us faces a personal challenge in deciding which media to access. Many people limit their exposure, choosing to view and listen only to what they particularly like and what supports the views they already hold. For instance, if you are conserva-

Communication Highlight

Convergence and Access

Convergence is a key to the future of technology. **Convergence** is the interconnectivity of various devices to each other and to the Internet or web. Bill Joy, Sun Microsystems' chief scientist, says convergence will relieve people of having to deal with many of the current difficulties in making technology work. According to Joy, in the near future, computers will work like small appliances—say, toasters or electric drills. When we buy computerized products, they will truly be "plug and play" (Sandberg, 1999).

But that's just half the story. The other half is abandoning the idea of a single PC in your home or office. Instead of that "old technology," says Bill Gates, we're moving quickly into the "PC-plus era" (Gates, 1999, p. 64). In the PC-plus era, people who can afford the newest technology will have multiple computerized devices, some of which will be connected to each other (for instance, when your computerized alarm clock rings, your computerized coffee maker will start) and all of which will all be linked to the net (for instance, the net will automatically reset your alarm clock and all other timer devices when you go on and off daylight savings time or after a power outage).

But a huge question remains: Who will have access to converging technologies, and who will not? If access is based on wealth, convergence will increase the divide between haves and have nots.

tive politically, you might read a conservative columnist in your daily paper and listen to conservative radio and television programs. The problem with that is that you don't expose yourself to criticisms of conservative policies and stances, and you don't give yourself the opportunity to learn about more liberal policies and positions. The same is true if you are politically liberal—you cannot be fully informed if you read, watch, and listen only to liberal sources. If you listen only to popular music, you'll never learn to understand, much less appreciate, classical music, jazz, or reggae. You cannot be informed about any issue or type of media unless you deliberately expose yourself to multiple, and even conflicting, sources of information and perspectives.

Exposing yourself to multiple media also means attending to more than entertainment. Television focuses primarily on entertainment, trends, and celebrities and officials in popular culture. One study of children ages 9 to 12 found that 98% of respondents knew who Michael Jordan and Michael Jackson were, but only 21% knew who Boris Yeltsin was, and only 20% recognized the name of Nelson Mandela ("Names & Faces," 1997). Tuning into celebrity culture is not sufficient for media literacy. So the access component of media literacy includes both being able to access mass communication and choosing to expose yourself to varied sources of information, opinion, and perspective.

Analyze Mass Communication

When we are able to analyze something, we understand how it works. If you aren't aware of English grammatical structure and rules, you can't write, read, or speak English effectively. If you are unaware of patterns that make up basketball, you will not be able to understand what happens in a game. If you don't understand how church or synagogue services are organized, you won't appreciate the meaning of those services. In the same way, if you don't understand patterns in media, you can't understand fully how music, advertising, programming, and so forth work. Learning to recognize patterns in media empowers you to engage media in critical and sophisticated ways.

James Potter (2001) points out that there are a few standard patterns that media use repeatedly. For example, despite the variety in music, media use a few basic chords, melody progressions, and rhythms. Even the content of music tends to follow stock patterns, most often love and sex (Christianson & Roberts, 1998). Most stories, whether in print, film, or television, open with some problem or conflict that progresses until it climaxes in final dramatic scenes. Romance stories typically follow a pattern in which we meet a main character who has suffered a bad relationship or has not had a serious relationship. The romance pattern progresses through meeting Mr. or Ms. Right, encountering complications or problems, resolving the problems, and living happily ever after (Riggs, 1999).

Just as media follow a few standard patterns for entertainment, they rely on basic patterns for presenting news. There are three distinct, but related features by which media construct the news (Potter, 2001).

- Selecting what gets covered: Only a minute portion of human activity is reported in the news. Gatekeepers in the media decide which people and events are newsworthy. By presenting stories on these events and people, the media make them newsworthy.

- Choosing the hook: Reporters and journalists choose how to focus a story, or how to "hook" people into a story. In so doing, they direct people's attention to certain aspects of the story. For example, in a story on a politician accused of sexual misconduct, the focus could be the charges made, the politician's denial, or the increase in sexual misconduct by public figures.

- Choosing how to tell the story: In the above story, media might tell it in a way that fosters sympathy for the person who claims to have been the target of sexual misconduct (interviews with the victim, references to other victims of sexual misconduct) or to tell it in a way that inclines people to be sympathetic toward the politician (shots of the politician with his or her family, interviews with colleagues who proclaim the politician's innocence). Each way of telling the story encourages people to think and feel distinctly about the story.

Critically Evaluate Messages from Mass Communication

Once you can analyze mass communication to understand how it works, you are prepared to take the next step: critically evaluating messages from mass media. When interacting with mass communication, you should use critical thought to assess what is presented. Rather than accepting news accounts unquestioningly, you should be thoughtful and skeptical. It's important to ask questions such as these:

- Why is this story getting so much attention? Whose interests are served, and whose are muted?

- What is the source of the statistics and other forms of evidence? Are the sources current? Do the sources have any interest in taking a specific position? (For example, tobacco companies have a vested interest in denying or minimizing the harms of smoking.)

- What's the hook for the story, and what alternative hooks might have been used?

Communication Highlight

Puffery: The Very Best of Its Kind!

One of the most popular advertising strategies is **puffery**, superlative claims that seem factual but are actually meaningless. For instance, what does it mean to state that a particular juice has "the most natural flavor"? Most natural in comparison to what—other juices, other drink products? Who judged it to have the most natural flavor: the corporation that produces it? A random sample of juice drinkers? What is the meaning of an ad that claims a car is "the new benchmark"? Who decided this was the new benchmark? To what is this car being compared? It's not clear from the ad, which is only puffery. And media literate people don't buy the claim or the product!

- Are stories balanced so that a range of viewpoints are given voice? For example, in a report on environmental bills pending in Congress, do news reports include statements from the Sierra Club, industry leaders, environmental scientists, and so forth?

- How are different people and viewpoints represented by gatekeepers (e.g., reporters, photographers, experts)?

It's equally important to be critical in interpreting other kinds of mass communication, such as music, magazines, billboards, and the web. When listening to popular music, ask what view of society, relationships, and so forth it portrays, who and what it represents as normal, and what views of women and men it fosters. Raise the same questions about the images in magazines and on billboards. When considering an ad, ask whether it offers meaningful evidence or merely puffery. Asking questions such as these allows you to be critical and careful in assessing what mass communication presents to you.

Respond Actively

People may respond actively or passively to mass communication and the worldviews that it portrays, depending on how media literate they are. If we respond passively, we mindlessly consume messages and the implicit values in them. On the other hand, if we respond actively, we recognize that the worldviews presented in mass communication are not unvarnished truth but partial, subjective perspectives that serve the interests of some individuals and groups while disregarding or misrepresenting the interests of others. Responding actively to mass communication includes choosing consciously how and when to use it, questioning what is presented, and involving yourself in controversies about media, particularly the newer technological forms.

Use Mass Communication Consciously Do you ever just turn on the TV and watch whatever is on? Do you ever get on the web and spend an hour or more surfing with no particular goal in mind? If so, you're not making a deliberate choice that allows you to select media to suit your needs and goals. Sophisticated media users realize that media serve many purposes, and they make deliberate choices that serve their goals and needs at particular times. For example, if you feel depressed and want to watch television, it might be better to watch a comedy or action drama than to watch a television movie about personal trauma and pain. If you have used all the money you budgeted for entertainment, don't check out pop-up ads for new CDs.

You can also use media to respond to media. Since the 1970s, the Guerrilla Girls have used media-savvy techniques to critique sexism and racism, particularly in the art world (Kollwitz & Kahlo, 2003). Some organizations now rely on virual e-mail to get their messages out to large numbers of people. A virual e-mail is not a virus that infects a computer, it is an e-mail that is so provocative or interesting that receivers are eager to send it to others, thus getting the message out. People from all walks of life call in to talk radio shows to express their opinions and to challenge those of others. And letters to the editor remain a way for people to respond to newspaper coverage.

–Manuel–

I was really angry about a story in the local paper. It was about Mexicans who come to the U.S. The story only mentioned Mexican Americans who get in trouble with the law, are on welfare, or are illegal residents. So I wrote a letter to the editor and said the story was biased and inaccurate. The editor invited me to write an article for the opinion page, and I did. In my article, I described many Mexican Americans who are hard-working, honest citizens who are making this country better. There were a lot of responses to my article, so I know I made a difference.

Manuel's experience demonstrates that assuming agency is not just personally empowering; it can also enrich cultural life. Don't succumb to thinking there's nothing you can do to affect mass media. There is a great deal that each of us can do on both the personal and the cultural level (Potter, 2002). People have an ethical responsibility to challenge messages of mass communication that they consider inaccurate or harmful.

To assume an active role in interacting with media, you must recognize that you are an agent who can affect what happens around you. Believing that we are powerless to control how mass communication affects us can become a self-fulfilling prophecy. Therefore, not recognizing your agency could induce you to yield the degree of control you could have.

Be Involved with Issues Surrounding Mass Media Responding actively is not just looking out for ourselves personally. It also requires us to become involved in thinking about how mass media influence social life and how, if at all, mass communication should be regulated. We've already discussed the escalation of violence in media, which can affect how people view violence and its appropriateness. But there are other issues, particularly in

Communication Highlight

Responding Actively

 If you want to learn more about gender and media, or if you want to become active in working against media that foster views of violence as normal, girls and women as subordinate, and buying as the route to happiness, visit these websites:

Action Coalition for Media Education:
http://www.acmecoalition.org

Center for Media Literacy: http://www.medialit.org

Children Now: http://www.childrennow.org

Media Watch: http://www.mediawatch.com

National Association for Family and Community Education:
http://www.nafce.org

National Coalition on Television Violence:
http://www.nctvv.org

TV Parental Guidelines Monitoring Board:
http://www.tvguidelines.org

the context of the Internet and the web, which reach mass audiences. What guidelines are reasonable? What guidelines infringe on freedom of speech and the press? We need to think carefully about what kinds of regulations we want and how to implement them.

Who should control the Internet and web (McGrath, 2002)? In his book *Silent Theft: The Private Plunder of Our Common Wealth,* David Bollier (2002) claims that the Internet belongs to the public and should not be controlled by wealthy, monopolistic companies. He uses the example of Microsoft, which Bollier claims tries to impose its platform and proprietary standards on PC users. But this is wrong, writes Bollier, because those private companies had nothing to do with developing the Internet that they now seek to control. The federal government, in partnership with universities, invested taxpayers' money to fund scientists who developed the Internet. Should private companies profit from regulating technologies whose development was supported by public funds? Are private companies correct in their claim that government regulation stifles innovation?

One form of communication on the Internet that irritates many people is advertising that they don't want and can't escape. The web is saturated with ads. If you go to a site to read a review of a movie, you may also get—without asking for them—offers to buy the soundtrack, video version, and other items connected with the movie (Rafter, 1999). Should ads on individuals' personal computers be regulated? Does the pervasiveness of advertising on the Internet blur the boundary between content and advertising? In addition to forcing their ads on us, many online advertisers collect information about you that you might not choose to release. Is this an invasion of your privacy?

Privacy is not the only issue at stake in questions of how to regulate electronic communication (if at all). Your physical health may also be at stake if some kinds of online communication are not regulated. A drug company set up a shop on the Internet and arranged for pharmacies in two states to ship prescription drugs to patients. The only problem was that the drug company needed doctors to write prescriptions, which are required for dispensing drugs that are not sold over the counter. The company hired doctors to review questionnaires submitted electronically by people who wanted prescriptions. One doctor who agreed to issue prescriptions online was cited by his state's medical quality assurance commission for unprofessional conduct; he was an orthopedic surgeon who was writing prescriptions for Viagra (used to treat male impotence) for patients he never examined ("Cyber-medicine," 1999). Prescribing medications online entails special dangers, including the possibility that patients have undetected conditions or are taking other medications that make particular drugs dangerous for them.

From the annoyance of unwelcome advertising to the dangers of indiscriminate prescriptions, much of mass communication, particularly on the web and the Internet, remains unregulated. We have an ethical responsibility to become involved in questions of whether regulations should be developed and, if so, who should develop and implement them.

Advertising saturates media.

© AP/Wide World Photos

Communication Highlight

Experiencing Communication in Our Lives

CASE STUDY: Power Zapper

The conversation scripted below is featured as a multimedia scenario on the *Communication in Our Lives* CD-ROM included with this book. Once you've launched the CD, click on the "Communication Scenarios" icon, and, from the Scenarios Menu, select "Power Zapper" to watch the video. Improve your own communication skills by reading, watching, listening to, critiquing, and analyzing this communication encounter.

Analyze the scenario by applying the principles covered in this chapter, and respond to the prompts that accompany the video, which you can access by clicking on "Analysis." After completing the conversation analysis and answering the questions, you can click on the "Done" button to compare your responses with the ones I suggest. Additional analysis questions are available in print at the end of this chapter and on the book's website.

Charles and Tina Washington are in the kitchen area of their great room working on dinner. At the other end of the room, their six-year-old son, Derek, is watching television.

Tina is tearing lettuce for a salad while Charles stirs a pot on the stove.

TINA: One of us is going to have to run by the store tomorrow. This is the last of the lettuce.

Charles: While we're at it, we'd better get more milk and cereal. We're low on those too.

TINA: I'll flip you for who has to make the store run.

Charles pulls a quarter out of his pocket, flips it in the air, and covers it with one hand when it lands on his other hand. "Call it."

TINA: Heads, you have to go by the store.

Charles removes the hand covering the quarter and grins. "Tails—it's your job."

She rolls her eyes and says, "Just can't win, some days."

Derek suddenly jumps up from his chair, points his finger at the chair in which he had been sitting, and shouts "Zap! You're dead! You're dead! I win!"

Charles goes to Derek. An advertisement for Power Zapper is just ending on the television, and Charles turns down the volume.

CHARLES: What's going on, Derek? Who's dead?

DEREK: The chair is. I zapped it with the Power Zapper, Mom. It's the coolest weapon.

Tina walks over to join Charles and Derek.

TINA: Power Zapper? What's a Power Zapper?

DEREK: It's the most popular toy in America, Mom! It's really cool!

TINA: Oh really? Who says so?

DEREK: They just said it on TV.

TINA: Does that mean it's true?

Derek points a finger at his mother and shouts, "Pow! I zapped you! You're dead!" At this point, Charles walks over and takes Derek's hand.

CHARLES: Hold on there, son. Don't go pointing at your mother.

DEREK: I was zapping her, Dad.

CHARLES: I see you were, but we don't hurt people, do we?

DEREK: I could if I had a Power Zapper. Can I have one for my birthday? Everybody else has one.

CHARLES: If everybody jumped off the roof, would you do that?

DEREK: I wouldn't need to if I had a Power Zapper because I could zap anyone who bothered me. I'd be so cool.

CHARLES: But zapping other people would hurt them. You wouldn't want to do that, would you?

TINA (to Charles): You're overreacting. It's just a toy.

CHARLES (to Tina): Kids learn from toys. I don't want Derek to learn that violence is cool.

TINA (to Charles): He isn't going to learn that with us as his parents. Don't get so worked up over a toy.

Chapter Summary

In this chapter, we have examined mass communication. We explored four theories that offer insight into how media operate and affect us. One theory asserts that people use mass communication to gratify their interests. Two other theories, agenda setting and cultivation theory, give greater emphasis to the ways in which mass communication influences what we think about (the agenda for public discussion) and how we perceive social life (the worldview that is cultivated by media). A final theory claims that mass communication functions to support dominant social relations, roles, and perspectives and to make them seem normal and right. Mass communication, along with other institutions and practices, creates, legitimizes, and sustains particular and partial views of social life that define the roles of specific groups within an overall culture. If you think about mass communication in your life, you'll probably realize that each of these theories has some merit.

The second section of the chapter focused on developing media literacy so that we can be informed, critical, and ethical citizens in a media-saturated world. The first step in developing media literacy is to realistically assess the power of mass communication. Media do not exist in isolation, nor do we as consumers of mass communication. Each of us participates in multiple and diverse social systems that shape our responses to mass communication and the worldviews it presents. To be responsible participants in social life, we need to question what is included—and what is made invisible—in mass communication.

Second, media literacy means being able to access mass communication. Access is both a personal and a collective issue. Personally, it means being able to use mass media competently and choosing to expose yourself to a range of media sources. Collectively, it means working to ensure that access to media is not more available to some people than to others.

Third, media literacy includes the ability to analyze how media work so that we can recognize patterns in news, entertainment, and advertising. Fourth, media-literate people do not accept media messages unthinkingly. Instead, they critically evaluate the messages. Fifth, media literacy requires us to respond actively to mass communication by being involved in personal decisions about media and in collective questions about its uses.

Sharpen Your Skill

Media Literacy in Action

In this chapter, you have learned about some of the ways that gatekeepers shape understanding, perspective, and attitudes. Apply what you've learned by identifying ways that I, as the author of this chapter, shaped the information presented to you.

Hook: Can you identify a hook that I used to get you interested in reading this chapter?

Gatekeeping: Whose points of view do I emphasize in discussing mass communication and media literacy? Are there other involved groups that I neglect or ignore?

Agenda setting: Which aspects of mass communication did I call to your attention? Which aspects of mass communication did I not emphasize or name?

 To further develop your skills as a literate media consumer complete Activity 12.2, "Critical Media Literacy," in your *Student Companion.*

We have an ethical responsibility to speak out against communication that we think is inaccurate, hurtful, or wrong. And speaking out can make a difference. In 1995, Calvin Klein discontinued an ad campaign because so many individuals and groups objected to the ads. Other companies have withdrawn ads and even products in response to voices of resistance.

Power relationships and social perspectives are never fixed in cultural life. They are always open to change and negotiation with voices that offer rival views of reality. One means of negotiating social meanings is by responding to mass communication. Without our consent and support, mass communication cannot exist.

Communication in Our Lives ONLINE

In addition to presenting the case studies' multimedia scenarios, the *Communication in Our Lives* CD-ROM provides quick access to the *Communication in Our Lives* website and InfoTrac College Edition. The website is online at http://communication.wadsworth.com/woodciol4, but you can only access this book's premium web content when you link to the site directly through the book's CD.

The *Communication in Our Lives* website features interactive tools for learning and reviewing the chapter's concepts and key terms, including electronic versions of the "For Further Reflection and Discussion" questions that appear below and a review quiz.

The website also provides updated web links and additional InfoTrac College Edition activities. If required, you can e-mail completed chapter activities or the quizzes to your instructor.

Key Concepts

agenda setting, *312*

convergence, *322*

cultivation, *315*

cultivation theory, *314*

gatekeeper, *312*

mainstreaming, *315*

mass communication, *308*

mass media, *308*

mean world syndrome, *318*

media literacy, *320*

puffery, *325*

resonance, *315*

uses and gratification theory, *311*

For Further Reflection and Discussion

1. As a class, discuss the four theories of mass communication covered in this chapter. How do your experiences support or challenge the claims of each theory?

2. Would it be ethical to exercise control over the violence presented in media? Do you think viewers, especially children, are harmed by the prevalence of violence in media? If you think there should be some controls, what groups or individuals would you trust to exercise them?

3. Choose "PowerTrac" on your InfoTrac College Edition, then select "Key Word" in the search index. Type "Women and Weight and Magazine Covers." Read the article "Women and Weight: Gendered Messages on Magazine Covers" by Amy Malkin, Kimberlie Wornian, and Joan Chrisler, which was published in a 1999 issue of the journal *Sex Roles*. Are the authors' findings consistent with your experiences? How well do the different theories of media functioning that we've discussed explain their findings about the influence of magazine covers and women's feelings about weight?

4. Sign on to InfoTrac College Edition. First select "PowerTrac," then "Author Index," then type "Beverly A. Browne." Read her 1998 article "Gender Stereotypes in Advertising on Children's Television in the 1990s: A Cross-National Sample." What does Browne report about how males and females are depicted in television advertising? Do her findings suggest that there have been substantial changes in how the sexes are represented?

5. Embrace the challenge advanced in this chapter by taking an active role in responding to mass communication. Write a letter to the editor of a local paper, or write to a manufacturer to support or criticize its product or the way it advertises its product. Visit the websites mentioned in the Communication Highlight box on page 326 to learn about your opportunities to become a more involved consumer and controller of mass media.

Experiencing Communication in Our Lives

Questions for Analysis and Discussion

Review the video of the scenario entitled "Power Zapper" that you watched when completing this chapter's case study (pages 328–329), or, if you haven't seen it yet, watch it for the first time. If you didn't previously finish the analysis questions included on the CD-ROM, do so now, and then respond to the following questions, which are also available on the book's website under "Activities for Chapter 12."

1. Identify an example of puffery in the advertisement for the Power Zapper.

2. Are Charles and Tina Washington teaching Derek to be a critical viewer of mass communication?

3. How does this scenario illustrate the process of mainstreaming?

4. Are you more in agreement with Charles or with Tina about whether toys teach important lessons to children?

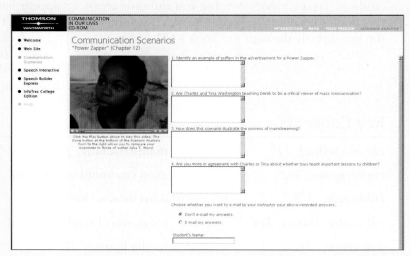

CHAPTER 13

Planning Public Speaking

Focus Questions

1. How is public speaking similar to conversation?

2. How can I pick a good topic for a speech?

3. How can I find out about my audience so that I can adapt my speech effectively?

4. What ethical responsibilities do speakers have when planning public speeches?

5. How can I listen critically to others' speeches?

Hank is a commercial artist at a public relations firm. On Thursday, Hank's supervisor asks him to prepare a 10-minute presentation for a client whose million-dollar account the firm hopes to get.

Bonnie belongs to a student group that opposes a planned tuition hike. Her group decides to attend an open meeting of the college President's Advisory Committee. During the meeting, a member of the advisory committee turns to Bonnie's group and asks, "Can you explain why you oppose the tuition increase?" Bonnie realizes that someone in the group needs to present their reasons for opposing the increase, and she rises to speak.

Miranda volunteers at the local animal protection society. The staff person who was scheduled to present an outreach program at a local high school calls in sick, and Miranda is asked to fill in.

Juan is a software designer who has created a number of innovative programs. Today, he is giving a 20-minute talk about a new program to people who have little experience with technologies.

At a public hearing on the location of a toxic waste dump, a representative of a chemical company claims that chemicals stored in the dump are safer than they really are. Kelly feels compelled to speak up so that listeners know the truth about the danger of the chemicals.

Although these people aren't professional speakers, each of them is called on to make oral presentations. Public speaking is part of most people's lives. If you are competent at public speaking, you increase your opportunities for professional effectiveness and advancement and your influence in community and society. Freedom to express our ideas in public is so basic to a free and democratic society that it is guaranteed by the First Amendment to the Constitution.

The role of public speaking in professional life is more obvious in some occupations than in others. If you plan to be an attorney, politician, salesperson, or educator, it's easy to see that speaking in public will be a routine part of your life. The importance of public speaking is less obvious, yet also present, in other careers. If you intend to be an accountant, city planner, counselor, doctor, or businessperson, you will have many opportunities to speak to small and large groups. Whatever profession you enter, skill in public speaking skills will be as asset to you.

The ability to present ideas effectively in public situations will also enhance your influence in civic, social, and political contexts. You'll have opportunities to voice your ideas at zoning meetings, neighborhood planning groups, and school boards. Public speaking is a basic communication skill that we all need if we want to have a voice in what happens in our workplaces, communities, and society.

Like other communication skills, effectiveness in public speaking can be developed with commitment and practice. Although some people may have

Communication Highlight

The First Amendment: Freedom of Religion, of Speech, and of the Press

"Congress shall make no law respecting an establishment of religion, or prohibiting the free exercise thereof; or abridging the freedom of speech, or of the press; or the right of people peaceably to assemble, and to petition the Government for a redress of grievances."

—Amendment I, The Constitution of the United States

more experience and perhaps even more aptitude for public speaking than others, everyone can learn to make effective presentations. In fact, much of what you have learned in previous chapters applies to public speaking. As we will see, many of the skills we've already discussed are relevant to effective public communication.

This chapter and the four that follow lead you through the process of planning, developing, and presenting public speeches. In this chapter, we'll first note similarities between public speaking and other kinds of communication we've studied. Next, we'll discuss foundations of effective public speaking: selecting and limiting topics, defining a general and specific purpose, and developing a thesis statement. The third section of the chapter emphasizes adapting speeches to particular speaking occasions and to particular listeners' orientations to topics and speakers.

The next four chapters build on material presented in this one. Chapter 14 identifies types of support for public speeches and discusses methods of conducting research. In Chapter 15, we'll learn about ways to organize and present public speeches, and we'll discuss the widespread concern of communication anxiety and ways to manage it. If you feel anxious about giving a public speech, you may want to read that section of Chapter 15 now. Chapter 16 focuses on informative public speeches, and Chapter 17 focuses on persuasive public speeches. As we discuss these topics, I'll show you partial and complete sample speeches to illustrate how the principles we discuss apply in actual speaking situations. After reading these five chapters, you should be able to plan, develop, and present an effective speech.

The ability to make effective presentations is critical to career advancement.

Public Speaking as Enlarged Conversation

Years ago, James Winans (1938), a distinguished professor of communication, remarked that effective public speaking is really enlarged conversation. Winans meant that the skills of successful public speaking are not so different from those we use in everyday conversations. As Michael Motley and Jennifer Molloy (1994, p. 52) explain, "Except for preparation time and turn-taking delay, public speaking has fundamental parallels to everyday conversation." Ethical considerations, such as honesty and avoidance of loaded and abusive language, are important in public speaking just as they are in social conversations. Furthermore, minor mistakes, such as stumbling over a phrase or forgetting a word, generally don't impair credibility or effectiveness (Motley, 1990). We make mistakes in everyday conversation and public speaking, and in neither case do they necessarily undercut our impact.

Effective public communication uses and builds on skills and principles we've discussed in earlier chapters. Whether we are talking with a couple of

Often, the most engaging public presentations are conversational in style.

friends or speaking to an audience of five hundred, we need to consider listeners' perspectives, create a good climate for communication, express our ideas clearly, organize what we say so that others can follow our thinking, explain and support our ideas, and present our thoughts in an engaging manner. Whether in social conversation or public speaking, we should use language and nonverbal behaviors that present our ideas clearly and ethically, and we should be sensitive to diversity in age, sex, race-ethnicity, religion, and so forth. In public speaking, as in everyday conversation, these are the skills of effective communication.

–Trina–

What I love about Oprah is that she always seems to be talking to me personally. I watch her show all the time and I've been to see her in person twice. She's always the same. No matter how many people are in an audience—even thousands—you feel like she's having a chat with you.

Thinking of public speaking as enlarged conversation reminds us that good public speaking is rarely stiff or exceedingly formal. In fact, the most effective public speakers tend to use an informal, personal style that invites listeners to feel as if they are being talked with, not lectured to. When I first taught a large lecture course, I learned that effective public speaking is much like conversation. For the first 10 years of my career, I taught classes of 20 to 35 students, and I relied on an interactive communication style that involved all of us. When I decided to teach a class of more than 100 students, I worried that I couldn't develop a teaching style effective in a large class. For half of that semester, I lectured in a fairly formal style because I thought that was appropriate with so many students. One day, a student asked a question that I answered by asking a question in return. He replied, then another student added her ideas, and an open discussion was launched. Both the students and I were more engaged with each other and the course material than we had been when I lectured formally. That's when I realized that effective teaching in large classes was enlarged conversation.

Sharpen Your Skill

Observing Presentational Style

Think about the speakers you have found most and least effective. For the most and least effective public speakers, answer these questions:

1. Did they use a formal or informal speaking style?

   ....

2. At the outset of speaking, did they give you a reason to listen?

   ....

3. Did the speakers give reasons for ideas and opinions they expressed?

   ....

4. Could you follow the speakers' trains of thought?

   ....

5. Did they adapt their ideas to your level of knowledge and your interests?

   ....

6. Did they seem excited about their ideas?

   ....

At its best, public speaking is enlarged conversation in which there is high personal engagement between listeners and speakers. With this background, we're now ready to consider the first steps in designing effective public presentations.

Choosing and Refining a Topic

A well-crafted speech begins with a limited topic, a clear purpose, and a concise thesis statement that listeners can grasp quickly and retain.

Choosing Your Topic

The first step in preparing a public speech is to select a topic. If you don't already have a topic in mind, you might consult sources such as *The Readers' Guide to Periodical Literature*, newspapers and news magazines, and current events programs on TV. Computerized databases allow you to search library holdings without actually going to the library. One database, Dialog Information Retrieval Service (DIRS), includes more than a million records from popular and academic sources.

Sharpen Your Skill

Generating Ideas for Speeches

What if you can't think of a topic for your speech? If thinking about your own experiences and interests doesn't suggest a topic, there are other resources. Read newspapers and magazines. Browse among books in your library or bookstores. These activities may remind you of topics that you care about. You can also search online at sites that feature idea generators. You can use the idea generators to search broad areas such as business, the arts, and education. Within each broad category are numerous more specialized topics. One good site is http://www.lib.odu.edu/libassist/idea.

Select a Topic That Matters to You When you are asked to speak, seize the chance to speak about a topic that matters to you. When we care about a topic, we have a head start in that we already know a fair amount about it. In addition, personal interest in the subject will make your delivery more engaging and dynamic. Perhaps you are a vegetarian and want to inform others of the moral, health, and economic reasons for vegetarianism. If you are committed to strong environmental policies, you might want to persuade your classmates to be more environmentally responsible. Maybe you have strong beliefs about the death penalty, inner-city crime, or other important social topics. A speech is the ideal opportunity to influence how others feel and think about important issues that matter to you.

Select a Topic Appropriate to the Speaking Occasion Personal knowledge and interest aren't the only criteria for selecting a topic. We should also consider the speaking occasion or situation. What are the expectations, demands, and constraints of particular speaking situations? Some contexts virtually dictate speaking content. For example, a rally for a political candidate demands speeches that praise the candidate, a ceremony honoring a person requires speakers to pay tribute to the person, a keynote speech at a professional conference should address the concerns of that profession, and funerals demand speeches that honor the person who has died and his or her life.

–Pat–

When we had our Phi Beta Kappa induction last spring, we had a very well-known scholar give the speech. He began by talking about how great our basketball team is and how we may win the championship this year. He talked about the team for about 5 minutes before he said anything else. It's not like I'm against sports or anything. I mean, I go to games and I think our team is way cool. But Phi Beta Kappa is the highest academic honor society on campus. It didn't seem the right situation to be leading a rally for the team.

Physical setting is also part of the speaking occasion. You know what your classroom is like and the time of day you will speak. In other speaking situations, it's appropriate to ask in advance about the physical setting. Is the room in which you will speak large or small? Is it well lit or dim? Are chairs comfortable or not? Is the temperature comfortable, hot and stuffy, or chilly? Will you present your speech at 10 A.M., after a heavy lunch, or midafternoon? Will listeners have sat through a long day of meetings and speeches? Each of these factors influences listeners' ability to listen and pay attention.

Communication Highlight

Connecting Yourself with Your Topic

One of the most powerful ways for speakers to enhance impact is to demonstrate personal involvement with their topics. Some good examples of speakers who show their personal involvement with topics come from acceptance speeches at Academy Awards ceremonies (Robinson, 2001). When Tom Hanks won the best actor award for his portrayal of an attorney with AIDS in *Philadelphia*, he used his speech to pay tribute to the millions of people who have died of HIV-related illnesses. He also paid tribute to a former teacher who was gay and who inspired his performance. That same year, a nonactress, Gerda Weisman Klein, won an award for her documentary film about the Holocaust, *One Survivor Remembers*. In accepting the award, Weisman said, "I've been in a place for six incredible years where winning meant a crust of bread and to live another day" (p. 16).

If possible, check the room in advance yourself. You might be able to control some possible hindrances such as temperature or seating arrangement. If there are undesirable aspects of the setting that are beyond your control (uncomfortable seating, speaking after listeners have had a big meal), you must do your best to compensate for them. A dynamic and engaging delivery can do much to surmount listeners' lethargy or discomfort.

Sometimes you won't know the physical setting in advance or won't be able to control it. In that case, you must adapt as best you can on the spot. Once, my partner, Robbie, was asked to give a keynote speech after dinner at a meeting of the North Carolina Student Sierra Club. In the past, he had given many keynote speeches at Sierra Club meetings. Based on past events, Robbie assumed that the dinner would be in a banquet room and that people would be dressed somewhat formally. He prepared a 30-minute speech, which he planned to deliver forcefully from a speaking podium. He dressed in a good suit and tie. When he got to the meeting, he discovered that the dinner was a cookout at a campsite—certainly appropriate for a Sierra Club group, but not what he was expecting! Robbie quickly adapted his appearance by taking off his jacket and tie and rolling up his shirtsleeves.

He then adapted the content of his speech and his delivery to the informal speaking situation in which he found himself. He decided to eliminate some of the quotations from environmental leaders because the light from the campfire would not be sufficient for him to read quotes from note cards, and he didn't want to risk misquoting others. And he adapted his planned forceful, podium delivery to a more conversational, storytelling style. Robbie would have been ineffective had he had not adapted himself and his speech to the physical setting.

Select a Topic Appropriate to Your Audience   Effective speakers also select topics that will appeal to the needs, interests, and situations of listeners. A public speech is not a chance primarily to showcase yourself by showing how smart, clever, funny, or knowledgeable you are. It is first and foremost a chance to affect others—that's the whole goal of speaking. And if you want to affect others, you begin by thinking about them in the first stages of planning a speech.

Speakers who don't consider listeners' perspectives may be perceived as self-centered and ineffective. In selecting a topic, ask what issues interest your listeners, how topics that matter to you are or can be relevant to them, what knowledge they have, and what experiences and concerns they are likely to share with you. We'll have more to say about considering listeners later in this chapter. For now, just realize that you should take listeners into account when choosing a topic as well as at every stage in planning and giving a speech.

Narrow Your Topic   Effective speakers limit their speeches to a manageable focus (McGuire, 1989). A speech on the broad topic of interpersonal communication could be narrowed to a more specific focus on managing conflict, listening effectively, or creating supportive climates. Any of these three topics could be discussed in a 10- to 20-minute speech. If you're interested in the general topic of health-care reform, you might narrow that to reducing the costs of drugs or increasing preventive medicine (wellness).

You can't competently discuss the broad topic of health care reform in a single speech, but you can cover a particular aspect of it.

Sharpen Your Skill

Selecting and Narrowing Your Topic

Identify three broad topics or areas that you care about.

Topic 1:...

Topic 2:...

Topic 3:...

Now list three subtopics for each one. The subtopics should be narrow enough to be covered well in a short speech.

Topic 1: 1...

2...

3...

Topic 2: 1...

2...

3...

Topic 3: 1...

2...

3...

Select one of the nine subtopics for your upcoming speech.

Another way to narrow your speaking purpose is to use a **mind map** (Jaffe, 1995; Wycoff, 1991). A mind map is a holistic record of information on a topic, which many visual thinkers prefer to an outline. You create a mind map by free-associating ideas in relation to a broad area of interest. For example, perhaps you want to speak on the general topic of the environment. To narrow that broad topic to a manageable focus for a single speech, you could brainstorm issues related to the topic. Figure 13.1 shows many specific issues that might occur to someone who creates a mind map on the topic of environment.

Defining Your General and Specific Purposes in Speaking

The second step in designing an effective speech is to define your purpose for speaking. This involves two steps. First, you should decide whether your general purpose is to persuade, entertain, or inform listeners. Second, you should refine your general purpose into a specific purpose.

General Purposes of Speaking   Traditionally, three general speaking purposes have been recognized: entertaining, informing, and persuading (Table 13.1). You probably realize that these purposes often overlap. For example, informative speeches routinely include humor or interesting com-

Figure 13.1
Mind Map

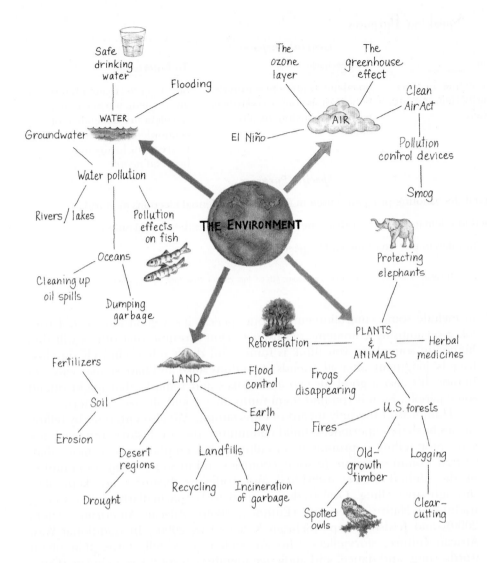

ments that aim to entertain listeners. Persuasive speeches typically contain much information about issues and solutions. Speeches intended to inform may also persuade listeners toward new beliefs, attitudes, or actions. Although speeches often involve more than one purpose, usually one purpose is primary.

One speaking goal is to entertain. In **speeches to entertain,** the primary objective is to engage, interest, amuse, or please listeners. You might think that speeches to entertain are presented only by accomplished comics and performers. Actually, in the course of our lives many of us will be involved in speaking to entertain. You might be asked to give an after-dinner speech, to present a toast at a friend's wedding, or to make remarks at a retirement party for a colleague. In each case, the primary goal is to entertain, although the entertainment might include information about the occasion, the couple being married, or the colleague who is retiring.

Even when your primary purpose in speaking is not to entertain, you'll want to interest listeners whom you intend to inform or persuade. If you want

Table 13.1: Speaking Purposes

	General Purposes	
To Inform	**To Persuade**	**To Entertain**
Speaking to define, instruct, explain, clarify, demonstrate, teach, or train	Speaking to influence attitudes, beliefs, or actions; to convince, motivate to action, inspire, or sell	Speaking to create interest, amusement, warm feelings; to celebrate, remember, or acknowledge others or events; to create or fortify ties between people

Specific Purposes

To understand the balloting procedure used in the 2000 presidential elections in Florida

To sign a petition demanding new voting systems for all districts in the United States

To laugh at my jokes in the "roast the CEO" speech

Adapted from Sprague, J. & Stuart, D. (1996). *The Speaker's Handbook*, 4th ed. (pp. 29–30). New York: Harcourt Brace.

to include some entertainment in your speech, it's a good idea to test your jokes or amusing comments in advance. Don't assume that others will find humor in something you think is funny, and don't rely exclusively on close friends' judgment; after all, friends often think alike and have similar senses of humor. It's also a good idea to avoid jokes and remarks that might offend some people. Even if you find them funny, they could alienate listeners.

Humor isn't the only means of entertaining. We also entertain by telling stories to share experiences, build community, pass on history, and teach lessons. Storytelling is prominent in cultures that emphasize oral, more than written, communication. In some countries and in some social communities in the United States, individual and collective histories are kept alive through storytelling. Oral traditions tend to be particularly strong among traditional Native Americans (Einhorn, 2000), African Americans (Fitch, 2000), and Jewish groups (Schram & Schwartz, 2000). In traditional West African culture, storytellers, who are called *griots,* tell stories that blend words, song, and dance, and audience members respond as a chorus (Cummings, 1993).

Storytelling, or narrative speaking, often occurs in families as parents share stories about their courtship, discuss their childhoods, and tell children about relatives. You probably heard many family stories as you were growing up. Narratives also socialize new employees into organizations. As long-time members of organizations tell "war stories" and recount significant moments in an organization's life, they introduce new members to key players in the organization and socialize the newcomers in the organization's history and core values (Pacanowski & O'Donnell-Trujillo, 1983).

Storytelling weaves groups and history together by telling stories that create common knowledge and understandings. Notice that although narrative speaking is considered primarily entertaining, it may also serve to inform or persuade. Think about some of the family stories you heard. Probably some of them informed you about what your parents and ancestors had done. They may also have persuaded you to endorse certain values, such as honesty and hard work.

Speaking to inform is a common presentational goal. **Speeches to inform** have the primary goal of increasing listeners' understanding, awareness, or knowledge about some topic. When you speak to inform, your goal is to tell listeners something they don't already know. Consider several situations that might call for informative speaking:

- To make listeners aware of a new way of thinking about a familiar topic
- To teach listeners how to do something new
- To correct listeners' misconceptions
- To increase listeners' understanding of a topic about which they know only a little
- To make listeners aware of issues or problems
- To inform listeners about important events
- To describe a new procedure or policy

A speaker might give an informative speech if she or he wants listeners to understand the philosophy of the Republican Party or existing programs for recycling. In both cases, the general purpose is to inform listeners. Speeches to inform may also take the form of demonstrations, in which the speaker shows how to do something while giving a verbal explanation. For instance, a demonstration speech might show listeners how to use a new computer program or how to distinguish poisonous from nonpoisonous mushrooms. Speeches to inform may also aim to teach listeners something entirely new. Sasha, a student in one of my classes, gave a speech on arranged marriages, which still occur in her native country. Her goal was for students to understand the history of arranged marriages and the reasons why they work for many people.

Storytelling is a powerful way to pass on history and strengthen familial and community bonds. It plays a central role in oral cultures.

Speeches to persuade have the purpose of changing people's attitudes, beliefs, or behaviors or motivating people to action. Persuasive goals are to influence attitudes, change practices, alter beliefs, and motivate action. Rather than an entertainer or teacher, the persuasive speaker is an advocate who argues for a cause, issue, policy, attitude, or action. Persuasive speeches aim to change how listeners think, feel, or act. To do so, they must do more than provide information, although information typically is part of persuasive speaking as well. The key goal of persuasive speeches is to strengthen listeners' existing attitudes or beliefs or to actually change what they think, believe, and do. Persuasive purposes include these:

- To convince listeners to do something they are not currently doing
- To show listeners they should believe in, or support, a specific policy, law, or organization
- To convince listeners to stop doing something
- To motivate listeners to take a specific action

- To convince listeners to buy a product
- To motivate listeners to vote for a candidate
- To inspire listeners to volunteer time or make donations to a worthy cause

In one of my classes, a student named Chris gave a speech to persuade other students to donate blood. He began by telling us that he was a hemophiliac and that his life depended on blood donations. This self-disclosure increased his credibility with listeners. He then informed listeners about the procedures for donating blood (a subordinate informational purpose) so that they would not be deterred by fear of the unknown. Next, he described the cases of several people who died because adequate supplies of blood weren't available. In the two weeks after his speech, more than one-third of the students who had been in the audience donated blood!

Specific Purposes of Speaking   Once you have decided on your general speaking purpose, you will want to define a **specific purpose,** which is a behavioral objective or observable response that will indicate that you have been effective in achieving your communication goal. Examples of specific speaking purposes are:

- I want 25% of listeners to sign up to donate blood.
- I want listeners to be able to give correct answers to questions about how HIV is and is not spread.
- I want listeners to know this candidate's stand on free trade.

Developing a Thesis Statement

Once you have selected and narrowed your speaking topic and defined your general and specific purpose, you're ready to develop the thesis statement of your speech. A **thesis statement** is the main idea of an entire speech. It concisely states the heart of your speech. It should capture the key message in a short and precise sentence that listeners can remember easily (Table 13.2).

A good thesis statement is one that listeners can grasp at the beginning of your talk and remember after you have finished. They may forget specific details and evidence you present, but you want them to remember the main idea. They are most likely to retain it if you create a concise thesis statement and repeat it several times during your talk. Chris's thesis statement for his informative speech was this: "Donating blood is painless, quick, and life-saving for others." Although Chris's listeners may have forgotten many of the specific points in his speech, they remembered his main idea: the thesis statement. When Chris gave his persuasive speech, his thesis statement was: "You should donate blood."

Table 13.2: Sample Thesis Statements

Ineffective	Effective
Think twice before you decide you're for gun control.	Gun control jeopardizes individual rights and safety.
Vegetarianism is a way of life.	Vegetarian diets are healthful and delicious.
Big businesses should get breaks.	Tax breaks for businesses are good for the economy.

Table 13.3: **Steps in Planning Public Speaking**

Step	Example
1. Identify the broad topic:	Education
2. Narrow the topic:	Continuing education
3. Define a general purpose:	To persuade
4. Specify a specific purpose:	To motivate listeners to take courses after graduating from college
5. Develop a thesis statement:	"I hope to convince you that taking courses after you graduate can enrich you, your life, and your professional success."

Speech Builder Express, which you can access directly through your *Communication in Our Lives* CD-ROM, includes a section on developing thesis statements that are appropriate and effective for the type of speech you're preparing.

Sharpen Your Skill

Defining Your Purpose and Thesis Statement

Write out the general purpose of your speech.

I want my speech to...

Define the specific purpose of your speech by specifying the observable response that will indicate you have succeeded:

At the end of my speech, I want listeners to...

Does your specific purpose require you to meet subordinate goals such as including information in a persuasive speech?

To achieve my specific purpose I need to [entertain, inform, or persuade]

....

  For additional practice in developing thesis statements, complete Activity 13.1, "Developing Effective Thesis Statements," in your *Student Companion* or online under "Activities for Chapter 13" at the *Communication in Our Lives* website.

Effective speakers choose and limit their topics. As we've seen, this requires you to select and narrow a topic that matters to you and your listeners, define your general and specific speaking purposes, and develop a clear, concise thesis statement (Table 13.3). We're now ready to consider the key process of adapting your speaking goals, content, and delivery to specific listeners and speaking contexts.

Analyzing Your Audience

A student named Harold gave a persuasive speech to convince listeners to support affirmative action. He was personally compelling and dynamic in his delivery, and his ideas were well organized. The only problem was that his audience had little background on affirmative action, and he didn't explain exactly what the policy does and does not involve. He assumed listeners understood how affirmative action works, and he focused on its positive effects. His listeners weren't persuaded, because Harold failed to give them information that might have secured their support. Harold's speech also illustrates our earlier point that speeches often combine more than one speaking purpose; in this case, giving information was essential to Harold's larger goal of persuading listeners.

Another student named Christie spoke passionately about the morality of vegetarianism. She provided dramatic evidence of the cruelty animals suffer as they are raised and slaughtered. When we polled listeners after her speech, only two of thirty had been persuaded to consider vegetarianism. Why was Christie ineffective? Because she didn't recognize and address listeners' beliefs that vegetarian foods are unhealthy and tasteless. Christie mistakenly assumed that listeners would know that it's easy to get sufficient protein, vitamins, and minerals without consuming meat, and she assumed they understood that vegetarian foods can be delicious. However, her listeners didn't know that, and they weren't about to consider a diet that they thought was neither nutritious nor appetizing.

Christie and Harold made the mistake of not adapting to their audiences. It's impossible to entertain, inform, or persuade people if we don't understand and accommodate their perspectives, interests, attitudes, beliefs, and experiences (Griffin, 2004). Speakers need to know what listeners already know and believe, as well as what reservations they might have about a topic (McGuire, 1989). To paraphrase the advice of an ancient Greek rhetorician, "The fool persuades me with his or her reasons, the wise person with my own." That is, effective speakers understand and work with listeners' reasons, values, knowledge, and concerns.

All communication, including public speaking, involves interaction between people. You must take your listeners' perspectives into account if you want them to consider your views, and you must present your views in ways that make sense to them. We consider our friends' perspectives when we talk with them. We take into account other's views when we engage in business negotiations. We use dual perspective when communicating with children, dates, parents, and neighbors. Thus, audience analysis is important to effectiveness in all types of communication, including public speeches. We'll discuss two methods of analyzing audiences.

Demographic Audience Analysis

You've heard the word *demographics* used to refer to common characteristics of people in a community or nation. **Demographic analysis** identifies general features common to a group of listeners. Demographic characteristics include age, sex, religion, cultural heritage, race, occupation, political allegiances, and educational level. Demographic information about listeners is useful in two ways.

First, demographic information can help you adapt your speech to your listeners. For example, if you know the age or age range of listeners, you know what experiences are likely to be part of their history. You could assume that 60-year-old listeners know a fair amount about the Vietnam War but that 20-year-olds might not. You can assume that 50-year-olds remember President John Kennedy and Martin Luther King, Jr., but that 18–22-year-old listeners will not remember them. In planning a speech, references to events, people, music and so forth should be appropriate to the ages of listeners. In many speaking situations, you will have listeners of different ages—sometimes of several generations. In those cases, you'll want either to restrict your references to ones that will be familiar to listeners of all ages or to explain any references that might not be understood by some listeners.

Age is also linked to persuadability. In general, as people age, they are less likely to change their attitudes, perhaps because they've held their attitudes longer than younger people or because they've acquired knowledge that supports their attitudes (Meyers, 1993). Thus, it's generally reasonable to expect to move older listeners less than younger listeners toward new beliefs, attitudes, or actions.

Other demographic information can also guide speakers in preparing presentations that will interest and involve particular listeners. Because we live in a multicultural world, effective speakers must be careful not to use examples that exclude some groups. For instance, using generic male language (*chairman,* the pronoun *he* to refer to a doctor) is likely to offend some listeners. Similarly, referring to the winter break from school as "the Christmas holiday" will not feel inclusive to listeners who are not Christian. If speaking to a predominantly African American audience, in some situations (churches, for example) a speaker might anticipate and invite listeners' active participation.

The educational background of listeners can suggest what kinds of language may be appropriate. Once, when I was serving as an expert witness in a trial, I was asked about an instrument that had been used to measure an employee's effectiveness. I had reviewed the instrument in advance and determined that it was invalid and unreliable. I stated that as my opinion in court. One of the attorneys then asked me what validity and reliability were. The judge and jury didn't have statistical training, so I couldn't explain the technical meaning of convergent, predictive, internal, and external validity, and I couldn't explain specialized indexes of reliability. After a few moments of thought, I answered that validity is a matter of whether an instrument measures what it claims to measure, and reliability is a matter of whether the instrument consistently measures what it claims to measure over time. Had I been speaking to a group of researchers, I would have offered a more technical answer that was tailored to their greater statistical expertise.

We also know that people who have cognitively complex thinking styles want to understand things. For them, it's not enough to know that something is the case. They also need to know *why* it's the case—what makes it so (Meyers, 1993). Cognitive complexity tends to increase with age and education, so we can make predictions about listeners' cognitive complexity based on these other factors. When preparing a speech for cognitively complex listeners, we should provide more detailed evidence and explanations for our assertions than might be appropriate for a less cognitively complex group of listeners.

Speakers also use demographic information to make inferences about what listeners are likely to believe and what values and attitudes they are likely to have. For example, assume you plan to give a speech on the general topic of health-care reform. If your listeners' average age is 68, they are likely to be more interested in containment of drug costs and in reasonable options for long-term care of older adults than in preventive care and vaccines for children. Listeners in their twenties, on the other hand, would be likely to perceive preventive health care as more immediately relevant than ensuring reasonable options for long-term care of older adults.

Knowing something about the general characteristics of listeners may also suggest what type of evidence and which authorities will be effective. Statistics bore many listeners, especially if presented in a dull manner, but they might be very interesting to an audience of economists or mathematicians. A quotation from George W. Bush is more likely to be effective with a Republican audience than with a Democratic one. Citing Sandra Day O'Connor or Ruth Bader Ginsburg might impress a group of women attorneys more than citing Clarence Thomas would. Although all three are members of the Supreme Court, they have different degrees of credibility with different groups.

Demographic information provides general insights into what and whom listeners may find credible. Yet it's important to remember that demographic information can provide only a general profile of a group. As we noted when we discussed stereotypes in Chapters 2 and 7, not all members of a particular social group conform to all features of that group. Although demographic analysis can give you some general information about groups of people, it doesn't offer precise insight into any particular individual.

Communication Highlight

Failing to Unify

George W. Bush assumed the presidency under extremely difficult circumstances. His opponent, Al Gore, had won the popular vote, but the electoral vote was less clear. Voting irregularities around the country, especially in Florida, called into question the legitimacy of his presidency. The Supreme Court ruled that Bush had won, but because he hadn't won a majority of votes, his mandate was weak.

The country was deeply divided, not just between allegiance to Gore and Bush but also over the fairness of the voting and the Supreme Court ruling. Thus, Bush needed to bring the nation together. At his inaugural ceremony, Bush spoke about unifying the nation, being a president for all of the people, and celebrating the diversity that makes America great.

Although Bush's speech acknowledged America's diversity, another part of the inauguration did not. The two prayers delivered as part of the ceremony were presented by Evangelical Christians. Both preachers paid homage to Christian values and praised Jesus specifically. This failed to connect with or include millions of Americans who are Jewish, Buddhist, Hindu, Muslim, and so forth.

Speakers may also draw on demographic information to create connections with their listeners. Politicians create points of identification with voters in diverse regions. In the South, a candidate might tell stories about growing up in southern towns; in New England, the candidate might reminisce about college years at Harvard or Dartmouth; in the Midwest, the candidate might speak about friends and family who live there. It is unethical for speakers to disguise or distort their background, ideas, or positions in order to build common ground with listeners. However, understanding the demographic characteristics of listeners helps a speaker decide which aspects of her or his life and interests to emphasize in a particular situation.

−Lamont−

A big filmmaker came to talk to our class, and I figured he was in a world totally different from ours. I mean, the man makes multimillion-dollar movies and knows all the big stars. But he started his talk by telling us about when he was in college, and he talked about his favorite classes, about a bar he went to on Fridays, and about the special friends he'd made at college. I felt like he understood what my life is about, like he wasn't so different from me after all.

Sharpen Your Skill

Demographic Analysis

Answer the following questions (or research the answers) about the listeners to whom you plan to speak (notice that categories for questions 3 and 4 are arranged alphabetically to minimize perceptions of bias):

1. How many women and men are in your audience?

   ....

2. What are the average age and the age range of your listeners?

   ....

3. How many of your listeners are

   A. atheist

   B. Buddhist

   C. Catholic

   D. Hindu

   E. Jewish

   F. Protestant

   G. other

   ....

4. How many of your listeners are

   A. African American

   B. Asian American

   C. European American

D. Hispanic American

E. Native American

F. other ethnic identity

....

5. What is the average educational level of your listeners?

....

6. How many of your listeners are

A. married

B. single

C. divorced

....

7. How many of your listeners live

A. in dormitories

B. in apartments

C. with their families of origin

D. with a spouse or children

E. in fraternity or sorority houses

....

8. How many of your listeners have

A. a high school diploma

B. some college

C. college degree

D. some graduate work

E. technical or professional training

....

9. What is the average income of your listeners' families?

A. under $10,000

B. between $10,001 and $30,000

C. between $30,001 and $50,000

D. between $50,001 and $100,000

E. over $100,000

....

Demographic analysis can provide useful general information about listeners. However, it's important to guard against stereotypes of groups of people. Although many college students are between 18 and 22 years old, some are older than 22. Thus, it would be inadvisable to design a speech to college students for an exclusively 18- to 22-year-old audience. Although many women work outside the home, not all do, so an audience of women should not be addressed as if no homemakers were present. Similarly, speakers shouldn't stereotype an audience of men as uninterested in child care, because many men are very involved parents.

Situational Audience Analysis

A second method of audience analysis is **situational audience analysis,** which seeks information about specific listeners that relates directly to the speaker's topic and purpose. Situational audience analysis allows a speaker to discover what listeners already know and believe about a topic, speaker, and occasion so that the speaker can adapt to his or her listeners.

Listeners' Orientation toward the Topic
Effective speakers develop their speeches with attention to their specific listeners' interest, knowledge, and attitudes toward the speech topic. In many cases, listeners are already interested in the speech topic—that's why they attend. However, if listeners do not begin with interest in your topic, your job is to pique their interest. You might make them aware of how the topic relates to them: How does it or how will it affect them? What's at stake for them? Why should they care about what you have to say? Emma, a student of mine, began an informative speech about breast cancer this way: "Looking around the room, I see there are 16 women here. According to statistics, 2 of you—1 in every 8 women—will develop breast cancer in her lifetime."

You also want to analyze listeners' knowledge about your topic so that you can adapt appropriately. What do they already know about the topic? How much information (or misinformation) do they have? Once you have assessed listeners' knowledge about your topic, you can decide how much information you need to provide and how detailed and technical you can be.

Finally, in assessing your listeners' orientation toward your topic, you want to know what attitudes they hold. If they already favor something you are proposing, you don't need to persuade them to a positive attitude. Instead, you may want to move them to action—to motivate them to act on what they already favor. On the other hand, if your listeners are against or indifferent to something you are proposing, your persuasive goal is to convince them to consider your point of view. You will need to provide more evidence than you will if they already favor your position.

Listeners' Orientation toward the Speaker
To be effective, speakers must recognize and adjust to listeners' attitudes toward them. Listeners' perceptions of a speaker shape how they respond to the message. The more credibility a speaker has with listeners, the more likely they are to believe what she or he says and to consider her or his proposals. Do the listeners already know who the speaker is? Do they respect the speaker's expertise on the topic? Do listeners believe a speaker cares about what is good for them? If not, the speaker needs to give listeners reasons to trust him or her and to believe that he or she is interested in their welfare.

If you do not have credentials that establish you as an expert on a topic, you will want to demonstrate to listeners that you know what you are talking about. Explain how you learned about it. Describe your experiences with the topic. Include research that shows you are knowledgeable. Similarly, you will want to convince listeners that you care about what is good for them. Connect what you are talking about with listeners, as Emma did in opening her speech on breast cancer. Show that you have thought about them. Demonstrate that what you say will benefit them—how will it affect their health or success?

Because a speaker's credibility is critical to effectiveness, we'll return to this topic when we discuss using evidence (Chapter 14), building a strong introduction to a speech (Chapter 15), and increasing credibility (Chapter 17).

Listener's Orientation toward the Speaking Occasion In the fall of 2002, Paul Wellstone, a Democratic senator from Minnesota, was killed in a plane crash. In addition to grieving for his tragic loss, Democrats were worried about the elections coming up in just a month. Wellstone had seemed assured of reelection. His sudden death meant the Republican candidate might win his seat in the United States Senate.

After late-night strategy sessions, the Democrats came up with a plan to keep Wellstone's seat Democratic: They would announce that Walter Mondale, a former vice president from Minnesota, was the Democratic candidate and would carry on Wellstone's legacy. Early polling showed that, even with a very late start in the race, Mondale would get more votes than the Republican candidate.

The nationally televised memorial service for Senator Wellstone and his family members who also died in the plane crash began with speeches honoring the fallen senator, as was expected on this occasion. However, after the opening speeches, the memorial service turned into a political rally for Mondale, the new Democratic candidate. Although many of the people at the service joined in the spirit of the rally, the reaction from the broader public was decidedly unfavorable. Viewers were shocked and offended by what they perceived as disrespect for Wellstone and his family and a blatant exploitation of a memorial service for political purposes. Mondale was defeated, and most political analysts cited the voting public's negative reaction to the memorial service as the key reason.

This example illustrates the importance of considering what listeners expect in a particular speaking situation and what they will consider appropriate and inappropriate. An effective speech is not something that can be canned and presented the same way in every situation. Instead, an effective speech respects the particular situation in which it occurs, as well as listeners' expectations and sense of what is and is not proper. Robbie's informal speech at the campsite worked in that context, but it would have been inappropriate in a formal banquet room.

Adapting to particular occasions also requires speakers to consider what length of speech is appropriate. At a wedding reception I once attended, guests were toasting the newlyweds. One old friend of the groom got up to "say a few words" and then spoke for fifteen minutes! That's way too long for a toast, and other guests were clearly uncomfortable with what they perceived as stage hogging. A speech introducing a main speaker should be short. Listeners will be displeased if a speech of introduction drags on, because they came to hear the main speaker. On the other hand, the main

speaker generally speaks at length; listeners would be disappointed by a six-minute speech from a featured speaker.

Occasion also influences the type of speech. In the example of the memorial service for Paul Wellstone, the occasion demanded speeches honoring Wellstone. Endorsement speeches for Walter Mondale violated what listeners considered appropriate for the occasion. After-dinner speeches generally should include some entertainment—jokes, stories, and so forth—and should not be overly somber or information packed.

Whereas politicians and corporations can afford to conduct sophisticated polls to discover what people know, want, think, and believe, most of us don't have the resources to do that. So how do ordinary people engage in situational audience analysis? One answer is observation. Often, a speaker has some experience interacting with his or her listeners. Drawing on past interactions, a speaker may be able to discern a great deal about the knowledge, attitudes, and beliefs of listeners.

It's also appropriate to gather information about listeners through conversations, interviews, or surveys. You might conduct a survey to learn about your classmates' knowledge of and attitudes toward your thesis statement. The results of your survey should give you sufficient insight into the opinions of students on your campus to enable you to adapt your presentation to the students in your class.

Using demographic and situational audience analysis provides you with direct knowledge of listeners and information from which you can draw additional inferences. Taking listeners into consideration allows you build a speech that is adapted to your particular listeners and thus likely to have impact.

Sharpen Your Skill

Critically Analyzing Public Communication

Preparing a speech and listening critically to others' speeches are two sides of the same coin. The skills that allow you to present effective, ethical speeches also allow you listen critically when others speak.

Critically analyzing speeches enables you to make wise choices about how to respond to public communication. When you engage in critical analysis, you examine a speech to judge its value. Critical listeners ask questions such as:

- Is there adequate evidence for claims?

- Is the evidence explained, and is its credibility established?

- What are the speaker's motives?

- Does the speaker appear to be informed and unbiased?

- Does the speaker reason well and without any fallacies?

- Does the speaker demonstrate awareness of and respect for you and other listeners?

As you analyze a speech, the answers to questions such as these give you a basis for understanding how the speech works and for evaluating its effectiveness and the extent to which you will let it affect you.

Critically analyzing others' speeches also enriches your understanding of what you need to do to be effective when you are speaking in public. As we continue our discussion of public speaking in the next four chapters, keep in mind that each principle we discuss both guides you in preparing effective speeches and teaches you how to listen critically to the speeches of others.

Experiencing Communication in Our Lives

CASE STUDY: A Model Speech of Introduction

The following speech is featured on the *Communication in Our Lives* CD-ROM included with this book. Once you've launched the CD, click on the "Speech Interactive" icon, and, from the Speech Menu, select "Speech of Introduction" to watch the audiovisual presentation of Dan's speech. To read a description of Dan's assignment, click on the "Assignment" button. Improve your own public speaking skills by reading, watching, listening to, evaluating, and critiquing this sample speech.

Analyze the speech by applying the principles covered in this chapter, and respond to the prompts that accompany the video, which you can access by clicking on "Evaluation" and "Critique." After answering the evaluation questions and writing a brief critique of the speech, you can click on the "Done" button to compare your responses with the ones I suggest. Additional analysis questions are available in print at the end of this chapter and on the book's website.

Dan's assignment was to present a speech of introduction in which he introduces his classmates to Dr. Evelyn Horton. Dr. Horton is a doctor who specializes in family medicine, the profession that Dan hopes to enter.

"If you don't listen to your patients, you'll never be able to provide them with good medical care." That was the first thing Dr. Evelyn Horton said to me when I asked her what kinds of communication are essential to her work. Last Monday, I interviewed her because I hope one day to be a doctor. I want to introduce you to Dr. Horton and to describe the role of communication in her work as a doctor. I'll focus on the importance of two communication skills that Dr. Horton emphasized: listening and building a supportive, trusting relationship.

The first communication skill that Dr. Horton emphasized is listening. She told me that one of the reasons she wanted to become a doctor is that she had encountered too many doctors who didn't listen to her when she was a patient. "How can a doctor treat you, if he or she doesn't listen to you?" asked Dr. Horton. Dr. Horton isn't alone in feeling that many doctors don't listen. The *Journal of the American Medical Association* reported last year that patients' biggest dissatisfaction with doctors is that they don't listen.

I asked Dr. Horton to explain what was involved in effective listening. She said, and I quote, "To be a good listener, I have to let my patients know I really want to hear what's going on with them. I have to give them permission to tell me how they are feeling and if anything is bothering them." Some of the ways that Dr. Horton does this are to repeat what patients tell her so that they will elaborate, and to keep eye contact with them when they are speaking.

So focusing on patients and encouraging them to talk openly with her are the keys to effective listening in Dr. Horton's practice. The second communication skill that Dr. Horton emphasized is building a supportive, trusting relationship with her patients. She told me about one of her patients who had an eating disorder. Dr. Horton suspected the problem, but she couldn't do much to treat it until her patient, a nineteen-year-old woman, was willing to admit she had a problem.

How did Dr. Horton gain the patient's trust? She told me that she showed the patient she wasn't going to judge her—that it was okay to say anything, and it would be confidential. When the patient made a small disclosure about being afraid of gaining weight, Dr. Horton recalled, and I quote, "I told her many women have that fear, and there are healthy ways to control weight." Later, the patient told her that sometimes she skipped meals. Dr. Horton responded, and again I quote her, "That's an understandable thing to do when you're afraid of gaining weight, but there are healthier ways to maintain a good weight." As Dr. Horton responded without judgment to the patient, the young woman gradually opened up and told Dr. Horton about her excessive dieting and exercise. Together, they worked out a better plan for managing the patient's weight.

Being nonjudgmental, then, is a key to building a trusting doctor-patient relationship. Now you've met Dr. Evelyn Horton, a doctor who knows the importance of communication to her work. For her, listening and building a supportive, trusting relationship with patients are the keys to being a good doctor. Let me close with one last statement Dr. Horton made. She told me, "To treat people, you have to communicate well with them."

Chapter Summary

In this chapter, we considered the nature of public speaking and the first steps in designing effective presentations. We began by noting that rather than differing radically from other kinds of communication, public speaking is enlarged conversation, in which a speaker interacts personally with listeners. To do this effectively, it's important to select and limit your topic, to define your general and specific purposes, and to develop a clear thesis statement. In addition, designing an effective presentation requires consideration of listeners. Effective speakers take into account what listeners know, believe, value, think, and feel about the topic, speaker, and occasion. When a speaker adapts to listeners, they are likely to be more receptive to the speaker's ideas.

In the next chapter, we'll discuss ways to conduct research and use research in public speaking. Building good arguments increases a speaker's credibility and enhances the power of ideas presented. Before proceeding to Chapter 14, complete the checklist on this page to make sure you've done the preliminary work to create a strong foundation for your speech.

Checklist for Planning a Public Speech

If you prefer, you may complete this checklist online under "Forms and Checklists for Chapter 13" at the *Communication in Our Lives* website.

In addition, you may want to use Speech Builder Express, to which you have free access through your *Communication in Our Lives* CD-ROM. At the end of this chapter, I've included a specific suggestion for using Speech Builder Express to begin planning your speech.

My speech topic is...

My general purpose is ....

My specific purpose is..

My thesis statement is ....

1. I know the following demographic information about the people who will listen to my speech:

    Age: ....

    Education: ....

    Political position: ....

    Sex ratio: ....

    Ethnicities: ....

    Other: ....

2. I know the following information about my particular listeners:

    Listeners' interest in my topic: ....

    Listeners' knowledge about my topic: ....

    Listeners' personal experience with my topic: ....

    Listeners' beliefs about my topic: ....

    Listeners' attitudes about my thesis: ....

    Listeners' expectations of the speaking occasion: ....

    Listeners' orientation toward me as a speaker: ....

Communication in Our Lives ONLINE

In addition to presenting the case studies' multimedia scenarios and speeches, the *Communication in Our Lives* CD-ROM provides quick access to the *Communication in Our Lives* website, Speech Builder Express, and InfoTrac College Edition. The website is online at http://communication.wadsworth.com/woodciol4, but you can only access this book's premium web content when you link to the site directly through the book's CD.

The *Communication in Our Lives* website features interactive tools for learning and reviewing the chapter's concepts and key terms, including electronic versions of the "For Further Reflection and Discussion" questions that appear below and a review quiz.

The website also provides updated web links and additional InfoTrac College Edition activities. If required, you can e-mail completed chapter activities or the quizzes to your instructor.

Key Concepts

demographic analysis, *346*	specific purpose, *344*	speeches to persuade, *343*
mind map, *340*	speeches to entertain, *341*	thesis statement, *344*
situational audience analysis, *351*	speeches to inform, *343*	

For Further Reflection and Discussion

1. Think about one presentation that you recently attended—perhaps a lecture in a class or a speaker at a campus event. To what extent did the speaker seem to take the audience into consideration? Identify specific factors that affect your perception of speaker's knowledge of you and other listeners. Did this make a difference in the speaker's effectiveness?

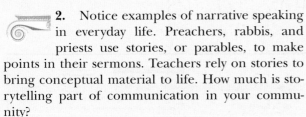 **2.** Notice examples of narrative speaking in everyday life. Preachers, rabbis, and priests use stories, or parables, to make points in their sermons. Teachers rely on stories to bring conceptual material to life. How much is storytelling part of communication in your community?

 3. Use your InfoTrac College Edition to search for topics for a speech. Check informational publications to stimulate

your thinking about a range of topics. Examples of good sources available through your InfoTrac College Edition are *Health News*, *World Economic Outlook*, and *World Press Review*.

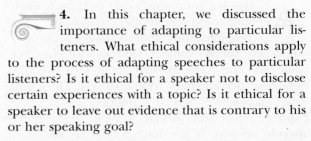 **4.** In this chapter, we discussed the importance of adapting to particular listeners. What ethical considerations apply to the process of adapting speeches to particular listeners? Is it ethical for a speaker not to disclose certain experiences with a topic? Is it ethical for a speaker to leave out evidence that is contrary to his or her speaking goal?

5. Check two databases for sources on a topic that interests you. Track down two sources from each database to read in detail.

Questions for Analysis and Discussion

Review the video of Dan's speech of introduction that you watched when completing this chapter's case study (pages 354–355), or, if you haven't seen it yet, watch it for the first time. If you didn't previously finish the "Evaluation" questions and "Critique" activity included on the CD-ROM, do so now, and then respond to the following questions, which are also available on the book's website under "Activities for Chapter 13."

1. Does Don's speech give you a sense of who Dr. Horton is?

2. Did Don's introduction catch your attention and give you a road map of what he would cover in his speech?

3. How did Don move you from one part of his speech to the next?

4. How did quotes and examples from Dr. Horton add to the speech?

5. Was Don's conclusion effective?

6. Which model of communication presented in Chapter 1 best describes Dr. Horton's communication with patients?

Speech Builder Express

This is a good time to get to know Speech Builder Express. It offers tools to help you complete your speech assignment. You can access Speech Builder Express with the user name and the password that came with the CD-ROM that accompanies your textbook. Once you have accessed Speech Builder Express, select the "Create a New Speech" section. If you have a title for your speech, type that in as the name of your file. If not, type a temporary name, such as "My First Speech." Next, select the Speech Timeline section on Speech Builder Express. Type in the date on which you will give your speech. Next, select "Goal/Purpose," and type in the specific purpose of your speech. Next, select "Thesis Statement," and type in the thesis statement for your speech (if you have developed it).

Save your file (Speech Title or "My First Speech") to your desktop, or e-mail it to your instructor if that is requested. You'll be adding to this file as you develop your speech using Chapters 14–17.

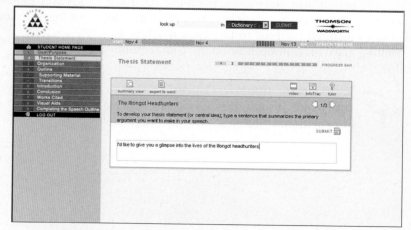

CHAPTER 14

Researching and Developing Support for Public Speeches

Focus Questions

1. What can I do to support the claims in my speech?

2. What ethical guidelines should I follow in selecting and using evidence?

3. How can I make statistics interesting to listeners?

4. How many visual aids should I use?

5. How do I credit sources in a speech?

6. How can I use computerized visuals effectively?

© The Image Bank/Getty Images

You are four times more likely to have a traffic accident when using a cell phone.	Drivers shouldn't use cell phones.
This isn't a hearing; it's a public lynching designed to persecute a Black man.	This hearing isn't fair.
Chief Seattle believed that human life is a web. He said, "Whatever we do to the web, we do to ourselves. All things are bound together."	People are connected to one another.

The sentences on the left have impact. They pack a punch and catch our attention. In contrast, the sentences on the right are flat and unmemorable. One difference between the sentences is that those on the left include support for ideas, whereas the ones on the right simply advance claims without backing them up with any evidence. Critical listeners will not accept unsupported claims, so speakers must use evidence to fortify the ideas they advance.

In the first statement, statistical evidence supports the claim that the chances of being in a traffic accident increase when drivers use cell phones. The second statement was made by Clarence Thomas in the 1991 Supreme Court confirmation hearings, regarding Anita Hill's charges that he had sexually harassed her. By using a metaphor equating the hearings with a lynching, Thomas induced some people to perceive the hearings not as an orderly judicial process but as a racist vendetta. The third statement draws on the credibility of a widely admired Native American to argue that humans are deeply interconnected. Each of these statements relies on support, or evidence. Effective use of supporting materials, such as statistics, analogies, and quotations, enhances the impact of speeches and the credibility of speakers.

In this chapter, we focus on conducting research and weaving evidence into a presentation. Throughout the process of researching and building support for a speech, it's important to conduct research and select evidence adapted to particular listeners. A speaker's success is tied directly to whether listeners understand, believe, and accept what she or he says. Your goal is not simply to use good evidence; rather, it is to use supporting materials that will be effective with your particular listeners.

Conducting Research

At the outset of developing a speech, you may already have a definite point of view and know a good deal about your topic. Mining your own knowledge and conducting further research will help you find additional information to increase your effectiveness. Initial research includes reading, thinking, talking with others, and perhaps conducting surveys. All these activities help you discover the range of information available on your topic. Then, you are ready to evaluate all the evidence you've found and decide which materials most effectively support the specific claims in your speech.

Research continues throughout the development of the speech. In the early stages of research, you may unearth information that leads you to modify your original thesis statement. As you continue, you may find evidence that convinces you to add additional points. We'll discuss four types of research in which speakers engage as they develop informative and persuasive presentations: library and online research, personal knowledge, interviews, and surveys.

Library and Online Research

Libraries and online services hold a wealth of information that can help you develop and support the ideas in your speech. Begin your research by paying a visit to the reference librarian at your library. Describe your speech topic to your reference librarian, and ask for suggestions on relevant print and electronic sources of information.

Internet As you probably know, the Internet offers an astounding amount of information on almost any topic. Using a search engine, you can type a key word or phrase and be presented with websites that may be relevant to your topic. For instance, I typed the key word "intercultural communication" into my search engine and was given a list of 78,235 sites.

Although the Internet offers a lot of information, that information isn't necessarily credible or reliable. Most magazines and newspapers have staff who check all information in articles before they go to press. Before this textbook was published, references were checked by a researcher, and proofreaders verified cross-references. Claims and evidence were evaluated by independent reviewers. In contrast, there is no systematic procedure for checking the accuracy of information posted on the Internet. Anyone can create a website and put any content on it. People who create or contribute to sites may not have sound backing for their claims. They may have vested interests in particular viewpoints. They may be trying to sell a product (many of the sites in my key word search were created by retailers to sell

Communication Highlight

Evaluating Online Sources for Speeches

 Material found online is not necessarily trustworthy. Remember, anyone can set up a website, and anyone can make claims on the Internet. Because Internet content is unregulated, you should be especially critical when evaluating it. To assess information found on the Internet, begin by applying the five standard tests for evidence summarized in Table 14.3 on page 383. In addition, ask the following questions:

1. Can you verify the material independently (by checking another source or consulting an expert)?

2. Does the source have the experience, position, or other credentials to be an authority?

3. Does the source have any vested interest in making the claim or presenting the alleged information?

4. Does the source acknowledge other sources, including ones that advance different points of view?

If you decide the online material is sound, you should cite it in your bibliography as well as your text, using the following format:

Hulme, M. & Peters, S. (2001). *Me, my phone, and I: The role of the mobile phone.* CHI 2001 Workshop: Mobile communications: Understanding users, adoption, and design, Seattle WA. Retrieved January 3, 2002, from http://www.cs.colorado.edu/~palen/chi_workshop.

Basic principles for evaluating material found on the web, and links to multiple sites that discuss the credibility of web information, can be found at http://www.uis.edu/~schroede/valid.htm.

books, programs, and other products). Information on the Internet may be out of date or presented out of context.

Indexes Libraries have indexes that summarize publications and backgrounds of individuals. Indexes of articles published in academic journals are important resources. *Psychological Abstracts,* for example, surveys articles published on psychological topics. If you want to know what research has been done on self-concept, simply look up "self-concept" in *Psychological Abstracts,* and you will find a list (probably a very long one) of published research on the topic. In addition, indexes of government documents summarize laws, policies, and regulations related to many topics.

Sharpen Your Skill

Gathering Information

Go to your campus library or the Internet and consult at least one index for information published on your topic.

The index I consulted is ....

I found .... publications on my topic.

I learned the following from three of the cited publications that I read in full:

1. ....
....

2. ....
....

3. ....
....

There are several good sources of background information on experts you may cite in your speech. Some of the more popular ones are *Who's Who in America, Who's Who in American Women, Biography Index,* and *Directory of American Scholars.* You enhance your own credibility and that of sources you cite when you provide detailed information about their qualifications and accomplishments.

Sharpen Your Skill

Background on Experts

Research the credentials of three authorities you plan to cite in your speech. Below write important information that contributes to their credibility.

1. .... holds the following titles: ....
.... and has the following experiences and qualifications: ....

2. .... holds the following titles: ....
.... and has the following experiences and qualifications: ....

3. .... holds the following titles: ....
.... and has the following experiences and qualifications: ....

Databases and Search Engines Databases allow you to search a library's or service's holdings from a computer terminal. One widely used database is Dialog Information Retrieval Service (DIRS), which includes more than 1 million records from popular and academic publications and news services. Two other superior information retrieval systems are Bibliographic Retrieval Service (BRS) and Wilsonline. InfoTrac is a fully searchable, online database that provides access to over 20 years of complete articles published in over 8,000 different periodicals. InfoTrac is updated daily, so it is also very current.

Communication in Our Lives is accompanied by InfoTrac College Edition, a version of the full database designed specifically for college students that itself features more than 10 million full-text articles from nearly 4,000 scholarly and popular sources. There are also specialized databases for fields such as medicine and law. A librarian can tell you which databases are available through your library.

To learn how to access DIRS, InfoTrac, or other online services, check with your campus computer center or a reference librarian. It's a good idea to begin library research by conducting a computer search to discover what information is available on your topic. Most college libraries have programs that can quickly identify all articles and books related to your topic.

Not only can you search the collections of your library from a computer terminal, but you can use online services to research holdings in other places. Most modern libraries allow you to search for data all over the world. Computer terminals with telephone links give you access to huge databases that can provide information for your speech. Search engines allow you to conduct subject-based searches. You might ask for information on education, and you would see a screen listing all the subcategories of education. You could then select the subcategory or subcategories that interest you and read the holdings in those subcategories to become familiar with current knowledge on the topic.

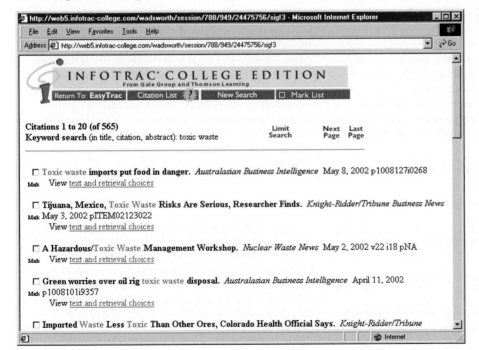

Figure 14.1
Using an Online Database to
Research Your Speech Topic

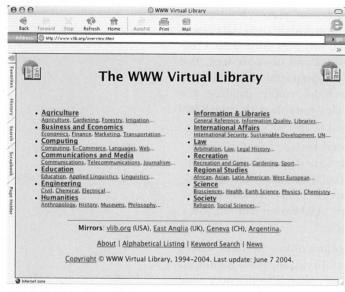

The WWW Virtual Library

- **Agriculture**
  Agriculture, Gardening, Forestry, Irrigation...
- **Business and Economics**
  Economics, Finance, Marketing, Transportation...
- **Computing**
  Computing, E-Commerce, Languages, Web...
- **Communications and Media**
  Communications, Telecommunications, Journalism...
- **Education**
  Education, Applied Linguistics, Linguistics...
- **Engineering**
  Civil, Chemical, Electrical...
- **Humanities**
  Anthropology, History, Museums, Philosophy...

- **Information & Libraries**
  General Reference, Information Quality, Libraries...
- **International Affairs**
  International Security, Sustainable Development, UN...
- **Law**
  Arbitration, Law, Legal History...
- **Recreation**
  Recreation and Games, Gardening, Sport...
- **Regional Studies**
  African, Asian, Latin American, West European...
- **Science**
  Biosciences, Health, Earth Science, Physics, Chemistry...
- **Society**
  Religion, Social Sciences...

Mirrors: vlib.org (USA), East Anglia (UK), Geneva (CH), Argentina.

About | Alphabetical Listing | Keyword Search | News

Copyright © WWW Virtual Library, 1994–2004. Last update: June 7 2004.

The Virtual Library is a valuable tool for conducting research. It provides a wealth of material and is updated frequently to ensure currency of information.

Print Reference Works Specialized references can save you hours of work by directing you to materials specifically on your topic. The *Reader's Guide to Periodical Literature* summarizes articles published in 125 popular magazines, including *Newsweek, Ebony, Working Woman,* and *Fortune.* The *Public Affairs Information Service Bulletin* indexes books, pamphlets, and other materials pertinent to public affairs. *American Demographics* is an amazing reservoir of information on Americans' patterns, behaviors, possessions, and so forth. It's the resource to check if you want to know how many televisions the average household has, how much sugar the average person consumes in a year, or how often most people eat out. *Facts on File* is a weekly publication that provides factual information and background on world news.

Personal Knowledge

Another source of information is yourself. What do you already know about your topic? How are you involved with it? What experiences have you had that qualify you to speak on the topic? Why does this topic matter to you? You will probably be comfortable and engaging when you talk about experi-

Communication Highlight

Caught in the Net

Conducting research on the Internet provides mountains of information, but it may also have another effect: addiction. According to Kimberly Young, a faculty member in the Psychology Department of the University of Pittsburgh, as many as 5 million Internet users may already be addicted. She likens Internet addiction to eating disorders, saying that both are prompted by emotional and psychological problems. Young has devised a self-test for Internet addiction (K. Young, 1998). Here are sample items from her test:

1. How often do you find that you stay online longer than you intended?

2. How often do you prefer the excitement of the Internet to intimacy with your partner?

3. How often do you form new relationships with fellow online users?

4. How often do you find yourself anticipating when you will go online again?

5. How often do you snap, yell, or act annoyed if someone bothers you while you are online?

Before you diagnose yourself as an Internet addict, be aware that distinguished scholars have questioned Young's work. Malcolm Parks, a member of the Speech Communication Department at the University of Washington, asserts that Young's research relies on instruments that are not valid. Furthermore, he criticizes her for relying too heavily on case studies and not conducting rigorous statistical comparisons of Internet addicts to nonaddicts (Kiernan, 1998). Whether or not *addiction* is too strong a term, it's clear that many people do become seriously absorbed with life on the net.

Use your InfoTrac College Edition to read Peter Mitchell's 2000 article "Internet Addiction: Genuine Diagnosis or Not?" In this article, Mitchell presents views of those who think Internet addiction is a myth and those, including Kimberly Young, who think it is a real and serious problem. After reading the article, what is your opinion of the validity of the concept of Internet addiction?

ences you have had and knowledge you have gained through personal involvement with a topic. A second reason to include personal content in a speech is that it tends to enhance your credibility. When you draw on your own experiences and knowledge, listeners are likely to perceive you as more credible than someone who is not personally involved with the topic.

Sharpen Your Skill

Using Your Expertise

List three experiences that directly involve you with the topic of your speech:

1. ....
   ....

2. ....
   ....

3. ....
   ....

   Explain why these experiences qualify you to speak on the topic.

Interviews

Interviews allow you to gather information, to check the accuracy of ideas you have, and to understand the perspective of people who are experts or who have special experience with your topic. Many community organizations have experts who can provide you with a wealth of information on specific topics. For example, the American Lung Association has chapters in most communities, and a staff person could furnish very recent information on the causes and frequency of lung disease and ways to reduce the toll on health and life. Other organizations, such as the Parent–Teacher Association, the Animal Protection Society, the Sierra Club, Habitat for Humanity, and Alcoholics Anonymous can provide up-to-date information and background in their respective areas.

You need to plan ahead for interviews because experts often have busy schedules. When you call to request an interview, identify yourself, explain the purpose of the interview, and state the approximate length of time you expect the interview to take. Prepare a list of questions in advance to increase the productivity of an interview and to ensure that you don't forget important questions. You may include both closed-ended questions, which ask for specific information ("How long have you held this position?" "How much does this program cost annually?" "When was the this survey conducted?"), and open-ended questions, which allow interviewees to give more elaborate responses ("What do you think would improve the system here?" "Can you describe how your organization identifies priorities?").

In addition to questions you prepare, you'll want to invite interviewees to initiate ideas. As experts, they may be aware of information and dimensions of a topic that haven't occurred to you. Furthermore, you have an ethical responsibility to respect an interviewee's priorities, concerns, and perspective. If an interviewee gives permission, it's acceptable to take notes during interviews. However, you should be careful to keep your primary attention on the interviewee. Audiotaping interviews is appropriate only if the interviewee agrees.

Possible Interviewees

List four people you might interview to gain expert perspective and information on your topic. For each person, list his or her name, title or position, and relevance to the topic.

	Name	Position or Title	Relevance to Topic
1.	....	....	....
2.	....	....	....
3.	....	....	....
4.	....	....	....

E-mail or phone two of the people on your list to ask for an interview.

Conducting interviews often increases a speaker's credibility. Quoting interviewees shows that a speaker has invested personal effort in researching a topic. In addition, listeners often find experts' opinions persuasive (Olson & Cal, 1984). To maximize the impact of testimony, speakers should identify the source's credentials and explain why the source qualifies as expert. It's naive to assume listeners will know a source's credentials, experience, and other bases of expertise. Thus, in your speech you should explain the credentials of anyone whom you quote or paraphrase. You may credit your sources in several ways:

> "Chris Brenner is the chief of police on our campus. He says, and I quote, . . ."

> "After 10 years in the position of chief of campus police, Chris Brenner says, and I quote, . . ."

> "In an interview I conducted with Chris Brenner, long-time chief of campus police, I learned that . . ."

> "To find out about crime on our campus, I interviewed the chief of campus police. According to Chief Brenner, . . ."

–Cole–

It was really effective when Joel told us he had interviewed police officers to find out their views about drivers who use cell phones. He had lots of good information from other sources, but what really impressed me was that he took the time to talk with police officers himself. I felt like that showed he cared enough to really learn about his topic in a personal way.

Surveys

Survey research involves asking a number of people about their opinions, views, values, actions, or beliefs. Surveys are useful in two situations. First, sometimes there's no published research on something important to your speech. Yumiko, a student taking his first speaking course, was concerned that many of his peers at the university had misperceptions about Japanese people and their traditions. He decided to use his speech as an opportunity to correct misperceptions. After two weeks of research, he was discouraged because he couldn't find any studies of American college students' views of Japanese people. We developed a short questionnaire on views of Japanese people that was handed out to 100 students on campus. This gave Yumiko some information about local students' perceptions. A survey such as the one Yumiko conducted is useful, but it has limits. Because casual surveys generally aren't random and don't meet other criteria for sound research, they must be reinforced with other forms of research.

For a speech on junk foods, one student surveyed seventy-five faculty, staff, and students to find out how often they ate various products. Another student surveyed her peers to find out how often they attended women's and men's basketball games. For a speech about the dangers of drinking, Justin surveyed his peers to find out how often and how much they drank each week. By gauging the attitudes and patterns of behavior of people like your listeners, you gain valuable insight into ways to adapt your presentation to your listeners' views, beliefs, and habits. The more directly your speech relates to your listeners and their lives, the more effective you will be (Table 14.1).

A second use of surveys is to learn about your audience's knowledge of and attitudes toward your topic. Although it isn't always feasible to survey your listeners, when it is possible this helps you find out what listeners know. Based on what you learn, you can include information they don't have and not bore them by telling them what they already know. Surveys of listeners also allow you to discover what personal experience they have pertinent to your topic. Attitudes based on direct experience are more difficult to change (Wu & Shaffer, 1988).

Sharpen Your Skill

Constructing a Survey

Prepare a list of five to ten questions to discover general attitudes and behaviors relevant to your speech topic.

1. ....
2. ....
3. ....
4. ....
5. ....
6. ....
7. ....
8. ....
9. ....
10. ....

Decide where you will distribute the survey. Try to avoid any obvious bias based on location. For example, administering the survey at local bars and at the campus library might involve very different kinds of respondents. Handing it out at a Christian church would likely exclude non-Christian respondents.

Table 14.1: Guidelines for Constructing Surveys

The following guidelines will help you construct a survey that will provide you with solid information.

1. Respondents should be chosen to reflect the population (or larger group) whose opinions you seek to understand. (Students may reflect students' opinions. However, students generally would not reflect homeowners' opinions.)

2. Respondents should be qualified to answer the questions. (Only people who are informed about inflation and living expenses have the information to answer this question: "How much should the cost-of-living adjustment be for Social Security recipients?")

3. Questions should be worded to avoid bias. ("You favor gun control, don't you?" is a leading question that biases respondents toward answering "yes." "Do you favor gun control?" is not biased. You will get different responses if you ask people if they favor "helping the poor" and if they favor "welfare.")

4. Each question should focus on only one issue. ("Do you favor Medicare and Medicaid?" asks respondents' opinions on two distinct issues. This question should be split into two separate questions.)

5. Questions should allow for all possible responses. (It would not be accurate to ask respondents whether they are Democrats or Republicans, because those two responses don't include other possible choices, such as Libertarians and Independents).

6. Questions should rely on language that will be clear to respondents. (For years, the Census Bureau asked people whether they worked "full-time," which the bureau defined as 35 hours a week or more. However, many respondents interpreted "full-time" to mean 40 hours a week or more. The bureau revised the wording of the question to remove the ambiguity.)

7. Avoid negative language in survey items; it tends to be confusing. (Respondents are likely to misunderstand this question: "Do you agree or disagree that the United States should not have socialized medicine?" The question is clearer when phrased this way: "Do you agree or disagree that the United States should have socialized medicine?")

Adapted from Babbie, 2001.

If you plan to speak on gun control, you might want to know whether your listeners are aware of existing legislation, whether they hunt, and whether they or members of their families own firearms for protection. For a speech on family leave practices, it would be helpful to find out whether listeners understand the limits of the Family Medical Leave Act and whether they are aware that the United States is the only industrialized nation that doesn't have guaranteed family leave for all workers.

Audience surveys can also help you learn what attitudes your listeners hold. At a minimum, you'll want to know whether your listeners agree or disagree with your position and how strong their attitudes are. If you want to argue for more severe sentences for convicted felons, and your listeners are strongly against that, then you might choose to limit your persuasive goal to reducing the strength of listeners' resistance to stronger sentencing. On the other hand, if they already agree with your position, you might try to move them toward action by asking them to write letters to senators or to vote for candidates who share their attitudes. What you can achieve in a given speech depends to a large extent on the starting beliefs and knowledge of your listeners (Wu & Shaffer, 1988).

Now that we have discussed ways to conduct research, we're ready to consider specific forms of support, or evidence.

Using Evidence to Support Ideas

Evidence is material used to support claims a speaker makes. You support an idea when you include material to clarify, prove, or demonstrate it. In addition, support may enhance interest and emotional response to ideas. Evidence serves a number of important functions in speeches. First, it can be used to make ideas clearer, more compelling, and more dramatic. Second, evidence fortifies a speaker's opinions, which are seldom sufficient by themselves to persuade intelligent listeners. Finally, evidence heightens a speaker's credibility. Speakers who use good evidence show that they are informed and prepared. Thus, including strong evidence allows speakers to build credibility.

The effectiveness of evidence depends directly on whether listeners understand and accept it. This reinforces the importance of audience analysis, which we discussed in Chapter 13. Remember that even if you quote a leading authority in support of your ideas, the evidence won't be effective if your listeners don't know the authority or don't find the authority credible (Olson & Cal, 1984). Consequently, your goal is to include support that your particular listeners will find credible, interesting, and convincing while also making sure your evidence is valid.

−Harihar−

Last week at the meeting of Nepalese Americans, a speaker talked to us about principles of ethical conduct. He quoted Jesus for principles such as loving your neighbors and being kind to others. But all of us in the group are Buddhist, and there are Buddhist precepts that say the same thing. For us, Buddha would have been a better person than Jesus to use for moral principles.

To decide when to use evidence in a speech, ask yourself, "Will my listeners understand and believe this claim on my say-so alone?" If not, then you'll want to include evidence.

Speech Builder Express, which you can access directly through your *Communication in Our Lives* CD-ROM, includes a section focused on selecting the amount and types of supporting material you may need, based on the main points of your speech.

The next decision you need to make is what type of evidence to use. Five forms of support are widely recognized, and each tends to be effective in specific situations and for particular goals. Before including any form of evidence in a speech, the speaker should check the accuracy of her or his material and the credibility of the source. When presenting evidence to listeners, speakers have an ethical responsibility to give credit to the source (an oral footnote) and tell listeners the date of the evidence.

Statistics

Statistics are numbers that summarize many individual cases or that demonstrate relationships between phenomena. Statistics allow us to state quickly a

Cartoon by Signe Wilkinson. Reprinted by permission of Cartoonists & Writers Syndicate/cartoonweb.com

large amount of information. For example, a speaker could demonstrate the prevalence of injuries caused by drivers who are under the influence of alcohol by stating, "According to the American Automotive Association, one in four people injured in traffic accidents is the victim of a driver who had been drinking." Statistics can also be used to document connections between two or more things. For instance, a speaker could tell listeners, "According to the Highway Patrol, you are 50% more likely to have an accident if you drink before driving." This draws listeners' attention to the link between drinking and automobile accidents.

Most Americans say that statistics enhance a speaker's credibility (Crossen, 1994). For that to happen, you must translate statistics into information that is meaningful to listeners. A National Geographic program (National Geographic, 1994) on environmental responsibility forcefully

Communication Highlight

Don't Put Your Audience to Sleep

Have you ever been lulled to sleep by a speaker who rattled off streams of numbers? If so, you're not alone. Used unimaginatively, statistics are likely to bore listeners. To avoid this fate when you are speaking, you may follow guidelines for using statistics effectively.

- First, limit the number of statistics you use in a speech. A few well-chosen numbers mixed with other kinds of support can be dramatic and persuasive, whereas a laundry list of statistics can be monotonous and ineffective.

- Second, round off numbers so that listeners can understand and retain them. We're more likely to

remember that "approximately 1 million Americans are homeless" than that "987,422 Americans are homeless."

- Third, select statistics that are timely. Occasionally, a very old statistic is still useful. For example, the number of people who died in the Great Plague is not likely to change over the years. In most cases, however, the most accurate statistics are recent. Remember that statistics are a numerical picture of how something was at a specific time. But things change, and speakers should get new snapshots when they do.

made the point that Americans overconsume natural resources: It was stated that "North Americans make up only 6% of the world's population, yet they consume 40% to 60% of the planet's resources." To describe a million homeless people in terms listeners will immediately understand, a student speaker said, "That's fifty times the number of students on our campus." Another student speaker translated this way the statistic that one in four college-age women will be raped in her lifetime: "Of the seventeen women students in this room today, four will probably be raped some time during their lives." Statistics aren't boring, but they can be poorly presented. With imagination and effort, you can make statistics interesting and powerful.

Sharpen Your Skill

Bringing Statistics Alive

Practice translating statistics into interesting and meaningful information. Here's an example.

Statistic: Americans annually spend $14 billion on alcohol, $9 billion on tobacco, $2 billion on pets, and $200 million on juvenile reform.

Translation: For every $1 spent on juvenile reform in America, $70 are spent on alcohol, $45 on tobacco, and $10 on pets.

Statistic: Children under 10 watch television an average of 50 hours each week.

Translation: ....

Statistic: The Stealth bomber program cost $40 billion and produced a total of twenty aircraft.

Translation: ....

Statistic: The number of working poor, people who make $13,000 or less a year, rose from 12% of the workforce in 1984 to 18% in 2004.

Translation: ....

Now, apply what you've learned to your own speech. Select three statistics you could use in your speech, and translate them into meaningful, interesting terms.

Statistic 1: ....
can be translated this way: ....

Statistic 2: ....
can be translated this way: ....

Statistic 3: ....
can be translated this way: ....

  For additional practice in bringing statistics alive, complete Activity 14.2, "Translating Statistics," in your *Student Companion* or online under "Activities for Chapter 14" at the *Communication in Our Lives* website.

Examples

Examples are single instances used to make a point, dramatize an idea, or personalize information. We'll consider four types of examples.

Undetailed Examples When speakers want to make a point quickly, undetailed examples are useful. These are brief references that quickly recount specific instances of something. In this chapter, I've used a number of undetailed examples of student speeches to give you a concrete idea of conceptual points we're discussing. Undetailed examples may also be used to remind listeners of information with which they're already familiar. One student opened a speech on the costs of textbooks by saying, "Remember standing in the long lines at the bookstore and paying for more than your tuition at the start of this term?" His listeners immediately identified with the topic of the speech.

Detailed Examples Detailed examples provide more elaborate information than undetailed ones, so they are valuable when listeners aren't familiar with an idea. A student included this detailed example in her speech on environmental justice:

> *Most of you haven't lived near a toxic waste dump, so you may not understand what's involved. In one community, the incidence of cancer is 150% higher than in the country as a whole. The skin on one man's hands was eaten away when he touched the outside of a canister that stored toxic waste. His skin literally dissolved when it came in contact with the toxin.*

Detailed examples create vivid pictures that can be moving and memorable. However, they take time to present, so they should be used sparingly.

Hypothetical Examples Sometimes speakers don't have a real example that adequately makes a point. In such cases, speakers can create a hypothetical example, which is not factual but can add clarity and depth to a speech. To be effective, hypothetical examples must be realistic illustrations of what you want to exemplify. Hypothetical examples often are used to portray average cases rather than to represent a single person or event. If you use a hypothetical example, you have an ethical responsibility to inform listeners that it is not a factual, real example.

Stories A final kind of example is the story, or anecdote. Stories included in speeches often are based on personal experiences. Presidents Reagan and Clinton routinely included several personal stories in their speeches to personalize their ideas and create identification with listeners. Religions rely on stories—parables in Christianity, teichos in Buddhism—to teach values and persuade people to follow them. Attorneys rely on stories to persuade judges and jurors, taking all the known facts in a case and weaving them together in a way that makes sense and supports their clients' accounts of events. The attorneys with whom I consult tell me that the key challenge in trial court is to create a story that covers all the facts and is more believable than the story created by the opposing council.

Speakers often tell a story to put a human face on abstract issues. To help middle-class listeners understand the personal meaning of poverty, a student told this story of a woman he interviewed to prepare his speech:

> *To start her day, Annie pours half a glass of milk and mixes it half and half with water so that the quart she buys each week will last. If she finds day-old*

Communication Highlight

The Typical American Family

John F. Kennedy was a powerful public speaker. He wove many kinds of support into his speeches to strengthen his credibility and increase the impact of his ideas.

On May 19, 1962, President John F. Kennedy used the following hypothetical example in his speech at the rally for the National Council of Senior Citizens at Madison Square Garden:

> Let's consider the case of a typical American family—a family which might be found in any part of the United States. The husband has worked hard all of his life, and now he has retired. He might have been a clerk or a salesman or worked in a factory. He always insisted on paying his own way. This man, like most Americans, wants to care for himself. He has raised his own family, educated his children, and he and his wife are drawing Social Security now. Then his wife gets sick, not just for a week, but for a very long time. First the savings go. Next, he mortgages his home. Finally, he goes to his children, who are themselves heavily burdened. Then their savings begin to go. What is he to do now? Here is a typical American who has nowhere to turn, so he finally will have to sign a petition saying he's broke and needs welfare assistance.

bread on sale at the market, she has toast, but she can't afford margarine. Annie coughs harshly and wishes this throat infection would pass. She can't afford to go to a doctor. Even if she could, the cost of drugs is beyond her budget. She shivers, thinking that winter is coming. That means long days in the malls so that she can be in heated places. It's hard on her and the kids, but the cost of heat is more than she can pay. Annie is only 28 years old, just a few years older than we are, but she looks well into her forties. Like you, Annie grew up expecting a pretty good life, but then her husband left her. He doesn't pay child support, and she can't afford a detective to trace him. Her children, both under 4, are too young to be left alone, so she can't work.

The story about Annie puts a human face on poverty. A story that has depth takes time, so speakers have to consider whether the point they want to make justifies the time a story will take. When developed with care, stories can provide valuable support to speakers' claims.

Comparisons

Comparisons are associations between two things that are similar in some important way or ways. **Similes** are explicit comparisons that typically use the word *like* or *as* to link two things: "A teacher is like a guide." "A politician is like an orchestra conductor." "Smoking is like giving away years of life." **Metaphors** are implicit comparisons that suggest likeness between two things that have something in common: "Life is a grand adventure." "Voting is

Communication Highlight

I Have a Dream

© Corbis

Martin Luther King, Jr., was a dynamic and eloquent public speaker who skillfully used sophisticated rhetorical techniques to shape his message.

The Reverend Martin Luther King, Jr.

We've come to our nation's capital to cash a check. When the architects of our republic wrote the magnificent words of the Constitution and the Declaration of Independence, they were signing a promissory note to which every American was to fall heir. The note was a promise that all men—yes, Black men as well as White men—would be guaranteed the unalienable rights of life, liberty and the pursuit of happiness.

It is obvious today that America has defaulted on this promissory note insofar as her citizens of color are concerned . . . America has given the Negro people a bad check; a check which has come back marked "insufficient funds." But we refuse to believe that there are insufficient funds in the great vaults of opportunity of this nation. So we've come to cash this check—a check that will give us upon demand the riches of freedom and security of justice.

 To read the full text of Martin Luther King, Jr.'s "I Have a Dream" speech, go to http://www.holidays.net/MLK/speech.htm.

Source: Reprinted by arrangement with The Estate of Martin Luther King, Jr., c/o Writer's House, Inc. as agent for the proprietor, New York, NY. Copyright 1963 Martin Luther King, Jr., copyright renewed 1991 Coretta Scott King.

being a good neighbor." "Education is a journey." A student speaker used this analogy in her speech about the college experience: "College is a journey from the known to the unknown. Each step in the process takes us farther from what we knew before and leads us to new understandings."

Comparisons can be powerful rhetorical devices because they invite listeners to see something familiar in a new light. In 1963, the Reverend Martin Luther King, Jr., delivered his eloquent "I Have a Dream" speech to more than 200,000 listeners. In it, he compared the United States' unfulfilled promises to African American citizens to a check for which funds must now be provided. This was a compelling metaphor that used the familiar idea of a check to explain civil rights promises that had been made but not yet kept by the country.

Quotations

Quotations, or testimony, are exact citations of statements made by others. Speakers often use quotations to clarify ideas or to make them more memorable. If someone has stated a point in an especially effective manner, then you may want to quote his or her words. In a speech on homeless citizens, a student quoted a metaphor used by a social worker: "Homelessness is a cancer that eats away at the vitality and decency of our society." To explain why many women of color don't identify with the feminist movement, a Latina student quoted her grandmother as saying, "White women aren't interested in the problems we face. They don't know our lives, and they don't represent our needs." Notice that in this case the woman quoted was both a layperson and an expert on the topic; her experience as a Latina qualified her to speak.

Quotations may also be used to substantiate ideas. Using an expert's testimony may be persuasive to listeners, but only if they respect the expert who is quoted. Thus, it's important to provide "oral footnotes" in which you identify the name, position, and qualifications of anyone whom you quote, as well as the date for the quoted statement. For example, in discussing preservation of wilderness, you might say, "Speaking in 1997, Tim Worth, former Colorado senator and current undersecretary of state for global affairs, warned that stronger environmental policies are needed if we want to preserve any wilderness land for the next generation."

From *The Wall Street Journal.* Reprinted by permission of Cartoon Features Syndicate.

"He's a great field dog, and is much in demand as a motivational speaker."

Whenever you quote another person, you are ethically obligated to give credit to that person just as you are for all other forms of evidence. This can be done by changing your tone of voice after stating an authority's name, or by telling listeners, "This authority stated that . . ." It is also acceptable to say "quote" at the beginning of a quotation and "end quote" at the end of it, although this method of citing sources becomes boring if it is used repeatedly in a speech.

To be effective with critical listeners, quotations must meet four criteria. First, as we've already noted, sources should be people whom listeners know and respect or whom they will respect once you identify credentials. You won't convince politically liberal listeners of anything by quoting Rush Limbaugh, and you'll never convince politically conservative listeners by quoting Edward Kennedy or Hillary Rodham Clinton. This point reinforces our previous discussion of the importance of keeping your listeners in mind at each step in the process of designing and delivering a speech.

A second criterion for testimony is that it should come from someone who is qualified to speak on the issue (Olson & Cal, 1984). Wall Street whiz Elaine Garazelli is qualified to offer informed opinions on investments. However, she exceeded her area of expertise when she testified to the quality of a certain brand of panty hose. Garazelli is not more qualified to judge this product than any other woman who wears panty hose. The hosiery company was counting on the **halo effect,** which involves assuming that an expert in one area is also an expert in other areas. The halo effect is also behind the use of athletic stars to advertise cereals and other products for the judgment of which they have no special qualifications (for example, Michael Jordan

Communication Highlight

The Seneca Falls Convention in 1848 formally launched the women's rights movement in the United States. In delivering a speech she coauthored with other women's rights advocates, Elizabeth Cady Stanton cleverly quoted the Declaration of Independence—with a few modifications in the original wording. Here's an excerpt (Campbell, 1989):

We hold these truths to be self-evident: that all men and all women are created equal; that they are endowed by their Creator with certain inalienable rights, that among these are life, liberty, and the pursuit of happiness.

for Hanes underwear). Although some people may fall prey to the halo effect, discerning listeners will not. Ethical speakers rely on authorities who are qualified, and they identify authorities' qualifications to enhance their credibility in listeners' minds.

Sharpen Your Skill

Sources Listeners Will Accept

List six people whom you could cite in your speech. These should be people whom you have interviewed or have encountered in other research on your topic.

1. ....
2. ....
3. ....
4. ....
5. ....
6. ....

Now, consider which of these people are most likely to be known and respected by the people who will listen to your speech. Put an asterisk (*) by the three you think would have the greatest credibility with your listeners.

Ethical quotations must also meet the criterion of accuracy. For instance, you should respect the context in which comments are made. It is unethical to take a statement out of context in order to make it more supportive of your ideas. Also, it's unethical to alter a direct quotation by adding or deleting words. Sometimes writers omit words and indicate this with ellipses: "Noted authority William West stated that 'there is no greater priority . . . than our children.'" In oral presentations, however, it is difficult to indicate omitted words in a smooth manner. When using quotations, speakers have an ethical responsibility to be accurate and fair in representing others and their ideas.

Finally, quotations should come from unbiased sources. It's hardly convincing when scientists paid by the tobacco industry tell us cigarettes don't cause cancer. For the same reason, it's not persuasive when spokespeople for Microsoft assure us that they are not trying to create a monopoly. These two sources are biased because they have a vested interest in a particular viewpoint. Their bias limits their credibility as believable authorities on tobacco and chemical waste products, respectively.

Visual Aids

Support also is provided by **visual aids,** such as charts, graphs, photographs, transparencies, computer graphics, and physical objects. Visual aids can increase listeners' understanding and retention of ideas presented in a speech (Hamilton, 1999; Hamilton & Parker, 2001). People are more likely to remember material that is presented both orally and visually. Visual aids also tend to increase listeners' interest in a presentation because they add variety to the message (Hamilton, 1999; Hamilton & Parker, 2001). Further, visual aids provide content cues to speakers, which reduces reliance on notes.

By using widely available computer technologies, it's often possible to prepare very sharp, effective visual aids. You may have software programs that allow you to design charts, graphs, and other visuals. Computer-generated visual aids can be transformed easily into transparencies, which are the most commonly used visual aid in most professional presentations (Hamilton, 1999). If you don't know how to design visuals on a computer, you might find it useful to check with your campus computer assistance office.

This speaker maintains eye contact with listeners while using a well-designed visual aid.

Visual aids can be used either to reinforce ideas presented verbally or to provide information in their own right. For example, Figure 14.2 is a bar graph that could effectively strengthen the statistics on juvenile reform we discussed earlier. Pie charts can forcefully emphasize contrasts and proportions (Figure 14.3). Many software programs allow you to generate attractive and informative graphs, charts, and other visual aids.

Diagrams or models help speakers explain complex concepts and unfamiliar topics. Especially in speeches of demonstration, a model or physical diagram can be very useful. One of my students prepared a diagram to show listeners how a nuclear reactor works. Maps help listeners understand geographic relationships and issues.

Photographs can be used to reinforce verbal messages or as messages in their own right. To fortify her argument that development is eroding coastal land, a student showed enlarged pictures of an island community before development, when healthy sand dunes existed, and after development, when the dunes had eroded. In a speech urging listeners to contribute to an organization that provides food to starving people in undeveloped countries, a student showed pictures of women, men, and children who were so starved they looked like skeletons. The old adage, "A picture is worth a thousand words" was true in this case because the student's picture spoke more compellingly about hunger than any words ever could have.

Figure 14.2
Bar Graphs Dramatize Statistics

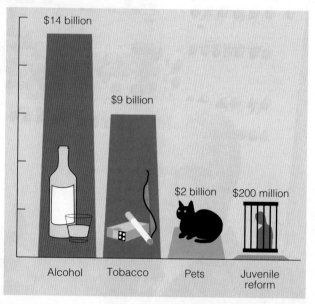

Figure 14.3
Pie Charts Clarify Proportions

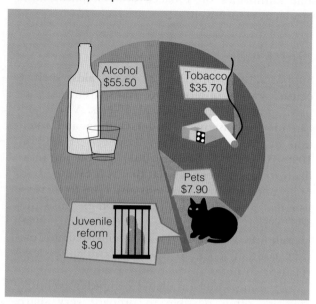

Handouts are also very useful visual aids. Because listeners can take handouts with them, they are particularly valuable when a speaker wants information to remain with listeners. After a speech encouraging students to vote for a bill currently under consideration by the state legislature, a student gave every listener a handout with the names, addresses, and phone numbers of their representatives. Another student, who spoke on the topic of the dangers of drinking, concluded her speech by handing out a list of agencies and phone numbers that could be called by people who thought they might have problems with alcohol. In both cases, the handouts ensured that listeners had critical information long after the speech was over. You may have noticed that in both examples of students who used handouts, the written materials were passed to listeners at the end of the speeches. This was an effective choice on the speakers' parts because it avoided breaking up a speech to pass out paper and listeners reading the handout while the speaker was talking. Because handouts may distract listeners, it's wise to save them until you have finished speaking.

Communication Highlight

Making PowerPoint Work for You

One of the most popular and useful presentational software programs is PowerPoint. Because computerized presentations can enhance speeches, many public speaking courses require students to learn PowerPoint or other presentational software. Communication scholars Joe Downing and Cecile Garmon (2001) wanted to know if hands-on instruction and online learning differed in effectiveness. They had one group of students learn PowerPoint through a users' guide available online. A second group of students were taught PowerPoint in the classroom. There was no difference in the two groups of students' confidence and competence in using PowerPoint.

 You can access an online guide to using PowerPoint at: http://www.actden.com/pp.

Creating Visual Aids

Think about the possibilities for visual aids to enhance your speech. Describe visual aids of each type that you could use. Don't worry that you might not actually include all of them. The point for now is to brainstorm possibilities to visually support your ideas.

Bar graph ....

Pie chart of ....

Photographs of ....

Diagram of ....

Map of ....

Handout on ....

Computerized visual of ....

You can also use technologies to create visual aids. You may want to use part of a film or create a videotape to dramatize a point in your speech. A student speaker showed parts of the Disney film *Pocahontas* to support her claim that the main character was very different from the historical figure. Visuals available on websites that can be shown to listeners sometimes are more effective than manually created ones.

Guidelines for Using Visual Aids   For visual aids to be effective, speakers should observe several guidelines (Williams, 1994). First, a visual aid should be large enough and clear enough to be seen clearly by all listeners. As obvious as this advice is, speakers routinely violate it by showing photographs, graphs, or PowerPoint slides that can be seen only by listeners in the front of the room. Make sure any numbers, words, or emblems can be seen clearly by listeners in the back of the room. Make sure that letters in major headings are at least 3 inches high and that letters in subpoints are at least 2 inches high. By using an overhead projector, a speaker can present transparencies and other material in enlarged form.

A second guideline is to keep visual aids simple and uncluttered. Detailed visuals with a great deal of information are more likely to confuse than clarify. Especially if you are presenting a series of slides (computerized or not), simplicity is important. You can create effective slides by following the guidelines in Table 14.2. A good basic rule for visual aids is to use them to highlight key information and ideas, not to summarize all content.

Many visual aids are verbal texts—main ideas of a speech, major points in a policy, or steps to action. When visual texts are used, certain guidelines apply. As a general rule, a visual text should have no more than six lines of words, should use phrases more than sentences, and should use a simple typeface. Color and variations in type size can be used to add emphasis to visual texts. This applies to handouts, overhead transparencies, and large visuals displayed at the front of a room. Although visual aids can be very effective, it's possible to have too much of a good thing. When speakers use too many visuals or too much variation in type color and style, listeners may

Communication Highlight

Merrie Spaeth served as White House director of media relations during President Reagan's administration. She advises speakers to use visual aids to add impact to words. Even simple visual aids can be effective, says Spaeth. For example, President Reagan often held up letters from which he read to audiences. He could have simply summarized what the letter said, but he added force by holding the actual sheet of paper (Spaeth, 1996).

Table 14.2: Guidelines for Using Slides in a Speech

Slides—whether computerized or not—enhance a speech only if they add to its impact. They don't enhance a speech when they confuse or frustrate listeners. To create effective slides for public speaking, follow these guidelines:

1. Each slide should focus on a single concept or point and key information to support that concept or point (phrases or key words generally are preferable to whole sentences or lengthy text).

2. Fonts should be large enough to be read by listeners at the back of the speaking room. Generally, main points should appear in 36-point type, supporting ideas should appear in 24- or 28-point type, and text should appear in type no smaller than 18 points.

3. Typefaces should be clean and clear. Avoid *script styles*, *overuse of italics*, or **TRENDY TYPEFACES**. They are distracting and can detract from clarity.

4. Mix uppercase and lowercase lettering. ALL CAPITAL LETTERS CAN BE HARD TO READ.

5. Use art to provide visual relief from text and enhance interest. If using a computerized presentation program, consider using clip art or pictures imported from the web.

6. Use one design consistently. Computerized programs such as PowerPoint have design templates. Stick with one design to provide visual continuity and transitions.

7. Select a color scheme that is visually strong but not overpowering. Especially if you are showing a series of slides, avoid glaring colors that can tire listeners. Occasionally, you may violate this guideline to adapt to your particular listeners. For instance, if you are speaking at the banquet of a company that has a teal and white logo, you might want a teal and white color scheme.

8. Use special effects sparingly. It may effective to have text zoom in from the right with a blaring sound on one slide, but it would be tiring and ineffective for text to zoom in slide after slide.

9. Use visual highlighting sparingly. It can be effective to **boldface** or highlight one particularly important idea. However, the impact of visual highlighting is lost when it is overdone.

10. Give credit to those who created any material you use. Acknowledge authors of quotations or other material. You should also get permission to use any materials that are not in the common domain.

11. Don't sacrifice content for flashy visuals. Visual aids, including computerized ones, should enhance your content, not substitute for it.

12. Make slides bright enough that you do not have to darken the room fully.

experience visual overload. As a guideline for deciding how many visuals to use in a speech, Cheryl Hamilton (1999) suggests this formula:

$$\frac{\text{Length of speech}}{2} + 1 = \text{Maximum number of visuals}$$

If you are preparing a 10-minute speech, you should include no more than six visual aids (10/2 + 1 = 6). Note that each slide in a series of slides counts as one visual aid.

Perhaps the biggest mistake speakers make with visual aids is giving them higher priority than they give content. You should develop the content of your presentation before you even consider visual aids. After developing your ideas, if you do want to use visual aids, focus on creating ones that reinforce content. They should never eclipse content or compensate for the lack of careful development of ideas. With the increasing ease of creating slick visual presentations, it has become common for glitzy visuals to disguise flimsy content (Zukerman, 1999).

There are also some mechanical guidelines for using visual aids effectively. First, remove or cover visual aids before and after you use them. A visual aid that's strong enough to be effective in supporting ideas will distract listeners' attention from what you are saying if it is left in view when not in use. Also, maintain visual contact with listeners when using visual aids. Novice speakers often make the mistake of facing their charts or pictures when discussing them. This breaks the connection between a speaker and listeners.

 To develop further skill in using evidence effectively and ethically, complete Activity 14.3, "Recognizing Ineffective Speaking," in your *Student Companion* or online under "Activities for Chapter 14" at the *Communication in Our Lives* website.

It's a good idea to keep an ongoing record of evidence you discover during the research process. There are two ways to do this. The traditional method is to write out each piece of evidence, preferably on separate note cards. By the end of researching your speech, you should have a deck of cards that contain evidence you might use in the final speech.

A mind map is an alternative method of keeping track of information that you find while you are researching a speech. In Chapter 13, we discussed mind maps as a way to narrow the focus of a broad topic. The same method can also help you record information. A mind map is a more holistic, less linear way to record information than the conventional note card

Communication Highlight

When Drama Is Too Dramatic

In an effort to add drama to presentations, speakers sometimes make unwise and even dangerous choices. Some visual aids are not appropriate for use in any circumstances. For example, a real, functional firearm is dangerous in public situations. In addition to the fact that "there's no such thing as an unloaded gun," firearms may frighten listeners, and that distracts them from listening to a speech.

Other visual aids that are risky and should be avoided include live animals, illegal substances, and chemicals that could react to one another. It's also unwise to use visual aids that might seriously upset or disgust listeners. The purpose of visuals is to enhance your speech, not to be so sensational that they take attention away from your ideas.

Figure 14.4
Mind Map of Evidence

Source: Jaffe, C. (2001). *Public Speaking: Concepts and Skills for a Diverse Society,* Third Edition, Belmont, CA: Wadsworth.

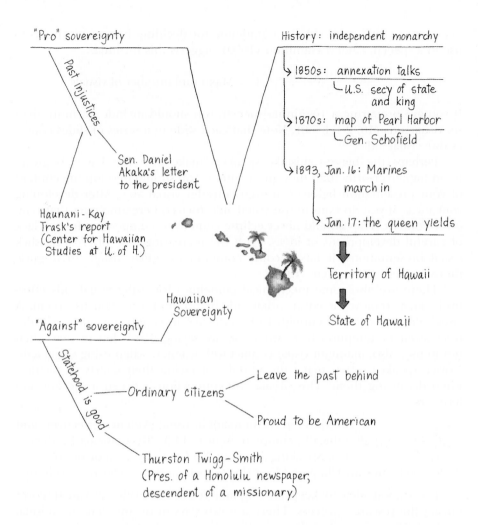

"Pro" sovereignty

Past injustices

Sen. Daniel Akaka's letter to the president

Haunani-Kay Trask's report (Center for Hawaiian Studies at U. of H.)

Hawaiian Sovereignty

History: independent monarchy

1850s: annexation talks
└ U.S. secy of state and king

1870s: map of Pearl Harbor
└ Gen. Schofield

1893, Jan. 16: Marines march in

Jan. 17: the queen yields

Territory of Hawaii

State of Hawaii

"Against" sovereignty

Statehood is good

Ordinary citizens
├ Leave the past behind
└ Proud to be American

Thurston Twigg-Smith (Pres. of a Honolulu newspaper, descendent of a missionary)

system. To construct a mind map for your speech, begin by writing the subject of your presentation in the center of a blank page. Then, draw a line from the center to each piece of evidence that you discover as you conduct your research. At this stage, you shouldn't try to determine which evidence you will use; for now, write down all the information you find. Once you have a complete record of information you've gathered, you can decide which evidence to include in your presentation. Figure 14.4 shows a mind map record of information for a speech on Hawaiian sovereignty.

Statistics, examples, comparisons, quotations, and visual aids support your ideas in different ways. Whereas evidence such as statistics, examples, and quotations can provide strong logical support, visual aids and analogies often are more powerful in adding clarity, interest, and emotional appeal to a speech. All forms of evidence, when carefully chosen and ethically used, tend to increase the credibility listeners confer on a speaker and the extent to which they retain the speaker's ideas (Table 14.3).

 To increase your familiarity with the different types of evidence we've discussed, complete Activity 14.1, "Identifying Evidence," in your *Student Companion* or online under "Activities for Chapter 14" at the *Communication in Our Lives* website.

Table 14.3: Testing Evidence

Five questions help speakers test whether evidence is ethical and effective. Each question addresses a specific criterion for assessing the worth of evidence:

1. Is there enough evidence to support a claim? (sufficiency)

2. Is the evidence accurately presented—quotations are verbatim, nothing is taken out of context? (accuracy)

3. Does the evidence relate directly to the claim it is intended to support? (relevance)

4. Is the evidence appropriately timely—are statistics, quotations, examples, and comparisons current or appropriate for the time discussed? (timeliness)

5. Is the evidence free of biases such as vested interest? (impartiality)

CASE STUDY: Using Evidence: Environmental Racism

The following speech is featured on the *Communication in Our Lives* CD-ROM included with this book. Once you've launched the CD, click on the "Speech Interactive" icon, and, from the Speech Menu, select "Evidence" to watch the audiovisual presentation of Shannon Navarro's speech entitled "Environmental Racism." To read a description of Shannon's assignment, click on the "Assignment" button. Improve your own public speaking skills by reading, watching, listening to, evaluating, and critiquing this sample speech.

Analyze the speech by applying the principles covered in this chapter, and respond to the prompts that accompany the video, which you can access by clicking on "Evaluation" and "Critique." After answering the evaluation questions and writing a brief critique of the speech, you can click on the "Done" button to compare your responses with the ones I suggest. Additional analysis questions are available in print at the end of this chapter and on the book's website.

Jason Harris/© 2001 Wadsworth

Now, first let's take a look at the effects environmental racism can pose for many low-income families, especially children. As I stated previously, the health problems residents in Daly City are battling are just an example of the many communities suffering from contamination, communities such as West Dallas. According to the article "Overcoming Racism in Environmental Decision Making" in the May 1994 edition of *Environment,* a study of the West Dallas Lead Smelters showed that cleanup crews were estimated to have removed 30,000 and 40,000 cubic yards of lead-contaminated soil from sites such as schools and even private homes, causing an epidemic of lead poisoning in school-age children suffering from lack of concentration, lack of hearing, and stunted growth. And according to the article "Making Connections in the Water Realm" in the March–April 1997 edition of *Sierra,* in Columbia, Mississippi, low-income schoolchildren play across the street from barrels full of poisons.

These incidences show that low-income schoolchildren are not receiving the same educational benefits as the elite, and they must suffer not only because they want to attend school but because their parents didn't happen to make enough money. But lead poisoning isn't all that these people must suffer from; nuclear plants every day are spreading carbon monoxide and sulfur dioxide, increasing the number of deaths from asthma. Skylene causes liver and kidney damage, as well as brain hemorrhaging. Ammonia, nitric acid, silicone, and many other deadly chemicals are guiltlessly being released into our oceans, air, sewers, and drinking water, causing countless health problems and epidemics.

According to the article "Environmental Racism: The Uneven Distribution of Risk," published by Reputation Management on their website, along an 85-mile-long corridor of chemical plants known as "Cancer Alley" in Monroeville, Louisiana, there is a community with an extremely large, low-income African American population. And according to the article "Overcoming Racism: Environmental Decision Making," all along the Rio Grande, nuclear plants dump toxic wastes into a river from which 95% of the region's residents get their drinking water. People began to notice that the incidence of anencephaly, also known as being born without a brain, is four times the U.S. national average in these areas.

But the thing is, it just doesn't affect these minorities, it affects us all. We all drink the same water, breathe the same air, and live on the same soil. After all, we do live in the same environment.

Chapter Summary

This chapter focused on ways to research speeches and support ideas to be presented. Just as when you are first planning a speech, your listeners should influence how you research and support it. Therefore, you need to ask yourself what kinds of research and what forms of support your particular listeners are most likely to find interesting and credible.

The process of researching a speech includes reviewing your personal experiences and knowledge about your topic, interviewing experts who can expand your insight into the subject, scouting libraries for evidence, and conducting surveys to find out about others' beliefs, practices, and knowledge relevant to your topic. It isn't unusual for speakers to revise the focus of a speech in the course of conducting research. This is appropriate when information you discover modifies or alters your knowledge or even your position.

Research for a speech provides speakers with different kinds of evidence that they can use to clarify, dramatize, and energize a speech. The five types of evidence we discussed are statistics, examples, comparisons, quotations, and visual aids. These are effective forms of support when they are used thoughtfully and ethically and when they are adapted to the interests, knowledge, attitudes, and experiences of listeners.

Now that you've gone through the phases of planning, researching, and finding support for speeches, we're ready to consider the final steps in designing effective presentations. Chapter 15 explains how to organize and present public speeches. Before you move on to Chapter 15, take a moment to fill in this chapter's checklist for researching and supporting your speech.

Checklist for Researching
and Supporting a Public Speech

If you prefer, you may complete this checklist online under "Forms and Checklists for Chapter 14" at the *Communication in Our Lives* website.

In addition, you may want to use Speech Builder Express, to which you have free access through your *Communication in Our Lives* CD-ROM. At the end of this chapter, I've included a suggestion for using Speech Builder Express to develop your speech.

1. I conducted the following research:

    A. Review of my personal experience showed that.....................................

    B. I interviewed (name/title):...

      (name/title):...

      (name/title):...

    C. I checked these three indexes:..

    D. I checked these three online sources:...

    E. I surveyed on the following issues:...

2. I found the following key evidence for my speech:

    A. Statistics:...

    B. Authorities I will quote:...

    C. Examples:...

    D. Comparisons:...

    E. Visual aids:..

3. I have all of the information to identify my sources appropriately and to explain why they are qualified and relevant to the ideas I will present.

    If you have not completed all items on this checklist, do so now before moving on to Chapter 15.

Communication in Our Lives ONLINE

In addition to presenting the case studies' multimedia scenarios and speeches, the *Communication in Our Lives* CD-ROM provides quick access to the *Communication in Our Lives* website, Speech Builder Express, and InfoTrac College Edition. The website is online at http://communication.wadsworth.com/woodciol4, but you can only access this book's premium web content when you link to the site directly through the book's CD.

The *Communication in Our Lives* website features interactive tools for learning and reviewing the chapter's concepts and key terms, including electronic versions of the "For Further Reflection and Discussion" questions following and a review quiz.

The website also provides updated web links and additional InfoTrac College Edition activities. If required, you can e-mail completed chapter activities or the quizzes to your instructor.

Key Concepts

For Further Reflection and Discussion

1. After you've interviewed two experts on your topic, reflect on what you learned. What did they explain, reveal, or show you that added to your knowledge of the topic?

2. How did the process of researching your speech affect your understandings, beliefs, and speaking goal? Explain what changed and why.

 3. Use your InfoTrac College Edition to find current evidence to support your speech. If you plan to speak on a health-related topic, use publications such as *World Health, Health News,* or *Healthfacts.* If you plan to speak on a public policy issue, check out publications such as *Public Welfare, Weekly Compilation of Presidential Documents,* and *Public Interest.* Type in the key words relevant to your topic.

 4. Pay attention to evidence in a speech on campus. Evaluate the effectiveness of evidence. Are visuals clear and uncluttered? Does the speaker explain the qualifications of sources cited, and are those sources adequately unbiased? What examples and comparisons are presented, and how effective are they? Evaluate the ethical quality of the evidence used. Did the speaker provide enough information for you to assess the expertise of any sources cited? Did the speaker show that the sources were not biased?

5. The web offers many sites that provide excellent information and evidence for speeches. To check out possibilities, visit some of the following websites and type in key words to define the search: http://excite.com; http://www.yahoo.com; http://www.ipl.org/reading/news (online newspapers from around the world).

6. Experiment with PowerPoint or other computerized software. Notice how different designs, colors, and special effects affect the clarity and impact of your slides.

Questions for Analysis and Discussion

 Review the video of Shannon's speech that you watched when completing this chapter's case study (pages 383–384), or, if you haven't seen it yet, watch it for the first time. If you didn't previously finish the "Evaluation" questions and "Critique" activity included on the CD-ROM, do so now, and then respond to the following questions, which are also available on the book's website under "Activities for Chapter 14."

1. Identify the types of evidence that the speaker used to develop the point in this excerpt from a speech.

2. Was the evidence effective? Did it meet the five tests for evidence?

3. Was the evidence ethical?

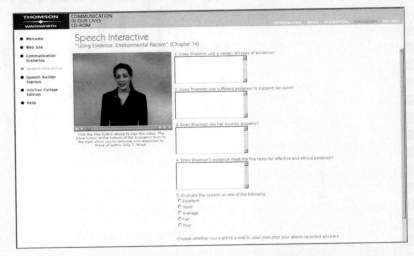

Speech Builder Express

 Access Speech Builder Express with the user name and the password that came with the CD-ROM that accompanies your textbook. Pull up the file you created after reading Chapter 13 (Speech Title or "My First Speech"). If you didn't give your speech a title earlier, do so now.

Select the "Supporting Material" section on Speech Builder Express. Type in evidence that you plan to use in your speech. Next, select "Works Cited," and type in the complete reference information for each source of evidence.

Save your file to your hard drive, or e-mail it to your instructor if that is requested. You'll add to this file as you develop your speech, using Chapters 15–17.

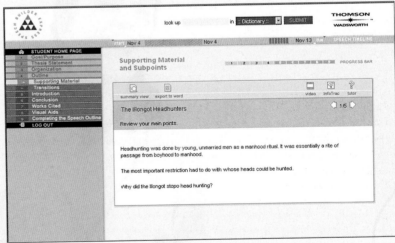

CHAPTER

15

Organizing and Presenting Public Speeches

Focus Questions

1. What is oral style?

2. How many main points can I cover effectively in a 7- to 10-minute speech?

3. What are my options for organizing my speech?

4. How do I prepare an effective outline for my speech?

5. Is it normal to feel apprehensive about public speaking?

6. How can I make my delivery dynamic and effective?

Millions of people have back problems in this country. It's hard to recover from back problems, particularly ruptures of discs. A lot of problems result from strains caused by lifting heavy objects. People could save themselves a lot of pain if they avoided doing things that hurt backs. It's important to take care of your back because a disc rupture can immobilize you for up to two weeks. Another way discs rupture is from unhealthy everyday habits such as sitting too long in one position or not using chairs that provide good support.

Millions of people in this country who suffer from back problems could save themselves a lot of pain by avoiding the two primary causes of back injury. One major cause is excessive strain, for example, from lifting heavy objects. A second cause is unhealthy everyday habits, such as sitting too long in one position or using chairs without good back support. It's important to take care of your back because a ruptured disc can immobilize you for up to two weeks.

Which of these paragraphs was easier for you to understand and follow? Which one made more sense to you? If you're like most people, the second paragraph seemed more logical and coherent. The content of the two paragraphs is the same. What differs is how they are organized. In the first paragraph the speaker wanders from discussing one cause (strain) of back problems, to noting the length of recuperation time and then back to discussing a second cause (unhealthy habits) of back problems.

In contrast, in the second paragraph the speaker tells us that there are two primary causes of back problems, so we're prepared at the outset to learn about two causes. The speaker next explains both causes, and only then does the speaker discuss the recuperation time we're in for if we don't take care of our backs. The organization of the second paragraph makes it easier to follow and retain the information presented.

This chapter guides you through the process of organizing your speech and practicing your delivery. In the pages that follow, we'll consider alternative ways to organize ideas, styles of delivery, and ways to practice effectively.

Organizing Speeches

We've all sat through speeches in which speakers seemed disorganized. They rambled or moved from one idea to the next in a way that was hard to follow. Perhaps they didn't tell us in advance what to expect, so we couldn't follow their thinking. Perhaps they submerged main ideas instead of making them stand out so that we'd retain them. Without strong organization, a speech will fail, no matter how good the ideas are and no matter how thoroughly it is researched and supported. If listeners cannot follow a presentation, they won't be informed, persuaded, or impressed. They also won't remember the ideas in the speech.

Effective organization of speeches relies on many of the principles covered in our discussion of perception in Chapter 2. For instance, you learned that people tend to notice what stands out, so you want to make your main ideas stand out. You also learned that our expectations shape perception, so at the outset of your speech you should tell your listeners what to expect.

Organization increases speaking effectiveness (Darnell, 1963; Spicer & Bassett, 1976) for several reasons. First, people like structure, and they expect ideas to come to them in an orderly way. Second, organization influences comprehension of ideas. Listeners can understand and remember a speech that is well organized because they grasp connections between ideas. Listeners are less likely to retain the key ideas in a poorly organized speech. Third, listeners are persuaded better by an organized speech than by a disorganized one (McCroskey & Mehrley, 1969). Finally, organization enhances a speaker's credibility, probably because a carefully structured speech reflects well on a speaker's preparation and respect for listeners (Baker, 1965). Listeners may perceive a speaker as incompetent or unprepared if a speech is disorganized.

Organizing an effective speech is not the same as organizing a good paper, although the two forms of communication benefit by some similar structural principles. Effective organization for oral and written communication differs in three key ways:

1. Oral communication requires more explicit organization.
2. Oral communication benefits from greater redundancy within the message.
3. Oral communication should rely on less complex sentence structures.

Unlike readers, listeners can't refer back to a previous passage if they become confused or forget an earlier point. To increase listeners' comprehension and retention, speakers should use simple sentences, provide signposts to highlight organization, and repeat key ideas (Woolfolk, 1987). Consistent with the need for redundancy in oral communication, good speeches follow the form of telling listeners what you're going to tell them, presenting your message, then reminding them of your main points. This translates into preparing an introduction, a body, and a conclusion for an oral presentation.

Effective organization begins with a good outline. We'll discuss different kinds of outlines and how each can help speakers organize their ideas. Next, we focus on organizing the body of a speech, because that is the substance of a presentation. After considering various methods of structuring the body of a speech, we'll discuss how to build an introduction and conclusion and how to weave in transitions to move listeners from one point to another.

Outlining Speeches

Once you've honed your speaking purpose and thesis, analyzed your audience, and collected your evidence, you are ready to create an outline. Beginning speakers often think that an outline is unnecessary, but they're mistaken. A good outline helps you organize your ideas and make sure that you have enough evidence to support your claims. A good outline also provides you with a safety net in case you forget what you intend to say or in case you are disrupted by some unforeseen event, such as a question or a disturbing noise. Speakers who wing it without outlines can be undermined if they have a lapse of memory; there's nothing to guide them back on track. There are three kinds of outlines: working, formal, and keyword.

The Working Outline
Speakers usually begin organizing their ideas by creating a **working outline** to give themselves a basic map of the speech. The working outline is just for the speaker; it is his or her sketch of the speech. In it, the speaker usually jots down main ideas to see how the ideas fit together. Once ideas are laid out in a basic structure, the speaker can tell where more evidence is needed, where ideas don't seem well connected,

and so forth. Working outlines usually evolve through multiple drafts as speakers see ways to improve speeches. Because working outlines aren't meant for others' eyes, they often include abbreviations and shorthand that make sense only to the speaker.

The Formal Outline   A **formal outline** includes all main points and subpoints, supporting materials, and transitions, along with a bibliography of sources. It should not be the whole speech unless you are giving a manuscript speech, which we will discuss later in this chapter. In most cases, speakers who write out entire speeches sound canned, and they tend to read the speech instead of communicating interactively with listeners.

An effective formal outline has main headings for the introduction, body, and conclusion. Under each main point are subpoints, references to supporting material, and abbreviated transitions. If your speech includes quotations, statistics, or other evidence that must be presented with absolute accuracy, you should write the evidence in full, either on your outline or on separate index cards. Your written evidence should include the source and date of the evidence so that you can provide oral footnotes to listeners. Full references should be listed as your bibliography or **Works Cited.** Table 15.1 presents guidelines for constructing formal outlines. Figure 15.1 shows a sample formal outline prepared by a student.

The Key Word Outline   Some speakers prefer a less detailed formal outline, called a **key word outline.** As the name implies, a key word outline includes only key words for each point. Its purpose is to trigger the speaker's memory of each point. Like the working outline, a key word outline is intended for the speaker's use. Therefore, it may include abbreviations and shorthand that make sense only to the speaker. For instance, to prompt your memory of a quote by Quincy Grady on the values of college sports, you might write this: "Grady—college sports." Although those three words might not make sense to anyone else, they would jog your memory of the quote you want to share with listeners. Figure 15.2 (page 396) shows a key word outline for a student speech.

Organizing the Body of a Speech

The body of a speech develops and supports the central idea, or thesis statement, by organizing it into several points that are distinct yet related. In short speeches of 5 to 10 minutes, no more than three points can be developed well, and two are often adequate. In longer speeches of 11 to 20 minutes, more points can be developed.

We'll discuss eight organizational patterns. As we discuss each pattern, you'll have the opportunity to think about how you might use it in your speech. Experiment with each structure for your presentation so that you see how the different patterns uniquely sculpt your ideas and their impact. In Chapter 17, we'll discuss one additional pattern that can be especially effective for persuasive speaking.

The Time Pattern   Time patterns (also called temporal and chronological patterns) organize ideas on the basis of temporal relationships. Listeners find it easy to follow a time pattern because we often think in terms of temporal order: what follows what, what comes first, and what comes next.

Table 15.1: Principles for Preparing a Formal Outline

1. Use full sentences for each point.

2. Each point or subpoint in a speech should have only one idea.

3. Use standard symbols and indentation for outlines.

   I. Roman numerals are used for main points.

      A. Capital letters are used for subpoints that support main points.

         1. Arabic numbers are used for material that supports subpoints.

            a. Lowercase letters are used for material that amplifies supporting material.

4. A point, subpoint, or supporting material should never stand alone. If you have a point I, you must have a point II (and possibly III). If you have a subpoint A, there must be a subpoint B (and possibly C). Outlines show how ideas are developed and related. If there is only one subpoint, you don't need to outline it—it's the main point.

5. Strive for parallelism when wording main points and subpoints. This adds to the coherence of a speech and makes it easier for listeners to follow. Here's an example of parallel wording of main and subpoints in a speech:

   I. Poor advising diminishes students' academic experiences.

      A. Students lose out by taking courses that don't interest them.

      B. Students lose out by missing courses that would interest them.

   II. Poor advising delays students' graduation.

      A. Some students have to return for a fifth year to graduate.

      B. Some students have to take extension courses to graduate.

      C. Some students have to attend summer school to graduate.

6. Include all references in your outline. These should be written as full citations according to the guidelines of a standard style manual such as those published by the Modern Language Association or the American Psychological Association, or *The Chicago Manual of Style*. Your instructor may specify the style guidelines that you should follow.

7. Cite sources using accepted style guidelines for research reports. Three widely used systems for citing sources in papers and speech outlines are APA (American Psychological Association), MLA (Modern Language Association), and CBE (Council of Biology Editors). You can learn how to cite your sources using each set of guidelines by visiting these websites:

    MLA: http://www.hccs.cc.tx.us/system/library/TipSheets/MLA

    APA: http://owl.english.purdue.edu/handouts/research/r_apa.html

    CBE: http://library.osu.edu/sites/guides/cbe.gd.html

Because time patterns emphasize progression, development, or change, they encourage listeners to perceive topics as a process.

Time patterns are useful for describing processes that take place over time, for explaining historical events, and for tracing sequences of action. Time patterns are also effective for presentations that create suspense and build to a climax. One student speaker led his listeners through the detec-

Figure 15.1
Formal Outline

I. Introduction
   A. **Attention:** Would you vote for a system in which half
      of us work only one job, the other half of us work two
      jobs, and everyone gets equal rewards? No? Well that's
      the system that most families in this country have today.
   B. **Thesis statement:** Women's double shift in the paid
      labor force and the home has negative effects on them
      personally and on marriages.
   C. **Preview:** In the next few minutes, I will show that the
      majority of married women work two jobs: one in the
      paid labor market and one when they get home. I will
      then trace the harmful effects of this inequitable division
      of labor.
II. Body
   A. The majority of married women today work two jobs:
      one in the paid labor market and a second one
      when they get home each day.
      1. Most families today have two wage earners.
         a. Only 17% of contemporary families have one
            earner.
         b. As married women have taken on full-time jobs
            outside of the home over the past three decades,
            husbands of working wives have increased the
            amount of housework and child care they do
            from 20% to 30%.
      2. Working wives do more "homework" than working
         husbands.
         a. Research shows that husbands tend to do the
            less routine chores while wives do most of the
            daily chores.

tive work of pharmaceutical research and development to the discovery of a
new drug for treating mood disorders. Another student traced how the
Industrial Revolution changed domestic roles in the United States. A third
student explained the past and present of electronic communication and
predicted what the future holds. In a persuasive speech opposing strip mining, a student described the progressive damage strip mining causes to the
environment.

Thesis: Immigration has been part of American life since the time of
Columbus.

Main Point 1: In 1492, Columbus brought the first immigrants to America.

Main Point 2: In the 1700s and 1800s, people from Europe and Asia
came to America to make it their home.

Main Point 3: Today, the largest group of immigrants comes from South
America.

Figure 15.1
Formal Outline
(*continued*)

  b. Husbands' reasons for not doing more work in the home are that they are tired after work, they don't feel men should do many home chores, and their wives don't expect them to help out more.

  3. Working wives tend to do more homemaking and child care chores, regardless of which spouse earns more in the job outside the home.

  a. Consider Jeremy and Nancy. She earns 65% of the family's income, and she does 80% of the child care and home chores.

  b. Sociologist Arlie Hochschild found that 2 out of 10 husbands in two-worker families do 50% of the work involved in homemaking and child care.

Transition: Now that we've seen what the double shift is, let's consider its effects.

B. The double shift harms women's health and creates marital stress.

  1. The double shift harms women's physical and psychological health.

  a. Research shows that women who work outside of the home and do most of the homemaking and child care suffer sleep deprivation, reduced immunity to infections, and increased susceptibility to illnesses.

  b. A recent study by the American Medical Association found that working women who do the majority of "homework" are more stressed, depressed, and anxious.

  2. The double shift also erodes marital satisfaction.

  a. Women resent husbands who don't contribute a fair share to home life.

Sharpen Your Skill

Using the Time Pattern

Think about how you might organize a speech using the time pattern. Write a thesis that reflects the time pattern and two or three main points that follow a temporal sequence.

Thesis:

1. ....

2. ....

3. ....

The Spatial Pattern Spatial patterns organize ideas according to physical relationships. This structure is especially appropriate for speeches that describe or explain layouts, geographic relationships, or connections

Figure 15.1
Formal Outline
(*continued*)

            b. Inequitable division of "homework" is linked to
               separations and divorces.
    Transition: Let me now pull together what the double shift
        is and how it harms women and marriages.
III. Conclusion
    A. **Summary:** I've shown you that the majority of wives
       today work a double shift while their husbands do not.
       This is not only unfair, it is also harmful to women's
       health and to marriages.
    B. **Final appeal:** Each of us who chooses to marry can
       create an equitable marriage. As I've shown you, the
       reward for making that choice is healthier wives and
       happier, more enduring marriages. That's a pretty good
       return on the investment of creating an equitable
       marriage.

between objects or parts of a system. Listeners find it natural to think in terms of left to right, top to bottom, north to south, and back to front.

Spatial patterns can be used to structure both informative and persuasive speeches. Student speakers have successfully used spatial patterns to inform listeners about the relationships between components of nuclear reactors, the layout of a new library, and the four levels of forest vegetation. In persuasive speeches, students have relied on spatial patterns to argue that solar energy is sufficient to heat homes, that urban sprawl is increasing in the United States, and that Buddhism has spread from its origins in Eastern cultures to Western societies.

Thesis: Our campus includes spaces for learning, socializing, and living.

Main Point 1: At the center of our campus are the classroom buildings.

Main Point 2: Surrounding the classroom buildings are places for students to eat and socialize.

Main Point 3: The south part of campus consists of dormitories and apartments for students with families.

Figure 15.2
Key Word Outline

I. Introduction
   A. Half work one, half work two
   B. Effects—personal, on marriage
   C. Majority of married women; effects of inequity
II. Body
   A. Majority of married women—two jobs
      1. Two wage earners standard
         a. 17% single wage earner
         b. 10% increase in husbands' contribution
      2. 20% husbands assume half
      3. Pattern varies
         a. Class
            i. Jacob and Ina
            ii. John and Jennifer
         b. Education
      4. Women's double shift not tied to salary
         a. Jeremy and Nancy
         b. Hochschild study (see card 1)
   B. Effects
      1. Physical and psychological
         a. Sleep, illness, infection
         b. Stress unhappiness
      2. Marital satisfaction erodes
         a. Resentment
            i. Marion
            ii. Study (see card 2)
         b. Marital stability
            i. Divorce statistics (see card 3)
            ii. Therapist quote (see card 4)
III. Conclusion
   A. Unfair + health harms + marital stability and satisfaction
   B. Your choice—return on investment

Sharpen Your Skill

Using the Spatial Pattern

Think about how you might organize a speech using the spatial pattern. Write a thesis that reflects a spatial pattern and two or three main points that would follow a spatial sequence.

Thesis:

1. ....

2. ....

3. ....

The Topical Pattern Topical patterns order a presentation into several categories, classes, or areas of discussion. The classification pattern is appropriate when your topic breaks down into two or three areas that aren't related temporally, spatially, causally, or otherwise. Although topical patterns don't

Communication Highlight

Creating a Sense of Time

The Reverend Martin Luther King, Jr., relied on a time pattern in his "I Have a Dream" speech (Cox, 1989). He opened with a reference to "today," then traced the history of African Americans in the United States. Next, he returned to the present to argue that the government's promises to African Americans should be kept. He concluded by quoting a Negro spiritual that envisioned a future when all people of all races would be free. Throughout the speech, he fortified the time structure by using words such as *now, today,* and *urgency* and by repeating the key phrase "Now is the time." Read the following excerpts from his speech to appreciate how King crafted his speech around a temporal theme.

I am happy to join with you today in what will go down in history as the greatest demonstration in the history of our nation . . .

Five score years ago, a great American, in whose symbolic shadow we stand today, signed the Emancipation Proclamation . . .

But one hundred years later, the Negro is still not free. One hundred years later, the life of the Negro is still sadly crippled by the manacles of segregation and the chains of discrimination . . .

We have come to this hallowed spot to remind Americans of the fierce urgency of now . . . . Now is the time to make real the promises of Democracy. Now is the time to rise from the dark and desolate valley of segregation to the sunlight of racial justice. Now is the

time to lift our nation from the quicksands of racial injustice to the solid rock of brotherhood. Now is the time to make justice a reality for all of God's children . . . .

Nineteen-sixty-three is not an end, but a beginning . . .

And as we walk, we must make a pledge that we shall always march ahead. We cannot turn back . . .

I say to you today, my friends, so even though we face the difficulties of today and tomorrow, I still have a dream . . . . I have a dream that one day this nation will rise up and live out the true meaning of its creed: "We hold these truths to be self-evident; that all men are created equal." This will be the day . . . This will be the day when all of God's children will be able to sing with new meaning, "My country 'tis of thee, sweet land of liberty, of thee I sing." . . .

We allow freedom to ring, when we let it ring from every village and every hamlet, from every state and every city, we will be able to speed up that day when all of God's children, black men and white men, Jews and Gentiles, Protestants and Catholics, will be able to join hands and sing in the words of the old Negro spiritual, "Free at last! Free at last! Thank God Almighty, we are free at last!"

Source: Reprinted by arrangement with The Estate of Martin Luther King, Jr., c/o Writer's House, Inc. as agent for the proprietor, New York, NY. Copyright 1963 Martin Luther King, Jr., copyright renewed 1991 Coretta Scott King.

---

have the organic power of structures that highlight relationships, they can effectively order points in a speech.

Using topical patterns, speakers have given informative speeches on the three branches of government, the social and academic activities funded by student fees, and the contributions of students, faculty, and staff to campus life. Notice how each of these informative topics can be logically divided into two or three subtopics that serve as the main points of a speech.

Topical patterns can also be effective for persuasive speeches. In a speech urging students to vote for a candidate, one student focused on the candidate's personal integrity, experience in public service, and commitment to the community. Another student designed a persuasive speech that extolled the value of studying the humanities, the natural sciences, and the social sciences.

Thesis: Student fees fund extracurricular, intellectual, and artistic activities on campus.

Main Point 1: Fully 40% of student fees is devoted to extracurricular organizations.

Main Point 2: Another 30% of student fees pays for lectures by distinguished speakers.

Main Point 3: The final 30% of fees supports concerts and art exhibits.

Sharpen Your Skill

Using the Topical Pattern

Think about how you might organize a speech using the topical pattern. Write a thesis that reflects the topical pattern and two or three main points that would follow a topical sequence.

Thesis:

1. ....

2. ....

3. ....

The Star Pattern The star pattern includes several main points that work together to support a speech's overall theme. As you might have noticed, the star pattern is a variation on the topical structure. Yet the star pattern is more organic (Jaffe, 2001) in tying each point to an overriding theme. The star pattern is also more flexible. A standard topical organization has two or three points that a speaker covers in the same order and to the same extent each time the speech is given. With a star pattern, however, a speaker might start with different points and give more or less attention to specific points when speaking to different audiences.

Good visual aids reinforce the organization of a presentation.

© Jose L. Pelaez/Corbis Stock Market

One of the most common uses of the star pattern is in political speeches. Most candidates for office have a standard stump speech that includes their key positions and proposals. The order in which a candidate presents points and the extent to which each point is developed varies from audience to audience. For example, a candidate's platform might include strong support for the environment, enhancing America's fiscal security, and ensuring adequate care for elderly citizens. When the candidate speaks to environmental activists, he or she would lead with the stand on the environment and elaborate it in detail. When the candidate speaks to older citizens, he or she would begin by emphasizing his commitment to their health and to shoring up Medicare and Medicaid. When the candidate speaks to young and middle-aged audiences, the first point would be ensuring America's fiscal security so young people aren't strapped with debt. Using the star pattern, the candidate could adapt the order of points and the emphasis placed on each one. It would not be ethical to misrepresent positions to suit different audiences, but it was both ethical and effective to adapt the order and emphasis on different points.

Thesis: Our campus reflects contributions of administrators, faculty, students, and staff.

Main Point 1: Administrators are in charge of planning and coordinating all aspects of campus life.

Main Point 2: Faculty take the lead in charting the academic character of college life.

Main Point 3: Students are the primary designers of extracurricular life on campus.

Main Point 4: Staff make sure that the initiatives of administrators, faculty, and students are implemented consistently.

$-$Anne$-$

I'm an orientation counselor, and I think I've been using the star pattern to talk to new students, but I didn't know you called it that. With each new group, I have to tell them about the campus and town and school policies and so forth. With first-year students, I start off by talking about school policies because not knowing them can get the kids in trouble. With junior transfers, I get to that last and just spend a little time on it. With out-of-state students, I spend more time talking about the town and even the region—how the South is, which some of them don't understand. I pretty much cover everything with each group, but how I do it varies a lot, depending on who is in the group.

Sharpen Your Skill

Using the Star Pattern

Think about how you might organize a speech using the star pattern. Write a thesis that reflects the star pattern and two or three main points that would be included in a star structure.

Thesis:

1. ....

2. ....

3. ....

The Wave Pattern Like waves in an ocean, the wave pattern consists of repetition. Each wave, or main idea, builds up from evidence, then crests in a main point. Then more evidence follows, leading to the crest of another wave (Jaffe, 2001; Zediker, 1993). Each crest repeats the main theme, using the same words or variations on them. Look again at the excerpt from Martin Luther King's "I Have a Dream" speech. King gave examples of injustices, then crested with the statement, "I have a dream." He then gave more examples, and crested again by repeating the key line. Between each crest in a speech using the wave pattern, speakers should present listeners with a flurry of evidence: multiple undetailed examples, a few well-chosen detailed examples, statistics, quotations, and so forth. The wave pattern is effective because it moves organically, pulling listeners into its rhythm.

Thesis: The key mission of higher education is complete literacy.

Main Point 1: All students who graduate should be literate in speaking, reading, and writing.

Main Point 2: All students who graduate should be literate in communication technologies.

Main Point 3: All students who graduate should be literate in cultural life.

Using the Wave Pattern

Think about how you might organize a speech using the wave pattern. Write a thesis that reflects a wave pattern and two or three main points that would follow a wave sequence.

Thesis:

1. ....

2. ....

3. ....

The Comparative Pattern   As the name suggests, comparative patterns compare two or more objects, people, situations, events, or other phenomena. This structure is also called comparison/contrast and analogical organization. It encourages listeners to be aware of similarities or differences between two or more things. It is particularly effective in helping listeners understand a new idea, process, or event in terms of one with which they're already familiar. Appropriate for both informative and persuasive presentations, the comparative pattern highlights likeness or difference. Notice that in organizing her speech, Mayumi relied on comparison as her overall pattern and created three topical areas that compared Japanese and American views.

–Mayumi–

I selected comparative organization for my informative speech about American and Japanese marriages because I wanted the class to understand how people from my country think differently about marriage than Americans do. I divided my speech into courtship, division of household work, and meaning of divorce to show the difference between Americans and Japanese in each area.

Informative speeches using the comparative structure might explain how computers are like (or not like) human brains, how research for new drugs is like a detective's investigation, or how fission and fusion are different means of creating energy. Students giving persuasive speeches have used the comparative pattern to argue that socialized medicine is inferior to or superior to the U.S. system, that computer literacy is as important as oral and written literacy, and that undergraduate education is different from career preparation. In each case, the comparative structure invites listeners to perceive how two or more phenomena are alike or different.

Thesis: Health maintenance organizations are inferior to private medical practices.

Main Point 1: Health maintenance organizations provide less individualized patient care than private practices do.

Main Point 2: Health maintenance organizations are less likely than private practices to authorize important diagnostic tests.

Main Point 3: Health maintenance organizations place less emphasis on preventive care than private medical practices do.

Sharpen Your Skill

Using the Comparative Pattern

Think about how you might organize a speech using the comparative pattern. Write a thesis that reflects the comparative pattern and two or three main points that would follow a comparative structure.

Thesis:

1. ....

2. ....

3. ....

The Problem–Solution Pattern This pattern divides a topic into two major areas: a problem and a solution. Usually a speaker begins by describing a problem and its severity and then proposes a solution. Occasionally, this sequence is inverted when a speaker begins by discussing a solution and then explains the problem it solves. The problem–solution structure can be used for informative presentations with thesis statements such as "Affirmative action (solution) is designed to rectify historical discrimination (problem)," or "The increased cost of running a university (problem) explains the rise in tuition costs (solution)," or "Deregulation (solution) is designed to prevent monopolies that are unfair to consumers (problem)."

The problem–solution pattern is also effective for persuasive speeches because it lends itself naturally to advocating policies, answers, and practices. Students have used this pattern effectively to persuade others that vegetarianism (solution) can reduce cruelty to animals and world hunger (problems), that thousands of injuries and deaths on the highway (problem) could be prevented if there were stronger sentences for people convicted of driving under the influence of alcohol and other drugs (solution), that many people who are severely ill or dying (problem) could be helped if more people were organ donors (solution), and that the overcrowding of jails and the backlog of court cases (problems) could be decreased if we made all victimless crimes misdemeanors (solution).

The power of this pattern derives from the sequential involvement it invites from listeners. If they accept a speaker's description of a problem and believe the problem is important or urgent, they hunger for a solution. The speaker who presents a solution that addresses the problem they've already acknowledged has a good chance of convincing listeners to endorse the recommended proposal.

Thesis: Victimless crimes should be reclassified as misdemeanors.

Main Point 1: Currently, courts across the nation are overwhelmed by cases in which there is no victim.

Main Point 2: Reclassifying victimless crimes as misdemeanors would dramatically ease the burden on our courts.

Using the Problem–Solution Pattern

Think about how you might organize a speech using the problem–solution pattern. Write a thesis and two main points that would focus on a problem and a solution.

Thesis:

1. ....

2. ....

The Cause–Effect and Effect–Cause Patterns   This pattern is used to argue a direct relationship between two things: a cause and an effect. In some instances, speakers want to inform people that a situation, policy, or practice (effect) results from certain previous choices or events (causes). In other cases, speakers argue that a specific action (cause) will lead to a desired or undesired effect.

Cause–effect and effect–cause patterns are appropriate for both informative and persuasive speeches. We use them for informative presentations when our goal is to explain why something is the case (this effect results from this cause). The cause–effect structure is effective for persuasive speeches when the goal is to advocate some course of action (cause) that will have a particular effect.

You should be aware that it is extremely difficult to prove direct causation. Even scientific researchers who are convinced that smoking causes cancer, emphysema, and other serious conditions cannot conclusively verify that smoking is the cause. What they can prove is that smoking is related to higher mortality and debilitating medical conditions. There is ample evidence to establish a relationship between smoking (or chewing tobacco) and the likelihood of developing cancer and other diseases. Although other factors, such as lifestyle and heredity, may increase or decrease the likelihood of developing dread diseases, smoking is one factor that is strongly related. However, the relationship between smoking and disease does not definitively prove that smoking causes diseases. Thus, although speakers can seldom, if ever, prove direct causation, they can demonstrate relationships, or correlations, between two things, and this is often persuasive to listeners.

> *Thesis:* Raising the minimum wage would be bad for our economy.
>
> *Main Point 1:* Raising the minimum wage would reduce worker productivity.
>
> *Main Point 2:* Raising the minimum wage would lead to greater unemployment.
>
> *Main Point 3:* Raising the minimum wage would decrease profits for businesses.

Using the Cause–Effect Pattern

Think about how you might organize your speech using the cause–effect pattern. Write a thesis and two main points that highlight a cause or causes and an effect or effects.

Thesis:

1. ....

2. ....

Now think about how you might organize a speech using an effect–cause structure. Write a thesis and two main points that identify one or more effects and one or more causes of the effect.

Thesis:

1. ....

2. ....

The eight patterns we've discussed represent different ways to organize public presentations. No one pattern is inherently superior to any other. Each one can be effective for certain speaking goals, topics, and listeners. To structure your speech effectively, you should consider how each of the eight patterns might shape the content and impact of your presentation. For example, a combination of wave and temporal patterns allowed Martin Luther King, Jr., to emphasize progress and change by highlighting past, present, and an imagined future of race relations in the United States.

Had he selected a problem–solution pattern, he might have focused on problems of racial inequity and ways in which government policies could address them. Using a topical pattern, he might have drawn listeners' attention to personal, community, and social effects of discrimination. Each pattern affects the overall meaning of a speech. In creating your own presentation, think about the meaning invited by various patterns, and select one that emphasizes your intent.

Designing the Introduction

The introduction to a speech is the first thing listeners hear. A good introduction accomplishes four goals: (1) It gets listeners' attention and motivates them to listen. (2) It presents a clear thesis statement. (3) It enhances the speaker's credibility. (4) It previews how the speech will be developed. That's a lot to accomplish in a short time, so careful thought is required to design a strong introduction.

Getting Listeners' Attention and Motivating Them to Listen

The first objective of an introduction is to gain listeners' attention and give them a reason to listen. Often speakers accomplish both of those objectives simultaneously because listeners are motivated to listen when something catches their attention.

There are many ways to gain listeners' attention and interest. You might begin with a dramatic piece of evidence, such as a stirring quotation, a striking visual aid, a strong example, or a startling statistic. Each of these forms of evidence can capture listeners' interest and make them want to hear more.

You may also open with a question that invites listeners to become involved with the topic. Rhetorical questions are ones that do not require a response from listeners, yet they get listeners thinking about a topic: "Do you know the biggest cause of death among college students?" "Would you like to know how to double your chances of getting a job offer?" Action

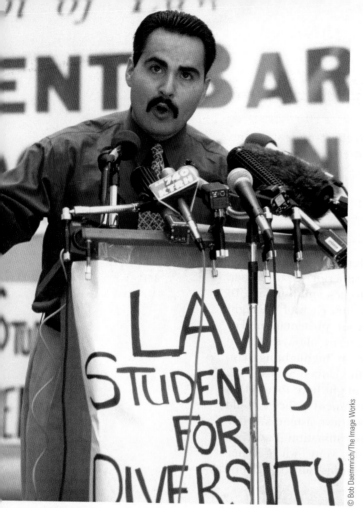

When preparing a speech, build connections between your ideas and listeners' expectations, attitudes, and knowledge.

© Bob Daemmrich/The Image Works

questions do require listeners to respond in some fashion, perhaps by nodding their heads or raising their hands: "How many of you wear seat belts when you drive?" "How many of you went home over fall break?" Both rhetorical and action questions engage listeners personally at the outset of a speech.

There are other ways to capture listeners' attention. For example, speakers sometimes refer to current events or experiences of listeners that are related to the topic of a speech. A student who spoke on homelessness immediately after fall break opened this way: "If you're like me, you went home over the break and enjoyed good food, a clean bed, and a warm, comfortable house—all of the comforts that a home provides. But not everyone has those comforts."

Another effective way to capture listeners' attention is to provide them with direct experience, which is a highly effective foundation for persuasion (Baron & Berne, 1994). For example, in a speech advocating a low-fat diet, a speaker began his presentation by passing out low-fat cookies he had baked. All of his listeners then had an immediate experience with delicious and healthful food.

When appropriate to speaking situations, humor can also be an effective way to open a speech, but only if it succeeds in amusing listeners. A joke that fails diminishes credibility and may arouse negative responses from listeners. Unless you're sure a joke will be funny to listeners, it's better to avoid using humor to open a speech. Thus, it's a good idea to try jokes out on people who are similar to your listeners.

Presenting a Clear Thesis Statement
The second function of an introduction is to state the main message of your speech, which is the thesis statement we discussed in Chapter 13. Your thesis should be a short, clear sentence that directly states the overall theme of your presentation. Remember that the thesis is not a full description of the content of your speech. Your thesis statement should only announce the key idea of your speech so that listeners have a clear understanding of your focus:

- "In the next few minutes, I will describe problems with advising on our campus and ask your help in solving them."
- "Today, I want to persuade you that we should protect the Arctic National Wildlife Refuge from development."
- "I want to inform you about your legal rights when interviewing for a job."
- "I will show you that the death penalty is ineffective and discriminatory."

Building Credibility
The third function of an introduction is to establish a speaker's credibility. Listeners regard a speaker as credible if she or he seems qualified to speak on a the topic, shows good will toward them, and demonstrates dynamism or involvement with the topic.

Communication Highlight

To show that they are qualified to speak on a topic, speakers may mention their personal experience with a topic to establish initial credibility: "I've spent the last three summers working with inmates in a prison." "I am a hemophiliac." Speakers may also explain how they gained expertise on their topics. "For the past two years, I have volunteered at the homeless shelter here in town." If you do not have personal experience with a topic, let listeners know that you have gained knowledge in other ways. "I interviewed ten people who work with abused children." "I learned about the problem of homelessness in two sociology classes that I took last year."

In addition to letting your listeners know that you are qualified to speak on your topic, you want to demonstrate that you have goodwill and are trustworthy. Doing so increases the likelihood that listeners will trust you and what you say. You might do this by explaining why you think your speech will help them. "What I'm going to tell you might save a life, perhaps your own." "My speech will give you information vital to making an informed choice when you vote next week."

Speakers confront a particular problem in establishing goodwill if they are advocating an unpopular position. They need to demonstrate they respect listeners' possible objections. One way to do this is to show that you once held their attitudes. "Some of you may think homeless people are just lazy and don't want to work. I thought so too, before I began volunteering at the local shelter and talked with some of them."

Rebecca Ewing gave a speech favoring graduated licensing, a system that gives new drivers incremental driving freedom. She knew that many of her listeners, who were students, would not initially agree with her position. To defuse potential hostility or resistance, Rebecca explained that she understood many of them would disagree with her—a statement that showed she understood how they might feel. In turn, many of the students who were listening were willing to hear why she advocated graduated licensing. If you'd like to see how Rebecca did this, read her speech or view the video that appears at the end of Chapter 17.

Previewing the Body   The final purpose of an introduction is to tell listeners about coming attractions. You want to preview your major points so that listeners understand how you will develop ideas and can follow you. The preview announces the main points of your speech. Typically, a preview enumerates, or lists, the main points. Here are examples from student speeches:

- "I will show you that there has been a marked decrease in advisors' accessibility and helpfulness to students. Then I will ask you to sign a petition that asks our provost to hire more advisors and provide ongoing training to them."

- "In discussing the Arctic National Wildlife Refuge, I will describe the Coastal Plain, which is the biological heart of the refuge, and then tell you about the porcupine caribou, who come there each year to calve."

- "To convince you that the death penalty should be abolished, I will first provide evidence that it is ineffective as a deterrent to crime. Second, I will demonstrate that the death penalty discriminates against minorities and people who are poor."

Notice how each of these previews directs listeners to think along the lines the speaker will follow in developing the speech. Thus, the previews succeed in increasing listeners' ability to understand, follow, and retain the speaker's ideas (Baird, 1974).

Sharpen Your Skill

Designing Your Introduction

Apply the principles we've discussed to develop an introduction to a speech you plan to give. Using the following outline, fill in full sentences for each element of your introduction.

I. Introduction

   A. Attention and motivation: ....

   B. Thesis: ....

   C. Credibility: ....

   D. Preview: ....

 To further enlarge your awareness of the elements in a good introduction, view the sample speech "Hate Crimes" on your *Communication in Our Lives* CD-ROM. Click the "Speech Interactive" icon, then click "Impromptu Speech."

An effective introduction gains listeners' attention and tells them what you will speak about and how you will develop ideas. Because the average introduction takes up less than 10% of speaking time, speakers need to plan carefully to achieve the three goals of introductions.

Crafting the Conclusion

The next step in organizing a speech is to craft a strong conclusion. As you may recall, we noted that effective public speaking includes deliberate redundancy to enhance listeners' retention of key ideas. The conclusion is a

Mariah Morgan speaks about the dangers of active ignorance.

speaker's last chance to drive home the main points of a presentation. An effective conclusion summarizes content and provides a memorable final thought. As you may realize, these two functions are similar to the attention and preview in introductions. In repeating key ideas and leaving the audience with a compelling final thought, a speaker provides psychological closure on the speech. Like introductions, conclusions are short, generally taking less than 5% of total speaking time. Thus, it's important to accomplish the two objectives of a conclusion very concisely (Miller, 1974).

To summarize the content of your speech, it's effective to restate your thesis and each major point. You can do this in a sentence or two. Here are examples from student speeches:

- "Today I've identified two key problems with advising: an insufficient number of advisers and inadequate training of advisers. Both of these problems can be solved if you will join me in urging our president to increase the number of advisers and the training they get."

- "If you believe, as I do, that Alaska's Arctic Wildlife Refuge should be protected from drilling, then please write or call your congressional representatives."

- "I hope my speech has informed you of your legal rights in interviews and what you can do if an interviewer violates them."

- "I've shown you that the death penalty doesn't prevent crime, and it discriminates against minorities and the poor."

After reviewing main points, a conclusion should offer listeners a final idea, ideally something particularly memorable or strong or an ending that returns to the opening idea to provide satisfying closure. In a speech on environmental activism, the speaker began with " 'One earth, one chance' is the Sierra Club motto" and ended with "We have one chance to keep our one earth. Let's not throw it away." This was effective because the ending returned to the opening words but gave them a slightly different twist. A student who argued that the death penalty should be abolished ended the speech with this statement: "We need to kill the death penalty before it kills anyone else." A third example, again from a student speaker, is this memorable closing: "I've given you logical reasons to be a blood donor, but let me close with something more personal: I am alive today because there was blood available for a massive transfusion when I had my automobile accident. Any one of us could need it tomorrow." Effective conclusions are short and focused. They highlight central ideas one last time and offer listeners a powerful or compelling concluding thought.

Speech Builder Express, which you can access directly through your *Communication in Our Lives* CD-ROM, includes extensive prompts and a clear framework for organizing and outlining different types of speeches.

Building in Transitions

The final organizational issue is **transitions,** which are words and sentences that connect ideas and main points in a speech so that listeners can follow a speaker. Transitions signal listeners that you are through talking about one idea and are ready to connect it to the next one. Effective transitions are like signposts for listeners. They tell listeners where you have been, where you are, and where you are heading (Wilson & Arnold, 1974).

Transitions may be words, phrases, or entire sentences. Within the development of a single point, it's effective to use transitional words or phrases such as *therefore, and so, for this reason, as this evidence suggests,* and *consequently.* To make transitions from one point to another in a speech, phrases can be used to signal listeners that you are starting to discuss a new idea:

- "My second point is . . ."
- "Now that we have seen how many people immigrate to America, let's consider what they bring to us."
- "In addition to the point I just discussed, we need to think about . . ."
- "Now that you understand the gravity of the problem, perhaps you're wondering what you can do to help."

To move from one to another of the three major parts of a speech (introduction, body, and conclusion), you can signal your audience with statements that summarize what you've said in one part and point the way to the next. For example, here's an internal summary and transition between the body of a speech and the conclusion:

- "I've now explained in some detail why we need stronger educational and health programs for new immigrants. Let me close by reminding you of what's at stake."

Transitions also may be nonverbal. For example, you might hold up one, two, and three fingers to reinforce your movement from the first to the second to the third main point in the body of your speech. Changes in vocal intensity, eye contact, and inflection can effectively mark movement from one idea to the next. For instance, you could conclude the final point of the

Communication Highlight

Whoops! Where's the Connection?

When good transitions are missing, a speech is likely to seem disjointed or even incoherent. A particularly glaring failure to create smooth transitions came when James Cameron accepted his award for directing *Titanic* at the 1997 Academy Awards (Robinson, 2001, p. 18). In his acceptance speech, Cameron said, "I'd like to do a few seconds of silence in remembrance of the 1,500 men, women, and children who died when the ship went down. Now, let's party 'til dawn!"

body of your speech with strong volume and then drop the volume to begin the conclusion. Silence is also effective in marking transitions. A pause after the introduction signals listeners that a speaker is going to a new place. Visual aids also help listeners move with a speaker.

Transitions are vital to effective speaking. If the introduction, body, and conclusion are the bones of a speech, the transitions are the sinew that holds the bones together. Without them, a speech may seem more like a laundry list of unconnected ideas than a coherent whole.

Sharpen Your Skill

Noticing Organization in Speeches

To increase your awareness of organizational patterns and their impact, study effective speeches that have been given. Two websites offer excellent collections of speeches. Visit one or both, identify the organizational structure used in three speeches, and evaluate whether the speaker made wise choices in organizing the speech. The PBS site Great American Speeches offers texts of more than ninety speeches. Background and audio or visual clips are available for some of these. Visit this site at http://www.pbs.org/greatspeeches.

The Online Speech Bank offers a wide variety of speeches, sermons, lectures, and interviews. Visit this site at http://www.americanrhetoric.com/speechbank.htm.

Communication Apprehension: Natural and Often Helpful

There are very few people who don't sometimes feel apprehensive about talking with others (Bostrom, 1988; Richmond & McCroskey, 1992). Virginia Richmond and James McCroskey (1995a) report that almost 95% of Americans surveyed said they had some degree of anxiety about communicating in some situations. As you prepare to present your speech, it's important for you to understand **communication apprehension** and how to manage it so that it doesn't detract from your effectiveness.

A degree of anxiety is natural and may actually improve communication. Both novice and seasoned speakers experience anxiety. Many politicians feel nervous before and during a presentation, even though they make hundreds of speeches. Likewise, teachers who have taught for years usually feel tension before meeting a class, and seasoned journalists such as Mike Wallace say they get butterflies when conducting interviews.

Some anxiety can be helpful. It makes us more alert, largely because our bodies produce adrenaline and extra blood sugar, which increase energy. You can channel the extra energy into purposeful gestures and movement when you are speaking. The energy produced in response to communication anxiety allows politicians, teachers, and journalists to be more dynamic and interesting.

Although a degree of anxiety about speaking is natural, too much can interfere with effectiveness. Anxiety strong enough to hinder our ability to interact with others is communication apprehension. The apprehension may be about real or anticipated communication encounters.

I'd Rather Lose Than Have to Give a Speech

© Bob Daemmrich/PhotoEdit, Inc.

Have you ever seen pro-golfer Annika Sorenstam interviewed? If so, you've probably noticed that she seems at ease speaking in public. That wasn't always the case. As a high school student, she was so afraid of speaking that she often deliberately played to win second place so that she wouldn't have to give the winner's speech (Morreale, 2003). Her confidence today reminds us that communication apprehension can be managed.

Causes of Communication Apprehension

There are two types of communication apprehension: situational and chronic. For many of us, certain situations spark anxiety. For instance, if you are scheduled to speak to a group that is known to be hostile to you or your ideas, anxiety is to be expected. In other cases, we feel apprehensive because real or imagined features of a situation worry us. Before a performance review, it's natural to be a little anxious about what your supervisor might say about areas in which you need to improve.

Research indicates that five situational factors often generate apprehension. First, we tend to be more anxious when communicating with people who are unfamiliar to us or who we think are different from us. Apprehension is also likely to be present in new or unusual situations, such as your first job interview. A third situational cause of apprehension is being in the spotlight. When we are the center of attention, we tend to feel self-conscious and anxious that we might embarrass ourselves. Fourth, we may feel apprehensive when we're being evaluated (Motley & Molloy, 1994).

A final situational reason for apprehension is a past failure or failures in a particular speaking situation. For example, my doctor called me one day to ask me to coach her for a speech she had to give to a medical society. Eleanor had last given a public speech eight years ago in medical school. Just before the speech, her first patient had died, and she was badly shaken. As a result, she was disorganized, flustered, and generally ineffective. That single incident, which followed a history of successful speaking, was so traumatic that Eleanor developed acute speaking anxiety.

Communication apprehension is more difficult to manage when it is chronic. Rather than feeling anxious, in specific situations, which is often appropriate, some people are generally apprehensive about communicating. People who have chronic communication anxiety learn to fear communication, just as some of us learn to fear heights or water (Beatty, Plax, & Kearney, 1985; DeFleur & Ball-Rokeach, 1989).

–Michael–

To this day, I have vivid memories of my father being sick, I mean throwing up sick, anytime he had to make a presentation to his work team. He would start getting edgy weeks before the presentation, then he'd get nervous, then he'd be unable to hold food down. By the day of a presentation, he was a basket case. That's probably why I was so fearful of speaking until I got help.

Sharpen Your Skill

Personal Report of Communication Apprehension

Instructions

Following are 24 statements about communicating. Don't worry if some of the following statements seem similar to other statements. In the space to the left of each item, indicate the extent to which you agree that this statement describes you. Please record your first impressions without analyzing statements closely. Use the following scale:

1 = strongly agree that this describes me

2 = agree that this describes me

3 = undecided how well this describes me

4 = disagree that this describes me

5 = strongly disagree that this describes me

.... 1. I dislike participating in group discussions.

.... 2. Generally, I am comfortable while participating in group discussions.

.... 3. I am tense and nervous while participating in group discussions.

.... 4. I like to get involved in group discussions.

.... 5. Engaging in group discussions with new people makes me tense and nervous.

.... 6. I am calm and relaxed while participating in group discussions.

.... 7. Generally, I am nervous when I have to participate in a meeting.

.... 8. Usually, I am calm and relaxed while participating in meetings.

.... 9. I am very calm and relaxed when I am called on to express an opinion at a meeting.

.... 10. I am afraid to express myself at meetings.

.... 11. Communicating at meetings usually makes me uncomfortable.

.... 12. I am very relaxed when answering questions at a meeting.

.... 13. While participating in a conversation with a new acquaintance, I feel very nervous.

.... 14. I have no fear of speaking up in conversation.

.... 15. Ordinarily, I am very tense and nervous in conversations.

.... 16. Ordinarily, I am very calm and relaxed in conversations.

.... 17. While conversing with a new acquaintance, I feel very relaxed.

.... 18. I'm afraid to speak up in conversations.

.... 19. I have no fear of giving a speech.

.... 20. Certain parts of my body feel very tense and rigid while I'm giving a speech.

.... 21. I feel relaxed while giving a speech.

.... 22. My thoughts become confused and jumbled when I am giving a speech.

.... 23. I face the prospect of giving a speech with confidence.

.... 24. While giving a speech, I get so nervous I forget facts I really know.

Computing Your Score

This test allows you to calculate your overall communication apprehension score and your communication apprehension scores for particular speaking situations.

Group score	Add scores for items 2, 4, and 6 Subtract scores for items 1, 3, and 5 Add 18 =
Meeting score	Add scores for items 8, 9, 12 Subtract scores for items 7, 10, 11 Add 18 =
Dyad score	Add scores for items 14, 16, 17 Subtract scores for items 13, 15, 18 Add 18 =
Public speaking score	Add scores for items 19, 21, and 23 Subtract scores for items 20, 22, 24 Add 18 =
Total score	Add the four subscores together

Total Communication Apprehension Score =

Total scores range from 24 to 120. (If your score is over 120 or under 24, you have calculated incorrectly.) Scores of 83 or more indicate high communication apprehension. People who score in this range tend to talk little and tend to be shy and somewhat withdrawn and nervous in some speaking situations. Scores of 55 or less indicate low communication apprehension. People who score in this range tend to enjoy being with others, like talking, and feel confident of their communication ability. You can complete this assessment online. To access the online PRCA instrument, use your CD-ROM to access the PRCA-24 survey on the Communication in Our Lives protected website.

Source: McCroskey, J. C. (1982). *Introduction to Rhetorical Communication* (4th ed.). Englewood Cliffs, NJ: Prentice Hall.

Reducing Communication Apprehension

Communication apprehension is learned. Therefore, it's reasonable to think it can also be unlearned—at least in many cases. Communication scholars have developed four methods of reducing communication apprehension. If you do not have significant communication apprehension, reading this section may help you understand people who do. If you have more communication apprehension than you would like, reading this section will give you ways to reduce your anxiety.

Systematic Desensitization   **Systematic desensitization** is a method of treating many fears, from fear of flying to fear of speaking. It focuses on reducing the tension that surrounds the feared event (Beatty & Behnke, 1991; Daly & McCroskey, 198F4). Systematic desensitization teaches people how to relax and thereby reduce the physiological features of anxiety. The goal is to learn to associate feeling relaxed with images of oneself in communication situations.

Cognitive Restructuring   **Cognitive restructuring** is a method of helping people change how they think about speaking situations (Motley & Molloy, 1994). According to this method, speaking is not the problem; rather, the problem is how we use irrational beliefs to interpret speaking situations. For example, if you think you must be perfect, totally engaging, and liked by everyone who hears you, then you've set yourself up for failure. You've created expectations that are impossible to meet, which might be why you feel emotionally uneasy about communicating. A key part of cognitive restructuring is teaching apprehensive people to identify and challenge negative self-statements, which we discussed in Chapter 3.

Positive Visualization   **Positive visualization** aims to reduce anxiety by guiding apprehensive speakers through imagined positive speaking experiences (Hamilton, 1999). Researchers report that positive visualization is especially effective in reducing chronic apprehension (Ayres & Hopf, 1990; Bourhis & Allen, 1992; Lau, 1989; Porter & Foster, 1986). In professional life, managers are coached to visualize successful negotiations and meetings. In the world of sports, athletes are taught to imagine playing well, and those who engage in positive visualization improve as much as athletes who physically practice their sport.

Sharpen Your Skill

Positive Visualization

First, imagine yourself speaking to three of your friends on a topic about which you care. Now visualize your friends nodding and asking questions that indicate they are interested in what you say. Notice that they are looking intently at you, and their postures are attentive.

Now imagine that someone you don't know joins your friends, and you continue speaking. It's okay if you feel a little anxious, but visualize the stranger becoming very attentive to your communication. Notice how the new person looks at you with admiration.

Next, imagine that you are asked to speak on the same topic to a student group, and you agree. Visualize the room in which you speak: a small conference room in the campus student union. The room seems warm and comfortable. When you enter, twenty people are there to hear you. Notice that they smile when you walk to the front of the room. See how they look at you expectantly because they are interested in your topic.

Visualize yourself starting your talk: You begin by telling the listeners that, like them, you are a student. Notice that they nod and acknowledge the connection between you and them. Feel yourself becoming relaxed and confident. Then you tell them what you will cover in your talk. Notice how your words flow easily and smoothly. See the nods and smiles of your listeners. As you speak, they stay engaged with you—interested, following your ideas, impressed by your knowledge. When you are through, the listeners break into spontaneous applause.

Skills Training **Skills training** assumes that lack of speaking skills causes us to be apprehensive about speaking. This method focuses on teaching people skills such as how to start conversations, organize ideas, build strong introductions, and support claims (Phillips, 1991).

You may be thinking that each of these methods seems useful. If so, your thinking coincides with research that indicates that a combination of all three methods is more likely to relieve speaking anxiety than any single method (Allen, Hunter, & Donahue, 1989). If you experience serious communication apprehension that interferes with your ability to express your ideas, ask your instructor to direct you to professionals who can work with you.

Presenting Public Speeches

We turn now to the final aspect of public speaking. Delivery, or oral style, affects every aspect of speaking effectiveness, from listeners' interest to listeners' judgments of a speaker's credibility. We'll first discuss oral style, pointing out how it differs from written style. Then, we'll consider alternative styles of delivery.

Oral Style

Oral style refers to speakers' visual, vocal, and verbal communication with listeners.

Visual delivery concerns a speaker's appearance, facial expressions, eye contact, posture, gestures, movement during a presentation, and visual aids. Vocal aspects of delivery include volume, pitch, pronunciation, articulation, inflection, pauses, and speaking rate. Verbal delivery consists of word choices and sentence structure.

A common mistake of speakers, both new and experienced, is to use written style rather than oral style. But a speech is not a spoken essay. There

are three primary qualities of effective oral communication (Wilson & Arnold, 1974). First, usually it is more informal than written communication. Thus, speakers use contractions and sentence fragments that would be inappropriate in a formal written document. Informality may also be evident in speaker's dress and posture—for instance, sitting on the edge of a table to talk to an audience. The informal character of oral style also means it's appropriate for speakers to use colloquial words and even slang in informal speaking contexts. However, speakers shouldn't use slang or jargon that might offend any listener or that might not be understood by some listeners.

Effective oral style also tends to be more personal than written style. It's generally effective for speakers to include personal stories and personal pronouns, referring to themselves as "I" rather than "the speaker." In addition, speakers should sustain eye contact with listeners and show that they are approachable. If you reflect on speakers you've found effective, you'll probably realize that they seemed personal and open to you.

Third, effective oral style tends to be more immediate and more active than written style. This is important because listeners must understand ideas immediately as they are spoken, whereas readers can take time to comprehend ideas. In oral presentations, simple sentences ("I have three points") and compound sentences ("I want to describe the current system of selling textbooks, and then I will propose a less costly alternative") are more appropriate than complex sentences ("There are many reasons to preserve the Arctic National Wildlife Refuge, some of which have to do with endangered species and others with the preservation of wilderness environment, yet our current Congress is not protecting this treasure").

Immediacy also involves moving quickly instead of gradually to develop ideas. Rhetorical questions, interjections, and redundancy also enhance the immediacy of a speech. Reread the excerpts from Martin Luther King, Jr.'s, speech on page 397, and notice his skill in repeating key phrases, such as, "Now is the time." Also note Dr. King's use of simple sentences and his emphasis on personal language (*I* and *we*). Contrast the communication style of speakers you find effective with the style of speakers you judge to be less effective. The latter group is likely to adopt a formal, impersonal, abstract style of communication.

Styles of Delivery

Throughout this book, we've seen that communication occurs in contexts that influence what will be effective and ineffective. This basic communication principle guides a speaker's choice of a style of presentation. The style of delivery that's effective at a political rally is different from the style appropriate for an attorney's closing speech in a trial; delivering a toast at a wedding requires a style different from that required in testifying before Congress. There are four presentational styles.

Effective oral style is generally informal, personal, and immediate.

© Taxi/Getty Images

Table 15.2: Guidelines for Effective Delivery

1. Adapt your appearance to your listeners. It's often effective for speakers to look similar to their listeners, probably because this suggests common ground.

2. Adapt your appearance to the speaking situation. Formal dress is likely to be appropriate for speech to executives that is given in an office or board room. However, if that same speech were given at a company retreat by the ocean, casual dress would be more appropriate.

3. Use gestures to enhance impact. Gestures can reinforce ideas and complement verbal messages. Moving your arm in an arc motion can suggest progression to reinforce a time pattern.

4. Adopt a confident posture. Stand erect, with your shoulders back and your feet slightly apart for optimum balance.

5. Use confident, dynamic body movement to communicate your enthusiasm and confidence. Walk to the speaking podium (or wherever you will speak) with assurance: head up, arms comfortably at your sides, at a pace that is neither hurried nor halting. As you speak, move away from the podium to highlight key ideas or to provide visual transitions from one point to the next.

6. Maintain good eye contact with listeners. Try to vary your visual zone so that you look at some listeners at one moment, then move your gaze to a different segment of listeners.

7. Use volume that is strong but not overpowering. The appropriate volume will vary, depending on the size of your audience. You need to speak louder to an audience of 200 than to an audience of 25. You also need to adapt your volume to the environment. If a noisy air conditioner is running, you'll need to increase your volume to be heard. Be careful not to let your volume drop off at the end of sentences, a common problem for beginning speakers. At the same time, avoid excessive volume; listeners don't appreciate feeling that a speaker is shouting at them.

8. Use your voice to enhance your message. Pitch, rate, volume, and articulation are vocal qualities that allow you to add emphasis to important ideas. As you practice your speech, decide which words and phrases you want to emphasize.

9. Use pauses for effect. It is often effective to pause for a second or two after stating an important point or presenting a dramatic example or statistic.

10. Do not let accent interfere with clarity. Most of us speak in ways that reflect our ethnic and regional heritage. For everyone but professional broadcasters, regional dialects are acceptable. However, your accent must be understandable to listeners.

11. Articulate clearly. Articulation is correctness of pronunciation. Speakers lose credibility when they mispronounce words or when they add or delete syllables. You should verify the pronunciation for all words in your speech. Common instances of added syllables are *cohabitate* for *cohabit*, *orientated* for *oriented*, *preventative* for *preventive*, and *irregardless* for *regardless*.

Impromptu Style **Impromptu speaking** involves little preparation. Speakers speak off the cuff, organizing ideas as they talk and working with evidence that is already familiar to them. You use an impromptu style when you make a comment in a class, answer a question you hadn't anticipated in an interview, or respond to a request to share your ideas on a topic. There is no time to prepare or rehearse, so you have to think on your feet.

Impromptu speaking is appropriate when you know a topic well enough to organize and support your ideas without a lot of advance preparation. For instance, the president of a company could speak off the cuff about the company's philosophy, goals, and recent activities. Similarly, politicians who have worked out their positions and familiarized themselves with evidence often speak in an impromptu style.

Impromptu speaking tends to be highly informal, personal, and immediate—the best qualities of oral style. Yet impromptu speaking has the disadvantage of allowing less time to research and organize. Consequently, this is not an effective style when speakers are not highly familiar with topics and at ease in speaking in public.

Sharpen Your Skill

Analyzing Impromptu Speaking

The CD-ROM that accompanies this book includes a sample impromptu speech by a student named Mariah, whose topic is hate crimes. You will find it listed as "Impromptu Speech" on the Speech Menu within "Speech Interactive" on the CD-ROM. View Mariah's speech and answer the following questions:

1. How would the speech differ if it had been extemporaneous instead of impromptu?

2. Was Mariah effective in using the off-the-cuff, impromptu style?

3. Was Mariah's delivery informal, immediate, and personal—the qualities associated with effective impromptu delivery?

Extemporaneous Style Probably the most common presentational style today, **extemporaneous speaking** relies on preparation and practice, but actual words and nonverbal behaviors aren't memorized. Extemporaneous speaking (also called extemp) requires speakers to do research, organize ideas, select supporting evidence, prepare visual aids, outline the speech, and practice delivery. Yet the speech itself is not written out in full. Instead, speakers construct an outline—usually a key word outline.

Effective extemporaneous speaking requires a fine balance between too little and too much practice. Not rehearsing enough may result in stumbling, forgetting key ideas, and not being at ease with the topic. On the other hand, too much practice tends to result in a speech that sounds canned. The idea is to prepare and practice just enough to be comfortable with the material yet still natural and spontaneous in delivery. Extemporaneous speaking involves a conversational and interactive manner that is generally very effective with listeners. This probably is why the extemporaneous style is the most popular presentational mode.

Manuscript Style As the name suggests, **manuscript style** involves speaking from the complete manuscript of a speech. After planning, researching, organizing, and outlining a presentation, a speaker then writes the complete word-for-word text and practices the presentation

Dr. Carberry has been showing much more originality in his sermons lately, hasn't he?

using that text or that text transferred to a teleprompter. The clear advantage of this style is that it provides total security to speakers. Even if a speaker gets confused when standing before an audience, she or he can rely on the full text.

The security provided by working with a full written text of a speech often is offset by several disadvantages of manuscript speaking. First, this style limits a speaker's ability to adapt on the spot to listeners. If someone looks puzzled, the extemporaneous speaker can elaborate an idea, but the manuscript speaker may be locked into the written text. This points to a second hazard of manuscript speaking: the tendency to read the speech. It's difficult to be animated and visually engaged with listeners when reading a manuscript.

–Brad–

Most of my professors are pretty good. They talk with us in classes, and they seem to be really involved in interacting with students. But I've had several professors who read their notes—like, I mean, every day. They'd just come in, open a file, and start reading. I had one professor who almost never looked at us. It didn't feel like a person was communicating with us. I'd rather have read his notes on my own.

A third disadvantage is that it's difficult to adopt oral style when relying on a written manuscript. Only veteran manuscript speakers or speech writers can write a speech that has oral flavor. More often, a manuscript speech adopts written style, so it isn't immediate, personal, and informal.

Manuscript speaking is appropriate, and perhaps necessary, in a few specific situations. When the content of a speech must be precise and there is no room for adapting or rewording ideas, then a manuscript is advisable. The situations that require this are few and not part of most people's everyday lives. Official declarations, diplomatic agreements, and formal press statements are examples of contexts in which manuscript speaking may be advisable.

Even in formal situations, openness and conversational style are appropriate. Notice the nonverbal behaviors of the speaker, Richard Gere.

Memorized Style The final presentational style is **memorized speaking,** which carries the manuscript style one step further. After going through all the stages of manuscript speaking (preparing, researching, organizing, outlining, writing out the full text, and practicing), a speaker commits the entire speech to memory and speaks from a manuscript that is in his or her head. The advantages of this style are the same as those for manuscript speaking: An exact text exists, so everything is prepared in advance. However, there are serious disadvantages to memorizing. Because memorized speaking is based on a full written speech, the presentation may reflect written rather than oral style. In addition, memorized speaking is risky because a speaker has no safety net in case of memory lapses. Speakers who forget a word or phrase may become rattled and unable to complete the presentation. Whereas a speaker using extemporaneous style and an outline would simply substitute a different word if the desired one didn't come to mind, a speaker who has memorized a speech may get stuck and be unable to continue if she or he forgets anything. Memorized style also can limit effective delivery. It is difficult for a speaker to sound spontaneous when she or he has memorized an entire speech. Because the speaker is preoccupied with remembering the speech, she or he can't interact fully with listeners. These drawbacks of memorized speaking explain why it isn't widely used or recommended.

Knowing the benefits and liabilities of each presentational style provides you with alternatives. For most speaking occasions, extemporaneous style is effective because it combines good preparation and practice with spontaneity. Although this style tends to be the most effective in the majority of speaking situations, there are exceptions. When deciding which style to use, carefully consider your own needs and speaking preferences, the nature of your presentation, the context in which you will deliver it, and your particular listeners.

Practice

Whichever presentational style you choose, practice is important. Ideally, you should begin practicing your speech several days before you plan to deliver it. During practice, you should rely on your outline as it will be when you actually deliver the speech. This ensures that you will be familiar with its layout and know where various materials are on the outline. You should also practice with visual aids and any other materials you plan to use in your speech so that you are comfortable working with them.

There are many ways to practice a speech. Usually, speakers prefer to practice alone initially so that they gain some confidence and comfort in presentation. You may find it helpful to practice in front of a mirror to see how you look and to keep your eyes focused away from the outline. Practicing before a mirror is especially helpful in experimenting with different nonverbal behaviors that can enhance your presentational impact.

Videotaping is another way to see practice. You can review the tape to see and hear yourself and to make decisions about how to refine your delivery. You might notice distracting gestures that you weren't conscious of as you spoke. You might realize that you are not making strong eye contact with listeners. You might recognize places where pauses or inflection would increase the impact of your presentation. If the videotape shows you pulling your

Practicing a speech in front of a mirror allows this speaker to monitor how he will appear to listeners.

© Dwayne Newton/PhotoEdit

hair, scratching your face, or not keeping eye contact, you can monitor these behaviors in additional practice. If you see that you look at your notes too much, you can work to increase your eye contact when speaking. Take breaks between practices so that you don't wind up memorizing the speech inadvertently.

When you've rehearsed enough to feel comfortable with the speech, it's a good idea to practice in front of others. Ask friends to listen, and invite their feedback on ways you can refine your presentation. Ask whether they can follow your organization; whether they find your evidence convincing; and whether they perceive your delivery as personal, immediate, and informal. Also ask your listeners to give you feedback on your nonverbal communication: Are you maintaining good eye contact? Are your gestures, facial expressions, and movements appropriate? Do you use vocal inflections, changes in volume, and pauses effectively to accent your ideas? Is it hard to understand any words you use in your speech?

Practice until you know your material well but haven't memorized it. *Then stop!* Overrehearsing is just as undesirable as not practicing enough. You want to preserve the freshness and spontaneity that is important in oral style.

Sharpen Your Skill

Rehearsing Your Speech

You'll need three 20-minute periods at different times to complete this activity.

1. After you have prepared the outline and note cards that you will use when you present your speech, find a quiet place where you will not be disturbed. Present the speech as you intend to deliver it to your class. As you rehearse, practice looking at different parts of the room as you will later engage in eye contact with your classmates.

2. Wait at least a few hours after your first practice to do the second one. This time, practice in the same room, but stand in front of a mirror; ideally it should be a full-length mirror so that you can see yourself as listeners will see you. Give your speech as you plan to deliver it to your classmates. As you speak, notice your posture and nonverbal communication. Are you using effective hand gestures, facial expressions, and changes in body posture and position?

3. Wait at least a few hours after your second practice to do the third one. You may want to invite several friends or classmates to join you in this practice session so that you have an audience. For this rehearsal, go to your classroom or another classroom that is set up similarly to yours. Sit down in the room as you would sit in your class. Imagine the teacher announcing that it is your turn to speak. Get up from your seat, go to the podium or front of the classroom, and present your speech as you plan to deliver it to your classmates. Practice looking at different areas of the room or at your friends as you will later engage in eye contact with classmates. If you have access to a video camera, you may tape this third rehearsal and then analyze your presentation.

CASE STUDY: Analyzing Delivery: Speech of Self-introduction

Jason Harris/© Wadsworth

The following speech is featured on the *Communication in Our Lives* CD-ROM included with this book. Once you've launched the CD, click on the "Speech Interactive" icon, and, from the Speech Menu, select "Delivery" to watch the audiovisual presentation of Adam Currier's speech of self-introduction. To read a description of Adam's assignment, click on the "Assignment" button. Improve your own public speaking skills by reading, watching, listening to, evaluating, and critiquing this sample speech.

Analyze the speech by applying the principles covered in this chapter, and respond to the prompts that accompany the video, which you can access by clicking on "Evaluation" and "Critique." After answering the evaluation questions and writing a brief critique of the speech, you can click on the "Done" button to compare your responses with the ones I suggest. Additional analysis questions are available in print at the end of this chapter and on the book's website.

Every year since I've remembered, we've gone back to Iowa and spent a week of that summer just being with my dad's parents, my grandparents. And each year, as I grew, I grew closer and closer to my grandfather. And it got to the point where I no longer just knew him as a relative but I knew him as a human being. Sitting outside on his porch one day, right before he died, he told me about his life. We were talking about what he had done, being in World War II, being a dentist, being a community leader, all the things he had ever achieved in his life—and it all sounded so perfect. I said, "Grandfather, what do you regret most in your life?" He said, "Adam, I regret not seeing more sunsets."

A couple months later, he passed on, and I realized that I didn't enjoy every single minute with him as much as I could've, and I didn't have the time with him that I thought that I had. So I look at my wall now, and I see the quotes on it and see the stories on it and the pictures on it and I realize that everyone I've come into contact with, everyone I've ever met, everything I've done, has all contributed to shaping the person that I am.

Chapter Summary

In this chapter, we focused on ways to organize and present public communication. We discussed different types of outlines that assist speakers in organizing material. Next, we considered eight patterns for ordering the ideas in a speech and explored how each pattern affects the residual message of a presentation. Which organizational structure is best depends on a variety of factors, including the topic, your speaking goal, and the listeners with whom you will communicate.

We also noted that communication apprehension is common, natural, and often helpful to speakers. If you understand why it occurs and how to manage any apprehension you have, you can be effective in making public presentations. We identified different presentational styles and saw that each one has potential advantages and liabilities. Effective delivery cannot be reduced to a universal formula. What is effective depends on particular speakers, contexts, listeners, and speaking goals. To make sure that you've thought through all important aspects of organizing, outlining, and delivery, review the checklist at the end of this chapter. Then you'll be ready to proceed to Chapter 16, in which we analyze the full text of a student speech to see how organization, evidence, and other facets of public speaking work in an actual presentation.

Checklist for Organizing and Presenting a Speech

Complete the checklist below. If you prefer, you may complete this checklist online under "Forms and Checklists for Chapter 15" at the *Communication in Our Lives* website.

In addition, you may want to use Speech Builder Express, to which you have free access through your *Communication in Our Lives* CD-ROM. At the end of this chapter, I've included a suggestion for using Speech Builder Express to help you organize your speech.

1. How could you structure your speech using each of the organizational patterns we discussed? Write out a thesis statement for each pattern.

    A. Time: ....

    B. Space: ....

    C. Topical: ....

    D. Star: ....

    E. Wave: ....

    F. Comparative: ....

    G. Problem–solution: ....

    H. Cause–effect: ....

    I. Effect–cause: ....

2. Which pattern have you decided to use?

    A. List the two or three main points into which you've divided your topic: ...., ..., and ....

3. Describe the three parts of your introduction:

    A. I will gain attention by ....

    B. My thesis statement: ....

    C. My preview is ....

4. Describe the transitions you've developed to move listeners from idea to idea in your speech.

    A. My transition from introduction to the body of the speech is ....

    B. My transitions between major points in the body are ....

C. My transition from the body to the conclusion of the speech is

....

5. Describe the two parts of your conclusion:

   A. Restatement of thesis and major points: ....

   B. Concluding emphasis: ....

6. The delivery style I will use is .... because ....

7. I've practiced my speech

   A. On my own

   B. In front of others

   C. In front of a mirror

   D. In the room where I will deliver it

   E. On videotape

 ## Communication in Our Lives ONLINE

In addition to presenting the case studies' multimedia scenarios and speeches, the *Communication in Our Lives* CD-ROM provides quick access to the *Communication in Our Lives* website, Speech Builder Express, and InfoTrac College Edition. The website is online at http://communication.wadsworth.com/woodciol4, but you can only access this book's premium web content when you link to the site directly through the book's CD.

 The *Communication in Our Lives* website features interactive tools for learning and reviewing the chapter's concepts and key terms, including electronic versions of the "For Further Reflection and Discussion" questions that appear here and a review quiz.

The website also provides updated web links and additional InfoTrac College Edition activities. If required, you can e-mail completed chapter activities or the quizzes to your instructor.

Key Concepts

cognitive restructuring, *413*

communication apprehension, *409*

extemporaneous speaking, *417*

formal outline, *391*

impromptu speaking, *416*

key word outline, *391*

manuscript style, *417*

memorized speaking, *418*

oral style, *414*

positive visualization, *413*

skills training, *414*

systematic desensitization, *413*

transitions, *407*

working outline, *390*

Works Cited, *391*

For Further Reflection and Discussion

1. Do you think that a speaker has an ethical responsibility to organize a speech well, or is organization strictly a strategic matter—something to help a speaker have impact? Does careful organization reflect ethical issues, such as respect for listeners?

2. Attend a public presentation and keep notes on how the speaker organizes the speech. What is the overall pattern of the presentation? Did the speaker make a wise choice? Identify transitions in the speech, and evaluate their effectiveness. Do the introduction and conclusion serve the appropriate speaking goals?

3. To appreciate the difference between written and oral styles, do this: Using library references, find a volume of famous speeches and select two to analyze. Then select two formal essays to analyze (the Declaration of Independence, for example). Check the essays and speeches against the features of oral style we discussed. Now deliver the essays orally. What happens? Are they effective as oral communication? Explain why or why not.

4. Give a 1- to 2-minute impromptu speech on your favorite activity or some other topic with which you are already familiar. Next, spend two days preparing an extemporaneous speech on the same topic. How do the two speeches differ in quality and effectiveness?

5. Use your *InfoTrac College Edition* to find the journal *Vital Speeches*. Read President George W. Bush's October 7, 2001, speech, "We Are at War against Terrorism: The Attack on the Taliban." In this speech, President Bush announced that America was launching a war against terrorism. Does he provide sufficient justification for going to war? How does the opening of his speech recognize and address American values?

Experiencing Communication in Our Lives

Questions for Analysis and Discussion

Review the video of Adam's speech that you watched when completing this chapter's case study (page 421), or, if you haven't seen it yet, watch it for the first time. If you didn't previously finish the "Evaluation" questions and "Critique" activity included on the CD-ROM, do so now, and then respond to the following questions, which are also available on the book's website under "Activities for Chapter 15."

1. Was the speaker dynamic—excited about the topic?

2. Was the speaker's language clear, immediate, and vivid?

3. Did the speaker use nonverbal communication to enhance effectiveness?

4. What style of speaking did the speaker use? Was this an appropriate choice for this speech, this occasion, and the particular listeners?

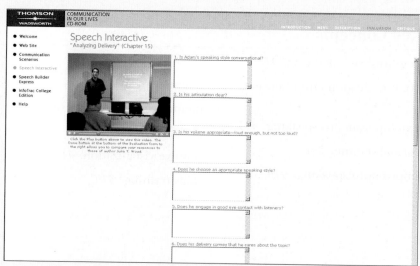

Speech Builder Express

Access Speech Builder Express with the user name and the password that came with the CD-ROM that accompanies your textbook. Click "Resume" to pull up the file for your speech.

Select "Organization" on the Express menu. Speech Builder Express will ask you how many main ideas you will include in your speech. Use the drop-down menu to click "2" or "3." Speech Builder Express will then provide you with a text box for each main idea. Type your main ideas, one in each of the provided boxes.

You will then be asked to select an organization pattern for your speech. As you learned in this chapter, there is no single best organizational pattern for all speeches. Review your thesis and main points to decide which organizational pattern will be most effective for your speech. Click that pattern on the list provided.

Now select "Outline" on the Express menu. Speech Builder Express will prompt you through the steps in outlining your speech: developing subpoints, designing internal summaries, creating transitions, developing the introduction and conclusion.

You're nearly done. Select "Completing the Speech Outline" on the Express menu. You can now review what you did in each of the preparation steps. You may also check for errors in spelling and formatting.

Save your file to your hard drive, and print it out so that you can work with it offline. You may also e-mail it to your instructor if that is requested. As you continue to think about your speech, you may return to Speech Builder Express at any time to modify your outline and notes.

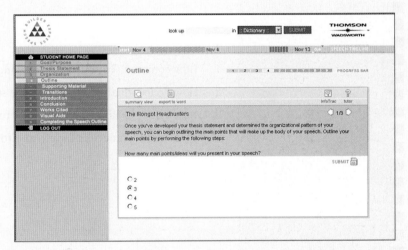

CHAPTER 16

Informative Speaking

Focus Questions

1. How common is informative speaking?
2. How do informative and persuasive speaking differ?
3. How can I increase listeners' desire to learn information?
4. What ethical guidelines apply to informative speaking?

O ur era has been called "the information age." To live and work effectively in this time, we need to know how to share information with others—in the workplace, in social situations, and in community and civic contexts (Maxwell & McCain, 1997). Skill at informative speaking is critical if you want to be effective personally, professionally, and socially.

This chapter focuses on informative speaking. Much of what you've learned from previous chapters applies to your study of informative speaking. In Part I of this book, you studied principles of effective verbal and nonverbal communication, how to understand and adapt to cultural differences, and how to foster friendly, supportive climates for interaction. In addition, Chapters 13, 14, and 15 introduced you to the basics of planning, researching, supporting, organizing and delivering speeches.

Building on what you've already learned, this chapter guides you through the process of developing and presenting an effective informative speech. We will first highlight the importance of this kind of speaking in everyday life and note how it differs from persuasive speaking, which we will cover in Chapter 17. Next, we'll discuss guidelines for effective informative speaking. To conclude the chapter, there is a sample informative speech.

The Nature of Informative Speaking

Informative speeches are presentations, the goal of which is to increase others' knowledge, understanding, or abilities. For instance, you might give an informative speech that aims to increase listeners' understanding of how campus elections work, add to their knowledge of political candidates, or teach them how to cast votes (Table 16.1). Competence in informative speaking is important if you plan to coach sports, be part of neighborhood and civic groups, and succeed in your profession (Morreale, Osborn, & Pearson, 2000).

Informative Speaking in Everyday Life

It's likely that you'll give a number of speeches in your life. Many of them—probably the majority—will be informative speeches. Some will be formal,

Communication Highlight

The Information Age

More people around the world have greater access to more information than ever before in human history (Maxwell & McCain, 1997; Wurman, 1989). Satellite connections let us see and hear real-time coverage of an earthquake in Japan, a terrorist attack in Iraq, a daring rescue of a climber trapped on Everest, and the birth of six babies to a mother in Canada. Computers allow us to access the web and the Internet to follow news stories, chat with people around the globe, order products and services, and research topics from routine to esoteric.

The wealth of information available today is a mixed blessing. It gives us access to unprecedented amounts of information. Yet we can easily feel overwhelmed by the endless stream of data that bombard us. This suggests that speakers need to help listeners sift and sort. Informative speeches should make it easy for listeners to follow ideas, connect bits of information, and recognize which information is most important.

Table 16.1: **Types of Informative Speeches**

Type	Sample Specific Purpose
Demonstration	To show listeners how to construct a speech outline
Instruction	To teach listeners how to perform CPR
Description	To describe the people and land of Nepal
Explanation	To explain why (or how) hurricanes form
Briefing	To summarize the results of a new marketing strategy
Reporting	To provide detailed information on the results of a new marketing strategy

many will be informal, but all will focus on conveying information to others. Consider these examples of everyday informative speaking:

- You need to explain a new procedure to a continuous quality improvement team at your company.
- You want to teach scouts how to start a fire without matches.
- You want to inform others in your neighborhood association about a Community Watch program that's decreased burglaries in other neighborhoods.
- Your supervisor asks you to brief stakeholders on the new strategic plan your firm is implementing.
- You want to describe a new offensive strategy to the Little League team you coach.
- You want to tell a civic group about traditions in your culture.
- You want to teach a group of friends how to prepare a complicated dessert.
- You want to report to your co-workers on what you learned at a conference so that so that they understand new developments in your field.

Sharpen Your Skill

Informative Speaking in Your Life

How common is informative speaking in your everyday life? For the next week, keep a record of the informative speeches you hear (those given by others), grouped into the four categories listed here. Remember that an informative speech need not be long—it may be just a couple of minutes in which someone teaches you how to do something or explains a new procedure, describes a rule or policy, or tells you the background of an issue.

1. Informative speaking in classes

2. Informative speaking on the job

3. Informative speaking with friends

4. Other informative speaking

Table 16.2: **Informative versus Persuasive Speaking**

1. Persuasive speeches tend to have more controversial purposes.

2. Persuasive speeches seek more powerful responses from listeners.

3. Persuasive speeches need greater degrees of proof.

4. Persuasive speeches require earning greater amounts of credibility.

Comparing Informative and Persuasive Speaking

Informative speaking and persuasive speaking are different from each other, yet they have much in common. Both require research, organization, supporting material, and delivery. There are also overlaps between informative and persuasive goals. For example, in an informative speech, you are trying to persuade listeners to attend to what you say and to care about learning. In **persuasive speeches,** you need to inform listeners about certain issues in order to influence their values, attitudes, or behaviors.

Four differences between informative and persuasive speaking are particularly important (See Table 16.2).

The Controversial Nature of the Purpose   Informative speeches tend to have less controversial purposes than persuasive speeches. Something is controversial when it can be debated or argued—in other words, when not everyone is likely to agree or accept it. Typically, informative presentations don't present highly controversial ideas. They generally aim to give listeners new information: to teach, explain, or describe a person, object, event, process, or relationship. Persuasive speeches, on the other hand, aim to change listeners' attitudes, beliefs, or behaviors.

Obviously, information can have persuasive impact, so it can be controversial. Yet the degree to which a purpose is controversial is much greater in persuasive speeches. An informative speech might have the specific purpose of describing the historical conditions that led to establishment of affirmative action policies. A persuasive speech on the same topic might have the specific purpose of persuading listeners to support or oppose affirmative action policies. Clearly, the latter purpose is more controversial than the former.

The Response Sought   Related to their differing purposes are the responses informative and persuasive speeches seek from listeners. In the affirmative action example, the speaker giving an informative speech wants listeners to understand certain historical conditions. The speaker giving a persuasive speech wants listeners to believe that affirmative action is right or wrong, justified or not justified, beneficial or harmful. The persuasive speaker might even want to persuade listeners to take specific actions to oppose or support affirmative action at local, regional, or national levels. In seeking to change listeners in some way, persuasive speeches seek a more powerful response: change rather than acceptance of new information.

The Degree of Evidence Needed   Because persuasive speeches tend to be more controversial and seek to convince listeners to change in some way, they generally need stronger supporting material than informative speeches do. This does not mean that informative speeches don't need proof. They do. If you give an informative speech on the historical conditions leading up to the establishment of affirmative action policies, you might present various evidence to help listeners understand the points in your speech: statistics and examples to document the extent of discrimination, quotations from people who faced discrimination, and analogies to compare racial discrimination to other kinds of discrimination. Each type of supporting material helps you achieve your purpose of informing listeners.

However, an effective persuasive speech on the same topic generally must include more supporting material. Why? Because listeners expect more evidence when they are being asked to think, feel, or act differently from when they are being asked only to understand something. Listeners will want convincing evidence not only that discrimination exists and is wrong but also that affirmative action policies are an effective response to the problem.

In persuasive speeches, speakers also have a responsibility to anticipate and address their listeners' reservations. Doing this effectively requires evidence. Perhaps in researching public opinions on affirmative action, you learn that the most common objection is based on the assumption that it lowers standards for admission to schools and professions. To persuade listeners to support affirmative action, you should present evidence that shows that standards have not declined in institutions that follow affirmative action policies.

–Vince–

Last week, I went to hear a speaker on capital punishment. He was trying to convince us that we should abolish it, but I wasn't convinced. What he mainly did was to inform us that there are cases where innocent people are convicted or even put to death. But he never showed us—or me, anyway—that abolishing capital punishment is the answer. Why can't we just reform it, like, require absolute proof of guilt before someone can be sentenced to die? And what about all the people who really are guilty of horrible things, like school killings or the Oklahoma bombing? Shouldn't they be sentenced to death? He never talked about that.

The Importance of Credibility   Credibility is important to any speaker's effectiveness. As with evidence, however, the credibility a speaker needs varies with the speaking purpose. In general, a speaker attempting to change people needs more credibility than a speaker who seeks only to inform them. The reason is simple: Because the persuasive speaker asks more of listeners than the informative speaker does, the listeners expect more credibility of the speaker.

Whereas an informative speech usually presents noncontroversial information, a persuasive speech asks listeners to think, feel, or act differently. Thus, persuasive speakers have a greater responsibility to convince listeners that they (the speakers) have the personal integrity and expertise to merit listeners' belief in them and what they advocate. Because credibility is so important in persuasive speaking, we will discuss it in depth in Chapter 17.

In summary, compared to informative speeches, persuasive presentations tend to have more controversial purposes, seek more powerful responses from listeners, need greater amounts of evidence, and require that speakers earn greater levels of credibility in listeners' minds. Each of these differences is a matter of degree, not an absolute contrast.

Guidelines for Effective Informative Speaking

Eight guidelines are particularly important for informative speeches.

Provide Listeners with a Clear Thesis Statement

As we noted in Chapter 13, listeners want to know why they are listening—what they are supposed to get out of the informative speech. Only then can they focus their listening. When giving an informative presentation, the speaker should state a simple, clear thesis that tells listeners what the speech will provide or do. The thesis should motivate listeners by alerting them that the information to come will be useful to them. As you'll recall from previous chapters, a good thesis is clear and direct: "At the end of my talk, you will understand the different citizen responsibilities and effects of three popular Neighborhood Watch programs used in our county." Upon hearing this thesis, listeners know exactly what the speaker plans to give them and what they should get out of listening.

Connect with Listeners' Values and Experiences

As with all communication, informative speeches should build connections with listeners. Speakers should learn what listeners know about a topic. This allows a speaker to avoid telling them what they already know and to connect the topic with listeners' values and experiences. For instance, in a speech with the specific purpose of describing alternative Neighborhood Watch programs, a speaker might open by saying, "I know we share a concern for safety in our neighborhood. What I want to do is describe the three Neighborhood Watch programs in our county so that we can make an informed choice about what is right for our community." This opening

This chef is giving an informative speech that includes humor.

This speaker uses nonverbal behaviors to connect with listeners.

establishes common ground between the speaker and listeners by noting that they "share a concern" and by using *we* language: "our neighborhood," "we can make," "our community." Another way the speaker could open the speech is by saying, "I know several of you have been burglarized in the last year." To connect with listeners' values, the speaker might say, "We all want to feel that our homes are safe from intrusion. We have a right to that."

Motivate Listeners to Want Information

Information is so pervasive today that we screen much of it out (Wurman, 1989). For an informative speech to be effective, listeners must be motivated to want what the speaker is providing. In some cases, listeners are motivated for their own reasons. For instance, listeners will attend a nonrequired CPR class because they want to learn how to perform CPR. They are already motivated.

In other cases, the speaker may need to motivate people to want information. For example, a supervisor may need to fuel employees' hunger for information on a new procedure that the company wants them to follow. In this situation, the supervisor might say, "I know we all get tired of learning new procedures, but the one I'm going to explain today will make your jobs easier and increase your productivity." This statement motivates employees to listen, especially if their pay is based on their productivity. Notice that the statement also recognizes that listeners have been asked to learn numerous procedures and that it can get tiring.

–Mandy–

I went to the placement office the other day for a workshop on interviewing. I wasn't really interested, but I thought I should go, so I was just kind of there but not really paying attention. Then the facilitator got us started. The first thing she said was that students who attended these workshops tended to get more and better job offers than students who don't. That definitely got my attention! From then on, I was listening very carefully and taking lots of notes.

Build Credibility with Listeners

As we've noted, for the speaker to be effective, listeners must perceive him or her as credible. When giving an informative speech, you should demonstrate that you have some expertise relevant to your topic. You may show you have personal experience ("I took a CPR course"). You may also demonstrate to listeners that you have gained information in other ways ("To prepare to talk to you today, I spoke with emergency room doctors about people who died but could have been saved with CPR").

You'll also want to show listeners that you care about them or that the information you are offering will help them in some way. You might say, "This information will come in handy when you start interviewing for jobs." You might also show goodwill by explaining how the information you are presenting has helped you, and let your listeners infer that it might help them too ("My sister would have drowned last year if I hadn't known how to give CPR. It can help any of us save lives").

Adapt to Diverse Listeners

In our diverse society, few audiences are homogeneous. For the informative speaker, this implies that it is important to speak in ways that include and respect diverse experiences, values, and viewpoints. People whose homes have been burglarized have an experience different from those whose homes have not been burglarized. People who believe in nonviolence as a way of life differ in key respects from people who believe that everyone has a right to use violence to protect themselves and their property. Citizens who were raised in highly communal cultures are likely to be more inclined toward communal efforts to protect a neighborhood than are people who were raised in highly individualistic cultures. Families without children may have different security concerns from families with children, especially young ones.

–Dimitri–

I am looking for a new car, so I went to a dealership. I was looking at a model that Consumer Reports *said has the highest safety rating. Then the salesman came over and started talking about the car I was looking at. His pitch was that it was cheap and fuel efficient. I asked him a couple of questions about safety issues, which are my primary concerns with cars, and he just brushed them back and kept telling me how economical it was. He lost that sale.*

A quotation from Jesus will have more impact with Christians than with Muslims. A quotation from Charlton Heston will carry more weight with conservatives than with liberals. Some people think more visually than others, so it's wise to include both visual aids and nonvisual supporting materials.

Organize So Listeners Can Follow Easily

From our discussion in Chapter 7, we know that listening is hard work. When giving an informative talk, a speaker should do all that she or he can to reduce the amount of work listeners have to invest. Applying the principles we discussed in Chapter 15, this means that you should structure your speech clearly. As we learned, your introduction should capture listeners' attention ("Would you like to increase your productivity and paychecks by 10%?"), provide a clear thesis ("I'm going to explain a new procedure that will increase your efficiency and income"), and preview what will be covered ("I will demonstrate a new method of sorting and routing stock and show how much faster and more accurate it is than the method you've been using").

Transitions should be woven throughout the speech to assist listeners in following the flow of ideas. The conclusion should summarize key points ("I've shown you how to increase your paycheck") and end

Few audiences today are homogeneous.

© Michael Newman/PhotoEdit

with a strong idea or punch ("In this case, what's good for the company IS also good for you").

The body of an informative speech should also be organized clearly (Table 16.3). Some of the patterns we discussed in Chapter 15 are especially well adapted to informative speeches. Time and spatial patterns can be very effective for speeches that aim to demonstrate, describe, explain, or teach ("In my speech, I will describe how fetuses develop in the first, second, and third trimesters"; "I want to explain how leg and arm positions at the keyboard affect the back and neck"). Topical patterns are commonly used for reports and briefings that address several areas of a topic ("I want to summarize developments in our sales and marketing divisions").

When introducing new or alternative ideas or procedures, the comparative pattern can be effective ("The new method of sorting and routing stock differs from our current method in two key ways").

Although they are less commonly used in informative presentations, problem–solution and cause–effect or effect–cause patterns can be good choices. For instance, an informative speech might explain how a new procedure for sorting and routing stock solves a problem. The same topic might be organized using a cause–effect pattern to show that the new procedure (cause) will increase productivity (effect).

Table 16.3: Organizing Informative Speeches

Specific Purpose	Thesis	Organizational Pattern
Listeners will learn how to recognize differences between poisonous and nonpoisonous plants.	I will teach you how to tell which plants are safe to eat.	Comparison/contrast
Team members will know management's response to our strategic plan.	I want to summarize the feedback from management on our goals and implementation strategies.	Topical
To teach friends how I make crème brûlée.	I am going to take you through the steps involved in making a perfect crème brûlée.	Time
Employees will understand the reasons for a new procedure for sorting and routing stock.	I want to explain how the new procedure we're going to start using solves problems that have frustrated us for years.	Problem–solution

Like all other types of speeches, effective informative presentations highlight key points so they stand out to listeners. Also, smooth transitions should be developed to connect points in a speech.

 Speech Builder Express, which you can access directly through your *Communication in Our Lives* CD-ROM, includes extensive prompts and a clear framework for organizing and developing speeches that incorporate a variety of informative strategies.

Design Your Speech to Enhance Learning and Retention

Much of the information that we need in order to do our jobs and live our lives is not particularly interesting. This poses a challenge for you when you give an informative speech. The informative speaker is responsible for making material interesting to listeners. In addition, information can be complex and difficult to grasp, particularly in oral presentations. This creates a second challenge for informative speakers: You must do all you can to increase the clarity of the information. Five strategies can help you make your information interesting and clear.

Limit the Information You Present Most of us can understand and remember only so much information at a time. By the time you are ready to give an informative speech, you know a great deal about the topic. It's your job to sort through all that you know to make good choices about two or three points you want to make. You may think five points are important. If you try to present all five, however, you risk having listeners remember none or the less important ones.

If you must cover more than two or three points to inform listeners fully, then you have two choices. You may give multiple informative talks, separated by time to allow listeners to absorb and apply the information you've provided before they get more. A second option is to rely on other principles of increasing clarity and interest that we discuss later in this chapter.

Move from Familiar to Unfamiliar   It's normal to feel uneasy when you are asked to understand new information or learn a new process or skill. Speakers can reduce this anxiety by starting with what is familiar to listeners and moving to what is new. For instance, the supervisor in our example might open an informative speech by saying, "All of you know the sorting and routing procedure we've used for years. The new procedure extends what you already know. What you've done in the past is to sort incoming stock into three piles. From now on, you'll be sorting it into four. It's the same process—just one more pile." Upon hearing this, listeners realize that their basic sorting process is not being abandoned; it is only getting more complex. The skills they already have will transfer.

Repeat Important Ideas   Repetition is a powerful way to increase retention (Thompson & Grundgenett, 1999). Have you ever been introduced to someone and not recalled the person's name 5 minutes later? That's because you heard it only once. The introduction probably was like this: "Pat, I'd like you to meet Leigh." If the person doing the introduction had wanted to help you remember Leigh's name, it would have been better to say this: "Pat, I'd like you to meet Leigh. Leigh and I go way back; we met in our sophomore year. We got together when Leigh and I were trying out for the chorus and Leigh got a place when I didn't." In that short introduction Leigh's name was mentioned four times. You'll probably remember it. You're more likely to remember something you hear three times than something you hear only once.

The same principle applies to informative speaking. As an illustration, let's return to our supervisor. It's important that employees retain the new classifications into which they will be sorting stock, so these bear repeating: "In the past you've sorted stock into new, returns, and used. As most of you know, the stock we've been putting in the return pile has really been of two types: stock that was missing something and stock that was defective. Now we're breaking returns into two separate piles: ones with missing parts and ones with defective parts. So we have missings and defects. The missing pile is for stock that is missing a part. We can fix these items by adding the missing part. The defect pile is for stock that has something wrong with it, usually a defective part. So missings and defects are the new piles we want to use." The repeated references to *missings* and *defects* increase listeners' ability to understand and retain the new classifications for stock.

Sharpen Your Skill

Practicing Repetition for Retention

Apply the principle of repetition in your daily activities for the next three days to see how it affects your retention of new information.

When you meet a new person, work his or her name into conversation at least three times in your initial interaction.

After each class you attend, repeat the main information provided three times. (Tip: Repeat the information out loud so that you hear it as well as see it in your notes.)

If you have a job, repeat what your supervisor or customers say to yourself. For instance, if you wait tables, mentally repeating customers' orders will help you remember them.

Highlight Key Material Do you become more attentive in class when a teacher says, "This next point is really important," or "You're likely to see this on the test"? Probably you do. That's what the teacher intends. He or she is highlighting key material to get your attention. In this example, the teacher highlighted by framing. "This material is important" is a frame that calls your attention to important material.

"This material is important."

MATERIAL

There are other ways to highlight key material. You might say something direct, such as, "Listen up. This is important." Or you might say, "I hope you'll really tune in to this next point." You could also say, "If you remember only one thing from my talk, it should be this: . . ." All of these give verbal clues to listeners that you are presenting especially important material.

You can also provide nonverbal clues to highlight key material. Raising volume or inflection tends to capture interest, so listeners are likely to listen more carefully when a speaker alters volume or inflection. Gestures can also emphasize the importance of key ideas. You can change your position— move from behind a podium to in front of it, move from sitting to standing—to draw listeners' attention.

Rely on Multiple Communication Channels If a speaker says, "Red berries often are poisonous," you might get the point. You'd be more likely to get it and retain it if the speaker made that statement and also showed you pictures of red berries or gave you red berries. When we use multiple channels to communicate, we increase the likelihood that listeners will learn and retain new information.

When you're presenting a lot of information or complex information, handouts can greatly increase listeners' retention and ability to use new information. Listeners both hear the talk and see the notes summarizing key points. Visual aids can also highlight information. The supervisor in our example might develop a visual aid to show the two new classifications that grow out of the one former one (Figure 16.1). Showing this while also talking about the two new classifications lets listeners learn and retain through two senses: eyes and ears. The visual aid would be especially effective if the two new classifications stood out visually. They might be larger or in a different, striking color.

Involve Listeners

Have you ever been a passenger when someone else was driving and later not been sure

Figure 16.1
Visual Aid to Illustrate a New Procedure

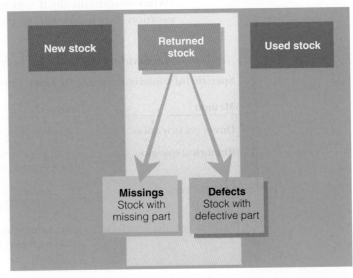

"Hard to believe he flunked public speaking."

how to get back to where the two of you went? If you drive yourself, there's a greater likelihood that you'll learn how to get to the place. This common experience reminds us that we learn best when we do something ourselves rather than just hear about it. Involvement generates active learning, and that's critical to effective informative speaking. There are many ways to involve listeners in informative speeches. We'll highlight four of the most effective.

Call for Participation You might give sticks to scouts and get them to try rubbing them together as you demonstrate how to do this to start a fire (but only if fire codes allow this and if you can control possible danger). You might let people try a new procedure at a demonstration stand you set up. You might bring plants that are poisonous and nonpoisonous so that listeners can see, smell, and touch them as you describe how they differ.

Sometimes speakers can't have listeners participate directly. Perhaps it isn't feasible to set up a model for the new sorting and routing procedure. Perhaps you can't let scouts try making fire because the fire code prevents this. In such cases, effective speakers involve listeners in other ways (Table 16.4).

Ask Rhetorical Questions One way to involve listeners when direct participation is impossible is to ask rhetorical questions. These are questions that a speaker doesn't actually expect listeners to answer. By asking them, however, a speaker invites listeners' mental participation: They are likely to answer rhetorical questions silently in their heads. This allows listeners to feel as if they are interacting with the speaker and personally involved with the topics. "How many of you have ever wished you had an extra $100?" "What would you do if you made 20% more each week? Would you take a vacation, buy a new car, or pay some bills?"

Table 16.4: Generating a Sense of Listener Participation

Specific Informative Purpose: To Teach Listeners How to Recognize Poisonous Plants.

Method	Example
Direct participation	I want each of you to smell the berries I'm handing out.
Rhetorical question	If you were stranded on a camping trip, would you know how to survive?
Poll listeners	How many of you have ever pulled a ripe berry off a bush and wondered if it was safe to eat?
Refer to specific listeners	Jane, remember when you watched Tom Hanks in *Castaway* and wondered how he knew what was safe to eat on the island?

Poll Listeners Another way to involve listeners is to ask questions that poll listeners to find out what they think, feel, or want or what experiences they have had. This allows you as a speaker to motivate them to want the information you are going to present. "How many of you have ever left your home for a vacation and worried about whether someone was going to break into it?" "How many of you would like to earn $100 more a week?" Speakers can ask for audible responses ("If you have had this experience, say 'yes'") or a show of hands ("Let me see the hands of everyone who has had this experience").

Refer to Specific Listeners To involve listeners you may also speak directly to or about particular members of your audience. Ethically, you must be careful not to speak to or about others in ways that could embarrass them or would reveal information they consider private. In many cases, you can honor this ethical principle and still speak to or about specific listeners to generate a sense of participation and community. "Bill and Sally, we've all heard about the break-in at your house." "Just the other day, I overheard Ed talking about what he'd do if he won the lottery. Well, Ed, I've got good news for you: You may not win the lottery, but you can get more money." Comments such as these create a sense of participation and interaction.

Use Effective and Ethical Supporting Materials

Figure 16.2
Visual Aid to Motivate Employees

To be effective in informing listeners, speeches must include supporting material that is both effective and ethical. Effective supporting materials add interest and clarity to a speech. Ethical supporting materials present accurate information fairly and without distortion (Lehman & DuFrene, 1999).

Returning to our previous example, the supervisor might create a bar graph to provide a vivid visual comparison of productivity using the current and new procedures for sorting and routing stock. Quotes from employees at other firms that use the new procedure would add additional support, particularly because listeners are likely to believe what peer-workers say about a new procedure. Statistics also can be effective if they are made interesting to listeners.

In our example, the speaker might take the average employee's salary and show how much it should go up using the new procedure. The speaker might develop a visual aid to show how that increase would multiply over a period of time (Figure 16.2). This

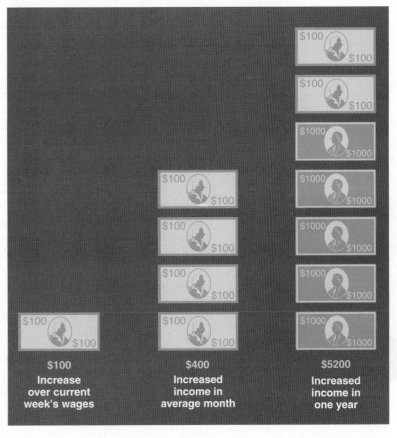

would add interest and motivate listeners to pay close attention and learn the new procedure.

To be ethical, supporting material should meet the criteria we discussed in Chapter 14 (see Table 14.3 on page 383). To review, supporting material should be sufficient to achieve the speaking purpose, such as teaching or describing (sufficiency); accurate, correct and complete, with sources cited, presented in its original context (accuracy); relevant to the topic and claims made (relevance); timely, usually current or in some cases historically situated (timeliness); and free of biases, such as vested interests (impartiality).

Using these criteria, it would be ethical for the speaker to tell employees that their wages should increase an average of 20% only if the speaker had adequate data to support that claim (the criterion of accuracy). If only 25% of employees who have used the new procedure increase their productivity, it would not be ethical to state that they could expect to increase their wages, because only one in four could reasonably expect that. If most employees do increase their productivity by 20% but only after 4 to 6 months of adjusting to the new procedure, the speaker would be ethically obligated to inform them of the time lag (the criterion of timeliness). If employees who use the new procedure at other plants have different working conditions and tools, the change in their productivity might not generalize to the listeners in this case (the criterion of relevance).

Experiencing Communication in Our Lives

CASE STUDY: Informative Speech: The Black Box

The following speech excerpt (and the rest of the speech from which it's taken) is featured on the *Communication in Our Lives* CD-ROM included with this book. Once you've launched the CD, click on the "Speech Interactive" icon, and, from the Speech Menu, select "Informative Speech" to watch the audiovisual presentation of Michael Daniels's speech. To read a full description of Michael's assignment, click on the "Assignment" button. Improve your own public speaking skills by reading, watching, listening to, evaluating, and critiquing this sample speech.

Analyze the speech by applying the principles covered in this chapter, and respond to the prompts that accompany the video, which you can access by clicking on "Evaluation" and "Critique." After answering the evaluation questions and writing a brief critique of the speech, you can click on the "Done" button to compare your responses with the ones I suggest. Additional analysis questions are available in print at the end of this chapter and on the book's website.

Michael delivered this speech at the California Community College Forensics Association Annual Tournament. Because this informative speech was presented outside of a class, references are not presented as they would be in a standard outline.

Jason Harris/© 2001 Wadsworth

The crew of Alaska Air 261 struggled desperately to correct a problem with the aircraft's horizontal stabilizers. But by the time they realized the true scope of the problem, it was too late, and the aircraft spiraled into the Pacific Ocean, killing all 88 people on board. But how do we know this? Certainly not from any eyewitness accounts—everybody on board the flight perished. The source of this information, according to *Newsweek*, February 14, 1999, is a device of which most people have heard but of which very few know very much. The source of this information is none other than the black box.

CNN, April 15, 1999, tells us that the black box has been responsible in literally thousands of air crashes, both in discovering their cause as well as in determining what must be done in the future so that the same failure is not repeated. My purpose today is first to explain some features and functions of the black box, second to explore its current status, and third to elucidate some of the new and upcoming developments stemming from its technology.

Chapter Summary

In this chapter, we've focused on informative speaking, which is part of most people's lives. We described the many types of informative speeches and noted how informative speaking differs from persuasive speaking. We then highlighted eight guidelines for effective informative speaking. Because these guidelines are at the heart of the impact of your informative presentations, we'll summarize them here:

1. Provide listeners with a clear thesis statement.
2. Connect with listeners' values and experiences.
3. Motivate listeners to want information.
4. Incorporate diverse perspectives.
5. Organize so listeners can follow easily.
6. Design your speech to enhance learning and retention.
7. Involve listeners.
8. Use effective and ethical supporting materials.

If you follow these eight guidelines and apply the principles we've discussed in previous chapters, you should be able to give effective informative speeches.

 ## Communication in Our Lives ONLINE

In addition to presenting the case studies' multimedia scenarios and speeches, the *Communication in Our Lives* CD-ROM provides quick access to the *Communication in Our Lives* website, Speech Builder Express, and InfoTrac College Edition. The website is online at http://communication.wadsworth.com/woodciol4, but you can access this book's premium web content only when you link to the site directly through the book's CD.

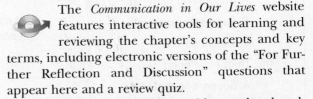 The *Communication in Our Lives* website features interactive tools for learning and reviewing the chapter's concepts and key terms, including electronic versions of the "For Further Reflection and Discussion" questions that appear here and a review quiz.

The website also provides updated web links and additional InfoTrac College Edition activities. If required, you can e-mail completed chapter activities or the quizzes to your instructor.

Key Concepts

For Further Reflection and Discussion

1. Use your InfoTrac College Edition to read Ruth Bader Ginsburg's speech (in *Vital Speeches*) "The Supreme Court," delivered on May 1, 2001. What organizational pattern does she use? Does the introduction capture attention and tell listeners what to expect in the speech? Is this speech informative, persuasive, or both?

2. Attend an informative speech on campus or in the community. Identify the thesis, organizational pattern. Evaluate the ethical and strategic quality of the speaker's evidence.

3. To find quotations that are relevant to your speech, visit the Quotations Home Page at http://usgeocities.yahoo.com/search?p=quotes.

4. Complete the outline on this page for your informative speech. Provide a complete citation for each source you use.

5. Use the evaluation form on page 443 to evaluate Michael Daniels's speech on black boxes.

Informative Speech Outline

General Purpose:

Specific Purpose:

Introduction

    I. Attention device

    II. Motivation for listening

    III. Thesis statement

    IV. Preview of speech

    Transition to body of speech

Body

    I. First main point

        A. Supporting material

        B. Supporting material

        C. Transition

    II. Second main point

        A. Supporting material

        B. Supporting material

        C. Transition

    III. Third main point

        A. Supporting material

        B. Supporting material

        C. Transition

    Transition to conclusion

You may have only two main points.

You may have more than two kinds of supporting material for main points.

Conclusion

    I. Summary of main points

    II. Strong closing statement

References

Evaluation Form for Informative Speeches

Speaker's Name: _____   Date: _____

Speech Topic: _____

_____

1. Did the speaker capture listeners' initial attention? _____

    _____

2. Did the speaker motivate listeners to want information? _____

    _____

3. Did the speaker state a clear thesis? _____

    _____

4. Did the speaker preview the body of the speech? _____

    _____

5. Was the speech structured clearly and appropriately? _____

    _____

6. Were strong transitions provided between parts of the speech and main points in the body of the speech?

    _____

7. Did the speaker provide effective supporting material? _____

    _____

8. Did the speaker use ethical supporting material? _____

    _____

9. Did the speaker involve listeners directly by polling them, asking rhetorial questions, or speaking to or about

    particular listeners? _____

10. Did the speaker use strategies to enhance listeners' learning and retention? _____

    _____

11. Did the speaker connect the topic to listeners' experiences and values? _____

    _____

12. Did the conclusion summarize main points of the speech? _____

    _____

13. Did the speech end on a strong note? _____

    _____

Experiencing Communication in Our Lives

Questions for Analysis and Discussion

 Review the video of Michael's speech that you watched when completing this chapter's case study (pages 440–441), or, if you haven't seen it yet, watch it for the first time. If you didn't previously finish the "Evaluation" questions and "Critique" activity included on the CD-ROM, do so now, and then respond to the following questions, which are also available on the book's website under "Activities for Chapter 16."

1. Did Michael Daniels effectively capture your attention at the beginning of his speech?

2. Did the preview forecast coverage adequately?

3. Did he provide effective and ethical evidence to support his ideas?

4. Were there good transitions between main points?

5. Did the conclusion summarize main points in the speech?

Speech Builder Express

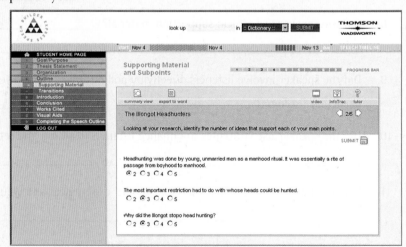

Access Speech Builder Express with the user name and the password that came with the CD-ROM that accompanies your textbook. Click "Resume" to pull up the file for your informative speech.

Review your speech outline, and refine it to reflect your ongoing work on the speech. Also review your references. Be sure to check for errors in spelling and formatting. You're ready to print out your outline and begin practicing your informative speech. As you practice, you may find you want to make further revisions. Just return to Speech Builder Express, type in the changes, and print out the new outline.

CHAPTER 17

Persuasive Speaking

Focus Questions

1. What are the three bases of persuasion?
2. What organizational structures are most effective for persuasive speeches?
3. When is a one-sided speech more persuasive than a two-sided?
4. How do speakers manage hostile audiences?

- You want to convince others to vote for a candidate in whom you believe deeply.

- You need to persuade your staff to embrace a new management philosophy.

- As the coach of a soccer team, you want to talk to the teenage players about the dangers of drugs and persuade them not to experiment.

- You want members of your fraternity to commit to a community service project.

- You want to persuade your friends to become organ donors.

- You want to convince the town council not to build a commercial center on the edge of your neighborhood.

Welcome to persuasive speaking. Although most of us won't give persuasive speeches regularly, nearly all of us will do so at times. In some cases, we'll be asked to make persuasive presentations. For instance, your manager might want you to persuade a potential client that your firm can provide the best service. In other cases, your values and commitments will compel you to speak in an effort to persuade others to ideas or actions that you think are right or desirable.

This chapter focuses on persuasive speaking. As you'll discover, much of what you've learned in previous chapters applies to persuasive speaking. Building on that knowledge, in this chapter we'll begin by defining persuasive speaking. Second, we'll discuss three cornerstones of persuasion and ways to build your credibility as a speaker. Next, we'll identify organizational patterns that are particularly effective for persuasive speeches. Fourth, we'll identify guidelines for effective persuasive speaking.

Understanding Persuasive Speaking

Persuasive speeches aim to change others by prompting them to think, feel, believe, or act differently. You may want to change people's attitudes toward policies, candidates for office, or groups of people. You may want to alter the strength of others' attitudes for or against particular issues. You may want to convince people to feel differently about the customs of immigrants. You may want to change how people act, perhaps convince them to quit smoking, to use seatbelts, to donate blood, or to volunteer for community service. In each case, your goal is persuasive: You aim to change the people with whom you speak.

In thinking about persuasive speaking, it's important to keep three characteristics in mind (Table 17.1). First, like all other communication, persuasive speaking involves multiple communicators. The transactional model of communication we discussed in Chapter 1 is as relevant to persuasive speaking as it is to other kinds of communication. Effective persuasion is not something speakers do to listeners. Instead, it is engagement between a speaker and listeners. Although the speaker may be in the spotlight, the listeners are very much part of effective persuasive speaking, from planning to delivery. Speakers should consider listeners' experiences, expectations, values, and attitudes when they first think about topics and how to approach them.

In developing strong persuasive speeches, speakers need to keep listeners in mind: What kinds of evidence will they find impressive? Which experts

Table 17.1: Qualities of Persuasive Speaking

- Speaker and listeners interact.
- It is not coercive.
- Its effect usually is incremental or gradual.

will they respect? What is likely to lead these particular listeners to respect the speaker? In delivering persuasive speeches, speakers need to establish and maintain visual and personal connections with listeners and respond to feedback. After a persuasive speech, listeners may ask questions. Effective speakers respond in an open-minded manner that demonstrates respect for listeners. Throughout persuasive speaking, then, speakers and listeners are engaged in transactional communication.

Second, remember that persuasion is not coercion or force. The great rhetorical scholar Aristotle distinguished between what he called inartistic proofs and artistic proofs. An inartistic proof doesn't require any art or skill on our part. We don't have to consider or respect others to get what we want using inartistic proofs. For instance, if you hold a gun to someone's head and say, "Give me your money or I'll shoot you," you may get the money. In that sense, you've been effective (although you might wind up in jail). However, you haven't been artistic, and you haven't engaged in persuasion. To do that, you would need to give the other person convincing reasons to give you the money. You would use reasons and words to motivate, not force, the other person to do what you want. Persuasion relies on artistic, not inartistic, proofs.

Third, persuasive impact usually is gradual and incremental. Although sometimes people's positions undergo rapid, radical shifts, usually we move gradually toward new ideas, attitudes, and actions. When we hear a persuasive speech, we compare its arguments with our experience and knowledge. If the speaker offers strong arguments, good evidence, and coherent organization, we may shift our attitudes or behaviors to some degree. If we later encounter

additional persuasion, we may shift our attitudes further. Over time and with repeated persuasion, we may change our attitude or behaviors.

Because persuasion tends to happen gradually and incrementally, speakers should understand the attitudes and behaviors of listeners and adapt their persuasive goals accordingly. For example, assume you believe that the role of the Electoral College, in national elections should be abandoned, and you want to persuade others to your point of view. How would an effective persuasive speech differ if you knew in advance that listeners strongly favored the current Electoral College system, or if you knew that they already had reservations about it?

Visual aids and dynamic extemporaneous delivery increase persuasive impact.

© Laimute Druskis/Stock Boston

In the first case, it would be unrealistic and ineffective to try to persuade listeners to support repeal of the Electoral College. A more realistic initial speaking goal would be to persuade listeners that there are some disadvantages to the current electoral system. In this instance, you would be effective if you could reduce the strength of their position favoring the Electoral College. Because the second group of listeners already has reservations, you can build on those and lead them closer to supporting repeal of the Electoral College.

The Three Cornerstones of Persuasion

Teachers in ancient Greece and Rome understood that effective speaking, especially persuasive speaking, is essential to democratic societies. Thus, learning to speak effectively and persuasively was central to the education of Greek and Roman citizens. These ancient teachers recognized three cornerstones of persuasion, which are also called three forms of proof, or reasons people are persuaded: These are **ethos, pathos,** and **logos** (Kennedy, 1991). Although these three forms of proof are also important in other kinds of speaking, they assume special prominence when we engage in persuasion (Figure 17.1).

Ethos

Ethos refers to the perceived personal character of the speaker. We are more likely to believe the words of people whom we trust. We tend to attribute high ethos to people if we perceive that

- they have integrity
- they can be trusted
- they have goodwill toward us
- they know what they are talking about
- they are committed to the topic (show enthusiasm, dynamism)

Figure 17.1
The Three Cornerstones of Persuasion

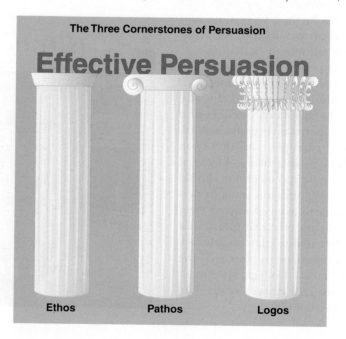

The Three Cornerstones of Persuasion

Effective Persuasion

Ethos   Pathos   Logos

Listeners will have confidence in you and what you say if they think you care about their welfare, are trustworthy, have relevant expertise, care about your topic, and have good character (Stiff, 1994). Conversely, listeners are likely not to place confidence in speakers they think are uniformed, uninvolved with the topic, untrustworthy, manipulative, or otherwise of poor character.

−Carl−

Last year, I had a teacher who didn't know anything about the subject. She made a lot of really vague statements, and when we tried to pin her down on specifics, she would blow off hot air—saying nothing at all. Nobody in the class thought she had any credibility.

Because ethos is critical to persuasive impact, you should do what you can to demonstrate to your listeners that you are of good character. Table 17.2 identifies specific ways that you can influence listeners' perceptions of your ethos.

Pathos

Pathos refers to emotional reasons for attitudes, beliefs or actions. Logic is not the only thing that affects what we believe. We are also influenced by our feelings: passions, fears, love, desire, personal values, shame, compassion, and so forth. Emotional proofs address the more subjective reasons for our beliefs in people, ideas, causes, and courses of action.

In preparing your persuasive presentation, develop ways to help your listeners not just understand your ideas but also feel a certain way about them. You may want them to feel positively about what you advocate. You may want them to feel negatively about some problem you are seeking to solve. You may want them to feel outraged about an injustice, compelled to help others,

Table 17.2: Demonstrating Ethos

Dimensions of Ethos	Ways to Demonstrate
Goodwill	Identify common ground between you and listeners.
	Show respect for listeners' attitudes and experiences.
	Show that what you're saying will benefit them.
Expertise	Provide strong support for your claims.
	Document sources of support.
	Address concerns about or objections to your position.
	Demonstrate personal knowledge of the topic.
Trustworthiness	Use supporting materials ethically.
	Address other points of view fairly.
	Demonstrate that you care about your listeners.
Dynamism	Use appropriate volume and vocal emphasis.
	Assume a confident posture.
	Use gestures and kinesics to enhance forcefulness.
	Be energetic in presentation.

Table 17.3: Enhancing Pathos

Way to Enhance Pathos in Persuasive Speaking	Example
Personalize the issue, problem, or topic.	Include detailed examples.
	Tell stories that give listeners a sense of being in situations, experiencing problems.
	Translate statistics to make them interesting and personal.
Appeal to listeners' needs and values.	Show how your position satisfies listeners' needs, is consistent with their values.
	Use examples familiar to listeners to tie your ideas to their values and experiences.
	Show listeners how doing or believing what you advocate helps them live up to their values.
	Include quotations from people whom listeners respect.
Bring material alive.	Use visual aids to give listeners vivid, graphic understanding of your topic.
	Use striking quotes from people involved with your topic.
	Use active, concrete language to paint verbal pictures.

or afraid of a policy or possibility. Feelings such as these add to the persuasive impact of your speech. Table 17.3 shows particular ways to enhance pathos.

–Melanie–

Last night, I saw an ad on television that asked viewers to help children who were starving in other countries. At first, I paid attention, but it just went over the top. The pictures were so heartbreaking that I just couldn't watch. I felt disgusted and guilty and mainly, mainly what I really felt was turned off.

As Melanie notes, appeals to emotions are powerful—and dangerous. They can easily alienate listeners instead of involving them. Fear and guilt are uncomfortable emotions, so speakers should be very cautious in arousing them. You may want your listeners to fear what will happen if they don't do what you advocate, but you don't want them to be so overwhelmed by fear that they are paralyzed and thus unable to act or to listen to you. Also, fear appeals can decrease a speaker's ethos if listeners are skeptical of the claimed dangers. If you appeal to listeners' fears, do so in moderation. Guilt can also be both aversive and disabling.

Generally, it's more effective to encourage listeners to do something they will feel good about (send money to help starving children overseas) than to berate them for what they are or aren't doing (eating well themselves while others starve). You want to appeal to listeners' emotions to persuade them, not to arouse their emotions for the sake of arousal itself.

Logos

The third reason for belief is logos, which is rational or logical proof. In persuasive speeches, logical proofs are arguments, reasoning, and evidence to support claims.

Forms of Reasoning   Most reasoning can be classified as one or the other of two basic forms. **Inductive reasoning** begins with specific examples and uses them to draw a general conclusion (Faigley & Selzer, 2000). **Deductive reasoning** begins with a conclusion and then supports it by giving specific examples. Suppose you want to present a speech arguing that global temperature change is damaging our environment. To reason inductively, you would start by citing specific places where global climate change is occurring and document the harm in each case. Then you would advance the general conclusion that global climate change threatens life on our planet. Reasoning deductively, you would reverse that order, beginning with the general conclusion and then showing how it is supported by specific cases.

The Toulmin Model   Another way to think about reasoning was originated by philosopher Stephen Toulmin (1958; Toulmin, Rieke, & Janik, 1984). Toulmin explained that logical reasoning consists of three primary components: claims, grounds for the claims, and warrants that connect the claims to the grounds for them. In addition to these three basic parts of logical reasoning, Toulmin's model includes qualifiers and rebuttals. Figure 17.2 shows the **Toulmin model of reasoning.**

The first component of Toulmin's model is the **claim,** which is an assertion. For instance, you might advance this claim: "The death penalty doesn't deter crime." On its own, that claim is not convincing.

To give persuasive impact to a claim, you need to provide some **grounds** for believing it. Grounds are evidence or data that support the claim. As we saw in Chapter 14, evidence includes examples, testimony, statistics, and

Communication Highlight

Inductive and Deductive Reasoning

Inductive	Deductive
	We must act to prevent further global climate change.
Ice is melting on Alaska's North Slope, causing increased temperatures on the plains.	
	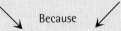 Because
The sea level is rising by 1 inch each year on the eastern coast. As it does, marshlands and barrier islands are being destroyed.	Melting ice on Alaska's North Slope is causing rising temperatures on the plains.
The ozone layer is thinning, allowing more harmful ultraviolet rays to get through. In turn, these cause skin cancer, cataracts, and weakened immune systems.	Rising sea levels on the east coast are destroying marshlands and barrier islands.
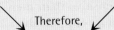 Therefore,	The ozone layer is thinning, allowing more harmful ultraviolet rays to get through. These rays cause skin cancer, cataracts, and weakened immune systems.
We must act to prevent further global climate change.	

analogies. Visual aids may be used to graphically represent examples, statistics, and so forth. For example, you might cite statistical evidence showing that crime did not diminished when certain states enacted the death penalty, or that crime did not rise when certain states repealed the death penalty.

Consider a second example. You assert, or claim, that global climate change is harming the planet. Grounds, or evidence, to support that claim might include statistics to document the occurrence of global climate change, detailed examples of people whose lives have been negatively affected by changes in the earth's temperature, the testimony of distinguished and unbiased scientists, or visual aids that show changes over time. All these kinds of evidence support your claim that global climate change is harming our planet.

Grounds are necessary to support claims. However, they aren't sufficient; the grounds must be justified. That justification is a **warrant,** which explains the relevance of the grounds to the claim. You've probably heard the word *warrant* in connection with law enforcement. If a police officer wants to search the home of Pat Brown, the officer must obtain a search warrant from a judge. The officer shows the judge evidence suggesting that Pat Brown has engaged in criminal activity. If the judge agrees that the evidence links Brown to criminal activity, a search warrant is issued. However, if the judge thinks the evidence is insufficient to link Brown to criminal activity, a warrant is not issued. Warrants operate the same way in persuasive speaking. If listeners perceive your evidence as relevant to and supportive of the claim, they're likely to believe your claim.

Figure 17.2
The Toulmin Model of Reasoning

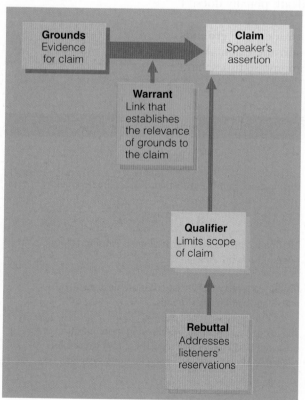

Let's return to a previous example. To support your claim that the death penalty does not deter crime, you provide statistics showing that crime rates did not increase when certain states repealed the death penalty. If the statistics were compiled by the Department of Justice, your listeners may perceive them as justifying the claim. On the other hand, if the statistics were compiled by an organization that opposes the death penalty, your listeners might perceive the source of the evidence as biased and therefore not trustworthy. In that case, there would not be a warrant to justify linking the evidence to the claim.

A **qualifier** is a word or phrase that limits the scope of your claim. "Women are more interpersonally sensitive than men" is a very broad claim—so broad that it is difficult to support. A more supportable claim would be qualified: "In general, women are more interpersonally sensitive than men," or "Some women are more sensitive than some men," or "In many situations, women tend to be more interpersonally sensitive than men." The three qualified claims are more supportable.

Finally, Toulmin's model includes **rebuttal,** which anticipates and addresses reservations that listeners are likely to have about claims. As we've noted repeatedly, effective speakers consider listeners. When you analyze your listeners, try to anticipate their reservations about or objections to your claims. You demonstrate respect for listeners when you acknowledge their reservations and address them in your speech.

In our example, the speaker might realize that listeners could say to themselves, "The death penalty may not deter all crimes, but I'll bet it deters serious crimes like homicide." If the speaker has reason to think listeners may resist the claim on this basis, the speaker would offer a rebuttal to the reservation. It would be effective for the speaker to cite the *New York Times* 2000 investigative report that shows that since 1976 states without the death penalty have had homicide rates no higher than those of states with the death penalty.

Careful reasoning and good evidence allow you to offer logical appeals that are sound, effective, and ethical. Later in this chapter, we'll discuss some of the most common kinds of logical fallacies so that you can avoid them when you make persuasive presentations.

Building Credibility

We've already introduced the term *ethos* and noted its importance to effectiveness in persuasive speaking. Now, we want to consider ethos in more depth because of its critical role in persuasion.

Understanding Credibility

Another word for ethos is **credibility,** which a speaker earns by convincing listeners that he or she has personal integrity, is positively disposed toward them, and can be trusted. Notice that credibility is tied to how others perceive a speaker. This means that a speaker's credibility doesn't reside in the speaker. Instead, it is conferred by listeners or not conferred if they find a speaker untrustworthy, uninformed, or lacking in goodwill.

In recent years, we've heard a lot about credibility gaps and the lack of credibility of some national figures. Many people have lost confidence in many politicians and other public figures. It's easy to understand why citizens don't find some national leaders credible. When a senator campaigns on a promise to restrict illegal immigration and then is found to employ an undocumented alien, credibility withers. Likewise, when congressional representatives proclaim the importance of fiscal responsibility and themselves bounce checks, they lose credibility as advocates of government financial responsibility. We believe in people who practice what they preach, and we grant credibility to people whose words and actions are consistent.

Most Americans perceive Colin Powell as highly credible.

© Bob Daemmrich/Stock Boston

–Soyana–

The greatest teacher I ever had taught a class in government policies and practices. Before coming to campus, he had been an adviser to three presidents. He had held a lot of different offices in government, so what he was teaching us was backed up by personal experience. Everything he said had so much more weight than what I hear from professors who've never had any practical experience.

Credibility arises from the three cornerstones of persuasion: ethos, pathos, and logos. Listeners are likely to find speakers credible if they demonstrate their personal integrity, establish emotional meaning for their topics, and present ideas logically and with good evidence.

Types of Credibility

Credibility is not static; it can change in the course of communication (Figure 17.3). Have you ever attended a public speech by someone you respected greatly and found the presentation disappointing? Did you think less of the speaker after the speech than before it? Have you ever gone to a presentation without knowing much about the speaker and found it so impressive that you changed an attitude or behavior? If so, then you know from personal experience that credibility can increase or decrease as a result of a speech.

Initial Credibility   Some speakers have high **initial credibility,** which is the expertise and trustworthiness listeners recognize before a presentation begins. Initial credibility is based on titles, positions, experiences, or achievements that are known to listeners before they hear a speech. For example, most listeners would grant General Colin Powell high initial credibility on issues of military goals and strategies. A former inmate of a state prison would have high initial credibility in a speech on prison conditions.

Derived Credibility   In addition to initial credibility, speakers may also gain **derived credibility,** which is the expertise and trustworthiness that listeners confer on speakers as a result of how speakers communicate during presentations. Speakers earn derived credibility by organizing ideas clearly and logically, including convincing and interesting evidence that connects with listeners, and demonstrating energy and involvement. Speakers who are

**Figure 17.3
Developing Credibility**

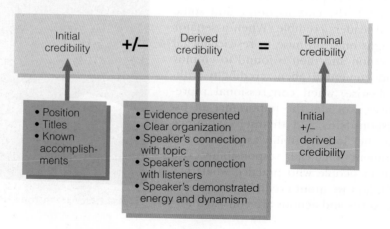

not well known tend not to have high initial credibility, so they must derive credibility from the quality of their presentations.

Terminal Credibility   The credibility of speaker at the end of a presentation is **terminal credibility.** It is the cumulative expertise, goodwill, and trustworthiness listeners attribute to a speaker—a combination of initial and derived credibility. Terminal credibility may be greater or less than initial credibility, depending on how effectively a speaker has communicated.

Enhancing Credibility

As you plan, develop, and present a persuasive speech, you should aim to enhance listeners' perceptions of your credibility. To summarize what we've discussed about credibility, here are ways to establish initial credibility and build derived and terminal credibility:

- State your qualifications for speaking on this topic: experiences you have had, titles or jobs you hold, research you have done.
- Show listeners that you care about them—that your speech is relevant to their welfare.
- Appeal to listeners' emotions, but be careful of overwhelming or alienating listeners with excessively dramatic appeals.
- Reason carefully, and avoid reasoning fallacies.
- Use effective, ethical supporting materials.
- Communicate both verbally and nonverbally that you care about the topic and are involved with it.
- Respond to questions fairly and with an open-mind.

Organizing Speeches for Persuasive Impact

In Chapter 15, we discussed ways to organize speeches. The principles you learned there apply to persuasive speaking:

- Your introduction should capture listeners' attention, provide a clear thesis statement, establish your credibility, and preview your speech.
- Your conclusion should summarize main points and end with a strong closing statement.

Communication Highlight

Goodwill and Credibility

More than 2,000 years ago, the ancient Greek rhetorician Aristotle wrote that a speaker's credibility depended on listeners' perceptions of the speaker's intelligence, character, and goodwill. Since Aristotle's time, research has established empirical support for strong links between credibility and perceived intelligence and character. But what about goodwill?

In a 1999 investigation, Jim McCroskey and Jason Teven found that perceived goodwill is positively linked to perceptions of likableness and believability. In other words,

when listeners think a speaker cares about them and has ethical intentions toward them, they are likely to trust and like the speaker. The practical implication of this study is that speakers who want to be judged credible should establish goodwill toward listeners.

According to McCroskey and Teven (1999), goodwill tends to be established in three ways: showing understanding of listeners' ideas, feelings, and needs; demonstrating empathy, or identification, with listeners' feelings; and being responsive to listeners while speaking.

- You should provide internal summaries of main points.
- You should provide smooth transitions between points and the parts of your speech.
- The body of your speech should be organized to reinforce your thesis and show listeners how your ideas cohere.

To build on these general principles for organizing public communication, we want to focus on special organizational concerns relevant to persuasive speaking. We will discuss two topics: the motivated sequence pattern, which is particularly well adapted to persuasive goals, and the relative merits of one-sided and two-sided presentations.

The Motivated Sequence Pattern

Any of the organizational patterns that we discussed in Chapter 15 can be used to structure persuasive speeches. Table 17.4 shows how each of the eight patterns we discussed could support a persuasive thesis.

In addition to the eight patterns we have already discussed, there is a ninth structure that can be highly effective in persuasive speaking. In the 1930s, public speaking scholar Alan Monroe developed the **motivated sequence pattern** for organizing speeches (Monroe, 1935). It has proven quite effective in diverse communication situations (Gronbeck et al., 1994; Jaffe, 1995). The primary reason for the effectiveness of the motivated sequence pattern is that it follows a natural pattern of human thought by gaining listeners' attention, demonstrating a need, offering a solution, and then helping them visualize and act on the solution. This pattern progressively increases listeners' motivation and personal involvement with a problem and its solution. The motivated sequence pattern includes five sequential steps, summarized in Table 17.5.

In the first step, listeners' attention is drawn to the subject. Here a speaker makes a dramatic opening statement ("Imagine this campus with no trees whatsoever"), shows the personal relevance of the topic ("The air you are breathing right now exists only because we have trees"), or otherwise catches listeners' attention. Later in this chapter, we'll discuss additional ways to capture listeners' initial attention.

The second step establishes need by showing that a real and serious problem exists ("Acid rain is slowly but surely destroying the trees of this planet"). Next is the satisfaction step, in which a speaker recommends a solution ("Stronger environmental regulations and individual efforts to use environmentally safe products can protect trees and thus the oxygen we breathe"). The fourth step, visualization, increases listeners' commitment to the solution identified in the satisfaction step by helping them imagine the results that would follow from adopting the recommended solution ("You will have ample air to breathe, and so will your grandchildren. Moreover, we'll all have the beauty of trees to enrich our lives").

Speech Builder Express, which you can access directly through your *Communication in Our Lives* CD-ROM, includes extensive prompts and a clear framework for organizing and developing speeches that incorporate a variety of persuasive strategies.

Finally, speakers move to the action step, which involves a direct appeal for concrete action on the part of listeners ("Refuse to buy or use any

Table 17.4: Organizing for Persuasion

Lloyd Bennett works for a public relations firm that wants to convince Casual Cruise Lines to become a client. Lloyd could use any of the eight basic organizational patterns to structure his speech to persuade the cruise line to hire his firm.

Pattern	Thesis and Main Points
Chronological	Our firm can move Casual Cruise Lines into the future. I. Originally, Casual Cruise Lines attracted customers whose average age was 58. II. In recent years, that customer base has shrunk. III. To thrive in the years ahead, Casual Cruise Lines needs to appeal to younger customers.
Spatial	Our proposal focuses on redesigning the space on cruise ships to appeal to the 30- to 45-year-old market. I. In the staterooms, we propose replacing the conventional seafaring motif with abstract, modernistic art. II. In the public area of the lower deck, we propose replacing the current coffee shops with sushi and espresso bars and adding fitness rooms. III. On the upper deck, we propose building hot tubs beside the pool.
Topical	Our firm has the most experience advertising cruise lines and the most innovative staff. I. Our firm has increased revenues for three other cruise lines. II. Our firm has won more awards for innovation and creativity than the others Casual Cruise Lines is considering for this account.
Star	Let's consider how younger customers might be attracted if we revamped ship decor, activities, and cuisine. I. Younger customers like modern decor. II. Younger customers want youthful activities. III. Younger customers want trendy foods.
Wave	The theme we propose is: "No shuffleboards and no kids—Casual Cruise Lines" I. If you're too young for shuffleboard, you're ready for a Casual Cruise. II. If you're too old to babysit, you're ready for a Casual Cruise.
Comparative	Casual Cruise Lines needs to adapt to younger customers whose needs and interests differ from those of older customers. I. We recommend 3-, 5-, and 7-day cruises because older people have the time for extended cruises, but 30- to 45-year-olds can usually spare a week or less at a time. II. Casual Cruise Lines should get rid of Bingo and shuffleboard and add dancing and nightclubs, which are favorite leisure activities of 30- to 45- year-olds. III. We recommend adding 24-hour espresso bars and onboard fitness rooms to meet the preferences of 30- to 45-year olds.
Problem–solution	We have a solution to Casual Cruise Lines' inability to attract younger customers. I. Casual Cruise Lines hasn't been able to get a substantial share of the lucrative 30- to 45-year-old market. II. Our advertising campaign specifically targets this market.
Cause–effect	The advertising campaign we propose will attract young, affluent customers by appealing to their interests and lifestyles. I. Our proposal's emphasis on luxury features of the cruise caters to this market's appreciation of extravagance. II. Our proposal to feature adults-only cruises caters to this market's demonstrated preferences. III. Our proposal to offer 2- to 4-day cruises meets this market's interest in long weekend getaways.

Table 17.5: The Motivated Sequence Pattern

1. Attention: Focus listeners' attention.

2. Need: Demonstrate that a real problem exists.

3. Satisfaction: Propose a solution to the demonstrated problem.

4. Visualization: Give listeners a vision of the impact of the solution.

5. Action: Ask listeners to think, feel, or act to bring the proposed solution into being.

aerosol products," "Sign this petition that I am sending to our senators in Washington, D.C."). The action step calls on listeners to take action to bring about the solution the speaker helped them visualize.

–Velma–

I've heard a lot of speeches on discrimination, but the most effective I ever heard was Cindy's in class last week. Other speeches I've heard focused on the idea that discrimination is wrong, but that's something I already believe, so they weren't helpful. Cindy, on the other hand, told me how to do something about discrimination. She showed me how I could act on what I believe.

Velma's commentary explains why the motivated sequence pattern is especially suited to persuasive speaking: It goes beyond identifying a problem and recommending a solution. In addition, it intensifies listeners' desire for a solution by helping them visualize what it would mean and gains their active commitment to being part of the solution. When listeners become personally involved with an idea and with taking action, they are more enduringly committed.

Sharpen Your Skill

Using the Motivated Sequence Pattern

Think about how you might organize a speech using the motivated sequence pattern. Write a thesis and five main points for a motivated sequence appeal.

Thesis:

1. Attention: ....

2. Need: ....

3. Satisfaction: ....

4. Visuallization: ....

5. Action: ....

One-sided and Two-sided Presentations Compared

Perhaps you are wondering whether it's more effective to present only your own point of view or both sides of an issue in a persuasive speech (the question generally is not relevant to informative speeches). That's an important question, and it's one that communication scholars have studied in depth.

Research conducted to discover whether one-sided or two-sided presentations are more effective suggests that the answer is, "It depends." More specifically, it depends on the particular people a speaker addresses, which reminds us again that good audience analysis is critical to effective public speaking. Decisions of whether to present one side of an issue or more than one side depend on the particular listeners for whom a speech is intended.

Listeners' Expectations   As we've noted before, effective speakers always try to learn what listeners expect so they don't fail to meet expectations. In educational settings, listeners are likely to expect speakers to discuss more than one side of an issue (Lasch, 1990). On the other hand, at campaign rallies candidates often present only their own side because they are speaking to committed supporters. Expectations may also be shaped by prespeech publicity. Imagine you decide to attend a speech after seeing a flyer for a presentation on the pros and cons of requiring all students at your school to purchase computers. You might be irritated if the speaker presented only the pros or only the cons of the proposed requirement.

Listeners' Attitudes   It makes a difference whether listeners are likely to be favorably disposed toward your ideas (Griffin, 1991). If they already favor your position, you may not need to discuss alternative positions in depth. However, if listeners favor a position different from yours, then it's essential to acknowledge and deal with their views. If your listeners oppose what you propose, it's unlikely that you will persuade them to abandon their position and adopt yours. With an audience hostile to your views, it's more reasonable to try to lessen their hostility to your ideas or to diminish the strength of their commitment to their present position (Trenholm, 1991).

Failure to consider listeners' opposing ideas diminishes a speaker's credibility because listeners may assume that the speaker either is uninformed of another side or is informed but trying to manipulate them by not discussing it. Either conclusion lessens credibility and the potential for impact on listeners. Speakers have an ethical responsibility to give respectful consideration to listeners' ideas and positions. Doing so encourages reciprocal respect from listeners for the ideas you present. R.J.'s commentary illustrates this.

Effective speakers adapt to listeners' experiences and expectations.

-R.J.-

In my ROTC unit, there's a lot of bad will toward the idea of gays in the military. Some of the guys have really strong feelings against it, so I was interested in what would happen at a required seminar last week with a guest speaker who was arguing that gays should be allowed in the services. He was really good! He spent the first ten minutes talking about all of the concerns, fears, and reasons why officers and enlisted personnel disapprove of having gays in the military, and he showed a lot of respect for those reasons. Then he presented his own ideas and showed how they answered most of the concerns people had. I won't say everyone was persuaded 100% that gays should be allowed in, but I will say he managed to get a full hearing with a group that I thought would

© Spencer Grant/PhotoEdit

just turn him off from the word go. Since he talked to us, I've heard some of the guys saying that maybe gays wouldn't be a problem.

Listeners' Knowledge What an audience already knows or believes about a topic should influence decisions of whether to present one or more sides of an issue. Listeners who are well informed about a topic are likely to be aware of more than one side, so your credibility will be enhanced if you include all sides in your presentation (Jackson & Allen, 1990). Also, highly educated listeners tend to realize that most issues have more than one side, so they may be suspicious of speakers who present only one point of view.

In some instances, speakers know that listeners will later be exposed to counterarguments, which are arguments that oppose those of a speaker. In such cases, it's advisable to inoculate listeners. **Inoculation** in persuasion is similar to inoculation in medicine. Vaccines give us limited exposure to diseases so that we won't contract them later. Similarly, persuasive inoculation "immunizes" listeners in advance against opposing ideas and arguments they may encounter in the future. If listeners later hear the other side, they have some resistance to arguments that oppose your position (Kiesler & Kiesler, 1971). For example, in political campaigns, candidates often make statements such as this: "Now, my opponent will tell you that we don't need to raise taxes, but I want to show you why that's wrong." By identifying and dispelling the opposing candidate's ideas in advance, the speaker improves the chance that listeners will agree with and later vote for her or him.

Listeners may be persuaded by arguments that oppose yours if you haven't inoculated them against those arguments. In fact, research indicates that of the three options—one-sided only, two-sided, or two-sided with refutation of the other side—generally the most persuasive strategy is to present both sides and refute arguments for the other side (Allen et al., 1990).

Sharpen Your Skill

Deciding Whether to Present One or Two Sides

Apply what you have learned to decide whether you should present one or two sides in your persuasive speech.

1. Are your listeners likely to expect to hear more than one side of the issue?

    A. How much education do they have?

    B. Has there been any prespeech publicity?

    C. Is there any reason to think that listeners do or do not care about hearing both sides?

2. What are your listeners' attitudes toward your topic?

    A. Do they have a position on the topic? If so, is it the same as yours?

    B. How strongly do listeners hold their opinions on the topic?

3. What level of knowledge about the topic do your listeners have?

    A. Do they know about more than one side of the issues?

    B. How much information about the topic have they already gained?

4. Are your listeners likely to hear counterarguments after your speech?

There is no quick and easy formula for deciding whether to present one-sided or two-sided discussions of a topic. Like most aspects of public speaking, this decision involves judgment on the speaker's part. That judgment should be informed by ethical considerations of what listeners have a right to know and what content is necessary to represent the issues fairly. In addition, judgments of whether to present more than one side should take into account listeners' expectations, attitudes, and knowledge and the likelihood that listeners have been or will be exposed to opposing arguments.

Guidelines for Effective Persuasive Speeches

In this chapter, we've already discussed some guidelines for effective persuasive speaking. For instance, we discussed the importance of developing a speech that includes the three cornerstones of persuasion: ethos, pathos, and logos. We also emphasized the importance of speaker credibility, and we identified specific ways to build yours when you speak. We extended our previous discussion of organizing speeches to discuss the motivated sequence pattern and the merits of presenting one or two sides of arguments. In addition to these guidelines, three other principles are important for effective persuasive speaking.

Create Common Ground with Listeners

In any communication context, common ground is important. That general principle has heightened importance in persuasive speaking. A persuasive speaker tries to move listeners to a point of view or action. It makes sense that they will be more likely to move with the speaker if they perceive some common ground with him or her. Listeners may think, "If we share all of these values and concerns, then maybe I should rethink my position on this one issue we disagree on."

Kenneth Burke (1950), a distinguished theorist of language, believed that people are divided from one another: They differ in experiences, attitudes, values, and so forth. At the same time, there is overlap between people: We share some experiences, values, language, and so forth. Burke viewed communication as the primary way in which people transcend their divisions and enlarge what is common to them. Burke saw finding common ground as a process of **identification,** or recognizing and enlarging commonalities between communicators.

Effective persuasive speakers seek out similarities between themselves and their listeners and bring those similarities into listeners' awareness. A few years ago, a student of mine wanted to persuade his listeners that fraternities are positive influences on members' lives. From polling students on campus, Steve knew that many held negative stereotypes of "frat men." He reasoned that

© David Young-Wolff/PhotoEdit

Effective speakers find common ground with listeners.

most of his listeners, who did not belong to Greek groups, would be likely to view him both negatively and as different from them. This is how he established common ground in opening his speech:

> You've probably heard a lot of stories about wild fraternity parties and "frat men" who spend most of their time drinking, partying, and harassing pledges. I confess, I've done all of that as a brother in Delta Sigma Phi. I've also spent every Sunday for the last semester volunteering in the Big Brother Program that helps underprivileged kids in the city. And I've built friendships with brothers that will last my entire life. Like many of you, I felt a little lost when I first came to this campus. I wanted to find a place where I belonged at college. Like you, I want to know people and be involved with projects that help me grow as a person. For me, being in a fraternity has done that.

This is an effective opening. Steve began by showing listeners that he realized they might hold some negative views of fraternity men. He went further and acknowledged that he personally fit some of those stereotypes. But then Steve challenged the adequacy of the stereotypes by offering some information that didn't fit with them. Volunteering as a Big Brother isn't part of the "party guy" image. Having recognized and challenged stereotypes his listeners were likely to hold, Steve then began to create common ground. Most of his listeners could remember feeling lost when they first came to college. Most of them could identify with wanting to belong and to grow as people. Steve's opening successfully identified similarities between himself and his listeners, so they were open to considering his argument that fraternities are valuable.

Adapt to Listeners

Effective persuasion focuses on particular listeners. A good persuasive speech is not designed for just anyone. Instead, it is adapted to specific listeners' knowledge, attitudes, motives, experiences, values, and expectations. The methods of audience analysis that we discussed in Chapter 13 should help you learn who your listeners are and what they know, believe, and expect in relation to your topic.

As a speaker, your job is to apply what you learn about your listeners as you develop and present your speech. In his speech on the values of fraternities, Steve adapted to his listeners by showing that he understood common stereotypes of "frat men" and that there was some truth to them. This enhanced Steve's credibility and his listeners' willingness to open their minds to what he had to say.

In 1998, Raymond W. Smith, chairperson of Bell Atlantic, spoke about hate speech on the Internet. Smith spoke at the Simon Wiesenthal Center, which is dedicated to human rights (Smith, 1998). Although Smith spoke against censoring hate speech on the Internet, he realized that his largely Jewish listeners had acute knowledge of the dangers of hate speech. In his opening remarks Smith said,

> Neo-Nazis and extremists of every political stripe who once terrorized people in the dead of night with burning crosses and painted swastikas are now sneaking up on the public—especially our kids—through the World Wide Web.

Although Smith went on to argue against censorship, he let his listeners know that he was well aware of hate speech and the harms it can cause. Within his speech, Smith further adapted to his listeners by quoting Jewish leaders, who had high credibility with listeners.

Knowing that many of his listeners favored censorship, Smith presented a two-sided speech. He began by considering the arguments of those who favor censorship, treating them thoroughly and respectfully. He then turned to the other side (the one he favored): not censoring hate speech on the Internet. Smith argued that censorship will not get to the source of the problem, which is hate. Instead, he said the solution is to teach tolerance and respect. In making this argument, Smith adapted to his listeners at the Wiesenthal Center by saying

> While cyberhate cannot be mandated or censored out of existence, it can be countered by creating hundreds of chat lines, home pages, bulletin boards, and websites dedicated to social justice, tolerance, and equality for all people. . . . Moral leadership can have a tremendous impact. Quite simply, we need more Simon Wiesenthal Centers.

To adapt to his listeners, Smith acknowledged their cultural history, quoted authorities they respected, and thoughtfully considered the argument for censorship. Therefore, his listeners were then willing to give an equally thoughtful hearing to Smith's argument against censorship.

Avoid Fallacious Reasoning

A **fallacy** is an error in reasoning. The word *fallacy* is derived from the Latin word *fallacia,* which means "deceit." Fallacies present false, or flawed, logic. Despite the original meaning, deceit, fallacies may be intentional or unintentional. Either way, they are not effective with educated or thoughtful audiences. They detract from a speaker's credibility because they suggest that the speaker is not ethical. To be effective and ethical, you should avoid using fallacies in your speeches. To be a critical listener, you should be able to recognize fallacies used by others. We'll discuss eight of the most common fallacies in reasoning. This should allow you to avoid these fallacies in your speaking and to identify and resist them if they are part of others' communication.

Ad Hominem Arguments In Latin, the word *ad* means "to," and *hominem* means "human being." Thus, **ad hominem arguments** are ones that go to the person instead of the idea. It is not ethical to argue for your point of view by attacking the integrity of someone who has taken a stand opposing yours.

"You can't trust what George Boxwood says about the importance of a strong military. After all, he never served a day in the military." Although it may be true that George Boxwood didn't serve in the military, that doesn't necessarily discredit his argument about the importance of a strong military. Mr. Boxwood may have researched the topic vigorously, interviewed military personnel, and studied historical effects of strong and weak military forces. Mr. Boxwood's own service—or lack thereof—is not directly relevant to the quality of his argument for a strong military. Unethical speakers sometimes try to undercut people whose positions oppose their own by attacking the people, not the arguments. Critical listeners recognize this fallacy and distrust speakers who engage in it.

Post Hoc, Ergo Propter Hoc

Post hoc, ergo propter hoc is a Latin phrase meaning "after this, therefore because of this." Sometimes when one thing follows another, we mistakenly think the first thing caused the second. Unethical speakers sometimes try to persuade us to think that a coincidental sequence is causal. For instance, the U.S. economy faltered and verged on recession after George W. Bush became president. Does that mean Bush and his administration caused the economic slowdown? Not necessarily. To support the claim that Bush caused the economic slowdown, a speaker would need to demonstrate that specific policies implemented by Bush hurt the economy.

Bandwagon Appeal

When I was a child, I often tried to persuade my parents that I should be allowed to do something because all of my friends were doing it. Invariably, my parents rejected that reason and replied, "If all of your friends jumped off the roof, would you do that?" At the time, that answer exasperated me. But my parents were right. They rejected the **bandwagon appeal,** which argues that because most people believe or act a particular way, you should too. Widely held attitudes are not necessarily correct, as Columbus and Galileo proved. Thoughtful listeners won't be persuaded to your point of view just because lots of other people have been. It's more ethical and more effective to give them good reasons why they should agree with you.

Slippery Slope

The **slippery slope** fallacy claims that once we take the first step, more and more steps inevitably will follow until some unacceptable consequence results. For example, an unethical speaker who wanted to argue against a proposal to restrict logging in a protected environmental area might state, "Restricting logging is only the first step. Next, the environmentalists are likely to want to prohibit any timber cutting. Pretty soon, we won't be able to build homes or furniture." The idea that we won't have lumber to build homes and furniture is extreme. It has little to do with the question of whether we should restrict logging in one particular area. Critical listeners don't find it credible when speakers reduce arguments to absurdities.

Hasty Generalization   A **hasty generalization** is a broad claim based on too limited evidence. It is unethical to assert a broad claim when you have only anecdotal or isolated evidence or instances. Consider these examples of hasty generalizations based on inadequate data:

- Three congressional representatives have had affairs. Therefore, members of Congress are adulterers.

- An environmental group illegally blocked loggers and workers at a nuclear plant. Therefore, environmentalists are radicals who take the law into their own hands.

- Four of our star basketball players left college for pro careers this year. Therefore, basketball players aren't serious students.

In each case, the conclusion is based on very limited evidence. In each case, the conclusion is hasty and fallacious.

Red Herring Argument   Years ago, fox hunters sometimes dragged a dead fish across the trail of a fox to see whether the dogs would be diverted in the wrong direction (Gass, 1999). They were trying to train the dogs not to let the smell of the fish, originally a herring, deflect them from hunting the fox. Speakers who try to deflect listeners from relevant issues engage in **red herring** arguments. They say something that is irrelevant to their topic or that doesn't really respond to a listener's question. The point is to divert the listener from something the speaker can't or doesn't want to address.

Either–Or Logic   What is wrong with this statement: "Either abolish fraternities on our campus or accept the fact that this is a party school where drinking is more important than learning." The fallacy in this statement is that it implies there are only two options: either get rid of fraternities altogether or allow partying to eclipse academics. Are there no other alternatives? Might it be possible to work with fraternities to establish policies limiting parties to weekends? Might it be possible to increase the quality of academics so that students are motivated to be more involved with learning? In most instances, **either–or** thinking is simplistic and fallacious.

Reliance on the Halo Effect   The **halo effect** occurs when we generalize a person's authority or expertise in a particular area to other areas that are irrelevant to the person's experience and knowledge. It is fallacious to think that because a person is knowledgeable on particular topics, he or she is knowledgeable on all topics. It's also unethical to quote someone you think the audience will respect when that person has no qualification as an expert on your topic. Politician Bob Dole urges men to use Viagra. Michael Jordan urges us to buy a particular brand of underwear. William Shatner and Lenard Nemoy, who played Captain Kirk and Mr. Spock on *Star Trek*, encourage us to use priceline.com. Well-known people appear in the mustache advertisements promoting milk. Are any of these people experts on the products they are urging us to buy and use?

To be effective and ethical, persuasive speakers should avoid fallacies in reasoning (Table 17.6). Likewise, effective critical listeners should be able to detect fallacies in reasoning and to resist being persuaded by them.

Table 17.6: Fallacies in Reasoning

Ad hominem attack	You can't believe what Jane Smith says about voting, because she doesn't vote.
Post hoc, ergo propter hoc	The new flextime policy is ineffective because more people have been late getting to work since it went into effect.
Bandwagon appeal	You should be in favor of the new campus meal plan because most students are.
Slippery slope	If we allow students to play a role in decisions about hiring and tenure of faculty, pretty soon students will be running the whole school.
Hasty generalization	People should not be allowed to own Rottweilers, because there have been three instances of Rottweilers attacking children.
Either–or	Tenure should be either abolished or kept exactly as it is.
Red herring argument	People who own Rottweilers should own cats instead. Let me tell you why cats are ideal pets.
Reliance on the halo effect	World-famous actor Richard Connery says that we should not restrict people's right to own firearms.

Experiencing Communication in Our Lives

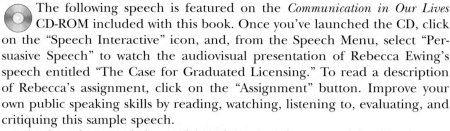

CASE STUDY: Persuasive Speech: The Case for Graduated Licensing

The following speech is featured on the *Communication in Our Lives* CD-ROM included with this book. Once you've launched the CD, click on the "Speech Interactive" icon, and, from the Speech Menu, select "Persuasive Speech" to watch the audiovisual presentation of Rebecca Ewing's speech entitled "The Case for Graduated Licensing." To read a description of Rebecca's assignment, click on the "Assignment" button. Improve your own public speaking skills by reading, watching, listening to, evaluating, and critiquing this sample speech.

Analyze the speech by applying the principles covered in this chapter, and respond to the prompts that accompany the video, which you can access by clicking on "Evaluation" and "Critique." After answering the evaluation questions and writing a brief critique of the speech, you can click on the "Done" button to compare your responses with the ones I suggest. Additional analysis questions are available in print at the end of this chapter and on the book's website.

Rebecca Ewing was a junior at the University of North Carolina at Chapel Hill when she presented her persuasive speech on graduated licensing. Below is the text of the introduction to her speech. Although Rebecca's speech is strong, it is not perfect. As you view it on your CD, consider how it could be made even more effective. Also think about different ways you might accomplish the speaker's objectives; can you identify alternative organizational structures, kinds of evidence, transitions, and so forth?

It was a typical Friday night in a small town in Florida just two short years ago. Two 13-year-old girls, Margaux and Crystal, were planning a night out at the mall. At around 7:30 P.M., Crystal and Margaux met up with seven other friends. The group decided to head to another friend's apartment.

One of the teenagers, Nick, who had just turned 16, agreed to drive the eight of them to the friend's apartment. Soon, two in the group were up front and the other seven were sardined in the back of Nick's Honda. None of the teens in the back seat could wear seat belts.

Once on the highway, Nick quickly picked up speed. Then the girls became frightened and told Nick to slow down. Instead of slowing, Nick accelerated to 85 miles per hour and began to tailgate other cars. Eventually, Nick lost control of his car and jumped the median into oncoming traffic, resulting in a head-on collision. What happened next is every parent's nightmare. Nick and the front-seat passenger survived due to airbags. However, of the seven teens crammed into the back seat, only two survived, and both were severely injured. Regrettably, Margaux and Crystal did not make it (Barr, 1998, p. 79).

Sixteen-year-olds are faced with an incredible responsibility when it comes time to get their driver's licenses. But are they equipped to handle difficult driving situations? Is a 16-year-old mature enough to handle such an awesome responsibility? Every year, so many teenagers have their lives cut short in tragic car accidents due to lack of proper training and too much freedom at too young an age.

Sixteen is just too young for people to be driving without adult supervision. I think that the evidence I will present to you today will convince you to agree with me that 16 is too young for unsupervised driving. After I've established the dangers of giving licenses to 16-year-olds, I will propose a solution that has already proven its effectiveness in eight states.

Chapter Summary

This chapter focused on persuasive speaking. After noting the many situations in which persuasive speaking occurs, we identified ethos, pathos, and logos and the cornerstones of effective persuasion, and we highlighted ways in which speakers can incorporate each into presentations. Extending this, we discussed credibility, which is especially important in persuasive speaking. We identified three types of credibility—initial, derived, and terminal—and discussed ways in which speakers can build their credibility during the process of planning, developing, and presenting persuasive speeches. The next section of the chapter reviewed general organizational principles and highlighted organizational concerns that are particularly relevant to persuasive speaking.

We introduced the motivated sequence pattern, which can be very powerful in moving listeners to accept and act on persuasive appeals. We also discussed the merits of one-sided and two-sided presentations, and we identified criteria for choosing which will be most effective in particular situations and with particular listeners.

The last section of the chapter provided guidelines for persuasive speaking. The first is to build common ground between a speaker and listener. The second is to adapt to particular listeners by tailoring a persuasive speech to their expectations, knowledge, experiences, motives, values, and attitudes. The third is to avoid fallacies in reasoning, which are usually ineffective and always unethical.

The advice presented in this and previous chapters should allow you to prepare and present a persuasive speech that has impact.

Communication in Our Lives ONLINE

In addition to presenting the case studies' multimedia scenarios and speeches, the *Communication in Our Lives* CD-ROM provides quick access to the *Communication in Our Lives* website, Speech Builder Express, and InfoTrac College Edition. The website is online at http://communication.wadsworth.com/woodciol4, but you can access this book's premium web content only when you link to the site directly through the book's CD.

The *Communication in Our Lives* website features interactive tools for learning and reviewing the chapter's concepts and key terms, including electronic versions of the "For Further Reflection and Discussion" questions that appear below and a review quiz.

The website also provides updated web links and additional InfoTrac College Edition activities. If required, you can e-mail completed chapter activities or the quizzes to your instructor.

Key Concepts

ad hominem argument, *463*

bandwagon appeal, *464*

claim, *451*

credibility, *453*

deductive reasoning, *451*

derived credibility, *454*

either–or, *465*

ethos, *448*

fallacy, *463*

grounds, *451*

halo effect, *465*

hasty generalization, *465*

identification, *461*

inductive reasoning, *451*

initial credibility, *454*

inoculation, *460*

logos, *448*

motivated sequence pattern, *456*

pathos, *448*

persuasive speeches, *446*

post hoc, ergo propter hoc, 464

qualifier, *452*

rebuttal, *452*

red herring, *465*

slippery slope, *464*

terminal credibility, *455*

Toulmin model of reasoning, *451*

warrant, *452*

For Further Reflection and Discussion

1. What do you consider particularly effective and ineffective choices made by Rebecca in her speech, which is featured on your CD-ROM? Explain your evaluations.

2. Was the problem–solution pattern an effective choice for Rebecca's speech? Why or why not? Would the speech have been as effective if it had followed a solution–problem organization?

3. Go to *Vital Speeches* in your InfoTrac College Edition. Select Suzanne Morse's January 1, 2001, speech, "The Rap of Change." Evaluate her effectiveness in selecting quotations to support ideas and add interest. How does she use time to shape the speech?

4. Reread this chapter's discussion of one-sided and two-sided persuasive speeches. When is it ethical to present only one side of a topic? When is it unethical? In answering this question, remember that ethical considerations are not necessarily the same as strategic ones. A speaker who uses unethical arguments or evidence might be effective in convincing listeners to think or do something.

5. Go to *Vital Speeches* in your InfoTrac College Edition. Select Daniel Rose's November 15, 2001, speech, "In the Days Ahead: New York and Boston After September 11." How does his speech adapt to the situation in America after the terrorist attacks? Which organizational pattern did Rose use in his speech?

Questions for Analysis and Discussion

 Review the video of Rebecca's speech that you watched when completing this chapter's case study (pages 466–467), or, if you haven't seen it yet, watch it for the first time. If you didn't previously finish the "Evaluation" questions and "Critique" activity included on the CD-ROM, do so now, and then respond to the following questions, which are also available on the book's website under "Activities for Chapter 17."

1. Did Rebecca provide a strong introduction with an attention device, a clear thesis, and a clear preview?

2. Are the sources of evidence credible? Why or why not? Is there any reason to suspect that the sources are biased?

3. What other kinds of evidence might the speaker have used to strengthen the persuasive impact of her message?

4. Did Rebecca's speech reflect awareness of ethos, pathos, and logos?

5. How did Rebecca adapt the message to listeners who were 19- to 24-year-old college students? Can you think of additional ways she might have adapted this message to these particular listeners?

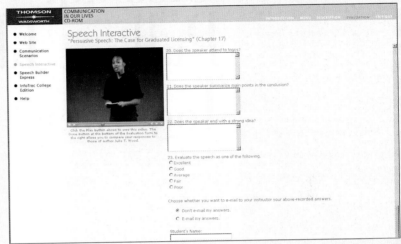

Speech Builder Express

Access Speech Builder Express with the user name and the password that came with the CD-ROM that accompanies your textbook. Click "Create a New Speech" on the Express Menu. Type in the title of your persuasive speech. If you haven't given it a title, just type in a keyword title such as "Environmental Awareness Speech."

Proceed through the steps in Speech Builder Express to develop your speech and to prepare your list of references (Works Cited). Speech Builder Express is designed so that you can log off and return to it frequently as you move through the process of developing your persuasive speech.

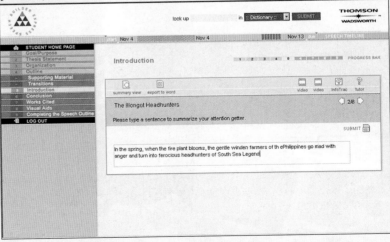

Closing:
Pulling Ideas
Together

As I reflect on all that we've explored in this book, I find a central theme that unifies the many topics we've discussed. The theme is that communication is an intricate tapestry woven from the threads of self, others, perceptions, relationships, contexts, culture, climate, listening, and verbal and nonverbal messages. Each thread has its own distinct character, and yet each thread is also woven into the complex, ever-changing tapestry of human communication. We've taken time to discuss each thread in its own right and then explored how it blends with other threads in particular communication situations.

Sometimes a particular thread stands out boldly, as individual threads sometimes do in woven fabric. For instance, the thread of delivery is quite prominent in public speaking, and the thread of listening is less visible. Yet, as we learned, in order to be effective, speakers must understand and adapt to their listeners because listeners decide how credible a speaker is and how effective public communication can be. Similarly, in group discussion the thread of leadership stands out more clearly than it does in the context of personal relationships. Yet, with friends and romantic partners, issues of leadership are also present, although they are less obvious than in group discussion or public speaking. Thus, even when threads of communication are restrained in particular interactions, they are present and important.

At other times, an individual thread blends so completely with other threads that we don't perceive it as separate from the overall pattern of the tapestry. Organization, for example, is present in interaction between friends as they decide what to talk about and how to sequence the topics. Yet in friends' conversation, the thread of organization is muted, and other threads, such as sensitive listening, stand out. Similarly, the thread of delivery is subdued in casual conversations, yet our communication with friends is affected by how we articulate our ideas—by vocal force, volume, pace, and other aspects of delivery. The many threads that make up the tapestry of communication vary in intensity and prominence from one point in the tapestry to another, yet all are part of the whole.

To conclude our study of the communication tapestry, let's review what we've discussed and what it means for us. The overall goal of this book is to increase your insight into the ways in which communication is an integral part of our everyday lives.

We launched our journey in Chapter 1, which described the range of human communication and the modern academic field that bears its name. Chapter 2 allowed us to delve into the complicated process of perception so that we could understand how perception, thought, and communication interact. We learned that we seldom, if ever, perceive the full, raw reality around us. Instead, we perceive selectively, noticing only some things and overlooking others. The labels we use to name, classify, and evaluate our perceptions reverberate in our consciousness to shape what we perceive and what it means to us. In fact, most of the time, how we think, feel, and act are based less on objective realities in the external world than on how we label our selective perceptions of it. This is normal, yet it can cause us trouble if we forget that we are responding to our labels, not to the world itself.

In Chapter 3, we traced the reciprocal relationship of communication and personal identity. As we interact with others and learn how they see us, we form initial concepts of who we are. At the same time, how we see ourselves influences how and with whom we communicate. In turn, the ways we interact and the people with whom we interact affect how our sense of self continues to evolve. The connection between identity and communication is continuous and reciprocal.

The elaborate and fascinating relationships between culture and communication were the focus of Chapter 4. There, we unmasked the subtle ways in which communication creates and sustains the beliefs, values, and practices that define cultures and social communities. Equally important, we saw that cultures shape the forms and content of communication by telling us what is and is not important and what are appropriate and inappropriate ways of interacting with others. Understanding differences between cultures and social communities allows us to appreciate the distinct character of each one and to enlarge our own repertoire of communication skills.

Chapters 5 through 7 focused on primary forms of communication: verbal communication, nonverbal behavior, and listening. As we considered each topic, we examined ways to improve our personal effectiveness as communicators. Particularly important to our understanding of these topics is the realization that people differ in their styles of listening and their verbal and nonverbal communication. Awareness of these differences helps us understand others on their terms. The principles and skills we discussed in these chapters should serve you well throughout your life as you seek to interact effectively and sensitively with others in personal, social, and professional contexts.

The second part of the book extended the first seven chapters by weaving basic communication concepts and skills into interpersonal, group and mass communication. In Chapters 8 and 9, we explored interpersonal communication in general and as it occurs in friendships and romantic relationships. The intimate bonds that grace our lives are communicative achievements because we create and sustain them largely through interaction and the meanings we assign to it. Communication is the lifeblood of intimacy. In dramatic forms, such as declarations of love and disclosure of secrets, and in everyday small talk, it is communication that continually breathes life and meaning into our relationships with others.

© Myrleen Ferguson Cate/PhotoEdit, Inc.

We moved to quite a different context in Chapters 10 and 11, which examined communication in small groups. There, we learned what types of communication facilitate and hinder effective group discussion and what communication responsibilities accompany effective membership and leadership. We also studied the standard agenda for problem solving, which gives participants an effective method of organizing group discussion.

Chapter 12 focused on mass communication, which permeates our lives. After exploring how mass communication works, we focused on ways to develop critical skills that enhance your media literacy.

Part Three of this book concentrated on public speaking. From the early stages of planning presentations to researching and developing evidence and finally to organizing, outlining, and practicing, public speaking involves skills that most of us already have and use in other communication situations. As is true for all interactions, good public speaking centers on others; the values, interests, knowledge, and beliefs of listeners guide what speakers can and cannot wisely say and how they develop and present their ideas. Effective public speaking, like effective everyday conversation, is a genuine interaction between people in which the views and values of all participants should be taken into account.

Whether we are talking to a friend, a co-worker on a task team, or an audience of five hundred, we rely on common basic ethical principles and communication skills. Among the most important is sensitivity to others and their perspectives. Another principle important in all communication situations is sensitive listening. When we listen mindfully to others, we gain insight into them and their perspectives so that we may communicate effectively with them.

Clarity and responsibility are earmarks of effective verbal and nonverbal communication. To be clear in our messages and to understand those of others, we must recognize the ambiguity and abstractness of communication and must find ways to check with others to make sure we share meanings. Responsibility involves following ethical principles in our communication. In addition to respecting others and their positions, we should be careful to be accurate in making claims, whether in public speech or private conversation. Any evidence we use to support our ideas should be sound, and anything we say should be respectful of others and their differences. Whether we're talking to one person in an intimate setting or to a thousand in a large auditorium, good communication is clear, responsible, and sensitive.

Throughout *Communication in Our Lives,* we've seen that people differ in their communication and in the meanings they attach to words and actions. The cornucopia of cultures and social communities in our world gives rise to a fascinating range of communication styles. No single way of communicating is inherently superior to any other; the differences result from diverse cultural heritages and practices.

Learning not to impose our own communication patterns and our culture's judgments on others and being open to styles of interaction that differ from our own allow us to enlarge and enrich who we are individually and collectively. Curiosity, appreciation, and openness to unfamiliar ways of communicating are the foundation of a healthy pluralistic society in which each of us preserves our own distinct identity while remaining part of and engaged with a larger whole.

If you have learned these principles and skills of human communication, then you have the foundation of effectiveness in personal, professional, and social settings. If you are committed to practicing and continually enlarging the principles and skills introduced in this book, then you can look forward to a life of personal growth, meaningful relationships, professional success, and social impact. What is more, you are on the threshold of a life filled with joy. I wish you all of that.

© Michael Newman/PhotoEdit

Appendix A
Annotated Sample Speeches

Civility without Censorship:
The Ethics of the Internet–Cyberhate

Transcript of address by Bell Atlantic Corporation Chairman Raymond W. Smith

Abstract: Smith believes that efforts to corrupt public discourse on race and ethnicity on the Internet should be stopped. He feels that the Internet should be used as a medium to promote positive experience and information. He also believes that racism has no place on the Internet.

Full Text: Address by RAYMOND W. SMITH, Former Chairman, Bell Atlantic Corporation.

Delivered at the Simon Wiesenthal Center/Museum of Tolerance, Los Angeles, California, December 1, 1998.

Thank you, Rabbi Cooper, for the gracious introduction . . . and let me acknowledge the tremendous contributions the Museum and the Center have made toward harmonizing race relations and advancing equality and justice. We're truly honored that you would include us in today's program.

> Graciously acknowledges sponsor.

For the past two years, I've been using the "bully pulpit" to alert various civil rights leaders and organizations (like Martin Luther King III and the NAACP) of the dangers posed by cyberhate. If not for the early groundbreaking work by the Simon Wiesenthal Center, I doubt whether I would have even known of this growing threat. Thank you for warning us—and now, for showing us—how extremists are using the Internet for their own purposes.

When thinking about this morning's topic, I can't help but mention a cartoon that recently appeared in the newspapers. Through the doorway, a mother calls out to her teenager—who is surrounded by high-tech equipment—"I hope you're not watching sex stuff on the Internet!" To which her son replies, "Naw, I'm getting it on TV!"

> Humor also foreshadows content.

Until recently, the chief concern of parents was pornography—kids' access to it over the web and the fear of sexual predators cruising cyberspace. Now, we're worried about hate mongers reaching out to our children in digital space.

As we have just seen and heard, neo-Nazis and extremists of every political stripe who once terrorized people in the dead of night with burning crosses and painted swastikas are now sneaking up on the public—especially our kids—through the World Wide Web.

> Anticipates listeners' concerns and addresses those first.

As cyberhate is nothing less than the attempt to corrupt public discourse on race and ethnicity via the Internet, many people see censorship of websites and Net content as the only viable way to meet this growing threat.

> Identifies one solution which listeners may favor.

I disagree.

Instead of fearing the Internet's reach, we need to embrace it—to value its ability to connect our children to the wealth of positive human experience and knowledge. While there is, to quote one critic, "every form of diseased intelligence" in digital space, we must remember that it comprises only a small fraction of cyberspace. The Internet provides our children unlimited possibilities for learning and education—the great libraries, cities, and cultures of the world also await them at just the click of a mouse key.

In short, we need to think about ways to keep cyberhate off the screen, and more about ways to meet it head on: which translates into fighting destructive rhetoric with constructive dialogue—hate speech with truth—restrictions with greater Internet access.

Thesis

This morning, then, I would like to discuss with you the options that are available to combat cyberhate that don't endanger our First Amendment guarantees—and that remain true to our commitment to free speech.

That people and institutions should call for a strict ban on language over the Web that could be considered racist, anti-Semitic, or bigoted is totally understandable. None of us was truly prepared for the emergence of multiple hate-group websites (especially those geared toward children), or the quick adoption of high technology by skinheads and others to market their digital cargo across state lines and international date lines at the speed of light.

One possible reason some people feel inclined to treat the Internet more severely than other media is that the technology is new and hard to understand. Also, the Internet's global reach and ubiquitous nature make it appear ominous. As Justice Gabriel Bach of Israel noted, this ability makes it especially dangerous. "I'm frightened stiff by the Internet," he said; "Billions of people all over the world have access to it."

Cites a source that is likely to have high credibility with his particular listeners.

My industry has seen all this before.

The clash between free speech and information technology is actually quite an old one. Nearly a century ago, telephone companies, courts, and the Congress debated whether "common carriers" (public phone companies) were obligated to carry all talk equally, regardless of content. And in the end—though some believed that the phone would do everything from eliminate Southern accents and increase Northern labor unrest—free speech won out in the courts.

Whatever the technology, be it the radio or the silver screen, history teaches us that white supremacists, anti-Semites, and others will unfortunately come to grasp, relatively early on, a new medium's potential.

Persuasive analogies add to Smith's derived credibility.

We simply can't condemn a whole technology because we fear that a Father Coughlin or a Leni Riefenstahl (early pioneers in the use of radio and film to advance anti-Semitism or Hitler's Reich) is waiting in the wings to use the latest technology to their own advantage. Nor can we expect the Congress, the federal government, or an international regulatory agency to tightly regulate cyberspace content in order to stymie language we find offensive.

The wisdom of further empowering such organizations and agencies like the FCC or the United Nations aside, it is highly doubtful, even if they had the authority, that they would have the ability to truly stem the flow of racist and anti-Semitic language on the World Wide Web.

Good arguments against bans and restrictions.

Anybody with a phone line, computer, and Internet connection can set up a website—even broadcast over the Net.

Even if discovered and banned, online hate groups can easily jump Internet service providers and national boundaries to avoid accountability. I think cyber guru Peter Huber got it right when he said, "To censor Internet filth at its origins, we would have to enlist the Joint Chiefs of Staff, who could start by invading Sweden and Holland."

Effective quotation

Then there is the whole matter of disguise. Innocent-sounding URLs (handles or website names) can fool even the most traveled or seasoned "cybernaut."

As for efforts on Capitol Hill and elsewhere to legislate all so-called "offensive" language off the Internet, here again we can expect the courts to knock down any attempts to curtail First Amendment rights on the Internet. As the Supreme Court ruled last year when it struck down legislation restricting the transmission of "indecent" material online: (To quote) "Regardless of the strength of the government's interest, the level of discourse reaching a mailbox simply cannot be limited to what is suitable for a sandbox."

In short, although the temptation is great to look to legislation and regulation as a remedy to cyberhate, our commitment to free speech must always take precedence over our fears.

So, cyberhate will not be defeated by the stroke of a pen.

Now, this is not to say that because we place such a high value on our First Amendment rights, we can't do anything to combat the proliferation of hate sites on the Internet or protect young minds from such threatening and bigoted language.

Law enforcement agencies and state legislators can use existing laws against stalking and telephone harassment to go after those who abuse e-mail. . . . Parents can install software-filtering programs (such as the Anti-Defamation League's HateFilter, or the one Bell Atlantic uses, CyberPatrol) to block access to questionable Internet sites. . . . Schools and libraries can protect children by teaching them how to properly use the Internet and challenge cyberhate. . . . And Internet service providers can voluntarily decline to host hate sites. (Bell Atlantic Internet Services, for instance, reserves the right to decline or terminate service which "espouses, promotes or incites bigotry, hatred, or racism.")

Given that today's panel has representatives from state government, law enforcement, the courts, and the Internet industry, we can discuss these initiatives later in more detail. The point is, there are other ways besides empowering national or international oversight agencies or drafting draconian legislation, to lessen the impact of cyberhate.

Freedom, not censorship, is the only way to combat this threat to civility. In short, more speech—not less—is needed on the World Wide Web.

In fact, the best answer to cyberhate lies in the use of information technology itself. As a reporter for *The Boston Globe* recently concluded, (quote) "The same technology that provides a forum for extremists enables civil rights groups and individuals to mobilize a response in unprecedented ways."

We totally agree.

Our prescription to combat cyberhate is therefore rather simple but far reaching in its approach:

The first component is access: If we're to get to a higher level of national understanding on racial and ethnic issues—and strike at the very roots of cyberhate—we must see that no minority group or community is left out of cyberspace for want of a simple Internet connection or basic computer.

At Bell Atlantic, we've been working very hard to provide the minority communities we serve with Internet access. Across our region, thousands of inner-city schools, libraries, colleges, and community groups are now getting connected to cyberspace through a variety of our foundation and state grant programs. Also, our employees have been in the forefront of volunteering their time and energy to wire schools to the Internet during specially designated "Net" days.

Internet access alone, however, won't build bridges of understanding between people—or level the playing field between cyberhaters and the targets of their hate.

The second thing we must do is make sure the web's content is enriched by minority culture and beliefs, and that there are more websites and home pages dedicated to meeting head-on the racist caricatures and pseudo-history often found in cyberspace.

Memorable language in quotation

Transition moves listeners to the proposal Smith advocates.

Undetailed examples support claim that existing laws protect us against hate speech.

Clear announcement of his proposal

Well-chosen quotation

"First" provides a clue so listeners can follow.

"Second" is a mini-transition to move listeners along.

While cyberhate cannot be mandated or censored out of existence, it can be countered by creating hundreds of chat lines, home pages, bulletin boards, and websites dedicated to social justice, tolerance, and equality—for all people regardless of race, nationality, or sexual orientation.

Over the past two years, Bell Atlantic has helped a number of minority and civil rights groups launch and maintain their websites (like the NAACP, the Leadership Council on Civil Rights, and the National Council of La Raza), and we've done the same for dozens of smaller cultural organizations (like the Harlem Studio Museum and El Museo del Barrio).

We believe that kind of moral leadership can have a tremendous impact. Quite simply, we need more Simon Wiesenthal Centers, Anti-Defamation Leagues, and Southern Poverty Law Centers monitoring and responding to cyberhate.

If we're to bring the struggle for human decency and dignity into cyberspace, we must see that the two most powerful revolutions of the twentieth century—those of civil rights and information technology—are linked even closer together.

Finally, we need to drive real-time, serious dialogue on the religious, ethnic, and cultural concerns that divide us as a nation—a task for which the Internet is particularly suited.

Precisely because it is anonymous, the Internet provides a perfect forum to discuss race, sexual orientation, and other similar issues. On the Internet, said one user, "you can speak freely and not have fears that somebody is going to attack you for what comes out of your heart." It's the kind of open and heartfelt discussion that we need to advance and sponsor online.

Already, a number of small groups and lone individuals are meeting the cyberhate challenge through simple dialogue between strangers. I'm talking about websites run by educators to inform parents about online hate materials . . . sites operated by "recovering" racists to engage skinheads and other misguided kids in productive debate . . . websites run by concerned citizens to bridge the gap in ignorance between ethnic, racial, and other communities.

The "Y? forum," also known as the National Forum on People's Differences, is a wonderful example of a website where readers can safely ask and follow discussions on sensitive cross-cultural topics without having to wade through foul language or "flame wars."

As a columnist from *The Miami Herald* described the appeal of these kinds of sites, "As long as we are mysteries, one to another, we face a perpetuation of ignorance and a feeding of fear. I'd rather people ask the questions than try to make up the answers. I'd rather they ask the questions than turn to myth and call it truth."

In closing, my company recognizes that the Internet doesn't operate in a vacuum. We agree that those who profit from information technology have a special responsibility to see that its promise is shared across class, race, and geographic boundaries.

That's why we're working with the public schools and libraries in our region to see that they're all equipped with the pens, pencils, and paper of the twenty-first century . . . why we're helping to further distance learning and telemedicine applications that serve the educational and health needs of the disabled and isolated . . . why we're helping minority groups and civil rights organizations use information technology to spread their vision and their values to the millions of people electronically linked to the global village.

And that's the way it should be.

Let me leave you with a personal story. . . .

When growing up, my Jewish friends and I often swapped theology-tales from the Hassidic Masters for stories from the *Lives of the Saints*. I remember from these discussions that one of the great rabbis noted that the first word of the Ten Commandments

Undetailed examples enhance the credibility of Smith and his company.

Gracious acknowledgment of sponsoring center

"Finally" signals listeners that this is the last point in his proposal.

Examples are effective in providing concrete illustrations of how this idea works.

Acknowledges his responsibility.

Uses examples to summarize his proposal.

Detailed example is likely to appeal to listeners.

is "I" and the last word is "neighbor." In typical Talmudic fashion, the rabbi was telling us that if we want to incorporate the commandments into our lives, we must move from a focus on ourselves to others.

At Bell Atlantic, the more we grow—in both scale and scope—the greater the emphasis we place on being a good corporate citizen, and the more we're driven to see that digital technology is used for purposes of enlightenment and education.

The Internet will fundamentally transform the way we work, learn, do commerce. It will also, if properly used and rightly taught, help bridge the gap in understanding between communities—becoming not a tool of hate but one of hope.

Restates thesis.

Thank you again for the invitation to join you this morning.

■ ■ ■

Mending the Body by Lending an Ear: The Healing Power of Listening

Transcript of speech delivered by Carol Koehler, assistant professor of communication and medicine, in Missouri on March 19, 1998

Abstract: Koehler explains the four important elements of doctor–patient relationships, namely, care, acknowledgment, response, and emotional control (CARE). Listening to patients' complaints and practicing CARE are valuable skills of health-care professionals.

Full Text: Address by CAROL KOEHLER, Ph.D., Assistant Professor of Communication and Medicine. Reprinted with permission from Carol Koehler.

Delivered to the International Listening Association Business Conference, at the Ritz-Carlton Hotel, Kansas City, Missouri, March 19, 1998.

I would like to start this morning by telling you two different stories. Each story has the same two characters and happens in the same location. Both stories occur within a twenty-four-hour period.

Over the Christmas holidays, my husband and I were invited to a formal black-tie wedding. This was to be an elegant event, so we put on our best evening clothes. Adding to that, I wore my mother's diamond jewelry and this fabulous mink coat that I inherited. Just before we left the house, I telephoned my 86-year-old mother-in-law for her daily checkup. When she answered, her voice sounded a little strange, so my husband and I decided to stop at her apartment to make sure she was all right before we went to the wedding.

When we arrived she seemed slightly disoriented (she was 86 years old but wonderfully healthy, sharp witted, and self-sufficient). We called her physician to ask his advice, and he said to bring her to the local emergency room and have her checked out. We did that. This was a Saturday night, so the emergency room was pretty active. When we arrived, I in my mink and my husband in his tux, we looked noticeably different from the general population in the waiting room. While my husband filled out forms, the doctors took my mother-in-law into a makeshift curtained room. When I noticed that the staff had removed both her glasses and her hearing aid, I realized she experienced some anxiety, so at that point I decided to stay with her to keep her from being frightened. As I went into the room, a young doctor said, "Ma'am, you can't go in there." Without missing a beat, I said, "Don't be ridiculous." With that, I went and found a chair in the waiting room, brought it into the examination room, and sat

Detailed story captures listeners' immediate interest and attention.

down. I remember thinking the staff looked a little bewildered, but no one challenged me at any time. When my mother-in-law's hands felt a little cool, I asked for a heated blanket and one was brought immediately. So it went for the entire evening; we missed the wedding but finally got my mother-in-law in a permanent room about 2 A.M.

The next day I went to the hospital about 10 o'clock in the morning dressed in tennis shoes, a sweat suit, and no makeup. As I arrived at my mother-in-law's room, an unfamiliar doctor was just entering. I introduced myself and asked him to speak up so my mother-in-law would be aware of why he was there and what he was doing. I told him that she tends to be frightened by the unexpected and without her glasses or hearing aid, she was already frightened enough. This thirty-something male doctor proceeded to examine my mother-in-law without raising his voice so that she could hear and without acknowledging me or my request in any way. Actually he never really looked at either one of us.

In both those scenarios, I was listened to, not by ears alone, but by eyes, by gender, by age judgments, and by social status assessments. That started me thinking. . . .

Credible sources establish the problem.

Why did a recent article in the *Journal of the American Medical Association* indicate high dissatisfaction in traditional doctor–patient appointments? Why is it *The Wall Street Journal* claims that perception of physician concern and not physician expertise is the deciding factor in the rising number of malpractice suits? Why did *The New England Journal of Medicine* report that the care and attention quotient is causing "alternative" medical practices to grow by leaps and bounds? Given this litany of events, what does it really mean to listen? And why, in the name of science, don't we produce better listeners in the medical profession?

"First," "second," and "third" help listeners follow Koehler's organization.

The reasons are so obvious that they are sometimes overlooked. First, listening is mistakenly equated with hearing, and since most of us can hear, no academic priority is given to this subject in either college or med school (this, by the way, flies in the face of those who measure daily time usage). Time experts say we spend 9% of our day writing, 16% reading, 30% speaking, and 45% listening—just the opposite of our academic pursuits. Second, we perceive power in speech. We put a value on those who have the gift of gab. How often have you heard the compliment, "He/she can talk to anyone"? Additionally, we equate speaking with controlling both the conversation and the situation. The third and last reason we don't listen is that we are in an era of information overload. We are bombarded with the relevant and the irrelevant, and it is easy to confuse them. Often it's all just so much noise.

Thesis is advanced.

How can we address this depressing situation? Dan Callahan, a physician and teacher, argues that primacy in health care needs to be given to the notion of care over cure. Caring as well as curing humanizes our doctor–patient relationships.

Inviting listeners to participate sustains their interest and involvement.

Let's talk about what that might mean for health care. What comes to mind when someone is caring? [The audience responded with the words *warm, giving, interested, genuine,* and *sincere.*] Now, what comes to mind when you think of the opposite of care? [The audience volunteered *cold, uninterested, egotistical, busy, distracted,* and *selfish.*]

What might a caring doctor be like? If we take the word CARE and break it down, we find the qualities that are reflective of a therapeutic communicator, in other words, someone who listens not with ears alone.

The four letters in CARE are used to organize main points.

C stands for *concentrate.* Physicians should hear with their eyes and ears. They should avoid the verbal and visual barriers that prevent real listening. It may be as simple as eye contact (some young doctors have told me they have a difficult time with looking people in the eye), and my advice is, when you are uncomfortable, focus on the patient's mouth and as the comfort level increases, move to the eyes. In the placement of office furniture, try and keep the desk from being a barrier between you and the patient. Offer an alternative chair for consultations—one to the side of your desk and one in front of the desk. Let the patient have some control and power to decide their own comfort level.

A stands for *acknowledge*. Show them that you are listening by using facial expressions, giving vocal prompts, and listening between the lines for intent as well as content. Listen for their vocal intonation when responding to things like prescribed medication. If you hear some hesitation in their voice, say to them, "I hear you agreeing, but I'm getting the sound of some reservation in your voice. Can you tell me why?" And then acknowledge their response. Trust them and they will trust you.

R stands for *response*. Clarify issues by asking, "I'm not sure what you mean." Encourage continuing statements by saying, "And then what?" or "Tell me more." The recurrent headache may mask other problems. Provide periodic recaps to focus information. Learn to take cryptic notes and then return your attention to the patient. (Note taking is sometimes used as an avoidance tactic, and patients sense this.) Use body language by leaning toward the patient. Effective listening requires attention, patience, and the ability to resist the urge to control the conversation.

Undetailed examples clarify ideas.

E stands for *exercise emotional control*. This means if your "hot buttons" are pushed by people who whine, and in walks someone who does that very thing, you are likely to fake interest in the patient. With your mind elsewhere, you will never really hear that person. Emotional blocks are based on previous experiences. They are sometimes activated by words, by tone of voice, by style of clothes or hair, or by ethnicity. It is not possible for us to be free of those emotional reactions, but the first step in controlling them is to recognize when you are losing control. One of the most useful techniques to combat emotional responses is to take a deep breath when confronted with the urge to interrupt. Deep breathing redirects your response, and as a bonus, it is impossible to talk when you are deep breathing. Who of us would not choose the attentive caring physician?

As it nears time for me to take that deep breath, I would just like to reiterate that listening is a learned skill, and learning to listen with CARE has valuable benefits for health-care professionals and patients. As a wise man named J. Isham once said, "Listening is an attitude of the heart, a genuine desire to be with another which both attracts and heals."

Summarizes key ideas.

Effective closing quotation

Thank you very much.

■ ■ ■

Witchcraft
Dana Wheeler

(Sample Informative Speech)

The following speech was presented by Dana Wheeler in November 1998. At the time, she was a student in a communication course taught by Dr. Lynette Long at James Madison University. The assignment was to prepare and present a 5-minute informative speech that included at least three references. Dana's choice of witchcraft as a topic was both original and interesting. In developing her speech, Dana made some effective choices. Her opening shows that she understood and addressed stereotypes of witchcraft that her listeners were likely to hold. Personally interviewing a real witch enhanced Dana's credibility, as did her careful use of respected sources.

The opening demonstrates that Dana is aware of common stereotypes of witches. By admitting she held some of these stereotypes, she creates identification with listeners.

The description of Silver Raven creates a strong visual impression of a normal woman.

Dana advances a clear, concise thesis.

Dana presents an effective preview of her speech so listeners can follow her.

To begin with signals listeners that she is introducing her first main point, a definition of witchcraft.

Reference to her interview of Silver Raven enhances Dana's credibility and creates a personal face for the abstraction of "witch."

A published analysis of witchcraft is used to support Silver Raven's description of it.

Dana provides a concise internal summary of her first point and uses *now* to signal that she is moving on to her next point.

She strengthens the credibility of her sources by alerting listeners that books by Reis, Summers, and Middleton are published by scholarly presses.

In an efficient internal summary of points 1 and 2, Dana uses *now* to signal listeners she is moving on to her third point.

Silver Raven's joke humanizes her to listeners.

Evil, wicked, spooky, followers of the devil. I was even thinking to myself, "Please do not sacrifice me tonight!" All of these things were going through my mind as I went to a real witch's house to interview her on Halloween night. Imagine that you were on your way to interview a witch. Would similar thoughts be going through your mind?

As I approached her house and knocked on the door, a very normal-looking woman answered. She had dark brown hair and green eyes. She was wearing a pair of Levis jeans with a Dodgers shirt, and she had no shoes on. Her name was Silver Raven. There were no broomsticks or black cats inside her home, and the house was decorated with the normal things seen in most homes. After researching witchcraft and interviewing a witch, I am here to inform you about what witchcraft is and is not. I want to correct misunderstandings that are sometimes associated with the witchcraft religion. Today, I will define witchcraft, tell you why people want to become witches and practice witchcraft, and talk about some of the ceremonies that are involved with it.

To begin with, I will define witchcraft. Many people misunderstand witchcraft as silly potions and evil spells to harm people. This is not true. Witchcraft is the study of Old Religion, and witches refer to their practice as the "Old Religion" or "The Craft." Now, people who practice Old Religion practice medicine through intimate knowledge of herbs and working of nature. Also, they use psychology through clever magic incantations that use words to evoke certain reactions in people. According to Silver Raven, the witch I interviewed, Wicca (another word for witchcraft) is an earth-based religion that works with the forces of the universe. It is not Satan worship, it is not the sacrifice of living things, and it is not evil. She said it is also one of the fastest-growing religions in the United States today. Hans Holzer, author of *The Truth about Witchcraft,* gives a similar definition to that of Silver Raven. He defines it as having belief in a spiritual life after death and reincarnation, which are the cornerstones of the witchcraft religion. Witches believe in life everlasting in immortality of the human spirit soul. They do not believe in the devil, hell, or heaven.

Now that you have been informed about the definition of witchcraft, you might be wondering why people want to get involved with witchcraft. According to Elizabeth Reis, author of *Spellbound: Women and Witchcraft in America,* which was published by Scholarly Resources, people get involved because they enjoy the exciting ceremonies that are part of witchcraft. Also, people believe in witchcraft because they can feel the positive power it produces in their lives. People in witchcraft feel a sense of belonging to a select group. They value the smallness and intimacy and the democratic process of being part of a group of witches. Montague Summers published *History of Witchcraft and Demonology* with University Books. In this book, he explains that people who want to practice witchcraft do not view it as a way to circumvent natural law but rather a way to learn more about the craft and perhaps in the process understand themselves a little better. In a book sponsored by the prestigious National History Press, author John Middleton explains that people are drawn to witchcraft to learn facts about mental powers and the secret workings of the universe. Finally, the biggest reason why people become involved in the witchcraft religion is because they can work spells and make things happen.

Now that I have defined witchcraft and explained why many people want to become involved in it, I want to inform you about some of the ceremonies and rituals that are important to witchcraft. During our interview, Silver Raven told me that each day before she goes to work to teach kids (she laughs, and says "no, not to eat them"), she begins with 15 to 30 minutes of meditation in the morning, and incense and white candles burn in the bathroom while she showers. Other ceremonies are performed among witches inside a consecrated circle to keep the power inside it. They wear only silver jewelry to represent "the moon goddess" and never wear gold. The bible of the witches, called *Book of Shadows,* is always present. Witches believe that dancing and chanting arouses "the power," which is an electric force emanating from their bodies.

A few of the holidays that ceremonies are performed [on] are May 1, celebration of fertility (particularly of the earth); June 21, powerful day for magic and healing; August 1, day of thanksgiving for earth's bounty; and September 21, celebration of the harvest (a day of balance). The most popular holiday is October 31, which is Halloween. Halloween is a day of mourning those a person has lost, a time of remembering and honoring, and a time of death and rebirth. It is the witches' new year because of the position of the moon, which makes the veil thinnest between the worlds of the living and the dead on this date, as Silver Raven explained it to me.

Undetailed examples of ceremonies show listeners that witchcraft does not focus on evil brews and destructive spells.

Now that I have given you a definition of witchcraft, explained why many people want to get involved, and described some of the key ceremonies, you should have a factual basis for understanding what witchcraft is and is not. Witchcraft is not out to convert anyone, as Silver Raven said in our interview. Witchcraft also is not evil or wicked, as some people think. It is just another form of religion being practiced in the United States. I hope the information I've provided today gives you a better understanding of witchcraft. Let me end my speech with the words Silver Raven spoke to me when we ended our interview, "Blessed be." (Reprinted by permission.)

Dana summarizes the three points of her speech and restates her thesis that popular stereotypes of witchcraft are misinformed.

Closing with Raven's quote, "Blessed be" effectively reinforces Dana's thesis that witchcraft is not evil.

References

Holzer, H. (1969). *The Truth about Witchcraft.* New York: Doubleday & Company, Inc.
Middleton, J. (1967). *Magic, Witchcraft, and Curing.* New York: The Natural History Press.
Murray, M. A. (1970). *The God of the Witches.* New York: Oxford University Press.
Reis, E. (1998). *Spellbound.* Delaware: Scholarly Resources Inc.
Summers, M. (1956). *The History of Witchcraft and Demonology.* New York: University Books Inc.
Wheeler, D. L. (1998, October 31). Interview with Silver Raven, witch practicing witchcraft.

Appendix B
Interviewing

Focus Questions

1. What are the purposes of interviewing?

2. Is there a standard pattern for interviews?

3. What topics are illegal in employment interviews?

4. How can you prepare to communicate effectively in hiring interviews?

5. What do companies include in their websites that might be helpful to you in an employment interview?

You've probably participated in a number of interviews during your life. It's likely that you have been an interviewee many times. Perhaps you were interviewed by committees that appoint students to leadership positions at your school or award scholarships to students. You may have had interviews with members of groups you sought to join. Probably you have interviewed more than once for part-time or full-time jobs.

You've probably been on the other side of the interviewing process too; you may have interviewed people who were applying to join organizations to which you belong. Perhaps you've had jobs that required you to conduct telephone or in-person interviews. You may have interviewed experts to gain information about a topic on which you were writing a paper or preparing a speech.

When the topic of interviewing comes up, many college students think immediately of hiring or employment interviews. Yet hiring is only one of many ways that interviews show up in our lives. As we shall see, interviews are part of professional, civic, and social life. Because interviews are common, learning to communicate effectively in interviews is important to your personal and professional success.

An **interview** is a communication transaction that emphasizes questions and answers (Lumsden & Lumsden, 2004, p. 266). In this section, we'll discuss various kinds of interviews. In this appendix, we will discuss interviewing and identify ways you can enhance your effectiveness as both interviewer and interviewee. First, we will identify a range of purposes or types of interviews. Second, we will discuss the typical structure and style of interviews. Third, we will describe different kinds of questions interviewers use. Then, we will identify challenges that are part of interviewing. We will focus on hiring interviews because those are particularly important to many college students. Our discussion will provide tips for preparing to interview and for dealing with inappropriate or illegal questions.

Understanding Communication in Interviews

Types and Purposes of Interviews

Communication scholars have identified distinct types of interviews. Each interview is defined by its primary purpose, although many interviews have multiple and sometimes conflicting purposes. For example, a job candidate may want both to be honest and to get a job offer, and the two goals may be at odds. An interviewer may want to gain information for a speech yet may be biased about the topic that he or she wants to support. We'll discuss eleven types of interviews.

Information-giving Interviews In the first type of interview, the interviewer provides information to the interviewee. Doctors engage in **information-giving interviews** when they explain to patients how to prepare for procedures, take medicines, follow exercise programs, and observe symptoms. Academic advisers give students information about curricular requirements and administrative processes. Team leaders often inform new members of a work unit about expectations and operating procedures.

Information-getting Interviews In this type of interview, the interviewer asks questions to learn about the interviewee's opinions, knowledge, attitudes, behaviors, and so forth. Public opinion polls, census taking, and research surveys are common examples of **information-getting interviews.** Physicians also use these to gain insight into patients' medical histories and current conditions (Farnill, Hayes, & Todisco, 1997). Journalists devote a great deal of time to information-getting interviews to obtain background material for stories they are writing and to learn about experts' opinions on newsworthy topics. Information-getting interviews are useful whenever we are trying to learn about something—perhaps to write a paper, prepare a speech, or enlarge our personal understanding of some issue.

Persuasive Interviews Interviews designed to influence attitudes or actions are **persuasive interviews.** The best-known example of these is the sales interview, in which a salesperson attempts to persuade a customer to buy a product or service. Persuasive interviews can sell more than products. They may also promote people (political candidates) and ideas (persuading an administrator to act on your team's report, convincing a company to implement environmental regulations).

Problem-solving Interviews When people need to solve some problem, they may engage in **problem-solving interviews.** Perhaps you have met with a professor to discuss difficulties in a course. The two of you may have collaborated to identify ways to improve your note taking, study habits, and writing. Supervisors sometimes hold problem-solving interviews with employees to discover and resolve impediments to maximally effective work. Colleagues often talk to each other to resolve problems in morale, productivity, or other work-related issues. By seeking each other's perspectives we can broaden our understanding of problems and our insight into potential solutions.

Counseling Interviews

Like problem-solving interviews, **counseling interviews** focus on a problem. In counseling interviews, however, the problem is not mutual. A client has a problem, such as stress, depression, or compulsiveness, that she or he wants to overcome. The counselor attempts to help the client understand the problem more fully and collaborates with the client to develop strategies for coping with or overcoming the difficulty (Evans, Coman, & Goss, 1996). Counseling interviews also occur outside the therapeutic setting: We may seek counseling from attorneys to address (or avoid) legal problems, from accountants to get help with financial matters, and from religious leaders to deal with spiritual issues.

Employment Interviews

The purpose of **employment interviews** is to allow employers and job candidates to assess each other and decide whether there is a good fit between them. Typically, employment interviews include periods of information giving and information getting as well as persuasive efforts on the part of both participants. The prospective employer wants to convince the job candidate of the quality of the company, and the candidate wants to convince the prospective employer of the quality of his or her qualifications. Ideally, both participants gain enough information to make a sound judgment of the fit between the candidate and the job.

Complaint Interviews

Complaint interviews allow people to register complaints about a product, service, or person. Many firms have departments whose sole purpose is to accept and respond to complaints. Of primary importance is showing the people who complain that their complaints are heard and that they matter. The interviewer (company representative) attempts to gain information about the customer's dissatisfaction: What was defective or disappointing about the product? Was service inadequate? What would it take to satisfy the customer now? The person conducting complaint interviews should call recurring complaints to the attention of those who can diagnose and solve underlying problems.

Performance Reviews

Most organizations require **performance reviews,** or performance appraisals, at regular intervals. By building performance appraisals into work life, organizations continually monitor employees' performance and foster their professional growth. The performance review is an occasion on which a supervisor comments on a subordinate's achievements and professional development, identifies any weaknesses or problems, and collaborates to develop goals for future performance. During the interview, subordinates should offer their perceptions of their strengths and weaknesses and participate actively in developing goals for professional development (Kikoski, 1998).

Reprimand Interviews

When a person's work is unsatisfactory or when the person is creating tensions with coworkers, a supervisor may conduct a **reprimand interview.** The goals are to identify lapses in professional conduct, determine sources of problems, and establish a plan for improving future performance. Because reprimands tend to evoke defensiveness, developing a constructive, supportive climate for these interviews is especially important. Supervisors may foster a good climate by opening the interview with assurances that the goal is to solve a problem together, not to punish the subordinate. Supervisors should also invite subordinates to express their perceptions and feelings fully.

Stress Interviews   **Stress interviews** are designed to create anxiety in respondents or interviewees. Although they may include gaining or giving information, hiring, or other interview purposes, stress interviews are unique in their deliberate intent to apply pressure. Frequently used communication techniques for inducing stress are rapid-fire questions, intentional misinterpretations and distortions of the interviewee's responses, and hostile or skeptical nonverbal expressions.

Why, you might ask, would anyone deliberately create a high-stress interview situation? Actually, stress interviews may be useful in several contexts. Attorneys may intentionally intimidate reluctant or hostile witnesses or people whose honesty is suspect. Similarly, prison administrators and police officers may communicate aggressively with people they think are withholding important information. This kind of interview also may be used in hiring people for high-stress jobs. By deliberately trying to rattle job candidates, interviewers can assess how well they manage and respond to stress.

Exit Interviews   In academic and professional life, **exit interviews** have become increasingly popular. The goal of this type of interview is to gain information, insights, and perceptions about a place of work or education from a person who is leaving. While people are in a job or learning environment, they may be reluctant to mention dissatisfactions or to speak against those who have power over them. When people are leaving an organization or school, however, they can offer honest insights and perceptions with little fear of reprisal. Thus, exit interviews can be especially valuable in providing information about policies, personnel, and organizational culture.

I routinely have exit interviews with graduate students when they complete their degrees in my department. From these conferences, I gain important information that allows me and my colleagues to refine our curriculum, program requirements, and opportunities for graduate students.

The Structure of Interviews

To be effective, interviews should follow a structure that builds a good communication climate and allows the interviewer and interviewee to deal with substantive matters. Experienced interviewers, even those without professional training, tend to organize interview communication into a three-stage sequence. Interviewees who understand the purpose of each stage in the sequence increase their ability to participate effectively.

The Opening Stage   The initial stage of an interview tends to be brief and aims to create an effective climate for interaction, clarify the purpose, and preview issues to be discussed (Wilson & Goodall, 1991). Typically, opening small talk encourages a friendly climate:

- "I see you're from Buffalo. Are the winters there still as harsh as they used to be?"
- "It's been 6 months since our last performance review. Any new developments in your life?"

- "I noticed you got your B.A. from State University. I graduated from there too. Did you ever take any courses with Doctor Bransford in anthropology?"

After opening small talk, effective interviewers state the purpose of the interview and how they plan to accomplish that purpose:

- "As you know, I'm on campus today to talk with liberal arts majors who are interested in joining Hodgeson Marketing. I'd like to ask you some questions about yourself and your background, and then I want to give you an opportunity to ask me anything you want about Hodgeson."
- "Pat, the reason I asked you to meet with me today is that there have been some complaints about your attitude from others on your work team. I know you are good at your job and have a fine history with the firm, so I want us to put our heads together to resolve this matter. Let's begin with me telling you what I've heard, and then I'd like to hear your perceptions of what's happening."

The Substantive Stage   The second stage of an interview, which generally consumes the bulk of time, deals with substance or content relevant to the purpose of the interview. For example, in reprimand interviews the substantive stage would zero in on identifying problem behaviors and devising solutions. In a hiring interview, the substantive stage might concentrate on the job candidate's background, experience, and qualifications.

Because the goal of the substantive stage is to exchange information, it takes careful planning and thought. Most interviewers prepare lists of topics or specific questions and use their notes to make sure they cover all the important topics. During the interview, they may also take notes of responses. Communication during this phase tends to progress from broad topic areas to increasingly narrow, detailed, and demanding questions within each topic. After introducing a topic, the interviewer may ask some initial general questions and then follow up with more detailed probes. Because the pattern of communication moves from broad to narrow, it has been called the **funnel sequence** (Cannell & Kahn, 1968; Moffatt, 1979). The interviewer may repeat the funnel sequence for each new topic area in an interview.

During the substantive stage, an interviewer may invite the interviewee to take the lead in communication, either by posing questions or by volunteering perceptions and ideas in response to what has been covered thus far. To be an effective interviewee, you should be prepared with questions and topics that you want to introduce. This portrays you as someone who is self-initiating and responsible. Research shows that it's also important to monitor your nonverbal communication. Interviewers tend to be most impressed with interviewees whose paralanguage and kinesics convey enthusiasm, confidence, and an outgoing personality (Mino, 1996).

The Closing Stage   Like the opening stage, the closing stage tends to be brief. Its purposes are to summarize what has been discussed, state what follow-up will occur, if any, and create good will in parting. Summarizing the content of the interview increases the likelihood that an accurate and complete record (written or in memory) of the interview will survive. If the interviewer overlooks any topics, the interviewee may appropriately offer a reminder. Interviewees also may ask about follow-up if interviewers fail to mention this.

Most interviews follow the three-step sequence we've discussed. Occasionally, they do not. Some interviewers are ineffective because they are disorganized, unprepared, and inadequately trained in effective interviewing. They may ramble for 15 minutes or more and fail to provide any closing other than "Gee, our time is up." In other instances, interviewers may deliberately violate the standard pattern to achieve their goals. For example, in stress interviews designed to test how well a person responds to pressure, the interviewer may skip opening comments and jump immediately into tough substantive questions. This allows the interviewer to assess how well the respondent copes with unexpected stress.

Styles of Interviewing

Like other forms of communication, interviews have climates that may be more or less open, egalitarian, supportive, and cooperative. The climate between participants in interviews is influenced by aspects of communication that we discussed in Part I of this book—for instance, the degree of confirmation provided, cultivation of a defensive or supportive climate, and effective or ineffective listening. Formality and balance of power also affect the climate of an interview.

Interviews may be more or less formal. In highly formal interviews, participants tend to stay within social and professional roles. The content of highly formal interviews tends to follow a standard format, often one that the interviewer has written to structure the interaction. Nonverbal communication provides further clues to formality: clothes, a formal meeting room, stilted postures, and a stiff handshake are all signs of formality.

In contrast, informal interviews are more relaxed, personal, and flexible. The interviewer attempts to engage the interviewee as an individual, not just a person in a general role. Typically, informal interviews aren't as rigidly structured as formal interviews. The interviewer may have a list of standard topics (either memorized or written down), but those provide only guidelines, not a straightjacket for communication. Informal interviews often include nonverbal cues such as smiling, relaxed postures, casual surroundings, and informal dress.

Most interviews fall between the extremes of formality and informality. Also, interviews may become more or less formal as a result of communication between participants. A person who communicates in a stilted manner is likely to encourage formality in the other person. Conversely, a person who communicates casually promotes a relaxed style of response.

Another influence on the communication climate in interviews is the balance of power between interviewer and interviewee. Power may be evenly balanced between participants or skewed toward the interviewer or the interviewee.

Interviewees have the greatest power to direct communication in **mirror interviews,** in which the interviewer consistently reflects the interviewee's comments to the interviewee. This may be done by restating verbatim what an interviewee says, paraphrasing an interviewee's comments, or making limited inferences about an interviewee's thoughts and feelings based on the communication. Skillful listening is essential for effectively using the mirror style (Banville, 1978). Consider this sample excerpt from a mirror interview:

INTERVIEWER: Tell me about your studies.

INTERVIEWEE: I'm a communication major.

INTERVIEWER: So you've studied communication?

INTERVIEWEE: Yes, especially organizational communication and leadership.

INTERVIEWER: Then you're particularly interested in leadership in organizations?

INTERVIEWEE: Yes. I think communication is the heart of effective leadership, so studying it has taught me a lot about how to lead well.

INTERVIEWER: So you see communication as the heart of effective leadership?

INTERVIEWEE: Well, I see leadership as motivating others and empowering them to achieve their goals. A person who knows how to communicate clearly, listen well, and establish rapport with others is most able to motivate them.

In this exchange, the interviewer lets the interviewee lead. What the interviewee says is the basis for the interviewer's subsequent questions and probes. Astute interviewees realize that mirror interviews give them significant opportunity to highlight their strengths and introduce topics they wish to discuss.

Distributive interviews are those in which power is equally divided (or distributed) between participants. Both ask and answer questions, listen and speak, and contribute to shaping the direction and content of communication. The distributive style of interviewing is generally used when participants are equal in professional or social standing. Distributive interviews may also be used between people with unequal power if the interviewer wants to create a relaxed exchange. Recruiters often use distributive styles to put job candidates at ease.

Authoritarian interviews are those in which the interviewer exercises primary control over interaction. The interviewer may avoid or quickly cut off discussion of any topics not on the list and may give the interviewee little or no opportunity to ask questions or initiate topics. Efficiency is the primary strength of the authoritarian style of interviewing: Many topics can be covered quickly. But the authoritarian style of interviewing can be frustrating to interviewees, and the interviewer may miss relevant information by failing to specifically seek it and by not giving the interviewee an opportunity to initiate topics.

In **stress interviews,** which we discussed earlier in this chapter, the interviewer has primary control, as in authoritarian interviews. Unlike authoritarian interviews, however, stress interviews are a deliberate attempt to create anxiety in the interviewee. Thus, the interviewer controls not only the pace and content of interaction but also the psychological agenda.

Interviewees have even less control than in authoritarian interviews because stress interviews often rely on trick questions, surprise turns in topic, and unsettling responses to interviewees. If you find yourself in a stress interview, recognize that it is probably a deliberate attempt to test your ability to cope with pressure. Stay alert and flexible to deal with unpredictable communication from the interviewer.

Forms of Questions in Interviews

Most interviews follow a question–answer pattern in which each person speaks only briefly before the other person speaks. Consequently, skill in asking and responding to questions is central to effectiveness. Skillful interviewers understand that different kinds of questions shape responses, and effective interviewees recognize the opportunities and constraints of distinct forms of questions. We'll consider eight of the most common types of questions and discuss the responses invited by each.

Open Questions Open questions are general queries that initiate new topics: "What can you tell me about yourself?" "What is your work experience?" Because open questions are broad, they allow interviewees a wide latitude of appropriate responses. Thus, interviewees have an opportunity to steer communication toward topics that interest or reflect well on them.

Closed Questions Closed questions call for specific, brief responses. Unlike open questions, they do not invite broad answers. Instead, they ask for a concrete, narrow reply, often in the form of "yes" or "no." Closed questions often are used to follow up on general replies to open questions. "How many business courses have you taken?" "What was your position at the summer camp?" "How did you handle that situation?" Closed questions call for short, direct answers, and an interviewer may interpret more general responses negatively.

Mirror Questions Mirror questions paraphrase or reflect the previous communication. If an interviewee says, "I have worked in a lot of stressful jobs," the interviewer might respond reflectively by saying, "So you can handle pressure, right?" At the content level of meaning, a mirror question seems pointless because it merely repeats what preceded it. At the relationship level of meaning, however, mirror questions say, "Elaborate; tell me more." Thus, they represent opportunities to expand on ideas.

Hypothetical Questions Hypothetical questions ask a person to respond to a speculative situation. The questioner may describe a hypothetical scenario and then ask the respondent to react. Recruiters often pose hypothetical questions to see how well job candidates can think on their feet. A student of mine provided the following example of a hypothetical question she was asked in a job interview: "Assume you are supervising an employee who is consistently late to work and sometimes leaves early. What would you do?" My student responded that her first course of action would be to talk with the employee to determine the reason for her tardiness and early departures. Next, she said, she would work with the employee to eliminate the source or, if company policies allowed it, to rearrange the schedule to accommodate the employee's circumstances.

This response showed that the job candidate was collaborative and supportive—precisely the qualities the recruiter wanted to assess. Hypothetical questions are designed to find out how you grasp and respond to complex situations. The content of your answer may be less important than the way you approach the situation (Gladwell, 2000).

Probing Questions When we probe something, we go beneath its surface to find out more about it. During interviews, probing questions go beneath the surface of a response to gather additional information and insight. Consider this example of several probing questions that follow an open question and a broad response:

> INTERVIEWER: Tell me about your work history.
>
> INTERVIEWEE: I've held ten jobs while I've been attending college.
>
> INTERVIEWER: Why have you held so many different jobs instead of sticking with one of them?
>
> INTERVIEWEE: I kept switching in the hope of finding one that would be really interesting.
>
> INTERVIEWER: What makes a job interesting to you?
>
> INTERVIEWEE: It would have to be challenging and have enough variety not to bore me.
>
> INTERVIEWER: Are you easily bored?

Note how the interviewer probes to learn more about the interviewee's responses. Each probe seeks more details about the interviewee's attitudes toward work.

Leading Questions Leading questions predispose a certain response. For example, "You believe in teamwork, don't you?" encourages "Yes" as a response, whereas "You don't drink on a regular basis, do you?" encourages "No" as a response. Leading questions generally are not a good way to get candid responses, because they suggest how you want a person to respond (Stewart & Cash, 1991). Leading questions can be useful, however, if an interviewer wants to test an interviewee's commitment to an idea. An acquaintance of mine who recruits employees for sales positions that require a lot of travel often poses this leading question: "After a year or two of travel, the novelty wears off. I assume you expect a permanent location after a year or so with us, right?" Applicants who answer "yes" do not get job offers, because travel is an ongoing part of the sales positions.

Loaded Questions Loaded questions are worded to reflect the emotions or judgments of the person asking the question. The language in the question is laden with emotion and may cause an interviewee to respond emotionally. "How do you feel about slackers who expect to leave work at 5 P.M. every day?" In this question, the word *slackers* suggests the interviewer's negative judgment of employees who expect to quit at 5 P.M. each day. An interviewee is likely to pick up on the bias in the question and reply, "I think an employee should work until the job is done, not until the clock strikes 5 P.M." But this may not reflect the interviewee's actual views, so the question isn't effective in probing the interviewee's attitudes.

Another version of the loaded question involves baiting an interviewee. The classic example of a loaded question is, "When did you stop beating your dog?" The question presumes something (in this case, that the interviewee at some point did beat her or his dog) that hasn't been established. This kind of loaded question is likely to foster defensiveness in an interviewee and to limit what an interviewer learns about the interviewee.

Summary Questions   A final kind of question is the summary question, which covers what has been discussed. Although summary questions often are phrased as statements, they function as questions. For example, "I believe we've covered everything" should be perceived as, "Do we need to discuss anything else?" "It seems we've agreed on expectations for your performance during the next quarter" should be perceived as, "Do you feel we have a common understanding of what's expected of you?" Communication that summarizes topics in an interview provides an opportunity for participants to check whether they agree about what they've discussed and what will follow.

What we've discussed gives us a foundation for discussing two important challenges for communicating in interviews.

Challenges When Communicating in Interviews

Like all other kinds of interaction, interviewing presents challenges that require communication skills. We will discuss two specific challenges: preparing to be interviewed and dealing with illegal questions. We will use the hiring interview to illustrate these challenges, but the ideas we'll discuss pertain to other kinds of interviews as well.

Preparing to Interview Effectively

My students have often told me that they can't prepare for interviews because they don't know what the interviewer will ask. Even without knowing exactly what questions will arise, you can do a great deal to prepare yourself for a successful interview. First, prepare a résumé that is concise, accurate in content and style (proofread carefully!), and professional in appearance. Your résumé is your first chance to "advertise yourself" to potential employers (Krannich & Banis, 1990).

Conduct Research   Every type of interview benefits from advance research, although the appropriate research varies according to the interview's purpose. Before performance appraisals, both the supervisor and the subordinate should review any previous performance appraisals. In addition, both participants should think about what has happened since the last appraisal: Have goals that were set been met? Have there been notable achievements, such as development of new skills or receipt of awards? It's also appropriate to talk with others to learn what is expected of employees at various stages in their careers.

Research is critical for effective employment interviewing. *Wall Street Journal* reporter Rochelle Sharpe (1995) notes that only about 5% of job applicants do any research on a company before interviewing for a job with it. Therefore, you can put yourself ahead of 95% of job applicants by doing advance research. To learn about a hiring organization, you'll want information about its products and services, self-image, history, benefits, organizational culture, and so forth. If you know someone who works for the company, ask that person to share perceptions and information with you. If you aren't personally acquainted with employees at the company, check for materials in your library or placement office or an online service. Standard references such as *Moody's Manuals* and *Standard & Poor's Index* provide information about the size, locations, salary levels, structure, employee benefits, and financial condition of many organizations.

The Internet and the World Wide Web are additional sources of information. Many companies have web pages that allow you to learn such things as how the company thinks of itself, the image it wants to project, and its size and geographic scope. Because websites are updated regularly, visiting a company's website is a good way to get the current information about a company that interests you.

Research enhances your effectiveness in two ways. First, the information you gather provides a basis for questions that show you've done your homework and understand the company. Second, when you know something about a company's or program's priorities, image, and goals, you can adapt your communication to acknowledge the expectations and norms of the company.

Engage in Person-centered Communication In Chapter 2, we discussed person-centered communication, in which one person recognizes and respects the perspective of another person. To prepare for an interview, ask yourself, "What would I want to know if I were interviewing me for this position?" Don't ask what you want to tell the interviewer about yourself or what you think is most important about your record. Instead, take the perspective of the interviewer as you anticipate the interaction.

You are not likely to know the interviewer personally, so you can't realistically expect to understand him or her as a unique individual. What matters is to recognize that in the interview situation the recruiter is a representative of a particular company with distinct goals, history, expectations, and culture. If you have researched the company, you will be able to adapt your communication to the interviewer's frame of reference.

Person-centered communication also requires sensitivity to cultural differences. For instance, people who were raised in some Asian cultures tend to be modest about personal achievements and abilities. Viewed from a Western perspective, such modesty might be misinterpreted as lack of confidence (Kikoski, 1998; U.S. Department of Labor, 1992).

Practice Responding One of the most common complaints of employment recruiters is that candidates are unprepared for interviews (DeVito, 1994). Examples of appearing unprepared include not bringing a résumé to the interview, not knowing about the company, and not recalling specific information, such as names of former supervisors and dates of employment. Ability to recall specific information shows you are prepared and knowledgeable. Yet many people fumble when asked about specifics. Why? Because they assume they know about themselves—after all, it's their life—so they don't bother to review details and practice responses.

You can avoid appearing unprepared by taking time before an interview to review your experiences and accomplishments and to remind yourself of key names, places, and dates. It's also a good idea to practice responding aloud to questions. You want your communication to reflect what employers look for—attentiveness, positive attitude, preparation, clarity, and motivation (Anderson & Killenberg, 1998; Farnill, Hayes, & Todisco, 1997; Peterson,

1. Why did you decide to attend this school?

2. Why did you choose _____ as your major?

3. What do you consider the best course you've taken? Why?

4. Why are you interested in our company (firm)?

5. How does your academic background pertain to this job?

6. What do you consider your most serious weakness?

7. What are your long-term professional goals?

8. Which of the jobs you've held has been most satisfying to you? Why?

9. What is the most difficult situation you have ever been in? How did you handle it?

10. Who has been the biggest influence in your life?

11. What are your hobbies? How do you spend spare time?

12. How do you define success in sales (marketing, management, training, etc.)?

13. Why should we hire you instead of another person?

14. What kind of people do you prefer to work with? Why?

15. Are you willing to travel?

16. Do you plan to pursue further education in the future?

17. What do you think of the president's budget proposal [or another current national issue]?

18. Describe your closest friend.

19. How long would you expect to remain with our company?

20. Do you think recent developments in technology are particularly relevant to our company? Why? How?

21. What can you do for this company?

22. What do you see as disadvantages of this job?

23. Define *teamwork*. Give me an example of a team on which you worked.

24. What do you expect your employer to do for you?

25. Tell me about yourself.

1997; Ramsay, Gallois, & Callan, 1997). Figure B.1 lists questions commonly asked during employment interviews.

Conducting research, engaging in person-centered communication, and practicing responses will not prepare you for everything that can happen in an interview. However, they will make you better prepared and more impressive than candidates who don't follow the guidelines we've discussed.

Managing Illegal Questions in Interviews

Just a couple of years ago, a student who was completing a professional degree was asked this question by a job recruiter: "What methods of birth control do you use?" Fortunately, this student knew the question was discriminatory, so she refused to answer and reported the interviewer to the campus placement service.

Know the Law   The Equal Employment Opportunity Commission (EEOC) is a federally created entity that monitors various kinds of discrimination in hiring decisions. In 1970, the EEOC issued initial guidelines pertinent to employment interviews, and these have been updated periodically. EEOC guidelines also apply to tests, application forms, and other devices used to screen job applicants.

EEOC regulations prohibit discrimination on the basis of criteria that are legally irrelevant to job qualifications. Because the EEOC is an arm of the federal government, it protects interviewees in all states from intrusive questions about race, ethnicity, marital status, age, sex, disability, and arrests. Individual states and institutions may impose additional limits on information about candidates that may be used in hiring decisions. For instance, my school has a policy against discrimination based on military service or sexual orientation.

An illegal question reflects either an interviewer's ignorance of the law or willful disregard of it. People who conduct interviews should review restrictions on questions in a good source such as Arthur Bell's 1989 book *The Complete Manager's Guide to Interviewing*. Whether interviewers intend to ask illegal questions or not, it's important for interviewees to know what questions are not legally permissible in employment interviews. If you don't understand the legal boundaries on questions, you cannot protect your rights.

Responding to Illegal Questions   Knowing which questions are out of bounds doesn't tell us what to do if we are asked an inappropriate question. You may choose to respond if it doesn't bother you. You also have the right to object and point out to an interviewer that a question is inappropriate. If you don't care about the job, this is a reasonable way to respond. But realize that even if you exercise your rights diplomatically, doing so may lessen an interviewer's interest in hiring you.

One effective way to respond to unlawful questions is to provide only information that may be sought legally. This strategy preserves a supportive climate in the interview by not directly reprimanding the interviewer with "You can't ask that question." For instance, if an employer asks whether you are a native Chinese speaker, you might respond, "I am fluent in both English and Chinese." If you are asked whether you belong to any political organizations, be wary because this is often an effort to determine your religion or political affiliation. You might answer, "The only organizations to which I belong that are relevant to this job are the Training and Development Association and the National Communication Association." If a diplomatic response, such as a partial answer, doesn't satisfy the interviewer, it is appropriate for you to be more assertive. You might ask, "How does your question pertain to qualifications for this job?" This more direct response can be effective in protecting your rights without harming the climate. It is possible to be both assertive and cordial, and this is generally advisable. Figure B.2 lists some questions that can and cannot legally be asked by employment interviewers.

It's legal to ask:

1. Are you a law-abiding person?
2. Do you have the physical strength to do this job?
3. Are you fluent in any languages other than English?
4. Could you provide proof that you are old enough to meet the age requirements for this job?
5. Your transcript shows you took a course in socialism. Did you find it valuable?

But illegal to ask:

1. Have you ever been convicted of a felony?
2. Are you physically disabled?
3. Are you a native speaker of English?
4. How old are you?
5. Are you a socialist?
6a. Would you be willing to live in a town without a temple/church/synagogue?
6b. Does your religion allow you to work on Saturdays?
7. May I have a picture to put with your file?
8. Do you have [plan to have] children?
9. Are you married?
10. Do you have reliable child care?
11. Do you own a car or a house?
12. What is your political affiliation?

Experiencing Communication in Our Lives

CASE STUDY: Tough Questions

The following conversation is featured on the *Communication in Our Lives* CD-ROM included with this book. Once you've launched the CD, click on the "Communication Scenarios" icon, and, from the Scenarios Menu, select "Tough Questions" to watch the video.

Elliott Miller is a second-semester senior who has double-majored in business and communication. Today, he is interviewing with Community Savings and Loan, which is recruiting managerial trainees. Elliott has dressed carefully. He is wearing his good suit, a light blue shirt, a conservative necktie, and wingtips. At 10 A.M. sharp, he knocks on the office door of Karen Bourne, the person with whom he will interview. She is in her mid-thirties and is dressed in a conservative navy blue suit. She opens the door and offers her hand to Elliott.

BOURNE: Mr. Miller, I see you're right on time. That's a good start. [They shake hands.]

MILLER: Thank you for inviting me to interview today.

BOURNE: Sit down. [He sits in the chair in front of her desk; she sits behind the desk.] So, you're about to finish college, are you? I remember that time in my own life—exciting and scary!

MILLER: It's definitely both for me. I'm particularly excited about the job here at Community Savings and Loan.

BOURNE: [smiles] Then there's a mutual interest. We had a lot of applications, but we're interviewing only eight of them. What I'd like to do is get a sense of your interests and tell you about our managerial trainee program here, so that we can see if the fit between us is as good as it looks on paper. Sound good to you?

MILLER: Great.

BOURNE: Let me start by telling you about a rather common problem we've had with our past managerial trainees. Many of them run into a problem—something they have trouble learning or doing right. That's normal enough—we expect that. But a lot of the trainees seem to get derailed when that happens. Instead of finding another way to approach the problem, they get discouraged and give up. So I'm very interested in hearing what you've done when you've encountered problems or roadblocks in your life.

MILLER: Well, I can remember one time when I hit a real roadblock. I was taking an advanced chemistry course, and I just couldn't seem to understand the material. I failed the first exam, even though I'd studied hard.

BOURNE: Good example of a problem. What did you do?

MILLER: I started going to all the tutorial sessions that grad assistants offer. That helped a little, but I still wasn't getting the material the way I should. So, I organized a study team and offered to pay for pizzas so that the students who were on top of the class would have a reason to come.

BOURNE: [nodding with admiration] That shows a lot of initiative and creativity. Did the study team work?

MILLER: [smiling] It sure did. I wound up getting a B in the course, and so did several other members of the study team who had been in the same boat I was in early in the semester.

BOURNE: So you don't mind asking for help if you need it?

MILLER: I'd rather do that than flounder, but I'm usually pretty able to operate independently.

BOURNE: So you prefer working on your own to working with others?

MILLER: That depends on the situation or project. If I have all that I need to do something on my own, I'm comfortable working solo. But there are other cases in which I don't have everything I need to do something well—maybe I don't have experience in some aspect of the job or I don't have a particular skill or I don't understand some perspectives on the issues. In cases like that, I think teams are more effective than individuals.

BOURNE: Good. Banking management requires the ability to be self-initiating and also the ability to work with others. Let me ask another question. As I was looking over your transcript and résumé, I noticed that you changed your major several times. Does that indicate you have difficulty making a commitment and sticking with it?

MILLER: I guess you could think that, but it really shows that I was willing to explore a lot of alternatives before making a firm commitment.

BOURNE: But don't you think that you wasted a lot of time and courses getting to that commitment?

MILLER: I don't think so. I learned something in all of the courses I took. For instance, when I was a philosophy major, I learned about logical thinking and careful reasoning.

That's going to be useful to me in management. When I was majoring in English, I learned how to write well and how to read others' writing critically. That's going to serve me well in management too.

BOURNE: So what led you to your final decision to double-major in business and communication? That's kind of an unusual combination.

MILLER: It seems a very natural one to me. I wanted to learn about business because I want to be a manager in an organization. I need to know how organizations work, and I need to understand different management philosophies and styles. At the same time, managers work with people, and that means I have to have strong communication skills.

Summary

Interviews are common in everyday life. They occur when we respond to pollsters' questions, apply for a job or promotion, conduct research, engage in counseling, and so forth. In this chapter, we have gained insight into the structure and processes involved in interviewing. We have learned that most interviews follow a three-part sequence and that different styles and forms of question are used to achieve different objectives in interview situations.

In the second section of this appendix, we focused on three guidelines for effective communication when interviewing, especially in the context of job seeking. The first guideline is to prepare by researching the company and the interviewer, by reviewing your qualifications and experience, and by practicing dealing with questions, including difficult ones. A second guideline for effectiveness in interviews is to be person-centered in your communication. Adapting the content and style of your communication to the person with whom you are interacting is important. A final suggestion is to become familiar with legal issues relevant to interviewing. Whether you are an interviewer or an interviewee, you should know and abide by laws governing what can and cannot be asked in interviews.

 ## Communication in Our Lives ONLINE

In addition to presenting the case studies' multimedia scenarios and speeches, the *Communication in Our Lives* CD-ROM provides quick access to the *Communication in Our Lives* website, Speech Builder Express, and InfoTrac College Edition. The website is online at http://communication.wadsworth .com/woodciol4, but you can access this book's premium web content only when you link to the site directly through the book's CD.

 The *Communication in Our Lives* website features interactive tools for learning and reviewing the chapter's concepts and key terms, including electronic versions of the "For Further Reflection and Discussion" questions following and a review quiz.

 The website also provides updated web links and additional InfoTrac College Edition activities. If required, you can e-mail completed chapter activities or the quizzes to your instructor.

Key Concepts

authoritarian interview, *A-16*	distributive interview, *A-16*	funnel sequence, *A-14*
complaint interview, *A-12*	employment interview, *A-12*	information-getting interview, *A-11*
counseling interview, *A-12*	exit interview, *A-13*	

For Further Reflection and Discussion

1. Arrange an information-seeking interview with a person in the field you hope to enter. Ask the person to tell you about the job—its advantages and disadvantages and the skills it requires.

2. Schedule an interview with a peer on a topic of mutual interest. During the interview experiment with different forms of questions (open-ended, closed, mirror, stress, hypothetical). How do the different types of questions affect the interviewee's comfort and responses?

3. Think about the ethical issues in choosing how to respond to illegal questions if the questions are not personally offensive or bothersome. For instance, Christians might think they have nothing to lose by responding honestly to the question, "Can you work on Saturdays?" If only members of minority religions refuse to answer questions about religion, how effective are the legal protections provided by EEOC guidelines? If all Protestants answer questions about religion honestly, are members of other religions jeopardized?

4. Identify a company that is of interest to you for future employment. Visit the company's website and record what is presented there. How does information on the website help you prepare for an effective job interview? Compare what you find on the website with what is available in printed materials (brochures, annual reports, etc.) about the company.

5. If you would like tips for how to be effective in a virtual interview, to go http://interview.monster.com/rehearsal/video.

6. Watch one television program that features interviews of newsmakers. *Face the Nation, Meet the Press,* and *Sixty Minutes* are programs that feature news interviews. Also watch one television program that features interviews with celebrities or people in the limelight. The talk show of Oprah Winfrey is an example of this genre. Identify the form of each question posed (open, extended, closed) and the response it generates. Do the different kinds of interviews rely on distinct types of questions? Why? What do you conclude about how the style of question affects responses?

Experiencing Communication in Our Lives

Questions for Analysis and Discussion

Review the case study "Tough Questions." Respond to the questions following and on the CD-ROM under "Conversation Analysis," and press the "Done" button at the end of the form to compare your answers with my suggested responses. These questions are also available on the *Communication in Our Lives* website under "Activities for Appendix B."

1. Did Ms. Bourne provide a good opening for the interview?

2. How effectively do you think Mr. Miller handled the tough questions that Ms. Bourne asked?

3. Did Mr. Miller seem well prepared for the interview?

4. Identify leading questions asked by Ms. Bourne, and evaluate how Mr. Miller responded to them.

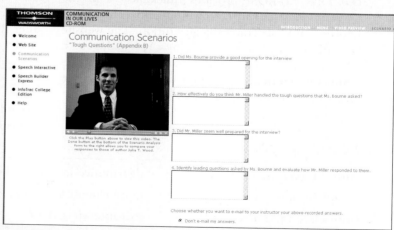

Glossary

abstract   Removed from concrete reality. Symbols are abstract because they are inferences and generalizations derived from a total reality.

acknowledgment   The second of three levels of interpersonal confirmation. Acknowledgment communicates that you have heard and understand another's feelings and thoughts.

ad hominem argument   From the Latin for "to the man," an argument that attacks the integrity of the person who has taken the opposing position.

agenda setting   Mass media's ability to select and call to the public's attention ideas, events, and people.

ambiguous   Subject to more than one interpretation. Symbols are ambiguous because their meanings vary from person to person and context to context.

ambushing   Listening carefully in order to attack a speaker.

arbitrary   Random; not determined by necessity. Symbols are arbitrary because there is no particular reason for any one symbol to stand for a certain referent.

artifacts   Personal objects we use to announce our identities and personalize our environments.

assimilation   The giving up of one's own ways for those of another culture.

attachment styles   Patterns of parenting that teach children who they are, who others are, and how to approach relationships.

attributions   Causal accounts that explain why things happen and why people act as they do.

authoritarian interview   An interviewing style in which the interviewer has and exerts greater power than the interviewee.

authoritarian leadership   A leadership style in which a leader provides direction, exerts authority, and confers rewards and punishments on group members.

authority rule   A group decision-making method in which some person or group with authority tells a group what to do and the group ratifies the authority's decision.

bandwagon appeal   The fallacious argument that because most people believe or act in a certain way, you should too.

beliefs   Assumptions about what is true, accurate, or factual. Beliefs may be false even though they are accepted as true.

brainstorming   A group technique for generating possible solutions to a problem. Brainstorming encourages ideas to flow freely without immediate criticism.

chronemics   A type of nonverbal communication concerned with how we perceive and use time to define identities and interaction.

claim   An assertion. A claim advanced in speaking requires grounds (evidence) and warrants (links between evidence and claims).

climate communication   One of three constructive forms of participation in group decision making. Climate communication focuses on creating and sustaining an open, engaged atmosphere for discussion.

closeness in dialogue   Interpersonal closeness created through communication.

closeness in the doing   Interpersonal closeness created by doing things with and for others.

cognitive complexity   The number of constructs used, how abstract they are, and how elaborately they interact to create perceptions.

cognitive restructuring   A method of reducing communication apprehension that involves teaching people to revise how they think about speaking situations.

cohesion   The degree of closeness or feeling of esprit de corps among members of a group.

commitment   A decision to remain with a relationship. Commitment is one of three dimensions of enduring romantic relationships, and it has more impact on relational continuity than does love alone. It is also an advanced stage in the process of escalation in romantic relationships.

communication   A systemic process in which people interact with and through symbols to create and interpret meanings.

communication apprehension   Anxiety associated with real or anticipated communication encounters. Communication apprehension is common and can be constructive.

communication climate The overall feeling or emotional mood between people.

communication rules Shared understandings of what communication means and what behaviors are appropriate in various situations.

comparisons A form of evidence that uses associations between two things that are similar in some important way.

complaint interview An interview that allows people to register complaints about a product, service, person, or company.

compromise A method of group decision making in which members work out a solution that satisfies each person's minimum criteria but may not fully satisfy all members.

conflict Exists when people who depend on each other express different views, interests, or goals and perceive their differences as incompatible or as opposed by the other.

consensus A decision-making method in which all members of a group support a decision.

constitutive rules Communication rules that define what communication means by specifying how certain communicative acts are to be counted.

constructivism The theory that we organize and interpret experience by applying cognitive structures called *schemata*.

content level of meaning One of two levels of meaning in communication. The content level of meaning is the literal, or denotative, information in a message.

convergence The interconnectivity of various devices to each other and to the Internet or World Wide Web.

counseling interview An interview in which one person with expertise helps another to understand a problem and develop strategies to overcome the difficulty or cope more effectively with it.

covert conflict Conflict that is expressed indirectly. Covert conflict generally is more difficult than overt conflict to manage constructively.

credibility The perception that a person is informed and trustworthy. Listeners confer it, or refuse to confer it, on speakers.

criteria Standards that group members use to evaluate alternative solutions or decisions. Criteria should be established during stage three of the standard agenda.

critical listening Attending to communication to analyze and evaluate the content of communication or the person speaking.

critical thinking Examining ideas reflectively and carefully in order to decide what you should believe, think, or do.

cultivation The cumulative process by which television fosters beliefs about social reality.

cultivation theory The theory that television promotes an inaccurate worldview that viewers nonetheless assume reflects real life.

cultural calamity Adversity that brings about change in a culture; one of four ways cultures change.

cultural relativism The idea that cultures vary in how they think, act, and behave as well as in what they believe and value; not the same as *moral relativism*.

culture Beliefs, understandings, practices, and ways of interpreting experience that are shared by a number of people.

deductive reasoning A form of reasoning that begins with a general premise and arrives at a conclusion about particulars.

defensive listening Perceiving personal attacks, criticisms, or hostile undertones in communication where none are intended.

democratic leadership A style of leadership that provides direction without imposing strict authority on a group.

demographic audience analysis A form of audience analysis that focuses on general features that characterize a group of listeners.

derived credibility The expertise and trustworthiness that listeners attribute to a speaker as a result of how the speaker communicates during a presentation.

diffusion The incorporation or integration of characteristics of one culture into another as a result of contact between the two. Diffusion is one of four ways cultures change.

direct definition Communication that explicitly tells us who we are by specifically labeling us and reacting to our behaviors. Direct definition usually occurs first in families and then in interaction with peers and others.

distributive interview A style of interviewing in which roughly equal power is held by interviewer and interviewee.

downers Someone who communicates negatively about us and reflects negative appraisals of our worth as individuals.

dual perspective The ability to understand another person's perspective, beliefs, thoughts, or feelings.

dyadic breakdown The first stage of relational decay. Dyadic breakdown involves degeneration of the established patterns, understandings, and routines that make up a relational culture and that sustain intimacy on a day-to-day basis.

dyadic processes The set of processes in relational deterioration in which established relationship patterns break down and partners discuss problems and alternative futures for the relationship.

dynamic   Evolving and changing over time.

ego boundaries   A person's internal sense of where he or she stops and the rest of the world begins.

egocentric communication   An unconstructive form of group contribution that is used to block others or to call attention to oneself.

either–or logic   The fallacy of suggesting or assuming that only two options or courses of action exist when in fact there may be more.

emotional intelligence   The ability to recognize which feelings are appropriate in which situations and the ability to communicate those feelings effectively.

empathy   The ability to feel with another person or to feel what that person feels in a situation.

employment interview   An interview in which employer and job candidate assess each other and decide whether there is a good fit between them.

endorsement   The third of three levels of interpersonal confirmation. Endorsement communicates acceptance of another's thoughts and feelings; not the same as agreement.

environmental factors   Elements of settings that affect how we feel and act. Environmental factors are a type of nonverbal communication.

ethnocentrism   The tendency to regard ourselves and our way of life as superior to other people and other ways of life.

ethos   The perceived personal character of the speaker.

evidence   Material used to interest, move, or persuade people.

Types of evidence are statistics, examples, comparisons, and quotations. Visual aids may be used to represent evidence graphically.

examples   A form of evidence; a single instance that makes a point, dramatizes an idea, or personalizes information. The four types of examples are undetailed, detailed, hypothetical, and anecdotal.

exit interview   An interview designed to gain information, insights, and perceptions about a place of work or education from a person who is leaving.

explorational communication   The stage in the escalation path of romantic relationships in which two people explore various common interests and backgrounds that might provide a basis for further interaction.

extemporaneous speaking   A presentational style that includes preparation and practice but not memorization words and nonverbal behaviors.

fallacy   An error in reasoning.

feedback   Response to a message; may be verbal, nonverbal, or both. In communication theory, the concept of feedback appeared first in interactive models of communication.

formal outline   A complete outline of a speech, including the parts of a speech, main points, supporting material, transitions, and citations for sources.

funnel sequence   A pattern of communication in interviews that moves from broad, general questions to progressively narrower, more probing questions.

gatekeeper   People and groups that decide which messages pass through the gates of media that control information flow to consumers.

grave dressing processes   A set of processes in the deterioration of

romantic relationships, in which partners put the relationship to rest.

grounds   Evidence that supports claims in a speech.

group   Three or more people who interact over time, are interdependent, and follow shared rules of conduct to reach a common goal. One type of group is a team.

groupthink   The cessation of critical, independent thought on the part of a group's members about ideas generated by the group.

halo effect   The assumption that an expert in one area is also an expert in other unrelated areas.

haptics   Nonverbal communication that involves physical touch.

hasty generalization   A broad claim based on too few examples or too-limited evidence.

hearing   A physiological activity that occurs when sound waves hit our eardrums. Unlike listening, hearing is a passive process.

hypothetical thought   Cognitive awareness of experiences and ideas that are not part of the concrete, present situation.

identification   Recognizing and enlarging common ground between communicators.

identity scripts   Guides to action based on rules for living and identity. Initially communicated in families, identity scripts define our roles, how we are to play them, and basic elements in the plot of our lives.

impromptu speaking   Public speaking that involves little preparation. Speakers think on their feet as they talk about ideas and positions with which they are familiar.

indexing   A technique of noting that statements reflect specific times and circumstances and may not apply to other times or circumstances.

individual　A person, characterized by unique needs, goals, experiences, and qualities that affect what he or she looks for in others and relationships.

individualism　A strongly held Western value that views each person as unique and important and recognizes individual activities and achievements.

inductive reasoning　A form of reasoning that begins with specific instances and forms general conclusions based on them.

informational listening　Listening to gain and understand information; tends to focus on the content level of meaning.

information-getting interview　An interview in which the interviewer asks questions to learn about the interviewee's qualifications, background, experience, opinions, knowledge, attitudes, or behaviors.

information-giving interview　An interview in which the interviewer provides information to the interviewee.

informative speech　A presentation that aims to increase listeners' knowledge, understanding, or abilities.

initial credibility　The expertise and trustworthiness that listeners attribute to a speaker before a presentation begins. Initial credibility is based on the speaker's titles, positions, experiences, or achievements known to listeners before they hear the speech.

inoculation　"Immunization" of listeners to opposing ideas and arguments that they may later encounter.

intensifying communication　The stage in the escalation of romantic relationships that increases the depth of a relationship by increasing personal knowledge and allow-

ing a couple to begin creating a private culture. Also called *euphoria*.

interpersonal climate　The overall feeling between people, shaped by communication.

interpersonal communication　Communication between people, usually in close relationships such as friendship and romance.

interpretation　The subjective process of evaluating and explaining perceptions.

interview　A communication transaction that emphasizes questions and answers.

intrapersonal communication　Communication with ourselves; self-talk.

intrapsychic processes　The first set of processes in disintegration of romantic relationships; involves brooding about problems in the relationship and dissatisfactions with a partner.

invention　The creation of tools, ideas, and practices; one of four causes of culture change.

investment　Something put into a relationship that cannot be recovered should the relationship end. Investments, more than rewards and love, increase commitment.

invitational communication　The second stage in the escalation phase of romantic relationships, in which people signal that they are interested in interacting and respond to invitations from others.

key word outline　An abbreviated speaking outline that includes only key words for each point in a speech. The key words trigger a speaker's memory of the full point.

kinesics　Body position and body motions, including those of the face.

laissez-faire leadership　From the French term meaning "allow to do," this style of leadership is

nondirective and sometimes leads to unproductive group work.

listening　A complex process that consists of being mindful, physically receiving messages, selecting and organizing information, interpreting, responding, and remembering.

literal listening　Listening only to the content level of meaning and ignoring the relational level of meaning.

loaded language　An extreme form of evaluative language that relies on words that strongly slant perceptions and hence meanings.

logos　Rational or logical proofs.

mainstreaming　The process by which mass communication stabilizes and homogenizes social perspectives; a concept in cultivation theory.

manuscript speaking　A presentational style that involves speaking from the complete manuscript of a speech.

mass communication　Messages that are transmitted by a source (for instance, the ABC Network) that uses a technology (for instance, audio and visual) through a mass medium (for instance, television) to a large group of people who may not be in direct contact with the source of the messages.

mass media　Channels of mass communication, such as television and radio.

meaning　The significance we attach to phenomena such as words, actions, people, objects, and events.

mean world syndrome　The belief that the world is a dangerous place, full of mean people who cannot be trusted and who are likely to harm us; part of cultivation theory.

media literacy　The abilities to understand the influence of mass media and to access, analyze, evaluate, and respond to mass media in informed, critical ways.

memorized speaking   A presentational style in which a speech is memorized word for word in advance.

metaphor   An implicit comparison of two different things that have something in common.

mindfulness   From Zen Buddhism, being fully present in the moment; the first step of listening and the foundation of all other steps.

mind map   A holistic record of information on a topic. Mind mapping is a method that can be used to narrow speech topics or to keep track of information gathered during research.

mind reading   Assuming that we understand what another person thinks or how another person perceives something.

minimal encouragers   Communication that, by expressing interest in hearing more, gently invites another person to elaborate.

mirror interview   A style of interviewing in which an interviewer's questions reflect previous responses and comments of the interviewee. Mirror interviews allow interviewees substantial power.

monopolizing   Continually focusing communication on oneself instead of on the person who is talking.

motivated sequence pattern   A pattern for organizing persuasive speeches, consisting of five steps: attention, need, satisfaction, visualization, and action.

multilingual   Able to speak and think in more than one language or from more than one cultural perspective.

neutralization   One of four responses to relational dialectics;

involves balancing or finding a compromise between two dialectical poles.

noise   Anything that interferes with intended communication.

nonverbal communication   All forms of communication other than words themselves; includes inflection and other vocal qualities as well as several other behaviors.

norms   Informal rules that guide how members of a group or culture think, feel, act, and interact. Norms define what is normal or appropriate in various situations.

oral style   Visual, vocal, and verbal aspects of the delivery of a public speech.

organizational culture   Understandings about identity and codes of thought and action that are shared by members of an organization.

overt conflict   Conflict expressed directly and in a straightforward manner.

paralanguage   Vocal communication that does not include actual words. Sounds, vocal qualities, accents, and inflection are examples of paralanguage.

paraphrasing   A method of clarifying others' meaning by restating their communication.

participation   A response to cultural diversity in which people incorporate some practices, customs, and traditions of other groups into their own lives.

particular others   One source of social perspectives that people use to define themselves and guide how they think, act, and feel. The perspectives of particular others are the viewpoints of people who are significant to the self.

passion   Intensely positive feelings and desires for another person. Passion is based on the rewards of involvement and is not equivalent to commitment.

pathos   Emotional proofs for claims.

perception   The process of actively selecting, organizing, and interpreting people, objects, events, situations, and activities.

performance review   An interview in which a supervisor comments on a subordinate's achievements and professional development, identifies any weaknesses or problems, and collaborates with the subordinate to develop goals for future performance. Subordinates should offer perceptions of their strengths and weaknesses and participate actively in developing goals for professional development. Also known as a *performance appraisal.*

personal constructs   A bipolar mental yardstick that allows us to measure people and situations along specific dimensions of judgment.

personal relationship   A relationship defined by uniqueness, rules, relational dialectics, and commitment and affected by contexts. Personal relationships, unlike social ones, are irreplaceable.

person-centered perception   The ability to perceive another as a unique and distinct individual apart from social roles and generalizations.

perspective of the generalized other   The collection of rules, roles, and attitudes endorsed by the whole social community in which we live.

persuasive interview   An interview designed to influence attitudes, beliefs, values, or actions.

persuasive speech   A presentation that aims to change listeners by prompting them to think, feel, or act differently.

physical appearance   Physical features of people and the values attached to those features; a type of nonverbal communication.

positive visualization A technique for reducing speaking anxiety, in which a person visualizes herself or himself communicating effectively in progressively challenging speaking situations.

post hoc, ergo propter hoc Latin phrase meaning "After this, therefore because of this." The fallacy of suggesting or assuming that because event B follows event A, event A has therefore caused event B.

power The ability to influence others; a feature of small groups that affects participation.

power over The ability to help or harm others. Power over others usually is communicated in ways that highlight the status and influence of the person using the power.

power to The ability to empower others to reach their goals. People who use power to help others generally do not highlight their own status and influence.

problem-solving interview An interview in which people collaborate to identify sources of a mutual problem and to develop ways to address or resolve it.

procedural communication One of three constructive ways of participating in group decision making. Procedural communication orders ideas and coordinates contributions of members.

process Something that is ongoing and continuously in motion, for which it is difficult to identify beginnings and endings. Communication is a process.

prototype A knowledge structure that defines the clearest or most representative example of some category.

proxemics A type of nonverbal communication that includes space and how we use it.

pseudolistening Pretending to listen.

psychological responsibility The responsibility for remembering, planning, and coordinating domestic work and child care. In general, women assume the psychological responsibility for child care and housework even if both partners share in the actual tasks.

puffery Advertising strategy that relies on superlative claims for a product that seem factual but are actually meaningless.

punctuation Defining the beginning and ending of interaction or interaction episodes.

qualifier A word or phrase that limits the scope of a claim. Common qualifiers are *most, usually,* and *in general.*

quality improvement team A group in which people from different departments or areas in an organization collaborate to solve problems, meet needs, or increase the quality of work life. Also called a *continuous quality improvement team.*

quotation A form of evidence that uses exact citations of statements made by others. Also called *testimony.*

rebuttal A response to listeners' reservations about a claim made by a speaker.

recognition The most basic kind of interpersonal confirmation; communicates awareness that another person exists and is present.

red herring argument An argument that is irrelevant to the topic; an attempt to divert attention from something the arguer can't or doesn't want to address.

reflected appraisal The process of seeing and thinking about ourselves in terms of the appraisals of us that others reflect.

reframing One of four responses to relational dialectics. The reframing response transcends the apparent contradiction between two dialectical poles and reinterprets them as not in tension.

regulative rules Communication rules that regulate interaction by specifying when, how, where, and with whom to talk about certain things.

relational culture A private world of rules, understandings, and patterns of acting and interpreting that partners create to give meaning to their relationship; the nucleus of intimacy.

relational dialectics Opposing forces or tensions that are normal parts of all relationships. The three relational dialectics are autonomy/connectedness, novelty/predictability, and openness/closedness.

relational listening Listening to support another person or to understand another person's feelings and perceptions; focuses on the relational level of meaning as much as on the content level of meaning.

relationship level of meaning One of two levels of meaning in communication; expresses the relationship between communicators.

reprimand interview An interview conducted by a supervisor with a subordinate to identify lapses in the subordinate's professional conduct, determine sources of problems, and establish a plan for improving future performance.

resistance A response to cultural diversity that attacks the cultural practices of others or proclaims that one's own cultural traditions are superior.

resonance The extent to which media representations are congruent with personal experience.

respect A response to cultural diversity in which one values others' customs, traditions, and values, even if one does not actively incorporate them into one's own life.

resurrection processes The final set of processes in relationship deterioration, in which ex–partners begin to live independent of the former relationship.

revising communication A stage in the escalation of romantic relationships that many but not all couples experience; involves evaluating a relationship and working out any obstacles or problems before committing for the long term.

rules Patterned ways of behaving and interpreting behavior; all relationships develop rules.

schemata Cognitive structures we use to organize and interpret experiences. Four types of schemata are prototypes, personal constructs, stereotypes, and scripts.

scripts One of four cognitive schemata. Scripts define expected or appropriate sequences of action in particular settings.

segmentation One of four responses to relational dialectics. Segmentation responses meet one dialectical need while ignoring or not satisfying the contradictory dialectical need.

selective listening Focusing on only selected parts of communication. We listen selectively when we screen out parts of a message that don't interest us or with which we disagree, and also when we rivet attention on parts of communication that do interest us or with which we agree.

self A multidimensional process that involves forming and acting from social perspectives that arise and evolve in communication with others and ourselves.

self-disclosure The sharing of personal information about ourselves that others are unlikely to discover in other ways.

self-fulfilling prophecy Expectations or judgments of ourselves that are brought about by our own actions.

self-sabotage Self-talk that communicates that we're no good, we can't do something, we can't change, and so forth. Undermines belief in ourselves and motivation to change and grow.

self-serving bias The tendency to attribute our positive actions and successes to stable, global, internal influences that we control and to attribute negative actions and failures to unstable, specific, external influences beyond our control.

separation One of four responses to relational dialectics. The separation response occurs when friends or romantic partners assign one pole of a dialectic to certain spheres of activities or topics and assign the contradictory dialectical pole to distinct spheres of activities or topics.

silence The lack of verbal communication or paralanguage; Silence is a type of nonverbal communication that can express powerful messages.

similes A direct comparison that typically uses either *like* or *as* to link two things.

situational audience analysis A method of audience analysis that seeks information about specific listeners that relates directly to a topic, speaker, and occasion.

skills training A method of reducing communication apprehension that assumes that anxiety results from lack of speaking skills and therefore can be reduced by learning skills.

slippery slope The fallacy of suggesting or assuming that once a certain step is taken, steps will inevitably follow that will lead to some unacceptable consequence.

social climbing The process of trying to increase personal status in a group by winning the approval of high-status members.

social community Groups of people who live within a dominant culture yet are also members of specific, nondominant groups that have distinctive experiences and foster distinctive patterns of communicating.

social comparison Comparing ourselves with others to form judgments of our own talents, abilities, qualities, and so forth.

social support processes A set of processes in relational disintegration in which partners figure out how to inform outsiders that the relationship is ending and look to friends and family for support during the trauma of breaking up.

social relationship Unlike personal relationships, social ones tend to follow broad social scripts and rules, and participants tend to assume conventional social roles in relation to one another. Social relationships, unlike personal ones, can be replaced.

specific purpose A behavioral objective or observable response that a speaker specifies as a gauge of effectiveness; reinforces a speaker's more general speaking goals.

speech to entertain A speech the primary goal of which is to amuse, interest, or engage listeners.

speech to inform A speech the primary goal of which is to increase listeners' understanding, awareness, or knowledge of some topic.

speech to persuade A speech the primary goal of which is to change listeners' attitudes, beliefs, or behaviors or to motivate listeners to action.

standard agenda A logical, seven-step method for making decisions.

standpoint theory The theory that a culture includes a number of social groups that differently shape the knowledge, identities, and opportunities of members of those groups.

static evaluation Assessments that suggest something is unchanging or static. "Bob is impatient" is a static evaluation.

statistics A form of evidence that uses numbers to summarize a great many individual cases or to demonstrate relationships between phenomena.

stereotypes A predictive generalization about people and situations.

stress interview A style of interviewing in which an interviewer deliberately attempts to create anxiety in the interviewee.

survey research Research that involves asking a number of people about their opinions, preferences, actions, or beliefs relevant to a speaking topic.

symbol An arbitrary, ambiguous, and abstract representation of a phenomenon. Symbols are the basis of language, much nonverbal behavior, and human thought.

synergy A special kind of energy in groups that combines and goes beyond the energies, talents, and strengths of individual members.

system A group of interrelated elements that affect one another. Communication is systemic.

systematic desensitization A method of reducing communication apprehension that teaches

people how to relax physiologically and then helps them practice feeling relaxed as they imagine themselves in progressively difficult communication situations.

task communication One of three constructive forms of participation in group decision making; focuses on giving and analyzing information and ideas.

team A special kind of group characterized by different and complementary resources of members and a strong sense of collective identity. All teams are groups, but not all groups are teams.

terminal credibility The cumulative expertise and trustworthiness listeners attribute to a speaker as a result of the speaker's initial and derived credibility; may be greater or less than initial credibility, depending on how effectively a speaker communicates.

thesis statement The main idea of an entire speech. It should capture the key message in a concise sentence that listeners can remember easily.

tolerance A response to diversity in which one accepts differences, although one may not approve of or even understand them.

totalizing Responding to people as if one aspect of them is the sum total of who they are.

Toulmin model A representation of effective reasoning that includes five components: claim, grounds (evidence), warrant (link between grounds and claim), qualifier, and rebuttal.

transitions Words and sentences that connect ideas and main points in a speech so that listeners can follow a speaker.

understanding A response to cultural diversity that assumes differences are rooted in cultural teachings and that no traditions,

customs, and behaviors are intrinsically more valuable than others.

upper Someone who communicates positively about us and confirms with positive appraisals our worth as individuals.

uses and gratification theory The theory that people choose to attend to mass communication in order to fulfill personal needs and preferences.

values Views of what is good, right, and important that are shared by members of a particular culture.

visual aids A way of presenting evidence that uses visual means such as charts, graphs, photographs, and physical objects to reinforce ideas presented verbally or to provide information.

voting A method of group decision making based on the support of a certain number of group members. Some groups have simple majority rule, whereas others require two-thirds or three-fourths support.

vulture The extreme form of a downer. Vultures attack a person's self-concept and sense of self-worth; may be someone else or the person her- or himself.

warrant A justification for grounds (evidence) and claims in persuasive speaking.

working outline A sketch of main ideas and their relationships; used by and intended for only the speaker.

works cited A list of sources used in preparing a speech.

References

Abdullah, H. (1999, January 22). Gender roles, new rules. *The Raleigh News & Observer*, pp. E1, E3.

Abelson, R. (2001, April 29). Online message boards getting nasty. *The Raleigh News & Observer*, p. 8A.

Acitelli, L. (1988). When spouses talk to each other about their relationship. *Journal of Social and Personal Relationships, 5*, 185–199.

Acitelli, L. (1993). You, me, and us: Perspectives on relationship awareness. In S. W. Duck (Ed.), *Understanding relationship processes, 1: Individuals in relationships* (pp. 144–174). Newbury Park, CA: Sage.

Adler, R., & Towne, N. (1993). *Looking out/looking in* (7th ed.). Fort Worth, TX: Harcourt Brace Jovanovich.

Afifi, W., & Burgoon, J. (2000). The impact of violations on uncertainty and the consequences for attractiveness. *Human Communication Research, 26*, 203–233.

Agee, W., Ault, P., & Emery, E. (1996). *Introduction to mass communications* (12th ed.). Reading, MA: Addison-Wesley.

Aires, E. (1996). *Men and women in interaction: Reconsidering differences*. New York: Oxford University Press.

Alcoff, L. (1991, Winter). The problem of speaking for others. *Cultural Critique*, pp. 5–32.

Allen, M., Hale, J., Mongeau, P., Berkowitz-Stafford, S., Stafford, S., Shanahan, W., Agee, P., Dillon, K., Jackson, R., & Ray, C. (1990). Testing a model of message sidedness: Three replications. *Communication Monographs, 37*, 275–291.

Allen, M., Hunter, J., & Donahue, W. (1989). Meta-analysis of self-report data on the effectiveness of public speaking anxiety treatment techniques. *Communication Education, 38*, 54–76.

Andersen, M. L., & Collins, P. H. (Eds.). (2001). *Race, class, and gender: An anthology* (4th ed.). Belmont, CA: Wadsworth.

Andersen, P. (1993). Cognitive schemata in personal relationships. In S. W. Duck (Ed.), *Understanding relationship processes, 1: Individuals in relationships* (pp. 1–29). Newbury Park, CA: Sage.

Andersen, P. (1999). *Nonverbal communication: Forms and functions*. Mountain View, CA: Mayfield.

Andersen, P., Hecht, M., Hoobler, G., & Smallwood, M. (2002). Nonverbal communication across cultures. In W. Gudykunst & B. Mody (Eds.), *The handbook of international and intercultural communication* (2nd ed., pp. 89–106). Thousand Oaks, CA: Sage.

Anderson, C., & Martin, M. (1995). The effects of communication motives, interaction, involvement, and loneliness on satisfaction: A model of small groups. *Small Group Research, 16*, 118–137.

Anderson, K., & Leaper, C. (1998). Meta-analyses of gender effects on conversational interruption: Who, when, where, and how? *Sex Roles, 39*, 225–252.

Anderson, P., & Guerrero, L. (Eds.). (1998). *Handbook of communication and emotion*. San Diego, CA: Academic Press.

Anderson, R., & Killenberg, G. (1998). *Interviewing: Speaking, listening, and learning for professional life*. Mountain View, CA: Mayfield.

Angelou, M. (1990). *I shall not be moved*. New York: Random House.

Arenson, K. (2002, January 13). The fine art of listening. *Education Life*, pp. 34–35.

Argyle, M., & Henderson, M. (1984). The rules of friendship. *Journal of Social and Personal Relationships, 1*, 211–237.

Argyle, M., & Henderson, M. (1985). The rules of relationships. In S. W. Duck & D. Perlman (Eds.), *Understanding personal relationships: An interdisciplinary approach* (pp. 63–84). Beverly Hills, CA: Sage.

Aries, E. (1987). Gender and communication. In P. Shaver (Ed.), *Sex and gender* (pp. 149–176). Newbury Park, CA: Sage.

Armas, G. (2001, June 20). "Multiracial" a youthful category. *The Raleigh News & Observer*, p. 9A.

Arnold, H., & Feldman, D. (1986). *Organizational behavior*. New York: McGraw-Hill.

Auer, P. (Ed.). (1998). *Code switching in conversation: Language, interaction, and identity*. London: Routledge.

Axtell, R. (1990a). *Dos and taboos around the world* (2nd ed.). New York: Wiley.

Axtell, R. (1990b). *Dos and taboos of hosting international visitors*. New York: Wiley.

Ayres, J., & Hopf, T. S. (1990). The long-term effect of visualization in the classroom: A brief research report. *Communication Education, 39*, 75–78.

Babbie, E. (2001). *The practice of social research* (9th ed.). Belmont, CA: Wadsworth.

Bachen, C., & Illouz, E. (1996). Imagining romance: Young people's cultural modes of romance and love. *Critical Studies in Mass Communication, 13*, 279–308.

Bailey, A. (1998, February 29). Daily bread. *The Durham Herald-Sun*, p. C5.

Baird, J. E., Jr. (1974). The effects of speech summaries upon audience comprehension of expository speeches of varying quality and complexity. *Central States Speech Journal, 25*, 124–135.

Baker, E. E. (1965). The immediate effects of perceived speaker disorganization on speaker credibility and audience attitude change in persuasive speaking. *Western Journal of Speech Communication, 29*, 148–161.

Ban on annoying, obscene e-mail upheld. (1999, April 20). *The Raleigh News & Observer*, p. 4A.

Banville, T. (1978). *How to listen: How to be heard*. Chicago: Nelson-Hall.

Baran, S., & Davis, D. (2003). *Mass communication theory* (3rd ed.). Belmont, CA: Wadsworth.

Bargh, J. (1997). *The automaticity of everyday life*. Mahwah, NJ: Erlbaum.

Bargh, J. (1999, January 29). The most powerful manipulative messages are hiding in plain sight. *The Chronicle of Higher Education*, p. B6.

Barker, L., Edwards, R., Gaines, C., Gladney, K., & Holley, F. (1981). An investigation of proportional time spent in various communication activities by college students. *Journal of Applied Communication Research, 8*, 101–109.

Barnes, M. K., & Duck, S. (1994). Everyday communicative contexts for social support. In B. Burleson, T. Albrecht, & I. Sarason (Eds.), *Communication of social support* (pp. 175–194). Thousand Oaks, CA: Sage.

Baron, R. A., & Berne, D. (1994). *Social psychology* (7th ed.). Boston: Allyn & Bacon.

Barry, B. (2001). *Culture and equality: An egalitarian critique of multiculturalism*. New Haven, CT: Harvard University Press.

Bartholomew, K., & Horowitz, L. M. (1991). Attachment styles among young adults: A test of a four-category model. *Journal of Personality and Social Psychology, 61*, 226–244.

Bartlett, T. (2003, March 7). Take my chair (please). *The Chronicle of Higher Education*, pp. A36–A38.

Bass, A. (1993, December 5). Behavior that can wreck a marriage. *The Raleigh News & Observer*, p. 8E.

Bass, B. M. (1990). *Bass and Stogdill's handbook of leadership: Theory, research, and managerial applications* (3rd ed.). New York: Free Press.

Bateson, M. C. (1990). *Composing a life*. New York: Penguin/Plume.

Battaglia, D., Richard, F., Datteri, D., & Lord, C. (1998). Breaking up is (relatively) easy to do: A script for the dissolution of close relationships. *Journal of Social and Personal Relationships, 15*, 829–845.

Baumister, R., & Leary, M. (1995). The need to belong: Desire for interpersonal attachments as a fundamental human motivation. *Psychological Bulletin, 117*, 497–529.

Baxter, L. A. (1984). Trajectories of relationship disengagement. *Journal of Social and Personal Relationships, 7*, 141–178.

Baxter, L. A. (1985). Accomplishing relational disengagement. In S. Duck & D. Perlman (Eds.), *Understanding personal relationships: An interdisciplinary approach* (pp. 243–265). Beverly Hills, CA: Sage.

Baxter, L. A. (1987). Symbols of relationship identity in relationship cultures. *Journal of Social and Personal Relationships, 4*, 261–279.

Baxter, L. A. (1990). Dialectical contradictions in relational development. *Journal of Social and Personal Relationships, 7*, 69–88.

Baxter, L. A. (1993). The social side of personal relationships: A dialectical perspective. In S. Duck (Ed.), *Understanding relationship processes, 3: Social context and relationships* (pp. 139–165). Newbury Park, CA: Sage.

Baxter, L. A., & Montgomery, B. (1996). *Relating: Dialogues and dialectics*. New York: Guilford Press.

Baxter, L. A., & Simon, E. P. (1993). Relationship maintenance strategies and dialectical contradictions in personal relationships. *Journal of Social and Personal Relationships, 10*, 225–242.

Beatty, M. J., & Behnke, R. R. (1991). Effects of public speaking trait anxiety and intensity of speaking task on heart rate during performance. *Human Communication Research, 18*, 147–176.

Beatty, M. J., Plax, T., & Kearney, P. (1985). Reinforcement vs. modeling theory in the development of communication apprehension: A retrospective analysis. *Communication Research Reports, 12*, 80–95.

Be civil. (1994, July 5). *The Wall Street Journal*, p. A1.

Beck, A. (1988). *Love is never enough*. New York: Harper & Row.

Becker, A., Burwell, R., Gilman, S., Herzog, D., & Hamburg, P. (2002). Eating behaviours and attitudes following prolonged exposure to television among ethnic Fijian adolescent girls. *British Journal of Psychiatry, 180*, 509–514.

Becker, C. S. (1987). Friendship between women: A phenomenological study of best friends. *Journal of Phenomenological Psychology, 18*, 59–72.

Begley, S. (1998, November 2). Living hand to mouth. *Newsweek*, p. 69.

Bell, A. (1989). *The complete manager's guide to interviewing*. Homewood, IL: Dow Jones-Irwin.

Bellah, R., Madsen, R., Sullivan, W., Swindler, A., & Tipton, S. (1985). *Habits of the heart: Individualism and commitment in American life*. Berkeley: University of California Press.

Bellamy, L. (1996, December 18). Kwanzaa cultivates cultural and culinary connections. *The Raleigh News & Observer*, pp. 1F, 9F.

Belsky, J., & Pensky, E. (1988). Developmental history, personality, and family relationships: Toward an emergent family system. In R. A. Hinde & J. Stevenson-Hinde (Eds.), *Relationships within families: Mutual influences* (pp. 193–217). Oxford, UK: Clarendon.

Benenson, J., Gordon, A., & Roy, R. (2000). Children's evaluative appraisals in competition in tetrads versus dyads. *Small Group Research, 31*, 635–652.

Benjamin, D., & Horwitz, T. (1994, July 14). German view: "You Americans work too hard—and for what?" *The Wall Street Journal*, pp. B1, B6.

Berg, J. H. (1987). Responsiveness and self-disclosure. In V. J. Derlega & J. H. Berg (Eds.), *Self-disclosure: Theory, research, and therapy*. New York: Plenum.

Berger, C. R., & Bell, R. A. (1988). Plans and the initiation of social relationships. *Human Communication Research, 15*, 217–235.

Bergner, R. M., & Bergner, L. L. (1990). Sexual misunderstanding: A descriptive and pragmatic formulation. *Psychotherapy, 27*, 464–467.

Berko, R., Wolvin, A., & Wolvin, D. (1992). *Communicating: A social and career focus* (5th ed.). Boston: Houghton Mifflin.

Berne, E. (1964). *Games people play*. New York: Grove.

Bertman, S. (1998). *Hyperculture: The human cost of speed*. Westport, CT: Praeger.

Bingham, S. (Ed.). (1994). *Conceptualizing sexual harassment as discursive practice*. Westport, CT: Praeger.

Birdwhistell, R. (1970). *Kinesics and context*. Philadelphia: University of Pennsylvania Press.

Bites. (1998, September 30). *The Raleigh News & Observer*, p. 1F.

Blanchard, K., Carlos, J., & Randolf, A. (1998). *Empowerment takes more than a minute.* San Francisco, CA: Berrett-Koehler.

Blind man finds gift of sight also a burden. (1999, February 1). *The Raleigh News & Observer,* p. 7A.

Blumer, H. (1969). *Symbolic interaction: Perspective and method.* Englewood Cliffs, NJ: Prentice Hall.

Bolger, N., & Eckenrode, J. (1991). Social relationships, personality, and anxiety during a major stressful event. *Journal of Personality and Social Psychology, 61,* 440–449.

Bolger, N., & Kelleher, S. (1993). Daily life in relationships. In S. Duck (Ed.), *Understanding relationship processes, 3. Social context and relationships* (pp. 100–108). Newbury Park, CA: Sage.

Bollier, D. (2002). *Silent theft: The private plunder of common wealth.* New York: Routledge.

Bolman, L., & Deal, T. (1992). What makes a team work? *Organizational Dynamics, 21,* 34–44.

Bolton, R. (1986). Listening is more than merely hearing. In J. Stewart (Ed.), *Bridges, not walls* (4th ed., pp. 159–179). New York: Random House.

Boneva, B., Kraut, R., & Frohlich, D. (2001). Using e-mail for personal relationships: The difference gender makes. *American Behavioral Scientist, 45,* 530–550.

Booth-Butterfield, M., & Booth-Butterfield, S. (1994). Communication anxiety and signing effectiveness: Testing an interference model among deaf communicators. *Journal of Applied Communication Research, 22,* 273–286.

Bordo, S. (1999). *The male body: A new look at men in public and in private.* New York: Farrar, Straus & Giroux.

Bornstein, M., & Bradley, R. (Eds.). (2003). *Socioeconomic status, parenting, and child development.* Mahwah, NJ: Erlbaum.

Bostrom, R. N. (1988). *Communicating in public: Speaking and listening.* Santa Rosa, CA: Burgess.

Bostrom, R. N. (1996). Aspects of listening. In O. Hargie (Ed.), *Handbook of communication skills* (2nd ed., pp. 236–259). London: Routledge.

Boudreau, J. (2000, August 6). Missed manners. *The Raleigh News & Observer,* pp. 23A, 26A.

Boulding, K. (1990). *Three faces of power.* Newbury Park, CA: Sage.

Bourhis, J., & Allen, M. (1992). Meta-analysis of the relationship between communication apprehension and cognitive performance. *Communication Education, 41,* 68–76.

Bowen, S. P., & Michal-Johnson, P. (1996). Gendered negotiation about safer sex. In J. T. Wood (Ed.), *Gendered relationships* (pp. 177–196). Mountain View, CA: Mayfield.

Bowlby, J. (1973). *Separation: Attachment and loss* (Vol. 2). New York: Basic Books.

Bowlby, J. (1988). *A secure base: Parent–child attachment and healthy human development.* New York: Basic Books.

Bowles, J. G. (1990, September 24). The human side of quality. *Fortune,* n.p.

Boyd, N. (2002). *Beast within: Why men are violent.* Vancouver, BC: Groundwood/Greystone Books.

Bozzi, V. (1986, February). Eat to the beat. *Psychology Today,* p. 16.

Bradbury, T. N., & Fincham, F. D. (1990). Attributions in marriage: Review and critique. *Psychological Bulletin, 107,* 3–33.

Braithwaite, D., & Braithwaite, C. (1997). Viewing persons with disabilities as a culture. In L. Samovar & R. Porter (Eds.), *Intercultural communication: A reader* (8th ed., pp. 154–164). Belmont, CA: Wadsworth.

Braxton, G. (1999, June 5). Minorities glaringly absent from fall television lineup. *Richmond Times-Dispatch,* pp. F8–F9.

Brehm, S., Miller, R., Perlman, D., & Campbell, S. (2001). *Intimate relations* (3rd ed.). New York: McGraw-Hill.

Breslau, K. (2000, September 18). Tomorrowland, today. *Newsweek,* pp. 52–53.

Brooks, D. (2001a). *Bobos in paradise.* New York: Touchstone.

Brooks, D. (2001b, April 30). Time to do everything except think. *Newsweek,* p. 71.

Brooks, R., & Goldstein, S. (2001). *Raising resilient children.* New York: Contemporary Books.

Brown, J., Steele, J., & Walsh-Childers, K. (Eds.). (2002). *Sexual teens, sexual media.* Mahwah, NJ: Erlbaum

Brown, L. (1997). *Two-spirit people.* Binghamton, NY: Haworth Press.

Buber, M. (1957). Distance and relation. *Psychiatry, 20,* 97–104.

Buber, M. (1970). *I and thou* (Walter Kaufmann, Trans.). New York: Scribner.

Burgoon, J. K., Buller, D. B., Hale, J. L., & deTurck, M. A. (1984). Relational messages associated with nonverbal behaviors. *Human Communication Research, 10,* 351–378.

Burgoon, J. K., Buller, D. B., & Woodhall, G. W. (1989). *Nonverbal communication: The unspoken dialogue.* New York: Harper & Row.

Burgoon, J. K., & Le Poire, B. (1999). Nonverbal cues and interpersonal judgments: Participant and observer perceptions of intimacy, dominance, and composure. *Communication Monographs, 66,* 105–124.

Burke, K. (1950). *A rhetoric of motives.* Englewood Cliffs, NJ: Prentice Hall.

Burley-Allen, M. (1995). *Listening: The forgotten skill.* New York: John Wiley.

Business bulletin. (1996, July 18). *Wall Street Journal,* p. A1.

Buunk, B., & Mutsaers, W. (1999). Equity perceptions and marital satisfaction in former and current marriage: A study among the remarried. *Journal of Social and Personal Relationships, 16,* 123–132.

Caldera, Y. M., Huston, A. C., & O'Brien, M. (1989). Social interactions and play patterns of parents and toddlers with feminine, masculine, and neutral toys. *Child Development, 60,* 70–76.

Campbell, K. K. (1989). *Man cannot speak for her.* New York: Praeger.

Campbell, R. (1999). *Media and culture: An introduction to mass communication.* New York: St. Martin's Press.

Can a long distance relationship work? (1998). *Jet, 94,* 22–26.

Canary, D., & Dainton, M. (Eds.). (2003). *Maintaining relationships through communication.* Mahwah, NJ: Erlbaum.

Canary, D., & Stafford, L. (Eds.). (1994). *Communication and relational maintenance.* New York: Academic Press.

Cancian, F. (1987). *Love in America.* Cambridge, UK: Cambridge University Press.

Cancian, F. (1989). Love and the rise of capitalism. In B. Risman & P. Schwartz (Eds.), *Gender in intimate relationships* (pp. 12–25). Belmont, CA: Wadsworth.

Cannell, C., & Kahn, R. (1968). Interviewing. In G. Lindzey & E. Aronson (Eds.), *The handbook of social psychology* (Vol. 2, 2nd ed., pp. 569–584). Reading, MA: Addison-Wesley.

Capella, J. N. (1991). The biological origins of automated patterns of human interaction. *Communication Theory, 1,* 4–35.

Carbaugh, D. (1998). "I can't do that! But I can actually see around the corners": American Indian students and the study of public communication. In J. Martin, T. Nakayama, & L. Flores (Eds.), *Readings in cultural context* (pp. 160–171). Mountain View, CA: Mayfield.

Carl, W. (1998). A sign of the times. In J. T. Wood, *But I thought you meant . . . : Misunderstandings in human communication* (pp. 195–208). Mountain View, CA: Mayfield.

Carletta, J., Garrod, S., & Fraser-Krauss, H. (1998). Placement of authority and communication patterns in workplace groups: The consequences for innovation. *Small Group Research, 29,* 531–559.

Carroll, J., & Russell, J. (1996). Do facial expressions signal specific emotions? Judging emotion from the face in context. *Journal of Personality and Social Psychology, 70,* 205–218.

Carron, A., & Spink, K. (1995). The group size–cohesion relationship in minimal groups. *Small Group Research, 26,* 86–105.

Caspi, A., & Harbener, E. S. (1990). Continuity and change: Assortive marriage and the consistency of personality in adulthood. *Journal of Personality and Social Psychology, 58,* 250–258.

Cassirer, E. (1944). *An essay on man.* New Haven, CT: Yale University Press.

Caughlin, J., & Vangelisti, A. (2000). An individual difference explanation of why married couples engage in the demand/withdraw pattern of conflict. *Journal of Social and Personal Relationships, 17,* 523–551.

Chan, Y. (1999). Density, crowding, and factors intervening in their relationship: Evidence from a hyper-dense metropolis. *Social Indicators Research, 48,* 103–124.

Chesebro, J. W. (1995). Communication technologies as cognitive systems. In J. T. Wood & R. B. Gregg (Eds.), *Toward the 21st century.* Cresskill, NJ: Hampton.

China: Behind the Great Wall (1998, October 7). Newspapers in education. A special supplement to *The Raleigh News & Observer,* pp. 1–15.

Christianson, P., & Roberts, D. (1998). *It's not only rock & roll: Popular music in the lives of adolescents.* Cresskill, NJ: Hampton Press.

Cissna, K. N. L., & Sieburg, E. (1986). Patterns of interactional confirmation and disconfirmation. In J. Stewart (Ed.), *Bridges, not walls* (4th ed., pp. 230–239). New York: Random House.

Civickly, J. M., Pace, R. W., & Krause, R. M. (1977). Interviewer and client behaviors in supportive and defensive interviews. In B. D. Ruben (Ed.), *Communication yearbook, 1* (pp. 347–362). New Brunswick, NJ: Transaction Books.

Clair, R. P. (1993). The use of framing devices to sequester organizational narratives: Hegemony and harassment. *Communication Monographs, 60,* 113–136.

Clark, R. A. (1998). A comparison of topics and objectives in a cross-section of young men's and women's everyday conversations. In D. Canary & K. Dindia (Eds.), *Sex differences and similarities in communication* (pp. 303–319). Mahwah, NJ: Erlbaum.

Clark, R., & Delia, J. (1997). Individuals' preferences for friends' approaches to providing support in distressing situations. *Communication Reports, 10,* 115–121.

Clement, C., & McLean, K. (2000). *Wired, not weird.* New York: Macmillan.

Clemetson, L. (2000, September 18). Love without borders. *Newsweek,* p. 62.

Cloven, D. H., & Roloff, M. E. (1991). Sense-making activities and interpersonal conflict: Communicative cures for the mulling blues. *Western Journal of Speech Communication, 55,* 134–158.

Cole, T., & Leets, L. (1999). Attachment styles and intimate television viewing: Insecurely forming relationships in a parasocial way. *Journal of Social and Personal Relationships, 16,* 495–511.

Collins, P. (1998). *Fighting words: Black women and the search for justice.* Minneapolis: University of Minnesota Press.

Condry, S. M., Condry, J. C., & Pogatshnik, L. W. (1983). Sex differences: A study of the ear of the beholder. *Sex Roles, 9,* 697–704.

Conrad, C. (1995). Was Pogo right? In J. T. Wood & R. B. Gregg (Eds.), *Toward the 21st century.* Cresskill, NJ: Hampton.

Conrad, C., & Poole, M. (2002). *Strategic organizational communication: Into the twenty-first century* (5th ed.). Fort Worth, TX: Harcourt Brace.

Cooley, C. H. (1912). Human nature and the social order. New York: Scribner.

Cooper, L. (1997). Listening competency in the workplace: A model for training. *Business Communication Quarterly, 60,* 75–84.

Cooper, L., Seibold, D., & Suchner, R. (1997). Listening in organizations: An analysis of error structures in models of listening competency. *Communication Research Reports, 14,* 3.

Cosby, P. (1973). Self-disclosure: A literature review. *Psychological Bulletin, 79,* 73–91.

Cose, E. (2000, January 1). Our new look: The colors of race. *Newsweek,* pp. 28–30.

Côté, J., & Levine, C. (2002). *Identity, formation, agency, and culture.* Mahwah, NJ: Erlbaum.

Cox, J. R. (1989). The fulfillment of time: King's "I have a dream" speech (August 28, 1963). In M. C. Leff & F. J. Kaufeld (Eds.), *Texts in context: Critical dialogues on significant episodes in American rhetoric* (pp. 181–204). Davis, CA: Hermagoras Press.

Cox, J. R. (2004). Personal communication.

Cozart, E. (1996, November 1997). *Feng shui. The Raleigh News & Observer,* p. D1.

Cragan, J., Wright, D., & Kasch, C. (2004). *Communication in small groups: Theory, process, skills,* (6th ed.). Belmont, CA: Wadsworth.

Crandall, F., & Wallace, M. (1998). *Work and rewards in the virtual workplace: A "new deal" for organizations and employees.* Wooster, OH: AMACOM.

Crane, D. (1987). Diagnosing relationships with spatial distance: An empirical test of a clinical principle. *Journal of Marriage and the Family, 13,* 307–310.

Crohn, J. (1995). *Mixed matches.* New York: Fawcett Columbine.

Cronen, V., Pearce, W. B., & Snavely, L. (1979). A theory of rule-structure and types of episodes and a study of perceived enmeshment in undesired repetitive patterns ("URPs"). In D. Nimmo (Ed.), *Communication Yearbook, 3.* New Brunswick, NJ: Transaction Books.

Crossen, C. (1994). *Tainted truth: The manipulation of fact in America.* New York: Simon & Schuster.

Crossen, C. (1997, July 10). Blah, blah, blah. *The Wall Street Journal,* pp. 1A, 6A.

Crowley, G. (1995, March 6). Dialing the stress-meter down. *Newsweek*, p. 62.

Crowley, G. (1998, March 16). Healer of hearts. *Newsweek*, pp. 50–55.

Cummings, M. (1993). Teaching the African American rhetoric course. In J. Ward (Ed.), *African American communication: An anthology in traditional and contemporary studies* (pp. 239–248). Dubuque, IA: Kendall/Hunt.

Cunningham, J. A., Strassberg, D. S., & Haan, B. (1986). Effects of intimacy and sex-role congruency on self-disclosure. *Journal of Social and Clinical Psychology, 4,* 393–401.

Cunningham, J. D., & Antill, J. K. (1995). Current trends in non-marital cohabitation: The great POSSLQ hunt continues. In J. T. Wood & S. W. Duck (Eds.), *Understanding relationship processes, 6: Understudied relationships: Off the beaten track* (pp. 148–172). Thousand Oaks, CA: Sage.

"Cybermedicine" raises ethical questions. (1999, June 28). *The Raleigh News & Observer*, p. 7A.

Daly, J., & McCroskey, J. (Eds.). (1984). *Avoiding communication: Shyness, reticence, and communication apprehension.* Beverly Hills, CA: Sage.

Darnell, D. K. (1963). The relationship between sentence order and comprehension. *Speech Monographs, 30,* 97–100.

Dash, K. (1998, July 26). Telecommuting takes a good road map. *The Raleigh News & Observer*, p. 6E.

Davis, F. (1991). *Moving the mountain: The women's movement in America since 1960.* New York: Simon & Schuster.

Davis, S., & Kieffer, J. (1998). Restaurant servers influence tipping behaviors. *Psychological Reports, 83,* 223–236.

Deal, T., & Kennedy, A. (1999). *The new corporate cultures: Revitalizing the workplace after downsizing, mergers, and reengineering.* Reading, MA: Perseus Books.

The Dean yell. (2004, January 21). *The Boston Globe*, p. 1A.

DeFleur, M. L., & Ball-Rokeach, S. (1989). *Theories of mass communication* (5th ed.). White Plains, NY: Longman.

DeFrancisco, V. (1991). The sounds of silence: How men silence women in marital relations. *Discourse and Society, 2,* 413–423.

Delia, J., Clark, R. A., & Switzer, D. (1974). Cognitive complexity and impression formation in informal social interaction. *Speech Monographs, 41,* 299–308.

Deming, W. E. (1982). *Out of the crisis.* Cambridge, UK: Cambridge University Press.

Dennis, A., Aronson, J., Heninger, W., & Walker, H. (1999). Structuring time and task in electronic brainstorming. *MIS Quarterly*, 95–108.

Derlega, V. J., & Berg, J. H. (1987). *Self-disclosure: Research, theory, and therapy.* New York: Plenum.

Desktop video interviews catch recruiters' eyes. (1995, November 21). *The Wall Street Journal*, p. 1A.

DeVito, J. (1994). *Human communication: The basic course* (6th ed.). New York: HarperCollins.

Dicks, D. (Ed.). (1993). *Breaking convention with intercultural romances.* Weggis, Switzerland: Bergili Books.

Dickson, F. (1995). The best is yet to be: Research on long-lasting marriages. In J. T. Wood & S. W. Duck (Eds.), *Understanding relationship processes, 6: Understudied relationships: Off the beaten track* (pp. 22–50). Thousand Oaks, CA: Sage.

Dieter, P. (1989, March). *Shooting her with video, drugs, bullets, and promises.* Paper presented at the meeting of the Association of Women in Psychology, Newport, RI.

Diggs, N. (1998). *Steel butterflies: Japanese women and the American experience.* New York: State University of New York Press.

Diggs, N. (2001). *Looking beyond the mask: When American women marry Japanese men.* New York: State University of New York Press.

Dindia, K. (1994). A multiphasic view of relationship maintenance strategies. In D. Canary & L. Stafford (Eds.), *Communication and relational maintenance* (pp. 91–112). New York: Academic Press.

Dindia, K. (2000). Sex differences in self-disclosure, reciprocity of self-disclosure, and self-disclosure and liking: Three meta-analyses reviewed. In S. Petronio (Ed.), *Balancing the secrets of private disclosures* (pp. 21–35). Mahwah, NJ: Erlbaum.

Dixson, M., & Duck, S. W. (1993). Understanding relationship processes: Uncovering the human search for meaning. In S. W. Duck (Ed.), *Understanding relationship processes, 1: Individuals in relationships* (pp. 175–206). Newbury Park, CA: Sage.

Domestic violence. (1998, March 28). *The Washington Post*, p. A21.

Donald, D. (1996, February 15). Leadership lessons from Abraham Lincoln. *Fortune*, pp. 13–14.

Donnellon, A. (1996). *Team talk.* Boston: Harvard Business School Press.

Downing, J., & Garmon, C. (2001). Teaching students in the basic course how to use presentation software. *Communication Education, 50,* 218–229.

Drummond, K., & Hopper, R. (1993). Acknowledgment tokens in series. *Communication Reports, 6,* 47–53.

Duck, S. (1982). A topography of relationship disengagement and dissolution. In S. W. Duck (Ed.), *Personal relationships, 4: Dissolving personal relationships* (pp. 1–30). New York: Academic Press.

Duck, S. W. (1990). Relationships as unfinished business: Out of the frying pan and into the 1990s. *Journal of Social and Personal Relationships, 7,* 5–24.

Duck, S. W. (1994a). *Meaningful relationships.* Thousand Oaks, CA: Sage.

Duck, S. W. (1994b). Steady as (s)he goes: Relational maintenance as a shared meaning system. In D. Canary & L. Stafford (Eds.), *Communication and relational maintenance* (pp. 45–60). New York: Academic Press.

Duck, S. W., & Wood, J. T. (Eds.). (1995). *Understanding relationship processes, 5: Confronting relationship challenges.* Thousand Oaks, CA: Sage.

Duck, S. W., & Wood, J. T. (in press). What goes up may come down: Gendered patterns in relational dissolution. In M. Fine & J. Harvey (Eds.), *The handbook of divorce and dissolution of romantic relationships.* Mahwah, NJ: Erlbaum.

Eadie, W. F. (1982). Defensive communication revisited: A critical examination of Gibb's theory. *Southern Speech Communication Journal, 47,* 163–177.

Egan, G. (1973). Listening as empathic support. In J. Stewart (Ed.), *Bridges, not walls.* Reading, MA: Addison-Wesley.

Einhorn, L. (2000). *The Native American or oral tradition: Voices of the spirit and soul.* Westport, CT: Praeger.

Ellis, A. (1988). *How to stubbornly refuse to make yourself miserable about anything—yes, anything.* New York: Lyle Stuart.

Ellis, A., & Harper, R. (1977). *A new guide to rational living.* North Hollywood, CA: Wilshire.

Emmons, S. (1998, February 3). The look on his face: Yes, it was culture shock. *The Raleigh News & Observer,* p. 5E.

Entman, R. M. (1994). African Americans according to TV news. *Media Studies Journal, 8,* 29–38.

Entman, R. M., & Rojecki, A. (2000). *The Black image in the White mind: Media and race in America.* University of Chicago Press.

Erbert, L. (2000). Conflict and dialectics: Perceptions of dialectical contradictions in marital conflict. *Journal of Social and Personal Relationships, 17,* 638–659.

Estes, W. K. (1989). Learning theory. In A. Lessold & R. Glaser (Eds.), *Foundations for a psychology of education.* Hillsdale, NJ: Erlbaum.

Evans, B., Coman, G., & Goss, B. (1996). Consulting skills training and medical students' interviewing efficiency. *Medical Education, 30,* 121–128.

Evans, D. (1993, March 1). The wrong examples. *Newsweek,* p. 10.

Fagan, E. (2001). *Cast your net.* Harvard Common Press.

Faigley, L., & Selzer, J. (2000). *Good reasons.* Needham Heights, MA: Allyn & Bacon.

FAIR. (2000). Pre-convention coverage white-washes police violence, distorts activists' agenda. FAIR-L@listserv .american.edu. Accessed July 25, 2000.

Faludi, S. (1991). *Backlash: The undeclared war against American women.* New York: Crown.

Faludi, S. (1999). *Stiffed: The betrayal of the American man.* New York: Morrow.

Farnill, D., Hayes, S., & Todisco, J. (1997). Interviewing skills: Self-evaluation by medical students. *Medical Education, 31,* 122–127.

Fears, D., & Deane, C. (2001, July 6). Interracial marriages increasingly gain acceptance, study shows. *The Raleigh News & Observer,* p. 10A.

Fehr, B. (1993). How do I love thee: Let me consult my prototype. In S. W. Duck (Ed.), *Understanding relationship processes, 1: Individuals in relationships* (pp. 87–122). Newbury Park, CA: Sage.

Fehr, B., & Russell, J. A. (1991). Concept of love viewed from a prototype perspective. *Journal of Personality and Social Psychology, 60,* 425–438.

Fein, E., & Schneider, S. (2002). *The rules for online dating.* New York: Simon & Schuster.

Feldman, C., & Ridley, C. (2000). The role of conflict-based communication responses and outcomes in male domestic violence toward female partners. *Journal of Social and Personal Relationships, 17,* 552–573.

Ferrante, J. (2000). *Sociology: A global perspective* (4th ed.). Belmont, CA: Wadsworth.

Fincham, F. D., & Beach, S. (2002). Forgiveness in marriage: Implications for psychological aggression and constructive communication. *Personal Relationships, 9,* 239–251.

Fincham, F. D., & Bradbury, T. N. (1987). The impact of attributions in marriage: A longitudinal analysis. *Journal of Personality and Social Psychology, 53,* 510–517.

Fisher, A. (1998, June 22). Don't blow your new job. *Fortune, 137,* 159–162.

Fisher, B. A. (1987). *Interpersonal communication: The pragmatics of human relationships.* New York: Random House.

Fisher, K. (2000). *Leading self-directed work teams: A guide to developing new team leadership skills.* New York: McGraw-Hill.

Fitch, N. (Ed.). (2000). *How sweet the sound: The spirit of African American history.* New York: Harcourt College.

Fitzpatrick, M. A. (1988). *Between husbands and wives: Communication in marriage.* Newbury Park, CA: Sage.

Fitzpatrick, M. A., & Best, P. (1979). Dyadic adjustment in relational types: Consensus, cohesion, affectional expression and satisfaction in enduring relationships. *Communication Monographs, 46,* 167–178.

Fitzpatrick, M. A., & Sollie, D. (1999). Influence of individual and interpersonal factors on satisfaction and stability in romantic relationships. *Personal Relationships, 6,* 337–350.

Flanagin, A., Farinola, W., & Metzger, M. (2000). The technical code of the Internet/World Wide Web. *Critical Studies in Media Communication, 17,* 409–428.

Fletcher, G. J., & Fincham, F. D. (1991). Attribution in close relationships. In G. J. Fletcher & F. D. Fincham (Eds.), *Cognition in close relationships* (pp. 7–35). Hillsdale, NJ: Erlbaum.

Ford Foundation (1998, October 6). Americans see many benefits to diversity in higher education, finds first ever national poll on topic. Press release via Business Wire.

Foss, K., & Edson, B. (1989). What's in a name: Accounts of married women's name choices. *Western Journal of Communication, 53,* 356–373.

Fox-Genovese, E. (1991). *Feminism without illusions.* Chapel Hill: University of North Carolina Press.

Franklin, M., & Ramage, J. (1999). Til a long-distance job do us part. *Kiplinger's Personal Finance, 53,* p. 56.

Fraser, N. (1992). Rethinking the public sphere: A contribution to the critique of actually existing democracy. In C. Calhoun (Ed.), *Habermas and the public sphere* (pp. 109–142). Cambridge, MA: MIT Press.

Freed, K. (2002, May 11). Deep literacy: A proposal to produce public understanding of our interactivity. *Media & Education: Media Visions Journal.* Retrieved March 26, 2003 from http://www.mediavisions.com/ed-deeplit.html.

Fussell, S. (Ed.). (2002). *The verbal communication of emotion.* Mahwah, NJ: Erlbaum.

Gaines, S., Jr. (1995). Relationships between members of cultural minorities. In J. T. Wood & S. W. Duck (Eds.), *Understanding relationship processes, 6: Understudied relationships: Off the beaten track* (pp. 51–88). Thousand Oaks, CA: Sage.

Gammage, K., Carron, A., & Estabrooks, P. (2001). Team cohesion and individual productivity: The influence of the norm for productivity and the identifiability of individual effort. *Small Group Research, 32,* 3–18.

Gandy, O. H., Jr. (1994). From bad to worse: The media's framing of race and risk. *Media Studies Journal* (Special issue: *Race: America's rawest nerve), 8,* 39–48.

Gangwish, K. (1999). *Living in two worlds: Asian-American women and emotions.* Paper presented at the National Communication Association, Chicago.

Gants, D. (1999, April 9). Peer review for cyberspace: Evaluating scholarly Web sites. *The Chronicle of Higher Education,* p. B8.

Garner, T. (1994). Oral rhetorical practice in African American culture. In M. Houston & V. Chen (Eds.), *Our voices: Essays in culture, ethnicity, and communication* (pp. 81–91). Los Angeles: Roxbury Press.

Gass, R. (1999). Fallacy list: SpCom 335. Advanced argumentation. California State University, Fullerton. Available online at http://commfaculty.fullerton.edu/rgass/fallacy31.htm.

Gastil, J. (1994). A meta-analytic review of the productivity and satisfaction of democratic and autocratic leadership. *Small Group Research, 25,* 384–410.

Gates, B. (1999, May 31). Why the PC will not die. *Newsweek,* p. 64.

Gates, H. L. (1992). *Loose canons: Notes on the culture wars.* New York: Oxford University Press.

George, L. (1995, December 26). Holiday's traditions are being formed. *The Raleigh News & Observer,* pp. C1, C3.

Gerbner, G. (1990). Epilogue: Advancing on the path of righteousness (maybe). In N. Signorielli & M. Morgan (Eds.), *Cultivation analysis: New directions in media effects research* (pp. 250–261). Thousand Oaks, CA: Sage.

Gerbner, G., Gross, L., Morgan, M., & Signorielli, N. (1986). Living with television: The dynamics of the cultivation process. In J. Bryant & D. Zillmann (Eds.), *Perspectives on media effects* (pp. 17–40). Mahwah, NJ: Erlbaum.

Gerstel, N., & Gross, H. (1985). *Commuter marriage.* New York: Guilford Press.

Gibb, C. (1969). Leadership. In G. Lindsey & E. Aronson (Eds.), *The handbook of social psychology* (2nd ed., pp. 205–282). Reading, MA: Addison-Wesley.

Gibb, J. R. (1961). Defensive communication. *Journal of Communication, 11,* 141–148.

Gibb, J. R. (1964). Climate for trust formation. In L. Bradford, J. Gibb, & K. Benne (Eds.), *T-group theory and laboratory method* (pp. 279–309). New York: Wiley.

Gibb, J. R. (1970). Sensitivity training as a medium for personal growth and improved interpersonal relationships. *Interpersonal Development, 1,* 6–31.

Gibbs, J. T. (1992). Young Black males in America: Endangered, embittered, and embattled. In M. L. Andersen & P. H. Collins (Eds.), *Race, class, and gender: An anthology* (pp. 267–276). Belmont, CA: Wadsworth.

Gilman, S. (1999a). *Creating beauty to cure the soul: Race and psychology in the shaping of aesthetic surgery.* Durham, NC: Duke University Press.

Gitlin, T. (1995). *The twilight of common dreams.* New York: Metropolitan Books.

Gitlin, T. (2002). *Media unlimited: How the torrent of images and sounds overwhelms us.* New York: Metropolitan Books.

Gladwell, M. (2000, May 29). The new-boy network: What do job interviews really tell us? *The New Yorker,* pp. 68–72, 84–86.

Glascock, N. (1998, February 22). Diversity within Latino arrivals. *The Raleigh News & Observer,* p. 9A.

Global Internet statistics. (2002, March 31). Global Reach. Retrieved March 26, 2003, from http://global-reach .biz/globalstats/index.php3.

Gochenour, T. (1990). *Considering Filipinos.* Yarmouth, ME: Intercultural Press.

Goldsmith, D., & Fulfs, P. (1999). You just don't have the evidence: An analysis of claims and evidence in Deborah Tannen's "You just don't understand." In M. Roloff (Ed.), *Communication Yearbook, 22* (pp. 1–49). Thousand Oaks, CA: Sage.

Goleman, D. (1990, December 25). The group and self: New focus on a cultural rift. *The New York Times,* p. 40.

Goleman, D. (1995). *Emotional intelligence.* New York: Bantam.

Goleman, D. (1998). *Working with emotional intelligence.* New York: Bantam.

Goleman, D., McKee, A., & Boyatzis, R. (2002). *Primal leadership: Realizing the power of emotional intelligence.* Cambridge, MA: Harvard Business School Press.

Goode, E. (2001, August 1). 20% of girls report abuse by a date. *The Raleigh News & Observer,* p. 10A.

Gordon, J. R. (1998). *Organizational behavior: A diagnostic approach* (6th ed.). Englewood Cliffs, NJ: Prentice Hall.

Gottman, J. (1993). The roles of conflict engagement, escalation, or avoidance in marital interaction: A longitudinal view of five types of couples. *Journal of Consulting and Clinical Psychology, 61,* 6–15.

Gottman, J. (1994a). *What predicts divorce? The relationship between marital processes and marital outcomes.* Hillsdale, NJ: Erlbaum.

Gottman, J. (1994b). Why marriages fail. *The Family Therapy Newsletter,* pp. 41–48.

Gottman, J. (1999). Seven principles for making marriages work. New York: Crown.

Gottman, J. M., & Carrère, S. (1994). Why can't men and women get along? Developmental roots and marital inequities. In D. Canary & L. Stafford (Eds.), *Communication and relational maintenance* (pp. 203–229). New York: Academic Press.

Gottman, J., Markman, H. J., & Notarius, C. (1977). The topography of marital conflict: A sequential analysis of verbal and nonverbal behavior. *Journal of Marriage and the Family, 39,* 461–477.

Gottman, J., & Silver, N. (1994). *Why marriages succeed or fail.* New York: Simon & Schuster.

Greene, K., Frey, L., & Derlega, V. (2002). Interpersonalizing AIDS: Attending to the personal and social relationships of individuals living with HIV and/or AIDS. *Journal of Social and Personal Relationships, 19,* 5–18.

Greenleaf, C. (1998). *Attention to detail: A gentleman's guide to professional appearance and conduct.* New York: Mass Market Press.

Griffin, C. (2004). *An invitation to public speaking.* Belmont, CA: Wadsworth.

Griffin, E. (1991). *A first look at communication theory.* New York: McGraw-Hill.

Gronbeck, B. E., McKerrow, R., Ehninger, D., & Monroe, A. H. (1994). *Principles and types of speech communication* (12th ed.). Glenview, IL: Scott, Foresman.

Gross, M. (2000, June). The lethal politics of beauty. *George,* pp. 53–59, 99–100.

Gudykunst, W., & Lee, C. (2002). Cross-cultural communication theories. In W. Gudykunst & B. Mody (Eds.), *The handbook of international and intercultural communication* (2nd ed., pp. 25–50). Thousand Oaks, CA: Sage.

Guerrero, L. (1996). Attachment style differences in intimacy and involvement: A test of the four-category model. *Communication Monographs, 63,* 269–292.

Guldner, G. (2003). *Long-distance relationships: The complete guide.* Corona, CA: JFMilne Publications.

Gupta, V., Hanges, P., & Dorfman, P. (2002). Cultural clusters: Methodology and findings. *Journal of World Business, 37,* 11–15.

Hacker, K., Goss, B., & Townley, C. (1998). Employee attitudes regarding electronic mail policies: A case study. *Management Communication Quarterly, 11,* 422–432.

Hager, M., & Springen, K. (1998, March 16). Is love the best drug? *Newsweek,* pp. 54–56.

Hagins, J. (1996). The inconvenient public interest: Policy challenges in the age of information. *Journal of Applied Communication Research, 24,* 83–92.

Hall, E. (1959). *The silent language*. Garden City, NY: Doubleday.

Hall, E. T. (1966). *The hidden dimension*. New York: Anchor.

Hall, E. T. (1968). Proxemics. *Current Anthropology, 9,* 83–108.

Hall, E. T. (1977). *Beyond culture*. New York: Doubleday.

Hall, J. A. (1987). On explaining gender differences: The case of nonverbal communication. In P. Shaver & C. Hendricks (Eds.), *Sex and gender* (pp. 177–200). Newbury Park, CA: Sage.

Hall, J. A., & Bernieri, F. J. (Eds.). (2001). *Interpersonal sensitivity: Theory and measurement*. Mahwah, NJ: Erlbaum.

Hall, S. (1986). The problem of ideology: Marxism without guarantees. *Journal of Communication Inquiry, 10,* 28–44.

Hall, S. (1989). Ideology and communication theory. In B. Dervin, L. Grossberg, B. O'Keefe, & E. Wartella (Eds.), *Rethinking communication theory* (Vol. 1, pp. 40–52). Thousand Oaks, CA: Sage.

Hamachek, D. (1992). *Encounters with the self* (3rd ed.). Fort Worth: Harcourt Brace Jovanovich.

Hamilton, C. (1999). *Successful public speaking*. Belmont, CA: Wadsworth.

Hamilton, C., & Parker, C. (2001). *Communicating for results* (6th ed.). Belmont, CA: Wadsworth.

Haraway, D. (1988). Situated knowledges: The science question in feminism and the privilege of partial perspective. *Signs, 14,* 575–599.

Harding, S. (1991). *Whose science? Whose knowledge? Thinking from women's lives*. Ithaca, NY: Cornell University Press.

Hargraves, O. (2001a). *Culture shock! Morroco*. Portland, OR: Graphic Arts Center Publishing.

Hargraves, O. (2001b). *London at your door*. Portland, OR: Graphic Arts Center Publishing.

Harris, T. J. (1969). *I'm OK, you're OK*. New York: Harper & Row.

Harter, S., Waters, P., Pettitt, L., Whitesell, N., & Kofkin, J. (1997). Autonomy and connectedness as dimensions of relationship styles in men and women. *Journal of Social and Personal Relationships, 14,* 147–164.

Hartzler, M., & Henry, J. (1998). *Tolls for virtual teams*. New York: McGraw-Hill.

Harvey, J., & Weber, A. (2002). *Odyssey of the heart*. Mahwah, NJ: Erlbaum.

Harvey, J., & Wenzel, A. (Eds.). (2001). *A clinician's guide to maintaining and enhancing close relationships*. Mahwah, NJ: Erlbaum.

Haubegger, C. (1999, July 12). The legacy of generation—. *Newsweek*, p. 61.

Haught, N. (2003, May 30). Beards mean different things to different cultures. *The Raleigh News & Observer*, p. 5E.

Hawkins, K. (1995). Effects of gender and communication content on leadership emergence in small task-oriented groups. *Small Group Research, 26,* 234–249.

Hayakawa, S. I. (1962). *The use and misuse of language*. New York: Fawcett.

Hayakawa, S. I. (1964). *Language in thought and action* (2nd ed.). New York: Harcourt Brace & World.

Hecht, M., Jackson, R., & Ribeau, S. (2003). *African American communication*. Mahwah, NJ: Erlbaum.

Hecht, M. L., Collier, M. J., & Ribeau, S. A. (1993). *African American communication: Ethnic identity and cultural interpretation*. Newbury Park, CA: Sage.

Hecht, M. L., Marston, P. J., & Larkey, L. K. (1994). Love ways and relationship quality in heterosexual relationships. *Journal of Social and Personal Relationships, 11,* 25–44.

Hegel, G. W. F. (1807). *Phenomenology of mind* (J. B. Baillie, Trans.). Germany: Wurzburg & Bamburg.

Heider, F. (1958). *The psychology of interpersonal relations*. New York: Wiley.

Helgesen, S. (1990). *The female advantage: Women's ways of leadership*. New York: Doubleday/Currency.

Hendrick, C., & Hendrick, S. (1988). Lovers wear rose-colored glasses. *Journal of Social and Personal Relationships, 5,* 161–184.

Hendrick, C., & Hendrick, S. (1996). Gender and the experience of heterosexual love. In J. T. Wood (Ed.), *Gendered relationships* (pp. 131–148). Mountain View, CA: Mayfield.

Hendrick, C., Hendrick, S., Foote, F. H., & Slapion-Foote, M. J. (1984). Do men and women love differently? *Journal of Social and Personal Relationships, 2,* 177–196.

Henley, N. M. (1977). *Body politics: Power, sex and nonverbal communication*. Englewood Cliffs, NJ: Prentice Hall.

Hershey, P., & Blanchard, K. (1993). *Management of organizational behavior: Utilizing human resources*. Englewood Cliffs, NJ: Prentice Hall.

Hewes, D. (Ed.). (1995). *The cognitive bases of interpersonal perception*. Mahwah, NJ: Erlbaum.

Hicks, J. (1998, February 12). Eating disorders screening offered. *The Raleigh News & Observer*, p. 2E.

Hickson, M. III, Stacks, D., & Moore, N. (2003). *Nonverbal communication: Studies and applications*, (4th ed.). Los Angeles: Roxbury.

Higginbotham, E. (1992). We were never on a pedestal: Women of color continue to struggle with poverty, racism, and sexism. In M. L. Andersen & P. H. Collins (Eds.), *Race, class, and gender: An anthology* (pp. 183–190). Belmont, CA: Wadsworth.

Higgins, B. (1996, November). How e-mail changed everything. *San Francisco Focus*, 59–67. Cited in Morreale, S., Spitzberg, B., & Barge, K. (2001). *Human communication: Motivation, knowledge, and skills*. Belmont, CA: Wadsworth.

Hirokawa, R., Cathcart, R., Samovar, L., & Henman, L. (Eds.). (2004). *Small group communication: Theory and practice (an anthology)* (8th ed.). Los Angeles: Roxbury.

Hochschild, A. (1997). *The time bind: When work becomes home and home becomes work*. New York: Metropolitan.

Hochschild, A., with Machung, A. (2003). *The second shift* (Rev ed.). New York: Viking.

Hodson, R., & Sullivan, T. A. (2002). *The social organization of work* (3rd ed.). Belmont, CA: Wadsworth.

Hofstede, G. (1980). *Cultural consequences: International differences in work-related values*. Beverly Hills, CA: Sage.

Hofstede, G. (1991). *Cultures and organizations: Software of the mind*. London: McGraw-Hill. *Journal of Clinical Psychology, 38,* 136–141.

Holtzman, L. (2000). *Media messages: What film, television, and popular music teach us about race, class, gender, and sexual orientation*. New York: M. E. Sharpe.

Honeycutt, J. M., Woods, B., & Fontenot, K. (1993). The endorsement of communication conflict rules as a function of engagement, marriage and marital ideology. *Journal of Social and Personal Relationships, 10,* 285–304.

hooks, b. (1995). *Killing rage: Ending racism in America*. New York: Henry Holt.

Hoover, J. (2002). *Effective small group and team communication*. New York: Harcourt.

House, R., Javidan, M., Hanges, P., & Dorfman, P. (2002). Understanding cultures and implicit leadership theories across the globe: An introduction to Project GLOBE. *Journal of World Business, 37*, 3–10.

Houston, M. (2003). When Black women talk with White women: Why dialogues are difficult. In A. González, M. Houston, & V. Chen (Eds.), *Our voices: Essays in culture, ethnicity, and communication* (3rd ed., pp. 98–104). Los Angeles: Roxbury.

Houston, M., & Wood, J. T. (1996). Difficult dialogues, expanded horizons: Communicating across race and class. In J. T. Wood (Ed.), *Gendered relationships* (pp. 39–56). Mountain View, CA: Mayfield.

Hunt, D. (1999). *O. J. Simpson facts and fictions: News rituals in the construction of reality.* Cambridge, UK: Cambridge University Press.

Huston, M., & Schwartz, P. (1995). Relationships of lesbians and gay men. In J. T. Wood & S. W. Duck (Eds.), *Understanding relationship processes, 6: Understudied relationships: Off the beaten track* (pp. 89–121). Thousand Oaks, CA: Sage.

Huston, M., & Schwartz, P. (1996). Gendered dynamics in the romantic relationships of lesbians and gay men. In J. T. Wood (Ed.), *Gendered relationships* (pp. 163–176). Mountain View, CA: Mayfield.

Huston, T. L., McHale, S. M., & Crouter, A. C. (1986). When the honeymoon is over: Changes in the marriage relationship over the first year. In R. Gilmour & S. Duck (Eds.), *The emerging field of personal relationships* (pp. 109–132). Hillsdale, NJ: Erlbaum.

Hyatt, D. E., & Ruddy, T. M. (1997). An examination of the relationship between work group characteristics and performance: Once more into the breach. *Personnel Psychology, 50*, 533–585.

Hyde, M. J. (1995). Human being and the call of technology. In J. T. Wood & R. B. Gregg (Eds.), *Toward the 21st century.* Cresskill, NJ: Hampton.

Hymowitz, C. (2000, February 8). Racing onto the Web, one manager's secret is simple: Listening. *The Wall Street Journal*, p. B1.

Imperato, G. (May 1999). The e-mail prescription. *Fast Company*, pp. 90–92.

Inman, C. C. (1996). Friendships among men: Closeness in the doing. In J. T. Wood (Ed.), *Gendered relationships* (pp. 95–110). Mountain View, CA: Mayfield.

International Listening Association. (1995, April). An ILA definition of listening. *ILA Listening Post, 53*, p. 4.

Isaacs, W. (1999). *Dialogue and the art of thinking together.* New York: Doubleday.

Jackson, S., & Allen, J. (1990). Meta-analysis of the effectiveness of one-sided and two-sided argumentation. Paper presented at the International Communication Association, Montreal, Canada.

Jacobson, N., & Gottman, J. (1998). *When men batter women.* New York: Simon & Schuster.

Jafe, C. (1995). *Public speaking: A cultural perspective.* Belmont, CA: Wadsworth.

Jaffe, C. (2001). *Public speaking: Concepts and skills for a diverse society* (3rd ed.). Belmont, CA: Wadsworth.

James, D., & Clarke, S. (1993). Women, men, and interruptions: A critical review. In D. Tannen (Ed.)., *Gender and conversational interaction* (pp. 281–312). New York: Oxford University Press.

James, N. (2000). When Miss America was always White. In A. González, M. Houston, & V. Chen (Eds.), *Our voices: Essays in culture, ethnicity, and communication* (pp. 42–46). Los Angeles: Roxbury.

Janis, I. L. (1977). *Victims of groupthink.* Boston: Houghton Mifflin.

Janis, I. L. (1989). *Crucial decisions: Leadership in policymaking and crisis management.* New York: Free Press.

Javidi, A., & Javidi, M. (1994). Cross-cultural analysis of interpersonal bonding: A look at East and West. In L. A. Samovar & R. E. Porter (Eds.), *Intercultural communication: A reader* (7th ed.). Belmont, CA: Wadsworth.

Jhally, S., & Katz, J. (2001, Winter). Big trouble, little pond. *UMass*, pp. 26–31.

Johnson, D., & Johnson, F. (1991). *Joining together: Group theory and group skills.* Englewood Cliffs, NJ: Prentice Hall.

Johnson, F. (2000). *Speaking culturally: Language diversity in the United States.* Thousand Oaks, CA: Sage.

Johnson, F. L. (1989). Women's culture and communication: An analytic perspective. In C. M. Lont & S. A. Friedley (Eds.), *Beyond the boundaries: Sex and gender diversity in communication.* Fairfax, VA: George Mason University Press.

Johnson, F. L. (1996). Friendships among women: Closeness in dialogue. In J. T. Wood (Ed.), *Gendered relationships* (pp. 79–94). Mountain View, CA: Mayfield.

Johnson, M. P. (2001). Conflict and control: Symmetry and asymmetry in domestic violence. In A. Booth, A. Crouter, & M. Clements (Eds.), *Couples in conflict* (pp. 95–104). Mahwah, NJ: Erlbaum.

Johnson, M. P., & Ferraro, K. J. (2000). Research on domestic violence in the 1990s: Making distinctions. *Journal of Marriage and the Family, 62*, 948–963.

Johnson, N., Roberts, M., & Warell, J. (Eds.). (2002). *Beyond appearance: A new look at adolescent girls.* Washington, DC: American Psychological Association.

Jones, E., & Gallois, C. (1989). Spouses' impressions of rules for communication in public and private marital conflicts. *Journal of Marriage and the Family, 51*, 957–967.

Jossi, F. (2001). Teamwork aids HRIS decision process. *HR Magazine, 46*, 165–173.

Justice, R. (1999). We're happily married and living apart. *Newsweek, 134*, p. 12.

Kantrowitz, B., & Wingert, P. (2001, May 28). Unmarried, with children. *Newsweek*, pp. 46–55.

Katzenbach, J., & Smith, D. (1993, March–April). The discipline of teams. *Harvard Business Review*, 111–120.

Kaye, L. W., & Applegate, J. S. (1990). Men as elder caregivers: A response to changing families. *American Journal of Orthopsychiatry, 60*, 86–95.

Keeley, M. P., & Hart, A. J. (1994). Nonverbal behavior in dyadic interaction. In S. W. Duck (Ed.), *Understanding relationship processes, 4: Dynamics of relationships* (pp. 135–162). Thousand Oaks, CA: Sage.

Kelley, D. (1998). The communication of forgiveness. *Communication Studies, 49*, 1–17.

Kelley, H. H. (1967). Attribution theory in social psychology. In D. Levine (Ed.), *Nebraska Symposium on Motivation:* Vol. 15 (pp. 192–238). Lincoln: University of Nebraska Press.

Kelley, T., & Littman, J. (2001). *The art of innovation.* New York: Doubleday.

Kelly, C., Huston, T. L., & Cate, R. M. (1985). Premarital relationship correlates of the erosion of satisfaction in marriage. *Journal of Social and Personal Relationships, 2,* 167–178.

Kelly, G. A. (1955). *The psychology of personal constructs.* New York: W. W. Norton.

Kennedy, G. (Ed. & trans.). (1991). *Aristotle on rhetoric.* London: Oxford University Press.

Keyes, R. (1992, February 22). Do you have the time? *Parade,* pp. 22–25.

Kiernan, V. (1998, May 29). Some scholars question research method of expert on Internet addiction. *The Chronicle of Higher Education,* pp. A25–A27.

Kiesler, C. A., & Kiesler, S. B. (1971). Role of forewarning in persuasive communications. *Journal of Abnormal and Social Psychology, 18,* 210–221.

Kikoski, J. (1998). Effective communication in the performance appraisal interview: Face-to-face communication for public managers in the culturally diverse workplace. *Public Personnel Management, 27,* 491–513.

Kilbourne, J. (1999). *Deadly persuasion: Why women and girls must fight the addictive power of advertising.* New York: Free Press.

Kimball, M. (1986). Television and sex-role attitudes. In T. M. Williams (Ed.), *The impact of television: A natural experiment in three communities* (pp. 256–301). Orlando, FL: Academic Press.

Klein, R. (2001). *Jewelry talks: A novel thesis.* New York: Pantheon.

Klein, R., & Milardo, R. (2000). The social context of couple conflict: Support and criticism from informal third parties. *Journal of Social and Personal Relationships, 17,* pp. 618–637.

Kohlberg, L. (1958). *The development of modes of thinking and moral choice in the years 10 to 16.* Unpublished doctoral dissertation, University of Chicago.

Kohls, L. R. (2001). *Survival kit for overseas living.* Yarmouth, ME: Nicholas Brealey Intercultural Press.

Köllwitz, K., & Kahlo, F. (2003). Women and the art world: Diary of the feminist masked avengers. In R. Morgan (Ed.), *Sisterhood is forever* (pp. 437–444). New York: Washington Square Press.

Korzybski, A. (1948). *Science and sanity* (4th ed.). Lakeville, CT: International Non-Aristotelian Library.

Kouzes, J., & Posner, B. (1999). *Encouraging the heart: A leader's guide to recognizing and rewarding others.* New York: Jossey-Bass.

Krannich, R., & Banis, W. (1990). *High-impact résumés and letters* (4th ed.). Woodridge, VA: Impact Publications.

Kruger, R., & Casey, M. (2000). *Focus groups: A practical guide for applied research.* Thousand Oaks, CA: Sage.

Kupfer, D., First, M., & Regier, D. (2002). *A research agenda for SSM-V.* Washington DC: American Psychiatric Press.

Kurdek, L. A. (1993). The allocation of household labor in gay, lesbian, and heterosexual married couples. *Journal of Social Issues, 49,* 127–139.

LaFasto, F. & Larson, C. (2001). *When teams work best: 6,000 team members and leaders tell what it takes to succeed.* Thousand Oaks, CA: Sage.

La Gaipa, J. J. (1982). Rituals of disengagement. In S. W. Duck (Ed.), *Personal relationships, 4: Dissolving personal relationship* (pp. 189–209). London: Academic Press.

Lakoff, G., & Johnson, M. (1980). *Metaphors we live by.* Chicago: University of Chicago Press.

Lancaster, H. (1996, January 14). That team spirit can lead your career to new victories. *The Wall Street Journal,* p. B1.

Lane, D., & Shelton, M. (2001). The centrality of communication education in classroom computer-mediated communication: Toward a practical and evaluative pedagogy. *Communication Education, 50,* 2241–2255.

Lane, R. (2000). *The loss of happiness in market democracies.* New Haven, CT: Yale University Press.

Langer, S. (1953). *Feeling and form: A theory of art.* New York: Scribner.

Langer, S. (1979). *Philosophy in a new key: A study in the symbolism of reason, rite, and art* (3rd ed.). Cambridge, MA: Harvard University Press.

Langfred, C. (1998). Is group cohesiveness a double-edged sword? *Small Group Research, 29,* 124–143.

Langston, D. (2001). Tired of playing monopoly? In M. L. Andersen & P. H. Collins (Eds.), *Race, class, and gender: An anthology* (4th ed. pp. 125–133). Belmont, CA: Wadsworth.

Lareau, A. (2003). *Unequal childhoods: Class, race, and family life.* Berkeley: University of California Press.

Larson, G., & Larson, D. (2004). *Communicating in groups and teams: Sharing leadership.* Belmont, CA: Wadsworth.

Lasch, C. (1990, Spring). Journalism, publicity and the lost art of argument. *Gannett Center Journal,* pp. 1–11.

Laswell, H. D. (1948). The structure and function of communication in society. In L. Bryson (Ed.), *The communication of ideas.* New York: Harper & Row.

Lau, B. (1989). Imagining your path to success. *Management Quarterly, 30,* 30–41.

Leaper, N. (1999). How communicators lead at the best global companies. *Communication World, 16,* 33–36.

Leathers, D. G. (1986). *Successful nonverbal communication: Principles and applications.* New York: Macmillan.

Lederman, L. (1990). Assessing educational effectiveness: The focus group interview as a technique for data collection. *Communication Education, 39,* 117–127.

Lee, J. A. (1973). *The colours of love: An exploration of the ways of loving.* Don Mills, Ontario, Canada: New Press.

Lee, J. A. (1988). Love-styles. In R. J. Sternberg & M. L. Barnes (Eds.), *The psychology of love* (pp. 38–67). New Haven, CT: Yale University Press.

Lee, W. (1994). On not missing the boat: A processual method for intercultural understandings of idioms and lifeworld. *Journal of Applied Communication Research, 22,* 141–161.

Lee, W. (2000). That's Greek to me: Between a rock and a hard place in intercultural encounters. In L. Samovar & R. Porter (Eds.), *Intercultural communication: A reader* (9th ed., pp. 217–224). Belmont, CA: Wadsworth.

Lehman, C., & DuFrene, D. (1999). *Business communication* (12th ed.). Cincinnati: South-Western.

Leo, J. (1999, September 27). And now . . . smut-see TV. *U.S. News & World Report,* p. 15.

Le Poire, B. A., Burgoon, J. K., & Parrott, R. (1992). Status and privacy restoring communication in the workplace. *Journal of Applied Communication Research, 4,* 419–436.

Le Poire, B. A., & Yoshimura, S. (1999). The effects of expectancies and actual communication on nonverbal adaptation and communication outcomes: A test of interaction adaptation theory. *Communication Monographs, 66,* 1–30.

Levine, R., & Norenzayan, A. (1999). The pace of life in 31 countries. *Journal of Cross-Cultural Psychology, 30,* 178–205.

Lewin, K., Lippitt, R., & White, R. K. (1939). Patterns of aggressive behavior in experimentally created "social climates." *Journal of Social Psychology, 10,* 271–299.

Lim, T. (2002). Language and verbal communication across cultures. In W. Gudykunst & B. Mody (Eds.), *The handbook of international and intercultural communication* (2nd ed., pp. 69–88). Thousand Oaks, CA: Sage.

Lorde, A. (1992). Age, race, class, and sex: Women redefining difference. In M. L. Andersen & P. H. Collins (Eds.), *Race, class, and gender: An anthology* (pp. 495–502). Belmont, CA: Wadsworth.

Luft, J. (1969). *Of human interaction.* Palo Alto, CA: Natural Press.

Lumsden, G., & Lumsden, D. (2004). *Communicating in groups and teams* (4th ed.). Belmont, CA: Wadsworth.

Lund, M. (1985). The development of investment and commitment scales for predicting continuity of personal relationships. *Journal of Social and Personal Relationships, 2,* 3–23.

Lustig, M., & Koester, J. (1999). *Intercultural competence: Interpersonal communication across cultures.* New York: Longman.

Lytton, H., & Romney, D. M. (1991). Parents' differential socialization of boys and girls: A meta-analysis. *Psychological Bulletin, 109,* 267–296.

Maclel, D., & Herrera-Sobek, M. (Eds.). (1998). *Culture across borders: Mexican immigration and popular culture.* Tucson: University of Arizona Press.

Major, B., Schmidlin, A. M., & Williams, L. (1990). Gender patterns in social touch: The impact of setting and age. In C. Mayo & N. M. Henley (Eds.), *Gender and nonverbal behavior* (pp. 3–37). New York: Springer-Verlag.

Malandro, L. A., & Barker, L. L. (1983). *Nonverbal communication.* Reading, MA: Addison-Wesley.

Maltz, D. N., & Borker, R. (1982). A cultural approach to male–female miscommunication. In J. J. Gumpertz (Ed.), *Language and social identity* (pp. 196–216). Cambridge, UK: Cambridge University Press.

Mander, M. (Ed.). (1999). *Framing friction: Media and social conflict.* Urbana: University of Illinois Press.

Mangan, K. (2002, July 5). Horse sense or nonsense? Critics decry what they consider the "softening" of medical education. *The Chronicle of Higher Education,* pp. A8–A10.

Manning, M. (2000). *Dispatches from the ebony tower: Intellectuals confront the African American experience.* New York: Columbia University Press.

Manusov, V., & Harvey, J. (2001). *Attribution, communication behavior, and close relationships.* Port Chester, NY: Cambridge University Press.

Mapstone, E. (1998). *War of words: Women and men argue.* London: Random House.

Marion, L. (1997, January 11). Recruiting students just got easier for many companies. *The Raleigh News & Observer,* p. 3A.

Martin, C., Fabes, R., Evans, S., & Wyman, H. (2000). Social cognition on the playground: Children's beliefs about playing with girls and boys and their relations to sex-segregated play. *Journal of Social and Personal Relationships, 17,* 751–771.

Matsumoto, D., Franklin, B., Choi, J., Rogers, D., & Tatani, H. (2002). Cultural influences on the expression and perception of emotion. In W. Gudykunst & B. Mody (Eds.), *The handbook of international and intercultural communication* (2nd ed., pp. 107–126). Thousand Oaks, CA: Sage.

Maugh, T. H. II (2002, February 26). Center says AIDS virus is nearly 1 million in U.S. *The Raleigh News & Observer,* p. 8B.

Maxwell, J. C. (2001). *The 17 indisputable laws of teamwork: Embrace them and empower your team.* Nashville, TN: Thomas Nelson.

Maxwell, L., & McCain, R. (1997, July). Gateway or gatekeeper: The implications of copyright and digitalization on education. *Communication Education, 46,* 141–157.

May, L. (1998). *Masculinity and morality.* Ithaca, NY: Cornell University Press.

McCarthy, M. (1991). *Mastering the information age.* Los Angeles: Jeremy P. Tarcher.

McCauley, C., & Van Velsor, E. (Eds.). (2003). *The Center for Creative Leadership handbook of leadership development,* (2nd ed.). Indianapolis, IN: Jossey-Bass/Wiley.

McChesney, R. (1999). *Rich media, poor democracy: Communication politics in dubious times.* Urbana: University of Illinois Press.

McCombs, M., & Ghanem, S. (2001). The convergence of agenda setting and framing. In S. Reese, O. Gandy, & A. Grant (Eds.), *Framing public life: Perspectives on media and our understanding of the social world* (pp. 240–279). Mahwah, NJ: Erlbaum.

McCroskey, J. C. (1977). Oral communication apprehension: A summary of recent theory and research. *Human Communication Research, 4,* 78–96.

McCroskey, J. C. (1982). *Introduction to rhetorical communication* (4th ed.). Englewood Cliffs, NJ: Prentice Hall.

McCroskey, J. C., & Mehrley, R. S. (1969). The effects of disorganization and nonfluency on attitude change and source credibility. *Speech Monographs, 36,* 13–21.

McCroskey, J., & Teven, J. (1999). Goodwill: A reexamination of the construct and its measurement. *Communication Monographs, 66,* 90–103.

McGrane, S. (2000, September 4). Absence makes the typing skills grow stronger. *The Raleigh News & Observer,* p. 5D.

McGrath, P. (2002, June 10). Public or private? *Newsweek,* p. 32R.

McGuire, W. J. (1989). *Theoretical foundations of campaigns.* In R. E. Rice & C. K. Atkin (Eds.), *Public communication campaigns* (2nd ed., pp. 43–65). Newbury Park, CA: Sage.

McKinney, B., Kelly, L., & Duran, R. (1997). The relationship between conflict message styles and dimension of communication competence. *Communication Reports, 10,* 185–196.

Meacham, J. (2000, September 18). The new face of race. *Newsweek,* pp. 38–41.

Mead, G. H. (1934). *Mind, self, and society.* Chicago: University of Chicago Press.

Meeks, B., Hendrick, S., & Hendrick, C. (1998). Communication, love, and satisfaction. *Journal of Social and Personal Relationships, 15,* 755–773.

Mehrabian, A. (1981). *Silent messages: Implicit communication of emotion and attitudes* (2nd ed.). Belmont, CA: Wadsworth.

Men use half a brain to listen, study finds. (2000, November 29). *The Raleigh News & Observer,* p. 8A.

Merritt, B. (2000). Illusive reflections: African American women on primetime television. In A. González, M. Houston, & V. Chen (Eds.), *Our voices: Essays in culture, ethnicity, and communication* (3rd ed., pp. 47–53). Los Angeles: Roxbury.

Messner, M. (2000). Barbie girls versus sea monsters: Children-constructing gender. *Gender and Society, 7,* 121–137.

Metts, S., Cupach, W. R., & Bejlovec, R. A. (1989). "I love you too much to ever start liking you": Redefining romantic relationships. *Journal of Social and Personal Relationships, 6,* 259–274.

Meyers, D. G. (1993). *Social psychology* (4th ed.). New York: McGraw-Hill.

Meyers, M. (1994). News of battering. *Journal of Communication, 44,* 47–62.

Meyers, M. (1997). *News coverage of violence against women: Engendering blame.* Thousand Oaks, CA: Sage.

Miell, D. E., & Duck, S. W. (1986). Strategies in developing friendship. In V. J. Derlega & B. A. Winstead (Eds.), *Friendship and social interaction.* New York: Springer-Verlag.

Miller, E. (1974). Speech introductions and conclusions. *Quarterly Journal of Speech, 32,* 118–127.

Miller, G. R., & Parks, M. R. (1982). Communication in dissolving relationships. In S. W. Duck (Ed.), *Personal relationships 4: Dissolving personal relationships* (pp. 127–154). London: Academic Press.

Miller, J. B. (1993). Learning from early relationship experience. In S. W. Duck (Ed.), *Understanding relationship processes, 2: Learning about relationships* (pp. 1–29). Newbury Park, CA: Sage.

Mino, M. (1996). The relative effects of content and vocal delivery during a simulated employment interview. *Communication Research Reports, 13,* 225–238.

Moffatt, T. (1979). *Selection interviewing for managers.* New York: Harper & Row.

Molloy, J. (1988). *The new dress for success.* New York: Warner.

Molloy, J. (1996). *The new woman's dress for success book.* New York: Warner.

Monastersky, R. (2001, July 6). Look who's listening. *The Chronicle of Higher Education,* pp. A14–A16.

Monastersky, R. (2002, March 29). Speak before you think. *The Chronicle of Higher Education,* pp. A17–A18.

Monroe, A. H. (1935). *Principles and types of speech.* Glenview, IL: Scott, Foresman.

Montgomery, B. M. (1988). Quality communication in personal relationships. In S. W. Duck (Ed.), *Handbook of personal relationships* (pp. 343–366). New York: Wiley.

Moran, R. (2001). *Interracial intimacy: The regulation of race and romance.* Chicago: University of Chicago Press.

Morreale, S. (2001, May). Communication important to employers. *Spectra,* p. 8.

Morreale, S. (2003, September). Importance of communication. *Spectra,* p. 14.

Morreale, S., Osborn, M., & Pearson, J. (2000). Why communication is important: A rationale for the centrality of the study of communication. *Journal of the Association for Communication Administration, 29,* 1–25.

Motley, M. (1990). Public speaking anxiety *qua* performance anxiety: A revised model and an alternative therapy. *Journal of Social Behavior and Personality, 5,* 85–104.

Motley, M., & Molloy, J. (1994). An efficacy test of a new therapy ("communication-orientation motivation") for public speaking anxiety. *Journal of Applied Communication Research, 22,* 48–58.

Mudrack, P. & Farrell, G. (1995). An estimation of functional role behavior and its consequences for individuals in group settings. *Small Group Research, 26,* 542–571.

Mulac, A., Wiemann, J. M., Widenmann, S. J., & Gibson, T. W. (1988). Male/female language differences and effects in same-sex and mixed-sex dyads: The gender-linked language effect. *Communication Monographs, 55,* 315–335.

Mullen, B. (1994). Group cohesiveness and quality of decision making. *Small Group Research, 25,* 189–204.

Murphy, B. O., & Zorn, T. (1996). Gendered interaction in professional relationships. In J. T. Wood (Ed.), *Gendered relationships* (pp. 213–232). Mountain View, CA: Mayfield.

Mwakalye, N., & DeAngelis, T. (1995, October). The power of touch helps vulnerable babies survive. *APA Monitor,* p. 25.

Nader, R. (1996, January 1). Imagine that! *The Nation,* p. 10.

Nakazawa, D. (2003a, July 6). A new generation is leading the way. *Parade,* pp 4–5.

Nakazawa, D. (2003b), *Does anybody else look like me? A parent's guide to raising multiracial children.* Oxford, UK: Perseus Press.

Names & faces. (1997, September 11). *The Santa Barbara News-Press,* p. B8.

Nanda, S. (2004). Multiple genders among North American Indians. In J. Spade & Catherine Valentine (Eds.), *The kaleidoscope of gender* (pp. 64–70). Belmont, CA: Wadsworth.

Natalle, E. (1996). Gendered issues in the workplace. In J. T. Wood (Ed.), *Gendered relationships* (pp. 253–274). Mountain View, CA: Mayfield.

National Coalition Against Domestic Violence. (1999). http://www.ncadv.org (accessed 10 July 1999).

National Communication Association (NCA). (2000). *Pathways to careers in communication.* Annandale, VA: National Communication Association.

National Conference of La Raza (1998). Don't blink: Hispanics in television entertainment. In S. Biagi & M. Kem-Foxworth (Eds.), *Facing difference: Race, gender, and mass media* (pp. 29–31). Thousand Oaks, CA: Sage.

National Geographic. (1994, November 5). Public Broadcasting Service, 7:30 P.M. EST.

National Televison Violence Study. (1996). Scientific report. Thousand Oaks, CA: Sage.

New wrinkles in casual dress codes. (1999, November). *Kiplinger's Personal Finance Magazine,* p. 28.

A New Year's Eve primer. (1997, December 31). *The Raleigh News & Observer,* pp. 1E, 3E.

Nichols, M. (1995). *The lost art of listening: How learning to listen can improve relationships.* New York: Guilford Press.

Nicotera, A., Clinkscales, M., & Walker, F. (2002). *Understanding organization through culture and structure.* Thousand Oaks, CA: Sage.

Noller, P. (1986). Sex differences in nonverbal communication: Advantage lost or supremacy regained? *Australian Journal of Psychology, 38,* 23–32.

Noller, P. (1987). Nonverbal communication in marriage. In D. Perlman & S. Duck (Eds.), *Intimate relationships: Development, dynamics, and deterioration* (pp. 149–176). Newbury Park, CA: Sage.

Numbers. (1999, August 16). *Time,* pp. 21, 76.

Nussbaum, J. E. (1992, October 18). Justice for women! *The New York Review of Books,* pp. 43–48.

Nyquist, M. (1992, Fall). Learning to listen. *Ward Rounds* (pp. 11–15). Evanston, IL: Northwestern University Medical School.

Oakley, A. (2002). *Gender on planet Earth.* New York: The New Press.

Okin, S. M. (1989). *Gender, justice, and the family.* New York: Basic Books.

Olson, J. M., & Cal, A. V. (1984). Source credibility, attitudes, and the recall of past behaviors. *European Journal of Social Psychology, 14,* 203–210.

O'Neill, M. (1997, January 12). Asian folk art of *feng shui* hits home with Americans. *The Raleigh News & Observer,* p. 6E.

Orbe, M. P. (1994). "Remember, it's always the Whites' ball": Descriptions of African American male communication. *Communication Quarterly, 42,* 287–300.

Orbe, M., & Harris, T. (2001). *Interracial communication: Theory into practice.* Belmont, CA: Wadsworth.

Orbuch, T., & Veroff, J. (2002). A programmatic review: Building a two-way bridge between social psychology and the study of the early years of marriage. *Journal of Social and Personal Relationships, 19,* 549–568.

Ornish, D. (1998). *Love and survival: The scientific basis for the healing power of intimacy.* New York: HarperCollins.

Ornish, D. (1999). *Love and survival: 8 pathways to intimacy and health.* New York: HarperCollins.

Ortiz, L. (1998). Union response to teamwork: The case of Open Spain. *Industrial Relations Journal, 29,* 42–57.

O'Sullivan, P. (1995). Computer networks and political participation: Santa Monica's teledemocracy project. *Journal of Applied Communication Research, 23,* 93–107.

Pacanowski, M., & O'Donnell-Trujillo, N. (1983). Organizational communication as cultural performance. *Communication Monographs, 30,* 126–147.

Park, M. (1979). *Communication styles in two different cultures: Korean and American.* Seoul, S. Korea: Han Shin.

Patterson, M. L. (1992). A functional approach to nonverbal exchange. In R. S. Feldman & B. Rime (Eds.), *Fundamentals of nonverbal behavior* (pp. 458–495). New York: Cambridge University Press.

Pearce, W. B., Cronen, V. E., & Conklin, F. (1979). On what to look at when analyzing communication: A hierarchical model of actors' meanings. *Communication, 4,* 195–220.

Pearson, J. C. (1985). *Gender and communication.* Dubuque, IA: Wm. C. Brown.

Peters, J. (2000). *Speaking into the air: A history of the idea of communication.* Chicago: University of Chicago Press.

Peterson, M. (1997). Personnel interviewers' perceptions of the importance and adequacy of applicants' communication skills. *Communication Education, 46,* 287–291.

Petronio, S. (1991). Communication boundary management: A theoretical model of managing disclosure of private information between married couples. *Communication Theory, 1,* 311–335.

Petronio, S. (Ed.). (2000). *Balancing the secrets of private disclosures.* Mahwah, NJ: Erlbaum.

Pfeffer, J. (1997). *The human equation: Building profits by putting people first.* Boston: Harvard Business School Press.

Phillips, G. M. (1991). *Communication incompetencies.* Carbondale: Southern Illinois University Press.

Piaget, J. (1932/1965). *The moral judgment of the child.* New York: Free Press.

Pierson, J. (1995, February 17). Form + function. The Wall Street Journal, p. B1.

Pierson, J. (1995, November 20). If sun shines in, workers work better, buyers buy more. *The Wall Street Journal,* pp. B1, B8.

Pinsonneault, A., & Barki, H. (1999). *Electronic brainstorming: The illusion of productivity.* Information Systems Research, 10, 110–133.

Planalp, S. (1999). *Communicating emotion: Social, moral, and cultural processes.* New York: Cambridge University Press.

Pollack, W. (2000). *Real boys: Rescuing ourselves from the myths of boyhood.* New York: Owl Books.

Porter, K., & Foster, J. (1986). *The mental athlete: Inner training for peak performance.* New York: Ballantine.

Poster, M. (2001). *What's the matter with the Internet?* Minneapolis: University of Minnesota Press.

Postman, N. (1985). *Amusing ourselves to death.* New York: Penguin.

Potter, J. (1997). The problem of indexing risk of viewing television aggression. *Critical Studies in Mass Communication, 14,* 228–248.

Potter, J. (2001). *Media literacy* (2nd ed.). Thousand Oaks, CA: Sage.

Potter, J. (2002). *The 11 myths of media violence.* Thousand Oaks, CA: Sage.

Public pillow talk. (1987, October). *Psychology Today,* p. 18.

Puka, B. (1990). The liberation of caring: A different voice for Gilligan's different voice. *Hypatia, 5,* 59–82.

Purdy, M. (1997). What is listening? In M. Purdy & D. Borisoff (Eds.), *Listening in everyday life: A personal and professional approach* (2nd ed., pp. 1–20). Lanham, MD: University Press of America.

Quality circles help sharpen competitive edge. (1991, Winter). *The Scorpion: The Official All-State Legal Supply Employee Publication,* pp. 7–9.

Rafter, M. (1999, August 2–9). Check it out. *The Industry Standard,* pp. 87–90.

Ramsay, S., Gallois, C., & Callan, V. (1997). Social rules and attributions in the personnel selection interview. *Journal of Occupational and Organizational Psychology, 70,* 189–203.

Rawlins, W. K. (1981). *Friendship as a communicative achievement: A theory and an interpretive analysis of verbal reports.* Unpublished doctoral dissertation. Philadelphia: Temple University.

Rawlins, W. K. (1994). Being there and growing apart: Sustaining friendships during adulthood. In D. Canary & L. Stafford (Eds.), *Communication and relational maintenance* (pp. 275–294). New York: Academic Press.

Reeder, H. (2000). "I like you . . . as a friend": The role of attraction in cross-sex friendship. *Journal of Social and Personal Relationships, 17,* pp. 329–348.

Reel, B. W., & Thompson, T. L. (1994). A test of the effectiveness of strategies for talking about AIDS and condom use. *Journal of Applied Communication Research, 22,* 127–141.

Reis, H. T., Senchak, M., & Solomon, B. (1985). Sex differences in the intimacy of social interaction: Further examination of potential explanations. *Journal of Personality and Social Psychology, 48,* 1204–1217.

Remland, M. (2000). *Nonverbal communication in everyday life.* Boston: Houghton Mifflin.

Ribeau, S. A., Baldwin, J. R., & Hecht, M. L. (1994). An African American communication perspective. In L. Samovar & R. Porter (Eds.), *Intercultural communication: A reader* (7th ed., pp. 140–147). Belmont, CA: Wadsworth.

Richmond, V. P., & McCroskey, J. C. (1992). *Communication: Apprehension, avoidance, and effectiveness* (3rd ed.). Scottsdale, AZ: Gorsuch Scarisbrick.

Richmond, V. P., & McCroskey, J. C. (1995a). *Communication: Apprehension, avoidance, and effectiveness.* Scottsdale, AZ: Gorsuch Scarisbrick.

Richmond, V. P., & McCroskey, J. C. (1995b). *Nonverbal communication in interpersonal relations* (3rd ed.). Boston: Allyn & Bacon.

Rideout, V., Foehr, U., Roberts, D., & Brodie, M. (1999). *Kids and media@ the new millennium*. Menlo Park, CA: The Kaiser Foundation.

Riessman, C. (1990). *Divorce talk: Women and men make sense of personal relationships*. New Brunswick, NJ: Rutgers University Press.

Riggs, D. (1999, February 28). True love is alive and well, say romance book writers. *The Tallahassee Democrat*, p. 3D.

Risman, B., & Godwin, S. (2001). Twentieth-century changes in economic work and family. In D. Vannoy (Ed.), *Gender mosaics* (pp. 134–144). Los Angeles: Roxbury.

Robinson, D. (1995). *An intellectual history of psychology*. Madison: University of Wisconsin Press.

Robinson, G. (2001, March 4). Sometimes a thank you is enough. *The New York Times*, pp. 16, 18.

Rodriguez, R. (2002). *Brown: The last discovery of America*. New York: Viking.

Rodriguez, R. (2003, September 12). "Blaxicans" and other reinvented Americans. *The Chronicle of Higher Education*, pp. B10–B11.

Rohlfing, M. (1995). Doesn't anybody stay in one place anymore? An exploration of the understudied phenomenon of long-distance relationships. In J. T. Wood & S. W. Duck (Eds.), *Understanding relationship processes, 6: Understudied relationships: Off the beaten track* (pp. 173–196). Thousand Oaks, CA: Sage.

Rollie, S. S., & Duck, S. W. (in press). Divorce and dissolution of romantic relationships: Stage models and their imitations. In M. Fine & J. Harvey (Eds.) *Handbook of divorce and dissolution of romantic relationships*. Mahwah, NJ: Erlbaum.

Root, M. P. (1990). Disordered eating habits in women of color. *Sex Roles, 22*, 525–536.

Rorty, R. (1998). *Achieving our country*. Cambridge, MA: Harvard University Press.

Rosenberg, M. (1979). *Conceiving the self*. New York: Basic Books.

Rothwell, J. D. (2004). *In mixed company: Small group communication* (5th ed.). Belmont, CA: Wadsworth.

Ruark, J. (1999, February 12). Redefining the good life: A new focus in the social sciences. *The Chronicle of Higher Education*, pp. A12–A15.

Ruberman, T. R. (1992, January 22–29). Psychosocial influences on mortality of patients with coronary heart disease. *Journal of the American Medical Association, 267*, 559–560.

Ruddick, S. (1989). *Maternal thinking: Towards a politics of peace*. Boston: Beacon Press.

Ruggiero, T. (2000). Uses and gratifications theory in the 21st century. *Mass Communication & Society, 31*, 3–37.

Rusbult, C. (1987). Responses to dissatisfaction in close relationships: The exit–voice–loyalty–neglect model. In D. Perlman & S. W. Duck (Eds.), *Intimate relationships: Development, dynamics, and deterioration* (pp. 109–238). London: Sage.

Rusbult, C. E., Johnson, D. J., & Morrow, G. D. (1986). Impact of couple patterns of problem solving on distress and nondistress in dating relationships. *Journal of Personality and Social Psychology, 50*, 744–753.

Rusbult, C. E., & Zembrodt, I. M. (1983). Responses to dissatisfaction in romantic involvement: A multidimensional scaling analysis. *Journal of Experimental Social Psychology, 19*, 274–293.

Rusbult, C. E., Zembrodt, I. M., & Iwaniszek, J. (1986). The impact of gender and sex-role orientation on responses to dissatisfaction in close relationships. *Sex Roles, 15*, 1–20.

Rusk, T., & Rusk, N. (1988). *Mind traps: Change your mind, change your life*. Los Angeles: Price Stern Sloan.

Saker, A. (1996, January 18). Focus groups becoming vital tool for N. C. lawyers. *The Raleigh News & Observer*, pp. 1A, 14A.

Salazar, A. (1995). Understanding the synergistic effects of communication in small groups. *Small Group Research, 26*, 169–199.

Salins, P. (1998). *Assimilation, American style*. New York: Basic.

Sallinen-Kuparinen, A. (1992). Teacher communicator style. *Communication Education, 41*, 153–166.

Salopek, J. (1999). Is anyone listening? *Training and Development, 53*, 58–59.

Samovar, L., & Porter, R. (1998). *Communication between cultures* (3rd ed.). Belmont, CA: Wadsworth.

Samovar, L., & Porter, R. (Eds.). (2000). *Intercultural communication: A reader* (6th ed.). Belmont, CA: Wadsworth.

Samovar, L., & Porter, R. (2001). *Communication between cultures* (4th ed.). Belmont, CA: Wadsworth.

Samuelson, R. (2001, April 9). Can America assimilate? *Newsweek*, p. 42.

Samuelson, R. (2002, March 25). Debunking the digital divide. *Newsweek*, p. 37.

Sandberg, J. (1999, May 31). The quiet genius who brings it all together. *Newsweek*, p. 63.

Scarf, M. (1987). *Intimate partners: Patterns in love and marriage*. New York: Random House.

Schaub, C. (1998, October 31). Beware the guy with the wine-bottle collection. *The Raleigh News & Observer*, p. 5E.

Scheufele, D. (2000). Agenda-setting, priming, and framing revisited: Another look at cognitive effects of political communication. *Mass Communication & Society, 3*, 197–316.

Schminoff, S. B. (1980). *Communication rules: Theory and research*. Newbury Park, CA: Sage.

Schmitt, E. (2001a, May 15). For first time, nuclear families drop below 25% of households. *The New York Times*, p. 1A.

Schmitt, E. (2001b, March 13). For 7 million people in census, one race category isn't enough. *The New York Times*, pp. A1, A14.

Schneider, A. (1999, March 26). Taking aim at student incoherence. *The Chronicle of Higher Education*, pp. A16–A18.

Schram, P., & Schwartz, H. (2000). *Stories within stories: From the Jewish oral tradition*. Leonia, NJ: Jason Aronson.

Schramm, W. (1955). *The process and effects of mass communication*. Urbana: University of Illinois Press.

Schütz, A. (1999). It was your fault! Self-serving bias in autobiographical accounts of conflicts in married couples. *Journal of Social and Personal Relationships, 16*, 193–208.

Schutz, W. (1966). *The interpersonal underworld*. Palo Alto, CA: Science and Behavior Books.

Schwartz, T. (1989, January/February). Acceleration syndrome: Does everyone live in the fast lane nowadays? *Utne Reader*, pp. 36–43.

Sedikides, C., Campbell, W., Reeder, G., & Elliot, A. (1998). The self-serving bias in relational context. *Journal of Personality and Social Psychology, 74*, 378–386.

Segrin, C. (1998). Interpersonal communication problems associated with depression and loneliness. In P. Andersen & L. Guerrero (Eds.), *Communication and emotion: Theory, research, and applications* (pp. 215–242). San Diego, CA: Academic Press.

Seligman, M. E. P. (1990). *Learned optimism*. New York: Simon & Schuster/Pocket Books.

Seligman, M. E. P. (2002). *Authentic happiness.* New York: The Free Press.

Shannon, C., & Weaver, W. (1949). *The mathematical theory of communication.* Urbana: University of Illinois Press.

Shanahan, J., & Jones, V. (1999). Cultivation and social control. In D. Demers & K. Viswanath (Eds.), *Mass media, social control, and social change* (pp. 89–116). Ames: Iowa State University Press.

Shapiro, J., & Kroeger, L. (1991). Is life just a romantic novel? The relationship between attitudes about intimate relationships and the popular media. *American Journal of Family Therapy, 19,* 226–236.

Sharlet, J. (1999, July 2). Beholding beauty: Scholars nip and tuck at our quest for physical perfection. *The Chronicle of Higher Education,* pp. A15–A16.

Sharpe, R. (1995, October 31). The checkoff. *The Wall Street Journal,* p. A1.

Shattuck, T. R. (1980). *The forbidden experiment: The story of the wild boy of Aveyron.* New York: Farrar, Straus & Giroux.

Sheehan, J. (1996, February). Kiss and well: How to smooch and seduce your way to health. *Longevity,* pp. 50–51, 93.

Shellenbarger, S. (1995, August 23). Telecommuter profile. *The Wall Street Journal,* p. B1.

Shenk, D. (1997). *Data smog.* New York: Harper-Edge.

Shim, J. (1997). The importance of ethnic newspapers to U. S. newcomers. In S. Biagi & M. Kem-Foxworth (Eds.), *Facing difference: Race, gender, and mass media* (pp. 250–255). Thousand Oaks, CA: Sage.

Shimanoff, S. B. (1980). *Communication rules: Theory and research.* Beverly Hills, CA: Sage.

Shotter, J. (1993). *Conversational realities: The construction of life through language.* Newbury Park, CA: Sage.

Signorielli, N. (1990). Television's mean and dangerous world: A continuation of the cultural indicators perspective. In N. Signorielli & M. Morgan (Eds.), *Cultivation analysis: New directions in media effects research* (pp. 85–106). Thousand Oaks, CA: Sage.

Signorielli, N., & Morgan, M. (Eds.). (1990). *Cultivation analysis: New directions in media effects research.* Thousand Oaks, CA: Sage.

Silverblatt, A. (2001). *Media literacy: Keys to interpreting media messages,* (2nd ed.). Westport, CT: Praeger.

Simon, S. B. (1977). *Vulture: A modern allegory on the art of putting oneself down.* Niles, IL: Argus Communications.

Simons, G. F., Vázquez, C., & Harris, P. R. (1993). *Transcultural leadership: Empowering the diverse workforce.* Houston, TX: Gulf.

Sixel, L. M. (1995, August 6). Companies do college interviews by video. *The Raleigh News & Observer,* p. 10F.

Smith, R. (1998, December 1). *Civility without censorship: The ethics of the Internet cyberhate.* Speech delivered at the Simon Wiesenthal Center/Museum of Tolerance, Los Angeles, CA.

Smith, S. (1999, February 11). Test a bevy of new words. *The Raleigh News & Observer,* p. 3E.

Snapp, C., & Leary, M. (2001). Hurt feelings among new acquaintants: Moderating effects of interpersonal familiarity. *Journal of Social and Personal Relationships, 18,* pp. 315–326.

Sommerville, D. (1999, May 26). Race, gender attitudes begin early. *The Raleigh News & Observer,* p. 3F.

Sonnentag, S. (2001). High performance and meeting participation: An observational study in software design teams. *Group Dynamics: Theory, Research, and Practice, 5,* 3–18.

Spaeth, M. (1996, July 1). "Prop" up your speaking skills. *The Wall Street Journal,* p. A15.

Spain, D. (1992). *Gendered spaces.* Chapel Hill: University of North Carolina Press.

Spano, S. (2003, June 1). Rude encounters versus cultural differences. *The Raleigh News & Observer,* pp. 1H, 5H.

Spear, W. (1995). Feng shui *made easy: Designing your life with the ancient art of placement.* New York: HarperCollins.

Spencer, T. (1994). Transforming personal relationships through ordinary talk. In S. W. Duck (Ed.), *Understanding relationship processes, 4: Dynamics of relationships* (pp. 58–85). Thousand Oaks, CA: Sage.

Spicer, C., & Bassett, R. E. (1976). The effect of organization on learning from an informative message. *Southern Speech Communication Journal, 41,* 290–299.

Spitzack, C. (1990). *Confessing excess.* Albany: State University of New York Press.

Spitzack, C. (1993). The spectacle of anorexia nervosa. *Text and Performance Quarterly, 13,* 1–21.

Sprague, J., & Stuart, D. (1996). *The speaker's handbook* (4th ed.). New York: Harcourt Brace.

Stafford, L., Dutton, M., & Haas, S. (2000). Measuring routine maintenance: Scale revision, sex versus gender roles, and the prediction of relational characteristics. *Communication Monographs, 67,* 306–323.

Stamp, G. H., & Sabourin, T. C. (1995). Accounting for violence: An analysis of male spousal abuse narratives. *Journal of Applied Communication Research, 23,* 284–307.

Stanton, E. C., Anthony, S. B., & Gage, M. J. (1881/1969 reprint). *History of woman suffrage, I.* New York: Arno and *The New York Times.*

Statistical Abstract of the United States: 2001. (2002). Washington, DC: Congressional Information Service.

Steil, J. (2000). Contemporary marriage: Still an unequal partnership. In C. Hendrick & S. Hendrick (Eds.), *Close relationships: A sourcebook* (pp. 124–136). Thousand Oaks, CA: Sage.

Steil, L. (1997). Listening training: The key to success in today's organizations. In M. Purdy & D. Borisoff (Eds.), *Listening in everyday life: A personal and professional approach* (2nd ed, pp. 213–237). Lanham, MD: University Press of America.

Stets, J. E. (1990). Verbal and physical aggression in marriage. *Journal of Marriage and the Family, 52,* 501–514.

Stewart, C., & Cash, W. (1991). *Interviewing: Principles and practices* (6th ed.). Dubuque, IA: Wm. C. Brown.

Stewart, L., Stewart, A., Friedley, S., & Cooper, P. (1990). *Communication between the sexes* (2nd ed.). Scottsdale, AZ: Gorsuch Scarisbrick.

Stiff, J. B. (1994). *Persuasive communication.* New York: Guilford, Press.

Stone, B. (1998, June 8). The keyboard kids. *Newsweek,* pp. 72–74.

Stone, R. (1992). The feminization of poverty among the elderly. In M. L. Andersen & P. H. Collins (Eds.), *Race, class, and gender: An anthology* (pp. 201–214). Belmont, CA: Wadsworth.

Strasser, M. (1997). *Legally wed: Same-sex marriage and the Constitution.* Ithaca, NY: Cornell University Press.

Strege, J. (1997). *Tiger: A biography of Tiger Woods*. New York: Bantam/Doubleday.

Strine, M. S. (1992). Understanding "how things work": Sexual harassment and academic culture. *Journal of Applied Communication Research, 20,* 391–400.

Stroup, K. (2001, April 30). Business connections: The wired way we work. *Newsweek,* pp. 59–61.

Study finds U.S. children spend a full work week using TV, computers, games. (1999, November 17). *Agence France Presse,* p. 2.

Surra, C., Arizzi, P., & Asmussen, L. (1988). The association between reasons for commitment and the development and outcome of marital relationships. *Journal of Social and Personal Relationships, 5,* 47–64.

Sutton, M. (2001). Long-distance romantic relationships. Research paper for Communication 91. University of North Carolina at Chapel Hill.

Swain, S. (1989). Covert intimacy: Closeness in men's friendships. In B. Risman & P. Schwartz (Eds.), *Gender and intimate relationships* (pp. 71–86). Belmont, CA: Wadsworth.

Swidler, A. (2001). *Talk of love: How culture matters*. Chicago: University of Chicago Press.

Swiss, T. (Ed.). (2001). *Unspun key concepts for understanding the World Wide Web*. New York: New York University Press.

Sypher, B. (1984). Seeing ourselves as others see us. *Communication Research, 11,* 97–115.

Sypher, B., Bostrom, R., & Siebert, J. (1989). Listening, communication abilities, and success at work. *Journal of Business Communication, 26,* 293–303.

Tanaka, J. (1997, April 28). Drowning in data. *Newsweek,* p. 85.

Tannen, D. (1990). *You just don't understand: Women and men in conversation*. New York: William Morrow.

Tashiro, T., & Frazier, P. (2003). "I'll never be in a relationship like that again": Personal growth following romantic relationship breakups. *Personal Relationships, 10,* 113–128.

Tavris, C. (1992). *The mismeasure of woman*. New York: Simon & Schuster.

Taylor, A., Wiley, A., Kuo, F., & Sullivan, W. (1998). Growing up in the inner city: Green spaces as places to grow. *Environment and Behavior, 30,* 3–27.

Taylor, B., & Conrad, C. (1992). Narratives of sexual harassment: Organizational dimensions. *Journal of Applied Communication Research, 4,* 401–418.

Teams become commonplace in U.S. companies. (1995, November 28). *The Wall Street Journal,* p. A1.

Thomas, J. (1999). Do you hear what I hear? *Women in Business, 51,* 1–14.

Thomas, V. G. (1989). Body-image satisfaction among Black women. *Journal of Social Psychology, 129,* 107–112.

Thompson, E. H., Jr. (1991). The maleness of violence in dating relationships: An appraisal of stereotypes. *Sex Roles, 24,* 261–278.

Thompson, F., & Grundgenett, D. (1999). Helping disadvantaged learners build effective learning skills. *Education, 120,* 130–135.

Tolhuizen, J. H. (1989). Communication strategies for intensifying dating relationships: Identification, use, and structure. *Journal of Social and Personal Relationships, 6,* 413–434.

Toulmin, S. (1958). *The uses of argument*. Cambridge, MA: Cambridge University Press.

Toulmin, S., Rieke, R., & Janik, A. (1984). *An introduction to reasoning* (2nd ed.). New York: Macmillan.

Trenholm, S. (1991). *Human communication theory* (2nd ed.). Englewood Cliffs, NJ: Prentice Hall.

Triandis, H. C. (1990). Cross-cultural studies of individualism and collectivism. In J. J. Berman (Ed.), *Cross-cultural perspectives* (pp. 41–133). Lincoln: University of Nebraska Press.

Trotter, R. J. (1975, October 25). "The truth, the whole truth, and nothing but . . ." *Science News, 108,* 269.

Tubbs, S. (1998). *A systems approach to small group communication* (6th ed.). New York: McGraw-Hill.

Tusing, K., & Dillard, J. (2000). The sounds of dominance: Vocal precursors of perceived dominance during interpersonal influence. *Human Communication Research, 26,* 148–171.

Unemployment rate for youths is lowest in thirty years. (August 27, 1999). *The St. Louis Dispatch,* p. 1A.

Upton, H. (1995, May 8). Peerless advice from small-business peers. *The Wall Street Journal,* p. A14.

Urgo, J. (2000). *The age of distraction*. Jackson: Mississippi University Press.

U.S. Bureau of the Census (2001). *Census 2001*. Washington, DC: Government Printing Office.

U.S. Bureau of the Census (2002). *Census 2002*. Washington, DC: Government Printing Office.

U.S. Bureau of the Census (2003). *Census 2003*. Washington, DC: Government Printing Office.

U.S. Department of Labor. (1992). *Cultural diversity in the workplace*. Washington, DC: Government Printing Office.

Vachss, A. (1998a, March 29). A hard look at how we treat children. *Parade,* pp. 4–5.

Vachss, A. (1998b). *Safe house*. New York: Knopf.

Valentin, E., Rogers, L. E., & Gutierrez, E. (1997). Patterns of relational control and nonverbal affect in clinic and nonclinic couples. *Journal of Social and Personal Relationships, 14,* 5–29.

Value of children's shows is questionable, study finds. (1999, June 28). *The Raleigh News & Observer,* p. 5A.

Van Oostrum, J., & Rabbie, J. (1995). Intergroup competition and cooperation within autocratic and democratic management regimes. *Small Group Research, 26,* 269–295.

Van Styke, E. (1999). *Listening to conflict: Finding constructive solutions to workplace disputes*. New York: AMA Communications.

View. (2001, November–December). *Utne Reader,* p. 24.

Villarosa, L. (1994, January). Dangerous eating. *Essence,* pp. 19–21, 87.

Vito, D. (1999). Affective self-disclosure, conflict resolution, and marital quality. (Doctoral dissertation), *Dissertation Abstracts International, 60* (3–B), 1319.

Vocate, D. (Ed.). (1994). *Intrapersonal communication: Different voices, different minds*. Hillsdale, NJ: Erlbaum.

Wade, C., & Tavris, C. (1990). *Learning to think critically: The case of close relationships*. New York: HarperCollins.

Walker, M. B., & Trimboli, A. (1989). Communicating affect: The role of verbal and nonverbal content. *Journal of Language and Social Psychology, 8,* 229–248.

Walsh, D. (1994). *Selling out America's children: How America puts profits before values—and what parents can do*. Minneapolis, MN: Fairview Press.

Watzlawick, P., Beavin, J., & Jackson, D. D. (1967). *Pragmatics of human communication*. New York: W. W. Norton.

Weber, S. N. (1994). The need to be: The socio-cultural significance of Black language. In L. Samovar & R. Porter (Eds.), *Intercultural communication: A reader* (7th ed., pp. 221–226). Belmont, CA: Wadsworth.

Wech, B., Mossholder, K., Streel, R., & Bennett, N. (1998). Does work group cohesiveness afflict indivduals' performance and organizational commitment? *Small Group Research, 29,* 472–494.

Weimann, G. (2000). *Communicating unreality: Modern media and the reconstruction of reality.* Newbury Park, CA: Sage.

Weinstock, J., & Bond, L. (2000). Conceptions of conflict in close friendships and ways of knowing among young college women: A developmental framework. *Journal of Social and Personal Relationships, 17,* 687–696.

Weisinger, H. (1996). *Anger at work.* New York: William Morrow.

Werner, C., Altman, I., & Oxley, D. (1985). Temporal aspects of homes: A transactional perspective. In I. Altman & C. M. Werner (Eds.), *Home environments, 8. Human behavior and environment: Advances in theory and research* (pp. 1–32). Beverly Hills, CA: Sage.

Werner, C. M., Altman, I., Brown, B. B., & Ginat, J. (1993). Celebrations in personal relationships: A transactional/dialectical perspective. In S. W. Duck (Ed.), *Understanding relational processes, 3: Social context and relationships* (pp. 109–138). Newbury Park, CA: Sage.

West, C. (1992). The new cultural politics of difference. In C. Lemert (Ed.), *Social theory: The multicultural and classic readings* (pp. 577–589). San Francisco: Westview.

West, C., & Zimmerman, D. H. (1987). Doing gender. *Gender and Society, 1,* 125–151.

West, J. (1995). Understanding how the dynamics of ideology influence violence between intimates. In S. W. Duck & J. T. Wood (Eds.), *Understanding relationship processes, 5: Confronting relationship challenges* (pp. 129–149). Thousand Oaks, CA: Sage.

Weston, K. (1991). *Families we choose: Lesbians, gays, kinship.* New York: Columbia University Press.

Wexner, L. B. (1954). The degree to which colors (hues) are associated with mood-tones. *Journal of Applied Psychology, 38,* 432–435.

What work requires of schools: A SCANS report for America 2000. (June, 1991). *The Secretary's Commission on Achieving Necessary Skills.* Washington, DC: U.S. Department of Labor.

Whitbeck, L. B., & Hoyt, D. R. (1994). Social prestige and assortive mating: A comparison of students from 1956 and 1988. *Journal of Social and Personal Relationships, 11,* 137–145.

White, R., & Lippitt, R. (1960). *Autocracy and democracy.* New York: Harper & Row.

Whitman, T., White, R., O'Mara, K., & Goeke-Morey, M. (1999). Environmental aspects of infant health and illness. In T. Whitman & T. Merluzzi (Eds.), *Life-span perspectives on health and illness* (pp. 105–124). Mahwah, NJ: Erlbaum.

Whorf, B. (1956). *Language, thought, and reality.* New York: MIT Press/Wiley.

Wiemann, J. M., & Harrison, R. P. (Eds.). (1983). *Nonverbal interaction.* Beverly Hills, CA: Sage.

Williams, G. (1995). *Life on the color line: The true story of a White boy who discovered he was Black.* New York: Dutton.

Williams, R. (1994). *The non-designer's design book: Design and typographic principles for the visual novice.* Berkeley, CA: Peachpit Press.

Wilmot, W., & Hocker, J. (2001). *Interpersonal Conflict.* New York: McGraw-Hill.

Wilson, C., & Gutiérrez, & Chao, L. (2003). *The rise of class communication in multicultural America,* (3rd ed.). Thousand Oaks, CA: Sage.

Wilson, G., & Goodall, H., Jr. (1991). *Interviewing in context.* New York: McGraw-Hill.

Wilson, J. F., & Arnold, C. C. (1974). *Public speaking as a liberal art* (4th ed.). Boston: Allyn & Bacon.

Winans, J. A. (1938). *Speechmaking.* New York: Appleton-Century-Crofts.

Windsor, J., Curtis, D., & Stephens, R. (1997). National preferences in business and communication education: An update. *Journal of the Association for Communication Administration, 3,* 170–179.

Wong, W. (1994). Covering the invisible "model minority." *Media Studies Journal* (Special issue: *Race: America's rawest nerve*), 8, 49–60.

Wood, A., & Smith, M. (2001). *Online communication: Linking technology, identity, and culture.* Mahwah, NJ: Erlbaum.

Wood, J. T. (1982). Communication and relational culture: Bases for the study of human relationships. *Communication Quarterly, 30,* 75–84.

Wood, J. T. (1986). Different voices in relationship crises: An extension of Gilligan's theory. *American Behavioral Scientist, 29,* 273–301.

Wood, J. T. (1992). Telling our stories: Narratives as a basis for theorizing sexual harassment. *Journal of Applied Communication Research, 4,* 349–363.

Wood, J. T. (1993a). Brining different voices into the classroom. *National Women's Studies Association, 5,* 82–93.

Wood, J. T. (1993b). Engendered relations: Interaction, caring, power, and responsibility in intimacy. In S. W. Duck (Ed.), *Understanding relationship processes, 3: Social context and relationships* (pp. 26–54). Newbury Park, CA: Sage.

Wood, J. T. (1993c). Enlarging conceptual boundaries: A critique of research on interpersonal communication. In S. P. Bowen & N. J. Wyatt (Eds.), *Transforming visions: Feminist critiques in communication studies* (pp. 19–49). Cresskill, NJ: Hampton.

Wood, J. T. (1993d). Gender and moral voice: From woman's nature to standpoint theory. *Women's Studies in Communication, 15,* 1–24.

Wood, J. T. (1994a). Engendered identities: Shaping voice and mind through gender. In D. Vocate (Ed.), *Intrapersonal communication: Different voices, different minds.* Hillsdale, NJ: Erlbaum.

Wood, J. T. (1994b). Gender and relationship crises: Contrasting reasons, responses, and relational orientations. In J. Ringer (Ed.), *Queer words, queer images: The construction of homosexuality.* New York: New York University Press.

Wood, J. T. (1994c). Saying it makes it so: The discursive construction of sexual harassment. In S. Bingham (Ed.), *Conceptualizing sexual harassment as discursive practice* (pp. 17–30). Westport, CT: Praeger.

Wood, J. T. (1994d). *Who cares? Women, care, and culture.* Carbondale: Southern Illinois University Press.

Wood, J. T. (1995a). Feminist scholarship and research on personal relationships. *Journal of Social and Personal Relationships, 12,* 103–120.

Wood, J. T. (1995b). The part is not the whole. *Journal of Social and Personal Relationships, 12,* 563–567.

Wood, J. T. (1996a) Dominant and muted discourses in popular representations of feminism. *Quarterly Journal of Speech, 82,* 171–185.

Wood, J. T. (Ed.). (1996b). *Gendered relationships.* Mountain View, CA: Mayfield.

Wood, J. T. (1998). *But I thought you meant . . . : Misunderstandings in human communication.* Mountain View, CA: Mayfield.

Wood, J. T. (2000). *Relational communication: Continuity and change in personal relationships* (2nd ed.). Belmont, CA: Wadsworth.

Wood, J. T. (2001a). A critical response to John Gray's Mars and Venus portrayals of men and women. *Southern Communication Journal, 67,* 201–210.

Wood, J. T. (2001b). The normalization of violence in heterosexual romantic relationships: Women's narratives of love and violence. *Journal of Social and Personal Relationships, 18,* 239–261.

Wood, J. T. (2004). *Interpersonal communication: Everyday encounters* (4th ed.). Belmont, CA: Wadsworth.

Wood, J. T. (2005). *Gendered lives: Communication, gender and culture* (6th ed.). Belmont, CA: Wadsworth.

Wood, J. T. (in press). Monsters and victims: Male felons' accounts of intimate partner violence. *Journal of Social and Personal Relationships.*

Wood, J. T., Dendy, L., Dordek, E., Germany, M., & Varallo, S. (1994). Dialectic of difference: A thematic analysis of intimates' meanings for differences. In K. Carter & M. Presnell (Eds.), *Interpretive approaches to interpersonal communication* (pp. 115–136). New York: State University of New York Press.

Wood, J. T., & Duck, S. W. (1995a). Off the beaten track: New shores for relationship research. In J. T. Wood & S. W. Duck (Eds.), *Understanding relationship processes, 6: Understudied relationships: Off the beaten track* (pp. 1–21). Thousand Oaks, CA: Sage.

Wood, J. T., & Duck, S. W. (Eds.). (1995b). *Understanding relationship processes, 6: Understudied relationships: Off the beaten track.* Newbury Park, CA: Sage.

Wood, J. T., & Inman, C. C. (1993). In a different mode: Masculine styles of communicating closeness. *Journal of Applied Communication Research, 21,* 279–295.

Wood, J. T., & Phillips, G. M. (1990). The pedagogy of group decision making: Teaching alternative strategies. In G. M. Phillips (Ed.), *Small group communication: Theory and pedagogy.* Norwood, NJ: Ablex.

Woolfolk, A. E. (1987). *Educational psychology.* Englewood Cliffs, NJ: Prentice Hall.

The wrong weight. (1997, November). *Carolina Woman,* p. 7.

Wu, C., & Shaffer, D. R. (1988). Susceptibility to persuasive appeals as a function of source credibility and prior experience with attitude object. *Journal of Personal and Social Psychology, 52,* 677–688.

Wurman, R. (1989). *Information anxiety.* New York: Doubleday.

Wycoff, J. (1991). *Mind mapping: Your personal guide to exploring creativity and problem solving.* New York: Basic Books.

Wydra, N. (1998). *Look before you love: Feng shui techniques for revealing anyone's true nature.* New York: Contemporary Books.

Yamato, G. (2001). Something about the subject makes it hard to name. In M. L. Andersen & P. H. Collins (Eds.), *Race, class, and gender: An anthology* (4th ed., pp. 91–94). Belmont, CA: Wadsworth.

Yanes, W. (1990, November 9). Forget consensus: Fight it out, stick with decision. *Investor's Business Daily,* p. 6.

Young, J. (1998, May 8). Skeptical audience sees peril in information technology. *The Chronicle of Higher Education,* pp. A29–A30.

Young, K. (1998). *Caught in the Net.* New York: Wiley.

Young, S., Wood, J., Phillips, G., & Pedersen, D. (2001). *Group discussion* (3rd ed.). Prospect Heights, IL: Waveland.

Yum, J. (2000). The impact of Confucianism on interpersonal relationships and communication patterns in East Asia. In L. Samovar & R. Porter (Eds.), *Intercultural communication: A reader* (9th ed., pp. 63–73). Belmont, CA: Wadsworth.

Zachary, P. (2002, January 21). The new America. *In These Times,* pp. 22–23.

Zediker, K. (1993, February). *Rediscovering the tradition: Women's history with a relational approach to the basic public speaking course.* Albuquerque, NM: Western States Communication Association.

Zorn, T. (1995). Bosses and buddies: Constructing and performing simultaneously hierarchical and close friendship relationships. In J. T. Wood & S. W. Duck (Eds.), *Understanding relationship processes, 6: Understudied relationships: Off the beaten track* (pp. 122–147). Thousand Oaks, CA: Sage.

Zuckerman, M. B. (1993, August 2). The victims of TV violence. *U.S. News & World Report,* p. 64.

Zukerman, L. (1999, April 17). Words go right to the brain, but can they stir the heart? *The New York Times,* p. 9.

Index

NOTE: Page numbers followed by *f* indicate a figure; page numbers followed by *t* indicate a table.